PEARSON

ALWAYS LEARNING

Compiled by Frank Gavin • Emily Donville
Dagmar Vavrusa and Denvil Buchanan
Revised by Denvil Buchanan

Effective Reading and Writing for COMM 170 and Beyond

Fourth Custom Edition for Centennial College

Taken from:

Quick Access Reference for Writers, Fifth Canadian Edition, Fifth Edition
by Lynn Quitman Troyka and Douglas Hesse

Four in One: Rhetoric, Reader, Research Guide and Handbook, Fifth Edition
by Edward A. Dornan and Robert Dees

Essay Writing for Canadian Students with Readings, Seventh Edition
by Roger Davis, Laura K. Davis, Kay L. Stewart, and Chris J. Bullock

The Canadian Writer's World: Paragraphs and Essays,
First Canadian Edition
by Lynne Gaetz, Suneeti Phadke, and Rhonda Sandberg

Reading Rhetorically, Fourth Edition
by John C. Bean, Virginia A. Chappell, and Alice M. Gillam

Spotlight on Critical Skills in Essay Writing, Second Edition
by Carole Anne May

 **PEARSON**   ISBN 10: 1-323-23889-1
ISBN 13: 978-1-323-23889-9

Copyright Acknowledgments

Contents

Writing Analytical Essays   229

Analyzing Your Reading and Writing Context   230

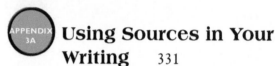

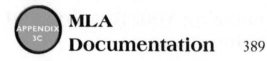
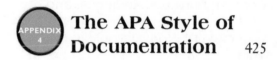

Part I:
About Reading

Strategies for Active Reading

CONTENTS

Effective reading is not a passive process, but requires the ongoing interaction of your mind and the printed page. Bringing your knowledge and experience to bear on a piece of writing can help you assess its ideas and conclusions. For example, an understanding of marriage, love, and conflict, as well as experience with divorce, can help readers comprehend an essay that explores divorce. As you read, try to understand each point that's made, consider how the various parts fit together, and anticipate the direction the writing will take. Active reading requires attention. Using specific reading strategies can help you take in more of what you read.

Orienting Your Reading

When reading for pleasure, you can read at any pace you choose, and break off reading when you feel distracted or bored. Reading for academic purposes, however, requires more focused attention. Before starting to read, ask yourself these questions:

- **Why am I reading this material?** Is it for a project you are working on? Is it for a class or an exam? Is it a building block to understanding more material?
- **How well do I need to know the material in the article?** Can you look back to the article as a reference? Is there only one main point you need to know? Are you going to be tested on much of the material in depth?
- **Is some material in the article more important to me than other material?** Sometimes in doing research you may be looking for a specific bit of information that is only one paragraph in a long article. If so, you can skim for the information. In most documents you read, certain sections are more

important than others. Often you can read to get the main points of the article and not focus on all the details. Other times, of course, you need to understand all the material in depth.

- **What will I do with the information in the article?** If you are looking for ideas for your own writing, you might read quickly. If you are responsible for writing a critique of the article, you need to read carefully and critically.
- **What kind of reading does the material suggest?** The significance, difficulty, and nature of the writing can all influence how you read. You may read an easy, humorous narrative quickly, but you may need to slow down when you read an argument for or against an important issue, paying careful attention to the main points put forward, perhaps even asking questions about them.

EXERCISE

Reading Activity *Look briefly at "The Appeal of the Androgynous Man" on pages 8–11. Identify three purposes you could have for reading this essay. Identify how these purposes would affect how you would read the essay and what you would look for in the essay.*

A First Reading

When going on a trip or an outing, you don't just jump in your car and take off. Usually you take some time to think about where you want to go. Sometimes you even have to check your route. The same is true of effective reading. Because of the challenging nature of most college-level reading assignments, you should plan on more than one reading. The goal of a good first reading is to orient yourself to the material.

Orient Yourself to the Background of the Essay   Before you begin, examine information accompanying the essay for clues about the essay's relevance. Scan the accompanying biographical sketch (if available) to determine the writer's expertise and biases on the topic. Read any notes by the author or editor about the process of researching or writing this essay. For professional essays, look for an abstract that provides a brief summary of the article. At this point, you may want to judge the credibility of the source.

Use the Title as a Clue   Most titles identify the topic and often the author's viewpoint as well. Thus, "The Sweet Smell of Success Isn't All That Sweet" suggests that the author isn't overly impressed with the conventional attitudes toward success.

Skim to Get the Gist of the Article   Sometimes you can just read the introductory and concluding paragraphs and the topic sentences (often the first or last sentences of paragraphs) to get the overall meaning of the article. Other times you will need to read the whole essay quickly. In your first reading, you can skim the more difficult sections without trying to understand them fully. Just try to get an idea of the essay's main thrust, the key ideas that support it, and the ways that they are organized.

Make Connections   When you've finished skimming the essay, think about what you have learned, and then express it in your own words. Until you can state its essence in your own words, you don't really understand what you've read, and you will be unlikely to remember it. Then make connections between the ideas.

Go back and underline the thesis statement, or, if there isn't one, try to formulate one in your own words. Identify what you already know about the topic, and examine your personal connection with the topic. You will read more effectively if you can connect what you read to your own knowledge and interests. Finally, jot down questions that the first reading raises in your mind.

Reading Activities

1. Using the author biography statement at the beginning of the article "The Appeal of the Androgynous Man" (page 8), identify what you can about the author's background, interests, and biases.
2. Before reading, write what you expect to be the essay's main idea, based on the title.
3. After skimming the essay, identify the main points of the essay and the thesis. Jot down at least two questions you have at the end of your first quick reading.

Second Readings

If you find the material difficult, or if thorough comprehension is essential, a second or even third reading may be necessary. On the second reading, you read more slowly than the first reading so that you can carefully absorb the writer's ideas.

Read Carefully and Actively   Read at a pace suitable to the material. Underline significant topic sentences as well as other key sentences and ideas or facts that you find important, but keep in mind that underlining in itself doesn't ensure comprehension. Restating the ideas in your own words is more effective. Depending on your purposes, you may also want to write down the main points in your own words or jot down ideas in the margins. As you proceed, examine the supporting sentences to see how well they back up the main idea. Keep an eye out for how the essay fits together.

Consider Reading as a Kind of Conversation with the Text   Develop the habit of asking questions about facts, reasons, ideas—practically anything in the essay. Jot down your queries and their answers in the margins. (On page 12, you can see how a student interacted with the first page of Amy Gross's essay, "The Appeal of the Androgynous Man.") Good writers anticipate questions and answer them somewhere in the essay. Moreover, because you have posed the questions yourself, you are more likely to see the connections in the text. If the author hasn't answered your questions anywhere in the essay, then you have discovered some weaknesses in the writing and research.

Master Unfamiliar Words   At times, unfamiliar words can hinder your grasp of the material. Whenever you encounter a new word, circle it, use context to help gauge its meaning, check the dictionary for the exact meaning, and then record the meaning in the margins or some other convenient place. If the writing is peppered with words you don't know, you may have to read the whole piece to figure out its general drift, then look up key words, and finally reread the material.

Take Conscious Steps to Understand Difficult Material   When the ideas of a single section prove difficult, write down the points of those sections you do understand. Then experiment by stating in your own words different interpretations of the problem section to see which one best fits the writing as a whole.

Sometimes large sections or entire texts are extremely difficult to understand. Use these strategies to improve your comprehension:

- State the ideas that are easier for you to understand and use them to unlock more difficult (but not unintelligible) meanings in related sections. Save the most difficult sections until last. But don't assume that you have to understand everything completely. Some works take a lifetime to fully understand.
- Discuss the essay with other students who are reading it.
- Read simpler material on the topic to get a basic knowledge of the topic.
- Ask your instructor for help. He or she may help you find background material that will make the selection easier to understand.

Pull the Entire Essay Together   Whenever you finish a major section of a lengthy essay, express your sense of what it means. Say it out loud or write it down. If you have difficulty seeing connections between the ideas, try representing them visually. You might make an outline that states the main points followed by subpoints. For a comparison paper, you might create a table with the main points of the comparison side by side. In addition, you can draw a diagram, list chronological steps, or write out main facts.

You can also use special techniques to strengthen your grasp of material that you may need to remember for a long time. Try restating the main points a couple of days after the second reading to test your retention. Sometimes it is helpful to explain the material to a sympathetic listener; then, if anything has become hazy or slipped your mind, reread the appropriate section(s). But if you must learn the material very thoroughly, make up a test and give it to yourself.

Mastering Reading Problems

Master the Problems That Interfere with Reading   If your environment is too noisy, if you are too tired, or if you have something on your mind, you can have difficulty reading. Do your reading at the time of day when you are most alert. Be sure you are in a well-lit environment that allows you to concentrate. Try to be rested and comfortable. If you get tired, take a short break or go for a short walk. If something else is bothering you, try to resolve the distraction or put it out of your mind. To avoid boredom, read more actively by connecting the topic to your interests and goals.

If you have extensive problems with your course reading, ask for help. Most universities offer courses in reading and provide tutors and workshops. Higher education usually requires a lot of reading, so take the steps necessary to become the most effective reader possible.

EXERCISE

Reading Activities

1. Reread "The Appeal of the Androgynous Man." Write more questions and notes in the margin as you deepen your understanding of the main points.

2. Create a table with two columns comparing the author's points about the "all-man" and those about the "androgynous man."

3. Find three difficult or unusual words in the essay. Determine their meaning from the context before checking them in a dictionary.

4. Try explaining the main ideas of the article to a friend or roommate.

Reading to Critique

In college, you usually read not only to understand but also to evaluate what you read. Your instructors want to know what you think about what you've read. Often you are asked whether you agree or disagree with a writer's argument. Sometimes you are asked to write an explicit critique of what you have read.

Your instructors want to see if you can distinguish facts and well-supported arguments from opinions and assumptions. Merely because information and ideas are in print does not mean that they are true or acceptable. For example, an essay might have faulty logic, unreasonable ideas, suspect facts, or unreliable authorities, despite its professional look. Don't hesitate to dispute the writer's information. Ask yourself these questions:

- Does the main point of the essay match your experience or prior learning about this subject?
- Does the evidence support the claim?
- Do the ideas appear reasonable?
- Do other works contradict these claims? Has the author omitted other pieces of evidence that might contradict the main points?
- Do the ideas connect in a logical way?

By knowing the principles of argumentation and various reasoning fallacies, you can critique any piece of writing.

EXERCISE

Reading Activities *Prepare your critique of "The Appeal of the Androgynous Man" by doing the following:*

1. Identify where and how the claims fail to match your experience.
2. Indicate where the evidence does not support the claims.
3. Indicate at least three places where the ideas do not appear reasonable.
4. Identify any evidence that seems to contradict the author's claims.
5. Evaluate whether the ideas connect in a logical way.

Reading Assignments Carefully

Many students could get better grades by simply reading their assignments more carefully. In assignments, instructors often indicate possible topics, suggest additional readings, identify the kinds of information that should and **should not** be included, set expectations on style and format, and establish procedures for the assignment such as the due date. You should read the assignment several times. Carefully note any specifications on topic, audience, organizational strategy, or style and format. Be sure to jot down procedures, such as due dates, in an assignment log or your calendar. Do not make assumptions. If you are not clear about a part of the assignment, ask your instructor.

Below is a very specific assignment; read it over carefully to determine what it requires.

OBJECTIVE DESCRIPTION SHORT ASSIGNMENT (50 POINTS)

Typed final draft following the class format guide is due in class September 12. This assignment page should be turned in with your completed description:

> The corner of Perry and King Street, near the Starr building, has been the scene of a terrible accident. The insurance company has asked you to write a brief objective description (approximately two pages double spaced) of the intersection for a report for possible use in court. Your description should not try to take a position about the relative danger of the intersection but rather provide as clear a picture as possible of the situation. The description should include the arrangement of the streets including the number of lanes, the businesses located immediately around the intersection, traffic and pedestrian flow, and the timing of the lights and the effect of that timing on traffic.

Checklist:

The description should:

1. Provide the general location of the intersection.
2. Indicate the streets' traffic function—i.e., major route from 131 into downtown Big Rapids.
3. Describe the actual roads.
4. Identify the businesses and their locations.
5. Describe traffic and pedestrian flow.
6. Detail the timing of the lights.
7. Maintain objective language.
8. Use clear, nontechnical language.

The assignment specifies the topic (a specific intersection), an audience (a court of law and an insurance company), key elements that are required as part of the description, a general style of writing (objective without taking a stance), and procedures including a deadline and format constraints. Clearly a short paper about the accident would not be acceptable since the assigned topic is the actual structure of the intersection. A style of writing that stressed the "horribly short lights that force students to scurry across like mice in front of a cat" would lose points since it takes a position and is not objective. Any description that left out any of the required elements (such as the timing of the lights) would also lose points.

Reading As a Writer

When you write, you can use reading as a springboard for improving your writing. Reading about the views of others, their experiences, and the information others present often deepens your understanding of yourself, your relationships, and your surroundings. In turn, this broadened perspective can supply you with writing ideas. When you get an idea from your reading, it's helpful to record possibilities by jotting down your thoughts or summarizing what you have read. You can also write down specific ideas, facts, and perhaps even a few particularly interesting quotations that you may want to use later. Be sure to record the source so that you can document it properly in order to avoid plagiarism.

When you read several sources that explore the same topic or related topics, you may notice connections among their ideas. Since these connections can be fertile ground for a paper of your own, don't neglect to record them. Once you have jotted down these ideas, circle or label the ideas they connect to. You can also draw lines linking different thoughts to each other and back to the main point. Then express your view of how these ideas fit together as a thesis statement. Interacting with multiple sources and using their ideas to advance the purpose of your writing is a form of synthesis. When you synthesize ideas into a new paper, review your information, determine the points you want to make, and experiment until you find the order that works best. As you write, use the material from your sources, but be careful to credit the authors properly in order to avoid plagiarism.

You can also learn new techniques and strategies from other writers. If you find an organizational pattern or a style you like, study the writer's technique. Perhaps you can use it yourself. Similarly, observe when a piece of writing fails and try to determine why.

EXERCISE

Reading Activities

1. Identify at least two strategies used in "The Appeal of the Androgynous Man" that you would find useful.
2. Identify at least two phrases that you found effective.
3. Identify at least two ideas that sparked ideas you could use in your own writing.

AMY GROSS

Does she favour androgynous men? What kind of appeal?

both male and female in one

The Appeal of the Androgynous Man

She will give a woman's perspective. She writes for and edits women's magazines.

Amy Gross, a native of Brooklyn, New York, earned a sociology degree at Connecticut College. Upon graduation, she entered the world of fashion publishing and has held writing or editorial positions at various magazines, including Talk, Mademoiselle, Good Housekeeping, Elle, *and* Mirabella. *She is the editor-in-chief of Oprah Winfrey's* O Magazine. *In our selection, which first appeared in* Mademoiselle *in 1976, Gross compares androgynous men favourably to macho "all-men."*

Seems as if she is going to talk about the advantages of androgynous men as compared to other men. Sees them as better.

1 James Dean was my first androgynous man.[1] I figured I could talk to him. He was anguished and I was 12, so we had a lot in common. With only a few exceptions, all the men I have liked or loved have been a certain kind of man: a kind who doesn't play football or watch the games on Sunday, who doesn't tell dirty jokes featuring broads or chicks, who is not contemptuous of conversations that are philosophically speculative, introspective, or otherwise

---

[1]James Dean (1931–1955) was a 1950s film star who gained fame for his portrayals of restless, defiant young men.

foolish according to the other kind of man. He is more self-amused, less inflated, more quirky, vulnerable and responsive than the other sort (the other sort, I'm visualizing as the guys on TV who advertise deodorant in the locker room). He is more like me than the other sort. He is what social scientists and feminists would call androgynous: having the characteristics of both male and female.

Attempt to counter stereotype? Can't androgynous men also be effeminate?

2   Now the first thing I want you to know about the androgynous man is that he is neither effeminate nor hermaphroditic. All his primary and secondary sexual characteristics are in order and I would say he's all-man, but that is just what he is not. He is more than all-man.

both male and female sex organs

3   The merely all-man man, for one thing, never walks to the grocery store unless the little woman is away visiting her mother with the kids, or is in the hospital having a kid, or there is no little woman. All-men men don't know how to shop in a grocery store unless it is to buy a 6-pack and some pretzels. Their ideas of nutrition expand beyond a 6-pack and pretzels only to take in steak, potatoes, scotch or rye whiskey, and maybe a wad of cake or apple pie. All-men men have absolutely no taste in food, art, books, movies, theatre, dance, how to live, what are good questions, what is funny, or anything else I care about. It's not exactly that the all-man's man is an uncouth illiterate. He may be educated, well-mannered, and on a first-name basis with fine wines. One all-man man I knew was a handsome individual who gave the impression of being gentle, affectionate, and sensitive. He sat and ate dinner one night while I was doing something endearingly feminine at the sink. At one point, he mutely held up his glass to indicate in a primitive, even ape-like, way his need for a refill. This was in 1967, before Women's Liberation. Even so, I was disturbed. Not enough to break the glass over his handsome head, not even enough to mutely indicate the whereabouts of the refrigerator, but enough to remember that moment in all its revelatory clarity. No androgynous man would ever brutishly expect to be waited on without even a "please." (With a "please," maybe.)

Suggests "all-men" men reject behaviours and interests they consider feminine, but isn't she stereotyping? Are all these men like this? She seems to be exaggerating.

4   The brute happened to be a doctor—not a hard hat—and, to all appearances, couth. But he had bought the whole superman package, complete with that fragile beast, the male ego. The androgynous man arrives with a male ego too, but his is not as imperialistic. It doesn't invade every area of his life and person. Most activities and thoughts have nothing to do with masculinity or femininity. The androgynous man knows this. The all-man man doesn't. He must keep a constant guard against anything even vaguely feminine (i.e., "sissy") rising up in him. It must be a terrible strain.

5   Male chauvinism is an irritation, but the real problem I have with the all-man man is that it's hard for me to talk to him. He's alien to me, and for this I'm at least half to blame. As his interests have not carried him into the sissy, mine have never taken me very far into the typically masculine terrains of sports, business and finance, politics, cars, boats and machines. But blame or no blame, the reality is that it is almost as difficult for me to connect with him as it would be to link up with an Arab shepherd or Bolivian sandalmaker. There's a similar culture gap.

6   It seems to me that the most masculine men usually end up with the most feminine women. Maybe they like extreme polarity. I like polarity myself, but the poles have to be within earshot. As I've implied, I'm very big on talking. I fall in love for at least three hours with anyone who engages me in a real conversation. I'd rather a man point out a paragraph in a book—wanting to share it with me—than bring me flowers. I'd rather a man ask what I think than tell me I look pretty. (Women who are very pretty and accustomed to hearing that they are pretty may feel differently.) My experience is that all-men men read books I don't want to see paragraphs of, and don't really give a damn what I or any woman would think about most issues so long as she looks pretty. They have a very limited use for women. I suspect they don't really like us. The androgynous man likes women as much or as little as he likes anyone.

7   Another difference between the all-man man and the androgynous man is that the first is not a star in the creativity department. If your image of the creative male accessorizes him with a beret, smock and artist's palette, you will not believe the all-man man has been seriously short-changed. But if you allow as how creativity is a talent for freedom, associated with imagination, wit, empathy, unpredictability, and receptivity to new impressions and connections, then you will certainly pity the dull, thick-skinned, rigid fellow in whom creativity sets no fires.

8   Nor is the all-man man so hot when it comes to sensitivity. He may be true-blue in the trenches, but if you are troubled, you'd be wasting your time trying to milk comfort from the all-man man.

9   This is not blind prejudice. It is enlightened prejudice. My biases were confirmed recently by a psychologist named Sandra Lipsetz Bem, a professor at Stanford University. She brought to attention the fact that high masculinity in males (and high femininity in females) has been "consistently correlated with lower overall intelligence and lower creativity." Another psychologist, Donald W. MacKinnon, director of the Institute of Personality Assessment and Research at the University of California in Berkeley, found that "creative males give more expression to the feminine side of their nature than do less creative men. . . . [They] score relatively high on femininity, and this despite the fact that, as a group, they do not present an effeminate appearance or give evidence of increased homosexual interests or experiences. Their elevated scores on femininity indicate rather an openness to their feelings and emotions, a sensitive intellect and understanding self-awareness and wide-ranging interests including many which in the American culture are thought of as more feminine. . . . "

10   Dr. Bem ran a series of experiments on college students who had been categorized as masculine, feminine, or androgynous. In three tests of the degree of nurturance—warmth and caring—the masculine men scored painfully low (painfully for anyone stuck with a masculine man, that is). In one of those experiments, all the students were asked to listen to a "troubled talker"—a person who was not neurotic but simply lonely, supposedly new in town and feeling like an outsider. The masculine men were the least supportive, responsive or humane. "They lacked the ability to express warmth, playfulness

and concern," Bem concluded. (She's giving them the benefit of the doubt. It's possible the masculine men didn't express those qualities because they didn't possess them.)

11 The androgynous man, on the other hand, having been run through the same carnival of tests, "performs spectacularly. He shuns no behavior just because our culture happens to label it as female and his competence crosses both the instrumental [getting the job done, the problem solved] and the expressive [showing a concern for the welfare of others, the harmony of the group] domains. Thus, he stands firm in his opinion, he cuddles kittens and bounces babies and he has a sympathetic ear for someone in distress."

12 Well, a great mind, a sensitive and warm personality are fine in their place, but you are perhaps skeptical of the gut appeal of the androgynous man. As a friend, maybe, you'd like an androgynous man. For a sexual partner, though, you'd prefer a jock. There's no arguing chemistry, but consider the jock for a moment. He competes on the field, whatever his field is, and bed is just one more field to him: another opportunity to perform, another fray. Sensuality is for him candy to be doled out as lure. It is a ration whose flow is cut off at the exact point when it has served its purpose—namely, to elicit your willingness to work out on the field with him.

13 Highly masculine men need to believe their sexual appetite is far greater than a woman's (than a nice woman's). To them, females must be seduced: Seduction is a euphemism for a power play, a con job. It pits man against woman (or woman against man). The jock believes he must win you over, incite your body to rebel against your better judgment: in other words—conquer you.

14 The androgynous man is not your opponent but your teammate. He does not seduce: he invites. Sensuality is a pleasure for him. He's not quite so goal-oriented. And to conclude, I think I need only remind you here of his greater imagination, his wit and empathy, his unpredictability, and his receptivity to new impressions and connections.

Writing about What You Read

Often in college, you are asked to write about what you read. Sometimes this assignment is a major research paper. However, sometimes you have to write shorter summaries and critiques. Though similar to the research paper, these shorter assignments focus on testing your ability to understand what you read.

Writing a Summary

A summary states the main points of an essay in your own words. A good summary lets someone who hasn't read the essay understand what it says. A summary can be one or more paragraphs. It should

- provide a context for the essay,
- introduce the author of the essay, and
- state the thesis.

These first three elements often form the introduction of a multiparagraph summary. Then

- state the main points of the essay (sometimes but not always based on the topic sentences), and
- conclude by summarizing the author's final point.

To prepare to write a summary, follow the steps in effective reading. Briefly outline the main points that make the writing easier. But avoid using the author's exact wording unless you use quotation marks. Also, don't interject your own views. A summary should reflect only the author's ideas.

A Sample Single-Paragraph Summary of "The Appeal of the Androgynous Man"

What kind of man should appeal to women? According to Amy Gross, the editor-in-chief of *O Magazine*, in "The Appeal of the Androgynous Man," the ideal is the "androgynous man," a man who shares the personality characteristics of both male and female. To make her point, Amy Gross contrasts the all-man man and the androgynous man. She believes that the all-man man does not share in activities like shopping, has no taste in the arts, is imperialistic, resists anything feminine, and is interested only in exclusively male topics. Worse, she points to studies that show that more masculine men are less creative. Further, she argues that the all-man man tends to see women as something to conquer rather than as partners. The androgynous man, by comparison, is very different. He does not resist things that are feminine and so shares in domestic activities, is comfortable with the arts, and can share interests with women. He is shown by studies to be more creative. Further, according to Gross, "The androgynous man is not your opponent but your teammate." As a result, she concludes that the androgynous man has the qualities that women should really look for in a man.

Writing a Critique

Often instructors ask you to give your views on an essay, indicating where you agree and disagree with the author's position. Keep in mind that you can agree with some points and still disagree with others. A critique combines a summary of the article with your thoughtful reaction. Most critiques consist of several paragraphs. A critique usually includes

- a description of the context of the essay
- an introduction of the author
- a statement of the essay's thesis
- the thesis for your critique
- a summary of the essay's main points
- a statement of the points with which you disagree
- a statement with reasons and evidence for your disagreement
- a conclusion

You are well prepared to write a critique if you follow the steps for reading effectively and reading critically.

A Sample Multiparagraph Critique of "The Appeal of the Androgynous Man"

1   What kind of man should appeal to women? According to Amy Gross, the editor-in-chief of *O Magazine*, in "The Appeal of the Androgynous Man," the ideal is the "androgynous man," a man who shares the personality characteristics typically considered masculine and feminine. But matters are not so simple. Amy Gross falsely divides men into two stereotyped categories. In fact, real men are much more complex.

2   To make her point, Amy Gross contrasts the all-man man and the androgynous man. She states that the all-man man does not share in activities like shopping, has no taste in the arts, is imperialistic, resists anything feminine, and is interested only in exclusively male topics. In addition, she points to studies that show that more masculine men are less creative. Further, she argues that the all-man man tends to see women as something to conquer rather than as partners. The androgynous man, by comparison, is very different. He does not resist things that are feminine and so shares in domestic activities, is comfortable with the arts, and can share interests with women. He is shown by studies to be more creative. Further, according to Gross, "The androgynous man is not your opponent but your teammate." As a result, she concludes that the androgynous man has the qualities that women should really look for in a man.

3   Gross would be correct if the all-man male were as she described him, because he would truly be undesirable. No woman should want a partner who takes her for granted, doesn't share her interests, or treats her simply as someone to conquer. But is that really what men are like? My brother plays football and loves to watch it on television. He also hunts and fishes. However, that isn't all he does. He plays with kittens, loves to cook, plays the guitar and sings, and secretly likes "chick flicks." As far as I can tell, he treats his girlfriend well. He seems genuinely concerned about her, will spend hours shopping with her, goes to events that interest her, and generally seems sensitive to her needs. Is he an "all-man man" or an "androgynous man"? Equally a man can write poetry, love Jane Austen, cook gourmet meals, and still take women for granted.

4   Gross presents evidence from psychological studies that show that more masculine men are less creative than more feminine men. But she doesn't provide enough evidence for the reader to assess the studies. How did the researchers actually measure masculinity and femininity? How many people were tested? What did they count as creativity? Certainly, the author, who was writing in the mid-70s, would have been influenced by the first wave of feminism, and by the rhetoric of the women's liberation movement. At this time, people were just beginning to question financial and social inequalities between men and women. However, much has changed since then. What was relevant in Gross's time is not necessarily relevant today.

5   Moreover, the fundamental mistake Gross makes is that she believes that women should select men according to types. They shouldn't. Women should date, love, and marry individual men. As a result, a woman should really be concerned about whether the man shares her interests, treats her well, has qualities she can love, and will be faithful. Where the man fits in a chart is far less important than the kind of man he is, regardless of whether he is "androgynous."

CHAPTER 2

Critical Thinking and Recognizing Fallacies

CONTENTS

Every aspect of our thinking is strongly affected by the fact that each of us sees experience from our own point of view—that is, we see experience through our unique frame of reference. Our frame of reference is composed of the intellectual and emotional knowledge and experience we each have accumulated throughout life. It's through the frame of reference that we understand or misunderstand new information. If, for instance, a fourteenth-century knight from King Arthur's court were suddenly to appear on a Los Angeles street corner today and a red Porsche roared up, he might perceive it to be a strange red beast and try to kill it with his sword. He couldn't possibly recognize a Porsche for what it is because automobiles would be outside his frame of reference.

By way of another example, imagine a human being who has been isolated in a room since birth without any knowledge of the outside world. On his eighteenth birthday, a television set is wheeled into his room and turned on. His frame of reference would not have the necessary information to process the experience. He might be delighted, completely lost, or perhaps even terrified at first. You can probably understand how essential your frame of reference is to your own perception by recalling experiences you now understand that you could not understand when you were younger because you lacked the necessary knowledge.

Taken from *Four in One: Rhetoric, Reader, Research Guide, and Handbook*, Fifth Edition, by Edward A. Dornan and Robert Dees.

At one time the traditional institutions of family, school, and church were the dominant institutions in people's lives. For better or worse, parents, teachers, and clergy members shaped personal and cultural perceptions by presenting a set of consistent values. Today, the mass media—television, radio, music, movies, newspapers, magazines, books, and the Internet—exert a powerful force in shaping what people think and how they behave.

As a result, throughout life you will have to sort through an onslaught of media images and public information, especially misleading information designed to influence your every choice. That's why it's important to have a rich and accurate frame of reference. In fact, false and inaccurate information in your frame of reference can be worse than no information at all. Remember that once white-skinned people believed that black-skinned people were mentally inferior (and thus were better off as slaves), that a woman's place was in the home, and that Asian countries would tumble into communism like falling dominos if the U.S. military withdrew from Vietnam.

Expanding your frame of reference is an important part of becoming a critical thinker. Keep this in mind: Thinking is as natural to all of us as flying is to birds or swimming is to fish, but thinking critically doesn't come naturally. Thinking critically must be learned.

Profile of a Critical Thinker

Critical thinkers share several key traits. Generally, critical thinkers vigorously pursue knowledge, especially knowledge that will help them make appropriate decisions for themselves. Because they are intellectually daring, critical thinkers tend to have a skeptical frame of mind, or as some might say, an attitude, which we like to characterize as a desire to think beyond the obvious.

Critical Thinkers Interrogate Cultural Values

Critical thinkers relentlessly question the dominant values of their culture. Every culture embraces what it considers normal, which is often referred to as *conventional wisdom*. But what is "normal"? It varies from age to age and from culture to culture. For example, it was once normal to believe that astrology could foretell a person's future. It was once normal to believe the Earth was the center of the universe and that its surface was flat, like a tabletop. It was once normal for children to work in fields and factories from dawn to dusk (and it still is in some parts of the world). And it was once normal for men to be paid more than women for the same work (and still seems to be in some professions).

Critical Thinkers Engage in Self-Analysis

Critical thinkers look into themselves to discover what they do and do not believe. When faced with making a decision, they objectively examine their values and then alter or stick with them, as appropriate. They also know that powerful experiences might have two levels of meaning: The *manifest* meaning, which they can understand intellectually, and the *latent* meaning, which influences them emotionally. In any case, self-analysis helps them make difficult decisions.

Critical Thinkers Keep an Open Mind

Critical thinkers are willing to consider information that opposes their own position. They remain objective while trying to understand why they react to a person or an experience in a certain way. They accept that their first reactions are tentative. When making a decision, a critical thinker might ask: Am I being overly influenced by a friend? A celebrity? A politician? A teacher? Parents? An unexamined value? Or perhaps by the emotional seduction of advertising or political rhetoric? By keeping an open mind, critical thinkers are always willing to modify their beliefs based on new information.

Critical Thinkers Build Consensus

Critical thinkers make an effort to "walk in the other person's shoes"; that is, they work at understanding other points of view. Although they might disagree with someone's beliefs, they don't concentrate on the disagreements. Instead, they attempt to keep communication open by identifying common ground to build agreement.

Become a Critical Thinker

Being a critical thinker doesn't mean conducting intellectual warfare by attacking the beliefs and opinions of everyone you encounter. It does mean approaching life thoughtfully with thinking skills that help you analyze, interpret, and evaluate information. You can begin to develop these skills by learning and employing several fundamental concepts.

Distinguish Between Facts and Opinions

Before you can evaluate information, you need to know whether the information is factual. A factual statement is one that can be verified through research, experiment, or observation. For example,

> Lance Armstrong won the Tour de France for the seventh time on July 24, 2005.
> American astronauts landed on the moon during the summer of 1969.
> Rock climbers run the risk that a rope will break.

All the above statements are simple, indisputable facts. Who would deny them? But not all facts are as clear as these statements. As a critical thinker, when you encounter murkier statements, you must look a little deeper by questioning how a fact was established. You might even consider the accuracy or the method used to determine its truth.

Statements are often backed up by *statistics*, that is, numerical facts. For example, the average American uses three gallons of paint a week. This adds up to more than a billion gallons of paint used in the United States every year, enough to fill a lake twenty feet deep, four miles long, and one mile wide.

Statistics are sometimes referred to as "alleged facts." An alleged fact can be misleading or intentionally deceitful. For example, the statement "The amount of junk mail Americans receive in one day could produce enough energy to heat 250,000 homes" may be a fact, but it is misleading. How would people produce energy from burning junk mail? The statement that an average American uses three gallons of paint a week is also misleading. Many Americans never lift a paintbrush, but the auto industry uses tens of thousands of gallons of paint every week.

You should always question the validity of facts when someone has something to gain from them. For decades, tobacco companies claimed that smoking was not unhealthful. They supported their position with scientific tests to prove they were right, but tobacco companies were funding the tests, thus controlling the outcome. Years later, objective research conducted by scientists independent of the tobacco companies proved the opposite—that smoking is a serious health hazard, not just to smokers but to those around them as well. As a critical thinker, you'll always keep your guard up. If a self-interested party is making a statement, then the statement is suspect.

Evaluating statements of opinion is tougher than determining the accuracy of facts. An *opinion*, unlike a fact, can't be objectively verified. Statements of opinion are statements that someone might believe but are not necessarily accurate.

A *preference* is an opinion that expresses personal taste—that is, what someone likes or dislikes. Such statements as *"CSI: Crime Scene Investigation* is my favorite television show" and "Dancing is a great exercise" express preferences, not facts. How can someone be wrong for liking a television show or a social activity? It makes no sense to challenge anyone's taste.

A controversial *judgment*, on the other hand, should be challenged. A judgment goes beyond personal preference. It is an opinion with a basis for support. Preferences can often be restated as judgments. For example, the statement *"CSI: Crime Scene Investigation* realistically portrays how crimes are solved through laboratory research" can be analyzed by comparing crime investigation as represented in the television series to actual crime investigation practices. The statement "An hour of dancing offers a more sustained aerobic workout than an hour of walking" creates the opportunity to compare the physical demands of dancing and walking. Both statements clearly reflect opinions that can be evaluated, though they are not very controversial.

Identify Assumptions Buried in Information

Assumptions are unstated beliefs that underlie opinions. When you closely examine an opinion, you will find that it usually rests on one or more assumptions, whether false or valid. For instance,

> AIDS is nature's way of punishing gay men and women for their sexual orientation.

Several assumptions are at work in this brief statement. First, it assumes that nature is a conscious entity and dispenses punishment. It also assumes that gay men and women are guilty in some respect and deserve to be punished. Finally, it assumes that sexual orientation is a choice, not a genetic given. Once the assumptions behind this statement are revealed, it loses its power.

Analyze Inferences for Reliability

An *inference* is an opinion based on a set of facts. It is a statement about what is not known based on what is known. A detective may infer from the evidence that a suspect is guilty. An arson investigator may infer from the ruins how a fire was ignited. A poker player may infer that an opponent has a better hand based on the opponent's betting patterns.

Inferences can be carefully or carelessly made. They may be made based on years of experience or made on a wild hunch. Inferences can be reliable or unreliable, that is, right or wrong. For example, suppose the following facts are true:

1. Your college classes are overcrowded.

2. No new instructors will be hired because of a budget shortfall.

3. A new apartment complex with 300 apartments is opening up before fall classes begin.

From these facts you may reasonably infer that in the fall semester your college classes will be even more crowded than they are now, and therefore there will be less individual attention from instructors.

But, as with all inferences, this one should be subjected to critical examination, which might reveal the following:

1. This year's graduating class is three times the size of any other graduating class, and the freshman class is the smallest of any entering class.

2. The college has not finalized the fall budget, so the shortfall is tentative.

3. The apartments are for senior citizens, not for college students.

These additional facts show that the original inference is unreliable.

Inference is closely related to *implication*. When someone says, "Most of the people who have lawns in this neighborhood are white and speak educated English, but most of the people who mow the lawns are brown and speak no English," he is implying that there is an injustice in this situation. When we hear such a statement, we infer that indeed there is an injustice. A speaker implies and a listener infers (and the two words are frequently misused).

Verify the Reliability of Interpretations

An *interpretation* examines facts and opinions to make sense of them. An interpretation is always speculative. It is often an attempt to think beyond the obvious to find a deeper meaning, the latent meaning. Personal experience, literary works, and cultural, political, and historical events often supply raw material for interpretation, and they can produce opposing interpretations.

For example, the Japanese military's surprise bombing of Pearl Harbor on December 7, 1941, took the United States into World War II. Later, some historians maintained that President Roosevelt had advance knowledge of the attack but did not warn our military. Their accusation was based mainly on the interpretation of one suspicious fact: By the summer of 1940, the United States had cracked Japan's top-secret diplomatic code, enabling intelligence agencies to monitor coded messages to and from Tokyo. Furthermore, they interpreted this to mean that President Roosevelt wanted to use the attack as a reason to involve the United States in World War II. To counter this interpretation, however, other historians have pointed out that the code-breaking intelligence could not have exposed the attack on Pearl Harbor because Japan sent no messages, coded or not coded, about the planned attack.

As the example shows, the reliability of an interpretation is only as good as the information it is based on. If the information is unreliable, then the interpretation will be unreliable, too.

Evaluate Information with Care

Generally, information will consist of facts, statistics, expert opinions, and personal examples. When evaluating the value of information, keep these five guidelines in mind:

1. Information should be relevant and should not be slanted to support someone's interests. Facts should be verifiable, and statistics should be current and come from independent sources.

2. Information should be complete; that is, it should include a full range of experiences and opinions. Expert opinions and personal observations should be typical, not exceptional.

3. Information should be sufficient. Generally, there should be enough information for a complete examination of the subject.

4. Information should be qualified. Beware of words like *all*, *always*, and *never*. Instead, information should be presented with words like *most*, *many*, *often*, *frequently*, *probably*, *infrequently*, and *seldom*.

5. Information must be accurate. Inaccurate information is misleading information.

Recognize Fallacies

Reasoning depends less on proving a claim than it does on finding evidence for that claim that readers will accept as valid. Logical fallacies, or kinds of faulty reasoning patterns, reflect a failure to provide sufficient evidence for a claim made by the writer.

Fallacies of logic

Begging the question	*Politicians are inherently dishonest because no honest person would run for public office.* The fallacy of begging the question occurs when the claim is restated and passed off as evidence.
Either–or	*Either we eliminate the regulation of businesses or else profits will suffer.* The either–or fallacy suggests that there are only two choices in a complex situation. Rarely, if ever, is this the case. (In this example, the writer ignores the fact that Enron was unregulated and went bankrupt.)
Hasty generalization	*We have been in a drought for three years; that's a sure sign of climate change.* A hasty generalization is a broad claim made on the basis of a few occurrences. Climate cycles occur regularly over spans of a few years; climate trends must be observed over centuries.
Non sequitur	*A university that can raise a billion dollars from alumni should not have to raise tuition.* A *non sequitur* (which is a Latin term meaning "it does not follow") ties together two unrelated ideas. In this case, the argument fails to recognize that the money for capital campaigns is often donated for special purposes such as athletic facilities and is not part of a university's general revenue.
Oversimplification	*No one would run stop signs if we had a mandatory death penalty for doing it.* This claim may be true, but the argument would be unacceptable to most citizens. More complex, if less definitive, solutions are called for.

Post hoc fallacy	*The stock market goes down when the AFC wins the Super Bowl in even years.* The post hoc fallacy (from the Latin post hoc ergo hoc, which means "after this, therefore this") assumes that things that follow in time have a causal relationship.
Rationalization	*I could have finished my paper on time if my printer had been working.* People frequently come up with excuses and weak explanations for their own and others' behaviour that often avoid actual causes.
Slippery slope	*If we decriminalize medical marijuana, then before long, everyone will be shooting up heroin on the street corners.* The slippery slope fallacy maintains that one thing inevitably causes something else (more serious) to happen.

Fallacies of emotion and language

Bandwagon appeals	*It doesn't matter if I copy a paper off the Web because everyone else does.* This argument suggests that everyone is doing it, so why shouldn't you? But on close examination, it may be that everyone really isn't doing it—and in any case, it may not be the right thing to do.
Name calling	Name calling is frequent in politics and among competing groups (*radical, terrorist, racist, fascist, separatist*). Unless these terms are carefully defined, they are meaningless.
Polarization	*All environmentalists are radicals.* Polarization, like name-calling, exaggerates positions and groups by representing them as extreme and divisive.
Straw man	*Environmentalists won't be satisfied until nobody is ever allowed to cut down a tree.* A straw man argument is a diversionary tactic that sets up another's position in a way that can be easily rejected. In fact, only a small percentage of environmentalists would make an argument even close to this one.

Write now Analyze fallacies in opinion writing

Examine writing that expresses opinions: blogs, discussion boards, editorials, advocacy websites, letters to the editor, or editorial pages of a local/national newspaper. Critically examine the opinion and identify any possible fallacies.

Select the example that has the clearest fallacy. Explain (in writing) the cause of the fallacy.

Part 2:
Readings

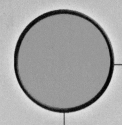

Don't You Think It's Time to Start Thinking?
Northrop Frye

Northrop Frye (1912–1991), one of Canada's most distinguished scholars, was reared in New Brunswick, and after attending school in Canada, received his MA from Oxford University, in England (1940). In 1939 Frye became a professor at the University of Toronto, where he wrote and taught until his death. His interests were literary criticism and school curriculum; his books include On Education *and* Myth and Metaphor. *The following essay insists that thinking happens only when a person writes down ideas "in the right words."*

1 A student often leaves high school today without any sense of language as a structure.

2 He may also have the idea that reading and writing are elementary skills that he mastered in childhood, never having grasped the fact that there are differences in levels of reading and writing as there are in mathematics between short division and integral calculus.

3 Yet, in spite of his limited verbal skills, he firmly believes that he can think, that he has ideas, and that if he is just given the opportunity to express them he will be all right. Of course, when you look at what he's written, you find it doesn't make any sense. When you tell him this he is devastated.

4 Part of his confusion here stems from the fact that we use the word "think" in so many bad, punning ways. Remember James Thurber's Walter Mitty who was always dreaming great dreams of glory. When his wife asked him what he was doing he would say, "Has it ever occurred to you that I might be thinking"?

5 But, of course, he wasn't thinking at all. Because we use it for everything our minds do, worrying, remembering, daydreaming, we imagine that thinking is something that can be achieved without any training. But again it's a matter of practice. How well we can think depends on how much of it we have already done. Most students need to be taught, very carefully and patiently, that there is no such thing as an inarticulate idea waiting to have the right words wrapped around it.

6 They have to learn that ideas do not exist until they have been incorporated into words. Until that point you don't know whether you are pregnant or just have gas on the stomach.

7 The operation of thinking is the practice of articulating ideas until they are in the right words. And we can't think at random either. We can only add one more idea to the body of something we have already thought about. Most of us spend very little time doing this, and that is why there are so few people whom we regard as having any power to articulate at all. When such a person appears in public life, like Mr. Trudeau, we tend to regard him as possessing a gigantic intellect.

"Don't You Think It's Time to Start Thinking?," by Northrop Frye from the *Toronto Star*,

A society like ours doesn't have very much interest in literacy. It is compulsory 8
to read and write because society must have docile and obedient citizens. We are
taught to read so that we can obey the traffic signs and to cipher so that we can
make out our income tax, but development of verbal competency is very much
left to the individual.

And when we look at our day-to-day existence we can see that there are strong 9
currents at work against the development of powers of articulateness. Young
adolescents today often betray a curious sense of shame about speaking articulately,
of framing a sentence with a period at the end of it.

Part of the reason for this is the powerful anti-intellectual drive which is 10
constantly present in our society. Articulate speech marks you out as an individual,
and in some settings this can be rather dangerous because people are often
suspicious and frightened of articulateness. So if you say as little as possible and
use only stereotyped, ready-made phrases you can hide yourself in the mass.

Then there are various epidemics sweeping over society which use 11
unintelligibility as a weapon to preserve the present power structure. By making
things as unintelligible as possible, to as many people as possible, you can hold the
present power structure together. Understanding and articulateness lead to its
destruction. This is the kind of thing that George Orwell was talking about, not
just in *Nineteen Eighty-Four*, but in all his work on language. The kernel of
everything reactionary and tyrannical in society is the impoverishment of the
means of verbal communication.

The vast majority of things that we hear today are prejudices and clichés, 12
simply verbal formulas that have no thought behind them but are put up as a
pretence of thinking. It is not until we realize these things conceal meaning, rather
than reveal it, that we can begin to develop our own powers of articulateness.

The teaching of humanities is, therefore, a militant job. Teachers are faced 13
not simply with a mass of misconceptions and unexamined assumptions. They
must engage in a fight to help the student confront and reject the verbal formulas
and stock responses, to convert passive acceptance into active, constructive power.
It is a fight against illiteracy and for the maturation of the mental process, for the
development of skills which once acquired will never become obsolete.

Questions about Meaning

1. Frye says that our minds can do many things besides thinking— worrying,
   remembering, and daydreaming, for example. Why does he say that these are
   not thinking?

2. What is the difference between reading to understand a traffic sign and reading
   to understand a play such as *Romeo and Juliet*? Why does Frye think that the
   distinction is so important?

3. Are the vast majority of things people hear prejudices and clichés? Frye says that
   they are and that people in power want it that way. Why does he think that this
   is true? Why does he refer to the novel *1984*?

4. In what ways are Frye's essay and message subversive?

5. Why are literacy skills so essential?

Questions about Style and Structure

1. The style of this essay is sometimes quite forceful, such as "you don't know whether you are pregnant or just have gas." Why does this kind of style help make Frye's point? What do we know about his feelings on the subject?

2. Frye uses a forceful style in this essay because he feels strongly about his subject and he wants teachers to see how important their job really is. Find words and phrases that show the power of his emotions, and explain those emotions.

The Twitter Trap

Bill Keller

The author was the Executive Editor of The New York Times from 2003 to 2011. This essay first appeared in the newspaper in 2011.

Last week my wife and I told our 13-year-old daughter she could join Facebook. Within a few hours she had accumulated 171 friends, and I felt a little as if I had passed my child a pipe of crystal meth.

I don't mean to be a spoilsport, and I don't think I'm a Luddite. I edit a newspaper that has embraced new media with creative, prizewinning gusto. I get that the Web reaches and engages a vast, global audience, that it invites participation and facilitates—up to a point—newsgathering. But before we succumb to digital idolatry, we should consider that innovation often comes at a price. And sometimes I wonder if the price is a piece of ourselves.

Joshua Foer's engrossing best seller **"Moonwalking With Einstein"** recalls one colossal example of what we trade for progress. Until the 15th century, people were taught to remember vast quantities of information. Feats of memory that would today qualify you as a freak—the ability to recite entire books—were not unheard of.

Then along came the Mark Zuckerberg of his day, Johannes Gutenberg. As we became accustomed to relying on the printed page, the work of remembering gradually fell into disuse. The capacity to remember prodigiously still exists (as Foer proved by **training himself to become a national memory champion**), but for most of us it stays parked in the garage.

Sometimes the bargain is worthwhile; I would certainly not give up the pleasures of my library for the ability to recite "Middlemarch." But Foer's book reminds us that the cognitive advance of our species is not inexorable.

My father, who was trained in engineering at M.I.T. in the slide-rule era, often lamented the way the pocket calculator, for all its convenience, diminished my generation's math skills. Many of us have discovered that navigating by G.P.S. has undermined our mastery of city streets and perhaps even impaired our innate sense of direction. Typing pretty much killed penmanship. Twitter and YouTube are nibbling away at our attention spans. And what little memory we had not already surrendered to Gutenberg we have relinquished to Google. Why remember what you can look up in seconds?

Robert Bjork, who studies **memory and learning at U.C.L.A.**, has noticed that even very smart students, conversant in the Excel spreadsheet, don't pick up patterns in data that would be evident if they had not let the program do so much of the work.

"Unless there is some actual problem solving and decision making, very little learning happens," Bjork e-mailed me. "We are not recording devices."

Foer read that Apple had hired a leading expert in heads-up display—the transparent dashboards used by pilots. He wonders whether this means that Apple is developing an **iPhone** that would not require the use of fingers on keyboards. Ultimately, Foer imagines, the commands would come straight from your cerebral cortex. (Apple refused to comment.)

10   "This is the story of the next half-century," Foer told me, "as we become effectively cyborgs."

Basically, we are outsourcing our brains to the cloud. The upside is that this frees a lot of gray matter for important pursuits like FarmVille and "Real Housewives." But my inner worrywart wonders whether the new technologies overtaking us may be eroding characteristics that are essentially human: our ability to reflect, our pursuit of meaning, genuine empathy, a sense of community connected by something deeper than snark or political affinity

The most obvious drawback of social media is that they are aggressive distractions. Unlike the virtual fireplace or that nesting pair of red-tailed hawks we have been **live-streaming on nytimes.com,** Twitter is not just an ambient presence. It demands attention and response. It is the enemy of contemplation. Every time my TweetDeck shoots a new tweet to my desktop, I experience a little dopamine spritz that takes me away from . . . from . . . wait, what was I saying?

My mistrust of social media is intensified by the ephemeral nature of these communications. They are the epitome of in-one-ear-and-out-the-other, which was my mother's trope for a failure to connect.

I'm not even sure these new instruments are genuinely "social." There is something decidedly faux about the camaraderie of Facebook, something illusory about the connectedness of Twitter. Eavesdrop on a conversation as it surges through the digital crowd, and more often than not it is reductive and redundant. Following an argument among the Twits is like listening to preschoolers quarreling: You did! Did not! Did too! Did not!

15   As a kind of masochistic experiment, the other day I **tweeted** "#TwitterMakesYouStupid. Discuss." It produced a few flashes of wit ("Give a little credit to our public schools!"); a couple of earnestly obvious points ("Depends who you follow"); some understandable speculation that my account had been hacked by a troll; a message from my wife ("I don't know if Twitter makes you stupid, but it's making you late for dinner. Come home!"); and an awful lot of nyah-nyah-nyah ("Um, wrong." "Nuh-uh!!"). Almost everyone who had anything profound to say in response to my little provocation chose to say it outside Twitter. In an actual discussion, the marshaling of information is cumulative, complication is acknowledged, sometimes persuasion occurs. In a Twitter discussion, opinions and our tolerance for others' opinions are stunted. Whether or not Twitter makes you stupid, it certainly makes some smart people *sound* stupid.

I realize I am inviting blowback from passionate Tweeters, from aging academics who stoke their charisma by overpraising every novelty and from colleagues at The Times who are refining a social-media strategy to expand the reach of our journalism. So let me be clear that Twitter is a brilliant device—a megaphone for promotion, a seine for information, a helpful organizing tool for everything from dog-lover meet-ups to revolutions. It restores serendipity to the flow of information. Though I am not much of a Tweeter and pay little attention to my Facebook account, I love to see something I've written neatly bitly'd and shared around the Twittersphere, even when I know—now, for instance—that the verdict of the crowd will be hostile.

The shortcomings of social media would not bother me awfully if I did not suspect that Facebook friendship and Twitter chatter are displacing real rapport and real conversation, just as Gutenberg's device displaced remembering. The things we may be unlearning, tweet by tweet—complexity, acuity, patience, wisdom, intimacy—are things that matter.

There is a growing library of credible digital Cassandras who have explored what new media are doing to our brains (**Nicholas Carr, Jaron Lanier, Gary Small and Gigi Vorgan, William Powers**, et al.). My own anxiety is less about the cerebrum than about the soul, and is best summed up not by a neuroscientist but by a novelist. In Meg Wolitzer's charming new tale, **"The Uncoupling,"** there is a wistful passage about the high-school cohort my daughter is about to join.

Wolitzer describes them this way: "The generation that had information, but no context. Butter, but no bread. Craving, but no longing."

Questions about Meaning

1. What did Johannes Gutenberg invent and why does Keller call him "the Mark Zuckerberg of his day"? Is Keller being ironic in making this comparison? If so, what is the effect of this irony?

2. What general point is the author making through the various examples in paragraph six?

3. What is the "trap" the title refers to? Is it associated just with Twitter?

Questions about Rhetorical Strategy and Style

1. Keller adopts a particular persona in the essay. What is it? Why do you think he adopts it? Is it effective?

2. What objection does Keller anticipate and how does he defend himself and his argument against it?

3. Why might Keller have chosen to conclude the essay not by quoting one of the "digital Cassandras" he mentions but a novelist? What does the quotation itself mean and is it effective?

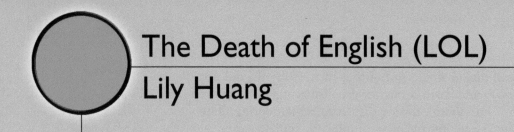

The Death of English (LOL)
Lily Huang

The author worked at Newsweek, a magazine in which this essay was first published in 2008. The article addresses the fear of English Language purists that text-messaging might help to damage the language.

1   The most hotly contested controversy sparked by the text-messaging phenomenon of the past eight years is over truant letters. "Textese," a nascent dialect of English that subverts letters and numbers to produce ultra-concise words and sentiments, is horrifying language loyalists and pedagogues. And their fears are stoked by some staggering numbers: this year the world is on track to produce 2.3 trillion messages—a nearly 20 percent increase from 2007 and almost 150 percent from 2000. The accompanying revenue for telephone companies is growing nearly as fast—to an estimated $60 billion this year. In the English-speaking world, Britain alone generates well over 6 billion messages every month. People are communicating more and faster than ever, but some worry that, as textese drops consonants, vowels and punctuation and makes no distinction between letters and numbers, people will no longer know how we're really supposed to communicate. Will text messaging produce generations of illiterates? Could this—OMG—be the death of the English language?

2   Those raising the alarm aren't linguists. They're teachers who have had to red-pen some ridiculous practices in high-school papers and concerned citizens who believe it their moral duty to write grammar books. The latter can be quite prominent, like John Humphrys, a television broadcaster and household name in Britain, for whom texting is "vandalism," and Lynne Truss, author of "Eats, Shoots and Leaves," who actually enjoys texting so much she never abbreviates. Britain, one of the first countries where texting became a national habit, has also produced some of the most bitter anti-texting vitriol; "textese," wrote John Sutherland in The Guardian, "masks dyslexia." But linguists, if anyone is paying attention, have kept quiet on this score—until now. In a new book, Britain's most prolific linguist finally sets a few things straight.

3   David Crystal's "Txtng: The Gr8 Db8" (Oxford) makes two general points: that the language of texting is hardly as deviant as people think, and that texting actually makes young people better communicators, not worse. Crystal spells out the first point by marshalling real linguistic evidence. He breaks down the distinctive elements of texting language—pictograms; initialisms, or acronyms; contractions, and others—and points out similar examples in linguistic practice from the ancient Egyptians to 20th-century broadcasting. Shakespeare freely used

elisions, novel syntax, and several thousand made-up words (his own name was signed in six different ways). Even some common conventions are relatively newfangled: rules for using the oft-abused apostrophe were set only in the middle of the 19th century. The point is that tailored text predates the text message, so we might as well accept that ours is a language of vandals. Who even knows what p.m. stands for? ("Post meridiem," Latin for "after midday," first recorded by a lazy delinquent in 1666.)

Where the naysayers see destruction, Crystal sees growth. He believes in the 4 same theory of evolution for language as some evolutionary biologists do for life: change isn't gradual. Monumental developments interrupt periods of stasis, always as a result of crucial external developments. The American Revolution had much greater consequences for the English language than texting has had thus far. The resulting differences between American and British English, Crystal says, are more pronounced than the differences between, say, the language of newspapers and text messages. (Interestingly, there are hardly any differences between American and British texting.)

As soon as linguists began to peer into the uproar over texting, researchers 5 examined the effects of texting experimentally. The results disproved conventional wisdom: in one British experiment last year, children who texted—and who wielded plenty of abbreviations—scored higher on reading and vocabulary tests. In fact, the more adept they were at abbreviating, the better they did in spelling and writing. Far from being a means to getting around literacy, texting seems to give literacy a boost. The effect is similar to what happens when parents yak away to infants or read to toddlers: the more exposure children get to language, by whatever means, the more verbally skilled they become. "Before you can write abbreviated forms effectively and play with them, you need to have a sense of how the sounds of your language relate to the letters," says Crystal. The same study also found the children with the highest scores to be the first to have gotten their own cell phones.

Which doesn't let the teenager who LOLs in a term paper off the hook—but 6 that's not so much a question of language ability as of judgment. It, too, should go the way of all slang ever inappropriately used in a classroom—rebuked with a red pen, not seized upon as a symptom of generational decline. Even if electronic communication engenders its own kind of carelessness, it's no worse than the carelessness of academic jargon or journalistic shorthand. It certainly doesn't engender stupidity. One look at the winners of text-poetry contests in Britain proves that the force behind texting is a penchant for innovation, not linguistic laziness. Electronic communication, Crystal says, "has introduced that kind of creative spirit into spelling once again." That heathen Shakespeare would have been onboard.

Questions about Meaning

1. How does Huang regard—and think we all should regard—the emergence and rapid spread of "Textese"? Why?

2. What limits on the use of "Textese" does Huang favour? Why does she do so? Do you agree there should be such limits?

3. The author refers to Shakespeare as a "heathen" in the essay's concluding sentence? What does the term mean and why do you think she uses it here?

Questions about Rhetorical Strategy and Style

1. What is the relationship between the title and Huang's thesis?

2. What tone does the title help to establish? Do you think the tone makes the essay more engaging and persuasive?

3. Are "pedagogues" (paragraph one) and "naysayers" (paragraph four) neutral or "loaded" terms? Explain. What effect do they have?

4. The author twice uses "Textese" in her essay. Why do you think she does this? Should she have used it more? Why or why not?

The Decline of Public Language
Margaret Wente

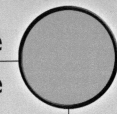

The author is a columnist with the Toronto-based **Globe and Mail** *where this first appeared in 2005.*

After they settled the hockey lockout,[1] I heard one of the players on the radio. He was saying that he welcomed the new rules that are supposed to make the action on the ice more exciting. "These changes will improve our product," he said.

Silly me. Sure, the NHL is a commercial enterprise with a bottom line in a competitive marketplace. But it was depressing to hear a superb athlete call his game a product. Who's going to get emotionally invested in a product? If hockey is the product, then what are fans? Do parents take their kids off to hockey practice at 6 a.m. so that the little tykes can sharpen their product skills? Maybe so. These days, it's not whether you win or lose. It's how you improve the product to capture greater market share.

No area of public life is safe from the language of the marketplace. Politics succumbed long ago. We no longer have political parties. We have brands, which have images to be either polished or tarnished, and policy platforms that, like toothpaste, are carefully tested beforehand on focus groups. Citizens are treated as consumers who either do or don't like the flavour of the candidate, also known as product. Stephen Harper[2] is said to be lousy at retail, which is why the poor man is being made to spend his summer hawking his wares at every small-town barbecue and Dairy Queen. Joan Rivers[3] shilling cubic zirconium on the Home Shopping Network has more dignity.

You might not expect better from politics. But what about good works? The charitable world also has a terminal case of management-speak. The new global CEO of Foster Parents Plan[4] (now known as Plan, for marketing simplicity) likes to talk about the importance of "brand awareness" in the voluntary sector. He's got ideas for better ways to "leverage dollars" and "compete for market share." As someone whose market share has been successfully captured by this group, I was relieved to learn that the little girls I sponsor in far-off lands are not simply passive recipients of aid. They are "development actors."

Every civic institution, arts organization and charity is obliged to use management-speak nowadays. That's because they need to reassure their multiple stakeholders that they operate on a businesslike model. They must demonstrate that they are effective and efficient, as well as accountable and transparent. It's not enough to help kids who live in poor countries, or treat sick people, or teach students. Every homeless shelter and hospital, every museum and university and branch of the civil service must have a vision, a mission, and a strategic plan. Their managers are made to go on long retreats with professional facilitators in order to come up with these things, which are then enshrined on plaques, highlighted in the annual report, and hung prominently in the main entrance of the institution for everyone to see.

6   Since everybody's vision and mission statement winds up sounding pretty much the same, this exercise may strike you as a phenomenal waste of time. But there's more. Everyone must also come up with tangible deliverables that have measurable outcomes. They must commit themselves to partner with their donors. They commit themselves to empower their clients, customers and, presumably, development actors. Above all, their institutions must be leaders, preferably world-class ones.

7   The decline of public language into sludge is the subject of a passionate polemic called *Death Sentences*, by Australian writer Don Watson.[5] Anyone who cares for words should read it. Mr. Watson thinks words ought to matter. He argues that the narrow, cliché-ridden vocabulary of managerialism has robbed the public language of elegance and gravity. "We use language to deal with moral and political dilemmas, but not this language," he fumes. "This language is not capable of serious deliberation. It could no more carry a complex argument than it could describe the sound of a nightingale. Listen to it in the political and corporate landscape, and you hear noises that our recent ancestors might have taken for Gaelic or Swahili, and that we ourselves often do not understand."

8   The language of management-speak has created a dark and impenetrable thicket. And once it gets into a place, it spreads like duckweed. "All kinds of institutions now cannot tell us about their services, including the most piddling change in them, without also telling us that they are contemporary, innovative and forward-looking, and committed to continuous improvement," he points out. Much of this abuse originates with management consultants, who, far from being jailed or sued for it, are richly rewarded. By far the worst offenders are HR practitioners, followed by those people who concoct recruitment ads.

9   "As President and CEO, you will provide vision, direction and inspiration," says an ad I saw the other day. They were looking for someone who could build market share for either soup or starving children; I can't remember. "A consummate communicator, strategist and leader, you have galvanized support for whatever corporate or charitable cause you've undertaken. Now you can leverage that presence and energy."

10   Like mission statements, all job ads sound the same. Everybody wants a "leader" who is "strategic," and preferably "visionary."

11   "You are highly strategic, analytical and collaborative in approach," reads another ad. "You are a visionary who is forward-looking with an innovative flair and a proven ability to move ideas from paper to practice. With well-honed leadership skills, [you will] execute a team-driven plan that will position this key functional area as one of excellence." What's the job? Well, it's CFO for a university. But it could be anything, really.

12   Anyone who cares about language, about meaning, about clarity, should revolt. Citizens are not customers, and democracy is not a product. If Barbra Streisand had sung "Customers . . . customers who need customers," would anyone have cared? If Martin Luther King had said, "I have a vision statement," would anyone have listened? Words matter more than we think. We need them to express our deepest values. As a wise man once said, what does it profit you if you gain market share but lose your soul? Or something like that.

Notes

1 When NHL team owners and players failed to agree on a new collective bargaining agreement in 2004, the owners refused to open arenas for the 2004–2005 season; hence a "lockout," the action employers take in a labour dispute to prevent workers from working, as opposed to a "strike." the action employees take by refusing to work.

2 In the spring of 2005, Paul Martin's minority Liberal government barely escaped facing two non-confidence votes: by the summer, then Conservative opposition leader Stephen Harper, who had lost to Martin in the 2004 election, was conducting an unofficial election campaign.

3 Joan Rivers is an American comedienne who promotes a line of jewelry for women, including pieces made with zirconium.

4 "CEO" stands for "chief executive officer," Foster Parents Plan (Plan) is a global charity matching individual Third World children with First World sponsors.

5 Don Watson was speechwriter to former Australian prime minister Paul Keating. Watson's *Death Sentences*, a critique of corporate and public jargon, has sold more than 85 000 copies since its publication in 2003.

Questions about Meaning

1. What is the "public language" Wente refers to in the essay? What other kind of language is there?

2. What is Wente's main objection to how public language is changing?

3. Who is the "wise man" Wente refers to in the final paragraph? Why not name him?

Questions about Rhetorical Strategy and Style

1. Why do you think Wente began by quoting a hockey player? Is it an effective way to begin?

2. What is the author doing in paragraph six? What is your own response to this kind of language?

3. Does Wente regard the problem she describes as a truly serious one? What in the essay indicates she does or does not?

I'm Not Racist, But . . .

Neil Bissoondath

Born in Trinidad, Neil Bissoondath (1955–) moved to Canada at age 18 to attend York University. Upon receiving a degree in French, Bissoondath taught both French and English before beginning his writing career. In choosing to be a full-time writer, he followed in the footsteps of his internationally known uncles, Shiva and V.S. Naipaul. Bissoondath's first book, the short story collection Digging Up the Mountains *(1985), received significant critical praise, and his nonfiction critique of multiculturalism,* Selling Illusions: The Cult of Multiculturalism in Canada *(1994), stirred a good deal of controversy. His book* The Innocence of Age *(1992) won the Canadian Authors Association Prize for fiction. Most of Bissoondath's work, both fiction and nonfiction, deals with the dislocation, alienation, and racial tension of non-white immigrants in Canadian society. In the following essay, the author questions the legitimacy of labeling all insensitive ethnic language as racism.*

1   Someone recently said that racism is as Canadian as maple syrup. I have no argument with that. History provides us with ample proof. But, for proper perspective, let us remember that it is also as American as apple pie, as French as croissants, as Jamaican as ackee, as Indian as aloo, as Chinese as chow mein, as. . . . Well, there's an entire menu to be written. This is not by way of excusing it. Murder and rape, too, are international, multicultural, as innate to the darker side of the human experience. But we must be careful that the inevitable rage evoked does not blind us to the larger context.

2   The word "racism" is a discomforting one: It is so vulnerable to manipulation. We can, if we so wish, apply it to any incident involving people of different colour. And therein lies the danger. During the heat of altercation, we seize, as terms of abuse, on whatever is most obvious about the person. It is, often, a question of unfortunate convenience. A woman, because of her sex, easily becomes a female dog or an intimate part of her anatomy. A large person might be dubbed "a stupid ox," a small person "a little" whatever. And so a black might become "a nigger," a white "a honky," an Asian "a paki," a Chinese "a chink," an Italian "a wop," a French-Canadian "a frog."

3   There is nothing pleasant about these terms; they assault every decent sensibility. Even so, I once met someone who, in a stunning surge of naiveté, used them as simple descriptives and not as terms of racial abuse. She was horrified to learn the truth. While this may have been an extreme case, the point is that the use of such patently abusive words may not always indicate racial or cultural distaste. They may indicate ignorance or stupidity or insensitivity, but pure racial hatred—such as the Nazis held for Jews, or the Ku Klux Klan for blacks—is a thankfully rare commodity.

Ignorance, not the willful kind but that which comes from lack of experience, is often indicated by that wonderful phrase, "I'm not racist but. . . ." I think of the mover, a friendly man, who said, "I'm not racist, but the Chinese are the worst drivers on the road." He was convinced this was so because the shape of their eyes, as far as he could surmise, denied them peripheral vision. 4

Or the oil company executive, an equally warm and friendly man, who, looking for an apartment in Toronto, rejected buildings with East Indian tenants not because of their race—he was telling me this, after all—but because he was given to understand that cockroaches were symbols of good luck in their culture and that, when they moved into a new home, friends came by with gift-wrapped cockroaches. 5

Neither of these men thought of himself as racist, and I believe they were not, deep down. (The oil company executive made it clear he would not hesitate to have me as a neighbour; my East Indian descent was of no consequence to him, my horror of cockroaches was.) Yet their comments, so innocently delivered, would open them to the accusation, justifiably so if this were all one knew about them. But it is a charge which would undoubtedly be wounding to them. It is difficult to recognize one's own misconceptions. 6

True racism is based, more often than not, on willful ignorance, and an acceptance of—and comfort with—stereotype. We like to think, in this country, that our multicultural mosaic will help nudge us into a greater openness. But multiculturalism as we know it indulges in stereotype, depends on it for a dash of colour and the flash of dance. It fails to address the most basic questions people have about each other. Do those men doing the Dragon Dance really all belong to secret criminal societies? Do those women dressed in saris really coddle cockroaches for luck? Do those people in dreadlocks all smoke marijuana and live on welfare? Such questions do not seem to be the concern of the government's multicultural programs, superficial and exhibitionistic as they have become. 7

So the struggle against stereotype, the basis of all racism, becomes a purely personal one. We must beware of the impressions we create. A friend of mine once commented that, from talking to West Indians, she has the impression that their one great cultural contribution to the world is in the oft-repeated boast that "We (unlike everyone else) know how to party." 8

There are dangers, too, in community response. We must be wary of the self-appointed activists who seem to pop up in the media at every given opportunity spouting the rhetoric of retribution, mining distress for personal, political and professional gain. We must be skeptical about those who depend on conflict for their sense of self, the non-whites who need to feel themselves victims of racism, the whites who need to feel themselves purveyors of it. And we must be sure that, in addressing the problem, we do not end up creating it. Does the *Miss Black Canada Beauty Contest* still exist? I hope not. Not only do I find beauty contests offensive, but a racially segregated one even more so. What would the public reaction be, I wonder, if every year CTV broadcast the *Miss White Canada Beauty Pageant?* We give community-service awards only to blacks: Would we be comfortable with such awards only for whites? In Quebec, there are The Association of Black Nurses, The Association of Black Artists, The Congress of Black Jurists. Play tit for tat: The Association of White Nurses, White Artists, White Jurists: visions of apartheid. Let us be frank, racism for one is racism for others. 9

Finally, and perhaps most important, let us beware of abusing the word itself. 10

Questions about Meaning

1. How does Bissoondath distinguish between what he considers simply unpleasant terms for ethnic minorities and true racism?

2. How does Bissoondath characterize the Canadian government's attempts to foster multiculturalism? Why, according to the author, do these attempts fail to address true racism?

3. What does Bissoondath mean when he says that "we must be sure that, in addressing the problem [of racism], we do not end up creating it"?

Questions about Rhetorical Strategy and Style

1. What is Bissoondath's definition of racism? To what extent does this definition strengthen his argument about the misuse of this term?

2. Cite two examples used in this essay and explain how they support the author's argument.

Don't Call Me That Word
Lawrence Hill

The author, best-known for his novel The Book of Negroes, *has written several book and articles on a variety of topics. He grew up in Don Mills and now live in Burlington, Ontario. This essay first appeared in* Maclean's *in 2002.*

Growing up in the 1960s in the affluent, almost all-white Don Mills, Ont., I was told by my black father that education and professional achievement were the only viable options for black people in North America. He laid down three rules as if they had been received from the mouth of God: 1) I was to study like the dickens; 2) anything less than complete success in school or at work was to be regarded as failure; 3) if anybody called me "nigger," I was to beat the hell out of him. 1

This is the legacy of being black in Canada. You overcompensate for the fluke of your ancestry, and stand on guard against those who would knock you down.[1] Over 400 years of black history here, we have had to overcome numerous challenges: the chains of slave vessels, the wrath of slave owners, the rules of segregation, the killing ways of police bullets, our own murderous infighting, and all the modern vicissitudes of polite Canadian oppression.[2] 2

Blacks in Canada, like our metaphorical brothers and sisters all over the world, have a vivid collective memory. We know what our ancestors have been through, and we know what our children still face. Most of us cringe when we hear the word "nigger." No other word in the English language distills hatred so effectively, and evokes such a long and bloody history. 3

These days, more people than ever are talking about the word "nigger," as a result of the publication this year of the book *Nigger: The Strange Career of a Troublesome Word*, by Randall Kennedy, a black American law professor at Harvard University. It's a fascinating read, but it raises a troublesome argument that I ultimately reject: Kennedy praises "African American innovators" (by which he means comedians and hip hop stylists)[3] for "taming, civilizing, and transmuting 'the filthiest, dirtiest, nastiest word in the English language.'" 4

Some misguided white people have bought into this same way of thinking. We have hit the pinnacle of absurdity when white teenagers sling their arms around black friends and ask, "Whassup my nigger"? And some white people seem to want a piece of that word, and feel the need to apply it to their own difficult experiences. The Irish have been referred to as "the niggers of Europe." In the 1970s, Québécois writer Pierre Vallieres titled one of his books *White Niggers of America*. And just the other night, when I visited a drop-in centre catering mostly to black junior high and high school students in Toronto's Kensington Market area, a white teenager decked out in baggy pants and parroting what he imagined 5 to be blackspeak complained that some kids accused him of being a "wigger"—an insulting term for whites who are trying to act black. Whatever that means.[4]

6   As Randall Kennedy rightly asserts, the word abounds in contemporary black urban culture. True, when it crops up in hip hop lyrics, it's not intended to carry the hate of the racist. It signals an in-group, brotherly, friendly trash talk. This is well known in American culture but it has penetrated black Canadian culture, too. Choclair, a leading black Canadian hip hop artist, uses the word "nigga"—a derivation of "nigger"—frequently in his lyrics.

7   Some people might say that the N-word is making a comeback. That the old-style, racist use of the word has faded into history and that it's now kosher to use the word in ordinary conversation. This argument fails on two counts. First, racists and racism haven't disappeared from the Canadian landscape. The comeback argument also fails because it suggests that reappropriating the word reflects a new linguistic trend.[5] This is naive. As a way of playing with the English language's most hateful word, black people—mostly young black males—have called themselves "nigger" for generations. The difference now is that these same young blacks have broadcast the word, via music and TV, to the whole world. In the middle-class black cultures I've encountered in Canada and the United States, such a young man usually gets slapped or tongue-lashed by his mother, at just about that point, and he learns that the only time it's safe to use that word is when he's chilling on the street with his buddies. Black people use the word "nigger" precisely because it hurts so much that we need to dance with our own pain, in the same way that blues music dives straight into bad luck and heartbreak. This is very much part of the black North American experience: we don't run from our pain, we roll it into our art.

8   But does that take the sting out of the word? No. And what's the proof of that? We don't use the word around our mothers, our teachers, the people we fall in love with, or our children. "Nigger" is a word that young black men use on each other. But the word still pains most black Canadians. Let me share an image of just how much the word hurts. A friend of mine—a black woman, community activist and graduate student—was dying to read Kennedy's book. She bought it last week, but couldn't bring herself to start devouring it on the subway to work until she had ripped off the cover: she wouldn't allow herself to be seen on the subway with the word "nigger" splashed on the cover of a book, so close to her face.

Notes

1   What is being echoed here?
2   What does Hill mean by "the modern vicissitudes of polite Canadian oppression"?
3   Who might Kennedy be referring to?
4   How does Hill effectively use syntax here?
5   What does *reappropriating* mean? Can you think of examples of other words that have been reappropriated?

Questions about Meaning

1. Why, according to Hill, do dome people, like Randall Kennedy, now think it is not only permissible but a good thing that more and more people are using the word "Nigger"?

2. In your own words, what are the "two counts" by which Hill thinks the argument by Randall Kennedy and others fails?

3. What at the end of paragraph five is the author indicating when he writes "Whatever that means" about the idea of "whites … trying to act black"?

Questions about Rhetorical Strategy and Style

1. What is the effect of using "That Word" rather than "Nigger" in the title?
2. To what is Hill alluding when he says that, being black, you have to "stand on guard" against potential assailants? What are the purpose and the effect of this allusion?
3. What is the effect of Hill's ending the essay by describing how his friend felt the need to rip the cover off Randall Kennedy's book before she would read it on the subway?

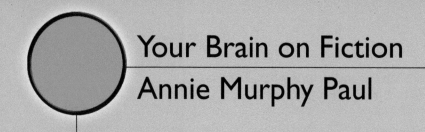

Your Brain on Fiction

Annie Murphy Paul

The author is a writer of magazine articles and books, including Origins: How the Nine Months Before Birth Shape the Rest of Our Lives. *This article first appeared in* The New York Times *in 2012.*

1   Amid the squawks and pings of our digital devices, the old-fashioned virtues of reading novels can seem faded, even futile. But new support for the value of fiction is arriving from an unexpected quarter: neuroscience.

2   Brain scans are revealing what happens in our heads when we read a detailed description, an evocative metaphor or an emotional exchange between characters. Stories, this research is showing, stimulate the brain and even change how we act in life.

3   Researchers have long known that the "classical" language regions, like Broca's area and Wernicke's area, are involved in how the brain interprets written words. What scientists have come to realize in the last few years is that narratives activate many other parts of our brains as well, suggesting why the experience of reading can feel so alive. Words like "lavender," "cinnamon" and "soap," for example, elicit a response not only from the language-processing areas of our brains, but also those devoted to dealing with smells.

4   In a 2006 study published in the journal NeuroImage, researchers in Spain asked participants to read words with strong odor associations, along with neutral words, while their brains were being scanned by a functional magnetic resonance imaging (fMRI) machine. When subjects looked at the Spanish words for "perfume" and "coffee," their primary olfactory cortex lit up; when they saw the words that mean "chair" and "key," this region remained dark. The way the brain handles metaphors has also received extensive study; some scientists have contended that figures of speech like "a rough day" are so familiar that they are treated simply as words and no more. Last month, however, a team of researchers from Emory University reported in Brain & Language that when subjects in their laboratory read a metaphor involving texture, the sensory cortex, responsible for perceiving texture through touch, became active. Metaphors like "The singer had a velvet voice" and "He had leathery hands" roused the sensory cortex, while phrases matched for meaning, like "The singer had a pleasing voice" and "He had strong hands," did not.

5   Researchers have discovered that words describing motion also stimulate regions of the brain distinct from language-processing areas. In a study led by the cognitive scientist Véronique Boulenger, of the Laboratory of Language Dynamics in France, the brains of participants were scanned as they read sentences like "John grasped the object" and "Pablo kicked the ball." The scans revealed activity in the motor cortex, which coordinates the body's movements. What's more, this activity

was concentrated in one part of the motor cortex when the movement described was arm-related and in another part when the movement concerned the leg.

The brain, it seems, does not make much of a distinction between reading 6 about an experience and encountering it in real life; in each case, the same neurological regions are stimulated. Keith Oatley, an emeritus professor of cognitive psychology at the University of Toronto (and a published novelist), has proposed that reading produces a vivid simulation of reality, one that "runs on minds of readers just as computer simulations run on computers." Fiction—with its redolent details, imaginative metaphors and attentive descriptions of people and their actions—offers an especially rich replica. Indeed, in one respect novels go beyond simulating reality to give readers an experience unavailable off the page: the opportunity to enter fully into other people's thoughts and feelings.

The novel, of course, is an unequaled medium for the exploration of human 7 social and emotional life. And there is evidence that just as the brain responds to depictions of smells and textures and movements as if they were the real thing, so it treats the interactions among fictional characters as something like real-life social encounters.

Raymond Mar, a psychologist at York University in Canada, performed an 8 analysis of 86 fMRI studies, published last year in the Annual Review of Psychology, and concluded that there was substantial overlap in the brain networks used to understand stories and the networks used to navigate interactions with other individuals—in particular, interactions in which we're trying to figure out the thoughts and feelings of others. Scientists call this capacity of the brain to construct a map of other people's intentions "theory of mind." Narratives offer a unique opportunity to engage this capacity, as we identify with characters' longings and frustrations, guess at their hidden motives and track their encounters with friends and enemies, neighbors and lovers.

It is an exercise that hones our real-life social skills, another body of research 9 suggests. Dr. Oatley and Dr. Mar, in collaboration with several other scientists, reported in two studies, published in 2006 and 2009, that individuals who frequently read fiction seem to be better able to understand other people, empathize with them and see the world from their perspective. This relationship persisted even after the researchers accounted for the possibility that more empathetic individuals might prefer reading novels. A 2010 study by Dr. Mar found a similar result in preschool-age children: the more stories they had read to them, the keener their theory of mind—an effect that was also produced by watching movies but, curiously, not by watching television. (Dr. Mar has conjectured that because children often watch TV alone, but go to the movies with their parents, they may experience more "parent-children conversations about mental states" when it comes to films.)

Fiction, Dr. Oatley notes, "is a particularly useful simulation because 10 negotiating the social world effectively is extremely tricky, requiring us to weigh up myriad interacting instances of cause and effect. Just as computer simulations can help us get to grips with complex problems such as flying a plane or forecasting the weather, so novels, stories and dramas can help us understand the complexities of social life."

These findings will affirm the experience of readers who have felt illuminated 11 and instructed by a novel, who have found themselves comparing a plucky young woman to Elizabeth Bennet or a tiresome pedant to Edward Casaubon. Reading great literature, it has long been averred, enlarges and improves us as human beings. Brain science shows this claim is truer than we imagined.

Questions about Meaning

1. According to the author, what is neuroscience now telling us about reading fiction and its effects?
2. What kind of metaphors seem to create the most brain activity? Why might this be the case and what lesson does this offer to us as writers?
3. Explain what "theory of mind" means and what its connection is to the reading of fiction.

Questions about Rhetorical Strategy and Style

1. What does the use of "of course" near the beginning of paragraph seven tell us about the writer's attitude toward her subject and her assumption about her readers?
2. In the final paragraph the author alludes to two characters from well-known 19th century novels: Elizabeth Bennet from Jane Austen's *Pride and Prejudice* and Edward Casaubon from George Eliot's *Middlemarch*. What do these references (that do not include the names of the authors or the names of the novels) tell us anything about who the writer presumes her readers are? Are the references a serious obstacle for those who have not read these novels or heard of these characters? Why or why not?

Kiddy Thinks

Alison Gopnik

The author is a professor of developmental psychology at the University of California. This essay first appeared in 2000 in **The Guardian Weekly** *in Great Britain and is an adaptation of a chapter in one of Gopnik's books,* **The Scientist in the Crib.**

When my son was a toddler his first question about a meal was always: "What's for dessert"? One day we had pineapple in kirsch. He spat it out, then looked at the adults devouring the stuff, and said: "Pineapple: it's yucky for me but it's yummy for you." For weeks afterwards, he would stop suddenly in the middle of a game and say: "Pineapple: yucky for me but yummy for you," as if he had discovered the most extraordinary fact of life. And in a sense he had: the realization that people think and feel differently is a profound one.

When we look around a room full of people, we don't see bags of skin and cloth draped over the furniture. We see other people, people with thoughts and emotions, desires and beliefs, sometimes like our own, sometimes not. And by the time they are 18 months old, this is what toddlers see as well. But how do such tiny children get from bags of skin to "other minds"?

In the past 30 years we have learned more about what young children know and how they learn than we did in the preceding 2,500 years. And this has revolutionised our view of children. For centuries, psychologists and philosophers agreed that babies were the opposite of adults. They were emotional and passive, dominated by perception and incapable of rational thought. John Locke[1] said they were "blank slates".

Today, scientists have only recently begun to appreciate just how much even the youngest babies know—and how much and how quickly they learn. There are three elements to this new picture. First, that children know a great deal, literally from the moment they are born. Second, that they are born with extremely powerful learning abilities. And, finally, that adults appear to be "programmed" to unconsciously teach babies and young children just the things they need to know.

In *How Babies Think*, my co-authors and I argue that very young children use the same strategies as scientists. They think, observe, formulate theories, make predictions, and do experiments. They also change their theories as they accumulate counter-evidence to their predictions.

But where scientists focus their attention on distant stars and invisible microbes, babies concentrate on everyday things: blocks, pet dogs, words and, most important: Mum and Dad and Aunt Ethel. In fact understanding other people seems to be one of the most crucial items in the scientific agenda of childhood, and it's a good illustration of how early learning takes place.

7   To begin with, children are born knowing that people are special. Newborn babies (the youngest tested was only 42 minutes old) can imitate facial expressions. There are no mirrors in the womb; newborns have never seen their own face. These tiny babies must somehow already understand the similarity between their own internal feeling (of, say, sticking out their tongue) and the external face they see (a round shape from which something pink protrudes). Newborn babies not only prefer faces to things but also recognise that those faces are *like their own face*. Nature, it seems, gives human beings a jump start on the Other Minds problem.

8   And what a jump start. By the time they are nine months old, babies can tell the difference between expressions of happiness, sadness and anger, and understand something about the emotions that produce those expressions. By the time they are one, they know that they will see something by looking where other people point; they know that they should do something by watching what others do; and they know how they should feel about something by seeing how others feel.

9   For instance, an adult can look in two boxes. She looks into one with an expression of joy and into the other with disgust. The baby will happily reach into the box that made her happy, but won't touch the box that disgusted her. The baby has discovered that its initial emotional rapport with other people extends to joint attitudes towards the world. In a simple way, one-year-olds already participate in a culture. But as babies learn that people usually have the same attitudes towards objects as they do, they are setting themselves up to learn something else, something more disturbing: they discover that sometimes people *don't* have the same attitudes.

10   Observe what happens when a baby reaches for a forbidden object—a lamp cord, say. It must seem perverse to the one-year-old: the more clearly she indicates her desire, the more adamantly her carer keeps it away. Even though the baby and the grown-up are reacting to the same object, their attitudes toward the object seem to be different.

11   By the time babies are about one-and-a-half, they start to understand the nature of these differences between people and become fascinated. If you offer a baby two bowls, one of biscuits, the other of raw broccoli, all the babies prefer the biscuits. But if the researcher indicates to the baby that she hates biscuits and loves broccoli, then hands the bowls to the baby and says: "Could you give me some"? something interesting happens. Fourteen-month-olds, with their innocent assumption that we all want the same thing, give her biscuits. But the wiser 18-month-olds give her broccoli, even though they themselves despise it. These tiny children have learned that other people's desires may conflict with their own.

12   This is also dramatically apparent in everyday life. Parents all know, and dread, the "terrible twos." While one-year-olds seem irresistibly drawn to forbidden objects (that lamp cord again), the two-year-olds seem deliberately bloody-minded. She doesn't even look at the lamp cord. Instead, her hand goes out to touch it as she looks, steadily, gravely, at you.

13   This demonic behaviour is quite rational, though. Our broccoli experiments show that children only begin to understand the differences in desires at 18 months. The terrible twos seem to involve a systematic exploration of that idea, like an experimental research programme. Toddlers are testing the extent to which their desires and those of others may conflict. The grave look is directed at you because you and your reaction, rather than the lamp cord, are the interesting thing. The terrible twos reflect a clash between children's need to understand other people and their need to live happily with them. If the child is a budding scientist, we parents are the laboratory rats.

Two-year-olds also have to learn how visual perception works. Toddlers love 14 hide and seek but aren't very good at it—a toddler will bury his head under the table with his bottom in view. In our lab, we explored when children learn how to hide things. Suppose I put a child on one side of a table and sit on the other. Then I put a screen and a toy on the table and ask the child to hide the toy from me. At 24 months, a toddler will put the toy on *my* side of the screen, so that it is actually hidden from them, but not from me. But 36-month-olds get this right. In fact, they'll often tell me they can see the toy but I can't. In the months in between, we observed many children experimenting. They would switch the toy from one side to the other, or come around to my side of the screen to make sure the toy really was hidden.

But this isn't the end of the story. Three-year-olds still have trouble with 15 another important fact about people. They know that we can see different things, but not that what we think about the world may be wrong.

In a classic experiment, you can give three-year-olds a shut chocolate box. 16 They open it and it turns out to have pencils inside. Then you ask them about another child in the nursery: "What will Nicky think is in the box: pencils or chocolates"? Three-year-olds report that Nicky will say there are pencils inside. They don't understand that Nicky will probably make the same mistake they made. Four-year-olds know that Nicky will be misled by the picture on the box.

Like scientists, children change their theories precisely because they make the 17 wrong predictions. In "mistaken belief" experiments, simply telling children the right answer makes no difference. Like scientists, children at first resist counter-evidence. Virginia Slaughter and I visited three-year-olds over several weeks and gave them examples of mistaken beliefs: a golf ball that turned out to be soap, a yellow duck that looked green when put behind blue plastic. Each time the child made the wrong prediction, we presented them with counter-evidence. After two weeks these three-year-olds understood a brand-new "mistaken belief" task, one they had never seen before, much better than a control group.

This experiment shows that even very young children are naturally able to 18 alter their predictions in the light of new evidence. But it also shows how important other people can be: our adult behaviour had helped the children to work out the correct answer. Of course, we're developmental psychologists.

Do grown-ups naturally help children learn in their everyday lives? The new 19 research suggests they do. One of the most dramatic examples of this is the sing-song voice adults use when they talk to babies. This speech style helps children sort out the sounds of language.

Similarly, the way that parents talk about the mind seems to influence their 20 children's everyday psychology. What are the consequences of this new view? The research *doesn't* mean there is some set of flashcards that will help babies be brighter. Babies are already as bright as can be. They learn through everyday play, and through the care and attention of adults around them. It also *doesn't* mean there is some "critical period" for learning in the first three years or some set of experiences children must have. Children and even adults keep learning throughout life. It definitely doesn't mean mothers should quit their jobs. Anyone who cares for small children and is sensitive to what interests them can teach them what they need to know.

On the other hand, the research does suggest that the everyday, unremunerated, 21 unremarkable work of caring for babies and young children is extremely important. Humans have managed to learn so much because generations of adults put effort into caring for children.

22   Ironically, this new scientific perspective comes when young children and parents are under enormous pressure. We still penalise parents for taking time off work to be with their children, instead of rewarding them. Most parents face agonising dilemmas as they balance jobs and children. If we really want babies to learn, we should ditch the videotapes and flashcards and work for paid parental leave, flexible work arrangements and publicly supported, high-quality childcare.

Note

1   English philosopher John Locke (1632–1704) believed that all of our knowledge comes from our senses. He thought that children were "blank slates" (that is, clean sheets of paper), passively acquiring knowledge through sensory impressions from the world around them.

Questions about Meaning

1. What are the ideas about babies and young children that Gopnik asserts new research has disproved?

2. What is the thesis of the essay? Where is it stated? Can you formulate it in your own words?

3. How, according to Gopnik, should parents and society at large apply what has recently been learned about babies and young children? How persuasive is she?

Questions about Rhetorical Strategy and Style

1. What is the effect of the anecdote with which Gopnik begins the essay? Why do you think she chose to introduce the essay this way?

2. How is the essay structured or organized? Does this make the content clearer and more accessible? Why or why not?

3. Why does Gopnik make explicit mention of what the research does *not* mean?

4. Gopnik is writing as both a scientist with expertise in child development and as a parent. Is the tone of the essay more reflective of one of these roles? Explain.

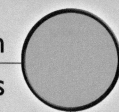

Salvation

Langston Hughes

Langston Hughes (1902–1967), a poet, short-story writer, essayist, and playwright, was born in Joplin, Missouri, and grew up in Kansas and Ohio. After graduating from high school (where he began writing poetry), Hughes spent 15 months in Mexico with his father, attended Columbia University for a year, worked as a seaman on cargo ships bound to Africa and Europe, and bused tables at a hotel in New York City. Later, he returned to school and graduated from Lincoln University (1929). Part of the "Harlem Renaissance" or "New Negro Renaissance"—and fiercely proud of his African-American heritage—Hughes often drew from Negro spirituals and blues and jazz in his literary work. Hughes was published in Amsterdam News, Crisis, The New Negro, *and many other periodicals. His books include the novel* Not Without Laughter *(1930); the short story collection* The Ways of White Folks *(1934); the play* The Mulatto *(1935); his autobiography* The Big Sea *(1940); and his poetry collections* The Weary Blues *(1926),* Shakespeare of Harlem *(1942),* Montage of a Dream Deferred *(1951), and* Ask Your Mama *(1961). This selection, which appeared first in* The Big Sea, *dramatizes an important event in Hughes's life.*

I was saved from sin when I was going on thirteen. But not really saved. It happened like this. There was a big revival at my Auntie Reed's church. Every night for weeks there had been much preaching, singing, praying, and shouting, and some very hardened sinners had been brought to Christ, and the membership of the church had grown by leaps and bounds. Then just before the revival ended, they held a special meeting for children, "to bring the young lambs to the fold." My aunt spoke of it for days ahead. That night I was escorted to the front row and placed on the mourners' bench with all the other young sinners, who had not yet been brought to Jesus. 1

My aunt told me that when you were saved you saw a light, and something happened to you inside! And Jesus came into your life! And God was with you from then on! She said you could see and hear and feel Jesus in your soul. I believed her. I had heard a great many old people say that same thing and it seemed to me they ought to know. So I sat there calmly in the hot, crowded church, waiting for Jesus to come to me. 2

The preacher preached a wonderful rhythmical sermon, all moans and shouts and lonely cries and dire pictures of hell, and then he sang a song about the ninety and nine safe in the fold, but one little lamb was left out in the cold. Then he said: 3

"Won't you come? Won't you come to Jesus? Young lambs, won't you come"? And he held out his arms to all us young sinners there on the mourners' bench. And the little girls cried. And some of them jumped up and went to Jesus right away. But most of us just sat there.

4   A great many old people came and knelt around us and prayed, old women with jet-black faces and braided hair, old men with work-gnarled hands. And the church sang a song about the lower lights are burning, some poor sinners to be saved. And the whole building rocked with prayer and song.

5   Still I kept waiting to *see* Jesus.

6   Finally all the young people had gone to the altar and were saved, but one boy and me. He was a rounder's son named Westley. Westley and I were surrounded by sisters and deacons praying. It was very hot in the church, and getting late now. Finally Westley said to me in a whisper: "God damn! I'm tired o' sitting here. Let's get up and be saved." So he got up and was saved.

7   Then I was left all alone on the mourners' bench. My aunt came and knelt at my knees and cried, while prayers and song swirled all around me in the little church. The whole congregation prayed for me alone in a mighty wail of moans and voices. And I kept waiting serenely for Jesus, waiting, waiting—but he didn't come. I wanted to see him, but nothing happened to me. Nothing! I wanted something to happen to me, but nothing happened.

8   I heard the songs and the minister saying: "Why don't you come? My dear child, why don't you come to Jesus? Jesus is waiting for you. He wants you. Why don't you come? Sister Reed, what is this child's name"?

9   "Langston," my aunt sobbed.

10   "Langston, why don't you come? Why don't you come and be saved? Oh, Lamb of God! Why don't you come"?

11   Now it was really getting late. I began to be ashamed of myself, holding everything up so long. I began to wonder what God thought about Westley, who certainly hadn't seen Jesus either, but who was now sitting proudly on the platform, swinging his knickerbockered legs and grinning down at me, surrounded by deacons and old women on their knees praying. God had not struck Westley dead for taking his name in vain or for lying in the temple. So I decided that maybe to save further trouble, I'd better lie, too, and say that Jesus had come, and get up and be saved.

12   So I got up.

13   Suddenly the whole room broke into a sea of shouting, as they saw me rise. Waves of rejoicing swept the place. Women leaped in the air. My aunt threw her arms around me. The minister took me by the hand and led me to the platform.

14   When things quieted down, in a hushed silence, punctuated by a few ecstatic "Amens," all the new young lambs were blessed in the name of God. Then joyous singing filled the room.

15   That night, for the last time in my life but one—for I was a big boy twelve years old—I cried. I cried, in bed alone, and couldn't stop. I buried my head under the quilts, but my aunt heard me. She woke up and told my uncle I was crying because the Holy Ghost had come into my life, and because I had seen Jesus. But I was really crying because I couldn't bear to tell her that I had lied, that I had deceived everybody in the church, that I hadn't seen Jesus, and that now I didn't believe there was a Jesus any more, since he didn't come to help me.

Questions about Meaning

1. Why did Hughes take so long to walk to the altar with the other children? Why did he wait so long to be "saved"?

2. Why did Hughes cry in bed after his experience at the revival? What had he come to believe about Jesus, about being "saved," and about himself?

3. What was the reaction of the adults in the congregation when Hughes finally walked to the altar? What does their reaction tell you about what salvation meant to the adults versus what it meant to the children?

Questions about Rhetorical Strategy and Style

1. How does Hughes define what it is to be "saved"? What example does he provide to support this definition?

2. How does Hughes use comparison and contrast in the dialogue he presents to reveal the differing mind-sets of the preacher and Westley? How did Westley's comments help convince Hughes to fake salvation?

3. Hughes's language creates rich imagery of the revival, such as a "rhythmical sermon, all moans and shouts and lonely cries and dire pictures of hell." Find other examples of his colorful, descriptive narrative. How would this selection be different without such language?

Growing Up Native

Carol Geddes

The author, a member of the Tlingit First Nations, has been a filmmaker, a teacher, an arts administrator, and a writer. This essay first appeared in Homemakers *magazine in 1990.*

1   I remember it was cold. We were walking through a swamp near our home in the Yukon bush. Maybe it was fall and moose-hunting season. I don't know. I think I was about four years old at the time. The muskeg was too springy to walk on, so people were taking turns carrying me—passing me from one set of arms to another. The details about where we were are vague, but the memory of those arms and the feeling of acceptance I had is one of the most vivid memories of my childhood. It didn't matter who was carrying me—there was security in every pair of arms. That response to children is typical of the native community. It's the first thing I think of when I cast my mind back to the Yukon bush, where I was born and lived with my family.

2   I was six years old when we moved out of the bush, first to Teslin, where I had a hint of the problems native people face, then to Whitehorse, where there was unimaginable racism. Eventually I moved to Ottawa and Montreal, where I further discovered that to grow up native in Canada is to feel the sting of humiliation and the boot of discrimination. But it is also to experience the enviable security of an extended family and to learn to appreciate the richness of the heritage and traditions of a culture most North Americans have never been lucky enough to know. As a film-maker, I have tried to explore these contradictions, and our triumph over them, for the half-million aboriginals who are part of the tide of swelling independence of the First Nations today.

3   But I'm getting ahead of myself. If I'm to tell the story of what it's like to grow up native in northern Canada, I have to go back to the bush where I was born, because there's more to my story than the hurtful stereotyping that depicts Indian people as drunken welfare cases. Our area was known as 12-mile (it was 12 miles from another tiny village). There were about 40 people living there—including 25 kids, eight of them my brothers and sisters—in a sort of family compound. Each family had its own timber plank house for sleeping, and there was one large common kitchen area with gravel on the ground and a tent frame over it. Everybody would go there and cook meals together. In summer, my grandmother always had a smudge fire going to smoke fish and tan moose hides. I can remember the cosy warmth of the fire, the smell of good food, and always having someone to talk to. We kids had built-in playmates and would spend hours running in the bush, picking berries, building rafts on the lake and playing in abandoned mink cages.

One of the people in my village tells a story about the day the old lifestyle 4 began to change. He had been away hunting in the bush for about a month. On his way back, he heard a strange sound coming from far away. He ran up to the crest of a hill, looked over the top of it and saw a bulldozer. He had never seen or heard of such a thing before and he couldn't imagine what it was. We didn't have magazines or newspapers in our village, and the people didn't know that the Alaska Highway was being built as a defence against a presumed Japanese invasion during the Second World War. That was the beginning of the end of the Teslin Tlingit people's way of life. From that moment on, nothing turned back to the way it was. Although there were employment opportunities for my father and uncles, who were young men at the time, the speed and force with which the Alaska Highway was rammed through the wilderness caused tremendous upheaval for Yukon native people.

It wasn't as though we'd never experienced change before. The Tlingit Nation, 5 which I belong to, arrived in the Yukon from the Alaskan coast around the turn of the century. They were the middlemen and women between the Russian traders and the Yukon inland Indians. The Tlingit gained power and prestige by trading European products such as metal goods and cloth for the rich and varied furs so much in fashion in Europe. The Tlingit controlled Yukon trading because they controlled the trading routes through the high mountain passes. When trading ceased to be an effective means of survival, my grandparents began raising wild mink in cages. Mink prices were really high before and during the war, but afterwards the prices went plunging down. So, although the mink pens were still there when I was a little girl, my father mainly worked on highway construction and hunted in the bush. The Yukon was then, and still is in some ways, in a transitional period—from living off the land to getting into a European wage-based economy.

As a young child, I didn't see the full extent of the upheaval. I remember a lot 6 of togetherness, a lot of happiness while we lived in the bush. There's a very strong sense of family in the native community, and a fondness for children, especially young children. Even today, it's like a special form of entertainment if someone brings a baby to visit. That sense of family is the one thing that has survived all the incredible difficulties native people have had. Throughout a time of tremendous problems, the extended family system has somehow lasted, providing a strong circle for people to survive in. When parents were struggling with alcoholism or had to go away to find work, when one of the many epidemics swept through the community, or when a marriage broke up and one parent left, aunts, uncles and grandparents would try to fill those roles. It's been very important to me in terms of emotional support to be able to rely on my extended family. There are still times when such support keeps me going.

Life was much simpler when we lived in the bush. Although we were poor 7 and wore the same clothes all year, we were warm enough and had plenty to eat. But even as a youngster, I began to be aware of some of the problems we would face later on. Travelling missionaries would come and impose themselves on us, for example. They'd sit at our campfire and read the Bible to us and lecture us about how we had to live a Christian life. I remember being very frightened by stories we heard about parents sending their kids away to live with white people who didn't have any children. We thought those people were mean and that if we were bad, we'd be sent away, too. Of course, that was when social workers were scooping up native children and adopting them out to white families in the south. The consequences were usually disastrous for the children who were taken away—alienation, alcoholism and suicide, among other things. I knew some of those kids. The survivors are still struggling to recover.

8   The residential schools were another source of misery for the kids. Although I didn't have to go, my brothers and sisters were there. They told stories about having their hair cut off in case they were carrying head lice, and of being forced to do hard chores without enough food to eat. They were told that the Indian culture was evil, that Indian people were bad, that their only hope was to be Christian. They had to stand up and say things like "I've found the Lord," when a teacher told them to speak. Sexual abuse was rampant in the residential school system.

9   By the time we moved to Whitehorse, I was excited about the idea of living in what I thought of as a big town. I'd had a taste of the outside world from books at school in Teslin (a town of 250 people), and I was tremendously curious about what life was like. I was hungry for experiences such as going to the circus. In fact, for a while, I was obsessed with stories and pictures about the circus, but then when I was 12 and saw my first one, I was put off by the condition and treatment of the animals.

10   Going to school in Whitehorse was a shock. The clash of native and white values was confusing and frightening. Let me tell you a story. The older boys in our community were already accomplished hunters and fishermen, but since they had to trap beaver in the spring and hunt moose in the fall, and go out trapping in the winter as well, they missed a lot of school. We were all in one classroom and some of my very large teenage cousins had to sit squeezed into little desks. These guys couldn't read very well. We girls had been in school all along, so, of course, we were better readers. One day the teacher was trying to get one of the older boys to read. She was typical of the teachers at that time, insensitive and ignorant of cultural complexities. In an increasingly loud voice, she kept commanding him to "Read it, read it." He couldn't. He sat there completely still, but I could see that he was breaking into a sweat. The teacher then said, "Look, she can read it," and she pointed to me, indicating that I should stand up and read. For a young child to try to show up an older boy is wrong and totally contrary to native cultural values, so I refused. She told me to stand up and I did. My hands were trembling as I held my reader. She yelled at me to read and when I didn't she smashed her pointing stick on the desk to frighten me. In terror, I wet my pants. As I stood there fighting my tears of shame, she said I was disgusting and sent me home. I had to walk a long distance through the bush by myself to get home. I remember feeling tremendous confusion, on top of my humiliation. We were always told the white teachers knew best, and so we had to do whatever they said at school. And yet I had a really strong sense of receiving mixed messages about what I was supposed to do in the community and what I was supposed to do at school.

11   Pretty soon I hated school. Moving to a predominantly white high school was even worse. We weren't allowed to join anything the white kids started. We were the butt of jokes because of our secondhand clothes and moose meat sandwiches. We were constantly being rejected. The prevailing attitude was that Indians were stupid. When it was time to make course choices in class—between typing and science, for example—they didn't even ask the native kids, they just put us all in typing. You get a really bad image of yourself in a situation like that. I bought into it. I thought we were awful. The whole experience was terribly undermining. Once, my grandmother gave me a pretty little pencil box. I walked into the classroom one day to find the word "squaw" carved on it. That night I burned it in the wood stove. I joined the tough crowd and by the time I was 15 years old, I

was more likely to be leaning against the school smoking a cigarette than trying to join in. I was burned out from trying to join the system. The principal told my father there was no point in sending me back to school so, with a Grade 9 education, I started to work at a series of menial jobs.

Seven years later something happened to me that would change my life forever. 12 I had moved to Ottawa with a man and was working as a waitress in a restaurant. One day, a friend invited me to her place for coffee. While I was there, she told me she was going to university in the fall and showed me her reading list. I'll never forget the minutes that followed. I was feeling vaguely envious of her and, once again, inferior. I remember taking the paper in my hand, seeing the books on it and realizing, Oh, my God, I've read these books! It hit me like a thunderclap. I was stunned that books I had read were being read in university. University was for white kids, not native kids. We were too stupid, we didn't have the kind of mind it took to do those things. My eyes moved down the list, and my heart started beating faster and faster as I suddenly realized I could go to university, too!

My partner at the time was a loving supportive man who helped me in every 13 way. I applied to the university immediately as a mature student but when I had to write Grade 9 on the application, I was sure they'd turn me down. They didn't. I graduated five years later, earning a bachelor of arts in English and philosophy (with distinction).

It was while I was studying for a master's degree in communications at McGill 14 a few years later that I was approached to direct my second film (the first was a student film). *Doctor, Lawyer, Indian Chief* (a National Film Board production) depicts the struggle of a number of native women—one who began her adult life on welfare, a government minister, a chief, a fisherwoman and Canada's first native woman lawyer. The film is about overcoming obstacles and surviving. It's the story of most native people.

Today, there's a glimmer of hope that more of us native people will overcome 15 the obstacles that have tripped us up ever since we began sharing this land. Some say our cultures are going through a renaissance. Maybe that's true. Certainly there's a renewed interest in native dancing, acting and singing, and in other cultural traditions. Even indigenous forms of government are becoming strong again. But we can't forget that the majority of native people live in urban areas and continue to suffer from alcohol and drug abuse and the plagues of a people who have lost their culture and have become lost themselves. And the welfare system is the insidious glue that holds together the machine of oppression of native people.

Too many non-native people have refused to try to understand the issues 16 behind our land claims. They make complacent pronouncements such as "Go back to your bows and arrows and fish with spears if you want aboriginal rights. If not, give it up and assimilate into white Canadian culture." I don't agree with that. We need our culture, but there's no reason why we can't preserve it and have an automatic washing machine and a holiday in Mexico, as well.

The time has come for native people to make our own decisions. We need to 17 have self-government. I have no illusions that it will be smooth sailing—there will be trial and error and further struggle. And if that means crawling before we can stand up and walk, so be it. We'll have to learn through experience.

While we're learning, we have a lot to teach and give to the world—a holistic 18 philosophy, a way of living with the earth, not disposing of it. It is critical that we all learn from the elders that an individual is not more important than a forest; we know that we're here to live on and with the earth, not to subdue it.

19   The wheels are in motion for a revival, for change in the way native people are taking their place in Canada. I can see that we're equipped, we have the tools to do the work. We have an enormous number of smart, talented, moral Indian people. It's thrilling to be a part of this movement.

20   Someday, when I'm an elder, I'll tell the children the stories: about the bush, about the hard times, about the renaissance, and especially about the importance of knowing your place in your nation.

Questions about Meaning

1. What were the chief characteristics of "growing up native," according to Geddes? How, does she imply, was her childhood different from the childhood of a non-native Canadian?

2. What is the significance of the incident in which the author was asked by a teacher to read aloud when an older boy in class could not?

3. How did going to university "change [the author's] life forever"?

Questions about Rhetorical Strategy and Style

1. What details of her own very early life does Geddes include? Were all the experiences positive ones that evoke pleasant memories?

2. Most of the essay is a narrative, but the last half dozen or so paragraphs are not. What is their relation to the narrative that precedes them? Is the connection clear and smooth?

Modern Cannibals of the Wilds
Basil Johnston

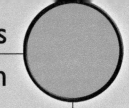

The author is a writer, storyteller, and teacher. Most of his books are about his—and his people's—Ojibway culture. This essay first appeared in The Globe and Mail *in 1991.*

Woods and forest once mantled most of this land, this continent. It was the home of the Anishinabek (Ojibway, Ottawa, Potowatomi, Algonquin), their kin and their neighbours. It was also the home of the moose, the deer, the caribou, the bear, their kindred and their neighbours. It was as well the home of the thrushes, the sparrows, the hawks, the tanagers, the ravens, the owls, their cousins and their neighbours. Mosquitoes, butterflies, caterpillars, ants, moths, their kin and their neighbours had a place therein. 1

Not only was it home, but a wellspring from which all drew their sustenance, medicine and knowledge. 2

Also dwelling in the woods and forests were weendigoes, giant cannibals who fed upon human flesh to allay their perpetual hunger. They stalked villages and camps, waiting for, and only for, the improvident, the slothful, the gluttonous, the promiscuous, the injudicious, the insatiable, the selfish, the avaricious and the wasteful, to be foolish enough to venture alone beyond the environs of their homes in winter. 3

But no matter how many victims a single weendigo devoured raw, he could never satisfy his hunger. The more he ate, the larger he grew, and the larger he grew, the greater his hunger. The weendigo's hunger always remained in proportion to his size. 4

Even though a weendigo is a mythical figure, he represents real human cupidity. What the old-time storyteller meant to project in the image of the weendigo was a universal and unchanging human disposition. But more learned people declared that no such monster ever existed, that he was a product of superstitious minds and imaginations. 5

As a result, the weendigo was driven from his place in Anishinabe traditions and culture, ostracized through disbelief and skepticism. It was assumed, and indeed it appeared as if, the weendigo and his brothers and sisters had passed into the Great Beyond, like many North American Indian beliefs and practices and traditions. 6

Actually, the weendigoes did not die out; they have only been assimilated and reincarnated as corporations, conglomerates and multinationals. They have taken on new names, acquired polished manners and renounced their craving for human flesh for more refined viands. But their cupidity is no less insatiable than their ancestors'. 7

8　　One breed subsists entirely on forests. When this breed beheld forests, its collective cupidity was stirred as it looked upon an endless, boundless sea of green—as in greenbacks. They saw beyond, even into the future. Money. Cash. Deposits. Bank accounts. Interest. Reserves. Investments, securities, bonds, shares, dividends, capital gains, assets, funds, deals, revenue, income, prosperity, opulence, profits, riches, wealth, comfort.

9　　They recruited woodsmen with axes, crosscut saws and Swede saws, sputters, shovels, cant hooks, grapples, chains, ropes, files and pikes, and sent them into the woods to fell, hew, saw, cut, chop, slash and level. The forests resounded with the clash of axes and the whine of saws as blades bit into the flesh of spruce, pine, cedar, tamarack and poplar to fill the demands of the weendigoes in Toronto, Montreal, Vancouver, New York, Chicago, Boston, wherever they now dwelt. Cries of "Timber!" echoed across the treetops, followed by the rip and tear of splintering trees, and thundering crashes.

10　　And as fast as woodsmen felled the trees, teamsters delivered sleighload after sleighload to railway sidings and to the rivers. Train after train, shipload after shipload of logs were delivered to the mills.

11　　Yet as fast as the woodsmen cut, as much as they cut, it was never fast enough. The quantity always fell short of the expectations of the weendigoes, their masters.

12　　"Is that all? Should there not be more? We demand a bigger return for our risks and our investments. Only more will satisfy us. Any amount will do, so long as it's more, and the more the better."

13　　The demands were met for more speed and more pulp, more logs and more timber. Axes, saws, woodsmen, horses and teamsters were replaced, and their blows and calls no longer rang in the forest. In their place, chainsaws whined, Caterpillar tractors with huge blades bulled and battered their way through the forest, uprooting trees to clear the way for automatic shearers that topped, limbed and sheared the trunks. These mechanical weendigoes gutted and desolated the forests, leaving death, destruction and ugliness where once there was life, abundance and beauty.

14　　Trucks and transports operated day and night delivering cargo with a speed and quantity that the horses and sleighs could never have matched.

15　　Yet the weendigoes wanted still more, and it didn't matter if their policies and practices of clear-cutting their harvest of timber and pulp resulted in violations of North American Indian rights or in the further impairment of their lives.

16　　Nor does it matter to them that their modus operandi permanently defiles hillside and mountainside by erosion. They are indifferent to the carnage inflicted upon bears, wolves, rabbits, thrushes, sparrows, warblers. Who cares if they are displaced? What possible harm has been done? Nor does it seem as if these modern weendigoes have any regard for the rights of future generations to the yield of Mother Earth.

17　　The new, reincarnated weendigoes are little different from their forebears. They are more omnivorous than their ancestors, however, and the modern breed wears elegant clothes and comports itself with an air of cultured and dignified respectability.

18　　Profit, wealth, comfort, power are the ends of business. Anything that detracts from or diminishes the anticipated return, be it taking pains not to violate the rights of others, or taking measures to ensure that the land remains fertile and productive for future generations, must, it seems, be circumvented.

And what has been the result of this self-serving, self-glutting disposition? In 19 10 short decades, these modern weendigoes have accomplished what at one time seemed impossible; they have laid waste immense tracts of forest that were seen as beyond limit as well as self-propagating, and ample enough to serve this generation and many more to come.

Now, as the forests are in decline, the weendigoes are looking at a future that 20 offers scarcity. Many others are assessing the weendigoes' accomplishments not in terms of dollars but in terms of damage—the damage they have inflicted on the environment and the climate and on botanical and zoological life.

Questions about Meaning

1. What kind of world does Johnston invoke in the first two paragraphs? Why is it important that readers understand the characteristics of that world at the outset?

2. What is the connection between the weendigo of myth and the modern weendigo? How are they alike and how are they different?

3. What kind of future does the conclusion of the reading anticipate? What is its relation to the world depicted in the introduction?

Questions about Rhetorical Strategy and Style

1. Why are there so many lists in the reading? Do they remind you of other lists in other readings? What effect do they have?

2. Is Johnston's ironic comment about "learned people" in paragraph five an example of gentle or sharp irony? What does the irony draw attention to and what is its effect?

3. Where does the essay change tone? How does the language change? What is the effect of these quite abrupt changes?

Seeing Red Over Myths

Drew Hayden Taylor

The author is an Ojibway from The Curve Lake First Nations in Ontario. He is also a playwright, columnist, film-maker, and lecturer. The essay was published in The Globe and Mail in March, 2001.

1   A year and a half ago, my Mohawk girlfriend and I (a fellow of proud Ojibway heritage) found ourselves in the history-rich halls of Europe, lecturing on Native issues, the propaganda and the reality, at a university deep in the heart of northeastern Germany. Then one young lady, a student at this former communist university, put up her hand and asked an oddly naïve question, something like, "Do Indian women shave their legs and armpits like other North American women"? This was not the strangest question I've had put to me. I keep a list, which includes, "I'm phoning from Edinburgh, Scotland, and am doing research on natives in the 1930s. Can you send information"? or "Where can I get my hands on some Inuit throat singers"?

2   But unbeknownst to me, the shaving of extremities in Europe is a largely unexplored area of female hygiene; evidently this topic warranted investigation as to its possible Aboriginal origin. But the question presented a rather obvious example of the issue that permeates North America: the myth of pan-Indianism. The young lady had begun her question with "Do Indian women . . . "? Sometimes the questioner substitutes First Nations/Native/Aboriginal/Indigenous for Indian. However it's worded, it reveals a persistent belief that we are all one people.

3   Within the borders of what is now referred to as Canada, there are more than fifty distinct and separate languages and dialects. And each distinct and separate language and dialect has emerged from a distinct and separate culture. I tried to tell this woman that her question couldn't be answered because, technically, there is no "Indian/First Nations/Aboriginal." To us, there is only the Cree, the Ojibway, the Salish, the Innu, the Shuswap, and so on.

4   I find myself explaining this point with annoying frequency, not just in Europe, but here in Canada, at the Second Cup, Chapters, or the bus station. The power of that single myth is incredible. When people ask me, "What do First Nations people want"? how do I answer? Some of the Mi'kmaq want to catch lobster, some of the Cree want to stop the flooding and logging of their territory in northern Manitoba, Alberta and Quebec, the Mohawk want the right to promote their own language, and I know bingo is in there somewhere.

5   That's why every time I see a TV news report talking about the plight of the Aboriginal people, I find myself screaming "Which people? Be specific!" That's why I never watch television in public.

6   Such is the power of myths. By their very definition, they're inaccurate or incomplete. Now you know why we as Native people (see, I do it myself) prefer

not to use the term "myth" when referring to the stories of our ancestors, as in "The Myths and Legends of Our People." There is something inherently wrong about starting a traditional story with "This is one of the myths that was passed down from our grandfathers. . . ." Literally translated, it means, "This is a lie that was handed down by our grandfathers. . . ."

The preferred term these days is *teachings*—as in, "Our teachings say. . . ." It's certainly more accurate because it recognizes the fact that most teachings exist for a purpose—that there's some nugget of metaphor or message within the subtext. And in the Native (there I go again!) way, we like to accentuate the positive. (Important note: The word *legend* can also be used instead of *teachings*, provided you have oral permission from a recognized elder, or written permission from an Aboriginal academic—any Nation will do.) 7

The myth of pan-Indianism is not the only one rooted in the Canadian psyche. A good percentage of Canadians believe that there's a strong Aboriginal tradition of alcoholism. In Kenora, a decade or so ago, someone told me that in one month alone there had been almost three hundred arrests of Aboriginals for alcohol-related offences. And Kenora's not that big a town. The statistic frightened me—until it was explained that rather than confirming the mind-boggling image of three hundred drunken Indians running through the Kenora streets, it signified the same dozen people who just got arrested over and over and over again. It's all in how you read the statistic. And nobody told me how many white people had been arrested over and over again. It's all in how you read that statistic. 8

While acknowledging that certain communities do, indeed, suffer from substance-abuse problems (like many non-Native communities, I might add), I can safely say that not myself, my girlfriend, my mother, my best friend, and most of the other people of Aboriginal descent I consider friends and acquaintances are alcoholics. I wonder why this myth is so persuasive. 9

It's also believed by a good percentage of Canadians that all Native people are poor. Unfortunately, many communities do suffer from mind-numbing poverty, as do many non-Native communities. But contrary to popular belief, capitalism was not a foreign concept to Canada's earliest inhabitants. There were levels of wealth and status back then; today, instead of counting their horses, the rich might count their horsepower. 10

Several weeks ago, a Toronto newspaper attacked a rumour about a coalition of Aboriginal people who had expressed interest in buying the Ottawa Senators [hockey team]. The columnist thought the idea preposterous: "These are the same people who can't afford to pay tax on a pack of smokes; the same people who are so poor they claim government policy is forcing them to live in neighbourhoods where a rusted car with more than one flat tire is considered a lawn ornament." Well, the ratio of rusted-car-on-lawn to no-rusted-car-on-lawn is so disproportionate it's hardly worth mentioning. 11

Yes, there are some wealthy Native people out there (I wish I knew more of them personally). But their existence is a hard idea to accept when the media only feature First Nations stories on the desperate and the tragic. 12

So where does this leave us? I was asked to write an essay on the "myths of a common Indian identity," which, as I translate it, means that I was asked to comment on lies about something that doesn't exist. That sounds more like politics to me. But if you're still curious about whether Indian women shave their legs and armpits, you'll have to ask one. I'm not telling. 13

Questions about Meaning

1. What is "the myth of pan-Indianism" and why does the author find it so objectionable?
2. When the author says he wonders "why the myth [about rates of alcoholism among "people of Aboriginal descent"] is so persuasive," do you think he is saying he really has no idea why this is so?

Questions about Rhetorical Strategy and Style

1. What is the effect of beginning the essay in the way the author does? What if he had begun, instead, by describing the time he was asked by someone to provide information about "natives in the 1930s"?
2. Why does the author draw attention to his own tendency to refer at times to "Indians," or "Natives," or "First Nations People"? What is the effect?
3. The author uses humour in several places in the essay. Does this mean he doesn't think the topic is especially serious? Why or why not?

What a Certain Visionary Once Said
Tomson Highway

The author, whose first language is Cree and who grew up in northern Manitoba, is best known for his plays, but he has also written novels and at least one opera libretto. This essay first appeared as an insert in **The Bank of Montreal Annual Report** *in 1992.*

As you travel north from Winnipeg, the flatness of the prairie begins to give way. And the northern forests begin to take over, forests of spruce and pine and poplar and birch. The northern rivers and northern rapids, the waterfalls, the eskers, the northern lakes—thousands of them—with their innumerable islands encircled by golden-sand beaches and flat limestone surfaces that slide gracefully into water. As you travel farther north, the trees themselves begin to diminish in height and size. And get smaller, until, finally, you reach the barren lands. It is from these reaches that herds of caribou in the thousands come thundering down each winter. It is here that you find trout and pickerel and pike and whitefish in profusion. If you're here in August, your eyes will be glutted with a sudden explosion of colour seldom seen in any southern Canadian landscape: fields of wild raspberries, cloudberries, blueberries, cranberries, stands of wild flowers you never believed such remote northern terrain was capable of nurturing. And the water is still so clean you can dip your hand over the side of your canoe and you can drink it. In winter, you can eat the snow, without fear. In both winter and summer, you can breathe, this is your land, your home.

Here, you can begin to remember that you are a human being. And if you take the time to listen—really listen—you can begin to hear the earth breathe. And whisper things simple men, who never suspected they were mad, can hear. Madmen who speak Cree, for one, can in fact understand the language this land speaks, in certain circles. Which would make madmen who speak Cree a privileged lot.

Then you seat yourself down on a carpet of reindeer moss and you watch the movements of the sky, filled with stars and galaxies of stars by night, streaked by endlessly shifting cloud formations by day. You watch the movements of the lake which, within one hour, can change from a surface of glass to one of waves so massive in their fury they can—and have—killed many a man. And you begin to understand that men and women can, within maybe not one hour but one day, change from a mood of reflective serenity and self-control to one of depression and despair so deep they can—and have—killed many a man.

You begin to understand that this earth we live on—once thought insensate, inanimate, dead by scientists, theologians and such—has an emotional, psychological and spiritual life every bit as complex as that of the most complex, sensitive and intelligent of individuals.

5   And it's ours. Or is it?

6   A certain ancient aboriginal visionary of this country once said: "We have not inherited this land, we have merely borrowed it from our children."

7   If that's the case, what a loan!

8   Eh?

Questions about Meaning

1. What does Highway mean when he suggests "madmen who speak Cree" are "a privileged lot"? Why must they be mad and why Cree?

2. Does the reading indicate that the earth is always benign? What in the essay tells us it is or is not?

3. In your own words restate the comment Highway attributes to the aboriginal visionary in paragraph six.

Questions about Rhetorical Structure and Style

1. The first paragraph is unusually long for an introductory paragraph. Why is it so long and what is the effect of all the details included in it?

2. What is the effect of Highway's directly addressing the reader as "you"?

3. Why might Highway have chosen to end the essay with "Eh"? Was it a good choice? Why or why not?

I'm a Banana and Proud of It

Wayson Choy

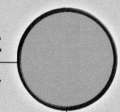

Wayson Choy (1939–) was born in Vancouver and now lives in Toronto, where he teaches at Humber College. His first novel, The Jade Peony *(1995), was awarded the Trillium Award for best book of 1996, an award he shared with Margaret Atwood. He has also published* Paper Shadows: A Chinatown Childhood *(2001), a book about growing up in Vancouver's Chinatown, and is currently at work on* The Ten Thousand Things, *a sequel to* The Jade Peony. *In the following essay, which first appeared in* The Globe and Mail, *Choy considers the significance of nicknames and their ability to appropriately reflect those who have them assigned to them.*

Because both my parents came from China, I look Chinese. But I cannot read or write Chinese and barely speak it. I love my North American citizenship. I don't mind being called a "banana," yellow on the outside and white inside. I'm proud I'm a banana.

After all, in Canada and the United States, native Indians are "apples" (red outside, white inside); blacks are "Oreo cookies" (black and white); and Chinese are "bananas." These metaphors assume, both rightly and wrongly, that the culture here has been primarily anglo-white. Cultural history made me a banana.

History: My father and mother arrived separately to the B.C. coast in the early part of the century. They came as unwanted "aliens." Better to be an alien here than to be dead of starvation in China. But after the Chinese Exclusion laws were passed in North America (late 1800s, early 1900s), no Chinese immigrants were granted citizenship in either Canada or the United States.

Like those Old China village men from *Toi San* who, in the 1850s, laid down cliff-edge train tracks through the Rockies and the Sierras, or like those first women who came as mail-order wives or concubines and who as bond-slaves were turned into cheaper labourers or even prostitutes—like many of those men and women, my father and mother survived ugly, unjust times. In 1917, two hours after he got off the boat from Hong Kong, my father was called "chink" and told to go back to China. "Chink" is a hateful racist term, stereotyping the shape of Asian eyes: "a chink in the armour," an undesirable slit. For the Elders, the past was humiliating. Eventually, the Second World War changed hostile attitudes against the Chinese.

During the war, Chinese men volunteered and lost their lives as members of the American and Canadian military. When hostilities ended, many more were proudly in uniform waiting to go overseas. Record Chinatown dollars were raised to buy War Bonds. After 1945, challenged by such money and ultimate sacrifices, the Exclusion laws in both Canada and the United States were revoked. Chinatown residents claimed their citizenship and sent for their families.

By 1949, after the Communists took over China, those of us who arrived here as young children, or were born here, stayed. No longer "aliens," we became legal citizens of North America. Many of us also became "bananas."

Historically, "banana" is not a racist term. Although it clumsily stereotypes many of the children and grandchildren of the Old Chinatowns, the term actually follows the old Chinese tendency to assign endearing nicknames to replace formal names, semicomic names to keep one humble. Thus, "banana" describes the generations who assimilated so well into North American life.

In fact, our families encouraged members of my generation in the 1950s and sixties to "get ahead," to get an English education, to get a job with good pay and prestige. "Don't work like me," Chinatown parents said. "Work in an office!" The *lao wahkiu* (the Chinatown old-timers) also warned, "Never forget—you still be Chinese!"

None of us ever forgot. The mirror never lied.

10   Many Chinatown teenagers felt we didn't quite belong in any one world. We looked Chinese, but thought and behaved North American. Impatient Chinatown parents wanted the best of both worlds for us, but they bluntly labelled their children and grandchildren "*juksing*" or even "*mo no.*" Not that we were totally "shallow bamboo butt-ends" or entirely "no brain," but we had less and less understanding of Old China traditions, and less and less interest in their village histories. Father used to say we lacked Taoist ritual, Taoist manners. We were, he said, "*mo li.*"

This was true. Chinatown's younger brains, like everyone else's of whatever race, were being colonized by "white bread" U.S. family television programs. We began to feel Chinese home life was inferior. We co-operated with English-language magazines that showed us how to act and what to buy. Seductive Hollywood movies made some of us secretly weep that we did not have movie-star faces. American music made Chinese music sound like noise.

By the 1970s and eighties, many of us had consciously or unconsciously distanced ourselves from our Chinatown histories. We became bananas.

Finally, for me, in my 40s or 50s, with the death first of my mother, then my father, I realized I did not belong anywhere unless I could understand the past. I needed to find the foundation of my Chinese-ness. I needed roots.

I spent my college holidays researching the past. I read Chinatown oral histories, located documents, searched out early articles. Those early citizens came back to life for me. Their long toil and blood sacrifices, the proud record of their patient, legal challenges, gave us all our present rights as citizens. Canadian and American Chinatowns set aside their family tongue differences and encouraged each other to fight injustice. There were no borders. "After all," they affirmed, "*Daaih ga tohng yahn . . .* We are all Chinese!"

15   In my book, *The Jade Peony,* I tried to recreate this past, to explore the beginnings of the conflicts trapped within myself, the struggle between being Chinese and being North American. I discovered a truth: these "between world" struggles are universal.

In every human being, there is "the Other"—something that makes each of us feel how different we are to everyone else, even to family members. Yet, ironically, we are all the same, wanting the same security and happiness. I know this now.

I think the early Chinese pioneers actually started "going bananas" from the moment they first settled upon the West Coast. They had no choice. They adapted. They initiated assimilation. If they had not, they and their family would have starved to death. I might even suggest that all surviving Chinatown citizens eventually became bananas. Only some, of course, were more ripe than others.

That's why I'm proudly a banana: I accept the paradox of being both Chinese and not Chinese.

Now at last, whenever I look in the mirror or hear ghost voices shouting, "You still Chinese!," I smile.

I know another truth: In immigrant North America, we are all Chinese.   20

Questions about Meaning

1. Choy distinguishes between nicknames and racist terms. Why does Choy consider "banana" not racist? How would you explain the difference between these two categories?

2. Many immigrants have written about the challenges of maintaining one's cultural heritage while simultaneously seeking assimilation. Why is this situation, in Choy's view, paradoxical?

3. What is genealogical research? Do you know your own family's history?

Questions about Strategy and Style

1. How would you characterize Choy's tone in this essay? Is it appealing? If so, why? What kind of person do you take him to be?

2. What effect does Choy's use of the term "banana" take on as it is repeated throughout? Do you think the author had a specific reason for using the term as often as he did?

3. Why did Choy write this essay? Who are his intended readers and what is he trying to accomplish with them? Why might the essay be important to his primary readers?

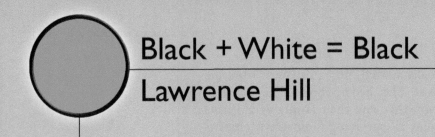

Black + White = Black

Lawrence Hill

The equation in Lawrence Hill's title, "Black + White = Black," neatly captures his struggle for identity growing up biracial in an upper middle-class white suburb of Toronto in the 1950's. This essay is an excerpt from Hill's book Black Berry, Sweet Juice: On Being Black and White in Canada *and appeared in* Maclean's *in 2001. Hill has published a variety of other works, notably the award-winning* The Book of Negroes *in 2007.*

1 My childhood was punctuated with sayings about black people. My father's relatives sometimes said, "The blacker the berry, the sweeter the juice." On one level, the meaning is obvious: a raspberry or strawberry that is full and dark and pregnant with its own ripeness is sweeter than its pink, prematurely plucked counterpart. But there is also a sexual undertone to the saying, a suggestion of the myth of the overcharged, overheated, high-performing black body. Presumably, the blacker berry tastes richer, more full and is juicier. The trouble with this expression is that it has always struck me as a limp-wristed effort to help black people believe that it was OK to be black. It seemed to me sad and pathetic that we even felt a need to pass around a saying like that.

2 But I wasn't the only one who found that the words itched more than they tickled. My father bombed the pious saying to smithereens with his own sarcastic version: "The blacker the berry/The sweeter the juice/But if you get too black/It ain't no use." I absolutely loved that variation. Why? Because it turned self-affirmation on its head with a mere 10 additional words, offering a bittersweet reminder of the hopelessness of being black in a society that doesn't love—or even like—black people. There were many other sayings, such as "If you're white/You're all right/If you're brown/Stick around/If you're black/Stay back." Black people said these words and laughed. All the sayings underscored the utter futility of being black.

3 I discovered, very early, that some people had strange ideas about the children of interracial unions, and seemed inclined to believe that life for us would be miserable. When I was 12, my best friend was a white girl, Marilyn (as I shall name her), whose mother would embarrass the dickens out of me by singing my praises to her own children. "Look how well Larry does in school. Why can't you be like that, Marilyn"? Astoundingly, this same mother who thought I was doing so well once took me aside and said, "Frankly, Larry, don't you think it is terrible, mixing races like that? It ruins the children! How are they to make their way in life"?

4 As a child, my own experience of race, including my concept of my own racial identity, was shaded quite differently from that of my parents. They were both born and raised in the United States, and their racial identities were clearly

delineated all their lives. The America of their youth and early adulthood was replete with laws that banned interracial marriages and upheld segregation in every domain of public life. One of the most telling details came to me from my mother, who was working as a secretary for a Democratic senator when she met my father in Washington in 1953: "When I started dating your father, even the federal government cafeterias were segregated." In the United States, there was never any doubt that my father was first and foremost a black man. Or that my mother was a white woman. And there is no question that, had my siblings and I been raised in the United States, we would have been identified—in school, on the street, in community centres, among friends—as black.

But my parents threw their unborn children a curveball. They came to Toronto   5 right after they married, had us and we all stayed here. They had had enough of racial divisions in their country of birth. And although they spent their lives at the forefront of the Canadian human-rights movement, they were also happy and relieved to set up in suburban, white, middleclass Toronto, where race faded (most of the time) into the background.

When I was growing up, I didn't spend much time thinking about who I was   6 or where I fit in. I was too busy tying my shoelaces, brushing my teeth, learning to spell, swinging baseball bats and shooting hockey pucks. But once in a while, just as my guard was down, questions of my own identity would leap like a cougar from the woods and take a bite out of my backside.

I found that race became an issue as a result of environmental factors. The   7 average white kid growing up in a white suburb didn't have to think of himself as white. Gradually, my environment started talking to me and making me aware that I could never truly be white. There's nothing like being called "nigger" to let you know that you're not white.

Learning that I wasn't white, however, wasn't the same as learning that I was   8 black. Indeed, for the longest time I didn't learn what I was—only what I wasn't. In the strange and unique society that was Canada, I was allowed to grow up in a sort of racial limbo. People knew what I wasn't—white or black—but they sure couldn't say what I was. I have black American cousins, of both lighter and darker complexions, who attended segregated schools and grew up in entirely black communities. They had no reason to doubt their racial identity. That identity was wrapped around them, like a snug towel, at the moment of birth.

In 1977, when I decided to take a year off university, I went to visit my cousins   9 in Brooklyn before flying to Europe, which must have appeared to them a quintessentially white thing to do. My cousin Richard Flateau took me under his wing, and was patient until I asked if he liked to play squash. An indignant retort exploded from his lips: "Larry! That's a white folks' game!" Today, looking back, I find irony in that memory. There I was, son of a black American Second World War veteran and a white American civil-rights activist, playing squash, a sport virtually unknown to inner-city blacks in the United States.

These days, I think of the factors that contributed to my sense of identity, and   10 of how malleable that sense of identity was and still is. There were days when I went straight from my exclusive, private boys' high school to family events populated by black relatives or friends who idolized the icons and heroes of my childhood— Angela Davis, with her intelligence and her kick-ass Afro; sprinters Tommie Smith and John Carlos, with their black-gloved fists raised on the Olympic podium in Mexico City; Muhammad Ali, who stood up to the white man and spoke the words that moved the world: "I ain't got no quarrel with the Viet Cong." I bounced back and forth between studying Latin, playing squash and revering black American cultural icons, but who exactly was I?

11   Lately, I have been looking at some family photos and mulling over what they mean to me. In my home office, I have some 30 framed shots of relatives. There are my three children, running, cavorting, picking apples. The eldest, Geneviève, is 11, and I wonder how she will come to see herself, racially, as she moves into adolescence. She has been a ballerina for six years, and you don't find a world much whiter than that, not even in Oakville, where we live. She knows who she is, and has had much contact with the black side of her family—but the girl has blue eyes and skin even lighter than mine, and I can see that if she is going to assert her own blackness one day, she may have to work hard at it. Nine-year-old Caroline, the middle child, is the darkest of my three, and has that uncanny middle-child ability to relate to anybody of any age. I have noticed that she already bonds vigorously with black women. Andrew, who is 7, is about as interested in race as he would be in nuclear physics. Interestingly, though, he has already called out a few times, "I'm not black, I'm white," and shot a look my way to test for a reaction. He looks white, too.

12   Would you like to know how my children would once have been categorized, racially? Quadroons. They have a father who is supposedly half-black and a mother who is white, and that parentage, according to the traditional racial definition blender, would have made them quadroons. Quadroons, of course, were most definitely black, and enslaved like the rest of us in Canada and the United States. Quadroon women were favoured by slave owners for features deemed exotic and sexy but not too black, thank you very much. I shudder to imagine children who looked just like mine dancing in the infamous Quadroon Balls in New Orleans, where hot-looking young women were bought and consumed until they were no longer young or beautiful.

13   Today in Canada, black people still contend with racism at every level of society. And yet, the way my children will define themselves, and be defined by others, remains up for grabs. Racial identity is about how you see yourself, about how you construct a sense of belonging, community, awareness and allegiance.

14   To this date, I have mostly seen myself as black. My black American relatives, who lived in Brooklyn, Washington, Baltimore and North Carolina, were much closer to us and much easier to visit than my mother's family. Apart from her twin, Dottie, whom we all adore, we never really got to know my mother's relatives. My mother spoke negatively of her brothers when we were young, describing how they gave her a hard time—one even questioned her sanity—when she announced that she would be marrying a black man. As a result, as a child I came to nourish a minor grudge against some of these relatives. On my father's side, however, family was like an extension of my own body and psyche.

15   My first sense of blackness, sprang from warm places. Our house boomed with jazz and blues on weekends. Dan, Karen and I watched—entranced, intrigued—as our parents danced in the living room to Ella Fitzgerald, Billie Holiday and Duke Ellington. Dad has an amazing voice. When he sang, he waltzed up and down the tunes with a playfulness and irreverence that we found absolutely infectious.

16   I remember being laid up with the flu when I was 5. My father asked: "Any musical requests, sir"? And I said, "Put on Joe Williams." *Every Day I Have the Blues* began to jump off the record player. I listened to my dad and Williams nailing the notes as Basie hammered the piano, and trumpets, trombones and saxophones erupted with glee. It's one of the happiest songs I've heard—even if it is about the blues. *Nobody loves me/nobody seems to care/between bad luck and trouble/well you know I've had my share.* Just about any words could have flown from Joe Williams's

lips and soared, ecstatically, as if to prove that nothing could keep this man from living and loving. Jazz and blues were already showing me the sweet alchemy of trouble and joy that defined black musical expression, and black people themselves.

I don't recall early moments with family members that gave me a negative 17 sense of race, but my siblings do. Perhaps because he was the firstborn, Dan had a rockier time with our father. Dan has no doubt that our father gave us mixed racial messages. When my brother was 11 or so, Dad gave him a stocking to wear on his head at night. The idea was to straighten out Dan's hair while he slept, or at the very least to keep it from getting too curly on the pillow. I asked Dan if Dad had told him why he had to wear it.

"It wasn't good to have curly hair. He'd pull a hair out of my head and put it 18 on the table and say, 'See? This is curly. It's not good to have curly hair.' And I remember feeling extremely hurt and ashamed, and I started wearing the stocking cap. I remember feeling very concerned that my hair was curly, and I remember being frantic about straightening it."

Dan now attributes the incident to the strange paradoxes of human nature. "I 19 think that kind of behavior is common among people like our father, who have worked in the field of human rights. Very often, people go into these fields as compensation for their own feelings of inadequacy. That way, they can still bring those feelings of inadequacy and self-hatred—self-racial-hatred—into the house."

Dan, Karen and I learned early that you can have a white parent and still be 20 considered black, but you can never have a black parent and be considered white. It ain't allowed. You'll be reminded of your "otherness" more times than you can shake a stick at it. This is one of the reasons why I self-identify as black. Attempts at pleasant symmetry, as in "half-white, half-black," trivialize to my eye the meaning of being black. This doesn't mean I don't love my mother. I love her as profoundly as I love any person on earth. But I just don't see myself as being the same race as she is. I raised this issue with my mother recently. "Listen," she told me, "when I married your father, I knew that our children would be black. I would have been an idiot to fail to see that. Look where we came from."

However, the suburb of Don Mills in which they eventually settled became as 21 suffocating for their children as D.C. had been for them. There were no blacks in my school, on my street. Because I looked so different from everyone else, I feared that I was ugly. I worried about having frizzy hair, big ears, a big nose and plump lips. When I looked in the mirror, I felt disgust. None of the people I admired looked the least bit like me. Listening to stories of my father's working world instilled in us a measure of black pride. We also derived a sense of connection from family moments around the television, which is odd because we weren't that interested in TV. But the late 1960s and the early 1970s featured big stand-up comedy numbers by Bill Cosby and Flip Wilson. When I watched these shows, I felt alive. I felt that there were people in the world who were speaking to me.

I had to find other ways to connect with them. So I ate up every bit of black 22 writing that I could find. Langston Hughes, Ralph Ellison, Richard Wright— whom I approached gingerly because my mother confessed that *Native Son* had upset her so much, it had made her vomit. James Baldwin. Eldridge Cleaver— now that cat fascinated me, especially when, in *Soul on Ice*, he speculated as to why black men and white women end up together. I read Alex Haley's *Autobiography of Malcolm X*, and had to struggle through the section of Malcolm X's life when he ardently believed that white people were the devil incarnate. I knew this to be false. My mother was white, and she was no devil.

23   Without knowing exactly what I was doing, I was forming my own sense of blackness and my own connection to the black diaspora. Soon, this exploration blossomed into creative writing. Every time I wrote, my mind wandered into the lives of black characters. Slowly, I was developing a sense of myself. These days, when I'm invited into schools with black students, I feel a tinge of nostalgia for a past not lived. I can't help wondering what it would have been like to have black people around me when I was young. I can't help wondering what it would have been like to go out with black girls, or to drift into a friend's home and find myself surrounded by black people. What a different life that would have been.

Questions about Meaning

1. Why did Hill's parents move to Toronto? What were the effects for Hill's family? Be sure to note both the positive and negative consequences.

2. What were the environmental and family influences that led to Hill's sense of identity?

3. The last sentence in this essay says that having been raised in a black community would have been "a different life" for Hill. Do you get the sense that he wishes he had grown up differently, or do you think that this "different life" would have been worse for him somehow?

Questions about Rhetorical Strategy and Style

1. The author opens this article with a discussion of a popular saying that is a metaphor that stereotypes black people as being more sexual than whites. The first few pages of this article continue to use figurative language (similes, metaphors and personification). Locate at least two other figures of speech in the first 8 paragraphs. Why would the author use these expressions? What do they add to the article?

2. In paragraph 12, Hill switches to the second person and asks "would you like to know how my children would once have been categorized, racially"? Why would the author reach out to the reader directly here? What does this tell us about the intended audience for this article?

Why My Mother Can't Speak English
Garry Engkent

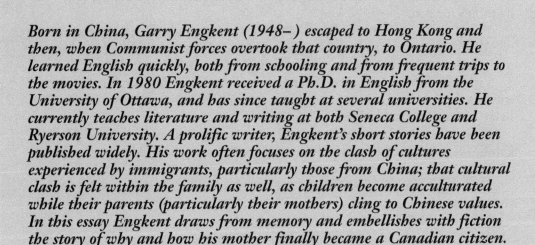

*Born in China, Garry Engkent (1948–) escaped to Hong Kong and
then, when Communist forces overtook that country, to Ontario. He
learned English quickly, both from schooling and from frequent trips to
the movies. In 1980 Engkent received a Ph.D. in English from the
University of Ottawa, and has since taught at several universities. He
currently teaches literature and writing at both Seneca College and
Ryerson University. A prolific writer, Engkent's short stories have been
published widely. His work often focuses on the clash of cultures
experienced by immigrants, particularly those from China; that cultural
clash is felt within the family as well, as children become acculturated
while their parents (particularly their mothers) cling to Chinese values.
In this essay Engkent draws from memory and embellishes with fiction
the story of why and how his mother finally became a Canadian citizen.*

My mother is seventy years old. Widowed for five years now, she lives alone in her
own house except for the occasions when I come home to tidy her household
affairs. She has been in *gum san*, the golden mountain, for the past thirty years. She
clings to the old-country ways so much so that today she astonishes me with this
announcement:

"I want to get my citizenship," she says as she slaps down the *Dai Pao*, "before
they come and take away my house."

"Nobody's going to do that. This is Canada."

"So everyone says," she retorts, "but did you read what the *Dai Pao* said? Ah,
you can't read Chinese. The government is cutting back on old-age pensions.
Anybody who hasn't got citizenship will lose everything. Or worse."

"The *Dai Pao* can't even typeset accurately," I tell her. Sometimes I worry
about the information Mother receives from the biweekly community newspaper.
"Don't worry—the Ministry of Immigration won't send you back to China."

"Little you know," she snaps back. "I am old, helpless, and without citizenship.
Reasons enough. Now, get me citizenship. Hurry!"

"Mother, getting citizenship papers is not like going to the bank to cash in
your pension cheque. First, you have to—"

"Excuses, my son, excuses. When your father was alive—"

"Oh, Mother, not again! You throw that at me every—"

"—made excuses, too." Her jaw tightens. "If you can't do this little thing for
your own mother, well, I will just have to go and beg your cousin to . . ."

Every time I try to explain about the ways of the *fan gwei*, she thinks I do not
want to help her. "I'll do it, I'll do it, okay? Just give me some time."

"That's easy for you," Mother snorts. "You're not seventy years old. You're not going to lose your pension. You're not going to lose your house. Now, how much *lai-shi* will this take"?

After all these years in *gum san* she cannot understand that you don't give government officials *lai-shi*, the traditional Chinese money gift to persons who do things for you.

"That won't be necessary," I tell her, "and you needn't go to my cousin."

15   Mother picks up the *Dai Pao* again and says: "Why should I beg at the door of a village cousin when I have a son who is a university graduate"?

I wish my father were alive. Then he would be doing this. But he is not here, and as a dutiful son, I am responsible for the welfare of my widowed mother. So I take her to Citizenship Court.

There are several people from the Chinese community waiting there. Mother knows a few of the Chinese women and she chats with them. My cousin is there too.

"I thought your mother already got her citizenship," he says to me. "Didn't your father—"

"No, he didn't."

20   He shakes his head sadly. "Still, better now than never. That's why I'm getting these people through."

"So they've been reading the *Dai Pao*."

He gives me a quizzical look, so I explain to him, and he laughs.

"You are the new generation," he says. "You didn't live long enough in *hon san*, the sweet land, to understand the fears of the old. You can't expect the elderly to renounce all attachments to China for the ways of the *fan gwei*, white devils. How old is she, seventy now? Much harder."

"She woke me up this morning at six and Citizenship Court doesn't open till ten."

25   The doors of the court finally open, and Mother motions me to hurry. We wait in line for a while.

The clerk distributes applications and tells me the requirements. Mother wants to know what the clerk is saying, so half the time I translate for her.

The clerk suggests that we see one of the liaison officers.

"Your mother has been living in Canada for the past thirty years and she still can't speak English"?

"It happens," I tell the liaison officer.

30   "I find it hard to believe that—not one word"?

"Well, she understands some restaurant English," I tell her. "You know, French fries, pork chops, soup, and so on. And she can say a few words."

"But will she be able to understand the judge's questions? The interview with the judge, as you know, is an important part of the citizenship procedure. Can she read the booklet? What does she know about Canada"?

"So you don't think my mother has a chance"?

"The requirements are that the candidate must be able to speak either French or English, the two official languages of Canada. The candidate must be able to pass an oral interview with the citizenship judge, and then he or she must be able to recite the oath of allegiance—"

35   "My mother needs to speak English," I conclude for her.

"Look, I don't mean to be rude, but why didn't your mother learn English when she first came over"?

I have not been translating this conversation, and Mother, annoyed and agitated, asks me what is going on. I tell her there is a slight problem.

"What problem"? Mother opens her purse, and I see her taking a small red envelope—*lai shi*—I quickly cover her hand.

"What's going on"? the liaison officer demands.

"Nothing," I say hurriedly. "Just a cultural misunderstanding, I assure you."   40

My mother rattles off some indignant words, and I snap back in Chinese: "Put that away! The woman won't understand, and we'll be in a lot of trouble."

The officer looks confused, and I realize that an explanation is needed.

"My mother was about to give you a money gift as a token of appreciation for what you are doing for us. I was afraid you might misconstrue it as a bribe. We have no intention of doing that."

"I'm relieved to hear it."

We conclude the interview, and I take Mother home. Still clutching the   45
application, Mother scowls at me.

"I didn't get my citizenship papers. Now I will lose my old-age pension. The government will ship me back to China. My old bones will lie there while your father's will be here. What will happen to me"?

How can I teach her to speak the language when she is too old to learn, too old to want to learn? She resists anything that is *fan gwei*. She does everything the Chinese way. Mother spends much time staring blankly at the four walls of her house. She does not cry. She sighs and shakes her head. Sometimes she goes about the house touching her favourite things.

"This is all your dead father's fault," she says quietly. She turns to the photograph of my father on the mantel. Daily, she burns incense, pours fresh cups of fragrant tea, and spreads dishes of his favourite fruits in front of the framed picture as is the custom. In memory of his passing, she treks two miles to the cemetery to place flowers by his headstone, to burn ceremonial paper money, and to talk to him. Regularly, rain or shine, or even snow, she does these things. Such love, such devotion, now such vehemence. Mother curses my father, her husband, in his grave.

When my mother and I emigrated from China, she was forty years old, and I, five. My father was already a well-established restaurant owner. He put me in school and Mother in the restaurant kitchen, washing dishes and cooking strange foods like hot dogs, hamburgers, and French fries. She worked seven days a week from six in the morning until eleven at night. This lasted for twenty-five years, almost to the day of my father's death.

The years were hard on her. The black-and-white photographs show a robust   50
woman; now I see a withered, frail, white-haired old woman, angry, frustrated with the years, and scared of losing what little material wealth she has to show for the toil in *gum san*.

"I begged him," Mother says. "But he would either ignore my pleas or say: 'What do you need to know English for? You're better off here in the kitchen. Here you can talk to the others in our own tongue. English is far too complicated for you. How old are you now? Too old to learn a new language. Let the young speak *fan gwei*. All you need is to understand the orders from the waitresses. Anyway, if you need to know something, the men will translate for you. I am here; I can do your talking for you.'"

As a conscientious boss of the young male immigrants, my father would force them out of the kitchen and into the dining room. "The kitchen is no place for you to learn English. All you do is speak Chinese in here. To survive in *gum san*, you have to speak English, and the only way you can do that is to wait on tables and force yourselves to speak English with the customers. How can you get your families over here if you can't talk to the immigration officers in English"?

A few of the husbands who had the good fortune to bring their wives over to Canada hired a retired school teacher to teach a bit of English to their wives. Father discouraged Mother from going to those once-a-week sessions.

"That old woman will get rich doing nothing. What have these women learned? *Fan gwei* ways—make-up lipstick, smelly perfumes, fancy clothes. Once she gets through with them, they won't be Chinese women any more—and they certainly won't be white either."

55   Some of the husbands heeded the words of the boss, for he was older than they, and he had been in the white devil's land longer. These wives stayed home and tended the children, or they worked in the restaurant kitchen, washing dishes and cooking *fan gwei* foods, and talking in Chinese about the land and the life they had been forced to leave behind.

"He was afraid that I would leave him. I depended on him for everything. I could not go anywhere by myself. He drove me to work and he drove me home. He only taught me how to print my name so that I could sign anything he wanted me to, bank cheques, legal documents . . ."

Perhaps I am not Chinese enough any more to understand why my mother would want to take in the sorrow, the pain, and the anguish, and then to recount them every so often.

Once, I was presumptuous enough to ask her why she would want to remember in such detail. She said that the memories didn't hurt any more. I did not tell her that her reminiscences cut me to the quick. Her only solace now is to be listened to.

My father wanted more sons, but she was too old to give him more. One son was not enough security he needed for old age. "You smell of stale perfume," she would say to him after he had driven the waitresses home. Or, to me, she would say: "A second mother will not treat you so well, you know," and, "Would you like another mother at home"? Even at that tender age, I knew that in China a husband could take a second wife. I told her that I didn't need another mother, and she would nod her head.

60   When my father died five years ago, she cried and cried. "Don't leave me in this world. Let me die with you."

Grief-stricken, she would not eat for days. She was so weak from hunger that I feared she wouldn't be able to attend the funeral. At his grave side, she chanted over and over a dirge, commending his spirit to the next world and begging the goddess of mercy to be kind to him. By custom, she set his picture on the mantel and burned incense in front of it daily. And we would go to the cemetery often. There she would arrange fresh flowers and talk to him in the gentlest way.

Often she would warn me: "The world of the golden mountain is so strange, *fan gwei* improprieties, and customs. The white devils will have you abandon your own aged mother to some old-age home to rot away and die unmourned. If you are here long enough, they will turn your head until you don't know who you are—Chinese."

My mother would convert the months and the days into the Chinese lunar calendar. She would tell me about the seasons and the harvests and the festivals in China. We did not celebrate any *fan gwei* holidays.

My mother sits here at the table, fingering the booklet from the Citizenship Court. For thirty-some years, my mother did not learn the English language, not because she was not smart enough, not because she was too old to learn, and not because my father forbade her, but because she feared that learning English would change her Chinese soul. She only learned enough English to survive in the restaurant kitchen.

65   Now, Mother wants *gum san* citizenship.

"Is there no hope that I will be given it"? she asks.

"There's always a chance," I tell her. "I'll hand in the application."

"I should have given that person the *lai shi*," Mother says obstinately.

"Maybe I should teach you some English," I retort. "You have about six months before the oral interview."

"I am seventy years old," she says. "*Lai shi* is definitely much easier."   70

My brief glimpse into Mother's heart is over, and it has taken so long to come about. I do not know whether I understand my aged mother any better now. Despite my mother's constant instruction, there is too much *fan gwei* in me.

The booklet from the Citizenship Court lies, unmoved, on the table, gathering dust for weeks. She has not mentioned citizenship again with the urgency of that particular time. Once in a while, she would say: "They have forgotten me. I told you they don't want old Chinese women as citizens."

Finally, her interview date is set. I try to teach her some ready-made phrases, but she forgets them.

"You should not sigh so much. It is bad for your health," Mother observes.

On the day of her examination, I accompany her into the judge's chamber. I   75
am more nervous than my mother.

Staring at the judge, my mother remarks: "*Noi yren.*" The judge shows interest in what my mother says, and I translate it: "She says you're a woman."

The judge smiles. "Yes. Is that strange"?

"If she is going to examine me," Mother tells me, "I might as well start packing for China. Sell my house. Dig up your father's bones, and I'll take them back with me."

Without knowing what my mother said, the judge reassures her. "This is just a formality. Really. We know that you obviously want to be part of our Canadian society. Why else would you go through all this trouble? We want to welcome you as a new citizen, no matter what race, nationality, religion, or age. And we want you to be proud—as a new Canadian."

Six weeks have passed since the interview with the judge. Mother receives a   80
registered letter telling her to come in three weeks' time to take part in the oath of allegiance ceremony.

With patient help from the same judge, my mother recites the oath and becomes a Canadian citizen after thirty years in *gum san*.

"How does it feel to be a Canadian"? I ask.

"In China, this is the eighth month, the season of harvest." Then she adds: "The *Dai Pao* says that the old-age pension cheques will be increased by nine dollars next month."

As we walk home on this bright autumn morning, my mother clutches her piece of paper. Citizenship. She says she will go up to the cemetery and talk to my father this afternoon. She has something to tell him.

Questions about Meaning

1. Why did the author's father refuse to allow his wife to learn English? How does the author suggest that his mother, at least at some level of consciousness, agreed with this reasoning?

2. What is the significance of the widow's mourning rituals for her dead husband? How do these rituals help readers understand Engkent's mother?

3. How does the judge interpret Mrs. Engkent's determination to be a Canadian citizen? What does this misperception suggest about other immigrants' motivations for citizenship?

Questions about Strategy and Style

1. Engkent chooses to deliver his narrative in the present tense. How does this choice affect the impact of his story? How would the story have been different had he used the more traditional past tense?

2. What have been the effects of not having learned English for the author's mother? In what ways do these effects seem to have been positive? In what ways negative?

3. Engkent presents a number of contrasts in this story: ways of dealing with Canadian as opposed to Chinese bureaucracy, men's and women's roles in Chinese culture, and his mother's devotion to and resentment of her husband, among others. Choose one significant contrast in the narrative and explain how it serves the author's purpose in relating his mother's story.

Being Canadian
Denise Chong

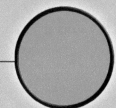

Denise Chong (1953–), the granddaughter of immigrants from China who were never able to vote or become Canadian citizens, was an economic advisor to Canadian Prime Minister Pierre Trudeau before she became a full-time writer. Among her books is a vivid and affecting memoir of her family's experience, **The Concubine's Children.** *Note that the text here was originally part of a speech she gave.*

I ask myself what it means to be a Canadian. I was lucky enough to be born in Canada [, so] I look back at the price paid by those who made the choice that brought me such luck. 1

South China at the turn of the century became the spout of the teapot that was China. It poured out middle-class peasants like my grandfather, who couldn't earn a living at home. He left behind a wife and child. My grandfather was 36 when exclusion came. Lonely and living a penurious existence, he worked at a sawmill on the mud flats of the Fraser River, where the Chinese were third on the pay scale behind "Whites" and "Hindus." With the door to Chinese immigration slammed shut, men like him didn't dare even go home for a visit, for fear Canada might bar their re-entry. With neither savings enough to go home for good, nor the means once in China to put rice in the mouths of his wife and child there, my grandfather wondered when, if ever, he could return to the bosom of a family. He decided to purchase a concubine, a second wife, to join him in Canada. 2

The concubine, at age 17, got into Canada on a lie. She got around the exclusion law in the only way possible: she presented the authorities with a Canadian birth certificate. It had belonged to a woman born in Ladner, British Columbia, and a middleman sold it to my grandfather at many times the price of the old head tax. Some years later, the concubine and my grandfather went back to China with their two Vancouver-born daughters. They lived for a time under the same roof as my grandfather's first wife. The concubine became pregnant. Eight months into her pregnancy, she decided to brave the long sea voyage back so that her third child could be born in Canada. [Her] false Canadian birth certificate would get her in. Accompanied by only my grandfather, she left China. Three days after the boat docked, on the second floor of a tenement on a back alley in Vancouver's Chinatown, she gave birth to my mother. 3

Canada remained inhospitable. Yet my grandparents *chose* to keep Canada in their future. Both gambled a heritage and family ties to take what they thought were better odds in the lottery of life. . . . 4

My own sense, four generations on, of being Canadian is one of belonging. I belong to a family. I belong to a community of values. I didn't get to choose my ancestors, but I can try to leave the world a better place for the generations that follow. The life I lead begins before and lingers after my time. 5

6   I am now the mother of two young children. I want to pass on a sense of what it means to be a Canadian. But what worries me as a parent, and as a Canadian, is whether we can fashion an enduring concept of citizenship that will be the glue that holds us together as a society. Curiously, Canadian citizenship elicits the most heartfelt response outside Canada. Any Canadian who has lived or travelled abroad quickly discovers that Canadian citizenship is a coveted possession. In the eyes of the rest of the world, it stands for an enlightened and gentle society.

7   Can we find a strong concept of citizenship that could be shared by all Canadians when we stand on our own soil? Some would say it is unrealistic to expect a symbol to rise out of a rather pragmatic past. We spilled no revolutionary blood, as did France—where the word *citoyen* was brought into popular usage—or America. Some lament the absence of a founding myth; we don't have the equivalent of a Boston Tea Party. Others long for Canadian versions of heroes to compete with the likes of American images that occupy our living rooms and our playgrounds. The one Canadian symbol with universal recognition is the flag. But where does the maple leaf strike a chord? Outside Canada. On the back packs of Canadian travellers. . . .

8   Some say Canadian citizenship is devalued because it is too easy to come here. But what sets Canadian society apart from others is that ours is an inclusive society. Canada's citizenship act remains more progressive than [the immigration laws of] many countries. Canadians by immigration have equal status with Canadians by birth. In contrast, in western Europe, guest workers, even if they descended from those who originally came, can be sent "home" any time. In Japan, Koreans and Filipinos have no claim to the citizenship of their birth. The plight of the Palestinians in Kuwait after the Gulf War gave the lie to a "free Kuwait."

9   Canadian citizenship recognizes differences. It praises diversity. It is what we as Canadians *choose* to have in common with each other. It is a bridge between those who left something to make a new home here and those born here. What keeps the bridge strong is tolerance, fairness, understanding, and compassion. Citizenship has rights and responsibilities. I believe one responsibility of citizenship is to use that tolerance, fairness, understanding, and compassion to leaf through the Canadian family album together. . . .

10   How we tell our stories is the work of citizenship. The motive of the storyteller should be to put the story first. To speak with authenticity and veracity is to choose narrative over commentary. It is not to glorify or sentimentalize the past. It is not to sanitize our differences. Nor [is it] to rail against or to seek compensation today for injustices of bygone times. In my opinion, to try to rewrite history leads to a sense of victimization. It marginalizes Canadians. It backs away from equality in our society, for which we have worked hard to find expression.

11   I believe our stories ultimately tell the story of Canada itself. In all our pasts are an immigrant beginning, a settler's accomplishments and setbacks, and the confidence of a common future. We all know the struggle for victory, the dreams and the lost hopes, the pride and the shame. When we tell our stories, we look in the mirror. I believe what we will see is that Canada is not lacking in heroes. Rather, the heroes are to be found within.

12   The work of citizenship is not something just for the week that we celebrate citizenship every year. It is part of every breath we take. It is the work of our lifetimes. . . .

13   If we do some of this work of citizenship, we will stand on firmer ground. Sharing experience will help build strength of character. It will explain our differences, yet make them less divisive. We will yell at each other less, and

understand each other more. We will find a sense of identity and a common purpose. We will have something to hand down to the next generation.

My grandfather's act of immigration to the new world and the determination 14 of my grandmother, the girl who first came here as a *kay toi neu*, to chance a journey from China back to Canada so that my mother could be born here, will stand as a gift to all future generations of my family. Knowing they came hoping for a better life makes it easy to love both them and this country.

In the late 1980s, I [found] myself in China, on a two-year stint living in Peking 15 and working as a writer. In a letter to my mother in Prince George, I confessed that, despite the predictions of friends back in Canada, I was finding it difficult to feel any "Chineseness." My mother wrote back: "You're Canadian, not Chinese. Stop trying to feel anything." She was right. I stopped such contrivances. I was Canadian; it was that which embodied the values of my life.

Questions about Meaning

1. According to the article, why is it difficult for Canadians to have a "strong concept of citizenship"?
2. What does Chong suggest we do to solidify our sense of what it means to be Canadian?
3. What kind of country was the Canada that Chong's grandfather first travelled to? Has it changed for Chong in the present? If so, what led to that change?
4. What are the benefits of sharing an identity as Canadians, according to Chong?

Questions about Rhetorical Strategy and Style

1. Why does the author mention other countries in paragraphs 8 and 9? Does this reduce or enhance the strength of her argument?
2. Why would the author have chosen to end her article with a personal story rather than a strong restatement of her argument? Is this an effective conclusion? Why or why not?

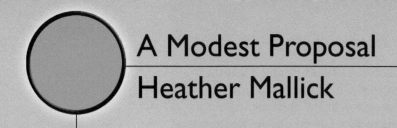

A Modest Proposal

Heather Mallick

The author is a columnist with **The Toronto Star.** *This essay first appeared on the CBC News website in 2010.*

1   Women in niqabs look like scary black crows as they flutter along a Canadian sidewalk. So what? Black crows are common enough birds. But they might as well be big red fire trucks when you consider the reactions of other Canadians, we who generally dress like drab sparrows: sensibly, comfortably and in shades of brown.

What is to be done?

In the latest standoff an immigrant from Egypt has refused to adjust her full-body niqab to uncover her mouth in the French-language class that the government hopes will help new Canadians fit into Quebec society. Told that it would be difficult to learn any language under those conditions, she spoke only when facing away from her male classmates and spoke to her female instructor one-on-one. Then she was reported to have asked the male students to move farther away from her.

The CEGEP de Saint-Laurent in Montreal was not happy. Neither was the Quebec government, which backed its immigration minister in saying that the woman, Naima Ahmed, could not remain in the class.

5   "This is the first time I felt racism [in Canada]," Ahmed told a newspaper in an interview after her story hit the headlines.

And I, a lifelong feminist—a stance that earns me almost daily hate mail—am pondering who I will most annoy with today's column.

What Ahmed calls racism is what I call feminism. Is Ahmed, as she says, protecting her modesty? If so, from what? Canadian men aren't easily inflamed by a mouth. Or a nose. Even the most crass men will remain reasonably polite when confronted by a female classmate with face, hair, ankles, the whole package.

Threat of Exposure

But Ahmed, 29, is new to this country. She has seen ill-treatment. She comes from a nation ranked by the World Economic Forum at the bottom of 58 countries in every aspect of women's rights: economic participation and opportunity, political power, education and health. Women in Cairo cannot walk on the street without enduring male assaults.

Ahmed's problem is that she thinks she'll endure the same problems in Montreal, not realizing that the niqab can seem threatening even to other women on a Canadian street.

This is how the great travel writer Jonathan Raban once described 10 the sight of Arab women visiting London while retaining their modesty, and I wouldn't call his description inaccurate: "It was the masks I noticed first. They made the women look like hooded falcons, and they struck me not as symbols of Islamic female modesty so much as objects of downright menace. Round every corner, one came upon these masks, and the black silk sheaths that encased the women as if they were corpses risen in their shrouds."

In Canada your face is your fortune. Along with clothing and speech, it is a way of quickly assessing another human being and figuring out a means of being social. Ahmed does not realize that if she doesn't adapt to this, she will never fit in Canadian society and will likely not work in her chosen field as a pharmacist, a job that requires clarity and obvious empathy.

On the other hand, immigrants' unwillingness to adapt to Canadian mores has also improved our lives immeasurably. I recall the shrimp cocktail, the iceberg lettuce salad, turkey served with marshmallows, boiled cabbage served on the plate like the earth humps on top of fresh graves. All classic Canadian cuisine.

At this immigrants did the equivalent of turning away from the class and gave us pizza, hummus, dim sum, tapas, boudin noir, Époisses, perogies, pickled herring, dal, pasteis de nata, vinho verde, burritos, polenta, baklava, etc. This has enhanced my life, given it an enchantment my Scottish mother and East Indian father, hardly foodies, never explored.

When Muslims offered us Shariah law, Muslim-Canadian feminists braved some very dire elderly imams and told us to turn our backs on it. So far we have and it has helped us all.

Canadians aim to welcome immigrants with courtesy and patience. Immigrants 15 come here because they like us. They bend; we bend; neither of us breaks.

Stigmatizing Assumptions

I have two daughters, which makes me a practical species of feminist with a meticulous interest in the daily lives of women. I want to hustle over to women in niqabs and whisper, "You don't have to wear that here." Politeness always triumphs and I have never done this. But I see myself from the black-cloaked woman's eyes— my tight clothing and exposed legs, long hair, lipstick, a real boldness with the men who are my equals—and I assume, perhaps unfairly, that she regards me as sluttish.

So women are at odds with each other over the niqab. It gets worse. A niqab inevitably insults all the men and women who encounter it, just by implication. I can take a niqab-wearer's incorrect assumptions about me personally, but I dislike her stigmatizing men, whose co-operation this feminist needs to build a society that will be fair to our daughters.

Ahmed is comfortable only in the company of females. She assumes that men are only at ease in the company of men (a reference to a brilliant Neil LaBute movie you may not wish to see).

But I believe all single-sex institutions are bad news. Book groups, single-sex schools, male top-heavy workplaces, police forces, armed forces, girl gangs, anywhere where one gender predominates or rules is headed for trouble. Am I alone in noticing that sexual segregation ends in tears and sometimes blood? Just read Margaret Atwood's novel *Cat's Eye* and study the mechanism.

Ahmed hopes that no man will ever see her face, and that men will never truly 20 interact or compete with her. We had that era in Canada, before the Persons

Case (and long after), when women were fired from their jobs when they married, when women, Jews and other undesirables couldn't get into good universities, when men ruled on sexual and reproductive matters, when society was compartmentalized to the extreme.

Ahmed wants Canada to give way and revert to an era of cruelty, nay perversion. Canada asks that she concede. Inevitably, both sides will adjust. But someone has to decide where it stops, and I believe niqabs are it.

Open and Shut Case

Here's a Canadian snapshot. Last night, I asked my male bus driver to let me off at my front door instead of the regular stop. It's a practice the Toronto transit system began years ago, when Paul Bernardo was capturing women as they got off the bus in order to rape and torture them. The rule was left in place after he was imprisoned.

The bus driver, a nice man, was happy to help. I was effusive in my thanks. In Cairo, a smart Ahmed wouldn't ride a bus at night. In fact, it was only in 2008 that Egyptian women were allowed even to apply for jobs driving buses.

In Egypt, the niqab might be practical. In Canada, it is nothing more than female self-harming. When anguished young women cut their arms and legs with knives to let out emotional pain, our health-care system sends them to doctors and counsellors.

25 I see no difference between hurting yourself in private with scissors and hurting yourself in public by rendering yourself both scary and invisible. The second course hurts the rest of us too.

I say we dispense with it, and with all the kindness and warmth I can offer, I welcome Naima Ahmed to this country.

Questions about Meaning

1. What is the proposal Malick is making in this essay? To whom is it addressed?
2. For what particular benefits does Mallick give credit to immigrants? What are some of the major benefits of immigration or contributions of immigrants that she has overlooked?
3. Paragraph seven begins with a bold statement: "What Ahmed calls racism is what I call feminism." What does this tell us about the author's view of Ahmed's claim that the Quebec's government's action was racist?

Questions about Rhetorical Strategy and Style

1. Another essay—very well-known, very highly regarded and included in this book—has the same title. Why might Mallick have chosen this title for this essay? Did the title influence your reading of the essay?
2. What is the effect of the simile Mallick uses in the essay's first sentence?
3. What is the tone of the essay's conclusion? What do you think Naima Ahmed's likely reaction to this welcome would be? Why?

Grinning and Happy

Joy Kogawa

Excerpted from Joy Kogawa's highly regarded 1981 novel **Obasan,**
"Grinning and Happy" tells the story of being Japanese-Canadian
during the Second World War and being classified as an "enemy
alien." The title nicely captures the ironic tension between perception
and reality.

There is a folder in Aunt Emily's package containing only one newspaper clipping   1
and an index card with the words "Facts about evacuees in Alberta." The newspaper
clipping has a photograph of one family, all smiles, standing around a pile of beets.
The caption reads: "Grinning and Happy."

Find Jap Evacuees Best Beet Workers   2
Lethbridge, Alberta, Jan. 22.
Japanese evacuees from British Columbia supplied the labour for 65%   3
of Alberta's sugar beet acreage last year, Phil Baker, of Lethbridge,
president of the Alberta Sugar Beet Growers Association, stated today.

"They played an important part in producing our all-time record   4
crop of 363,000 tons of beets in 1945," he added.

Mr. Baker explained Japanese evacuees worked 19,500 acres of beets   5
and German prisoners of war worked 5,000 acres. The labour for the
remaining 5,500 acres of Alberta's 30,000 acres of sugar beets was
provided by farmers and their families. Some of the heaviest beet yields
last year came from farms employing Japanese evacuees.

Generally speaking, Japanese evacuees have developed into most   6
efficient beet workers, many of them being better than the transient
workers who cared for beets in southern Alberta before Pearl Harbor. . . .

Facts about evacuees in Alberta? The fact is I never got used to it and I cannot,   7
I cannot bear the memory. There are some nightmares from which there is no
waking, only deeper and deeper sleep.

There is a word for it. Hardship. The hardship is so pervasive, so inescapable,   8
so thorough it's a noose around my chest and I cannot move any more. All the oil
in my joints has drained out and I have been invaded by dust and grit from the fields
and mud is in my bone marrow. I can't move anymore. My fingernails are black
from scratching the scorching day and there is no escape.

Aunt Emily, are you a surgeon cutting at my scalp with your folders and your   9
filing cards and your insistence on knowing all? The memory drains down the
sides of my face, but isn't enough, is it? It's your hands in my abdomen, pulling the
growth from the lining of my walls, but bring back the anaesthetist turn on the ether

clamp down the gas mask bring on the chloroform when will this operation be over Aunt Em?

10   Is it so bad?

11   Yes.

12   Do I really mind?

13   Yes, I mind. I mind everything. Even the flies. The flies and flies and flies from the cows in the barn and the manure pile—all the black flies that curtain the windows, and Obasan with a wad of toilet paper, spish, then with her bare hands as well, grabbing them and their shocking white eggs and the mosquitoes mixed there with the other insect corpses around the base of the gas lamp.

14   It's the chicken coop "house" we live in that I mind. The uninsulated unbelievable thin-as-a-cotton-dress hovel never before inhabited in winter by human beings. In summer it's a heat trap, an incubator, a dry sauna from which there is no relief. In winter the icicles drip down the inside of the windows and the ice is thicker than bricks at the ledge. The only place that is warm is by the coal stove where we rotate like chickens on a spit and the feet are so cold they stop registering. We eat cloves of roasted garlic on winter nights to warm up.

15   It's the bedbugs and my having to sleep on the table to escape the nightly attack, and the welts over our bodies. And all the swamp bugs and the dust. It's Obasan uselessly packing all the cracks with rags. And the muddy water from the irrigation ditch which we strain and settle and boil, and the tiny carcasses of water creatures at the bottom of the cup. It's walking in winter to the reservoir and keeping the hole open with the axe and dragging up the water in pails and lugging it back and sometimes the water spills down your boots and your feet are red and itchy for days. And it's everybody taking a bath in the round galvanized tub, then Obasan washing clothes in the water after and standing outside hanging the clothes in the freezing weather where everything instantly stiffens on the line.

16   Or it's standing in the beet field under the maddening sun, standing with my black head a sun-trap even though it's covered, and lying down in the ditch, faint, and the nausea in waves and the cold sweat, and getting up and tackling the next row. The whole field is an oven and there's not a tree within walking distance. We are tiny as insects crawling along the grill and there is no protection anywhere. The eyes are lidded against the dust and the air cracks the skin, the lips crack, Stephen's flutes crack and there is no energy to sing any more anyway.

17   It's standing in the field and staring out at the heat waves that waver and shimmer like see-through curtains over the brown clods and over the tiny distant bodies of Stephen and Uncle and Obasan miles away across the field day after day and not even wondering how this has come about.

18   There she is, Obasan, wearing Uncle's shirt over a pair of dark baggy trousers, her head covered by a straw hat is held on by a white cloth tied under her chin. She is moving like a tiny earth cloud over the hard clay clods. Her hoe moves rhythmically up down up down, tiny as a toothpick. And over there. Uncle pauses to straighten his back, his hands on his hips. And Stephen farther behind, so tiny I can barely see him.

19   It's hard, Aunt Emily, with my hoe, the blade getting dull and mud-caked as I slash out the Canada thistle, dandelions, crab grass, and other nameless non-beet plants, then on my knees, pulling out the extra beets from the cluster, leaving just one to mature, then three hand spans to the next plant, whack whack, and down on my knees again, pull, flick flick, and on to the end of the long long row and the next and the next and it will never be done thinning and weeding and weeding and weeding. It's so hard and so hot that my tear glands burn out.

And then it's cold. The lumps of clay mud stick on my gumboots and weight 20 my legs and the skin under the boots beneath the knees at the level of the calves grows red and hard and itchy from the flap flap of the boots and the fine hairs on my legs grow coarse there and ugly.

I mind growing ugly. 21

I mind the harvest time and the hands and the wrists bound in rags to keep the 22 wrists from breaking open. I lift the heavy mud-clotted beets out of the ground with the hook like an eagle's beak, thick and heavy as a nail attached to the top of the sugar-beet knife. Thwack. Into the beet and yank from the shoulder till it's out of the ground dragging the surrounding mud with it. Then crack two beets together till most of the mud drops off and splat, the knife slices into the beet scalp and the green top is tossed into one pile, the beet heaved onto another, one more one more one more down the icy line. I cannot tell about this time, Aunt Emily. The body will not tell.

We are surrounded by a horizon of denim-blue sky with clouds clear as spilled 23 milk that turn pink at sunset. Pink I hear is the colour of llama's milk. I wouldn't know. The clouds are the shape of our new prison walls—untouchable, impersonal, random.

There are no other people in the entire world. We work together all day. At 24 night we eat and sleep. We hardly talk anymore. The boxes we brought from Slocan are not unpacked. The King George/Queen Elizabeth mugs stay muffled in the *Vancouver Daily Province*. The camera phone does not sing. Obasan wraps layers of cloth around her feet and her torn sweater hangs unmended over her sagging dress.

Down the miles we are obedient as machines in this odd ballet without 25 accompaniment of flute or song.

"Grinning and happy" and all smiles standing around a pile of beets? That is 26 one telling. It's not how it was.

Questions about Meaning

1. The narrator, closely modeled on the author, tells us that the memory of her childhood experiences is painful. What was Kogawa's purpose in writing this? How do the introduction and conclusion explain this purpose?

2. What do the details in paragraph 24 tell the reader about the author and her family? In what way do they change the meaning of the author's experience?

3. What metaphors does Kogawa use to describe the concept of "memory" in paragraph 9? What do these comparisons tell us about her memories?

Questions about Rhetorical Strategy and Style

1. Kogawa is a poet. What evidence of this do you see in her writing? Find at least two metaphors and two similes. Why would the author choose to write about real historical events using poetic diction?

2. This narrative relies heavily on concrete, sensory detail. List at least one example each of the author's appeal to sight, sound, taste, touch and smell. What emotions do these sensory details evoke?

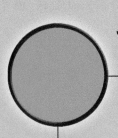

Just Walk On By: A Black Man Ponders His Power to Alter Public Space

Brent Staples

Brent Staples (1951-), an African American journalist, grew up not expecting to continue his education beyond high school. Spurred by unexpected encouragement, he earned a Ph.D. in psychology from The University of Chicago and wrote a prize-winning memoir, Parallel Time: Growing Up in Black and White *(1994). For many years now he has been an editorial writer for* The New York Times. *He wrote this essay, which continues to be much anthologized, for* Harper's Magazine *in 1986. The essay is still relevant in the light of the ongoing and simmering tension in American race relations.*

1   My first victim was a woman—white, well-dressed, probably in her early twenties. I came upon her late one evening on a deserted street in Hyde Park, a relatively affluent neighborhood in an otherwise mean, impoverished section of Chicago. As I swung onto the avenue behind her, there seemed to be a discreet, uninflammatory distance between us. Not so. She cast back a worried glance. To her, the youngish black man—a broad six feet two inches with a beard and billowing hair, both hands shoved into the pockets of a bulky military jacket— seemed menacingly close. After a few more quick glimpses, she picked up her pace and was soon running in earnest. Within seconds she disappeared into a
2   cross street.

   That was more than a decade ago. I was 22 years old, a graduate student newly arrived at the University of Chicago. It was in the echo of that terrified woman's footfalls that I first began to know the unwieldy inheritance I'd come into—the ability to alter public space in ugly ways. It was clear that she thought herself the quarry of a mugger, a rapist, or worse. Suffering a bout of insomnia, however, I was stalking sleep, not defenseless wayfarers. As a softy who is scarcely able to take a knife to raw chicken—let alone hold it to a person's throat—I was surprised, embarrassed, and dismayed all at once. Her flight made me feel like an accomplice in tyranny. It also made it clear that I was indistinguishable from the muggers who occasionally seeped into the area from the surrounding ghetto. The first encounter, and those that followed, signified that a vast, unnerving gulf lay between nighttime pedestrians—particularly women—and me. And I soon gathered that being perceived as dangerous is a hazard in itself. I only needed to turn a corner into a dicey situation, or crowd some frightened, armed person in a foyer somewhere, or make an errant move after being pulled over by a policeman. Where fear and weapons
3   meet—and they often do in urban America—there is always the possibility of death.

   In that first year, my first away from my hometown, I was to become thoroughly familiar with the language of fear. At dark, shadowy intersections in Chicago, I could cross in front of a car stopped at a traffic light and elicit the *thunk, thunk, thunk, thunk* of the driver—black, white, male, or female—hammering down the door locks. On less traveled streets after dark, I grew accustomed to but never comfortable with people who crossed to the other side of the street rather than pass me. Then there were the standard unpleasantries with police, doormen, bouncers, cab drivers, and others whose business it is to screen out troublesome individuals *before* there is any nastiness.   4

I moved to New York nearly two years ago and I have remained an avid night walker. In central Manhattan, the near-constant crowd cover minimizes tense one-on-one street encounters. Elsewhere—visiting friends in SoHo, where sidewalks are narrow and tightly spaced buildings shut out the sky—things can get very taut indeed.   5

Black men have a firm place in New York mugging literature. Norman Podhoretz in his famed (or infamous) . . . essay, "My Negro Problem—And Ours," recalls growing up in terror of black males; they "were tougher than we were, more ruthless," he writes—and as an adult on the Upper West Side of Manhattan, he continues, he cannot constrain his nervousness when he meets black men on certain streets. Similarly, a decade later, the essayist and novelist Edward Hoagland extols a New York where once "Negro bitterness bore down mainly on other Negroes." Where some see mere panhandlers, Hoagland sees "a mugger who is clearly screwing up his nerve to do more than just *ask* for money." But Hoagland has "the New Yorker's quick-hunch posture for broken-field maneuvering," and the bad guy swerves away.   6

I often witness that "hunch posture," from women after dark on the warrenlike streets of Brooklyn where I live. They seem to set their faces on neutral and, with their purse straps strung across their chests bandolier style, they forge ahead as though bracing themselves against being tackled. I understand, of course, that the danger they perceive is not a hallucination. Women are particularly vulnerable to street violence, and young black males are drastically overrepresented among the perpetrators of that violence. Yet these truths are no solace against the kind of alienation that comes of being ever the suspect, against being set apart, a fearsome entity with whom pedestrians avoid making eye contact.   7

It is not altogether clear to me now how I reached the ripe old age of 22 without being conscious of the lethality nighttime pedestrians attributed to me. Perhaps it was because in Chester, Pennsylvania, the small, angry industrial town where I came of age in the 1960s, I was scarcely noticeable against a backdrop of gang warfare, street knifings, and murders. I grew up one of the good boys, had perhaps a half-dozen fist fights. In retrospect, my shyness of combat has clear sources.   8

Many things go into the making of a young thug. One of those things is the consummation of the male romance with the power to intimidate. An infant discovers that random flailings send the baby bottle flying out of the crib and crashing to the floor. Delighted, the joyful babe repeats those motions again and again, seeking to duplicate the feat. Just so, I recall the points at which some of my boyhood friends were finally seduced by the perception of themselves as tough guys. When a mark cowered and surrendered his money without resistance, myth and reality merged—and paid off. It is, after all, only manly to embrace the power to frighten and intimidate. We, as men, are not supposed to give an inch of our lane on the highway; we are to seize the fighter's edge in work and in play and even in love; we are to be valiant in the face of hostile forces.   9

Unfortunately, poor and powerless young men seem to take all this nonsense literally. As a boy, I saw countless tough guys locked away; I have since buried several, too. They were babies, really—a teenage cousin, a brother of 22, a childhood friend in his mid-twenties—all gone down in episodes of bravado played out in the

10 streets. I came to doubt the virtues of intimidation early on. I chose, perhaps even unconsciously, to remain a shadow—timid, but a survivor.

The fearsomeness mistakenly attributed to me in public places often has a perilous flavor. The most frightening of these confusions occurred in the late 1970s and early 1980s when I worked as a journalist in Chicago. One day, rushing into the office of a magazine I was writing for with a deadline story in hand, I was mistaken for a burglar. The office manager called security and, with an ad hoc posse, pursued me through the labyrinthine halls, nearly to my editor's door. I had

11 no way of proving who I was. I could only move briskly toward the company of someone who knew me.

Another time I was on assignment for a local paper and killing time before an interview. I entered a jewelry store on the city's affluent Near North Side. The proprietor excused herself and returned with an enormous red Doberman pinscher straining at the end of a leash. She stood, the dog extended toward me, silent to my questions, her eyes bulging nearly out of her head. I took a cursory look around, nodded, and bade her good night. Relatively speaking, however, I never fared as badly as another black male journalist. He went to nearby Waukegan, Illinois, a couple of summers ago to work on a story about a murderer who was born there. Mistaking the reporter for the killer, police hauled him from his car

12 at gunpoint and but for his press credentials would probably have tried to book him. Such episodes are not uncommon. Black men trade tales like this all the time.

In "My Negro Problem—And Ours," Podhoretz writes that the hatred he feels for blacks makes itself known to him through a variety of avenues—one being his discomfort with that "special brand of paranoid touchiness" to which he says blacks are prone. No doubt he is speaking here of black men. In time, I learned to smother the rage I felt at so often being taken for a criminal. Not to do so

13 would surely have led to madness—via that special "paranoid touchiness" that so annoyed Podhoretz at the time he wrote the essay.

I began to take precautions to make myself less threatening. I move about with care, particularly late in the evening. I give a wide berth to nervous people on subway platforms during the wee hours, particularly when I have exchanged business clothes for jeans. If I happen to be entering a building behind some people who appear skittish, I may walk by, letting them clear the lobby before I return,

14 so as not to seem to be following them. I have been calm and extremely congenial on those rare occasions when I've been pulled over by the police.

And on late-evening constitutionals along streets less traveled by, I employ what has proved to be an excellent tension-reducing measure: I whistle melodies from Beethoven and Vivaldi and the more popular classical composers. Even steely New Yorkers hunching toward nighttime destinations seem to relax, and occasionally they even join in the tune. Virtually everybody seems to sense that a mugger wouldn't be warbling bright, sunny selections from Vivaldi's *Four Seasons*. It is my equivalent of the cowbell that hikers wear when they know they are in bear country.

Questions about Meaning

1. What are the effects on the author of having been stereotyped?

2. According to Staples, what has caused the stereotyping of black men as dangerous?

3. What is the "male romance" Staples writes about in paragraph 8? How does he feel about this "romance"?

4. How did Staples react to the violence of his childhood neighbourhood?

5. What solutions does Staples apply to his problem of being perceived as dangerous? Do these seem like reasonable solutions to you?

Questions about Rhetorical Strategy and Style

1. Why would the author use the word "victim" in the opening paragraph? What expectation does it set up for the reader? How does this help to reinforce his point?

2. What are the metaphors and similes Staples uses to describe how black men are seen by the public? What do they say about the black male stereotype?

3. What tone does the author establish in this essay? Is it angry, sad, thoughtful, ironic or something else? Support your answer with specific references to the essay.

The Seat Not Taken

John Edgar Wideman

The author, born in 1941, is a novelist, a memoirist, and a professor at Brown University. This essay first appeared in The New York Times *in 2010.*

1   At least twice a week I ride Amtrak's high-speed Acela train from my home in New York City to my teaching job in Providence, R.I. The route passes through a region of the country populated by, statistics tell us, a significant segment of its most educated, affluent, sophisticated and enlightened citizens.

2   Over the last four years, excluding summers, I have conducted a casual sociological experiment in which I am both participant and observer. It's a survey I began not because I had some specific point to prove by gathering data to support it, but because I couldn't avoid becoming aware of an obvious, disquieting truth.

3   Almost invariably, after I have hustled aboard early and occupied one half of a vacant double seat in the usually crowded quiet car, the empty place next to me will remain empty for the entire trip.

4   I'm a man of color, one of the few on the train and often the only one in the quiet car, and I've concluded that color explains a lot about my experience. Unless the car is nearly full, color will determine, even if it doesn't exactly clarify, why 9 times out of 10 people will shun a free seat if it means sitting beside me.

5   Giving them and myself the benefit of the doubt, I can rule out excessive body odor or bad breath; a hateful, intimidating scowl; hip-hop clothing; or a hideous deformity as possible objections to my person. Considering also the cost of an Acela ticket, the fact that I display no visible indications of religious preference and, finally, the numerous external signs of middle-class membership I share with the majority of the passengers, color appears to be a sufficient reason for the behavior I have recorded.

6   Of course, I'm not registering a complaint about the privilege, conferred upon me by color, to enjoy the luxury of an extra seat to myself. I relish the opportunity to spread out, savor the privacy and quiet and work or gaze at the scenic New England woods and coast. It's a particularly appealing perk if I compare the train to air travel or any other mode of transportation, besides walking or bicycling, for negotiating the mercilessly congested Northeast Corridor. Still, in the year 2010, with an African-descended, brown president in the White House and a nation confidently asserting its passage into a postracial era, it strikes me as odd to ride beside a vacant seat, just about every time I embark on a three-hour journey each way, from home to work and back.

7   I admit I look forward to the moment when other passengers, searching for a good seat, or any seat at all on the busiest days, stop anxiously prowling the quiet-car aisle, the moment when they have all settled elsewhere, including the ones

who willfully blinded themselves to the open seat beside me or were unconvinced of its availability when they passed by. I savor that precise moment when the train sighs and begins to glide away from Penn or Providence Station, and I'm able to say to myself, with relative assurance, that the vacant place beside me is free, free at last, or at least free until the next station. I can relax, prop open my briefcase or rest papers, snacks or my arm in the unoccupied seat.

But the very pleasing moment of anticipation casts a shadow, because I can't   8 accept the bounty of an extra seat without remembering why it's empty, without wondering if its emptiness isn't something quite sad. And quite dangerous, also, if left unexamined. Posters in the train, the station, the subway warn: if you see something, say something.

Questions about Meaning

1. What is the "obvious, disquieting truth" Wideman refers to in the second paragraph?
2. What is the connection between the election of Barack Obama, which the author alludes to in the essay, and the author's experience on the train?
3. What kind of things are the posters Wideman mentions in the last paragraph likely intended to encourage people to report when they see them? What is he suggesting by mentioning these posters and their message at the end of the essay?

Questions about Rhetorical Strategy and Style

1. The title echoes, deliberately or not, the title of one of Robert Frost's most famous poems, "The Road Not Taken." Read the poem and consider whether it and the essay might have a connection.
2. Wideman's calling the seat beside his own "free, free at last" echoes a phrase Martin Luther King, Jr. used at the very end of his famous "I Have a Dream" speech: "Free at last! Free at last! Thank God Almighty, we are free at last!" Why might Wideman have chosen to do this? What is the effect?

Chicken-Hips*

Catherine Pigott

Catherine Pigott, producer for the Canadian Broadcasting Corporation's **This Morning,** *became aware of women's issues when she taught English in Gambia in the early 1980s. Since then she has continued to champion women's concerns, recently serving on the Advisory Committee to the Afghan Women's Organization and producing the 1998 Canadian project and report "Muslim Women in the Media." The idea for* **Chicken Hips** *occurred to Pigott after she watched Katherine Gilday's documentary on eating disorders entitled* **The Famine Within.** *Soon after an interview with Gilday, Pigott was moved to pen the following essay.*

1 The women of the household clucked disapprovingly when they saw me. It was the first time I had worn African clothes since my arrival in tiny, dusty Gambia, and evidently they were not impressed. They adjusted my head-tie and pulled my *lappa*, the ankle-length fabric I had wrapped around myself, even tighter. "You're too thin," one of them pronounced. "It's no good." They nicknamed me "Chicken-hips."

2 I marvelled at this accolade, for I had never been called thin in my life. It was something I longed for. I would have been flattered if those ample-bosomed women hadn't looked so distressed. It was obvious I fell far short of their ideal of beauty.

3 I had dressed up for a very special occasion—the baptism of a son. The women heaped rice into tin basins the size of laundry tubs, shaping it into mounds with their hands. Five of us sat around one basin, thrusting our fingers into the scalding food. These women ate with such relish, such joy. They pressed the rice into balls in their fists, squeezing until the bright-red palm oil ran down their forearms and dripped off their elbows.

4 I tried desperately, but I could not eat enough to please them. It was hard for me to explain that I come from a culture in which it is almost unseemly for a woman to eat too heartily. It's considered unattractive. It was even harder to explain that to me thin is beautiful, and in my country we deny ourselves food in our pursuit of perfect slenderness.

5 That night, everyone danced to welcome the baby. Women swivelled their broad hips and used their hands to emphasize the roundness of their bodies. One needed to be round and wide to make the dance beautiful. There was no place for thinness here. It made people sad. It reminded them of things they wanted to forget, such as poverty, drought and starvation. You never knew when the rice was going to run out.

*Editor's title

I began to believe that Africa's image of the perfect female body was far more 6
realistic than the long-legged leanness I had been conditioned to admire. There, it is beautiful—not shameful—to carry weight on the hips and thighs, to have a round stomach and heavy, swinging breasts. Women do not battle the bulge, they celebrate it. A body is not something to be tamed and moulded.

The friends who had christened me Chicken-hips made it their mission to 7
fatten me up. It wasn't long before a diet of rice and rich, oily stew twice a day began to change me. Every month, the women would take a stick and measure my backside, noting with pleasure its gradual expansion. "Oh Catherine, your buttocks are getting nice now!" they would say.

What was extraordinary was that I, too, believed I was becoming more beautiful. 8
There was no sense of panic, no shame, no guilt-ridden resolves to go on the miracle grape-and-water diet. One day, I tied my *lappa* tight across my hips and went to the market to buy beer for a wedding. I carried the crate of bottles home on my head, swinging my hips slowly as I walked. I felt transformed.

In Gambia, people don't use words such as "cheating," "naughty," or "guilty" 9
when they talk about eating. The language of sin is not applied to food. Fat is desirable. It holds beneficial meanings of abundance, fertility and health.

My perception of beauty altered as my body did. The European tourists on the 10
beach began to look strange and skeletal rather than "slim." They had no hips. They seemed devoid of shape and substance. Women I once would have envied appeared fragile and even ugly. The ideal they represented no longer made sense.

After a year, I came home. I preached my new way of seeing to anyone who 11
would listen. I wanted to cling to the liberating belief that losing weight had nothing to do with self-love.

Family members kindly suggested that I might look and feel better if I slimmed 12
down a little. They encouraged me to join an exercise club. I wandered around the malls in a dislocated daze. I felt uncomfortable trying on clothes that hung so elegantly on the mannequins. I began hearing old voices inside my head: "Plaid makes you look fat. . . . You're too short for that style. . . . Vertical stripes are more slimming. . . . Wear black."

I joined the club. Just a few weeks after I had worn a *lappa* and scooped up rice 13
with my hands, I was climbing into pink leotards and aerobics shoes. The instructor told me that I had to set fitness goals and "weigh in" after my workouts. There were mirrors on the walls and I could see women watching themselves. I sensed that even the loveliest among them felt they were somehow flawed. As the aerobics instructor barked out commands for arm lifts and leg lifts, I pictured Gambian women pounding millet and dancing in a circle with their arms raised high. I do not mean to romanticize their rock-hard lives, but we were hardly to be envied as we ran like fools between two walls to the tiresome beat of synthesized music.

We were a roomful of women striving to reshape ourselves into some kind of 14
pubertal ideal. I reverted to my natural state: one of yearning to be slimmer and more fit than I was. My freedom had been temporary. I was home, where fat is feared and despised. It was time to exert control over my body and my life. I dreaded the thought of people saying, "She's let herself go."

If I return to Africa I am sure the women will shake their heads in bewildered 15
dismay. Even now, I sometimes catch my reflection in a window and their voices come back to me. "Yo! Chicken-hips!"

Questions on Meaning

1. Pigott tells the reader how it feels to have cultural assumptions questioned. How do the Gambian women make Pigott feel about herself?

2. How does Pigott's attitude change during her time in Gambia? Use specific references to the text in your answer.

3. What happens to Pigott when she returns to Canada from Africa? Why does she conform to the starvation and exercise cult?

Questions on Strategy and Style

1. Pigott compares the attitudes of Gambian women to those of Canadian women. How does this comparison explain the point the essay is making?

2. The descriptions of Gambian food are lush and vivid—red grease on balls of rice, for example. How do these descriptions affect the reader?

3. What sensory information does Pigott use to contrast the culture at home with that of Gambia? What do Pigott's descriptions suggest about the two societies and how might that be misleading? Does she address that issue anywhere in her text?

Feel Like a Wallflower?
Maybe It's Your Facebook Wall

Jenna Wortham

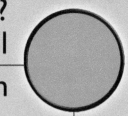

The author writes regularly about popular culture, music, and social media for Girl Crush Zine *and* The New York Times *where this essay first appeared in 2011.*

1 One recent rainy night, I curled up on my couch with popcorn and Netflix Instant, ready to spend a quiet night at home. The peace was sweet—while it lasted. Soon, my iPhone began flashing with notifications from a handful of social networking sites, each a beacon of information about what my friends were doing.

2 As the alerts came in, my mind began to race. Three friends, I learned, had arrived at a music venue near my apartment. But why? What was happening there? Then I saw pictures of other friends enjoying fancy milkshakes at a trendy restaurant. Suddenly, my simple domestic pleasures paled in comparison with the things I could be doing.

3 The flurry of possibilities set off a rush of restlessness and indecision. I was torn between nesting in my cozy roost or rallying for an impromptu rendezvous, and I just didn't know what to do.

4 My problem is emblematic of the digital era. It's known as FOMO, or "fear of missing out," and refers to the blend of anxiety, inadequacy and irritation that can flare up while skimming social media like Facebook, Twitter, Foursquare and Instagram. Billions of Twitter messages, status updates and photographs provide thrilling glimpses of the daily lives and activities of friends, "frenemies" co-workers and peers.

5 The upside is immeasurable. Viewing postings from my friends scattered around the country often makes me feel more connected to them, not less. News and photographs of the bike rides, concerts, dinner parties and nights on the town enjoyed by people in my New York social circle are invaluable as an informal to-do list of local recommendation.

6 But, occasionally, there is a darker side.

7 When we scroll through pictures and status updates, the worry that tugs at the corners of our minds is set off by the fear of regret, according to Dan Ariely, author of "Predictably Irrational" and a professor of psychology and behavioral economics at Duke University. He says we become afraid that we've made the wrong decision about how to spend our time.

8 Streaming social media have an immediacy that is very different from, say, a conversation over lunch recounting the events of the previous weekend. When you see that your friends are sharing a bottle of wine without you—and at that very moment—"you can imagine how things could be different," Professor Ariely said.

9   It's like a near miss in real life. "When would you be more upset"? he asked. "After missing your flight by two minutes or two hours?

10   "Two minutes, of course," he said, "You can imagine how things could have been different, and that really motivates us to behave in strange ways."

11   Fear of missing out does not apply only to those with a hyperactive nightlife.

12   A friend who works in advertising told me that she felt fine about her life—until she opened Facebook. "Then I'm thinking, 'I am 28, with three roommates, and oh, it looks like you have a precious baby and a mortgage' " she said. "And then I wanna die."

13   On those occasions, she said, her knee-jerk reaction is often to post an account of a cool thing she has done, or to upload a particularly fun picture from her weekend. This may make her feel better—but it can generate FOMO in another unsuspecting person.

14   Caterina Fake, co-founder of Flickr, the photo-sharing service, and of Hunch, a recommendation engine, said, "Social software is both the creator and the cure of FOMO." adding, "It's cyclical."

15   Some creators of social apps say they have constructed their services to make people keep coming back for more, but not for any insidious purpose.

16   "No one likes to perform in a vacuum," said Kevin Systrom, the chief executive of Instagrarm, a mobile photo-sharing application, which allows users to make comments about pictures. The more creative or striking a photograph, the more likely it is to attract favorable attention.

17   The feedback, Mr. Systrom said, can be slightly addictive. People using Instagram "are rewarded when someone likes it and you keep coming back," he said.

18   Whatever angst people may feel when they see someone else having a good time, he said, is probably exaggerated by the overall effect of so many new social data streams pouring into browsers and mobile phones at once.

19   "We aren't used to seeing the world as it happens," he said. "We as humans can only process so much data."

20   Of course, fear of missing out is hardly new. It has been induced throughout history by such triggers as newspaper society pages, party pictures and annual holiday letters—and e-mail—depicting people at their festive best. But now, Ms. Fake said, instead of receiving occasional polite updates, we get reminders around the clock, mainlined via the device of our choosing.

21   Sherry Turkle, a professor at the Massachusetts Institute of Technology and author of "Alone Together," says that as technology becomes ever more pervasive, our relationship to it becomes more intimate, granting it the power to influence decisions, moods and emotions.

22   "In a way, there's an immaturity to our relationship with technology," she said. "It's still evolving."

23   We are struggling with the always-on feeling of connection that the Internet can provide, she said, and we still need to figure out how to limit its influence on our lives. I asked Professor Turkle what people could do to deal with this stress-inducing quandary. She said she tell herself to "get a grip and separate myself from my iPhone."

24   Easier said than done. I've tried, but turning off my phone is nearly impossible—I'm not yet ready for that step.

25   That evening, though, I flipped the phone over to hide its screen. That helped me ignore what my friends were doing. I settled back to enjoy the evening, deciding not to venture out into the cold and misty night.

Questions about Meaning

1. What is it about new technology that, according to Jenna Wortham, makes it so powerful or even unsettling when it conveys information about what others are doing?
2. What response to the never-ending flood of updates does Wortham seem to be recommending, at least implicitly? What indicates this?

Questions about Rhetorical Strategy and Style

1. How does Jenna Wortham begin her essay? What do we immediately know about her? Might the introduction make some readers less likely to read further? Which readers and why?
2. How does Wortham make sure readers understand that her concerns are not simply her own? Did one of the quotations she used strike you as particularly insightful? Which one and why?

Distorted Images
Susan McClelland

The author is Canadian writer whose work has appeared in many newspapers and magazines around the world. Her book, **Bite of the Mango,** *is about a girl's journey from war victim in Sierra Leone to a UNICEF Special Representative. This article first appeared in* **Maclean's in August, 2000.**

1   When Zahra Dhanani was just seven years old, her four-foot frame already packed 100 lb.—so her mother, Shahbanu, put her on her first diet. "My mother, a fat woman, daughter of another fat woman, thought if I was skinny, different from her, I would be happy," says Dhanani. The diet, and many after, did not have the desired effect. By 13, Dhanani was sporadically swallowing appetite suppressants; at 17, she vomited and used laxatives to try to keep her weight under control. There were times when she wanted to die. "I had so much self-hate," recalls the 26-year-old Toronto immigration lawyer, "I couldn't look in the mirror without feeling revulsion."

2   The hate reflected more than just weight. "It was race," says Dhanani, who had moved with her family to Canada from East Africa when she was 4. "I was straightening my hair—doing anything to look white." Her recovery only began when, at age 19, she started to identify with women in other cultures. "I came to realize that there were people who revered large women of colour," says Dhanani, who now says she loves all of her 200 lb. She blames part of her earlier eating disorders on the images in western media: "When you have no role models to counteract the messages that fat is repulsive, it's hard to realize that you are a lovable human being."

3   Body image may be one of the western world's ugliest exports. Thanks to television, magazines, movies and the Internet, rail-thin girls and steroid-built beef-boys are being shoved in the faces of people all over the world. As a result, experts say, cultures that used to regard bulk as a sign of wealth and success are now succumbing to a narrow western standard of beauty. And that, in turn, is leading to incidences of eating disorders in regions where anorexia and bulimia had never been seen before. But body-image anxiety in ethnic cultures runs much deeper than weight. In South Africa, almost six years after the end of apartheid, black women still use harmful skin-bleaching creams in the belief that whiter is prettier. "We're seeing a homogenization and globalization of beauty ideals," says Niva Piran, a clinical psychologist at the University of Toronto. "It's white. It's thin. And the result is that people come to identify less with their own cultures and more with an image in the media."

4   In most cultures, bigger was considered better until the 19th century. "The larger a man's wife, the more he was seen as a good provider," says Joan Jacobs

Brumberg, a professor of American women's history at Cornell University and author of *Fasting Girls: The History of Anorexia Nervosa*. That began to change during the Industrial Revolution, she says, as women in the United States and Great Britain began to see thinness as a way to differentiate themselves from the lower classes. By the 1920s, fat was seen as unhealthy. And in the burgeoning magazine, movie and fashion industries, the women depicted as being successful in love, career and finances were slim and almost always white.

Still, eating disorders are not a modern affliction. Records of women starving themselves (anorexia) date back to the medieval period (1200 to 1500). As Brumberg notes in *Fasting Girls*, during this time, a woman who did not eat was admired for having found some other form of sustenance than food, like prayer. Yet, until the last century, the number of women who fasted was low. But, particularly over the past 30 years, the number of anorexics and women who self-induce vomiting (bulimia) or use laxatives has increased dramatically. "It's generally this obsession with the body, constant weight-watching, that introduces a person to these behaviours," says Merryl Bear of the Toronto-based National Eating Disorder Information Centre. It was commonly believed, however, that sufferers came predominantly from white, middle- and upper-class backgrounds. Experts thought ethnic minorities were immune because of their strong ties to communities that emphasize family and kinship over looks alone.

Studies done in the United States with Hispanic, black and Asian college students, however, show that women who are alienated from their minority cultures and integrated into mainstream society are prone to the same pressures of dieting as their white counterparts. In a recent study of South-Asian girls in Peel, Ont., 31 percent responded that they were not comfortable with their body shape and size. Fifty-eight percent compared their appearance with others, including fashion models—and 40 percent wanted to look like them.

Some of the most compelling research comes from Harvard Medical School psychiatrist Anne Becker, who was in Fiji in 1995 when the government announced that TV, including western programs, would be introduced. "Fijians revere a body that is sturdy, tall and large—features that show that the body is strong, hardworking and healthy," says Becker, "Thinness and sudden weight loss was seen as some kind of social loss or neglect."

In 1998, Becker returned to Fiji and found that this had all changed. Her studies showed that 29 percent of the girls now had symptoms of eating disorders. Many said they vomited to lose weight. But what was most alarming were the girls' responses about the role of television in their lives. "More than 80 percent said that watching TV affected the way they felt about their bodies," Becker says. "They said things such as, 'I watched the women on TV, they have jobs. I want to be like them, so I am working on my weight now.' These teenagers are getting the sense that as Fiji moves into the global economy, they had better find some way to make wages and they are desperate to find role models. The West to them means success, and they are altering their bodies to compete."

Cheryl McConney has felt the pressures to alter her body, too. The black 32-year-old native of Richmond Hill, Ont., co-hosts a daytime talk show on cable TV. And although it has not been difficult for her to get where she is in her career, she is concerned about how to navigate her next step. "Looking at Canadian television, I don't see many people who look like me on air," she says. At five-foot-five, and weighing about 145 lb., McConney has never been told she should lose weight. Still, in 1998, she went on a six-month, high-protein, low-carbohydrate diet, hoping to look better in front of the camera. She shed 20 lb. "I felt good.

People in the studio thought I looked great, but it wasn't easy to maintain." Within a year, she had gained it all back.

10   For McConney, race has been more of an issue. An industry insider jokingly told her that she would do better if she dyed her hair blond. And just a few months ago, she was discouraged from applying for another on-air host position because of what the casting agents said they were looking for. "They wanted the 'girl next door' and 'peaches-and-cream' pretty, not chocolate and cream," says McConney, adding: "It was pretty clear some women were not invited to participate because of their skin colour." As to the girl-next-door part: "I said it just depends where you live."

11   While McConney says she is determined to make it on air despite the barriers, Linda, who requested *Maclean's* not use her real name, may not be around to see her success. The 19-year-old—part South African and part East Indian—has anorexia. She says trying to fit into a Canadian suburban community played a big role in her illness. "I was never proud of my different religion, different skin colour," she says. "I would put white baby powder on my cheeks just to make me look white." What alarms her now, Linda says, is that with her skin pale from malnutrition and her weight fluctuating between 75 and 85 lb„ other young women often come up to her and say, "You look so good, I wish I looked like you." But she adds: "What they don't know is that my body is decaying. People glamorize eating disorders. But what it is is a lifetime of hospitalization and therapy." As long as the western media promote thinness and whiteness as the pinnacle of beauty, stories like Linda's will remain all too familiar.

Questions about Meaning

1. What, according to the article, is different about eating disorders in our modern world from eating disorders centuries ago?

2. According to the author, what caused the change from thinking of bigger as better to thinking one can never be too thin? What kind of evidence does she provide to support her view?

3. According to the article, what are the effects on non-white women, especially those who aren't thin, of a single idea of how a beautiful or attractive woman should look?

Questions about Rhetorical Strategy and Style

1. What is the effect of beginning and ending the article with short narratives about particular women? Why do you think the author chose these particular women? What kinds of details are provided about them?

2. Are there women, including some well-known ones, who might have complicated the picture or even contradicted the article's thesis if they had been mentioned and perhaps quoted?

Why I Want a Wife

Judy Brady

Judy Brady (1937–), born in San Francisco, studied painting and received a B.F.A. in 1962 in art from the University of Iowa. Then she married and raised a family in a traditional housewife role. She later commented that her male professors had talked her out of pursuing a career in education. In the late 1960s, she became active in the women's movement and began writing articles on feminism and other social issues. In 1990, she was the editor of Women and Cancer, *an anthology by women. The essay "Why I Want a Wife" appeared in the first issue of Ms. magazine in 1972.*

1 I belong to that classification of people known as wives. I am A Wife. And, not altogether incidentally, I am a mother.

2 Not too long ago a male friend of mine appeared on the scene fresh from a recent divorce. He had one child, who is, of course, with his ex-wife. He is looking for another wife. As I thought about him while I was ironing one evening, it suddenly occurred to me that I, too, would like to have a wife. Why do I want a wife?

3 I would like to go back to school so that I can become economically independent, support myself, and, if need be, support those dependent upon me. I want a wife who will work and send me to school. And while I am going to school I want a wife to take care of my children. I want a wife to keep track of the children's doctor and dentist appointments. And to keep track of mine, too. I want a wife to make sure my children eat properly and are kept clean. I want a wife who will wash the children's clothes and keep them mended. I want a wife who is a good nurturing attendant to my children, who arranges for their schooling, makes sure that they have an adequate social life with their peers, takes them to the park, the zoo, etc. I want a wife who takes care of the children when they are sick, a wife who arranges to be around when the children need special care, because, of course, I cannot miss classes at school. My wife must arrange to lose time at work and not lose the job. It may mean a small cut in my wife's income from time to time, but I guess I can tolerate that. Needless to say, my wife will arrange and pay for the care of the children while my wife is working.

4 I want a wife who will take care of *my* physical needs. I want a wife who will keep my house clean, a wife who will pick up after me. I want a wife who will keep my clothes clean, ironed, mended, replaced when need be, and who will see to it that my personal things are kept in their proper place so that I can find what I need the minute I need it. I want a wife who cooks the meals, a wife who is a *good* cook. I want a wife who will plan the menus, do the necessary grocery shopping, prepare the meals, serve them pleasantly, and then do the cleaning up while I do my studying. I want a wife who will care for me when I am sick and sympathize

with my pain and loss of time from school. I want a wife to go along when our family takes a vacation so that someone can continue to care for me and my children when I need a rest and change of scene.

5   I want a wife who will not bother me with rambling complaints about a wife's duties. But I want a wife who will listen to me when I feel the need to explain a rather difficult point I have come across in my course of studies. And I want a wife who will type my papers for me when I have written them.

6   I want a wife who will take care of the details of my social life. When my wife and I are invited out by friends, I want a wife who will take care of the babysitting arrangements. When I meet people at school that I like and want to entertain, I want a wife who will have the house clean, will prepare a special meal, serve it to me and my friends, and not interrupt when I talk about the things that interest me and my friends. I want a wife who will have arranged that the children are fed and ready for bed before my guests arrive so that the children do not bother us. I want a wife who takes care of the needs of my guests so that they feel comfortable, who makes sure that they have an ashtray, that they are passed the hors d'oeuvres, that they are offered a second helping of the food, that their wine glasses are replenished when necessary, that their coffee is served to them as they like it. And I want a wife who knows that sometimes I need a night out by myself.

7   I want a wife who is sensitive to my sexual needs, a wife who makes love passionately and eagerly when I feel like it, a wife who makes sure that I am satisfied. And, of course, I want a wife who will not demand sexual attention when I am not in the mood for it. I want a wife who assumes the complete responsibility for birth control, because I do not want more children. I want a wife who will remain sexually faithful to me so that I do not have to clutter up my intellectual life with jealousies. And I want a wife who understands that *my* sexual needs may entail more than strict adherence to monogamy. I must, after all, be able to relate to people as fully as possible.

8   If, by chance, I find another person more suitable as a wife than the wife I already have, I want the liberty to replace my present wife with another one. Naturally, I will expect a fresh, new life; my wife will take the children and be solely responsible for them so that I am left free.

9   When I am through with school and have a job, I want my wife to quit working and remain at home so that my wife can more fully and completely take care of a wife's duties.

10   My God, who *wouldn't* want a wife?

Questions about Meaning

1. Do you know any wives such as Brady describes? Describe one of them. If Brady's description seems unrealistic, describe a more realistic wife.

2. At first the essay seems to deplore a double standard. Does it really? What does the essay suggest about the origin and extent of male/female differences?

Questions on Rhetorical Strategy and Style

1. Satire commonly uses exaggeration both for humorous effect and to make a point. Analyze the exaggeration you see in this essay and explain how it enriches the reading experience.

2. What is the effect of Brady's use of great detail throughout the essay, including such things as filling the guests' wine glasses and taking the children to the zoo? Find other examples of detail to support your opinion.

3. If you substituted the word "husband" for "wife" throughout the essay, how would a contemporary reader react?

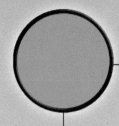

The Case for Marriage

Linda J. Waite and Maggie Gallagher

This essay is from a book of the same name published in 2001. Linda Waite (1947–) is a professor of sociology at the University of Chicago where she has focused her research on marriage, the family, and aging. Maggie Gallagher (1960–) is a writer and social commentator who now leads the Institute for Marriage and Public Policy.

1 In the 1950s, the rules were clear: first love, next marriage, and only then the baby carriage. Who could have imagined the tsunami ahead? In a rapid blur came the Pill, the sexual revolution, gay pride, feminism, the mass move of married mothers into the workplace, no-fault divorce, and an unexpected orgy of unmarried child-bearing. Without warning, the one firm understanding that marriage is a cornerstone of our society had all but disappeared.

2 Marriage, its detractors contend, can trap women and men in unhealthy relationships, pressuring them with irrational taboos to live in a way that does nobody any good. Preferences for marriage, special benefits for married couples— once viewed as common-sense supports for a vital social institution—are de-nounced as discriminatory. Some say marriage is financially unfair to men and frustrates their sexual needs. Others argue that it benefits men at the expense of women's independence, gratification, physical safety, and even sanity. Marriage "protects men from depression and makes women more vulnerable," [contends] Neil Jacobson, University of Washington psychologist and author of the 1998 book *When Men Batter Women*. . . .

3 From this perspective, divorce is perceived as a great social boon. And far from being cause for alarm and reform, the astonishing growth of births out of wedlock— from about five percent of total births in 1960 to a third of all births today—is seen as welcome proof of the emancipation of women from marital restrictions.

4 Even our language betrays the new attitudes toward marriage. A reluctance even to use the word seems to be sweeping the West. The Marriage Guidance Council of Australia recently changed its name to Relationships Australia. Britain's National Marriage Guidance Council metamorphosed into Relate. A popular sex education manual for children does not mention the M-word, although it acknowledges, vaguely, that "there are kids whose mothers and fathers live together."

5 But here is the great irony: if you ask the right questions, there is plenty of evidence suggesting that marriage is a vital part of overall well-being. Contrary to what many Americans now believe, getting and staying married is good for men, women, and children. Marriage, it turns out, is by far the best bet for ensuring a healthier, wealthier, and sexier life.

6 Imagine, for example, a group of men and women all 48 years old and as alike in background as social scientists can make them. How many will be alive at age 65? According to a study we did, of those men who never married or are divorced,

only 60 percent will still be around. By contrast, 90 percent of the married [men] will survive. Similarly, 90 percent of married women will reach 65, compared to 80 percent of single and divorced women.

It's not just a matter of mortality. Among men and women nearing retirement 7 age, wives are almost 40 percent less likely than unmarried women to say their health is poor. Even in old age married women are less likely to become disabled, and married people of both sexes are much less likely to enter nursing homes.

How can a mere social contract have such far-reaching effects? For one thing, 8 new research suggests that marriage might improve immune system functioning, as married people are shown to be less susceptible than singles to the common cold. For another, married people tend to pursue healthier lifestyles. The evidence is clear: spousal nagging works. A wife feels licensed to press her husband to get checkups or eat better. And a man responds to a wife's health consciousness in part because he knows that she depends on him as he depends on her. Statistics show that getting married leads to a dramatic reduction in smoking, drinking, and illegal drug use for both men and women, while just moving in together typically does not. And according to Justice Department data, wives are almost four times less likely than single women to fall victim to violent crime.

Then there's the question of domestic violence. Many commentators talk as 9 if the institution of marriage itself is at fault. Two eminent scholars, for example, title their influential essay on rates of domestic violence "The Marriage License as Hitting License." And Jacobson declares flatly that "marriage as an institution is still structured in such a way as to institutionalize male dominance, and such dominance makes high rates of battering inevitable." Even the best researchers tend to use *wife abuse* and *domestic violence* interchangeably, strongly implying that getting married can put women at special risk.

But the truth is that women who live with men out of wedlock are in much 10 greater danger. Cohabiting men are almost twice as likely as husbands to engage in domestic violence. To look at it another way, women who have never married are more than four times more likely than wives—and divorced women more than seven times more likely—to be the victims of intimate violence.

The kids' health can also benefit from marriage. Children are 50 percent more 11 likely to develop health problems due to a parental separation, and those in female-headed single-parent homes are more likely to be hospitalized or to suffer chronic health conditions such as asthma. And for babies marriage can mean the difference between life and death. Those born to single mothers are much more likely to die in the first year. Even among groups with the lowest risk of infant mortality, marriage makes a big difference: babies born to college-educated single mothers are 50 percent more likely to die than babies born to married couples. What's more, the health advantage of having married parents can be long-lasting.

If marriage can benefit health, how about its effect on the pocketbook? Recent 12 research suggests that getting and keeping a wife may be as important to a man's financial portfolio as getting a good education. Depending on which study you cite, husbands earn anywhere from 10 percent to 40 percent more than single men, and the longer men stay married, the greater the gap.

Like men, women get an earnings boost from marriage. But children change 13 the picture. One study finds that having a child reduces a woman's earnings by almost four percent and that two or more reduce her pay by almost 12 percent. Women get a marriage premium, but also pay a substantial motherhood penalty.

Still, there are countervailing benefits. Married couples manage their money 14 more wisely than singles and are less likely to report signs of economic hardship.

And the longer they stay married, the more wealth they build. By retirement, the average married couple has accumulated assets worth about $410,000, compared to $167,000 for those never married and $154,000 for the divorced.

15   Arguably, marriage itself is a form of wealth. Because they can share both the labor and the goods of life, husbands and wives produce more with less effort and cost. And having a partner who promises to care for you in good times and bad is also valuable—equal, according to one recent estimate, to a 12 percent increase in wealth for a 30-year-old spouse, and a whopping 33 percent for 75-year-old married people.

16   In theory, unmarried people who live together might enjoy the same economies. In practice, however, things work out differently. In *American Couples*, Philip Blumstein and Pepper Schwartz describe how a typical cohabiting couple thinks about money. Jane is a pediatrician living with Morton, a lawyer. "Morton was not particularly thrilled when I took the bonus and traded in the Volvo for the Alfa. Well, too bad. I let him alone and I expect him to let me alone." Morton agrees, somewhat wistfully: "I would not always make the same decisions she does. I would save and invest more. But it's her money, and I don't dare interfere."

17   By contrast, Lisa, a homemaker married to machinist Al, has no problems interfering with her husband's spending habits, because the money he makes is not "his" but "theirs." "He doesn't control it," Lisa says of her husband's spending, "so we have to stop quite often and discuss our budget and where did all this money go to. Why are you broke? Where did it go to? If it went to good causes, I can find 10 dollars more," she says confidently—the money manager for both of them. "If it didn't, tough."

18   Some experts try to de-emphasize the apparent benefits of marriage as a cover for the "real" problems plaguing children of divorce: poverty, family conflict, and poor parenting. As scholar Arlene Skolnick put it in a recent family studies textbook, "Family structure—the number of parents in the home or the fact of divorce—is not in itself the critical factor in children's well-being. In both intact and other families, what children need most is a warm, concerned relationship with at least one parent."

19   But three decades of evidence have made it clear that divorce dramatically increases economic hardship and puts new stress on the parent–child bond, thus exacerbating precisely the problems Skolnick decries. In the face of the hard data, it is almost impossible to argue that having married parents is not a critical factor in a child's well-being.

20   All right: so marriage trumps being single as far as health, wealth, and the kids' well-being goes. But surely the single person enjoys better sex? Wedding cake, in the old joke, is the best food to curb your sexual appetite. "What is it about marriage," wonders Dalma Heyn in *Marriage Shock*, "that so often puts desire at risk"?

21   Surprisingly, the truth is just the opposite: married people have better sex lives than singles. Indeed, married people are far more likely to have sex lives in the first place. Married people are about twice as likely as unmarried people to make love at least two or three times a week.

22   And that's not all: married sex is more fun. Certainly, at least, for men: forty-eight percent of husbands say sex with their partners is extremely satisfying, compared to just 37 percent of cohabiting men.

23   When it comes to creating a lasting sexual union, marriage implies at least a promise of permanence, which may be why cohabiting men are four times more likely to cheat, and cohabiting women eight times more likely, than husbands and wives.

That is doubtless one reason why married men and women, on average, tend   24
to be emotionally and mentally healthier—less depressed and anxious or
psychologically distressed than single, divorced, or widowed Americans. One study
that followed 14,000 adults over a 10–year period found that marital status was one
of the single most important predictors of personal happiness.

Marriage, we'd like to argue, is not just one of many kinds of relationships   25
that are all "equally valid"—equally likely to advance health and happiness of men,
women, and children. Of course we don't suggest that people should be dragooned
into marrying against their will, or that some marriages should not end. But we
do say that what enables marriage to deliver its powerful life-enhancing benefits
is that it is not just a private lifestyle, an arrangement whose success or failure
concerns the lover alone.

Marriage creates powerful positive changes in couples' lives because it is a   26
public relationship, living proof that interdependence, faithfulness, obligation,
responsibility, and union are more fruitful over the long run than choices that may
seem more immediately gratifying.

Helping people imagine that long run, then making it come true, is what   27
marriage still does best.

Questions about Meaning

1. What are some of the advantages to being married, according to the article?
2. What is the most surprising statistic the authors use in this article? Why is this
   such a surprise?
3. What is the thesis of this article? Where is it? Can you put it into your own
   words?

Questions on Rhetorical Strategy and Style

1. Why do the authors spend the opening paragraphs listing the counterarguments
   to their thesis? What does this tell us about their intended audience?
2. What kind of evidence do the authors use most often to support their
   arguments? Is this the most effective way to build this argument? Explain your
   answer.

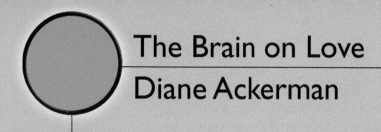

The Brain on Love
Diane Ackerman

The author is a poet, essayist, and naturalist. Her many books include A Nature History of the Senses. *This essay first appeared in The New York Times in 2012.*

1   A relatively new field, called interpersonal neurobiology, draws its vigor from one of the great discoveries of our era: that the brain is constantly rewiring itself based on daily life. In the end, what we pay the most attention to defines us. How you choose to spend the irreplaceable hours of your life literally transforms you.

2   All relationships change the brain — but most important are the intimate bonds that foster or fail us, altering the delicate circuits that shape memories, emotions and that ultimate souvenir, the self.

3   Every great love affair begins with a scream. At birth, the brain starts blazing new neural pathways based on its odyssey in an alien world. An infant is steeped in bright, buzzing, bristling sensations, raw emotions and the curious feelings they unleash, weird objects, a flux of faces, shadowy images and dreams—but most of all a powerfully magnetic primary caregiver whose wizardry astounds.

4   Brain scans show synchrony between the brains of mother and child; but what they can't show is the internal bond that belongs to neither alone, a fusion in which the self feels so permeable it doesn't matter whose body is whose. Wordlessly, relying on the heart's semaphores, the mother says all an infant needs to hear, communicating through eyes, face and voice. Thanks to advances in neuroimaging, we now have evidence that a baby's first attachments imprint its brain. The patterns of a lifetime's behaviors, thoughts, self-regard and choice of sweethearts all begin in this crucible.

5   We used to think this was the end of the story: first heredity, then the brain's engraving mental maps in childhood, after which you're pretty much stuck with the final blueprint.

6   But as a wealth of imaging studies highlight, the neural alchemy continues throughout life as we mature and forge friendships, dabble in affairs, succumb to romantic love, choose a soul mate. The body remembers how that oneness with Mother felt, and longs for its adult equivalent.

7   As the most social apes, we inhabit a mirror-world in which every important relationship, whether with spouse, friend or child, shapes the brain, which in turn shapes our relationships. Daniel J. Siegel and Allan N. Schore, colleagues at the University of California, Los Angeles, recently discussed groundbreaking work in the field at a conference on the school's campus. It's not that caregiving changes genes; it influences how the genes express themselves as the child grows. Dr. Siegel, a neuropsychiatrist, refers to the indelible sense of "feeling felt" that we learn as

infants and seek in romantic love, a reciprocity that remodels the brain's architecture and functions.

Does it also promote physical well-being? "Scientific studies of longevity, 8 medical and mental health, happiness and even wisdom," Dr. Siegel says, "point to supportive relationships as the most robust predictor of these positive attributes in our lives across the life span."

The supportive part is crucial. Loving relationships alter the brain the most 9 significantly.

Just consider how much learning happens when you choose a mate. Along 10 with thrilling dependency comes glimpsing the world through another's eyes; forsaking some habits and adopting others (good or bad); tasting new ideas, rituals, foods or landscapes; a slew of added friends and family; a tapestry of physical intimacy and affection; and many other catalysts, including a tornadic blast of attraction and attachment hormones — all of which revamp the brain.

When two people become a couple, the brain extends its idea of self to include 11 the other; instead of the slender pronoun "I," a plural self emerges who can borrow some of the other's assets and strengths. The brain knows who we are. The immune system knows who we're not, and it stores pieces of invaders as memory aids. Through lovemaking, or when we pass along a flu or a cold sore, we trade bits of identity with loved ones, and in time we become a sort of chimera. We don't just get under a mate's skin, we absorb him or her.

Love is the best school, but the tuition is high and the homework can be 12 painful. As imaging studies by the U.C.L.A. neuroscientist Naomi Eisenberger show, the same areas of the brain that register physical pain are active when someone feels socially rejected. That's why being spurned by a lover hurts all over the body, but in no place you can point to. Or rather, you'd need to point to the dorsal anterior cingulate cortex in the brain, the front of a collar wrapped around the corpus callosum, the bundle of nerve fibers zinging messages between the hemispheres that register both rejection and physical assault.

Whether they speak Armenian or Mandarin, people around the world use the 13 same images of physical pain to describe a broken heart, which they perceive as crushing and crippling. It's not just a metaphor for an emotional punch. Social pain can trigger the same sort of distress as a stomachache or a broken bone.

But a loving touch is enough to change everything. James Coan, a neuroscientist 14 at the University of Virginia, conducted experiments in 2006 in which he gave an electric shock to the ankles of women in happy, committed relationships. Tests registered their anxiety before, and pain level during, the shocks.

Then they were shocked again, this time holding their loving partner's hand. 15 The same level of electricity produced a significantly lower neural response throughout the brain. In troubled relationships, this protective effect didn't occur. If you're in a healthy relationship, holding your partner's hand is enough to subdue your blood pressure, ease your response to stress, improve your health and soften physical pain. We alter one another's physiology and neural functions.

However, it's not all sub rosa. One can decide to be a more attentive and 16 compassionate partner, mindful of the other's motives, hurts and longings. Breaking old habits isn't easy, since habits are deeply ingrained neural shortcuts, a way of slurring over details without having to dwell on them. Couples often choose to rewire their brains on purpose, sometimes with a therapist's help, to ease conflicts and strengthen their at-one-ness.

While they were both in the psychology department of Stony Brook 17 University, Bianca Acevedo and Arthur Aron scanned the brains of long-married couples who described themselves as still "madly in love." Staring at a picture of a spouse lit up their reward centers as expected; the same happened with those newly in love (and also with cocaine users). But, in contrast to new sweethearts and cocaine addicts, long-married couples displayed calm in sites associated with fear and anxiety. Also, in the opiate-rich sites linked to pleasure and pain relief, and those affiliated with maternal love, the home fires glowed brightly.

18   A happy marriage relieves stress and makes one feel as safe as an adored baby. Small wonder "Baby" is a favorite adult endearment. Not that romantic love is an exact copy of the infant bond. One needn't consciously regard a lover as momlike to profit from the parallels. The body remembers, the brain recycles and restages.

19   So how does this play out beyond the lab? I saw the healing process up close after my 74-year-old husband, who is also a writer, suffered a left-hemisphere stroke that wiped out a lifetime of language. All he could utter was "mem." Mourning the loss of our duet of decades, I began exploring new ways to communicate, through caring gestures, pantomime, facial expressions, humor, play, empathy and tons of affection—the brain's epitome of a safe attachment. That, plus the admittedly eccentric home schooling I provided, and his diligent practice, helped rewire his brain to a startling degree, and in time we were able to talk again, he returned to writing books, and even his vision improved. The brain changes with experience throughout our lives; it's in loving relationships of all sorts—partners, children, close friends—that brain and body really thrive.

20   During idylls of safety, when your brain knows you're with someone you can trust, it needn't waste precious resources coping with stressors or menace. Instead it may spend its lifeblood learning new things or fine-tuning the process of healing. Its doors of perception swing wide open. The flip side is that, given how vulnerable one then is, love lessons—sweet or villainous—can make a deep impression. Wedded hearts change everything, even the brain.

Questions about Meaning

1. According to Ackerman, what does "interpersonal neurobiology" add to our understanding of love? Does this change your own understanding of love and its effects??

2. What does the author say this new field does to our understanding of what happens when a once loving relationship ends? Does this make sense to you?

3. What does the author say are the benefits of a long-term intimate loving relationship?

4. What does the author mean when she refers to the self as "the ultimate souvenir"?

5. What is the "mirror world" that Ackerman writes about in paragraph seven?

Questions about Rhetorical Strategy and Style

1. How would you characterize the language of the essay? Why do you think the author chose to use such words and expressions? How effective did you find the author's language?

2. What does the author's description of her own and her husband's experience contribute to the essay? Did it affect your own response?

Stupid Jobs Are Good to Relax With

Hal Niedzviecki

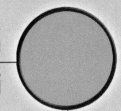

This essay was first published in This Magazine *in 1998. Its author, Hal Niedzviecki (1971–), is a prolific writer of both fiction and non-fiction, an editor, and a cultural commentator. You can find out what he's up to at www.SmellIt.ca*

Springsteen kicked off his world tour at Toronto's Massey Hall a while back. Along with record company execs and those who could afford the exorbitant prices scalpers wanted for tickets, I was in attendance. As Bruce rambled on about the plight of the itinerant Mexican workers, I lolled in the back, my job, as always, to make myself as unapproachable as possible—no easy feat, trapped as I was in paisley vest and bow-tie combo. Nonetheless, the concert was of such soporific proportions and the crowd so dulled into pseudo-reverence, I was able to achieve the ultimate in ushering—a drooping catatonia as close as you can get to being asleep while on your feet at a rock concert.

But this ushering nirvana wouldn't last long. For an usher, danger takes many forms, including vomiting teens and the usher's nemesis: the disruptive patron. And yes, to my semi-conscious horror, there she was: well-dressed, blond, drunk and doped up, swaying in her seat and . . . clapping. Clapping. In the middle of Springsteen's solo dirge about Pancho or Pedro or Luisa, she was clapping.

Sweat beaded on my forehead. The worst was happening. She was in my section. Her clapping echoed through the hall, renowned for its acoustics. The Boss glared from the stage, his finger-picking folksiness no match for the drunken rhythm of this fan. Then, miracle of miracles, the song ended. The woman slumped back into her seat. Bruce muttered something about how he didn't need a rhythm section. Placated by the adoring silence of the well-to-do, he launched into an even quieter song about an even more desperate migrant worker.

I lurked in the shadows, relaxed the grip I had on my flashlight (the usher's only weapon). Springsteen crooned. His guitar twanged. It was so quiet you could hear the rats squirrelling around the ushers' subterranean change rooms. The woman roused herself from her slumber. She leaned forward in her seat, as if suddenly appreciating the import of her hero's message. I wiped the sweat off my brow, relieved. But slowly, almost imperceptibly, she brought her arms up above her head. I stared, disbelieving. Her hands waved around in the air until . . . boom! Another song ruined, New York record execs and L.A. journalists distracted from their calculations of Bruce's net worth, the faint cry of someone calling, "Usher! Do something!"

For several years now, I have relied on stupid jobs to pay my way through the world. This isn't because I am a stupid person. On the contrary, stupid jobs are a way to avoid the brain-numbing idiocy of full-time employment. They are the next best thing to having no job at all. They will keep you sane, and smart.

6   I'm lazy sometimes. I don't always feel like working. On the stupid job, you're allowed to be lazy. All you have to do is show up. Hey, that's as much of an imposition on my life as I'm ready to accept. Does The Boss go to work every day? I don't think so. He's The Boss.

7   Understanding the stupid job is the key to wading your way through the muck of the working week and dealing with such portentous concepts as The Youth Unemployment Crisis and the Transformation of the Workplace. So sit back and let me explain. Or, as I used to say behind the scowl of my shining grin: "Hi, how are you this evening? Please follow me and I will show you to your seat."

8   "Out of Work: Is there Hope for Canada's Youth"? blurted the October 1997 issue of *Canadian Living*. My answer? There is more hope than ever. I'm not talking about ineffectual governments and their well-intentioned "partners," the beneficent corporations, all banding together to "create" jobs. After all, what kind of jobs do you think these corporations are going to create? Jobs that are interesting, challenging and resplendent with possibilities? Hardly. These are going to be stupid jobs. Bring me your college graduates, your aspiring business mavens, your literature lovers and we will find them rote employment where servility and docility are the best things they could have learned at university.

9   But hope, hope is something altogether different. Hope is the process whereby entire generations learn to undervalue their work, squirm out of the trap of meaningless employment, work less, consume less and actually figure out how to enjoy life.

10   I hope I'm right about this, because the reality of the underemployed, overeducated young people of Canada is that the stupid job is their future. As the middle-aged population continues to occupy all the "real" jobs, as the universities continue to hike tuition prices (forcing students to work and study part time), as the government continues to shore up employment numbers with make-work and "retraining," there will be more stupid jobs than ever. And these stupid jobs won't be reserved for the uneducated and poor. The fertile growth of the stupid job is already reaping a crop of middle-class youngsters whose education and upbringing have, somehow, given way to (supposedly) stalled prospects and uncertain incomes.

11   These are your grandchildren, your children, your sisters, your cousins, your neighbours. Hey, that might very well be a multi-coloured bow-tie wrapped around your neck.

12   I took a few tenuous steps down the aisle. All around me, luxurious people hissed in annoyance and extended their claws. Clapping woman was bouncing in her seat. She was smiling. Her face was flushed and joyous. The sound of her hands coming together was deafening. I longed for the floor captain, the front-of-house manager, the head of security, somebody to come and take this problem away from me. I hit her with a burst of flashlight. Taking advantage of her momentary blindness, I leaned in: "Excuse me Miss," I said. "You can't do that." "What"? she said. "That clapping," I said. "Listen," she slurred. "I paid $300 to see this. I can do what I want."

13   My flashlight hand wavered. Correctly interpreting my silence for defeat, she resumed her clapping. Springsteen strummed louder, unsuccessful in his attempt to drown out the beat of luxury, the truth of indulgence. I faded away, the darkness swallowing me up. For a blissful moment, I was invisible.

A lot of young people think their stupid jobs are only temporary. Most of them are   14
right, in a way. Many will move on from being, as I have been, an usher, a security
guard, a delivery boy, a data coordinator, a publishing intern. They will get
marginally better jobs, but what they have learned from their stupid jobs will stay
with them forever. Hopefully.

If I'm right, they will learn that the stupid job—and by extension, all jobs—   15
must be approached with willing stupidity. Set your mind free. It isn't necessary,
and it can be an impediment. While your body runs the maze and finds the cheese,
let your mind go where it will.

Look at it this way: you're trading material wealth and luxury for freedom and   16
creativity. To simplify this is to say that while you may have less money to buy
things, you will have a lot more time to think up ways to achieve your goals without
buying things. It is remarkable how quickly one comes to value time to just sit
and think. Oddly, many of us seem quite proud of having absolutely no time to
think about anything. The words "I'm so busy" are chanted over and over again
like a mantra, an incantation against some horrible moment when we realize
we're not so busy. In the stupid job universe, time isn't quantifiable. You're making
so many dollars an hour, but the on-job perks include daydreams, poems scribbled
on napkins, novels read in utility closets and long conversations about the sexual
stamina of Barney Rubble. How much is an idea worth? An image? A moment of
tranquility? A bad joke? The key here is to embrace the culture of anti-work.

Sometime after the Springsteen debacle, I was on delivery job dropping off   17
newspapers at various locales. I started arguing with my co-worker, the van driver,
about work ethic. I suggested we skip a drop-off or two, claiming that no one would
notice and even if they did, we could deny it and no one would care. He responded
by telling me that no matter what job he was doing, if he accepted the work, he was
compelled to do it right. I disagreed. Cut corners, I argued. Do less for the same
amount of pay. That's what they expect us to do, I said. Why else would they pay
us so little? Not that day, but some weeks later, he came to see things my way.

What am I trying to tell you? To be lazy? To set fire to the corporation?   18

Maybe. Our options might be limited, but they are still options. Somewhere   19
in the bowels of Massey Hall it has probably been noted in my permanent record
that I have a bad attitude. That was a mistake. I wasn't trying to have a bad attitude.
I was trying to have no attitude. . . .

What I should have told my friend in the delivery van was that when working the   20
stupid job, passivity is the difference between near slavery and partial freedom.
It's a mental distinction. Your body is still in the same place for the same amount
of time (unless you're unsupervised), but your mind is figuring things out. Figuring
out how many days you need to work to afford things like hard-to-get tickets to
concerts by famous American icons. Or figuring out why it is that at the end of the
week, most people are too busy or too tired to do anything other than spend their
hard-earned dollars on fleeting moments of cotton candy ecstasy as ephemeral as
lunch hour. Personally, I'd take low-level servitude over a promotion that means
I'll be working late the rest of my life. You want me to work weekends? You better
give me the rest of the week off. . . .

Montreal has one of the highest unemployment rates of any city in Canada. Young   21
people in that city are as likely to have full-time jobs as they are to spend their
nights arguing about Quebec separation. Not coincidentally, some of the best
Canadian writers, comic artists and underground periodicals are from that city.

We're talking about the spoken-word capital of North America here. Creativity plus unemployment equals art.

22   The burgeoning stupid job aesthetic is well documented in another youth culture phenomenon, the vaunted 'zine (photocopied periodicals published by individuals for fun, not money). Again, it doesn't take a genius to make the connection between the youth culture of stupid jobs and the urgency and creativity zine publishers display when writing about their lives. "So why was I dishonest and subversive"? asks Brendan Bartholomew in an article in the popular Wisconsin zine *Temp Slave*. "Well, I've been sabotaging employers for so long, it's become second nature. It's in my blood. I couldn't stop if I wanted to."

23   Slacking off, doing as little as possible, relishing my lack of responsibility, this is what the workplace has taught me to do. This is the stupid job mantra. It isn't about being poor. The stupid job aesthetic is not about going hungry. Canada is a country of excess. You cannot have a stupid job culture where people are genuinely, truly, worried that they are going to starve in the streets.

24   Nevertheless, the tenets of the stupid job revolution are universal: work is mainly pointless; if you can think of something better to do, you shouldn't have to work; it's better to have a low-paying job and freedom than a high-paying job and a 60-hour workweek. It was Bruce's drunken fan who highlighted the most important aspect of what will one day be known as the stupid job revolution: with money, you think you can do whatever you want, but you rarely can; without money, you can be like Bartholomew—a postmodern rat, a stowaway writing his diaries from the comfort of his berth at the bottom of the sinking ship.

25   My father's plight is a familiar one. He started his working life at 13 in Montreal. He's 55 now. His employer of 12 years forced him to take early retirement. The terms were great, and if he didn't own so much stuff (and want more stuff) he could live comfortably without ever working again. But he feels used, meaningless, rejected.

26   On his last day, I helped him clean out his office. The sight of him stealing staplers, blank disks and Post-it note pads was something I'll never forget. It was a memo he was writing to his own soul (note: they owe me).

27   But the acquisition of more stuff is not what he needs to put a life of hard work behind him. I wish that he could look back on his years of labour and think fondly of all the hours he decided not to work, those hours he spent reading a good book behind the closed door of his office, or skipping off early to take the piano lessons he never got around to. Instead of stealing office supplies, he should have given his boss the finger as he walked out the door. Ha ha. I don't care what you think of me. And by the way, I never did.

28   Despite his decades of labour and my years of being barely employed (and the five degrees we have between us), we have both ended up at the same place. He feels cheated. I don't.

Questions about Meaning

1. What are the advantages to having a stupid job, according to the article? Do you agree? Why or why not?
2. Niedzviecki's argument rests on the idea that most jobs are a form of mindless servitude. What evidence does he provide to support his point of view?
3. What is the thesis of this article? Can you paraphrase it?

Questions about Rhetorical Strategy and Style

1. What purpose does the story about the Springsteen concert serve? Why do you think the author goes back to this story in paragraphs 12 and 13?
2. How would you describe Niedzviecki's diction in this article? What purpose does it serve?

It's Not About You

David Brooks

The author is a columnist for The New York Times *where this first appeared in May (graduation month in the U.S.) 2011.*

1. Over the past few weeks, America's colleges have sent another class of graduates off into the world. These graduates possess something of inestimable value. Nearly every sensible middle-aged person would give away all their money to be able to go back to age 22 and begin adulthood anew.

2. But, especially this year, one is conscious of the many ways in which this year's graduating class has been ill served by their elders. They enter a bad job market, the hangover from decades of excessive borrowing. They inherit a ruinous federal debt.

3. More important, their lives have been perversely structured. This year's graduates are members of the most supervised generation in American history. Through their childhoods and teenage years, they have been monitored, tutored, coached and honed to an unprecedented degree.

4. Yet upon graduation they will enter a world that is unprecedentedly wide open and unstructured. Most of them will not quickly get married, buy a home and have kids, as previous generations did. Instead, they will confront amazingly diverse job markets, social landscapes and lifestyle niches. Most will spend a decade wandering from job to job and clique to clique, searching for a role.

5. No one would design a system of extreme supervision to prepare people for a decade of extreme openness. But this is exactly what has emerged in modem America. College students are raised in an environment that demands one set of navigational skills, and they are then cast out into a different environment requiring a different set of skills, which they have to figure out on their own.

6. Worst of all, they are sent off into this world with the whole baby-boomer theology ringing in their ears. If you sample some of the commencement addresses being broadcast on C-Span these days, you see that many graduates are told to: Follow *your* passion, chart *your* own course, march to the beat of *your* own drummer, follow *your* dreams and find *your*self. This is the litany of expressive individualism, which is still the dominant note in American culture.

7. But, of course, this mantra misleads on nearly every front.

8. College grads are often sent out into the world amid rapturous talk of limitless possibilities. But this talk is of no help to the central business of adulthood, finding serious things to tie yourself down to. The successful young adult is beginning to make sacred commitments — to a spouse, a community and calling — yet mostly hears about freedom and autonomy.

9. Today's graduates are also told to find their passion and then pursue their dreams. The implication is that they should find themselves first and then go off

and live their quest. But, of course, very few people at age 22 or 24 can take an inward journey and come out having discovered a developed self.

Most successful young people don't look inside and then plan a life. They look 10 outside and find a problem, which summons their life. A relative suffers from Alzheimer's and a young woman feels called to help cure that disease. A young man works under a miserable boss and must develop management skills so his department can function. Another young woman finds herself confronted by an opportunity she never thought of in a job category she never imagined. This wasn't in her plans, but this is where she can make her contribution.

Most people don't form a self and then lead a life. They are called by a problem, 11 and the self is constructed gradually by their calling.

The graduates are also told to pursue happiness and joy. But, of course, when 12 you read a biography of someone you admire, it's rarely the things that made them happy that compel your admiration. It's the things they did to court unhappiness — the things they did that were arduous and miserable, which sometimes cost them friends and aroused hatred. It's excellence, not happiness, that we admire most.

Finally, graduates are told to be independent-minded and to express their 13 inner spirit. But, of course, doing your job well often means suppressing yourself. As Atul Gawande mentioned during his countercultural address last week at Harvard Medical School, being a good doctor often means being part of a team, following the rules of an institution, going down a regimented checklist.

Today's grads enter a cultural climate that preaches the self as the center of a 14 life. But, of course, as they age, they'll discover that the tasks of a life are at the center. Fulfillment is a byproduct of how people engage their tasks, and can't be pursued directly. Most of us are egotistical and most are self-concerned most of the time, but it's nonetheless true that life comes to a point only in those moments when the self dissolves into some task. The purpose in life is not to find yourself. It's to lose yourself.

Questions about Meaning

1. Brooks is writing about how well or how poorly "America's colleges" have prepared their new graduates. How are "Canada's colleges" or "Ontario's colleges" different and just how different are they? Have you been encouraged to "follow your passion, chart your own course, ... "?

2. What is the author's chief criticism of American colleges? Is it just colleges he is faulting?

3. What is Brooks saying about happiness and the pursuit of happiness? Do you agree?

Questions about Rhetorical Strategy and Style

1. Who are the main intended readers of the essay? What indicates this?

2. Why might Brooks have chosen to refer to "baby-boomer theology" in paragraph six rather than, say, to "baby-boomer philosophy"?

3. Brooks often uses parallelism to sharpen a contrast or highlight a key point. What are some examples? Do they ever serve to exaggerate or oversimplify a difference?

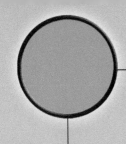

Cri de Coeur*

Lt.-Gen. Roméo Dallaire, with Major Brent Beardsley

Canadian Lieutenant-General Roméo Dallaire was the commander of the United Nations peacekeeping force in Rwanda during the 1994 genocide. This selection is the introduction to Dallaire's 2003 memoir **Shake Hands with the Devil: The Failure of Humanity in Rwanda.** *It is, as the title suggests, "a cry from the heart."*

1 It was an absolutely magnificent day in May 1994. The blue sky was cloudless, and there was a whiff of breeze stirring the trees. It was hard to believe that in the past weeks an unimaginable evil had turned Rwanda's gentle green valleys and mist-capped hills into a stinking nightmare of rotting corpses. A nightmare we all had to negotiate every day. A nightmare that, as commander of the UN peacekeeping force in Rwanda, I could not help but feel deeply responsible for.

2 In relative terms, that day had been a good one. Under the protection of a limited and fragile ceasefire, my troops had successfully escorted about two hundred civilians—a few of the thousands who had sought refuge with us in Kigali, the capital of Rwanda—through many government- and militia-manned checkpoints to reach safety behind the Rwandese Patriotic Front (RPF) lines. We were seven weeks into the genocide, and the RPF, the disciplined rebel army (composed largely of the sons of Rwandan refugees who had lived over the border in camps in Uganda since being forced out of their homeland at independence), was making a curved sweep toward Kigali from the north, adding civil war to the chaos and butchery in the country.

3 Having delivered our precious cargo of innocent souls, we were headed back to Kigali in a white UN Land Cruiser with my force commander pennant on the front hood and the blue UN flag on a staff attached to the right rear. My Ghanaian sharpshooter, armed with a new Canadian C-7 rifle, rode behind me, and my new Senegalese aide-de-camp, Captain Ndiaye, sat to my right. We were driving a particularly dangerous stretch of road, open to sniper fire. Most of the people in the surrounding villages had been slaughtered, the few survivors escaping with little more than the clothes on their backs. In a few short weeks, it had become a lonely and forlorn place.

4 Suddenly up ahead we saw a child wandering across the road. I stopped the vehicle close to the little boy, worried about scaring him off, but he was quite unfazed. He was about three years old, dressed in a filthy, torn T-shirt, the ragged remnants of underwear, little more than a loincloth, drooping from under his distended belly. He was caked in dirt, his hair white and matted with dust, and he

*Cri de coeur: Editor's title, in French meaning "a cry from the heart."

was enveloped in a cloud of flies, which were greedily attacking the open sores that covered him. He stared at us silently, sucking on what I realized was a high-protein biscuit. Where had the boy found food in this wasteland?

I got out of the vehicle and walked toward him. Maybe it was the condition I   5
was in, but to me this child had the face of an angel and eyes of pure innocence. I had seen so many children hacked to pieces that this small, whole, bewildered boy was a vision of hope. Surely he could not have survived all on his own? I motioned for my aide-de-camp to honk the horn, hoping to summon up his parents, but the sound echoed over the empty landscape, startling a few birds and little else. The boy remained transfixed. He did not speak or cry, just stood sucking on his biscuit and staring up at us with his huge, solemn eyes. Still hoping that he wasn't all alone, I sent my aide-de-camp and the sharpshooter to look for signs of life.

We were in a ravine lush with banana trees and bamboo shoots, which created   6
a dense canopy of foliage. A long straggle of deserted huts stood on either side of the road. As I stood alone with the boy, I felt an anxious knot in my stomach: this would be a perfect place to stage an ambush. My colleagues returned, having found no one. Then a rustling in the undergrowth made us jump. I grabbed the boy and held him firmly to my side as we instinctively took up defensive positions around the vehicle and in the ditch. The bushes parted to reveal a well-armed RPF soldier about fifteen years old. He recognized my uniform and gave me a smart salute and introduced himself. He was part of an advance observation post in the nearby hills. I asked him who the boy was and whether there was anyone left alive in the village who could take care of him. The soldier answered that the boy had no name and no family but that he and his buddies were looking after him. That explained the biscuit but did nothing to allay my concerns over the security and health of the boy. I protested that the child needed proper care and that I could give it to him: we were protecting and supporting orphanages in Kigali where he would be much better off. The soldier quietly insisted that the boy stay where he was, among his own people.

I continued to argue, but this child soldier was in no mood to discuss the   7
situation and with haughty finality stated that his unit would care and provide for the child. I could feel my face flush with anger and frustration, but then noticed that the boy himself had slipped away while we had been arguing over him, and God only knew where he had gone. My aide-de-camp spotted him at the entrance to a hut a short distance away, clambering over a log that had fallen across the doorway. I ran after him, closely followed by my aide-de-camp and the RPF child soldier. By the time I had caught up to the boy, he had disappeared inside. The log in the doorway turned out to be the body of a man, obviously dead for some weeks, his flesh rotten with maggots and beginning to fall away from the bones.

As I stumbled over the body and into the hut, a swarm of flies invaded my   8
nose and mouth. It was so dark inside that at first I smelled rather than saw the horror that lay before me. The hut was a two-room affair, one room serving as a kitchen and living room and the other as a communal bedroom; two rough windows had been cut into the mud-and-stick wall. Very little light penetrated the gloom, but as my eyes became accustomed to the dark, I saw strewn around the living room in a rough circle the decayed bodies of a man, a woman and two children, stark white bone poking through the desiccated, leather-like covering that had once been skin. The little boy was crouched beside what was left of his mother, still sucking on his biscuit. I made my way over to him as slowly and quietly as I could and, lifting him into my arms, carried him out of the hut.

9   The warmth of his tiny body snuggled against mine filled me with a peace and serenity that elevated me above the chaos. This child was alive yet terribly hungry, beautiful but covered in dirt, bewildered but not fearful. I made up my mind: this boy would be the fourth child in the Dallaire family. I couldn't save Rwanda, but I could save this child.

10   Before I had held this boy, I had agreed with the aid workers and representatives of both the warring armies that I would not permit any exporting of Rwandan orphans to foreign places. When confronted by such requests from humanitarian organizations, I would argue that the money to move a hundred kids by plane to France or Belgium could help build, staff and sustain Rwandan orphanages that could house three thousand children. This one boy eradicated all my arguments. I could see myself arriving at the terminal in Montreal like a latter-day St. Christopher° with the boy cradled in my arms, and my wife, Beth, there ready to embrace him.

11   That dream was abruptly destroyed when the young soldier, fast as a wolf, yanked the child from my arms and carried him directly into the bush. Not knowing how many members of his unit might already have their gunsights on us, we reluctantly climbed back into the Land Cruiser. As I slowly drove away, I had much on my mind.

12   By withdrawing, I had undoubtedly done the wise thing: I had avoided risking the lives of my two soldiers in what would have been a fruitless struggle over one small boy. But in that moment, it seemed to me that I had backed away from a fight for what was right, that this failure stood for all our failures in Rwanda.

13   Whatever happened to that beautiful child? Did he make it to an orphanage deep behind the RPF lines? Did he survive the following battles? Is he dead or is he now a child soldier himself, caught in the seemingly endless conflict that plagues his homeland?

14   That moment, when the boy, in the arms of a soldier young enough to be his brother, was swallowed whole by the forest, haunts me. It's a memory that never lets me forget how ineffective and irresponsible we were when we promised the Rwandans that we would establish an atmosphere of security that would allow them to achieve a lasting peace. It has been almost nine years since I left Rwanda, but as I write this, the sounds, smells and colours come flooding back in digital clarity. It's as if someone has sliced into my brain and grafted this horror called Rwanda frame by blood-soaked frame directly on my cortex. I could not forget even if I wanted to. For many of these years, I have yearned to return to Rwanda and disappear into the blue-green hills with my ghosts. A simple pilgrim seeking forgiveness and pardon. But as I slowly begin to piece my life back together, I know the time has come for me to make a more difficult pilgrimage: to travel back through all those terrible memories and retrieve my soul.

15   I did try to write this story soon after I came back from Rwanda in September 1994, hoping to find some respite for myself in sorting out how my own role as Force Commander of UNAMIR interconnected with the international apathy, the complex political manoeuvres, the deep well of hatred and barbarity that resulted in a genocide in which over 800,000 people lost their lives. Instead, I plunged into a disastrous mental health spiral that led me to suicide attempts, a medical release from the Armed Forces, the diagnosis of post-traumatic stress disorder, and dozens upon dozens of therapy sessions and extensive medication, which still have a place in my daily life.

16   It took me seven years to finally have the desire, the willpower and the stamina to begin to describe in detail the events of that year in Rwanda. To recount, from

°St. Christopher: A fearless martyr of the third century, patron saint of travellers.

my insider's point of view, how a country moved from the promise of a certain peace to intrigue, the fomenting of racial hatred, assassinations, civil war and genocide. And how the international community, through an inept UN mandate and what can only be described as indifference, self-interest and racism, aided and abetted these crimes against humanity—how we all helped create the mess that has murdered and displaced millions and destabilized the whole central African region.

A growing library of books and articles is exploring the tragic events in Rwanda 17 from many angles: eyewitness accounts, media analyses, assaults on the actions of the American administration at the time, condemnations of the UN's apparent ineptitude. But even in the international and national inquiries launched in the wake of the genocide, the blame somehow slides away from the individual member nations of the UN, and in particular those influential countries with permanent representatives on the Security Council, such as the United States, France and the United Kingdom, who sat back and watched it all happen, who pulled their troops or didn't offer any troops in the first place. A few Belgian officers were brought to court to pay for the sins of Rwanda. When my sector commander in Kigali, Colonel Luc Marchal, was court-martialled in Brussels, the charges against him were clearly designed to deflect any responsibility away from the Belgian government for the deaths of the ten Belgian peacekeepers under my command. The judge eventually threw out all the charges, accepting the fact that Marchal had performed his duties magnificently in a near-impossible situation. But the spotlight never turned to the reasons why he and the rest of the UNAMIR force were in such a dangerous situation in the first place.

It is time that I tell the story from where I stood—literally in the middle of the 18 slaughter for weeks on end. A public account of my actions, my decisions and my failings during that most terrible year may be a crucial missing link for those attempting to understand the tragedy both intellectually and in their hearts. I know that I will never end my mourning for all those Rwandans who placed their faith in us, who thought the UN peacekeeping force was there to stop extremism, to stop the killings and help them through the perilous journey to a lasting peace. That mission, UNAMIR, failed. I know intimately the cost in human lives of the inflexible UN Security Council mandate, the pennypinching financial management of the mission, the UN red tape, the political manipulations and my own personal limitations. What I have come to realize as the root of it all, however, is the fundamental indifference of the world community to the plight of seven to eight million black Africans in a tiny country that had no strategic or resource value to any world power. An overpopulated little country that turned in on itself and destroyed its own people, as the world watched and yet could not manage to find the political will to intervene. Engraved still in my brain is the judgment of a small group of bureaucrats who came to "assess" the situation in the first weeks of the genocide: "We will recommend to our government not to intervene as the risks are high and all that is here are humans."

My story is not a strictly military account nor a clinical, academic study of the 19 breakdown of Rwanda. It is not a simplistic indictment of the many failures of the UN as a force for peace in the world. It is not a story of heroes and villains, although such a work could easily be written. This book is a *cri de coeur* for the slaughtered thousands, a tribute to the souls hacked apart by machetes because of their supposed difference from those who sought to hang on to power. It is the story of a commander who, faced with a challenge that didn't fit the classic Cold War–era peacekeeper's rule book, failed to find an effective solution and witnessed, as if in punishment, the loss of some of his own troops, the attempted annihilation of an ethnicity, the butchery of children barely out of the womb, the stacking of severed limbs like cordwood, the mounds of decomposing bodies being eaten by the sun.

20   This book is nothing more nor less than the account of a few humans who were entrusted with the role of helping others taste the fruits of peace. Instead, we watched as the devil took control of paradise on earth and fed on the blood of the people we were supposed to protect.

Questions about Meaning

1. What value do individual human beings have for the international community, according to Dallaire? What value do they have for Dallaire?

2. Why did Dallaire establish the rule disallowing international adoptions? Does this seem like a reasonable rule? Why did he want to break it?

3. What does the word "genocide" literally mean? Whom does Dallaire blame for the genocide? Does his reasoning seem logical?

Questions about Rhetorical Strategy and Style

1. Why would the author have chosen to describe the horrors of war in such detail? Does it contribute to or take away from his purpose in writing?

2. What percentage of his article does the author spend on the story of the one boy he failed to rescue? Was it effective for him to spend that much time on that one example?

Why We Crave Horror Movies
Stephen King

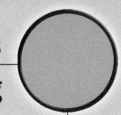

Stephen King (1947–) was born in Portland, Maine. After graduating from the University of Maine in 1970, King held a number of jobs—knitting mill worker, janitor, high school English teacher—before gaining fame and fortune as a mystery writer. A prolific and widely popular writer (his book sales have surpassed 20 million copies), King has become synonymous with horror stories and movies. His many books include **Carrie** *(1974),* **Salem's Lot** *(1975),* **The Shining** *(1977),* **The Dead Zone** *(1979),* **Firestarter** *(1980),* **Christine** *(1983),* **Pet Sematary** *(1983),* **The Tommyknockers** *(1984),* **Misery** *(1987),* **Needful Things** *(1991),* **Insomnia** *(1994),* **Bag of Bones** *(1998),* **The Green Mile** *(2000),* **The Plant** *(2000)—a serial novel which he published online,* **The Colorado Kid** *(2005), and* **Cell** *(2006). First published in* **Playboy** *in 1982, this essay explains, in the master's words, why we crave good horror shows.*

1   I think that we're all mentally ill; those of us outside the asylums only hide it a little better—and maybe not all that much better, after all. We've all known people who talk to themselves, people who sometimes squinch their faces into horrible grimaces when they believe no one is watching, people who have some hysterical fear—of snakes, the dark, the tight place, the long drop . . . and, of course, those final worms and grubs that are waiting so patiently underground.

2   When we pay our four or five bucks and seat ourselves at tenth-row center in a theater showing a horror movie, we are daring the nightmare.

3   Why? Some of the reasons are simple and obvious. To show that we can, that we are not afraid, that we can ride this roller coaster. Which is not to say that a really good horror movie may not surprise a scream out of us at some point, the way we may scream when the roller coaster twists through a complete 360 or plows through a lake at the bottom of the drop. And horror movies, like roller coasters, have always been the special province of the young; by the time one turns 40 or 50, one's appetite for double twists or 360-degree loops may be considerably depleted.

4   We also go to re-establish our feelings of essential normality; the horror movie is innately conservative, even reactionary. Freda Jackson as the horrible melting woman in *Die, Monster, Die!* confirms for us that no matter how far we may be removed from the beauty of a Robert Redford or a Diana Ross, we are still light-years from true ugliness.

5   And we go to have fun.

6   Ah, but this is where the ground starts to slope away, isn't it? Because this is a very peculiar sort of fun indeed. The fun comes from seeing others menaced—sometimes killed. One critic has suggested that if pro football has become the

voyeur's version of combat, then the horror film has become the modern version of the public lynching.

7   It is true that the mythic, "fairy-tale" horror film intends to take away the shades of gray. . . . It urges us to put away our more civilized and adult penchant for analysis and to become children again, seeing things in pure blacks and whites. It may be that horror movies provide psychic relief on this level because this invitation to lapse into simplicity, irrationality and even outright madness is extended so rarely. We are told we may allow our emotions a free rein . . . or no rein at all.

8   If we are all insane, then sanity becomes a matter of degree. If your insanity leads you to carve up women like Jack the Ripper or the Cleveland Torso Murderer, we clap you away in the funny farm (but neither of those two amateur-night surgeons was ever caught, heh-heh-heh); if, on the other hand, your insanity leads you only to talk to yourself when you're under stress or to pick your nose on your morning bus, then you are left alone to go about your business . . . though it is doubtful that you will ever be invited to the best parties.

9   The potential lyncher is in almost all of us (excluding saints, past and present; but then, most saints have been crazy in their own ways), and every now and then, he has to be let loose to scream and roll around in the grass. Our emotions and our fears form their own body, and we recognize that it demands its own exercise to maintain proper muscle tone. Certain of these emotional muscles are accepted—even exalted—in civilized society; they are, of course, the emotions that tend to maintain the status quo of civilization itself. Love, friendship, loyalty, kindness— these are all the emotions that we applaud, emotions that have been immortalized in the couplets of Hallmark cards and in the verses (I don't dare call it poetry) of Leonard Nimoy.

10   When we exhibit these emotions, society showers us with positive reinforcement; we learn this even before we get out of diapers. When, as children, we hug our rotten little puke of a sister and give her a kiss, all the aunts and uncles smile and twit and cry, "Isn't he the sweetest little thing"? Such coveted treats as chocolate-covered graham crackers often follow. But if we deliberately slam the rotten little puke of a sister's fingers in the door, sanctions follow—angry remonstrance from parents, aunts and uncles; instead of a chocolate-covered graham cracker, a spanking.

11   But anticivilization emotions don't go away, and they demand periodic exercise. We have such "sick" jokes as, "What's the difference between a truckload of bowling balls and a truckload of dead babies"? (You can't unload a truckload of bowling balls with a pitchfork . . . a joke, by the way, that I heard originally from a ten-year-old.) Such a joke may surprise a laugh or a grin out of us even as we recoil, a possibility that confirms the thesis: If we share a brotherhood of man, then we also share an insanity of man. None of which is intended as a defense of either the sick joke or insanity but merely as an explanation of why the best horror films, like the best fairy tales, manage to be reactionary, anarchistic, and revolutionary all at the same time.

12   The mythic horror movie, like the sick joke, has a dirty job to do. It deliberately appeals to all that is worst in us. It is morbidity unchained, our most base instincts let free, our nastiest fantasies realized . . . and it all happens, fittingly enough, in the dark. For those reasons, good liberals often shy away from horror films. For myself, I like to see the most aggressive of them—*Dawn of the Dead*, for instance— as lifting a trap door in the civilized forebrain and throwing a basket of raw meat to the hungry alligators swimming around in that subterranean river beneath.

13   Why bother? Because it keeps them from getting out, man. It keeps them down there and me up here. It was Lennon and McCartney who said that all you need is love, and I would agree with that.

14   As long as you keep the gators fed.

Questions on Meaning

1. What is King's succinct, five-word explanation for why we crave horror movies? What are the three reasons that he gives to elaborate upon this explanation?

2. What does King—who contends that everyone is mentally ill— mean by the comment, "sanity becomes a matter of degree"?

3. What are the elements of horror films that cause "good liberals" to avoid them?

Questions on Rhetorical Strategy and Style

1. What tone does King set with his opening comment? Explain why you believe that King was being serious, exaggerating, or simply toying with his readers. What was your reaction to that comment when you *completed* the essay?

2. Reread paragraphs 1–6. How does King introduce tension into his piece with the comment, "Ah, but this is where the ground starts to slope away, isn't it"? What suggestions is he placing in the minds of his readers when he begins to speak of "a very peculiar sort of fun"?

3. Explain the metaphor that King uses for our "anticivilization emotions" and the demands that those emotions make of us.

4. This narrative relies heavily on concrete, sensory detail. List at least one example each of the author's appeal to sight, sound, taste, touch and smell. What emotions do these sensory details evoke?

The Scar*
Kildare Dobbs

Kildare Dobbs is a prolific writer of essays, short fiction, and poetry. "The Scar," from Dobbs' 1968 essay collection Reading the Times, *graphically depicts the horrors of war, as reported to him by Emiko Okamoto, a survivor of the 1945 nuclear bombing of Hiroshima.*

1   This is the story I was told in 1963 by Emiko Okamoto, a young Japanese woman who had come to live in Toronto. She spoke through an interpreter, since at that time she knew no English. It is Emiko's story, although I have had to complete it from other sources.

2   But why am I telling it? Everyone knows how terrible this story is. Everyone knows the truth of what von Clausewitz said: "Force to meet force arms itself with the inventions of art and science." First the bow-and-arrow, then Greek fire, gunpowder, poison-gas—and so on up the lethal scale. These things, we're told, should be considered calmly. No sweat—we should think about the unthinkable, or so Herman Kahn suggests, dispassionately. And he writes: "We do not expect illustrations in a book of surgery to be captioned 'Good health is preferable to this kind of cancer.' Excessive comments such as 'And now there is a lot of blood' or 'This particular cut really hurts' are out of place. . . . To dwell on such things is morbid." Perhaps the answer to Herman Kahn is that if surgeons hadn't dwelt on those things we wouldn't now have anaesthetics, or artery forceps either, for the matter.

3   To think about thermonuclear war in the abstract is obscene. To think about any kind of warfare with less than the whole of our mind and imagination is obscene. This is the worst treason.

4   Before that morning in 1945 only a few conventional bombs, none of which did any great damage, had fallen on the city. Fleets of U.S. bombers had, however, devastated many cities round about, and Hiroshima had begun a program of evacuation which had reduced its population from 380,000 to some 245,000. Among the evacuees were Emiko and her family.

5   "We were moved out to Otake, a town about an hour's train-ride out of the city," Emiko told me. She had been a fifteen-year-old student in 1945. Fragile and vivacious, versed in the gentle traditions of the tea ceremony and flower arrangement, Emiko still had an air of the frail school-child when I talked with her. Every day, she and her sister Hideko used to commute into Hiroshima to school. Hideko was thirteen. Their father was an antique-dealer and he owned a house in the city, although it was empty now. Tetsuro, Emiko's thirteen-year-old brother, was at the Manchurian front with the Imperial Army. Her mother was kept busy looking after the children, for her youngest daughter Eiko was sick with heart trouble, and rations were scarce. All of them were undernourished.

*Editor's title.

134

The night of August 5, 1945, little Eiko was dangerously ill. She was not 6
expected to live. Everybody took turns watching by her bed, soothing her by
massaging her arms and legs. Emiko retired at 8:30 (most Japanese people go to
bed early) and at midnight was roused to take her turn with the sick girl. At 2 a.m.
she went back to sleep.

While Emiko slept, the *Enola Gay*, a U.S. B-29 carrying the world's first 7
operational atom bomb, was already in the air. She had taken off from the Pacific
island of Iwo Jima at 1:45 a.m., and now Captain William Parsons, U.S.N.
ordinance expert, was busy in her bomb-hold with the final assembly of Little
Boy. Little Boy looked much like an outsize T.N.T. block-buster but the crew
knew there was something different about him. Only Parsons and the pilot,
Colonel Paul Tibbets, knew exactly in what manner Little Boy was different.
Course was set for Hiroshima.

Emiko slept. 8

On board the *Enola Gay* co-pilot Captain Robert Lewis was writing up his 9
personal log. "After leaving Iwo," he recorded, "we began to pick up some low
stratus and before very long we were flying on top of an under-cast. Outside of a
thin, high cirrus and the low stuff, it's a very beautiful day."

Emiko and Hideko were up at six in the morning. They dressed in the uniform 10
of their women's college—white blouse, quilted hat, and black skirt—breakfasted
and packed their aluminum lunch-boxes with white rice and eggs. These they
stuffed into their shoulder bags as they hurried for the seven-o'clock train to
Hiroshima. Today there would be no classes. Along with many women's groups,
high school students, and others, the sisters were going to work on demolition. The
city had begun a project of clearance to make fire-breaks in its downtown huddle
of wood and paper buildings.

It was a lovely morning. 11

While the two young girls were at breakfast, Captain Lewis, over the Pacific, 12
had made an entry in his log. "We are loaded. The bomb is now alive, and it's a
funny feeling knowing it's right in back of you. Knock wood!"

In the train Hideko suddenly said she was hungry. She wanted to eat her lunch. 13
Emiko dissuaded her: she'd be much hungrier later on. The two sisters argued, but
Hideko at last agreed to keep her lunch till later. They decided to meet at the
main station that afternoon and catch the five-o'clock train home. By now they had
arrived at the first of Hiroshima's three stations. This was where Hideko got off,
for she was to work in a different area from her sister. "Sayonara!" she called.
"Goodbye." Emiko never saw her again.

There had been an air-raid at 7 a.m., but before Emiko arrived at Hiroshima's 14
main station, two stops farther on, the sirens had sounded the all-clear. Just after
eight, Emiko stepped off the train, walked through the station, and waited in the
morning sunshine for her streetcar.

At about the same moment Lewis was writing in his log. "There'll be a short 15
intermission while we bomb our target."

It was hot in the sun. Emiko saw a class-mate and greeted her. Together they 16
moved back into the shade of a high concrete wall to chat. Emiko looked up at the
sky and saw, far up in the cloudless blue, a single B-29.

It was exactly 8:10 a.m. The other people waiting for the streetcar saw it too 17
and began to discuss it anxiously. Emiko felt scared. She felt that at all costs she
must go on talking to her friend. Just as she was thinking this, there was a
tremendous greenish-white flash in the sky. It was far brighter than the sun. Emiko
afterwards remembered vaguely that there was a roaring or a rushing sound as
well, but she was not sure, for just at that moment she lost consciousness.

18   "About 15 seconds after the flash," noted Lewis, 30,000 feet high and several miles away, "there were two very distinct slaps on the ship from the blast and the shock wave. That was all the physical effect we felt. We turned the ship so that we could observe the results."

19   When Emiko came to, she was lying on her face about forty feet away from where she had been standing. She was not aware of any pain. Her first thought was: "I'm alive!" She lifted her head slowly and looked about her. It was growing dark. The air was seething with dust and black smoke. There was a smell of burning. Emiko felt something trickle into her eyes, tasted it in her mouth. Gingerly she put a hand to her head, then looked at it. She saw with a shock that it was covered with blood.

20   She did not give a thought to Hideko. It did not occur to her that her sister who was in another part of the city could possibly have been in danger. Like most of the survivors, Emiko assumed she had been close to a direct hit by a conventional bomb. She thought it had fallen on the post-office next to the station. With a hurt child's panic, Emiko, streaming with blood from gashes in her scalp, ran blindly in search of her mother and father.

21   The people standing in front of the station had been burned to death instantly (a shadow had saved Emiko from the flash). The people inside the station had been crushed by falling masonry. Emiko heard their faint cries, saw hands scrabbling weakly from under the collapsed platform. All around her the maimed survivors were running and stumbling away from the roaring furnace that had been a city. She ran with them toward the mountains that ring the landward side of Hiroshima.

22   From the *Enola Gay*, the strangers from North America looked down at their handiwork. "There, in front of our eyes," wrote Lewis, "was without a doubt the greatest explosion man had ever witnessed. The city was nine-tenths covered with smoke of a boiling nature, which seemed to indicate buildings blowing up, and a large white cloud which in less than three minutes reached 30,000 feet, then went to at least 50,000 feet."

23   Far below, on the edge of this cauldron of smoke, at a distance of some 2,500 yards from the blast's epicentre, Emiko ran with the rest of the living. Some who could not run limped or dragged themselves along. Others were carried. Many, hideously burned, were screaming with pain; when they tripped they lay where they had fallen. There was a man whose face had ripped open from mouth to ear, another whose forehead was a gaping wound. A young soldier was running with a foot-long splinter of bamboo protruding from one eye. But these, like Emiko, were the lightly wounded.

24   Some of the burned people had been literally roasted. Skin hung from their flesh like sodden tissue paper. They did not bleed but plasma dripped from their seared limbs.

25   The *Enola Gay*, mission completed, was returning to base. Lewis sought words to express his feelings, the feelings of all the crew. "I might say," he wrote, "I might say 'My God! What have we done?'"

26   Emiko ran. When she had reached the safety of the mountain she remembered that she still had her shoulder bag. There was a small first-aid kit in it and she applied ointment to her wounds and to a small cut in her left hand. She bandaged her head.

27   Emiko looked back at the city. It was a lake of fire. All around her the burned fugitives cried out in pain. Some were scorched on one side only. Others, naked and flayed, were burned all over. They were too many to help and most of them were dying. Emiko followed the walking wounded along a back road, still delirious, expecting suddenly to meet her father and mother.

The thousands dying by the roadside called feebly for help or water. Some of 28
the more lightly injured were already walking in the other direction, back towards
the flames. Others, with hardly any visible wounds, stopped, turned ashy pale, and
died within minutes. No one knew then that they were victims of radiation.

Emiko reached the suburb of Nakayama. 29

Far off in the *Enola Gay*, Lewis, who had seen none of this, had been writing, 30
"If I live a hundred years, I'll never get those few minutes out of my mind. Looking
at Captain Parsons, why he is as confounded as the rest, and he is supposed to
have known everything and expected this to happen. . . ."

At Nakayama, Emiko stood in line at a depot where riceballs were being 31
distributed. Though it distressed her that the badly maimed could hardly feed
themselves, the child found she was hungry. It was about 6 p.m. now. A little farther
on, at Gion, a farmer called her by name. She did not recognize him, but it seemed
he came monthly to her home to collect manure. The farmer took Emiko by the
hand, led her to his own house, where his wife bathed her and fed her a meal of
white rice. Then the child continued on her way. She passed another town where
there were hundreds of injured. The dead were being hauled away in trucks.
Among the injured a woman of about forty-five was waving frantically and
muttering to herself. Emiko brought this woman a little water in a pumpkin leaf.
She felt guilty about it; the schoolgirls had been warned not to give water to the
seriously wounded. Emiko comforted herself with the thought that the woman
would die soon anyway.

At Koi, she found standing-room in a train. It was heading for Otake with a 32
full load of wounded. Many were put off at Ono, where there was a hospital; and
two hours later the train rolled into Otake station. It was around 10 p.m.

A great crowd had gathered to look for their relations. It was a nightmare, 33
Emiko remembered years afterwards; people were calling their dear kinfolk by
name, searching frantically. It was necessary to call them by name, since most were
so disfigured as to be unrecognizable. Doctors in the town council offices stitched
Emiko's head-wounds. The place was crowded with casualties lying on the floor.
Many died as Emiko watched.

The town council authorities made a strange announcement. They said a new 34
and mysterious kind of bomb had fallen in Hiroshima. People were advised to
stay away from the ruins.

Home at midnight, Emiko found her parents so happy to see her that they 35
could not even cry. They could only give thanks that she was safe. Then they
asked, "Where is your sister"?

For ten long days, while Emiko walked daily one and a half miles to have her 36
wounds dressed with fresh gauze, her father searched the rubble of Hiroshima for
his lost child. He could not have hoped to find her alive. All, as far as the eye could
see, was a desolation of charred ashes and wreckage, relieved only by a few jagged
ruins and by the seven estuarial rivers that flowed through the waste delta. The
banks of these rivers were covered with the dead and in the rising tidal waters
floated thousands of corpses. On one broad street in the Hakushima district the
crowds who had been thronging there were all naked and scorched cadavers. Of
thousands of others there was no trace at all. A fire several times hotter than the
surface of the sun had turned them instantly to vapour.

On August 11 came the news that Nagasaki had suffered the same fate as 37
Hiroshima; it was whispered that Japan had attacked the United States mainland
with similar mysterious weapons. With the lavish circumstantiality of rumor, it
was said that two out of a fleet of six-engined trans-Pacific bombers had failed to

return. But on August 15, speaking for the first time over the radio to his people, the Emperor Hirohito announced his country's surrender. Emiko heard him. No more bombs! she thought. No more fear! The family did not learn till June the following year that this very day young Tetsuro had been killed in action in Manchuria.

38   Emiko's wounds healed slowly. In mid-September they had closed with a thin layer of pinkish skin. There had been a shortage of antiseptics and Emiko was happy to be getting well. Her satisfaction was short-lived. Mysteriously she came down with diarrhoea and high fever. The fever continued for a month. Then one day she started to bleed from the gums, her mouth and throat become acutely inflamed, and her hair started to fall out. Through her delirium the child heard the doctors whisper by her pillow that she could not live. By now the doctors must have known that ionizing radiation caused such destruction of the blood's white cells that victims were left with little or no resistance against infection.

39   Yet Emiko recovered.

40   The wound on her hand, however, was particularly troublesome and did not heal for a long time.

41   As she got better, Emiko began to acquire some notion of the fearful scale of the disaster. Few of her friends and acquaintances were still alive. But no one knew precisely how many had died in Hiroshima. To this day the claims of various agencies conflict.

42   According to General Douglas MacArthur's headquarters, there were 78,150 dead and 13,083 missing. The United States Atomic Bomb Casualty Commission claims there were 79,000 dead. Both sets of figures are probably far too low. There's reason to believe that at the time of the surrender Japanese authorities lied about the number of survivors, exaggerating it to get extra medical supplies. The Japanese welfare ministry's figures of 260,000 dead and 163,263 missing may well be too high. But the very order of such discrepancies speaks volumes about the scale of the catastrophe. The dead were literally uncountable.

43   This appalling toll of human life had been exacted from a city that had been prepared for air attack in a state of full wartime readiness. All civil-defence services had been overwhelmed from the first moment and it was many hours before any sort of organized rescue and relief could be put into effect.

44   It's true that single raids using so-called conventional weapons on other cities such as Tokyo and Dresden inflicted far greater casualties. And that it could not matter much to a victim whether he was burnt alive by a fire-storm caused by phosphorus, or by napalm or by nuclear fission. Yet in the whole of human history so savage a massacre had never before been inflicted with a single blow. And modern thermonuclear weapons are upwards of 1,000 times more powerful and deadly than the Hiroshima bomb.

45   The white scar I saw on Emiko's small, fine-boned hand was a tiny metaphor, a faint but eloquent memento.

Questions about Meaning

1. In his thesis, Dobbs states that it is "treason" to think about nuclear war "in the abstract". What does this mean? Who is being betrayed in that act?

2. Compare the two accounts of the day of the bombing: the story of the pilots and Emiko's experience. What are the main differences? Are there any similarities?

3. Most accounts of important historical events do not relate the small details of the lives of individuals like Emiko. Why does Dobbs consider these details to be as important as the details of the soldiers on the plane delivering the bomb?

4. Explain the concluding paragraph. What is the scar a metaphor for?

Questions about Rhetorical Strategy and Style

1. Analyze the diction of the passages where Emiko's story is told and the passages where the pilots' story is told. What is the difference?

2. Why does the author switch back and forth between Emiko's and the pilots' stories? Would the article be different if the two accounts were presented one after the other?

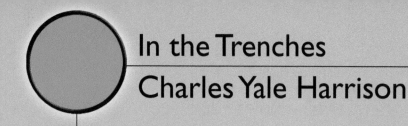

In the Trenches

Charles Yale Harrison

Charles Yale Harrison (1898–1954) served in the Canadian Army in World War One and is best known for his anti-war novella, **Generals Die in Bed.**

1   We leave the piles of rubble that was once a little Flemish peasant town and wind our way, in Indian file, up through the muddy communication trench. In the dark we stumble against the sides of the trench and tear our hands and clothing on the bits of embedded barbed wire that runs through the earth here as though it were a geological deposit.

Fry, who is suffering with his feet, keeps slipping into holes and crawling out, all the way up. I can hear him coughing and panting behind me.

I hear him slither into a water-filled hole. It has a green scum on it. Brown and I fish him out.

"I can't go any farther," he wheezes. "Let me lie here, I'll come on later."

5   We block the narrow trench and the oncoming men stumble on us, banging their equipment and mess tins on the sides of the ditch. Some trip over us. They curse under their breaths.

Our captain, Clark, pushes his way through the mess. He is an Imperial, an Englishman, and glories in his authority.

"So it's you again," he shouts. "Come on, get up. Cold feet, eh, getting near the line"?

Fry mumbles something indistinctly. I, too, offer an explanation. Clark ignores me.

"Get up, you're holding up the line," he says to Fry.

10   Fry does not move.

"No wonder we're losing the bloody war," Clark says loudly. The men standing near-by laugh. Encouraged by his success, the captain continues:

"Here, sergeant, stick a bayonet up his behind—that'll make him move." A few of us help Fry to his feet, and somehow we manage to keep him going.

We proceed cautiously, heeding the warnings of those ahead of us. At last we reach our positions.

It is midnight when we arrive at our positions. The men we are relieving give us a few instructions and leave quickly, glad to get out.

15   It is September and the night is warm. Not a sound disturbs the quiet. Somewhere away far to our right we hear the faint sound of continuous thunder. The exertion of the trip up the line has made us sweaty and tired. We slip most of our accouterments off and lean against the parados. We have been warned that the enemy is but a few hundred yards off, so we speak in whispers. It is perfectly still. I remember nights like this in the Laurentians. The harvest moon rides overhead.

Our sergeant, Johnson, appears around the corner of the bay, stealthily like a ghost. He gives us instructions:

"One man up on sentry duty! Keep your gun covered with the rubber sheet! No smoking!"

He hurries on to the next bay. Fry mounts the step and peers into No Man's Land. He is rested now and says that if he can only get a good pair of boots he will be happy. He has taken his boots off and stands in his stockinged feet. He shows us where his heel is cut. His boots do not fit. The sock is wet with blood. He wants to take his turn at sentry duty first so that he can rest later on. We agree.

Cleary and I sit on the firing-step and talk quietly.

"So this is war."   20

"Quiet."

"Yes, just like the country back home, eh"?

We talk of the trench; how we can make it more comfortable.

We light cigarettes against orders and cup our hands around them to hide the glow. We sit thinking. Fry stands motionless with his steel helmet shoved down almost over his eyes. He leans against the parapet motionless. There is a quiet dignity about his posture. I remember what we were told at the base about falling asleep on sentry duty. I nudge his leg. He grunts.

"Asleep"? I whisper.   25

"No," he answers, "I'm all right."

"What do you see"?

"Nothing. Wire and posts."

"Tired"?

"I'm all right."   30

The sergeant reappears after a while. We squinch our cigarettes.

"Everything O.K. here"?

I nod.

"Look out over there. They got the range on us. Watch out."

We light another cigarette. We continue our aimless talk.   35

"I wonder what St. Catherine Street looks like—"

"Same old thing, I suppose—stores, whores, theaters—"

"Like to be there just the same—"

"Me too."

We sit and puff our fags for half a minute or so.   40

I try to imagine what Montreal looks like. The images are murky. All that is unreality. The trench, Cleary, Fry, the moon overhead—this is real.

In his corner of the bay Fry is beginning to move from one foot to another. It is time to relieve him. He steps down and I take his place. I look into the wilderness of posts and wire in front of me.

After a while my eyes begin to water. I see the whole army of wire posts begin to move like a silent host towards me.

I blink my eyes and they halt.

I doze a little and come to with a jerk.   45

So this is war, I say to myself again for the hundredth time. Down on the firing-step the boys are sitting like dead men. The thunder to the right has died down. There is absolutely no sound.

I try to imagine how an action would start. I try to fancy the preliminary bombardment. I remember all the precautions one has to take to protect one's life. Fall flat on your belly, we had been told time and time again. The shriek of the shell, the instructor in trench warfare said, was no warning because the shell traveled faster than its sound. First, he had said, came the explosion of the shell—then came the shriek and then you hear the firing of the gun. . . .

From the stories I heard from veterans and from newspaper reports I conjure up a picture of an imaginary action. I see myself getting the Lewis gun in position. I see it spurting darts of flame into the night. I hear the roar of battle. I feel elated. Then I try to fancy the horrors of the battle. I see Cleary, Fry and Brown stretched out on the firing-step. They are stiff and their faces are white and set in the stillness of death. Only I remain alive.

An inaudible movement in front of me pulls me out of the dream. I look down and see Fry massaging his feet. All is still. The moon sets slowly and everything becomes dark.

50 The sergeant comes into the bay again and whispers to me:

"Keep your eyes open now—they might come over on a raid now that it's dark. The wire's cut over there—" He points a little to my right.

I stand staring into the darkness. Everything moves rapidly again as I stare. I look away for a moment and the illusion ceases.

Something leaps towards my face.

I jerk back, afraid.

55 Instinctively I feel for my rifle in the corner of the bay.

It is a rat.

It is as large as a tom-cat. It is three feet away from my face and it looks steadily at me with its two staring, beady eyes. It is fat. Its long tapering tail curves away from its padded hindquarters. There is still a little light from the stars and this light shines faintly on its sleek skin. With a darting movement it disappears. I remember with a cold feeling that it was fat, and why.

Cleary taps my shoulder. It is time to be relieved.

Over in the German lines I hear quick, sharp reports. Then the red-tailed comets of the *minenwerfer*° sail high in the air, making parabolas of red light as they come towards us. They look pretty, like the fireworks when we left Montreal. The sergeant rushes into the bay of the trench, breathless. "Minnies," he shouts, and dashes on.

60 In that instant there is a terrific roar directly behind us.

The night whistles and flashes red.

The trench rocks and sways.

Mud and earth leap into the air, come down upon us in heaps.

We throw ourselves upon our faces, clawing our nails into the soft earth in the bottom of the trench.

65 Another!

This one crashes to splinters about twenty feet in front of the bay.

Part of the parapet caves in.

We try to burrow into the ground like frightened rats.

The shattering explosions splinter the air in a million fragments. I taste salty liquid on my lips. My nose is bleeding from the force of the detonations.

70 SOS flares go up along our front calling for help from our artillery. The signals sail into the air and explode, giving forth showers of red, white and blue lights held aloft by a silken parachute.

The sky is lit by hundreds of fancy fireworks like a night carnival.

The air shrieks and cat-calls.

Still they come.

I am terrified. I hug the earth, digging my fingers into every crevice, every hole.

°*minenwerfer:* Mine-throwing trench mortars.

A blinding flash and an exploding howl a few feet in front of the trench.   75
My bowels liquefy.

Acrid smoke bites the throat, parches the mouth. I am beyond mere fright. I am frozen with an insane fear that keeps me cowering in the bottom of the trench. I lie flat on my belly, waiting. . . .

Suddenly it stops.

The fire lifts and passes over us to the trenches in the rear.

We lie still, unable to move. Fear has robbed us of the power to act. I hear Fry   80 whimpering near me. I crawl over to him with great effort. He is half covered with earth and débris. We begin to dig him out.

To our right they have started to shell the front lines. It is about half a mile away. We do not care. We are safe.

Without warning it starts again.

The air screams and howls like an insane woman.

We are getting it in earnest now. Again we throw ourselves face downward on the bottom of the trench and grovel like savages before this demoniac frenzy.

The concussion of the explosions batters against us.   85

I am knocked breathless.

I recover and hear the roar of the bombardment.

It screams and rages and boils like an angry sea. I feel a prickly sensation behind my eyeballs.

A shell lands with a monster shriek in the next bay. The concussion rolls me over on my back. I see the stars shining serenely above us. Another lands in the same place. Suddenly the stars revolve. I land on my shoulder. I have been tossed into the air.

I begin to pray.   90

"God—God—please. . ."

I remember that I do not believe in God. Insane thoughts race through my brain. I want to catch hold of something, something that will explain this mad fury, this maniacal congealed hatred that pours down on our heads. I can find nothing to console me, nothing to appease my terror. I know that hundreds of men are standing a mile or two from me pulling gun-lanyards, blowing us to smithereens. I know that and nothing else.

I begin to cough. The smoke is thick. It rolls in heavy clouds over the trench, blurring the stabbing lights of the explosion.

A shell bursts near the parapet.

Fragments smack the sandbags like a merciless shower of steel hail.   95

A piece of mud flies into my mouth. It is cool and refreshing. It tastes earthy.

Suddenly it stops again.

I bury my face in the cool, damp earth. I want to weep. But I am too weak and shaken for tears.

We lie still, waiting. . . .

Questions about Meaning

1. What is the narrator's attitude towards war? Make specific reference to the text to support your answer.

2. Why does the author choose to relate so many small, seemingly unimportant details about the experience of being a soldier? What do these teach us?

3. What does the conclusion contribute to the essay? Why end on such an ambiguous note?

Questions about Rhetorical Strategy and Style

1. Why would the author choose to write this narrative of past events in the first person, in the present tense? What effect do these choices have on the reader?

2. Why does the author sometimes choose to use plain diction, like in paragraph 15, to describe events and poetic diction to describe others? Do you see any pattern in his choices?

Wheels: The Car as a Cultural Driving Force

Pierre Berton

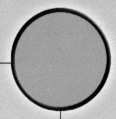

Pierre Berton (1920–2004) was the author of several books that could be said to define the term "popular history." They include The Last Spike, The National Dream, Flames across the Border, *and* Vimy. *He was also prominent as a newspaper columnist, radio commentator, and television personality.*

The astonishing thing about the automobile is that there are people still living who can remember a time when there weren't any. I am not one; but I can remember a place where at one time there were scarcely any. The northern community in which I was raised boasted three livery stables and a blacksmith shop, but in the winter only one motor car was to be seen on the roads. It was the milkman's Model-T Ford and I remember him having to hand-crank it at every stop. 1

In the summer a few more cars took to the gravel streets. As befitted his station, Judge Macaulay had the poshest automobile in town, a black Studebaker with fabric top known then as a "tour car". That was a great word in the 1920s. Few of us owned a car but we all played the popular Parker card game, *Touring*. 2

Of course we lived in a backwater. For in 1926—that was the first year I can remember squatting in Billy Bigg's blacksmith shop watching him hammer horseshoes into shape—the world beyond the Yukon had gone car crazy. We did not know it, but the greatest social transformation in history was under way. 3

We realize now that, more than any other invention, the automobile has changed our lives. It has affected the way we think, the way we act, the way we talk. It has up-ended the class system, sounded the death knell of Main Street, and played hell with the Lord's Day. As a precursor of the sexual revolution, it has been as important as the Pill. It has telescoped time and squeezed geography. It is both our slave and our master. For even as it has liberated us, it has made us its prisoner. 4

There was a time when transportation was the prerogative of the rich. Before the automobile arrived, the carriage, the coach-and-four, the private railway car and the hansom cab were accepted modes of travel, but only for the well-to-do. We are reminded of that era today when the Governor General rides to Parliament in an open landau. 5

The motor car changed all that. It has been the great leveller in terms of social distance as well as physical space. The factory worker, sensing the surge of power under the gas pedal of his truck, feels himself the equal of the businessman in his Dodge convertible. As Marshall McLuhan pointed out, it is the pedestrian who has become a second-class citizen. 6

7   The car gave the masses geographical mobility; and that meant social mobility, for the ability to choose is a concomitant of class. With the invention of the automobile, the poor could escape the confines of city tenements and narrow villages. In fact, the development of new mass-production techniques—the legacy of Henry Ford—blurred caste distinctions, creating in North America a vast middle class, most of whom owned cars.

8   The car brought to a settled world a glorious spontaneity that was not possible in the age of the horse and the railroad. Horses required long rest periods; they could not manage steep inclines without assistance. Railroads ran on schedule to predetermined destinations. But with the coming of the automobile, car owners could leap into their vehicles on impulse and take off in any direction. This ability to control the time and direction of travel marked for millions the beginning of a new freedom. It is also the reason why most wage earners today get a paid vacation.

9   With this independence came privacy. Alone in their cars people can sing, shout, talk to themselves or quietly plan their day, free from importuning associates or carping relatives. This human desire to be alone is, I believe, the chief reason why the idea of the car pool has never really taken hold in Canada. The highway are crowded with five-and six-passenger automobiles, most carrying only a driver.

10   As examples of the way the motor car has affected our lives, one need look only at such basics as health care, religion and education. The ambulance has brought swift medical aid to everyone; the bus has done away with the little red schoolhouse; and rural Canada is littered with boarded-up churches because the car, which made it possible to travel longer distances to worship, also may have made it too attractive to skip worship in favour of a Sunday drive.

11   Since the early days of the Tin Lizzie we have talked the language of cars. Just as words and phrases such as *free wheeling, green light, fast lane, going like sixty* and *step on it* indicate the swifter pace of the automobile era, so words like *car hop, motel, passion pit* and *drive-in* suggest a totally different lifestyle.

12   Urban sprawl, urban rot and urban renewal all spring out of the motor-car era and hint at the problems created by the suburban explosion, perhaps the single most important demographic change wrought by the automobile. The car made possible the escape from Shelley's "smoky populous cities"; and from the very outset this was seen as its greatest liberating force.

13   As a 1908 advertisement for the Sears motor car put it: "The Sears is the car for the businessman who has tired of home life in a congested neighbourhood and yearns for a cottage in the suburb for his family." Such blandishments were remarkably prescient, even though reality does not quite mesh with the fantasy. The countryside of 1989 is no facsimile of that of the century's first decade. One problem was that the people who escaped from the city insisted on bringing the city with them.

14   It has been determined that, apart from vacations, the trip to work is the longest regular journey most car owners are prepared to make. With the growth of superhighways and faster cars, that trip lengthened in distance but not in time. Business followed the commuters with such amenities as shops, theatres and department stores. The result was the suburban shopping centre.

15   It was the shopping centre that helped squeeze out that great Canadian institution Eaton's catalogue. It sucked the life blood from the main street of thousands of small towns. It turned the cores of such cities as Edmonton into virtual population deserts after work hours. It changed shopping habits and shopping hours. It encouraged the growth of retail chains, dooming individual merchant enterprises and contributing to the depersonalization and the conformity of the nation.

None of this, of course, could have been envisaged in 1900 when the automotive age can be said to have begun. That was the year when the early self-propelled vehicles began to look less like motorized buggies and more like motor cars, with a proper steering wheel instead of a tiller, a hood and a side door, and a speed that could reach a terrifying 40 miles an hour.

The universal phrase "get a horse!" suggests the derision in which early   16
automobiles were held. In 1890, the horse was the pivot around which a vast industry revolved, an industry doomed to oblivion within 20 years. There were at least 16 million horses in the United States, perhaps two million in Canada. Harness shops and carriage factories ran full blast. Thousands of wheelwrights and blacksmiths depended on the horse for their livelihood. An entire industry thrived on nails manufactured for horseshoes. Hay was one of the biggest cash crops. Every town had its livery stable, hitching post and horse trough.

Today, we think of pollution in terms of automobile exhaust. We forget that   17
in the city of Toronto, in 1890, tons of manure had to be swept off the streets every day. The stench of urine and the clouds of flies rising from the roadway plagued pedestrians and drivers alike. Women crossing the stinking wooden cobbles at Yonge and College streets were forced to raise their skirts and expose their ankles to prevent lumps of dung from sticking to their hems.

Nor is the traffic jam unique to our era. Photographs of Manhattan in the last   18
century show traffic brought to a standstill by trams, carts, drays, carriages and buggies.

As was the carriage, the early motor car was a toy for the wealthy, nothing   19
more. After the turn of the century, John Craig Eaton of the Toronto department store family acquired a Wilton. Billy Cochrane, the famous Alberta rancher, bought a Locomobile. R. B. Bennett, then a rising Calgary lawyer, had an Oldsmobile. Automobile owners were considered eccentric and their cars examples of what many considered "conspicuous waste" (Thorstein Veblen had just coined the phrase). In 1906, Woodrow Wilson, then president of Princeton University, termed the motor car "a picture of arrogant wealth" and announced that "nothing has spread a socialistic feeling more than the use of the automobile". Only a minority saw the automobile as a boon. Generally, it was reviled.

Like many later 20th-century institutions—movies, radio, television—the motor   20
car was seen initially as a symbol of the sickness of contemporary society. In his book *The Condition of England*, published in 1909, C. F. C. Masterman wrote that "wandering machines, travelling at an incredible rate of speed, scramble and smash along all the rural ways. You can see the evidence of their activity in the dust-laden hedges of the south country road, a grey, mud colour, with no evidence of green; in the ruined cottage gardens of the south country villages". The motor car, in short, was destroying the very countryside it also made available to the urbanites.

To the Canadian farmer, the car was also an anathema. It scared livestock and   21
killed poultry. "It is not time something was done to stop the automobile business"? the Newcastle, Ont. *Independent* asked in 1904. "They are becoming such a curse to the country that we cannot stand it. . . ."

If some saw the auto as the wrecker of rural life, others saw it as a means of   22
bringing the joys of the countryside to city dwellers. But it was one thing to extol those joys and quite another to enjoy them in the early automobile. The roads were almost impassable—a tangle of ruts and mudholes that sucked cars down to their axles. Signposts did not exist. Even towns could not be identified: the villagers knew where *they* lived. Local post officers often bore the sign Post Office with no other identification. The treadless tires blew easily and often (they were rarely

good for more than 3,000 miles), while changing one was a nightmare. A rear end projecting from beneath a hood on a country lane was a typical spectacle in pre-World War I days. Engines failed so often that one popular song of the era was "Get Out and Get Under".

23   The early motor car was also a repair shop on wheels. One store sold an automobile repair kit weighing 18 pounds. Driving was an experience akin to mountain climbing. The Damascus Hatcher, a patented device, was advertised, with enormous optimism, as follows: "When the wheel drops out of sight in the mud, get out the Damascus, cut a pole for a lever, right things up, and then on your way again."

24   Touring even required special clothing—linen duster, cap and goggles for men; and for women, long skirts, sleeves fastened at the wrist with elastic bands, motor coats, and turbans or wide-brimmed hats tied under the chin.

25   Of course women were expected to be mere passengers. It was believed that they could never act with speed in an emergency or muster the strength to push in a clutch or struggle with a gear shift. These myths were shattered in 1909 when Alice Huyler Ramsay drove across the continent in a green Maxwell, without male help.

26   Such ocean-to-ocean trips marked the beginning of the end of the era of the motor car as a toy. Soon it was to become as essential as the telephone. Its change in stature was rapid and complete by the early 1920s, thanks to a succession of ingenious devices that transformed what was essentially a motor-driven buggy into the family car of the mid-century. In 1911, the Dunlop company developed the anti-skid tire; within three years it was outselling its treadless counterpart. In the same year, the electric self-starter was an option, signaling the ultimate demise of the hand crank. The all-steel body also arrived in 1911, a forerunner to the closed car of the early 1920s, "a power-driven room on wheels—storm proof, lockable . . . its windows (closed) against dust or rain". And in 1914, the introduction of the spare wheel eliminated the ghastly business of tire repairing.

27   But the greatest revolution was Henry Ford's introduction, in 1908, of the cheap car—the famous Model-T—followed by the company's development in 1914 of the assembly line. The affordable car had arrived. In 1908, a Model-T runabout cost $825. By 1916, the Ford assembly line was turning out the same vehicle for $345.

28   The assembly line dealt a lethal blow to the old concept of craftsmanship based on long apprenticeship. Young, unskilled men with no previous training could master the simple techniques in a few weeks. To quote a pair of contemporary social observers: "As to machinists, old-time, all-round men, perish the thought. The Ford Motor Company has no use for experience, in the working ranks, anyway. It desires and prefers machine tool operators who have nothing to unlearn, who have no theories of perfect surface speeds for metal finishing, and who will simply do what they are told to do, over and over again, from bell-time to bell-time."

29   Individuality gave way to conformity with results that none could have foreseen. Since experience was not a precondition, immigrants and other unemployables soon found work on the assembly line—and that changed the demographic make-up of the continent. But the deadly monotony of the line (more easily endured by some than others) also required a much better wage rate and a shorter working day. Ford's $5, eight-hour day brought about the dominance of the middle class.

30   Again, because work was now seen to be boring and unfulfilling, mass production techniques—lampooned in Chaplin's movie, *Modern Times*—brought

the Protestant work ethic into disrepute. Since work was no longer satisfying, leisure took on a new importance, aided and abetted by the shorter work week. People began to live for their off-hours.

Mass production was also responsible for the youth cult that has been feature 31 of North American life in our era. Unskilled 19-year-olds were quicker on the assembly line than their fathers and therefore more valued. As the craftsmen of one generation lost status to the blue-collar workers of the next, respect for age and parental authority began to decline. As the sociologist James J. Fink has pointed out, "maleness" was also to suffer with the slow realization that women could fill any job on the line as easily as a man. Mere strength was no longer a criterion.

As the 1920s dawned, it became clear that the horse had become the toy and the 32 automobile the necessity. Robert and Helen Lynd, the two sociologists who wrote a study on an American community they called Middletown, came up with some interesting revelations about the motor car. Families, they found, were mortgaging their homes to buy one—and most were buying on time payments. The automobile industry had helped launch the revolution in credit that marks this century.

"We'd rather do without clothes than give up the car," a mother of nine told 33 the Lynds. "I'll go without food before I'll give up the car," said another. Pursuing their research, the Lynds asked people in rundown homes: "Do you have a bathtub? Do you own a car"? Of 26 persons questioned who had no bathtubs, 21 owned a car. As one woman is said to have remarked, "You can't go to town in a bathtub."

The car, the Lynds concluded, had revolutionized the concept of leisure. The 34 Sunday stroll, once a feature of the Lord's Day, was abandoned, replaced by the Sunday drive. And the car was the main device holding the family together. One mother declared, "I never feel as close to my family as when we are all together in the car."

The idea of a summer vacation was beginning to take hold because of the 35 automobile. In the 1890s people worked the year round, "never took a holiday", as some boasted. But, by the 1920s, a two-week vacation had become standard among the business class. The blue-collar workers had yet to achieve that status but the rise of unionism in the automobile plants made it simply a matter of time.

The car was the perfect symbol for a restless decade, the quintessential artifact of 36 the Roaring Twenties whose hallmarks were speed, sleekness and glamour. The music was fast and the girls, it was claimed, were faster. So were the cars. The Tin Lizzie had become a joke—a chariot for rubes. The Stutz Bearcat in flaming red and yellow symbolized the era. The Canadian Good Roads Association, founded in 1919 in Montreal to lobby for better highways, was by 1927 also lobbying to cure the "speed mania".

No woman, dressed in the cumbersome styles of 1919, could feel comfortable 37 in one of the new, closed automobiles. Overnight, to the horror of their elders, the bright young flappers chopped off their tresses, flung away their stays, hiked their skirts above the knee and piled into the rumble seat. "The auto," one American judge groaned, "has become a house of prostitution on wheels".

It had also become a symbol of sudden success. Each new model was awaited 38 with national anticipation. No celebrity had arrived until he or she was pictured beside a custom-built car or at the wheel of a straight twelve: Clara Bow, wheeling down Sunset Boulevard in an open Kissel; Gary Cooper dominated by his gigantic red and yellow Duesenberg. The gangster, too, were motorized and glamourized: Capone with his bullet-proof Cadillac; Dillinger in his Ford (the Number One

Public Enemy even wrote a personal testimonial to Henry). The car chase became a cinema staple; "taken for a ride" was the catch phrase of the era.

39   But for most of the continent, the motor car was something more than a glamorous status symbol. It could now be used to drive to work, to go shopping, to visit friends, to drive the kids to school or the dentist, to take the family picnicking. "I do not know of any other invention," Thomas Edison declared, "that has added to the happiness of the most people more than the automobile."

40   When the new million-dollar Automotive Building opened at the Canadian National Exhibition in Toronto in the fall of 1929, it set the seal on a car-oriented decade. This was the largest and finest structure anywhere devoted exclusively to the display of automobiles and accessories. Here one could glimpse the tip of the industrial iceberg being created by the invention of the motor car. For behind the shiny new models, with their running boards and big headlamps, stood dozens of other industries, businesses and services: oil refining, rubber manufacturing, retail sales, used-car lots, gas stations, auto supply stores, car washes, metal and paint and glass industries, taxi companies; and, in the future, car radios, drive-in theatres, motels, driving schools, car rental firms, and a vast array of roadside fast-food franchises that would turn the entrance to almost every city and town on the map into a true "Gasoline Alley".

41   Within a matter of weeks, Wall Street crashed and the Depression had arrived. Ironically, its greatest symbol of both hope and despair was a car—in the United States, the decrepit Hudson in which the Joad family in the movie *The Grapes of Wrath* moved from the dust bowl of Oklahoma to the fruit orchards of California; in Canada, the "Bennett buggy" (after Prime Minister R. B. Bennett) of the drought era, a car without an engine, drawn by a horse. For, as the Lynds found when they returned to their Middletown in the midst of the Depression, people refused to give up their cars.

42   The Joads' western pilgrimage symbolized the gypsy aspects of North American society, a restlessness that goes back to the days of the immigrant ships, the covered wagon and the Red River cart. The automobile arrived just after the frontier had been tamed. It fulfilled the ancestral urge to move on. And its symbol became the motel, the lineal descendant of the wayside inn.

43   The "auto tourist camp" of the early 1920s—not much more than a park with washroom facilities, and handy to a garage—became, in 1925, the tourist cabin and the auto court. The tiny, Spartan cabins grew more luxurious as the years went by but the lure was always the same; you could park your car at the front door of the motel room. Today, the small-town railway hotel, with its gloomy beer parlour, is all but obsolete; and in the cities, the major hostelries have had to change their entrances to accommodate the car. Who uses the front door of the Hotel Vancouver or Toronto's Royal York nowadays?

44   The auto court also flourished in the 1930s because people could not afford hotels, any more than they could afford a biannual model change. For 15 years of depression and war, the auto industry was stalled. Cars were sleeker, certainly. "Streamlining" was a word on everyone's lips. The traffic light arrived. People talked of "knee action" and "free wheeling". The roadster, the runabout and the rumble seat became obsolete. But when war came and people could again afford new models, they found there were none. Then, with the introduction of the flamboyant new Studebaker after 1945, the dam burst. The car became more than a workhorse. To quote a Buick ad in the mid-1950s: "It makes you feel like the man you are."

People went car crazy. They cared not a hoot for performance, efficiency or safety. What they wanted was power, glamour and status. The car was seen by psychologists as an extension of the owner's personality. Cadillac drivers were proud, flashy salesmen. DeSoto drivers were conservative, responsible members of the upper middle class. Studebaker owners were neat, sophisticated young intellectuals.

"One of the most costly blunders in the history of merchandising," Vance Packard 45 wrote in *The Hidden Persuaders*, "was the Chrysler Corporation's assumption that people buy automobiles on a rational basis." The company decided, in the early 1950s, that the public wanted a car in tune with the times: sturdy, easy to park, no frills—a compact with a shorter wheelbase. That decision almost wrecked Chrysler, but in hindsight we can see that the company was 20 years ahead of its time. The car it thought the public of the 1950s wanted became the status symbol of the late 1970s. The idea of the car as a reverse status symbol—compact, gas-efficient, devoid of tail fin or chrome, and not obviously expensive—derives from a massive about-face of attitudes toward the automobile and what it signifies. The change was spurred, of course, by government decree after the oil shortage, by traffic snarls, by a rising toll of highway deaths, by inner city rot and untrammeled suburban growth, and a consumer attitude that, for the want of a better word, we could call Naderism.

As the chairman of General Motors, James Roche, said in 1971, "the American 46 love affair with the car is over". After half a century, the car was again seen as a villain, polluting the air, destroying the countryside, causing death and mutilation, wasting money, time and gasoline, and fomenting a casual attitude to planned obsolescence.

Critics pointed to the car as the least-efficient means of transportation. In 47 1965, Elinor Guggenheimer, a New York City planning commissioner, pointed out that in 1911 a horse-drawn lorry could travel across Manhattan at an average speed of 11 miles per hour, while a modern taxi then could only achieve six.

Street and parking lots, it was discovered, gobbled up between 35 and 50 48 percent of the available space in a large city. Nine miles of freeway could destroy 24 acres of farmland; the average interchange took up 80 acres. Radio stations began to report daily on the pollution index in major cities, with the car as a leading culprit. And car manufacturers ceased boasting about "big car comfort". Foreign compacts became chic. Businessmen and housewives began to boast about how many miles their new car got to the gallon. North America's "Big Three" reeled under these blows and retooled. A new era had begun.

The new era has seen a return to the cities. People want to live downtown. Toronto 49 has virtually no apartment space left in the inner city, but there are For Sale signs blossoming in the suburbs. There is even talk of closing the city centres to all cars except taxis, an experiment that has been tried in some European communities. Does this mean that Marshall McLuhan was right when he predicted that the car is finished? The guru of the 1960s insisted that the home computer would so diversify the work force that commuting would be unnecessary, that the car culture would die.

What he failed to realize, as all critics of the car have failed to realize, is that 50 the automobile's greatest attraction is not as a commuter vehicle or as an aid to shopping. The former suburbanites who got rid of their cars when they moved to the inner city still line up on weekends to rent them. For when all is said and done, the major appeal of the motor car, with all its faults and weaknesses, is still what it was at the turn of the century: a liberating force. People want the freedom to move off at will without waiting for the horse to recover or a taxi to arrive, without standing in line for a streetcar or looking up rail or air schedules. In that sense the car remains the genie in the bottle. Release it carelessly and it becomes our master. Guard it vigilantly and it remains what it was always intended to be, a slave ready to serve us at our whim.

Questions about Meaning

1. Why was the widespread use of the car "the greatest social transformation in history"? Name some of the effects it has had on Canadian society, according to the article.
2. Why does Berton argue that the car has leveled out distinctions between classes? Is this still true today?
3. Why was the automobile criticized in its early days? Are any of those criticisms still valid?
4. In what way is the car our slave? How is it our master?

Questions about Rhetorical Strategy and Style

1. Berton is a historian. Compare this essay to an encyclopedia entry on the history of the automobile. How is Berton's history told differently? What does he include that an academic historian might leave out? What do these additions add to our knowledge or understanding of the times he writes about?
2. This essay is divided into 11 sections. What is the logic behind Berton's organization of this historical piece?

Killing Machines*
Linda McQuaig

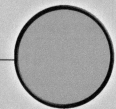

Journalist and author Linda McQuaig has written extensively in her books and numerous articles for the Globe and Mail, The National Post, *and the* Toronto Star *of the corruption and greed in big business and politics. "Killing Machines," excerpted from her 2004 book* It's the Crude, Dude: War, Big Oil, and the Fight for the Planet, *exemplifies McQuaig's wit and lively style as she examines the popularity of the SUV.*

Having paid insufficient attention to car advertisements in the 1990s, I somehow   1
didn't get the concept of an SUV. I didn't realize, for instance, that is was a symbol of
a bold, adventurous, sporty kind of life, driven by people with a tendency to go off-
road—just as, elsewhere in their lives, they have a tendency to break with the pack,
to do things their way, to think outside the box. To show how far out of the loop
I was, I didn't even know there was a difference between an SUV and a minivan.
They both just seemed like awkward, bulky, oversized versions of a car—useful,
no doubt, for those trips to Price Chopper when one comes home laden with
several extra cases of Coke and a year's supply of toilet paper.

Of course, I was dead wrong. I've learned that there's a world of difference   2
between a utilitarian minivan, which is designed for the Price Chopper trip as well
as carting around children's soccer equipment, and an SUV, which is not only bold
and adventurous but also glamorous, the car of choice these days among
Hollywood stars and others with limitless resources. Still, one can appreciate the
role advertising has played in making this sort of distinction clear to people, in
establishing the SUV as the symbol of everything chic. The sheer brilliance of
this advertising coup can perhaps best be measured by the extent of the image
transformation the SUV has undergone since its first incarnation as a vehicle
with few uses outside the funeral business. As Keith Bradsher has noted in his
book *High and Mighty*, the forerunner of the SUV—the Chevy Suburban—dates
back to the 1930s, and it managed to survive in the early decades largely because
its body was the perfect height and width for the easy loading and unloading of
coffins. This feature is retained today but omitted from SUV advertising.

So effective has the advertising campaign been that the public seems largely   3
unaware that SUVs are generally difficult to handle, with poor agility and
manoeuvrability—exactly the opposite of the sports car, which of course, used to
be the sexy car of choice. While a sports car, with its low-slung body and road-
gripping tires, can zip around corners at great speed, the rigid, high-set body of
the SUV makes its way around corners with considerably more difficulty, which
explains why ads typically show SUVs motionless at the top of a mountain or

*Editor's title.

charging straight ahead (got to get straight home with all that toilet paper), rather than driving on the kind of winding, exotic cliffside roads typically seen in sports car ads.

4   Much of the appeal of today's SUV may have less to do with sportiness and glamour, and more to do with security in an age of fear. Huge and growing ever larger, the SUV offers its riders a massive, wraparound steel exterior with the feel of a tank—a mobile version of a gated community. Bradsher reports that this is deliberate, that the tough, even menacing-looking appearance of many SUVs is intentionally and consciously designed by automakers for an era when civility on the roads has been replaced with unabashed hostility, a kind of me-first aggressiveness. In the age of everything from road rage to anthrax to SARS, you can't have too much steel between you and the rest of what's driving around out there.

5   And it's true: SUVs *are* a threat to others on the road—a fact that was appreciated as early as thirty years ago by researchers trying to draw attention to the dangers of designing vehicles with the sort of stiff, high front ends that are the hallmark of the SUV. In an accident, an SUV is two and a half times more likely than a mid-size car to kill the occupants of the other vehicle, due to the fact that SUVs are heavier (by a thousand pounds on average), stiffer and taller. These characteristics effectively turn SUVs into "battering rams in collisions with other vehicles," notes a recent report by the Union of Concerned Scientists. When an SUV hits a car from behind, it is more likely to ride up over the car's bumper, leaving the car (and its occupants) essentially defenseless. When an SUV hits a car from the side, it can ride up over the car's door frame and right into the passenger compartment. (Well, hello there!) This mismatch of sizes has been dubbed "vehicle incompatibility," but another possible name would be "vehicle homicide." And one-on-one against an unarmed pedestrian, an SUV is more lethal still, hitting the pedestrian higher up on the body, closer to vital organs, than a regular car does. Yet this greater height, stiffness and body weight seems to be something of a selling point, rather than a signal that perhaps something is seriously wrong with these oversized killing machines.

6   Even if the thought of killing others isn't a deterrent, one would think the thought of killing oneself and one's loved ones would count for something. But apparently not. SUV sales have skyrocketed despite the fact that they are also a danger to their own passengers because, with their considerable height, they have a tendency to roll over. More than 51,500 occupants of SUVs (and light trucks) died in rollovers from 1991 to 2001. The overall fatality rate for SUVs was 8 percent worse than for cars in 2000.

7   But the more far-reaching problem with SUVs—at least in terms of the survival of the planet—is the devastating amount of greenhouse gases they spew out into the air. An SUV produces roughly 40 percent more greenhouse gas emissions than a regular car does, and with SUV sales soaring—sales have increased seventeen-fold in the past two decades—their emissions have become a significant part of the problem of global warming. At a time when the dangers of global warming are blatantly evident and of serious concern to people all over the world, the breezy marketing of SUVs in North America makes a mockery of any claim that we are addressing the problem. While common sense would call for a special effort to move away from these over-emitting vehicles, exactly the opposite has been happening. Both the U.S. and Canadian governments have contributed to the SUV problem by offering SUVs regulatory controls far looser than those applied to regular cars. (The regulations were established in the U.S., but Canada has

effectively adopted matching standards, which the automakers have agreed to deliver on a voluntary basis.) The extraordinary growth in SUV sales over the last two decades, then, can be attributed as much to government favouritism as to the massive advertising campaign that has left prospective SUV buyers thinking of off-road adventure rather than the ease of moving coffins.

The story of the SUV is in many ways a microcosm of the human folly that   8
has led us to the brink of a climate change disaster. Perhaps it seems unfair to pick on the SUV. After all, it isn't, by any means, the only source of greenhouse gas emissions. It is, however, one of the fastest-growing sources. SUVs now account for an astonishing 24 percent of all new cars sold, up from just 2 percent in 1980. (Overall, the transportation sector accounts for 26 percent of U.S. greenhouse gas emissions. Along with coal-fired power plants, transportation is one of the key sources of the global warming problem.)

I'm picking on the SUV partly because it somehow serves as a metaphor for   9
the absurdity of the situation we find ourselves in, if for no other reason than that these enormous, awkward vehicles seem so…well…unnecessary. There's another aspect to this story that makes it emblematic of the saga of global warming: how easily the problem could be corrected if there were any serious political will. The technology exists to make enormous strides in cutting back the greenhouse gas emissions currently spewing out of SUVs (and other vehicles, but particularly SUVs) on highways across North America. I'm not talking about exotic space-age cars that run on hydrogen in some dream scenario (that's likely a couple of decades or so down the road), but about technology that already exists—and currently sits on shelves—in the offices of our big automakers. This, then, is the story of how Luddites° in the auto sector, fearful of risking their dominant market position, have declined to take us to where any sane person can see we must go, hiding behind claims of technological "can't do," hoping the public won't realize that what we have here is, in fact, a tale of technological "won't do."

Questions about Meaning

1. According to the author, why do people buy SUVs?
2. What is the role of advertising in the popularity of SUVs?
3. What negative consequences are there to driving SUVs?
4. What point does the author make in her conclusion? Is she fair? Why or why not?

Questions about Rhetorical Strategy and Style

1. What metaphors and similes does the author use to describe SUVs? What do they tell us about her attitude towards them?
2. Why does the author mention the selling point of the Suburban, that it could easily move coffins?
3. How would you describe the tone of this article? Is it a balanced argument? Why or why not?

°Luddites: In 1811 in Nottingham, England, textile workers led by Ned Ludd revolted against factory owners who were replacing craftsmen with new technology. They smashed the weaving machines, to protect their own jobs, until authorities put down the uprising. Since then, those who oppose new technology have often been called "Luddites."

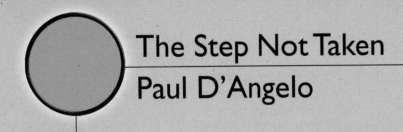

The Step Not Taken

Paul D'Angelo

In this cause and effect essay, Paul D'Angelo expresses his regret at doing "the big-city thing" instead of the "right thing," the "human thing" in his emotional encounter with a crying young man on an elevator. Published in the Globe and Mail *in 1995, this essay elicited dozens of responses from readers who had similar experiences and identified with D'Angelo's "confession."*

1 A few weeks ago I was followed into an office-building elevator by a well-dressed young man carrying a briefcase. He looked very sharp. Very buttoned-down. Wearing gold wire-frame glasses, he was of medium height and build with neatly trimmed brown hair and, I would guess, in his mid-20s. Typical junior executive material. There was nothing about him that seemed unusual. Nothing at all to indicate what was about to take place.

2 The elevator had only one control panel, and I excused myself as I leaned over to his side of the car and pushed the button for the 10th floor. He pushed the button for the 15th. The doors of the elevator closed and we began to ascend. Employing typical Toronto elevator etiquette, I stood staring up at the row of floor numbers above the doors while purposely ignoring my fellow passenger. Then it happened. A sudden strained gasp. Turning toward the noise, I was astonished to see the young man drop his briefcase and burst into tears. Our eyes met for a split second and, as if slapped, he averted his face from me, leaned his head against the wood-panelled wall of the elevator and continued to weep.

3 And what I did next still shames me.

4 The elevator stopped at the 10th floor and, without looking back, I stepped out. I stood in the hallway, a bundle of mixed emotions, wondering what to do. A combination of guilt and uncertainty washed over me. Should I go up to the 15th floor and make sure he's okay? Should I search him out from office to office? Should I risk the embarrassment it might cause him? Is he mentally disturbed? A manic depressive, perhaps? Is he a suicide just waiting to happen?

5 I didn't know what to do. So I did nothing.

6 And now he haunts me. Not with fear, of course, but with a sense of regret. I see his face crumbling before he turns to the wall. I see his shoulders heave as he sobs in a combination of sorrow and shame. I wonder now what brought him to that moment in time. How long had he been holding his pain inside before he could no longer contain it? What could possibly have overwhelmed him to such an extent that he was unable to keep from crying out?

7 Had he just visited the doctor and been told that he had an incurable disease? Was he having marital problems? Was his wife ill? His child? Had someone dear recently died? Was he being laid off? Was he looking for a job and meeting with

no success? Was he having financial woes? Was he without friends in the city and crushed by loneliness?

The sorrows of this world are endless.   8

The few people I have told about the incident all say I did the proper thing,   9
the best thing, by leaving the young man alone.

But they are wrong.   10

Like so many things in life, I know now what I should have done then. I should   11
have thrown caution to the winds and done the right thing. Not the big-city thing.
The right thing. The human thing. The thing I would want someone to do if they
ever found my son crying in an elevator. I should have given him the opportunity
to unload his sadness onto my shoulders. I should have reached out a hand and
patted him on the back. I should have said something like, "Why don't you let me
buy you a cup of coffee and you can tell me all your problems. There's no reason
to feel self-conscious. I'll listen for as long as you want to talk."

What would his reaction have been to that? Would he have turned even further   12
to the wall? Or would he have turned on me? Cursing me? Telling me to mind my
own damned business? Would he have lashed out at me? Sorrow and insecurity
turning to rage? Would he have physically attacked me? Or would he have gone
with me for that cup of coffee?

I don't know. I'll never know. All I can be certain of is that I left him in that   13
elevator with tears streaming down his face. And that he was alone. All alone.

I hope that somehow he gets to read these words, because I want him to know   14
that I'm pulling for him. That I hope things are looking up for him. That I hope
his sorrow is in the past. That I hope he is never again burdened with such awful
despair. That I am thinking of him. That I said a prayer for him. That I was wrong,
dreadfully wrong, not to step forward in his time of need.

That I'm sorry.   15

Questions about Meaning

1. What is D'Angelo's purpose in writing this article?
2. Why does the author feel shame for his actions in the elevator?
3. The author says that ignoring the man's pain is "the big city thing". What does
    he mean?

Questions about Rhetorical Strategy and Style

1. Why does the author describe the young man's appearance in such detail in the
    introduction?
2. What tone is established by the series of questions in the middle of the article?
    Would the article have been as effective if these had been simple statements?
3. Why does D'Angelo include a one-sentence conclusion? What effect does this
    have on the reader?

Thanks for Not Killing My Son

Rita Schindler

All we know about Rita Schindler is what she herself says in her letter. It was a student who noticed "Thanks for Not Killing My Son" in the "Have Your Say" feature of the December 30, 1990 Toronto Star. He tore it out and brought it to his writing teacher, exclaiming what a fine argument it was. The teacher agreed. By the time the editor of this book tried to reach Ms. Schindler, though, the Star had discarded her address. None of the many Schindlers listed in the Toronto phone book knew her, and the hospital mentioned in her letter would not divulge information. As this new edition was being put together we tried again to find her, but could not. Finally, Access Canada, the Canadian Copyright Licensing Agency, gave permission to reprint the letter, as it can do in such cases. We sincerely believe that Ms. Schindler would want her eloquent and highly principled argument made available to more persons of her son's generation. If you happen to know her, please show her this book and ask her to contact the publisher, who will direct her to the agency office where her author's fee is waiting.

1   I hope you will print my letter of gratitude to the strangers who have affected our lives.

2   Sometime between 1:30 p.m., Dec. 8, and 1 a.m., Dec. 9, a young man was viciously attacked—beaten and kicked unconscious for no apparent reason other than walking by you on a public sidewalk.

3   He was left lying in a pool of blood from an open head wound—in the Victoria Park-Terraview area. He was found around 1 a.m. and taken to Scarborough General Hospital where ironically his mother spent 48 hours in labor before giving him birth, 23 years earlier.

4   His mother is angry of course, but thankful for the following reasons.

5   First of all—his eye socket was shattered and hemorrhaging but his eyesight will not be affected. Thank you.

6   His ear canal was lacerated internally from a tremendous blow to the side of his head. The cut could not be stitched and the bleeding was difficult to stop. But his eardrum seems to be undamaged—thank you.

7   He required numerous stitches to his forehead, temple and face but your boots didn't knock one tooth out—thank you. His head was swollen almost twice its size—but Mom knew that his brain was intact—for he held her hand for six hours as he lay on a gurney, by the nurses station, I.V. in his arm—his head covered and crusted with dried blood—waiting for x-ray results and the surgeon to stitch him up.

8   So, thank you for this eyesight, his hearing and his hands which you could have easily crushed.

His hands—human hands—the most intricately beautiful and complex   9
instruments of incredible mechanism—the result of billions of years of evolution—
and you people used yours to beat another human being. Five guys and two girls
to beat one person. Who do I thank? Did you know he was a talented young
musician with a budding career—and that playing his keyboards and piano mean
more to him than my words can say.

And when his friends were talking about revenge, I heard him say, "No, I don't   10
want someone else's mother to go through what mine has." That's who you were
kicking in the head. And so—I thank you for not causing the most horrible and
devastating thing that can happen to any parent—that is—the untimely tragic loss
of a child—at any age.

You could have kicked him to death but you only left him to die, thank you.   11
A person found him and called for help.

I am his mother—and I have been given a second chance—thanks to you.   12

I hope that someday you'll have children and love them as much as I love   13
mine—but I wouldn't wish on your child what you did to mine.

Rita Schindler   14
Scarborough   15

Questions about Meaning

1. What is the author's purpose in writing this letter? Explain.
2. What argument is the author making in paragraph 9? Put it in your own words.
3. What is the purpose of the concluding paragraph? Do you think the author is sincere in her tone here? Why or why not?

Questions about Rhetorical Strategy and Style

1. What is the effect of the repetition of the words "thank you"?
2. What is the tone of this letter? Refer to specific words in the letter to support your answer.
3. Why would the author have used so much specific, concrete detail in describing her son's injuries? What effect does this have on the reader?

Forgiveness

June Callwood

In "Forgiveness," June Callwood, one of Canada's foremost social activists, explores through numerous examples the difficulties and benefits of being able to forgive. The essay was published in **The Walrus** *in April 2007 when Callwood was 82 and draws upon her personal experiences and those of others.*

1   A small boy in an industrial city in Ontario was beaten severely many times by his father, to the extent that the boy not infrequently required a doctor to stitch up the wounds. His father, a policeman, sincerely believed that if he beat his son with chains, belts, sticks, and his fists, the boy would not grow up to be gay. That boy, now in his thirties and indelibly a gay man, says he will never forgive his father.

2   "What he did is not forgivable," the man says with composure. "How can it ever be all right to abuse a child? But I have let it go."

3   And a woman, raised on the Prairies in a Finnish home, married a black man and had a son. She showed the infant proudly to her mother, whose reaction was a look of naked disgust. Her mother and that son, now a charming and successful adult, have since developed an affectionate relationship, but the daughter has not forgotten or forgiven the expression on her mother's face.

4   "The best I can do," she says, "is that I have stopped hating her."

5   The ability to forgive is a central tenet of every major religion in the world—Christian, Judaic, Hindu, Buddhist, and Islamic. Those faiths urge followers to forgive their enemies and, indeed, even to find a way to love those who wrong them. As the twenty-first century dawns, however, the world is making a spectacular mess of such pious admonitions. Instead of goodwill, this is the age of anger, the polar opposite of forgiveness. Merciless ethnic, tribal, and religious conflicts dominate every corner of the planet, and in North America individuals live with high levels of wrath that explode as domestic brutality, road rage, vile epithets, and acts of random slaughter.

6   Many people, like the gay man or the woman in a biracial marriage, find forgiveness an unreasonable dictate. Some assaults on the body or soul are unconscionable, they feel, and forgiveness is simply out of the question. It satisfies the requirements of their humanity that they gradually ease away from the primitive thoughts of revenge that once obsessed them.

7   When Simon Wiesenthal, the famed Nazi hunter, was in a German concentration camp, he found himself in strange situation. He was taken to the bedside of a dying SS officer, a youth who had killed many Jews, and the young man asked him, a Jew, for forgiveness. Wiesenthal was silent and left the room, but was haunted ever after. Thirty years later, he contacted some of the world's great thinkers and asked, what

should I have done? Theologians such as Bishop Desmond Tutu and the Dalai Lama gently hinted that he should have been forgiving, for his own sake, but others, notably philosopher Herbert Marcuse, said that great evil should never be forgiven. In *The Sunflower*, a collection of fifty-three responses to Wiesenthal's question, Marcuse wrote sternly that forgiveness condones the crime.

The moral vacuum left by the pervasive disuse and misuse of religious tenets has   8
allowed a secular forgiveness industry to spring into being. People who yearn desperately to rid themselves of an obsession for vengeance will seek help in curious places. Since 1985, the University of Wisconsin–Madison has offered forgiveness studies, and an International Forgiveness Institute was founded there. Four years ago, the world's first international conference on forgiveness drew hundreds of delegates to Madison. Stanford University has a forgiveness research project and people in California, a state on the cutting edge of self-absorption, are taking part in studies on the art and science of forgiveness. Self-help shelves in bookstores abound in titles such as *Forgive Your Parents: Heal Yourself.*

An odious US daytime television show, *Forgive or Forget*, features guests who   9
say they owe someone an apology. They describe their offence, and then, *ta-dah*, the injured party appears on the appropriately tacky set and either grants or withholds forgiveness. Will the former foes embrace one another? The titillated audience can't wait.

Apologies are iffy because often they are contrived or coerced. Apologies   10
extracted by judges, mediators, and parents are thin gruel for the wronged person. One familiar genre of apology, the one which commences, "I am sorry you are feeling badly," is particularly counterproductive because there is no admission of any responsibility; it is the other person's problem for being thin-skinned. A sincere and remorseful acceptance of blame, however, can close a wound.

Psychologists are engrossed by the topic and so are theologians, philosophers,   11
psychiatrists, and—surprise—cardiologists. Unforgiving people, some studies show, are three times more likely to have heart disease as people who don't carry grudges. These findings raise the suspicion that the researchers may have the cart before the horse. Heart attacks occur more often in blow-top people who have unfortified egos, the very ones most apt to be relentlessly unforgiving. On the other hand, people who hold tolerant views of human nature and don't seem to nurse grievances unduly tend to have blood pressures in the normal range.

Clergy, counsellors, and people who lecture and write books about forgiveness   12
all preach reductionism as a strategy for overcoming hot resentment of someone's nasty behaviour. They say that people who have been harmed should see the hurtful as deeply flawed human beings working out nameless aggressions. Pitiable and inferior, they are examples of failure to thrive. Adults still distressed by abuse, neglect, or rejection in childhood are urged to consider what happened in their parents' childhoods—often, bad parenting comes from being badly parented. The theory is that understanding the reasons for their parents' limitations will enable the offspring to acquire a measure of compassion.

Maybe it works. Hillary Clinton apparently forgave her sleazy husband because   13
she knows he had an unhappy childhood.

This technique can be applied to almost any injustice and falls within the   14
rapists-were-beaten-as-children, *poor them* school of thought, which for some skeptics veers perilously close to non-accountability. The law and common sense hold that adults are responsible for what they do. While empathy may help people appreciate why others behave badly, the exercise is somewhat patronizing. The

offender is reduced to a contemptible hive of neuroses and ungovernable aberrations, which accordingly elevates the injured party to a morally superior person.

15   Demonizing the enemy is a common coping mechanism in times of adversity. In military terms, it captures the high ground.

16   Catastrophes such as divorce, job loss, rape, robbery, infidelity, and slander are all assaults on personal dignity and self-respect. A sense of being intact—*safe*— has been violated, and people are dismayed to find themselves for some time emotionally crippled by anger and grief. Betrayal and loss take big chunks out of people's confidence and leave them feeling excruciatingly vulnerable to random harm.

17   The starting place, some therapists say, is to accept that something appalling has happened, and it hurts. Denial, a recourse more favoured by men than by women, won't help. The next step, they say, is to develop an off switch. When fury threatens to make the brain reel, people should grasp for distractions. Brooding about revenge only serves to unhinge reason. If people don't rid themselves of wrath, personal growth stops cold. The hard part comes at the end of the process. The choices are to enter a state of forgiveness, which is a triumph of generosity, or just to put the matter in a box, cover it with a lid, place a brick on the lid, and move on. In healthy people, a perverse state of mind eventually wears itself out.

18   In yoga, they say that it takes six years of regularly practising meditation to gain spiritual insight. Forgiveness of great wrong may take longer. The process can't even begin until the injured person stops crying.

19   Some people are marvellously unbroken by great injustices. Nelson Mandela smiled gently at his adversaries after twenty-seven years of brutal imprisonment. A worldwide figure of wonder, he even invited his white jailer to his inauguration as South Africa's president. In Cambodia, a pastor whose family had been wiped out by the Khmer Rouge baptized and forgave a notorious Khmer Rouge leader known as Duch. A university professor in Virginia had an urge to kill the intruder who beat his mother to death, but stopped himself with the thought, "Whose heart is darker"? And the father of a young girl casually murdered in a street encounter with a teenager she didn't know attended the trial and sat quietly throughout the appalling testimony. He said he would visit the youth in prison. "I do not think I can forgive him," he explained, "but perhaps if I know him I will not hate him."

20   Forgiveness is hard work. A woman, a devout Roman Catholic who forgave the man who tortured and killed her seven-year-old daughter, said, "Anyone who says forgiveness is for wimps hasn't tried it." The reward for giving up scalding thoughts of reprisal is peace of mind. It is worth the candle.

Questions about Meaning

1. What is the difference between the examples the author uses at the beginning of the article and those she uses at the end of the article? What can we learn from these examples?

2. According to the article, who benefits from forgiveness – the giver, the receiver, or both?

3. What is Callwood's thesis? Put it in your own words.

Questions about Rhetorical Strategy and Style

1. Why does the author use so many examples throughout her article? What do they add to the argument?

2. How does Callwood's satire on a "reality T.V." show fit into her argument?

3. Why is the article divided into 4 separate sections? Does this make the article easier to understand?

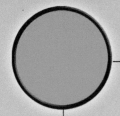

The Seven-Minute Life of Marc Lépine*

Nathalie Petrowski

Translated from the French by Ronald Conrad

Born 1954 in Paris and educated in Montreal, Nathalie Petrowski is a radio and TV personality, and one of Quebec's favourite print journalists—quirky, personal, satirical. In 1995 she also published **Maman Last Call,** *and wrote the script for the book's feature film version released in 2005. In her newspaper column for* Le Devoir *of December 16, 1989 Petrowski had a special challenge: ten days before, 25-year-old Marc Lépine had walked into an engineering class at the University of Montreal's École Polytechnique, shouted at the women students "You're all a bunch of feminists, and I hate feminists," ordered the men to leave—then lifted his rifle and shot the women. Six died. During the next minutes of terror he roamed the building, shooting. Altogether he gunned down 27 students, killing 14, all women. Then Lépine had turned the weapon on himself and died too. Canada felt a shock wave of anger and remorse, for this was the worst one-day mass murder in the nation's history, and its selectivity seemed to express a general sexism in society. In the next days, as the flag over Parliament flew at half-mast, citizens learned that Lépine's father had beat him and divorced the mother, and that the boy, though intelligent, had problems both academically and socially. He loved war movies, and from a paratrooper uncle had learned to handle firearms. His unemployment benefits were running out, the army would not take him, and the Polytechnique had refused him admission to its engineering program. Now on December 6 of every year, ceremonies across the nation honour the 14 young women, training for a profession still dominated by men, who were killed by a man whose suicide note blamed feminists for ruining his life. The essay that follows (originally entitled "Pitié pour les salauds") has a special poignancy, for Nathalie Petrowski wrote it in shock, as she and the nation first struggled to see meaning in the event.*

1   Pardon if I insist, pardon if I don't just mourn and forget, but it's stronger than I am, for a week I can't stop thinking about Marc Lépine. A psychoanalyst would say I'm identifying with the aggressor. But I'd say that inside every aggressor, every villain, there hides a victim.

2   I think of Marc Lépine to block out all the talk that just confuses things: Rambo, television, violence towards women, pornography, abortion, and firearms in display windows.

3   I think of Marc Lépine, still wondering what happened and exactly when the hellish countdown of his act was unleashed. Was it the morning of December 6, was it November 21 when he bought his rifle or September 4, when he applied for

the firearm permit? Was it the day of his birth, the first time his father beat him, the day his parents divorced, the week when he suddenly quit all his courses, the night a girl didn't want to dance with him? What about all the hours, the days, the weeks, the years that passed before the bomb inside him went off?

Still, journalists have told us everything: where he lived, the schools he went 4 to, the names of teachers and students he knew. We know how much he paid for his rifle and how he loved war movies. But once all this has been said, nothing has been said.

We know nothing of the ache that consumed him, of the torture inside him. 5 We know nothing of the evil path he slipped into smiling the cruel smile of the angel of destruction, no longer himself, knowing only that he was put on earth to destroy.

I think of Marc Lépine but equally of Nadia,° his sister who was beaten, too, 6 for singing out loud in the morning, Nadia who came from the same family but didn't fall prey to the same madness. Why Marc and not Nadia, why Marc and not another? That's what I ask myself when facts only deepen the mystery, when social criticism only confuses things.

No one remembers him from grade school, or from Sainte-Justine Hospital 7 where he spent a year in therapy with his mother and sister. Until last week Marc Lépine did not exist. He was an unknown quantity, a number, an anonymous face in the crowd, a nobody who no one would even look at or give the least warmth, the slightest affection. In a few moments he went from a nothing to one of a kind, a pathological case who the experts claim in no way represents the society where he was born and grew up.

For a week I've been talking with these experts, hoping to understand. For a 8 week all I've seen is that there is no one answer, there are a thousand. For a week I've dealt with the official and professional voices who keep their files under key who keep repeating that there's no use wanting to know more, that Marc Lépine is dead, that he can no longer be healed or saved, that it's too late to do anything at all. Sometimes their excuses and justifications sound like lies.

But I refuse to hear the silence of death that falls like snow, the shameful silence 9 that freezes my blood. Somewhere deep in the ruins of our private space we hide the truth, we try to protect ourselves saying that families—ours, his, the victims'— have been traumatized.

Forget about the past, say the authorities, let's move on and not let Marc 10 Lépine's act dictate our choices. Yet the surest way to let this act dictate our choices is to hide it, to let it become a medical, psychological and criminal secret, to push it into the smallest hollow of our collective memory till it's erased and we can say it never existed at all.

In this province where memory is reduced to a slogan on a licence plate,* we 11 want to forget Marc Lépine like we forget all events that can disturb us and make us think. Though I know nothing of Marc Lépine's story, I've met enough young people in the high schools and colleges to know that chance as well as reasons, randomness as well as all the wrong conditions in one person's life, caused this act. His tragic destiny looks more and more like a tangle of shattered hopes, of frustrated dreams, of hopeless waits on a long and cold road without a single hand extended to help, and no guardrail.

°Nadia: Lépine's sister Nadia Garbi later became a drug addict. In 1993 she died of cardiac arrest from an overdose.

*a slogan on a licence plate; Quebec licence plates bear the motto *"Je me souviens"* ("I remember") Quebeckers consider this a reference to their history, and specially the Conquest.

12   Marc Lépine died the evening of December 6, but unlike his victims, he had died long before. In the end his life lasted just seven minutes. Before and after, he was forgotten.

13   So pardon my pessimism, but I cannot help believing that somewhere, at this moment, there are other Marc Lépines who won't ask for anything because they don't even know what to ask for—other children turned into monsters by abusive fathers and impersonal schools systems, by a society so intent on excellence that every day it hammers the nail of Defeat further in, and plants seeds of frustration and violence in the fragile spirits of its children.

14   Though nothing can be done now for Marc Lépine, something can still be done for the others, whose inner clock has already begun the terrible countdown. It would be a mistake to forget them.

Questions about Meaning

1. What is Petrowski's thesis? Does she effectively support that thesis through the course of her essay? Explain your answer using specific references to the text.

2. What possible reasons does Petrowski present in her article for Lepine's turn to violent crime?

3. Does the author blame Lepine for his actions? Justify your answer.

Questions about Rhetorical Strategy and Style

1. Why would the author ask for pardon in the opening paragraph? Whom is she speaking to?

2. In paragraphs 3 and 11, the author uses metaphors to make her point. What are the images used and what effect do they have on the reader?

What I Have Lived For

Bertrand Russell

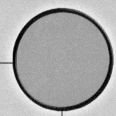

Bertrand Russell (1872–1970) wrote this concise and illuminating prologue to his autobiography when he was 84. The author was a distinguished mathematician, logician, and philosopher and a well-known and often controversial pacifist, atheist, and campaigner against what he saw as outmoded social conventions, especially those having to do with sex and marriage.

Three passions, simple but overwhelmingly strong, have governed my life: the longing for love, the search for knowledge, and unbearable pity for the suffering of mankind. These passions, like great winds, have blown me hither and thither, in a wayward course, over a deep ocean of anguish, reaching to the very verge of despair. 1

I have sought love, first, because it brings ecstasy—ecstasy so great that I would often have sacrificed all the rest of life for a few hours of this joy. I have sought it, next, because it relieves loneliness—that terrible loneliness in which one shivering consciousness looks over the rim of the world into the cold unfathomable lifeless abyss. I have sought it, finally, because in the union of love I have seen, in a mystic miniature, the prefiguring vision of the heaven that saints and poets have imagined. This is what I sought, and though it might seem too good for human life, this is what—at last—I have found. 2

With equal passion I have sought knowledge. I have wished to understand the hearts of men. I have wished to know why the stars shine. And I have tried to apprehend the Pythagorean power by which number holds sway above the flux. A little of this, but not much, I have achieved. 3

Love and knowledge, so far as they were possible, led upward toward the heavens. But always pity brought me back to earth. Echoes of cries of pain reverberate in my heart. Children in famine, victims tortured by oppressors, helpless old people a hated burden to their sons, and the whole world of loneliness, poverty, and pain make a mockery of what human life should be. I long to alleviate the evil, but I cannot, and I too suffer. 4

This has been my life. I have found it worth living, and would gladly live it again if the chance were offered me. 5

Questions about Meaning

1. Which sentence is the thesis statement?
2. What understanding of human beings and their place in the world is communicated by the introduction to this essay, especially the poetic diction of the second sentence? Is this vision of the relative power of humans supported or contradicted by paragraph 4?

3. What are the three reasons the author wanted to find love? Put them in your own words.
4. Is there any answer to the problem the author faces in paragraph 4? How can one live a happy life knowing that others suffer?
5. The author died in 1970, so this essay is at least 40 years old. Are the points Russell makes still relevant today? Why or why not?

Questions about Rhetorical Strategy and Style
1. Why would the author have put his three points in this order? Is he building to a climax, or starting with his most important point?
2. Locate the three topic sentences. How do they relate to the thesis statement?
3. Does this essay deviate in any way from the typical 5 paragraph essay taught in high school and college? If so, how?

The Dimensions of a Complete Life
Martin Luther King, Jr.

Dr. Martin Luther King, Jr. (1929-1968) wrote this essay when he was in his late twenties and before he became well-known as a champion of civil rights. A Baptist minister, King was eager to challenge as well as inspire his readers.

Many, many centuries ago, out on a lonely, obscure island called Patmos, a man by the name of John caught a vision of the new Jerusalem descending out of heaven from God. One of the greatest glories of this new city of God that John saw was its completeness. It was not partial and one-sided, but it was complete in all three of its dimensions. And so, in describing the city in the twenty-first chapter of the book of Revelation, John says this: "The length and the breadth and the height of it are equal." In other words, this new city of God, this city of ideal humanity, is not an unbalanced entity but it is complete on all sides. 1

Now John is saying something quite significant here. For so many of us the book of Revelation is a very difficult book, puzzling to decode. We look upon it as something of a great enigma wrapped in mystery. And certainly if we accept the book of Revelation as a record of actual historical occurrences it is a difficult book, shrouded with impenetrable mysteries. But if we will look beneath the peculiar jargon of its author and the prevailing apocalyptic symbolism, we will find in this book many eternal truths which continue to challenge us. One such truth is that of this text. What John is really saying is this: that life as it should be and life at its best is the life that is complete on all sides. 2

There are three dimensions of any complete life to which we can fitly give the words of this text: length, breadth, and height. The length of life as we shall think of it here is not its duration or its longevity, but it is the push of a life forward to achieve its personal ends and ambitions. It is the inward concern for one's own welfare. The breadth of life is the outward concern for the welfare of others. The height of life is the upward reach for God. 3

These are the three dimensions of life, and without the three being correlated, working harmoniously together, life is incomplete. Life is something of a great triangle. At one angle stands the individual person, at the other angle stand other persons, and at the top stands the Supreme, Infinite Person, God. These three must meet in every individual life if that life is to be complete. 4

Now let us notice first the length of life. I have said that this is the dimension of life in which the individual is concerned with developing his inner powers. It is that dimension of life in which the individual pursues personal ends and ambitions. This is perhaps the selfish dimension of life, and there is such a thing as moral and rational self-interest. If one is not concerned about himself he cannot be totally concerned about other selves. 5

6   Some years ago a learned rabbi, the late Joshua Liebman, wrote a book entitled *Peace of Mind*. He has a chapter in the book entitled "Love Thyself Properly." In this chapter he says in substance that it is impossible to love other selves adequately unless you love your own self properly. Many people have been plunged into the abyss of emotional fatalism because they did not love themselves properly. So every individual has a responsibility to be concerned about himself enough to discover what he is made for. After he discovers his calling he should set out to do it with all of the strength and power in his being. He should do it as if God Almighty called him at this particular moment in history to do it. He should seek to do his job so well that the living, the dead, or the unborn could not do it better. No matter how small one thinks his life's work is in terms of the norms of the world and the so-called big jobs, he must realize that it has cosmic significance if he is serving humanity and doing the will of God.

7   To carry this to one extreme, if it falls your lot to be street-sweeper, sweep streets as Raphael painted pictures, sweep streets as Michelangelo carved marble, sweep streets as Beethoven composed music, sweep streets as Shakespeare wrote poetry. Sweep streets so well that all the hosts of heaven and earth will have to pause and say, "Here lived a great street-sweeper who swept his job well." In the words of Douglas Malloch:

> If you can't be a highway, just be a trail;
> If you can't be the sun, be a star
> For it isn't by size that you win or you fail—
> Be the best of whatever you are.

When you do this, you have mastered the first dimension of life—the length of life.

8   But don't stop here; it is dangerous to stop here. There are some people who never get beyond this first dimension. They are brilliant people; often they do an excellent job in developing their inner powers; but they live as if nobody else lived in the world but themselves. There is nothing more tragic than to find an individual bogged down in the length of life, devoid of the breadth.

9   The breadth of life is that dimension of life in which we are concerned about others. An individual has not started living until he can rise above the narrow confines of his individualistic concerns to the broader concerns of all humanity.

10   You remember one day a man came to Jesus and he raised some significant questions. Finally he got around to the question, "Who is my neighbor"? This could easily have been a very abstract question left in mid-air. But Jesus immediately pulled that question out of mid-air and placed it on a dangerous curve between Jerusalem and Jericho. He talked about a certain man who fell among thieves. Three men passed; two of them on the other side. And finally another man came and helped the injured man on the ground. He is known to us as the good Samaritan. Jesus says in substance that this is a great man. He was great because he could project the "I" into the "thou."

11   So often we say that the priest and the Levite were in a big hurry to get to some ecclesiastical meeting and so they did not have time. They were concerned about that. I would rather think of it another way. I can well imagine that they were quite afraid. You see, the Jericho road is a dangerous road, and the same thing that happened to the man who was robbed and beaten could have happened to them. So I imagine the first question that the priest and the Levite asked was this: "If I stop to help this man, what will happen to me"? Then the good Samaritan came by, and by the very nature of his concern reversed the question: "If I do not stop

to help this man, what will happen to him"? And so this man was great because he had the mental equipment for a dangerous altruism. He was great because he could surround the length of his life with the breadth of life. He was great not only because he had ascended to certain heights of economic security, but because he could condescend to the depths of human need.

All this has a great deal of bearing in our situation in the world today. So often 12 racial groups are concerned about the length of life, their economic privileged position, their social status. So often nations of the world are concerned about the length of life, perpetuating their nationalistic concerns, and their economic ends. May it not be that the problem in the world is that individuals as well as nations have been overly concerned with the length of life, devoid of the breadth? But there is still something to remind us that we are interdependent, that we are all involved in a single process, that we are all somehow caught in an inescapable network of mutuality. Therefore whatever affects one directly affects all indirectly.

As long as there is poverty in the world I can never be rich, even if I have a 13 billion dollars. As long as diseases are rampant and millions of people in this world cannot expect to live more than twenty-eight or thirty years, I can never be totally healthy even if I just got a good check-up at Mayo Clinic. I can never be what I ought to be until you are what you ought to be. This is the way our world is made. No individual or nation can stand out boasting of being independent. We are interdependent. So John Donne placed it in graphic terms when he affirmed, "No man is an island entire of itself. Every man is a piece of the continent, a part of the main." Then he goes on to say, "Any man's death diminishes me because I am involved in mankind, and therefore never send to know for whom the bell tolls; it tolls for thee." When we discover this, we master the second dimension of life.

Finally, there is a third dimension. Some people never get beyond the first 14 two dimensions of life. They master the first two. They develop their inner powers; they love humanity, but they stop right here. They end up with the feeling that man is the end of all things and that humanity is God. Philosophically or theologically, many of them would call themselves humanists. They seek to live life without a sky. They find themselves bogged down on the horizontal plane without being integrated on the vertical plane. But if we are to live the complete life we must reach up and discover God. H.G. Wells was right: "The man who is not religious begins at nowhere and ends at nothing." Religion is like a mighty wind that breaks down doors and makes that possible and even easy which seems difficult and impossible.

In our modern world it is easy for us to forget this. We so often find ourselves 15 unconsciously neglecting this third dimension of life. Not that we go up and say, "Good-by, God, we are going to leave you now." But we become so involved in the things of this world that we are unconsciously carried away by the rushing tide of materialism which leaves us treading in the confused waters of secularism. We find ourselves living in what Professor Sorokin of Harvard called a sensate civilization, believing that only those things which we can see and touch and to which we can apply our five senses have existence.

Something should remind us once more that the great things in this universe 16 are things that we never see. You walk out at night and look up at the beautiful stars as they bedeck the heavens like swinging lanterns of eternity, and you think you can see all. Oh, no. You can never see the law of gravitation that holds them there. You walk around this vast campus and you probably have a great esthetic experience as I have had walking about and looking at the beautiful buildings, and you think you see all. Oh, no. You can never see the mind of the architect who drew the blueprint. You can never see the love and the faith and hope of the individuals who made it so. You look at me and you think you see Martin Luther King. You don't see Martin Luther King; you see my body, but, you must understand, my body can't think, my body can't reason. You don't see the me that makes me me. You can never see my personality.

17   In a real sense everything that we see is a shadow cast by that which we do not see. Plato was right: "The visible is a shadow cast by the invisible." And so God is still around. All of our new knowledge, all or our new developments, cannot diminish his being one iota. These new advances have banished God neither from the microcosmic compass of the atom nor from the vast, unfathomable ranges of interstellar space. The more we learn about this universe, the more mysterious and awesome it becomes. God is still here.

18   So I say to you, seek God and discover him and make him a power in your life. Without him all our efforts turn to ashes and our sunrises into darkest nights. Without him, life is a meaningless drama with the decisive scenes missing. But with him we are able to rise from the fatigue of despair to the buoyancy of hope. With him we are able to rise from the midnight of desperation to the daybreak of joy. St. Augustine was right—we were made for God and we will be restless until we find rest in him.

19   Love yourself, if that means rational, healthy, and moral self-interest. You are commanded to do that. That is the length of life. Love your neighbor as you love yourself. You are commanded to do that. That is the breadth of life. But never forget that there is a first and even greater commandment, "Love the Lord thy God with all thy heart and all thy soul and all thy mind." This is the height of life. And when you do this you live the complete life.

20   Thank God for John who, centuries ago, caught a vision of the new Jerusalem. God grant that those of us who still walk the road of life will catch this vision and decide to move forward to that city of complete life in which the length and the breadth and the height are equal.

Questions about Meaning

1. According to King, why is it good to have a measure of selfishness?
2. Why is it "tragic" to ignore the people around us?
3. Why does King assert that a complete life must include a religious dimension?
4. What is King's answer to those who would say that scientific knowledge leads us away from faith?
5. What logic is behind the organization of King's points in this essay?

Questions about Rhetorical Strategy and Style

1. Who is the intended audience of this essay? How do you know?
2. King uses a lot of poetic diction in his essay. Find at least two metaphors and two similes. What do these devices add to his argument? Why are there more of them towards the end of the essay?
3. Why does King allude to so many writers in his essay? Who are these writers?

Why I Like to Pay My Taxes
Neil Brooks

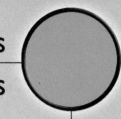

This piece, which challenges the widespread view that taxes are bad and should be resented by all who pay them, originally appeared in the Toronto Star in 2006. The author, a law professor, has taught tax policy and law at Osgoode Hall in Toronto for many years.

I like paying taxes. Taxes allow us to pursue our aspirations collectively and thus greatly enrich the quality of life for the average Canadian family. Taxes have brought us high-quality public schools that remain our democratic treasure, low tuition at world-class universities, freedom from fear of crippling health bills, excellent medical services, public parks and libraries, and liveable cities. None of these things comes cheaply.   1

Taxes also assist us in spreading our incomes over our lifetimes to maximize our well being by, for example, transferring income from our high-income years to our retirement years, from times when we are supporting children to times when we are not, and from periods when we are well and able to take care of our own needs to periods when we are ill or suffering from a disability.   2

Just as importantly, the public goods and services that we purchase with taxes leave working people more secure, healthier, better educated, more economically secure and therefore better protected against business threats, and thus more able to win their fair share of the national income that we all collectively produce.   3

Taxes also allow us to discharge our moral obligations to one another. They enable us to establish democratically controlled public institutions that attempt to prevent exploitation in market exchanges and family relations; to ensure mutuality in our interdependence upon each other; to compensate those who are inevitably harmed through no fault of their own by the operation of a dynamic market economy that we all benefit from; to ensure a more socially acceptable distribution of income and wealth than that which results from market forces alone; to strive for gender and racial equality; and to provide full entitlement and open access to those services essential to human development. As a result, taxes buy us a relatively high level of social cohesion and social equality and therefore the benefits of community existence. What would any of us have without community?   4

In spite of the fact that they enable us to collectively provide our most valuable goods and services, no one likes paying taxes. There is a good deal of public misunderstanding about the role of taxes in modern democratic states. In large part, this misunderstanding has been fostered by business interests and others who would like to roll back the economic and social borders of the public sector so that they can exercise unhindered power in our society through private markets. Part of   5 their deliberate and clever strategy has been to use language and concepts in discussing taxes that make it appear self-evident that, while citizens can afford more private goods and services, which businesses produce, they are deluding themselves and living beyond their means if they think they can afford more public goods and services produced by government. Examples of such misleading characterizations of taxes abound. Here are three:

6   **Increased taxes cannot be afforded.** This common and compelling-sounding refrain is patently nonsense. Many public goods provided by government and financed by taxes, such as health and education services, are necessities. Therefore, reducing the government supply of these services will not mean that people are no longer paying for them, it will simply mean that they are paying for them in the form of prices demanded by private providers instead of taxes paid to finance their provision through the public sector.

7   Similarly, when people say that we cannot afford to pay taxes to provide child and elderly care services, presumably they are not saying that we can no longer afford to look after our children or the elderly. What they must mean is that instead of spreading the cost of these services equitably, through the tax system, across the entire population, we should leave them to be borne by women, by and large, who provide these services unpaid in their own homes.

8   Thus, often when business interests assert that taxes should be reduced it is not because they think we can no longer afford the services that governments provide, but because they want to shift the cost of providing them from themselves and other high-income individuals to low-income families and women working in their homes at tasks that we all benefit from but for which they are not paid.

9   **Taxes are a burden.** This common description of taxes is equally misleading. Taxes are the price that we pay for goods and services produced in the public sector from which we all benefit. They are equivalent to amounts we pay as prices for goods and services produced in the private sector. Compounding the deception, at the same time as they speak of public goods as being financed by the "imposition of taxes," business interests often speak of private goods as being financed by "the dollar votes of consumers." Here rational understanding is stood on its head. The vote, which is the symbol of democracy, is assigned to a marketplace transaction, while taxes, which are democratically determined, are treated as being amounts people have no control over but that are imposed on them.

10   **Taxes restrict freedom.** This common objection to taxes subtly reinforces the idea that the public sector simply consumes whatever it purchases with tax money, instead of using the money to deliver goods and services that benefit citizens. Taxes, in fact, increase the amount of freedom in society.

11   In a market economy, to have money is to have freedom. The government transfers over 65 per cent of the taxes it receives to families in need in the form of pensions, child allowances, social assistance, and compensation for work-related injuries or loss of employment. Thus, while it might be said that taxes restrict the freedom of some, they greatly enlarge the freedom of others.

12   Taxes increase our freedoms in other ways, including for example, the freedom to travel by using publicly financed roads and other transportation systems, the freedom to learn and think critically, freedom from concerns over crippling health bills, and the freedom to enjoy public libraries, beaches and parks.

To promise, as some politicians are doing, that they are going to cut taxes in   13
order "to allow Canadians to keep more of their hard-earned dollars" is simply a
way of saying "forget about recognizing your moral obligations to one another, to
heck with pursuing your most noble aspirations collectively and do not worry
about securing the blessings of real freedom." These people need a civics lesson. As
a famous U.S. jurist noted, taxes are the price we pay for civilization.   14

Ultimately, what is at stake is the question of who will exercise power in our
society. Will important sources of power be controlled by a small number of
people through private markets? Or will important sources of power remain in the
control of the majority of Canadians through democratically elected institutions?

Questions about Meaning

1. What are some of the advantages to paying taxes, according to the article?
2. What is the thesis of this article? Where is it? Can you put it into your own
   words?
3. What are the three misunderstandings about taxes that Brooks comments on?
   How does he argue against them?

Questions about Rhetorical Strategy and Style

1. Who do you think is the intended audience for this article? Explain your answer.
2. Why does Brooks include questions in his conclusion? Is this an effective
   strategy for argumentation? Why or why not? Support your answer with
   specific reference to the text.

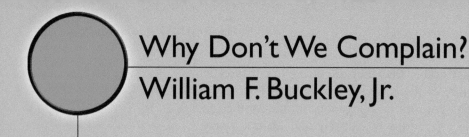

Why Don't We Complain?
William F. Buckley, Jr.

William F. Buckley, Jr. (1925–2008) was born in New York. One of ten children of a lawyer who had earned great wealth from Texas oil, Buckley was educated as a youth at St. Thomas More School in London and Millbrook School in New York. After a stint in the Navy during World War II, he attended Yale University, where he wrote for The Yale Daily News *and was a member of the debating team. Shortly after his graduation from Yale, he published* God and Man at Yale *(1951), a memoir in which he discusses his conservative political philosophy and basic Christian principles. An erudite and articulate spokesman for American conservatives, Buckley has published a number of books on politics and government, including* Happy Days Were Here Again: Reflections of a Libertarian Journalist *(1993); written a syndicated newspaper column; founded and edited a magazine expounding conservative viewpoints,* The National Review; *and hosted a weekly television program,* Firing Line. *He has also written novels and books on sailing, another passion. Buckley received the Presidential Medal of Freedom in 1991 from President Bush. Although liberals disagree vociferously with some of his viewpoints, they just as strongly respect his intelligence and forthrightness. The following essay, written in 1961, reflects not only Buckley's verbal precision, but also his trademark wry sense of humor.*

1   It was the very last coach and the only empty seat on the entire train, so there was no turning back. The problem was to breathe. Outside, the temperature was below freezing. Inside the railroad car the temperature must have been about 85 degrees. I took off my overcoat, and a few minutes later my jacket, and noticed that the car was flecked with the white shirts of the passengers. I soon found my hand moving to loosen my tie. From one end of the car to the other, as we rattled through Westchester County, we sweated; but we did not moan.

2   I watched the train conductor appear at the head of the car. "Tickets, all tickets, please!" In a more virile age, I thought, the passengers would seize the conductor and strap him down on a seat over the radiator to share the fate of his patrons. He shuffled down the aisle, picking up tickets, punching commutation cards. *No one addressed a word to him.* He approached my seat, and I drew a deep breath of resolution. "Conductor," I began with a considerable edge to my voice. . . . Instantly the doleful eyes of my seatmate turned tiredly from his newspaper to fix me with a resentful stare: what question could be so important as to justify my sibilant intrusion into his stupor? I was shaken by those eyes. I am incapable of making a

discreet fuss, so I mumbled a question about what time were we due in Stamford (I didn't even ask whether it would be before or after dehydration could be expected to set in), got my reply, and went back to my newspaper and to wiping my brow.

The conductor had nonchalantly walked down the gauntlet of eighty sweating American freemen, and not one of them had asked him to explain why the passengers in that car had been consigned to suffer. There is nothing to be done when the temperature *outdoors* is 85 degrees, and indoors the air conditioner has broken down; obviously when that happens there is nothing to do, except perhaps curse the day that one was born. But when the temperature outdoors is below freezing, it takes a positive act of will on somebody's part to set the temperature *indoors* at 85. Somewhere a valve was turned too far, a furnace overstocked, a thermostat maladjusted: something that could easily be remedied by turning off the heat and allowing the great outdoors to come indoors. All this is so obvious. What is not obvious is what has happened to the American people.

It isn't just the commuters, whom we have come to visualize as a supine breed who have got on to the trick of suspending their sensory faculties twice a day while they submit to the creeping dissolution of the railroad industry. It isn't just they who have given up trying to rectify irrational vexations. It is the American people everywhere.

A few weeks ago at a large movie theatre I turned to my wife and said, "The picture is out of focus." "Be quiet," she answered. I obeyed. But a few minutes later I raised the point again, with mounting impatience. "It will be all right in a minute," she said apprehensively. (She would rather lose her eyesight than be around when I make one of my infrequent scenes.) I waited, it was *just* out of focus—not glaringly out, but out. My vision is 20–20, and I assume that is the vision, adjusted, of most people in the movie house. So, after hectoring my wife throughout the first reel, I finally prevailed upon her to admit that it *was* off, and very annoying. We then settled down, coming to rest on the presumption that: a) someone connected with the management of the theatre must soon notice the blur and make the correction; or b) that someone seated near the rear of the house would make the complaint in behalf of those of us up front; or c) that—any minute now—the entire house would explode into catcalls and foot stamping, calling dramatic attention to the irksome distortion.

What happened was nothing. The movie ended, as it had begun, *just* out of focus, and as we trooped out, we stretched our faces in a variety of contortions to accustom the eye to the shock of normal focus.

I think it is safe to say that everybody suffered on that occasion. And I think it is safe to assume that everyone was expecting someone else to take the initiative in going back to speak to the manager. And it is probably true even that if we had supposed the movie would run right through the blurred image, someone surely would have summoned up the purposive indignation to get up out of his seat and file his complaint.

But notice that no one did. And the reason no one did is because we are all increasingly anxious in America to be unobtrusive, we are reluctant to make our voices heard, hesitant about claiming our rights; we are afraid that our cause is unjust, or that if it is not unjust, that it is ambiguous; or if not even that, that it is too trivial to justify the horrors of a confrontation with Authority; we will sit in an oven or endure a racking headache before undertaking a head-on, I'm-here-to-tell-you complaint. That tendency to passive compliance, to a heedless endurance, is something to keep one's eyes on—in sharp focus.

9   I myself can occasionally summon the courage to complain, but I cannot, as I have intimated, complain softly. My own instinct is so strong to let the thing ride, to forget about it—to expect that someone will take the matter up, when the grievance is collective, in my behalf—that it is only when the provocation is at a very special key, whose vibrations touch simultaneously a complexus of nerves, allergies, and passions, that I catch fire and find the reserves of courage and assertiveness to speak up. When that happens, I get quite carried away. My blood gets hot, my brow wet, I become unbearably and unconscionably sarcastic and bellicose; I am girded for a total showdown.

10   Why should that be? Why could not I (or anyone else) on that railroad coach have said simply to the conductor, "Sir"—I take that back: that sounds sarcastic—"Conductor, would you be good enough to turn down the heat? I am extremely hot. In fact I tend to get hot every time the temperature reaches 85 degr—" Strike that last sentence. Just end it with the simple statement that you are extremely hot, and let the conductor infer the cause.

11   Every New Year's Eve I resolve to do something about the Milquetoast in me and vow to speak up, calmly, for my rights, and for the betterment of our society, on every appropriate occasion. Entering last New Year's Eve I was fortified in my resolve because that morning at breakfast I had had to ask the waitress three times for a glass of milk. She finally brought it—after I had finished my eggs, which is when I don't want it any more. I did not have the manliness to order her to take the milk back, but settled instead for a cowardly sulk, and ostentatiously refused to drink the milk—though I later paid for it—rather than state plainly to the hostess, as I should have, why I had not drunk it, and would not pay for it.

12   So by the time the New Year ushered out the Old, riding in on my morning's indignation and stimulated by the gastric juices of resolution that flow so faithfully on New Year's Eve, I rendered my vow. Henceforward I would conquer my shyness, my despicable disposition to supineness. I would speak out like a man against the unnecessary annoyances of our time.

13   Forty-eight hours later, I was standing in line at the ski repair store in Pico Peak, Vermont. All I needed, to get on with my skiing, was the loan, for one minute, of a small screwdriver, to tighten a loose binding. Behind the counter in the workshop were two men. One was industriously engaged in serving the complicated requirements of a young lady at the head of the line, and obviously he would be tied up for quite a while. The other—"Jiggs," his workmate called him—was a middle-aged man, who sat in a chair puffing a pipe, exchanging small talk with his working partner. My pulse began its telltale acceleration. The minutes ticked on. I stared at the idle shopkeeper, hoping to shame him into action, but he was impervious to my telepathic reproof and continued his small talk with his friend, brazenly insensitive to the nervous demands of six good men who were raring to ski.

14   Suddenly my New Year's Eve resolution struck me. It was now or never. I broke from my place in line and marched to the counter. I was going to control myself. I dug my nails into my palms. My effort was only partially successful:

15   "If you are not too busy," I said icily, "would you mind handing me a screwdriver"?

16   Work stopped and everyone turned his eyes on me, and I experienced the mortification I always feel when I am the center of centripetal shafts of curiosity, resentment, perplexity.

17   But the worst was yet to come. "I am sorry, sir," said Jiggs defensively, moving the pipe from his mouth. "I am not supposed to move. I have just had a heart attack." That was the signal for a great whirring noise that descended from heaven.

We looked, stricken, out the window, and it appeared as though a cyclone had suddenly focused on the snowy courtyard between the shop and the ski lift. Suddenly a gigantic army helicopter materialized, and hovered down to a landing. Two men jumped out of the plane carrying a stretcher, tore into the ski shop, and lifted the shopkeeper onto the stretcher. Jiggs bade his companion good-by, was whisked out the door, into the plane, up to the heavens, down—we learned—to a near-by army hospital. I looked up manfully—into a score of man-eating eyes. I put the experience down as a reversal.

18   As I write this, on an airplane, I have run out of paper and need to reach into my briefcase under my legs for more. I cannot do this until my empty lunch tray is removed from my lap. I arrested the stewardess as she passed empty-handed down the aisle on the way to the kitchen to fetch the lunch trays for the passengers up forward who haven't been served yet. "Would you please take my tray"? "Just a *moment, sir!*" she said, and marched on sternly. Shall I tell her that since she is headed for the kitchen *anyway*, it could not delay the feeding of the other passengers by more than two seconds necessary to stash away my empty tray? Or remind her that not fifteen minutes ago she spoke unctuously into the loudspeaker the words undoubtedly devised by the airline's highly paid public relations counselor: "If there is anything I or Miss French can do for you to make your trip more enjoyable, *please* let us—" I have run out of paper.

19   I think the observable reluctance of the majority of Americans to assert themselves in minor matters is related to our increased sense of helplessness in an age of technology and centralized political and economic power. For generations, Americans who were too hot, or too cold, got up and did something about it. Now we call the plumber, or the electrician, or the furnace man. The habit of looking after our own needs obviously had something to do with the assertiveness that characterized the American family familiar to readers of American literature. With the technification of life goes our direct responsibility for our material environment, and we are conditioned to adopt a position of helplessness not only as regards the broken air conditioner, but as regards the overheated train. It takes an expert to fix the former, but not the latter; yet these distinctions, as we withdraw into helplessness, tend to fade away.

20   Our notorious political apathy is a related phenomenon. Every year, whether the Republican or the Democratic Party is in office, more and more power drains away from the individual to feed vast reservoirs in far-off places; and we have less and less say about the shape of events which shape our future. From this alienation of personal power comes the sense of resignation with which we accept the political dispensations of a powerful government whose hold upon us continues to increase.

21   An editor of a national weekly news magazine told me a few years ago that as few as a dozen letters of protest against an editorial stance of his magazine was enough to convene a plenipotentiary meeting of the board of editors to review policy. "So few people complain, or make their voices heard," he explained to me, "that we assume a dozen letters represent the inarticulated views of thousands of readers." In the past ten years, he said, the volume of mail has noticeably decreased, even though the circulation of his magazine has risen.

22   When our voices are finally mute, when we have finally suppressed the natural instinct to complain, whether the vexation is trivial or grave, we shall have become automatons, incapable of feeling. When Premier Khrushchev first came to this country late in 1959 he was primed, we are informed, to experience the bitter resentment of the American people against his tyranny, against his persecutions, against the movement which is responsible for the great number of American

deaths in Korea, for billions in taxes every year, and for life everlasting on the brink of disaster; but Khrushchev was pleasantly surprised, and reported back to the Russian people that he had been met with overwhelming cordiality (read: apathy), except, to be sure, for "a few fascists who followed me around with their wretched posters, and should be horsewhipped."

23   I may be crazy, but I say there would have been lots more posters in a society where train temperatures in the dead of winter are not allowed to climb to 85 degrees without complaint.

Questions about Meaning

1. What is the author's answer to the question in the title? In which paragraph/s is it located?

2. Buckley feels that the "reluctance" of Americans to complain is partly related to a "sense of helplessness" related to the "age of technology"—this written nearly 20 years before the first personal computer. Have computer technology and Internet communications weakened or enhanced our ability to complain?

3. Although the Russian premier is only mentioned at the end of the essay, how is Buckley's concern with passive Americans ultimately a political concern? Given that this essay was written during the cold war with the Soviet Union, what danger is symbolized by sweating, compliant commuters?

Questions about Rhetorical Strategy and Style

1. Buckley confesses that he is loud when he does complain—"I am incapable of making a discreet fuss" and "I cannot complain softly," he says. Reread his description of what happens when he *does* complain in the ski shop. Why does he include this incident in the essay?

2. Buckley was a highly educated man. How does his sophisticated vocabulary affect the reader?

Sit Down and Shut Up or Don't Sit by Me
Dennis Dermody

Dennis Dermody is a New York film critic who writes mainly for **Paper Magazine** *where this piece first appeared in 1993.*

All right, I admit it: I'm a tad neurotic when it comes to making it to the movies on time. I have to be there at least a half hour before the feature begins. Not that I'm worried about long lines at the box office, either. The movies I rush off to see are generally so sparsely attended you can hear crickets in the audience. It's just a thing I do. 1

Of course, sitting for 30 minutes watching a theater fill up is pretty boring, but through the years I've amused myself with a Margaret Mead—like study of the way people come in and take their seats and their antics during a movie. I felt I should share my impressions lest you find yourself succumbing to these annoying traits. 2

Right off the bat: Leave the kids at home. We're not talking about *Aladdin* or *Home Alone 2*—that I understand—but recently I went to see *Body of Evidence*, and it looked like a day-care center in the theater. Strollers were flying down the aisle, children were whining for candy, restless and audibly bored (especially during the hot-wax-dripping sequence), and eventually the day-care atmosphere caused fights among the adults. "Shut your kid up!" prompted a proud parent to slug a fellow patron, and before you knew it there were angry skirmishes all over the theater and the police had to be brought in. So either leave them at home with a sitter or tie them up to a fire hydrant outside the theater. 3

For some people, choosing a seat takes on moral and philosophical implications. Sometimes they stand in the middle of the aisle juggling coats, popcorn, and Cokes, seemingly overwhelmed by the prospect of choice. Should I sit down front, or will that be too close? Is this too far back? That man seems awfully tall, I bet I couldn't see the movie if I sat behind him. I'd love to sit somewhere in the middle but would I be too close to that group of teenagers shooting heroin into their necks? If I sit on this side, will the angle be too weird to watch the movie? Is that seat unoccupied because it's broken? Good Lord, the lights are dimming and I haven't made up my mind and now I won't be able to see where I'm going. 4

Many, upon choosing their seats, find they are unsatisfied and have to move. I've watched many couples go from one spot to another more than a dozen times before settling down—it's like watching a bird testing different spots to build a nest. 5

As the lights begin to dim and the annoying theater-chain logo streaks across the screen, lo and behold, here come the *latecomers*! Their eyes unaccustomed to the dark, in a panic they search for friends, for assistance, for a lonely seat. Just the other day, I watched an elderly woman come into the darkened theater 10 minutes 6 after the movie had begun and say out loud, "I can't see anything!" She then proceeded to inch her way down the aisle, grabbing onto what she thought were seats but were actually people's heads. I saw her sit down right in the lap of someone who shrieked in shock. After the woman stumbled back into the aisle, chattering wildly, someone mercifully directed her to an empty seat. Then, after a great flourish of getting out of her bulky coat, she asked spiritedly of the grumbling souls around her, "What did I miss"?

7   I also must address the behavior of people *during* the movie. The *chatterers* comment blithely on everything that is happening on the screen. Like Tourette's syndrome sufferers unable to control what they blurt out, these people say anything that comes into their heads. "What a cute puppy," they say when they spy an animal ambling off to the side of the frame. "I have that lamp at home," they exclaim. And add, five minutes later, "But mine is red."

8   The *krinklers* wander down the aisle with a million shopping bags and wait for a key sequence, then begin to forage in their bags for the perfect and most annoying plastic wrap, which they use to make noise with sadistic relish. You try to focus on the screen but the racket starts up again with a wild flourish. I've seen grown men leap to their feet with tears streaming down their face and scream, "Will you stop shaking that motherfucking bag!"

9   The *unending box of popcorn* people sit directly behind you and start masticating during the opening credits. It's bad enough having the smell of cooked corn wafting around you, but the sound is enough to drive you mad. You tell yourself that eventually they'll finish, but they never do. They keep chewing and chewing and chewing and you're deathly afraid that next they'll start on a four-pound box of malted milk balls.

10   So in summary: Get to the movie theater early and scout out the territory. It's a jungle in there, filled with a lot of really stupid animals. Know the telltale signs and act accordingly. And then sit down and shut up.

Questions about Meaning

1. The author has identified several varieties of movie goers and their before and during movie behaviours. How many categories can you identify?
2. There are many different problems Dermody has with various movie goers. Can you see any pattern in the behaviours he talks about? What do all of these disturbing movie goers have in common?

Questions about Rhetorical Strategy and Style

1. How would you describe the tone of this article? Make specific reference to the text to support your answer.
2. Who is the intended audience of this article? What is Dermody's purpose in writing?

The Truth about Lying
Judith Viorst

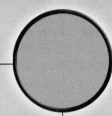

*Judith Viorst (1931–) is perhaps best known as an author of literature for children (**The Tenth Good Thing about Barney**), but she is also a poet and psychoanalysis researcher.*

I've been wanting to write on a subject that intrigues and challenges me: The subject of lying. I've found it very difficult to do. Everyone I've talked to has a quite intense and personal but often rather intolerant point of view about what we can—and can never *never*—tell lies about. I've finally reached the conclusion that I can't present any ultimate conclusions, for too many people would promptly disagree. Instead, I'd like to present a series of moral puzzles, all concerned with lying. I'll tell you what I think about them. Do you agree?

SOCIAL LIES

Most of the people I've talked with say that they find social lying acceptable and necessary. They think it's the civilized way for folks to behave. Without these little white lies, they say, our relationships would be short and brutish and nasty. It's arrogant, they say, to insist on being so incorruptible and so brave that you cause other people unnecessary embarrassment or pain by compulsively assailing them with your honesty. I basically agree. What about you?

Will you say to people, when it simply isn't true, "I like your new hairdo," "You're looking much better," "It's so nice to see you," "I had a wonderful time"?

Will you praise hideous presents and homely kids?

Will you decline invitations with "We're busy that night—so sorry we can't come," when the truth is you'd rather stay home than dine with the So-and-sos?

And even though, as I do, you may prefer the polite evasion of "You really cooked up a storm" instead of "The soup"—which tastes like warmed-over coffee—"is wonderful," will you, if you must, proclaim it wonderful?

There's one man I know who absolutely refuses to tell social lies. "I can't play that game," he says; "I'm simply not made that way." And his answer to the argument that saying nice things to someone doesn't cost anything is, "Yes, it does—it destroys your credibility." Now, he won't, unsolicited, offer his views on the painting you just bought, but you don't ask his frank opinion unless you want *frank*, and his silence at those moments when the rest of us liars are muttering, "Isn't it lovely"? is, for the most part, eloquent enough. My friend does not indulge in what he calls "flattery, false praise and mellifluous comments." When others tell fibs he will not go along. He says that social lying is lying, that little white lies are still lies. And he feels that telling lies is morally wrong. What about you?

1

5

PEACE-KEEPING LIES

Many people tell peace-keeping lies; lies designed to avoid irritation or argument; lies designed to shelter the liar from possible blame or pain; lies (or so it is rationalized) designed to keep trouble at bay without hurting anyone.

I tell these lies at times, and yet I always feel they're wrong. I understand why we tell them, but still they feel wrong. And whenever I lie so that someone won't disapprove of me or think less of me or holler at me, I feel I'm a bit of a coward, I feel I'm dodging responsibility, I feel . . . guilty. What about you?

10 Do you, when you're late for a date because you overslept, say that you're late because you got caught in a traffic jam?

Do you, when you forget to call a friend, say that you called several times but the line was busy?

Do you, when you didn't remember that it was your father's birthday, say that his present must be delayed in the mail?

And when you're planning a weekend in New York City and you're not in the mood to visit your mother, who lives there, do you conceal—with a lie, if you must—the fact that you'll be in New York? Or do you have the courage—or is it the cruelty?—to say, "I'll be in New York, but sorry—I don't plan on seeing you"?

(Dave and his wife Elaine have two quite different points of view on this very subject. He calls her a coward. She says she's being wise. He says she must assert her right to visit New York sometimes and not see her mother. To which she always patiently replies: "why should we have useless fights? My mother's too old to change. We get along much better when I lie to her.")

15 Finally, do you keep the peace by telling your husband lies on the subject of money? Do you reduce what you really paid for your shoes? And in general do you find yourself ready, willing and able to lie to him when you make absurd mistakes or lose or break things?

"I used to have a romantic idea that part of intimacy was confessing every dumb thing that you did to your husband. But after a couple of years of that," says Laura, "have I changed my mind!"

And having changed her mind, she finds herself telling peace-keeping lies. And yes, I tell them, too. What about you?

PROTECTIVE LIES

Protective lies are lies folks tell—often quite serious lies—because they're convinced that the truth would be too damaging. They lie because they feel there are certain human values that supersede the wrong of having lied. They lie, not for personal gain, but because they believe it's for the good of the person they're lying to. They lie to those they love, to those who trust them most of all, on the grounds that breaking this trust is justified.

They may lie to their children on money or marital matters.

20 They may lie to the dying about the state of their health.

They may lie about adultery, and not—or so they insist—to save their own hide, but to save the heart and the pride of the men they are married to.

They may lie to their closest friend because the truth about her talents or son or psyche would be—or so they insist—utterly devastating.

I sometimes tell such lies, but I'm aware that it's quite presumptuous to claim I know what's best for others to know. That's called playing God. That's called manipulation and control. And we never can be sure, once we start to juggle lies, just where they'll land, exactly where they'll roll.

And furthermore, we may find ourselves lying in order to back up the lies that are backing up the lie we initially told.

And furthermore—let's be honest—if conditions were reversed, we certainly 25 wouldn't want anyone lying to us.

Yet, having said all that, I still believe that there are times when protective lies must nonetheless be told. What about you?

If your Dad had a very bad heart and you had to tell him some bad family news, which would you choose: to tell him the truth or lie?

If your former husband failed to send his monthly child support check and in other ways behaved like a total rat, would you allow your children—who believed he was simply wonderful—to continue to believe that he was wonderful?

If your dearly beloved brother selected a wife whom you deeply disliked, would you reveal your feelings or would you fake it?

And if you were asked, after making love, "And how was that for you"? would 30 you reply, if it wasn't too good, "Not too good"?

Now, some would call a sex lie unimportant, little more than social lying, a simple act of courtesy that makes all human intercourse run smoothly. And some would say all sex lies are bad news and unacceptably protective. Because, says Ruth, "a man with an ego that fragile doesn't need your lies—he needs a psychiatrist." Still others feel that sex lies are indeed protective lies, more serious than simple social lying, and yet at times they tell them on the grounds that when it comes to matters sexual, everybody's ego is somewhat fragile.

"If most of the time things go well in sex," says Sue, "I think you're allowed to dissemble when they don't. I can't believe it's good to say, 'Last night was four stars, darling, but tonight's performance rates only a half.'"

I'm inclined to agree with Sue. What about you?

TRUST-KEEPING LIES

Another group of lies are trust-keeping lies, lies that involve triangulation, with *A* (that's you) telling lies to *B* on behalf of *C* (whose trust you'd promised to keep). Most people concede that once you've agreed not to betray a friend's confidence, you can't betray it, even if you must lie. But I've talked with people who don't want you telling them anything that they might be called on to lie about.

"I don't tell lies for myself," says Fran, "and I don't want to have to tell them 35 for other people." Which means, she agrees, that if her best friend is having an affair, she absolutely doesn't want to know about it.

"Are you saying," her best friend asks, "that if I went off with a lover and I asked you to tell my husband I'd been with you, that you wouldn't lie for me, that you'd betray me"?

Fran is very pained but very adamant. "I wouldn't want to betray you so . . . don't ask me."

Fran's best friend is shocked. What about you?

Do you believe you can have close friends if you're not prepared to receive their deepest secrets?

Do you believe you must always lie for your friends? 40

Do you believe, if your friend tells a secret that turns out to be quite immoral or illegal, that once you've promised to keep it, you must keep it?

And what if your friend were your boss—if you were perhaps one of the President's men—would you betray or lie for him over, say, Watergate?

As you can see, these issues get terribly sticky.

It's my belief that once we've promised to keep a trust, we must tell lies to keep it. I also believe that we can't tell Watergate lies. And if these two statements strike you as quite contradictory, you're right—they're quite contradictory. But for now they're the best I can do. What about you?

45   Some say that truth will out and thus you might as well tell the truth. Some say you can't regain the trust that lies lose. Some say that even though the truth may never be revealed, our lies pervert and damage our relationships. Some say . . . well, here's what some of them have to say.

"I'm a coward," says Grace, "about telling close people important, difficult truths. I find that I'm unable to carry it off. And so if something is bothering me, it keeps building up inside till I end up just not seeing them any more."

"I lie to my husband on sexual things, but I'm furious," says Joyce "that he's too insensitive to know I'm lying."

"I suffer most from the misconception that children can't take the truth," says Emily. "But I'm starting to see that what's harder and more damaging for them is being told lies, is *not* being told the truth."

"I'm afraid," says Joan, "that we often wind up feeling a bit of contempt for the people we lie to."

50   And then there are those who have no talent for lying.

"Over the years, I tried to lie," a friend of mine explained, "but I always got found out and I always got punished. I guess I gave myself away because I feel guilty about any kind of lying. It looks as if I'm stuck with telling the truth."

For those of us, however, who are good at telling lies, for those of us who lie and don't get caught, the question of whether or not to lie can be a hard and serious moral problem. I liked the remark of a friend of mine who said, "I'm willing to lie. But just as a last resort—the truth's always better."

"Because," he explained, "though others may completely accept the lie I'm telling, I don't."

I tend to feel that way too.

55   What about you?

Questions about Meaning

1. What is the difference between a moral puzzle and an argument? Is it effective for Viorst to have chosen to present moral puzzles? Why or why not?

2. What contrast does Viorst establish in her introduction between common attitudes about dishonesty and the approach taken in her essay? How does this contrast help Viorst to make her point?

3. What does the author reveal in her conclusion? What is her stance on lying in general?

Questions about Rhetorical Strategy and Style

1. Why does the author use the second person point of view? What is the effect on the reader?

2. Are the subtitles used in the essay necessary? Why or why not?

3. Is there a pattern to the organization of the sections of this essay? What is it?

A Hanging

George Orwell

George Orwell is the pen name used by the British author Eric Blair (1903–1950). Orwell was born in the Indian village of Motihari, near Nepal, where his father was stationed in the Civil Service. India was then part of the British Empire; Orwell's grandfather too had served the Empire in the Indian Army. From 1907 to 1922 Orwell lived in England, returning to India and Burma and a position in the Imperial Police, which he held until 1927. This is the period about which he writes in "A Hanging." Thereafter he lived in England, Paris, Spain, and elsewhere, writing on a wide range of topics. He fought in the Spanish Civil War and was actively engaged in several political movements, always against totalitarianism of any kind. He is best known today for two novels of political satire: **Animal Farm** *(1945) and* **1984** *(1949). He was also a prolific journalist and essayist, with his essays collected in five volumes. "A Hanging" was published in the collection of essays* **Shooting an Elephant** *in 1950. This essay reads very much like a story, using the rhetorical strategy of narration, but Orwell does have a point to make here, which emerges from a rather subtle approach.*

It was in Burma, a sodden morning of the rains. A sickly light, like yellow tinfoil, was slanting over the high walls into the jail yard. We were waiting outside the condemned cells, a row of sheds fronted with double bars, like small animal cages. Each cell measured about ten feet by ten and was quite bare within except for a plank bed and a pot for drinking water. In some of them brown, silent men were squatting at the inner bars, with their blankets draped round them. These were the condemned men, due to be hanged within the next week or two. 1

One prisoner had been brought out of his cell. He was a Hindu, a puny wisp of a man, with a shaven head and vague liquid eyes. He had a thick, sprouting mustache, absurdly too big for his body, rather like the mustache of a comic man in the films. Six tall Indian warders were guarding him and getting him ready for the gallows. Two of them stood by with rifles and fixed bayonets, while the others handcuffed him, passed a chain through his handcuffs and fixed it to their belts, and lashed his arms tight to his sides. They crowded very close about him, with their hands always on him in a careful, caressing grip, as though all the while feeling him to make sure he was there. It was like men handling a fish which is still alive and may jump back into the water. But he stood quite unresisting, yielding his arms limply to the ropes, as though he hardly noticed what was happening. 2

Eight o'clock struck and a bugle call, desolately thin in the wet air, floated from the distant barracks. The superintendent of the jail, who was standing apart 3

From *Shooting an Elephant and Other Essays* by George Orwell. Published by Harcourt Brace from the rest of us, moodily prodding the gravel with his stick, raised his head at the sound. He was an army doctor, with a grey toothbrush mustache and a gruff voice. "For God's sake, hurry up, Francis," he said irritably. "The man ought to have been dead by this time. Aren't you ready yet"?

4   Francis, the head jailer, a fat Dravidian in a white drill suit and gold spectacles, waved his black hand. "Yes sir, yes sir," he bubbled. "All iss satisfactorily prepared. The hangman iss waiting. We shall proceed."

5   "Well, quick march, then. The prisoners can't get their breakfast till this job's over."

6   We set out for the gallows. Two warders marched on either side of the prisoner, with their rifles at the slope; two others marched close against him, gripping him by arm and shoulder, as though at once pushing and supporting him. The rest of us, magistrates and the like, followed behind. Suddenly, when we had gone ten yards, the procession stopped short without any order or warning. A dreadful thing had happened—a dog, come goodness knows whence, had appeared in the yard. It came bounding among us with a loud volley of barks and leapt around us wagging its whole body, wild with glee at finding so many human beings together. It was a large woolly dog, half Airedale, half pariah. For a moment it pranced around us, and then, before anyone could stop it, it had made a dash for the prisoner, and jumping up tried to lick his face. Everybody stood aghast, too taken aback even to grab the dog.

7   "Who let that bloody brute in here"? said the superintendent angrily. "Catch it, someone!"

8   A warder, detached from the escort, charged clumsily after the dog, but it danced and gambolled just out of his reach, taking everything as part of the game. A young Eurasian jailer picked up a handful of gravel and tried to stone the dog away, but it dodged the stones and came after us again. Its yaps echoed from the jail walls. The prisoner, in the grasp of the two warders, looked on incuriously, as though this was another formality of the hanging. It was several minutes before someone managed to catch the dog. Then we put my handkerchief through its collar and moved off once more, with the dog still straining and whimpering.

9   It was about forty yards to the gallows. I watched the bare brown back of the prisoner marching in front of me. He walked clumsily with his bound arms, but quite steadily, with that bobbing gait of the Indian who never straightens his knees. At each step his muscles slid neatly into place, the lock of hair on his scalp danced up and down, his feet printed themselves on the wet gravel. And once, in spite of the men who gripped him by each shoulder, he stepped lightly aside to avoid a puddle on the path.

10   It is curious, but till that moment I had never realized what it means to destroy a healthy, conscious man. When I saw the prisoner step aside to avoid the puddle, I saw the mystery, the unspeakable wrongness, of cutting a life short when it is in full tide. This man was not dying, he was alive just as we are alive. All the organs of his body were working—bowels digesting food, skin renewing itself, nails growing, tissues forming—all toiling away in solemn foolery. His nails would still be growing when he stood on the drop, when he was falling through the air with a tenth-of-a-second to live. His eyes saw the yellow gravel and the grey walls, and his brain still remembered, foresaw, reasoned—even about puddles. He and we were a party of men walking together, seeing, hearing, feeling, understanding the same world; and in two minutes, with a sudden snap, one of us would be gone—one mind less, one world less.

11   The gallows stood in a small yard, separate from the main grounds of the prison, and overgrown with tall prickly weeds. It was a brick erection like three

sides of a shed, with planking on top, and above that two beams and a crossbar with the rope dangling. The hangman, a greyhaired convict in the white uniform of the prison, was waiting beside his machine. He greeted us with a servile crouch as we entered. At a word from Francis the two warders, gripping the prisoner more closely than ever, half led, half pushed him to the gallows and helped him clumsily up the ladder. Then the hangman climbed up and fixed the rope around the prisoner's neck.

We stood waiting, five yards away. The warders had formed in a rough circle round the gallows. And then, when the noose was fixed, the prisoner began crying out to his god. It was a high, reiterated cry of "Ram! Ram! Ram! Ram!" not urgent and fearful like a prayer or cry for help, but steady, rhythmical, almost like the tolling of a bell. The dog answered the sound with a whine. The hangman, still standing on the gallows, produced a small cotton bag like a flour bag and drew it down over the prisoner's face. But the sound, muffled by the cloth, still persisted, over and over again: "Ram! Ram! Ram! Ram! Ram!" 12

The hangman climbed down and stood ready, holding the lever. Minutes seemed to pass. The steady, muffled crying from the prisoner went on and on, "Ram! Ram! Ram!" never faltering for an instant. The superintendent, his head on his chest, was slowly poking the ground with his stick; perhaps he was counting the cries, allowing the prisoner a fixed number—fifty, perhaps, or a hundred. Everyone had changed colour. The Indians had gone grey like bad coffee, and one or two of the bayonets were wavering. We looked at the lashed, hooded man on the drop, and listened to his cries—each cry another second of life; the same thought was in all our minds; oh, kill him quickly, get it over, stop that abominable noise! 13

Suddenly the superintendent made up his mind. Throwing up his head he made a swift motion with his stick. "Chalo!" he shouted almost fiercely. 14

There was a clanking noise, and then dead silence. The prisoner had vanished, and the rope was twisting on itself. I let go of the dog, and it galloped immediately to the back of the gallows; but when it got there it stopped short, barked, and then retreated into a corner of the yard, where it stood among the weeds, looking timorously out at us. We went round the gallows to inspect the prisoner's body. He was dangling with his toes pointed straight downwards, very slowly revolving, as dead as a stone. 15

The superintendent reached out with his stick and poked the bare brown body; it oscillated slightly. "*He's* all right," said the superintendent. He backed out from under the gallows, and blew out a deep breath. The moody look had gone out of his face quite suddenly. He glanced at his wrist-watch. "Eight minutes past eight. Well, that's all for this morning, thank God." 16

The warders unfixed bayonets and marched away. The dog, sobered and conscious of having misbehaved itself, slipped after them. We walked out of the gallows yard, past the condemned cells with their waiting prisoners, into the big central yard of the prison. The convicts, under the command of warders armed with lathis, were already receiving their breakfast. They squatted in long rows, each man holding a tin pannikin, while two warders with buckets marched around ladling out rice; it seemed quite a homely, jolly scene, after the hanging. An enormous relief had come upon us now that the job was done. One felt an impulse to sing, to break into a run, to snigger. All at once everyone began chattering gaily. 17

The Eurasian boy walking beside me nodded towards the way we had come, with a knowing smile: "Do you know, sir, our friend (he meant the dead man) when he heard his appeal had been dismissed, he pissed on the floor of his cell. From fright. Kindly take one of my cigarettes, sir. Do you not admire my new 18 silver case, sir? From the boxwallah, two rupees eight annas. Classy European style."

19   Several people laughed—at what, nobody seemed certain.

20   Francis was walking by the superintendent, talking garrulously: "Well, sir, all has passed off with the utmost satisfactoriness. It was all finished—flick! Like that. It iss not always so—oah, no! I have known cases where the doctor was obliged to go beneath the gallows and pull the prissoner's legs to ensure decease. Most disagreeable!"

21   "Wriggling about, eh? That's bad," said the superintendent.

22   "Ach, sir, it iss worse when they become refractory! One man, I recall, clung to the bars of hiss cage when we went to take him out. You will scarcely credit, sir, that it took six warders to dislodge him, three pulling at each leg. We reasoned with him, 'My dear fellow,' we said, 'think of all the pain and trouble you are causing to us!' But no, he would not listen! Ach, he wass very troublesome!"

23   I found that I was laughing quite loudly. Everyone was laughing. Even the superintendent grinned in a tolerant way. "You'd better all come out and have a drink," he said quite genially. "I've got a bottle of whisky in the car. We could do with it."

24   We went through the big double gates of the prison into the road. "Pulling at his legs!" exclaimed a Burmese magistrate suddenly, and burst into a loud chuckling. We all began laughing again. At that moment Francis' anecdote seemed extraordinarily funny. We all had a drink together, native and European alike, quite amicably. The dead man was a hundred yards away.

Questions on Meaning

1. Why doesn't Orwell tell the reader the crime for which the prisoner is being executed?

2. When the narrator comments that now he realizes "what it means to destroy a healthy, conscious man," what does he really mean? Explain in your own words the insight he seems to experience at that moment.

3. The dog functions as a character in the essay, appearing at least three key times. What role does the dog play in Orwell's essay?

4. Why do the narrator and the officials laugh and have an amicable drink together after the execution?

Questions on Rhetorical Strategy and Style

1. Orwell uses two phrases in the essay, "bloody brute" and "classy European style," that have a meaning beyond their immediate reference. Explain the wider implications of these two phrases.

2. What is the tone of the essay, and what is its relationship to the subject matter? Support your answer with specific references to the text.

3. How long does the actual process of the execution take? Why does it seem to take so much longer? What is the purpose of Orwell's very detailed description of the execution?

A Modest Proposal

Jonathan Swift

Born in Dublin, Ireland, Jonathan Swift (1667–1745) entered the clergy after his education at Trinity College and Oxford University. Through his long life he wrote in a wide range of genres, including poetry, religious pamphlets, essays, and satires on various social and political themes. His best-known work is Gulliver's Travels, *a combination of children's story and social satire. Swift was always a supporter of Irish causes, as can be seen in "A Modest Proposal," which was published anonymously in 1729. In this ironic essay, the speaker— the "I"—is not Swift himself but a persona, a fictional voice who gives his proposal to cure the ills of contemporary Ireland. It is true that Ireland at this time had the problems described by this persona: poverty, unemployment, a failing economy, exploitation by the wealthy classes, conflict between the Anglican and Catholic churches, and so on. This is the serious subject Swift addresses through his satire. If you have not read or heard of his "proposal" previously, read slowly and attentively: you might be greatly surprised to learn the nature of his proposition.*

1   It is a melancholy object to those who walk through this great town or travel in the country, when they see the streets, the roads, and cabin doors, crowded with beggars of the female sex, followed by three, four, or six children, all in rags and importuning every passenger for an alms. These mothers, instead of being able to work for their honest livelihood, are forced to employ all their time in strolling to beg sustenance for their helpless infants, who, as they grow up, either turn thieves for want of work, or leave their dear native country to fight for the Pretender in Spain, or sell themselves to the Barbadoes.

2   I think it is agreed by all parties that this prodigious number of children in the arms, or on the backs, or at the heels of their mothers, and frequently of their fathers, is in the present deplorable state of the kingdom a very great additional grievance; and therefore whoever could find out a fair, cheap, and easy method of making these children sound, useful members of the commonwealth would deserve so well of the public as to have his statue set up for a preserver of the nation.

3   But my intention is very far from being confined to provide only for the children of professed beggars; it is of a much greater extent, and shall take in the whole number of infants at a certain age who are born of parents in effect as little able to support them as those who demand our charity in the streets.

4   As to my own part, having turned my thoughts for many years upon this important subject, and maturely weighed the several schemes of other projectors, I have always found them grossly mistaken in their computation. It is true, a child just dropped from its dam may be supported by her milk for a solar year, with

little other nourishment; at most not above the value of two shillings, which the mother may certainly get, or the value in scraps, by her lawful occupation of begging; and it is exactly at one year old that I propose to provide for them in such a manner as instead of being a charge upon their parents or the parish, or wanting food and raiment for the rest of their lives, they shall on the contrary contribute to the feeding, and partly to the clothing, of many thousands.

5   There is likewise another great advantage in my scheme, that it will prevent those voluntary abortions, and that horrid practice of women murdering their bastard children, alas, too frequent among us, sacrificing the poor innocent babes, I doubt, more to avoid the expense than the shame, which would move tears and pity in the most savage and inhuman breast.

6   The number of souls in this kingdom being usually reckoned one million and a half, of these I calculate there may be about two hundred thousand couples whose wives are breeders; from which number I subtract thirty thousand couples who are able to maintain their own children, although I apprehend there cannot be so many under the present distresses of the kingdom; but this being granted, there will remain an hundred and seventy thousand breeders. I again subtract fifty thousand for those women who miscarry, or whose children die by accident or disease within the year. There only remain an hundred and twenty thousand children of poor parents annually born. The question therefore is, how this number shall be reared and provided for, which, as I have already said, under the present situation of affairs, is utterly impossible by all the methods hitherto proposed. For we can neither employ them in handicraft nor agriculture; we neither build houses (I mean in the country) nor cultivate land. They can very seldom pick up livelihood by stealing till they arrive at six years old, except where they are of towardly parts; although I confess they learn the rudiments much earlier, during which time they can however be looked upon only as probationers, as I have been informed by a principal gentleman in the county of Cavan, who protested to me that he never knew above one or two instances under the age of six, even in a part of the kingdom so renowned for the quickest proficiency in that art.

7   I am assured by our merchants that a boy or a girl before twelve years old is no salable commodity; and even when they come to this age, they will not yield above three pounds, or three pounds and half a crown at most on the Exchange; which cannot turn to account either to the parents or the kingdom, the charge of nutriment and rags having been at least four times that value.

8   I shall now therefore humbly propose my own thoughts, which I hope will not be liable to the least objection.

9   I have been assured by a very knowing American of my acquaintance in London, that a young healthy child well nursed is at a year old a most delicious, nourishing, and wholesome food, whether stewed, roasted, baked, or boiled; and I make no doubt that it will equally serve in a fricassee or a ragout.

10   I do therefore humbly offer it to public consideration that of the hundred and twenty thousand children, already computed, twenty thousand may be reserved for breed, whereof only one fourth part to be males, which is more than we allow to sheep, black cattle, or swine; and my reason is that these children are seldom the fruits of marriage, a circumstance not much regarded by our savages, therefore one male will be sufficient to serve four females. That the remaining hundred thousand may at a year old be offered in sale to the persons of quality and fortune through the kingdom, always advising the mother to let them suck plentifully in the last month, so as to render them plump and fat for a good table. A child will make two dishes at an entertainment for friends; and when the family dines alone, the

fore or hind quarter will make a reasonable dish, and seasoned with a little pepper or salt will be very good boiled on the fourth day, especially in winter.

I have reckoned upon a medium that a child just born will weigh twelve pounds, 11 and in a solar year if tolerably nursed increaseth to twenty-eight pounds.

I grant this food will be somewhat dear, and therefore very proper for 12 landlords, who, as they have already devoured most of the parents, seem to have the best title to the children.

Infant's flesh will be in season throughout the year, but more plentiful in 13 March, and a little before and after. For we are told by a grave author, an eminent French physician, that fish being a prolific diet, there are more children born in Roman Catholic countries about nine months after Lent, than at any other season; therefore, reckoning a year after Lent, the markets will be more glutted than usual, because the number of popish infants is at least three to one in this kingdom; and therefore it will have one other collateral advantage, by lessening the number of Papists among us.

I have already computed the charge of nursing a beggar's child (in which list 14 I reckon all cottagers, laborers, and four fifths of the farmers) to be about two shillings per annum, rags included; and I believe no gentleman would repine to give ten shillings for the carcass of a good fat child, which, as I have said, will make four dishes of excellent nutritive meat, when he hath only some particular friend or his own family to dine with him. Thus the squire will learn to be a good landlord, and grow popular among the tenants; the mother will have eight shillings net profit, and be fit for work till she produces another child.

Those who are more thrifty (as I must confess the times require) may flay the 15 carcass; the skin of which artificially dressed will make admirable gloves for ladies, and summer boots for fine gentlemen.

As to our city of Dublin, shambles may be appointed for this purpose in the 16 most convenient parts of it, and butchers we may be assured will not be wanting; although I rather recommend buying the children alive, and dressing them hot from the knife as we do roasting pigs.

A very worthy person, a true lover of his country, and whose virtues I highly 17 esteem, was lately pleased in discoursing on this matter to offer a refinement upon my scheme. He said that many gentlemen of his kingdom, having of late destroyed their deer, he conceived that the want of venison might be well supplied by the bodies of young lads and maidens, not exceeding fourteen years of age nor under twelve, so great a number of both sexes in every county being now ready to starve for want of work and service; and these to be disposed of by their parents, if alive, or otherwise by their nearest relations. But with due deference to so excellent a friend and so deserving a patriot, I cannot be altogether in his sentiments; for as to the males, my American acquaintance assured me from frequent experience that their flesh was generally tough and lean, like that of our schoolboys, by continual exercise, and their taste disagreeable; and to fatten them would not answer the charge. Then as to the females, it would, I think with humble submission, be a loss to the public, because they soon would become breeders themselves; and besides, it is not improbable that some scrupulous people might be apt to censure such a practice (although indeed very unjustly) as a little bordering upon cruelty; which, I confess, hath always been with me the strongest objection against any project, how well soever intended.

But in order to justify my friend, he confessed that this expedient was put into 18 his head by the famous Psalmanazar, a native of the island Formosa, who came from thence to London above twenty years ago, and in conversation told my friend that in his country when any young person happened to be put to death, the executioner sold the carcass to persons of quality as a prime dainty; and that in his time the body of a plump girl of fifteen, who was crucified for an attempt to poison the emperor, was sold to his Imperial Majesty's prime minister of state, and other great mandarins of the court, in joints from the gibbet, at four hundred crowns. Neither indeed can I deny that if the same use were made of several plump young girls in this town, who without one single groat to their fortunes cannot stir abroad without a chair, and appear at the playhouse and assemblies in foreign fineries which they never will pay for, the kingdom would not be the worse.

19   Some persons of a desponding spirit are in great concern about that vast number of poor people who are aged, diseased, or maimed, and I have been desired to employ my thoughts what course may be taken to ease the nation of so grievous an encumbrance. But I am not in the least pain upon that matter, because it is very well known that they are every day dying and rotting by cold and famine, and filth and vermin, as fast as can be reasonably expected. And as to the younger laborers, they are now in almost as hopeful a condition. They cannot get work, and consequently pine away for want of nourishment to a degree that if any time they are accidentally hired to common labor, they have not strength to perform it; and thus the country and themselves are happily delivered from the evils to come.

20   I have too long digressed, and therefore shall return to my subject. I think the advantages by the proposal which I have made are obvious and many, as well as of the highest importance.

21   For first, as I have already observed, it would greatly lessen the number of Papists, with whom we are yearly overrun, being the principal breeders of the nation as well as our most dangerous enemies; and who stay at home on purpose to deliver the kingdom to the Pretender, hoping to take their advantage by the absence of so many good Protestants, who have chosen rather to leave their country than to stay at home and pay tithes against their conscience to an Episcopal curate.

22   Secondly, the poorer tenants will have something valuable of their own, which by law may be made liable to distress, and help to pay their landlord's rent, their corn and cattle being already seized and money a thing unknown.

23   Thirdly, whereas the maintenance of an hundred thousand children, from two years old and upwards, cannot be computed at less than ten shillings a piece per annum, the nation's stock will be thereby increased fifty thousand pounds per annum, besides the profit of a new dish introduced to the tables of all gentlemen of fortune in the kingdom who have any refinement in taste. And the money will circulate among ourselves, the goods being entirely of our own growth and manufacture.

24   Fourthly, the constant breeders, besides the gain of eight shillings sterling per annum by the sale of their children, will be rid of the charge of maintaining them after the first year.

25   Fifthly, this food would likewise bring great custom to taverns, where the vintners will certainly be so prudent as to procure the best receipts for dressing it to perfection, and consequently have their houses frequented by all the fine gentlemen, who justly value themselves upon their knowledge in good eating; and a skillful cook, who understands how to oblige his guests, will contrive to make it as expensive as they please.

26   Sixthly, this would be a great inducement to marriage, which all wise nations have either encouraged by rewards or enforced by laws and penalties. It would increase the care and tenderness of mothers toward their children, when they were sure of a settlement for life to the poor babes, provided in some sort by the public, to their annual profit instead of expense. We should see an honest emulation among the married women, which of them could bring the fattest child to the

market. Men would become as fond of their wives during the time of pregnancy as they are now of their mares in foal, their cows in calf, or sows when they are ready to farrow; nor offer to beat or kick them (as is too frequent a practice) for fear of a miscarriage.

Many other advantages might be enumerated. For instance, the addition of 27 some thousand carcasses in our exportation of barreled beef, the propagation of swine's flesh, and improvement in the art of making good bacon, so much wanted among us by the great destruction of pigs, too frequent at our tables, which are no way comparable in taste or magnificence to a well-grown, fat, yearling child, which roasted whole will make a considerable figure at a lord mayor's feast or any other public entertainment. But this and many others I omit, being studious of brevity.

Supposing that one thousand families in this city would be constant customers 28 for infants' flesh, besides others who might have it at merry meetings, particularly weddings and christenings, I compute that Dublin would take off annually about twenty thousand carcasses, and the rest of the kingdom (where probably they will be sold somewhat cheaper) the remaining eighty thousand.

I can think of no one objection that will possibly be raised against this proposal, 29 unless it should be urged that the number of people will be thereby much lessened in the kingdom. This I freely own, and it was indeed one principal design in offering it to the world. I desire the reader will observe; that I calculate my remedy for this one individual kingdom of Ireland and for no other that ever was, is, or I think ever can be upon earth. Therefore, let no man talk to me of other expedients: of taxing our absentees at five shillings a pound: of using neither clothes nor household furniture except what is of our own growth and manufacture: of utterly rejecting the materials and instruments that promote foreign luxury: of curing the expensiveness of pride, vanity, idleness, and gaming in our women: of introducing a vein of parsimony, prudence, and temperance: of learning to love our country, in the want of which we differ even from Laplanders and the inhabitants of Topinamboo: of quitting our animosities and factions, nor acting any longer like the Jews, who were murdering one another at the very moment their city was taken: of being a little cautious not to sell our country and conscience for nothing: of teaching landlords to have at least one degree of mercy toward their tenants: lastly, of putting a spirit of honesty, industry, and skill into our shopkeepers; who, if a resolution could now be taken to buy only our native goods, would immediately unite to cheat and exact upon us in the price, the measure, and the goodness, nor could ever yet be brought to make one fair proposal of just dealing, though often and earnestly invited to it.

Therefore, I repeat, let no man talk to me of these and the like expedients, till 30 he hath at least some glimpse of hope that there will ever be some hearty and sincere attempt to put them in practice.

But as to myself, having been wearied out for many years with offering vain, 31 idle, visionary thoughts, and at length utterly despairing of success, I fortunately fell upon this proposal, which, as it is wholly new, so it hath something solid and real, of no expense and little trouble, full in our own power, and whereby we can incur no danger in disobliging England. For this kind of commodity will not bear exportation, the flesh being of too tender a consistence to admit a long continuance in salt, although perhaps I could name a country which would be glad to eat up our whole nation without it.

After all, I am not so violently bent upon my own opinion as to reject any 32 offer proposed by wise men, which shall be found equally innocent, cheap, easy, and effectual. But before something of that kind shall be advanced in contradiction to my scheme, and offering a better, I desire the author or authors will be pleased maturely to consider two points. First, as things now stand, how they will be able to find food and raiment for an hundred thousand useless mouths and backs. And secondly, there being a round million of creatures in human figure throughout this kingdom, whose sole subsistence put into a common stock would leave them in debt two millions of pounds sterling, adding those who are beggars by profession to the bulk of farmers, cottagers, and laborers, with their wives and children who are beggars in effect; I desire those politicians who dislike my overture, and may perhaps be so bold to attempt an answer, that they will first ask the parents of these mortals whether they would not at this day think it a great happiness to have been sold for food at a year old in this manner I prescribe, and thereby have avoided such a perpetual scene of misfortunes as they have since gone through by the oppression of landlords, the impossibility of paying rent without money or trade, the want of common sustenance, with neither house nor clothes to cover them from the inclemencies of the weather, and the most inevitable prospect of entailing the like or greater miseries upon their breed forever.

33   I profess, in the sincerity of my heart, that I have not the least personal interest in endeavoring to promote this necessary work, having no other motive than the public good of my country, by advancing our trade, providing for infants, relieving the poor, and giving some pleasure to the rich. I have no children by which I can propose to get a single penny; the youngest being nine years old, and my wife past childbearing.

Questions on Meaning

1. Some readers, unfamiliar with satire and perhaps misled by a different use of the English language in another culture almost 300 years ago, read this essay through to the end thinking the author is seriously proposing eating human infants. Indeed, that perfectly serious tone is partly why this essay is so successful and is still read today, as Swift avoids "giving away" the joke by going too far in his exaggeration. Yet even a reader unfamiliar with satire should discern the many ways the essay shows Swift's sympathy with the plight of the poverty-stricken people of whom he writes. Reread the essay and look for several examples of this sympathy.

2. Given the severity of the social problem Swift is reacting to, one might think he should have taken a more direct approach in addressing it. Why do you think Swift chose irony and what does this method add to the meaning of the essay?

Questions on Rhetorical Strategy and Style

1. At what point did you begin to realize the irony of the essay? Reread the first three paragraphs and underline words and phrases that begin to build the satire from the very beginning. How does Swift continue to build the satire gradually up to the proposal itself in paragraph 10?

2. In this form of irony, meaning is apt to be the opposite of what is said. In particular, the "fine gentlemen" and landlords mentioned throughout the essay are not actually being praised. Find as many references as you can in the essay to this ruling class, and consider how they, as cannibals, bear the true brunt of Swift's satire.

3. A prominent characteristic of Swift's style in this essay is his use of detail, such as the exact numbers of children and percentages for breeding, specific recipes and seasonings, and exact monetary values versus costs. What does this specificity contribute to the essay?

4. Find the paragraph near the end of the essay in which Swift reveals his serious suggestions for solving Ireland's problems. How can you tell these are serious, not ironic, proposals?

5. Swift in this essay uses persuasive rhetorical strategies, even though he turns them upside-down with his satire. A persuasive essay may typically describe a problem, offer a solution, explain the benefits of the solution, and argue the superiority of this solution over others. Identify these strategies in Swift's essay and explain how he uses them.

The Westernization of the World

Paul Harrison

Published in 1979, this essay by Paul Harrison, sociologist and Christian ethicist, is concerned with the process and results of European cultural imperialism. It features many examples of the colonial mentality and, Harrison deeply regrets, "growing world uniformity."

"The bourgeoisie has, through its exploitation of the world market, given a cosmopolitan character to production and consumption in every country."

—Karl Marx

1 In Singapore, Peking opera still lives, in the back streets. On Boat Quay, where great barges moor to unload rice from Thailand, raw rubber from Malaysia, or timber from Sumatra, I watched a troupe of traveling actors throw up a canvas-and-wood booth stage, paint on their white faces and lozenge eyes, and don their resplendent vermilion, ultramarine, and gold robes. Then, to raptured audiences of bent old women and little children with perfect circle faces, they enacted tales of feudal princes and magic birds and wars and tragic love affairs, sweeping their sleeves and singing in strange metallic voices.

2 The performance had been paid for by a local cultural society as part of a religious festival. A purple cloth temple had been erected on the quayside, painted papier-mâché sculptures were burning down like giant joss sticks, and middle-aged men were sharing out gifts to be distributed among members' families: red buckets, roast ducks, candies, and moon cakes. The son of the organizer, a fashionable young man in Italian shirt and gold-rimmed glasses, was looking on with amused benevolence. I asked him why old people and children were watching the show.

3 "Young people don't like these operas," he said. "They are too old fashioned. We would prefer to see a high-quality Western variety show, something like that."

4 He spoke for a whole generation. Go to almost any village in the Third World and you will find youths who scorn traditional dress and sport denims and T-shirts. Go into any bank and the tellers will be dressed as would their European counterparts; at night the manager will climb into his car and go home to watch TV in a home that would not stick out on a European or North American estate. Every capital city in the world is getting to look like every other; it is Marshall McLuhan's global village, but the style is exclusively Western. And not just in consumer fashions: the mimicry extends to architecture, industrial technology, approaches to health care, education, and housing.

5 To the ethnocentric Westerner or the Westernized local, that may seem the most natural thing in the world. That is modern life, they might think. That is the way it will all be one day. That is what development and economic growth are all about.

Yet the dispassionate observer can only be puzzled by this growing world 6
uniformity. Surely one should expect more diversity, more indigenous styles and
models of development. Why is almost everyone following virtually the same
European road? The Third World's obsession with the Western way of life has
perverted development and is rapidly destroying good and bad in traditional
cultures, flinging the baby out with the bathwater. It is the most totally pervasive
example of what historians call cultural diffusion in the history of mankind.

Its origins, of course, lie in the colonial experience. European rule was 7
something quite different from the general run of conquests. Previous invaders
more often than not settled down in their new territories, interbred, and assimilated
a good deal of local culture. Not so the Europeans. Some, like the Iberians or the
Dutch, were not averse to cohabitation with native women; unlike the British, they
seemed free of purely racial prejudice. But all the Europeans suffered from the
same cultural arrogance. Perhaps it is the peculiar self-righteousness of Pauline
Christianity that accounts for this trait. Whatever the cause, never a doubt entered
their minds that native cultures could be in any way, materially, morally, or
spiritually, superior to their own, and that the supposedly benighted inhabitants
of the darker continents needed enlightening.

And so there grew up, alongside political and economic imperialism, that more 8
insidious form of control—cultural imperialism. It conquered not just the bodies,
but the souls of its victims, turning them into willing accomplices.

Cultural imperialism began its conquest of the Third World with the 9
indoctrination of an elite of local collaborators. The missionary schools sought
to produce converts to Christianity who would go out and proselytize among their
own people, helping to eradicate traditional culture. Later the government schools
aimed to turn out a class of junior bureaucrats and lower military officers who
would help to exploit and repress their own people. The British were subtle about
this, since they wanted the natives, even the Anglicized among them, to keep their
distance. The French, and the Portuguese in Africa, explicitly aimed at the
"assimilation" of gifted natives, by which was meant their metamorphosis into
model Frenchmen and Lusitanians, distinguishable only by the tint of their skin.

The second channel of transmission was more indirect and voluntary. It worked 10
by what sociologists call reference-group behavior, found when someone copies
the habits and lifestyle of a social group he wishes to belong to, or to be classed
with, and abandons those of his own group. This happened in the West when the
new rich of early commerce and industry aped the nobility they secretly aspired
to join. Not surprisingly the social climbers in the colonies started to mimic their
conquerors. The returned slaves who carried the first wave of Westernization in
West Africa wore black woolen suits and starched collars in the heat of the dry
season. The new officer corps of India were molded into what the Indian writer
Nirad Chaudhuri has called "imitation, polo-playing English subalterns," complete
with waxed mustaches and peacock chests. The elite of Indians, adding their own
caste-consciousness to the class-consciousness of their rulers, became more British
than the British (and still are).

There was another psychological motive for adopting Western ways, deriving 11
from the arrogance and haughtiness of the colonialists. As the Martiniquan political
philosopher, Frantz Fanon, remarked, colonial rule was an experience in racial
humiliation. Practically every leader of the newly independent state could recall
some experience such as being turned out of a club or manhandled on the street
by whites, often of low status. The local elite were made to feel ashamed of their
color and of their culture. "I began to suffer from not being a white man," Fanon

wrote, "to the degree that the white man imposes discrimination on me, makes me a colonized native, robs me of all worth, all individuality. . . . Then I will quite simply try to make myself white: that is, I will compel the white man to acknowledge that I am human." To this complex Fanon attributes the colonized natives' constant preoccupation with attracting the attention of the white man, becoming powerful like the white man, proving at all costs that blacks too can be civilized. Given the racism and culturism of the whites, this could only be done by succeeding in their terms, and by adopting their ways.

12   This desire to prove equality surely helps to explain why Ghana's Nkrumah built the huge stadium and triumphal arch of Black Star Square in Accra. Why the tiny native village of Ivory Coast president Houphouët-Boigny has been graced with a four-lane motorway starting and ending nowhere, a fivestar hotel and ultramodern conference center. Why Sukarno transformed Indonesia's capital, Jakarta, into an exercise in gigantism, scarred with sixlane highways and neofascist monuments in the most hideous taste. The aim was not only to show the old imperialists, but to impress other Third World leaders in the only way everyone would recognize: the Western way.

13   The influence of Western lifestyles spread even to those few nations who escaped the colonial yoke. By the end of the nineteenth century, the elites of the entire non-Western world were taking Europe as their reference group. The progress of the virus can be followed visibly in a room of Topkapi, the Ottoman palace in Istanbul, where a sequence of showcases display the costumes worn by each successive sultan. They begin with kaftans and turbans. Slowly elements of Western military uniform creep in, until the last sultans are decked out in brocade, epaulettes, and cocked hats.

14   The root of the problem with nations that were never colonized, like Turkey, China, and Japan, was probably their consciousness of Western military superiority. The beating of these three powerful nations at the hands of the West was a humiliating, traumatic experience. For China and Japan, the encounter with the advanced military technology of the industrialized nations was as terrifying as an invasion of extraterrestrials. Europe's earlier discovery of the rest of the world had delivered a mild culture shock to her ethnocentric attitudes. The Orient's contact with Europe shook nations to the foundations, calling into question the roots of their civilizations and all the assumptions and institutions on which their lives were based.

15   In all three nations groups of Young Turks grew up, believing that their countries could successfully take on the West only if they adopted Western culture, institutions, and even clothing, for all these ingredients were somehow involved in the production of Western technology. As early as the 1840s, Chinese intellectuals were beginning to modify the ancient view that China was in all respects the greatest civilization in the world. The administrator Wei Yüan urged his countrymen to "learn the superior technology of the barbarians in order to control them." But the required changes could not be confined to the technical realm. Effectiveness in technology is the outcome of an entire social system. "Since we were knocked out by cannon balls," wrote M. Chiang, "naturally we became interested in them, thinking that by learning to make them we could strike back. From studying cannon balls we came to mechanical inventions which in turn lead to political reforms, which lead us again to the political philosophies of the West." The republican revolution of 1911 attempted to modernize China, but her subjection to the West continued until another Young Turk, Mao Tse-tung, applied that alternative brand of Westernization: communism, though in a unique adaptation.

The Japanese were forced to open their border to Western goods in 1853, 16 after a couple of centuries of total isolation. They had to rethink fast in order to survive. From 1867, the Meiji rulers Westernized Japan with astonishing speed, adopting Western science, technology, and even manners: short haircuts became the rule, ballroom dancing caught on, and *moningku* with *haikara* (morning coats and high collars) were worn. The transformation was so successful that by the 1970s the Japanese were trouncing the West at its own game. But they had won their economic independence at the cost of losing their cultural autonomy.

Turkey, defeated in the First World War, her immense empire in fragments, 17 set about transforming herself under that compulsive and ruthless Westernizer, Kemal Atatürk. The Arabic script was abolished and replaced with the Roman alphabet. Kemal's strange exploits as a hatter will probably stand as the symbol of Westernization carried to absurd lengths. His biographer, Lord Kinross, relates that while traveling in the West as a young man, the future president had smarted under Western insults and condescension about the Turkish national hat, the fez. Later, he made the wearing of the fez a criminal offense. "The people of the Turkish republic," he said in a speech launching the new policy, "must prove that they are civilized and advanced persons in their outward respect also. . . . A civilized, international dress is worthy and appropriate for our nation and we will wear it. Boots or shoes on our feet, trousers on our legs, shirt and tie, jacket and waistcoat— and, of course, to complete these, a cover with a brim on our heads. I want to make this clear. This head covering is called a hat."

Questions about Meaning

1. What are the negative effects of cultural assimilation (of one country's people adopting the culture of another country's people)? Do these outweigh the positive effects of "westernization"?

2. According to the article, why is western culture so attractive to people from other countries even when it is clearly not appropriate, like in the examples in paragraphs 10 and 12?

3. How do Harrison's language and tone—for example, his use of the words "virus" or "perversion"—reflect his attitude?

4. Harrison describes three different kinds of imperialism: political, economic and cultural. Which does he think is the most damaging to societies around the world? Why?

Questions about Rhetorical Strategy and Style

1. How does Harrison introduce his article? Is it effective?

2. What is the effect of the final example Harrison provides in paragraph 17?

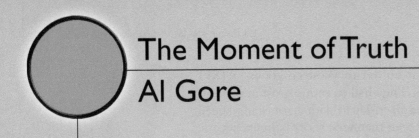

The Moment of Truth

Al Gore

The author was the Vice-President of the United States from 1993 to 2001. He won the Nobel Peace Prize in 2007 for his campaign to raise awareness of climate change. This essay first appeared in Vanity Fair *in 2006.*

1 Clichés are, by definition, over used. But here is a rare exception—a certifiable cliché that warrants more exposure, because it carries meaning deeply relevant to the biggest challenge our civilization has ever confronted. The Chinese expression for "crisis" consists of two characters: 危機. The first is a symbol for "danger"; the second is a symbol for "opportunity."

2 The rapid accumulation of global-warming pollution in the Earth's atmosphere is now confronting human civilization with a crisis like no other we have ever encountered. This climate crisis is, indeed, extremely dangerous, but it also presents unprecedented opportunities. Before we can get to the opportunities, however, it is crucial to define the danger, and to discuss how it is that we in the United States seem to be having such difficulty perceiving that danger.

危

3 The climate crisis may at times appear to be happening slowly, but in fact it is a true planetary emergency. The voluminous evidence suggests strongly that, unless we act boldly and quickly to deal with the causes of global warming, our world will likely experience a string of catastrophes, including deadlier Hurricane Katrinas° in both the Atlantic and Pacific."

4 We are melting virtually all of the mountain glaciers in the world—including those in the Rockies, the Sierras, the Andes, and the Alps—and, more ominously, the massive ice field on the roof of the world, on the enormous Tibetan Plateau, which has 100 times more ice than the Alps, and which supplies up to half of the drinking water of 40 percent of the world's people, through seven river systems that all originate there: the Indus, the Ganges, the Brahmaputra, the Salween, the Mekong, the Yangtze and the Yellow.

5 Even more important, we are rapidly melting the vast, but relatively thin, floating ice cap that covers the Arctic Ocean. For the first time, scientists are finding significant numbers of polar bears that have died by drowning, as the distance from the shores of the Arctic to the edge of the ice cap has stretched in places to 60 kilometers or more. At present, the North Polar cap helps to cool the planet by reflecting the vast majority of the sunlight that hits the Arctic during six months of the year. It is like a gigantic mirror larger than the entire United States. But the growing areas of open water left as the ice cap melts are absorbing the vast majority of the energy coming from the Sun, raising temperatures at the top of our planet far more rapidly than anywhere else.

We are beginning to melt—and possibly de-stabilize—the enormous, 10,000-   6
foot-thick mound of ice on top of Greenland and the equally enormous mass of
ice of West Antarctica, which is propped up precariously against the tops of islands,
poised to slip into the sea. Either of these massive, land-based ice sheets would, if
it melted or broke up and slid into the ocean, raise the sea level worldwide by
more than 20 feet. The largest ice mass of all on the planet—East Antarctica—was
long thought to be still growing. Until recently, that is, when a new, in-depth
scientific survey showed that it, too, may be beginning to melt.

Since the entire climate system of Earth is formed by the planetwide pattern   7
of wind and ocean currents, which redistribute heat from the tropics to the poles,
there is growing concern that the relatively stable pattern that has persisted for
11,000 years—since the last ice age and before the first appearance of cities—
may now be on the verge of radical and disruptive changes. The Gulf Stream, the
monsoon cycle in the Indian Ocean, the El Niño/La Niña cycle in the Eastern
Pacific, and the jet streams, among the other circulatory phenomena, are all at
risk of being pushed into new and unfamiliar patterns.

Global warming, together with the cutting and burning of forests and the   8
destruction of other critical habitats, is causing the loss of living species at a rate
comparable to that of the extinction of dinosaurs 65 million years ago. Most
scientists theorize that that event, by the way, was caused by a giant asteroid
colliding with the Earth. This time it is not an asteroid wreaking havoc; it is us.
We are recklessly dumping so much carbon dioxide into the Earth's atmosphere
that we have literally changed the relationship between the Earth and the Sun,
altering the balance of energy between our planet and the rest of the universe, so
the buildup of heat energy that should be re-radiated by the Earth is beginning to
wilt, melt, dry out, and parch delicate components of the planet's living systems.

More than 70 percent of the planet's surface is covered by ocean, and a series   9
of new, comprehensive studies show that the amount of CO_2 being absorbed into
the oceans is about one-third of what we have put into the environment with the
burning of fossil fuels. As a result, the oceans of the world are becoming more
acid, and the total amount of carbonic acid—even though it is a relatively weak
acid—is beginning to change the mix of carbonate and bicarbonate ions in the
oceans. This interferes with the ability of corals to form their calcium-carbonate
skeletons, which constitute the base of many food chains in the oceans. Even more
ominously, the amounts of carbonic acid we are continuing to sink into the oceans
will, if we don't change the current reckless pattern, make it more difficult for
many ocean creatures, large and tiny, to make shells, because the shells would
instantly dissolve in the newly acid ocean water, the way chalk (also calcium
carbonate) dissolves in vinegar. Continuing on our current path will return the
oceans to a chemical pH balance that last existed 300 million years ago—when
the Earth was a very different planet from the one that gave birth to and nurtured
the human species.

All of this, incredibly, could be set in motion in the lifetime of the children   10
already living—unless we act boldly and quickly. Even more incredibly, some of
the leading scientific experts are now telling us that without dramatic changes we
are in grave danger of crossing a point of no return within the next ten years! So
the message is unmistakable. This crisis means danger!

But in order to move through the danger to seize the opportunity, we have first   11
to recognize that we are in fact facing a crisis. So why is it that our leaders seem
not to hear such clarion° warnings? Are they resisting the truth because they know
that the moment they acknowledge it they will face a moral imperative to act? Is

it simply more convenient to ignore the warnings? Perhaps, but inconvenient truths do not go away just because they are not seen. Indeed, when they are not responded to, their significance doesn't diminish; it grows.

12   For example, the Bush administration was warned on August 6, 2001, of an attack by al-Qaeda: "Bin Ladin Determined to Strike in US," said the intelligence community in a message so important that it was the headline of the president's daily briefing that day, five weeks before the attacks of September 11. Didn't he see that clear warning? Why were no questions asked, meetings called, evidence marshaled, clarifications sought?

13   The Bible says, "Where there is no vision, the people perish."

14   Four Augusts later, as Hurricane Katrina was roaring across the unusually warm water of the Gulf of Mexico and growing into a deadly monster that was less than two days away from slamming into New Orleans, the administration received another clear warning: the levees—which had been built to protect the city against smaller, less powerful hurricanes—were in grave danger. But once again an urgent warning was ignored. The videotapes of one session make clear that the president heard the warnings but, again, asked not a single question.

15   This is not a partisan analysis. A recent report by Republicans in the House of Representatives called the White House reaction a "blinding lack of situational awareness." Republican representative Tom Davis of Virginia, the chairman of the House Committee on Government Reform, which produced the report, added, "The White House failed to act on the massive amounts of information at its disposal." Coupled with "disjointed decision making," the report continued, the president's failure to see the danger "needlessly compounded and prolonged Katrina's horror."

16   Where there is a blinding lack of situational awareness, the people perish.

17   Nearly 70 years ago, when a horrible and unprecedented storm of another kind was gathering in Europe, British prime minister Neville Chamberlain[0] found it inconvenient to see the truth about the nature of the evil threat posed by the Nazis. In criticizing his government's blinding lack of awareness, Winston Churchill[0] said, "So they go on in strange paradox, decided only to be undecided, resolved to be irresolute, adamant for drift, solid for fluidity, all-powerful to be impotent." After the appeasement° at Munich, Churchill said, "This is only the first sip, the first foretaste, of a bitter cup which will be proffered to us year by year—unless by supreme recovery of moral health and martial vigor we rise again and take our stand for freedom." Then he warned prophetically that "the era of procrastination, of half measures, of soothing and baffling expedients, of delays, is coming to a close. In its place, we are entering a period of consequences."

18   Today, there are dire warnings that the worst catastrophe in the history of human civilization is bearing down on us, gathering strength as it comes. And these warnings have also been met with a blinding lack of awareness, by the Congress as well as by the administration.

19   After the tragedy of Hurricane Katrina, many Americans now believe that we have entered a period of consequences—that Katrina, as horrible as it was, may have been the first sip of a bitter cup which will be proffered to us over and over again until we act on the truth we have wished would go away. And they are beginning to demand that the administration open its eyes and look at the truth, no matter how inconvenient it might be for all of us—not least for the special interests that want us to ignore global warming.

20   As Abraham Lincoln° said during our time of greatest trial, "We must disenthrall° ourselves, and then we shall save our country." America is beginning to awaken. And now we will save our planet.

機

So it is time for the good news: we can solve this crisis, and as we finally do 21
accept the truth of our situation and turn to boldly face down the danger that is
stalking us, we will find that it is also bringing us unprecedented opportunity. I'm
not referring just to new jobs and new profits, though there will be plenty of both.
Today we have all the technologies we need to start the fight against global
warming. We can build clean engines. We can harness the sun and wind. We can
stop wasting energy. We can use the Earth's plentiful coal resources without heating
the planet.

The procrastinators and deniers would have us believe that this will be painful 22
and impossibly expensive. But in recent years dozens of companies have cut
emissions of heat-trapping gases and saved money. Some of the world's largest
companies are moving aggressively to capture the enormous economic
opportunities in a clean-energy future.

But there's something far more precious than the economic gains that will be 23
made. This crisis is bringing us an opportunity to experience what few generations
in history ever have had the privilege of knowing: a generational mission; the
exhilaration of a compelling moral purpose; a shared and unifying cause; the thrill
of being forced by circumstances to put aside the pettiness and conflict that so
often stifle the restless human need for transcendence; the opportunity to rise.

When we do rise, it will fill our spirits and bind us together. Those who are 24
now suffocating in cynicism and despair will be able to breathe freely. Those who
are now suffering from a loss of meaning in their lives will find hope. When we
rise, we will experience an epiphany as we discover that this crisis is not really
about politics at all. It is a moral and spiritual challenge.

What is at stake is the survival of our civilization and the habitability of the 25
Earth. Or as one eminent scientist put it, the pending question is whether an
opposable thumb and a neocortex° are a viable combination on this planet.

The new understanding we will gain—about who we really are—will give us 26
the moral capacity to comprehend the true nature of other, related challenges that
are also desperately in need of being defined as moral imperatives with practical
solutions: HIV/AIDS and other pandemics that are ravaging large parts of
humankind, global poverty, the ongoing redistribution of the world's wealth from
the poor to the rich, the ongoing genocide in Darfur, famines in other parts of
Africa, chronic civil wars, the destruction of ocean fisheries, families that don't
function, communities that don't commune, the erosion of democracy in America,
and the re-feudalization of the public forum.

Consider once again what happened during the crisis of global Fascism°. When 27
England and then America and our allies ultimately did rise to meet the threat, we
won two wars simultaneously, in Europe and in the Pacific. And by the end of
those terrible wars, the Allies had gained the moral authority and vision to create
the Marshall Plan°—and persuade the taxpayers to pay for it! They had gained
the spiritual capacity and wisdom to rebuild Japan and Europe and launch the
renewal of the very nations they had just defeated in the war. In the process, they
laid the foundation for 50 years of peace and prosperity. One of their commanders,
General Omar Bradley, said at the end of World War II, "It is time we steered by
the stars and not by the lights of each passing ship."

And now so must we. For this, too, is a critical moment. Ultimately, it is not 28
about any scientific discussion or political dialogue; it is about who we are as
human beings. It is about our capacity to transcend our limitations, to rise to this
new occasion. To see with our hearts, as well as our heads, the response that is
now called for. This is a moral, ethical, and spiritual challenge.

29   Just as we can no longer ignore this challenge, neither should we fear it. Instead, we should welcome it. Both the danger and the opportunity. And then we will meet it because we must. We have accepted and met other great challenges in the past. We declared our liberty and then won it We designed a new form of government. We freed the slaves. We gave women the right to vote. We took on Jim Crow° and segregation. We cured polio and helped eradicate smallpox, we landed on the moon, we brought down Communism, and we helped end apartheid. We even solved a global environmental crisis—the hole in the stratospheric ozone layer—because Republicans and Democrats, rich nations and poor nations, businessmen and scientists, all came together to shape a solution.

30   And now we face a crisis with unprecedented danger that also presents an opportunity like no other. As we rise to meet this historic challenge, it promises us prosperity, common purpose, and the renewal of our moral authority.

31   We should not wait. We cannot wait. We must not wait.

32   The only thing missing is political will. But in our democracy, political will is a renewable resource.

Questions about Meaning

1. What is the cliché that Gore says is "deeply relevant to the biggest challenge our civilization has ever encountered"? Why does he seem somewhat uncomfortable about using the cliché?

2. Why, according to the author, does the United States, "have such difficulty perceiving that danger" the essay is about?

3. What does the scientist Gore refers to in paragraph 25 mean by saying "the pending question is whether an opposable thumb and a neocortex are a viable combination on this planet"?

Questions about Rhetorical Strategy and Style

1. What role is the author assuming by quoting the Hebrew Bible, "Where there is no vision the people perish"? Explain.

2. Why does Gore mention the warning the Bush administration was given on August 6, 201 about a possible al-Qaeda attack on the U.S.? Is he simply trying to embarrass the man who defeated him in the contested 2000 presidential election? What in the essay indicates his purpose?

Behind the Formaldehyde Curtain

Jessica Mitford

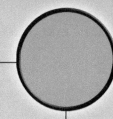

Jessica Mitford (1917–1996) was born in England, a member of the gentry. In 1939, she immigrated to the United States, where she became a communist and a naturalized citizen. Mitford is known for her sharp exposés of American institutions—such as funeral homes, television, prisons, diet camps, and the Famous Writers' School. She was published widely, including major nonfiction works, such as Kind and Usual Punishment: The Prison Business *(1973) and* The Trial of Dr. Spock *(1970); an anthology of her articles,* Poison Penmanship: The Gentle Art of Muckracking *(1979); two autobiographies, including* Daughters and Rebels *(1960); and various memoirs, such as* Grace Had an English Heart: The Story of Grace Darling, Heroine and Victorian Superstar *(1988). Mitford achieved literary notoriety in 1963, at age 46, when* The American Way of Death, *a ruthless attack on the funeral business, was published. This essay, which came from that book, illustrates her trademark trenchant black humor.*

The drama begins to unfold with the arrival of the corpse at the mortuary. 1

Alas, poor Yorick! How surprised he would be to see how his counterpart of 2 today is whisked off to a funeral parlor and is in short order sprayed, sliced, pierced, pickled, trussed, trimmed, creamed, waxed, painted, rouged and neatly dressed— transformed from a common corpse into a Beautiful Memory Picture. This process is known in the trade as embalming and restorative art and is so universally employed in the United States and Canada that the funeral director does it routinely, without consulting corpse or kin. He regards as eccentric those few who are hardy enough to suggest that it might be dispensed with. Yet no law requires embalming, no religious doctrine commends it, nor is it dictated by considerations of health, sanitation, or even of personal daintiness. In no part of the world but in North America is it widely used. The purpose of embalming is to make the corpse presentable for viewing in a suitably costly container; and here too the funeral director routinely, without first consulting the family, prepares the body for public display.

Is all this legal? The processes to which a dead body may be subjected are 3 after all to some extent circumscribed by law. In most states, for instance, the signature of next of kin must be obtained before an autopsy may be performed, before the deceased may be cremated, before the body may be turned over to a medical school for research purposes; or such provision must be made in the decedent's will. In the case of embalming, no such permission is required nor is it ever sought. A textbook, *The Principles and Practices of Embalming*, comments on this: "There is some question regarding the legality of much that is done within the preparation room." The author points out that it would be most unusual for a responsible member of a bereaved family to instruct the mortician, in so many words, to "embalm" the body of a deceased relative. The very term *embalming* is so seldom used that the mortician must rely upon custom in the matter. The author concludes that unless the family specifies otherwise, the act of entrusting the body to the care of a funeral establishment carries with it an implied permission to go ahead and embalm.

4   Embalming is indeed a most extraordinary procedure, and one must wonder at the docility of Americans who each year pay hundreds of millions of dollars for its perpetuation, blissfully ignorant of what it is all about, what is done, how it is done. Not one in ten thousand has any idea of what actually takes place. Books on the subject are extremely hard to come by. They are not to be found in most libraries or bookshops.

5   In an era when huge television audiences watch surgical operations in the comfort of their living rooms, when, thanks to the animated cartoon, the geography of the digestive system has become familiar territory even to the nursery school set, in a land where the satisfaction of curiosity about almost all matters is a national pastime, the secrecy surrounding embalming can, surely, hardly be attributed to the inherent gruesomeness of the subject. Custom in this regard has within this century suffered a complete reversal. In the early days of American embalming, when it was performed in the home of the deceased, it was almost mandatory for some relative to stay by the embalmer's side and witness the procedure. Today, family members who might wish to be in attendance would certainly be dissuaded by the funeral director. All others, except apprentices, are excluded by law from the preparation room.

6   A close look at what does actually take place may explain in large measure the undertaker's intractable reticence concerning a procedure that has become his major *raison d'être*. Is it possible he fears that public information about embalming might lead patrons to wonder if they really want this service? If the funeral men are loath to discuss the subject outside the trade, the reader may, understandably, be equally loath to go on reading at this point. For those who have the stomach for it, let us part the formaldehyde curtain. . . .

7   The body is first laid out in the undertaker's morgue—or rather, Mr. Jones is reposing in the preparation room—to be readied to bid the world farewell.

8   The preparation room in any of the better funeral establishments has the tiled and sterile look of a surgery, and indeed the embalmer-restorative artist who does his chores there is beginning to adopt the term "dermasurgeon" (appropriately corrupted by some mortician-writers as "demi-surgeon") to describe his calling. His equipment, consisting of scalpels, scissors, augers, forceps, clamps, needles, pumps, tubes, bowls and basins, is crudely imitative of the surgeon's, as is his technique, acquired in a nine- or twelve-month post-high school course in an embalming school. He is supplied by an advanced chemical industry with a bewildering array of fluids, sprays, pastes, oils, powders, creams, to fix or soften tissue, shrink or distend it as needed, dry it here, restore the moisture there. There are cosmetics, waxes and paints to fill and cover features, even plaster of Paris to replace entire limbs. There are ingenious aids to prop and stabilize the cadaver: A Vari-Pose Head Rest, the Edwards Arm and Hand Positioner, the Repose Block (to support the shoulders during the embalming), and the Throop Foot Positioner, which resembles an old-fashioned stocks.

9   Mr. John H. Eckels, president of the Eckels College of Mortuary Science, thus describes the first part of the embalming procedure: "In the hands of a skilled

practitioner, this work may be done in a comparatively short time and without mutilating the body other than by slight incision—so slight that it scarcely would cause serious inconvenience if made upon a living person. It is necessary to remove the blood, and doing this not only helps in the disinfecting, but removes the principal cause of disfigurements due to discoloration."

Another textbook discusses the all-important time element: "The earlier this 10 is done, the better, for every hour that elapses between death and embalming will add to the problems and complications encountered. . . ." Just how soon should one get going on the embalming? The author tells us, "On the basis of such scanty information made available to this profession through its rudimentary and haphazard system of technical research, we must conclude that the best results are to be obtained if the subject is embalmed before life is completely extinct—that is, before cellular death has occurred. In the average case, this would mean within an hour after somatic death." For those who feel that there is something a little rudimentary, not to say haphazard, about this advice, a comforting thought is offered by another writer. Speaking of fears entertained in early days of premature burial, he points out, "One of the effects of embalming by chemical injection, however, has been to dispel fears of live burial." How true; once the blood is removed, chances of live burial are indeed remote.

To return to Mr. Jones, the blood is drained out through the veins and replaced 11 by embalming fluid pumped in through the arteries. As noted in *The Principles and Practices of Embalming*, "every operator has a favorite injection and drainage point— a fact which becomes a handicap only if he fails or refuses to forsake his favorites when conditions demand it." Typical favorites are the carotid artery, femoral artery, jugular vein, subclavian vein. There are various choices of embalming fluid. If Flextone is used, it will produce a "mild, flexible rigidity. The skin retains a velvety softness, the tissues are rubbery and pliable. Ideal for women and children." It may be blended with B. and G. Products Company's Lyf-Lyk tint, which is guaranteed to reproduce "nature's own skin texture . . . the velvety appearance of living tissue." Suntone comes in three separate tints: Suntan; Special Cosmetic Tint, a pink shade "especially indicated for female subjects"; and Regular Cosmetic Tint, moderately pink.

About three to six gallons of a dyed and perfumed solution of formaldehyde, 12 glycerin, borax, phenol, alcohol and water is soon circulating through Mr. Jones, whose mouth has been sewn together with a "needle directed upward between the upper lip and gum and brought out through the left nostril," with the corners raised slightly "for a more pleasant expression." If he should be bucktoothed, his teeth are cleaned with Bon Ami and coated with colorless nail polish. His eyes, meanwhile, are closed with flesh-tinted eye caps and eye cement.

The next step is to have at Mr. Jones with a thing called a trocar. This is a 13 long, hollow needle attached to a tube. It is jabbed into the abdomen, poked around the entrails and chest cavity, the contents of which are pumped out and replaced with "cavity fluid." This done, and the hole in the abdomen sewn up, Mr. Jones's face is heavily creamed (to protect the skin from burns which may be caused by leakage of the chemicals), and he is covered with a sheet and left unmolested for a while. But not for long—there is more, much more, in store for him. He has been embalmed, but not yet restored, and the best time to start the restorative work is eight to ten hours after embalming, when the tissues have become firm and dry.

The object of all this attention to the corpse, it must be remembered, is to 14 make it presentable for viewing in an attitude of healthy repose. "Our customs require the presentation of our dead in the semblance of normality . . . unmarred by the ravages of illness, disease or mutilation," says Mr. J. Sheridan Mayer in his *Restorative Art*. This is rather a large order since few people die in the full bloom of health, unravaged by illness and unmarked by some disfigurement. The funeral industry is equal to the challenge: "In some cases the gruesome appearance of a mutilated or disease-ridden subject may be quite discouraging. The task of restoration may seem impossible and shake the confidence of the embalmer. This is the time for intestinal fortitude and determination. Once the formative work is begun and affected tissues are cleaned or removed, all doubts of success vanish. It is surprising and gratifying to discover the results which may be obtained."

15   The embalmer, having allowed an appropriate interval to elapse, returns to the attack, but now he brings into play the skill and equipment of sculptor and cosmetician. Is a hand missing? Casting one in plaster of Paris is a simple matter. "For replacement purposes, only a cast of the back of the hand is necessary; this is within the ability of the average operator and is quite adequate." If a lip or two, a nose or an ear should be missing, the embalmer has at hand a variety of restorative waxes with which to model replacements. Pores and skin texture are simulated by stippling with a little brush, and over this cosmetics are laid on. Head off? Decapitation cases are rather routinely handled. Ragged edges are trimmed, and head joined to torso with a series of splints, wires and sutures. It is a good idea to have a little something at the neck— a scarf or a high collar—when time for viewing comes. Swollen mouth: Cut out tissue as needed from inside the lips. If too much is removed, the surface contour can easily be restored by padding with cotton. Swollen necks and cheeks are reduced by removing tissue through vertical incisions made down each side of the neck. "When the deceased is casketed, the pillow will hide the suture incisions. . . . As an extra precaution against leakage, the suture may be painted with liquid sealer."

16   The opposite condition is more likely to present itself—that of emaciation. His hypodermic syringe now loaded with massage cream, the embalmer seeks out and fills the hollowed and sunken areas by injection. In this procedure the backs of the hands and fingers and the under-chin area should not be neglected.

17   Positioning the lips is a problem that recurrently challenges the ingenuity of the embalmer. Closed too tightly, they tend to give a stern, even disapproving expression. Ideally, embalmers feel, the lips should give the impression of being ever so slightly parted, the upper lip protruding slightly for a more youthful appearance. This takes some engineering, however, as the lips tend to drift apart. Lip drift can sometimes be remedied by pushing one or two straight pins through the inner margin of the lower lip and then inserting them between the two front upper teeth. If Mr. Jones happens to have no teeth, the pins can just as easily be anchored in his Armstrong Face Former and Denture Replacer. Another method to maintain lip closure is to dislocate the lower jaw, which is then held in its new position by a wire run through holes which have been drilled through the upper and lower jaws at the midline. As the French are fond of saying, *il faut souffrir pour être belle* (you have to suffer to be beautiful).

18   If Mr. Jones had died of jaundice, the embalming fluid will very likely turn him green. Does this deter the embalmer? Not if he has intestinal fortitude. Masking pastes and cosmetics are heavily laid on, burial garments and casket interiors are color-correlated with particular care, and Jones is displayed beneath rose-colored lights. Friends will say "How *well* he looks." Death by carbon monoxide, on the other hand, can be rather a good thing from the embalmer's viewpoint: "One advantage is the fact that this type of discoloration is an exaggerated form of a natural pink coloration." This is nice because the healthy glow is already present and needs but little attention.

The patching and filling completed, Mr. Jones is now shaved, washed and   19
dressed. Cream-based cosmetic, available in pink, flesh, suntan, brunette and
blond, is applied to his hands and face, his hair is shampooed and combed (and,
in the case of Mrs. Jones, set), his hands manicured. For the horny-handed son of
toil special care must be taken; cream should be applied to remove ingrained grime,
and the nails cleaned. "If he were not in the habit of having them manicured in life,
trimming and shaping is advised for appearance—never questioned by kin."

Jones is now ready for casketing (this is the present participle of the verb "to   20
casket"). In this operation his right shoulder should be depressed slightly "to turn
the body a bit to the right and soften the appearance of lying flat on the back."
Positioning the hands is a matter of importance, and special rubber positioning
blocks may be used. The hands should be cupped slightly for a more lifelike,
relaxed appearance. Proper placement of the body requires a delicate sense of
balance. It should lie as high as possible in the casket, yet not so high that the lid,
when lowered, will hit the nose. On the other hand, we are cautioned, placing the
body too low "creates the impression that the body is in a box."

Jones is next wheeled into the appointed slumber room where a few last touches   21
may be added—his favorite pipe placed in his hand or, if he was a great reader, a
book propped into position. (In the case of little Master Jones a Teddy bear may
be clutched.) Here he will hold open house for a few days, visiting hours 10 a.m.
to 9 p.m.

All now being in readiness, the funeral director calls a staff conference to make   22
sure that each assistant knows his precise duties. Mr. Wilber Kriege writes "This
makes your staff feel that they are a part of the team, with a definite assignment
that must be properly carried out if the whole plan is to succeed. You never heard
of a football coach who failed to talk to his entire team before they go on the field.
They have drilled on the plays they are to execute for hours and days, and yet the
successful coach knows the importance of making even the bench-warming third-
string substitute feel that he is important if the game is to be won." The winning
of *this* game is predicated upon glass-smooth handling of the logistics. The funeral
director has notified the pallbearers whose names were furnished by the family, has
arranged for the presence of clergyman, organist, and soloist, has provided
transportation for everybody, has organized and listed the flowers sent by friends.
In *Psychology of Funeral Service* Mr. Edward A. Martin points out: "He may not
always do as much as the family thinks he is doing, but it is his helpful guidance
that they appreciate in knowing they are proceeding as they should. . . . The
important thing is how well his services can be used to make the family believe they
are giving unlimited expression to their own sentiment."

The religious service may be held in a church or in the chapel of the funeral   23
home; the funeral director vastly prefers the latter arrangement, for not only is it
more convenient for him but it affords him the opportunity to show off his
beautiful facilities to the gathered mourners. After the clergyman has had his say,
the mourners queue up to file past the casket for a last look at the deceased. The
family is *never* asked whether they want an open-casket ceremony; in the absence
of their instruction to the contrary, this is taken for granted. Consequently, well
over 90 percent of all American funerals feature the open casket—a custom
unknown in other parts of the world. Foreigners are astonished by it. An English
woman living in San Francisco described her reaction in a letter to the writer:

> I myself have attended only one funeral here—that of an elderly fellow
> worker of mine. After the service I could not understand why everyone
> was walking towards the coffin (sorry, I mean casket), but thought I had

better fellow the crowd. It shook me rigid to get there and find the casket open and poor old Oscar lying there in his brown tweed suit, wearing a suntan makeup and just the wrong shade of lipstick. If I had not been extremely fond of the old boy, I have a horrible feeling that I might have giggled. Then and there I decided that I could never face another American funeral—even dead.

24   The casket (which has been resting throughout the service on a Classic Beauty Ultra Metal Casket Bier) is now transferred by a hydraulically operated device called Porto-Lift to a balloon-tired, Glide Easy casket carriage which will wheel it to yet another conveyance, the Cadillac Funeral Coach. This may be lavender, cream, light green— anything but black. Interiors, of course, are color-correlated, "for the man who cannot stop short of perfection."

25   At graveside, the casket is lowered into the earth. This office, once the prerogative of friends of the deceased, is now performed by a patented mechanical lowering device. A "Lifetime Green" artificial grass mat is at the ready to conceal the sere earth, and overhead, to conceal the sky, is a portable Steril Chapel Tent ("resists the intense heat and humidity of summer and the terrific storms of winter . . . available in Silver Grey, Rose or Evergreen"). Now is the time for the ritual scattering of earth over the coffin, as the solemn words "earth to earth, ashes to ashes, dust to dust" are pronounced by the officiating cleric. This can today be accomplished "with a mere flick of the wrist with the Gordon Leak-Proof Earth Dispenser. No grasping of a handful of dirt, no soiled fingers. Simple, dignified, beautiful, reverent! The modern way!" The Golden Earth Dispenser (at $5) is of nickel-plated brass construction. It is not only "attractive to the eye and long wearing"; it is also "one of the 'tools' for building better public relations" if presented as "an appropriate non-commercial gift" to the clergyman. It is shaped something like a saltshaker.

26   Untouched by human hand, the coffin and the earth are now united.

27   It is in the function of directing the participants through the maze of gadgetry that the funeral director has assigned to himself his relatively new role of "grief therapist." He has relieved the family of every detail, he has revamped the corpse to look like a living doll, he has arranged for it to nap for a few days in a slumber room, he has put on a well-oiled performance in which the concept of *death* has played no part whatsoever—unless it was inconsiderately mentioned by the clergyman who conducted the religious service. He has done everything in his power to make the funeral a real pleasure for everybody concerned. He and his team have given their all to score an upset victory over death.

Questions on Meaning

1. According to Mitford, what legal requirements are involved in dealing with a recently deceased person? Where does embalming fit into these requirements? In her first four paragraphs, what does she imply about the reasons for the almost universal practice of embalming in North America?

2. What is Mitford saying in this essay? That funeral homes are a ripoff? That funeral directors lack respect for the dead? That the funeral process circumvents death and grieving?

3. Keeping Mitford's message in mind, consider her tone. Do the level of detail and biting comments help support her arguments, or do you find that her tone

gets in the way of her message? Support your answer with specific references to the text.

4. Mitford quotes several times from publications about embalming. What is her attitude toward these publications? How do you know?

Questions on Rhetorical Strategy and Style

1. After introductory comments, Mitford shifts to a description of the funeral home's process of working with the corpse. How necessary is the background material that precedes the description of what happens to a corpse?

2. Biting wit is a hallmark of Mitford's exposés. Find three examples of her dry, sarcastic, black humor.

3. This essay well exemplifies how different rhetorical strategies can be used simultaneously. Find the point where Mitford uses comparison and contrast. What other rhetorical strategies are at work at this point?

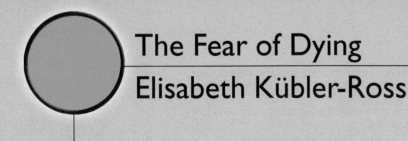

The Fear of Dying

Elisabeth Kübler-Ross

Written as the introduction to her influential book, **On Death and Dying** *(1969), this essay by Elisabeth Kübler-Ross suggests that dying patients are often treated inhumanely in modern hospitals. In spite of our increasing scientific prowess, she emphasizes how dying remains a mysterious and fearful process and requires special care-giving techniques.*

1   The ancient Hebrews regarded the body of a dead person as something unclean and not to be touched. The early American Indians talked about the evil spirits and shot arrows in the air to drive the spirits away. Many other cultures have rituals to take care of the "bad" dead person, and they all originate in this feeling of anger which still exists in all of us, though we dislike admitting it. The tradition of the tombstone may originate in this wish to keep the bad spirits deep down in the ground, and the pebbles that many mourners put on the grave are left-over symbols of the same wish. Though we call the firing of guns at military funerals a last salute, it is the same symbolic ritual as the Indian used when he shot his spears and arrows into the skies.

2   I give these examples to emphasize that man has not basically changed. Death is still a fearful, frightening happening, and fear of death is a universal fear even if we think we have mastered it on many levels.

3   What has changed is our way of coping and dealing with death and dying and our dying patients.

4   Having been raised in a country in Europe where science is not so advanced, where modern techniques have just started to find their way into medicine, and where people still live as they did in this country half a century ago, I may have had an opportunity to study a part of the evolution of mankind in a shorter period.

5   I remember as a child the death of a farmer. He fell from a tree and was not expected to live. He asked simply to die at home, a wish that was granted without questioning. He called his daughters into the bedroom and spoke with each one of them alone for a few minutes. He arranged his affairs quietly, though he was in great pain, and distributed his belongings and his land, none of which was to be split until his wife should follow him in death. He also asked each of his children to share in the work, duties, and tasks that he had carried on until the time of the accident. He asked his friends to visit him once more, to bid good-bye to them. Although I was a small child at the time, he did not exclude me or my siblings. We were allowed to share in the preparations of the family just as we were permitted to grieve with them until he died. When he did die, he was left at home, in his own beloved home which he had built, and among his friends and neighbors who went to take a last look at him where he lay in the midst of flowers in the place he had lived in and loved so much. In that country today there is still no make-believe

slumber room, no embalming, no false makeup to pretend sleep. Only the signs of very disfiguring illnesses are covered up with bandages and only infectious cases are removed from the home before the burial.

Why do I describe such "old-fashioned" customs? I think they are an indication 6 of our acceptance of a fatal outcome, and they help the dying patient as well as his family to accept the loss of a loved one. If a patient is allowed to terminate his life in the familiar and beloved environment, it requires less adjustment for him. His own family knows him well enough to replace a sedative with a glass of his favorite wine; or the smell of a home-cooked soup may give him the appetite to sip a few spoons of fluid which, I think, is still more enjoyable than an infusion. I will not minimize the need for sedatives and infusions and realize full well from my own experience as a country doctor that they are sometimes life-saving and often unavoidable. But I also know that patience and familiar people and foods could replace many a bottle of intravenous fluids given for the simple reason that it fulfills the physiological need without involving too many people and/or individual nursing care.

The fact that children are allowed to stay at home where a fatality has stricken 7 and are included in the talk, discussions, and fears gives them the feeling that they are not alone in the grief and gives them the comfort of shared responsibility and shared mourning. It prepares them gradually and helps them view death as part of life, an experience which may help them grow and mature.

This is in great contrast to a society in which death is viewed as taboo, 8 discussion of it is regarded as morbid, and children are excluded with the presumption and pretext that it would be "too much" for them. They are then sent off to relatives, often accompanied with some unconvincing lies of "Mother has gone on a long trip" or other unbelievable stories. The child senses that something is wrong, and his distrust in adults will only multiply if other relatives add new variations of the story, avoid his questions or suspicions, shower him with gifts as a meager substitute for a loss he is not permitted to deal with. Sooner or later the child will become aware of the changed family situation and, depending on the age and personality of the child, will have an unresolved grief and regard this incident as frightening, mysterious, in any case very traumatic experience with untrustworthy grownups, which he has no way to cope with.

We would think that our great emancipation, our knowledge of science and 9 of man, has given us better ways and means to prepare ourselves and our families for this inevitable happening. Instead the days are gone when a man was allowed to die in peace and dignity in his own home.

The more we are making advancements in science, the more we seem to fear 10 and deny the reality of death. How is this possible?

We use euphemisms, we make the dead look as if they were asleep, we ship the 11 children off to protect them from the anxiety and turmoil around the house if the patient is fortunate enough to die at home, we don't allow children to visit their dying parents in the hospitals, we have long and controversial discussions about whether patients should be told the truth—a question that rarely arises when the dying person is tended by the family physician who has known him from delivery to death and who knows the weaknesses and strengths of each member of the family.

I think there are many reasons for this flight away from facing death calmly. 12 One of the most important facts is that dying nowadays is more gruesome in many ways, namely, more lonely, mechanical, and dehumanized; at times it is even difficult to determine technically when the time of death has occurred.

Dying becomes lonely and impersonal because the patient is often taken out 13 of his familiar environment and rushed to an emergency room. Whoever has been very sick and has required rest and comfort especially may recall his experience of being put on a stretcher and enduring the noise of the ambulance siren and hectic rush until the hospital gates open. Only those who have lived through this may appreciate the discomfort and cold necessity of such transportation which is only the beginning of a long ordeal—hard to endure when you are well, difficult to express in words when noise, light, bumps, and voices are all too much to put up with. It may well be that we might consider more the patient under the sheets and blankets and perhaps stop our well-meant efficiency and rush in order to hold the patient's hand, to smile, or to listen to a question. I include the trip to the hospital as the first episode in dying, as it is for many. I am putting it exaggeratedly in contrast to the sick man who is left at home—not to say that lives should not be saved if they can be saved by a hospitalization but to keep the focus on the patient's experience, his needs and his reactions.

14   When a patient is severely ill, he is often treated like a person with no right to an opinion. It is often someone else who makes the decision if and when and where a patient should be hospitalized. It would take so little to remember that the sick person too has feelings, has wishes and opinions, and has—most important of all—the right to be heard.

15   Well, our presumed patient has now reached the emergency room. He will be surrounded by busy nurses, orderlies, interns, residents, a lab technician perhaps who will take some blood, an electrocardiogram technician who takes the cardiogram. He may be moved to X-ray and he will overhear opinions of his condition and discussions and questions to members of the family. He slowly but surely is beginning to be treated like a thing. He is no longer a person. Decisions are made often without his opinion. If he tries to rebel he will be sedated and after hours of waiting and wondering whether he has the strength, he will be wheeled into the operating room or intensive treatment unit and become an object of great concern and great financial investment.

16   He may cry for rest, peace, and dignity, but he will get infusions, transfusions, a heart machine, or tracheotomy if necessary. He may want one single person to stop for one single minute so that he can ask one single question—but he will get a dozen people around the clock, all busily preoccupied with his heart rate, pulse, electrocardiogram or pulmonary functions, his secretions or excretions but not with him as a human being. He may wish to fight it all but it is going to be a useless fight since all this is done in the fight for his life, and if they can save his life they can consider the person afterwards. Those who consider the person first may lose precious time to save his life! At least this seems to be the rationale or justification behind all this—or is it? Is the reason for this increasingly mechanical, depersonalized approach our own defensiveness? Is this approach our own way to cope with and repress the anxieties that a terminally or critically ill patient evokes in us? Is our concentration on equipment, on blood pressure, our desperate attempt to deny the impending death which is so frightening and discomforting to us that we displace all our knowledge onto machines, since they are less close to us than the suffering face of another human being which would remind us once more of our lack of omnipotence, our own limits and failures, and last but not least perhaps our own mortality?

17   Maybe the question has to be raised: Are we becoming less human or more human? Though this book is in no way meant to be judgmental, it is clear that whatever the answer may be, the patient is suffering more—not physically, perhaps, but emotionally. And his needs have not changed over the centuries, only our ability to gratify them.

Questions on Meaning

1. What is the author's attitude towards the advances we have made in medical science? Be sure to support your answer with specific references to the text. Do you agree with her point of view? Why or why not?
2. What are the meanings of "taboo," "euphemism," and "slumber room"?
3. Kubler-Ross discusses children at length in this article. What point is she trying to make about children and death?

Questions on Rhetorical Strategy and Style

1. In this article, Kubler-Ross compares two possible ways of dealing with a dying patient: she tells the story of the local farmer she knew as a child and that of the typical patient who dies in a hospital. What are the main points of comparison the author makes between these two scenarios? What does the comparison show us about the author's attitude towards death?
2. What effect is created by the author's use of rhetorical questions near the end of the essay?

The Right to Die
Norman Cousins

The title to this essay implies that suicide may be a human right. As some people decline into complete dependency, should suicide be legalized? Cousins's 1975 essay uses the suicide of eminent Protestant theologian Henry P. Van Dusen and his wife, Elizabeth, to make this case.

1   The world of religion and philosophy was shocked recently when Henry P. Van Dusen and his wife ended their lives by their own hands. Dr. Van Dusen had been president of Union Theological Seminary; for more than a quarter-century he had been one of the luminous names in Protestant theology. He enjoyed world status as a spiritual leader. News of the self-inflicted death of the Van Dusens, therefore, was profoundly disturbing to all those who attach a moral stigma to suicide and regard it as a violation of God's laws.

2   Dr. Van Dusen had anticipated this reaction. He and his wife left behind a letter that may have historic significance. It was very brief, but the essential point it made is now being widely discussed by theologians and could represent the beginning of a reconsideration of traditional religious attitudes toward self-inflicted death. The letter raised a moral issue: does an individual have the obligation to go on living even when the beauty and meaning and power of life are gone?

3   Henry and Elizabeth Van Dusen had lived full lives. In recent years, they had become increasingly ill, requiring almost continual medical care. Their infirmities were worsening, and they realized they would soon become completely dependent for even the most elementary needs and functions. Under these circumstances, little dignity would have been left in life. They didn't like the idea of taking up space in a world with too many mouths and too little food. They believed it was a misuse of medical science to keep them technically alive.

4   They therefore believed they had the right to decide when to die. In making that decision, they weren't turning against life as the highest value; what they were turning against was the notion that there were no circumstances under which life should be discontinued.

5   An important aspect of human uniqueness is the power of free will. In his books and lectures, Dr. Van Dusen frequently spoke about the exercise of this uniqueness. The fact that he used his free will to prevent life from becoming a caricature of itself was completely in character. In their letter, the Van Dusens sought to convince family and friends that they were not acting solely out of despair or pain.

6   The use of free will to put an end to one's life finds no sanction in the theology to which Pitney Van Dusen was committed. Suicide symbolizes discontinuity; religion symbolizes continuity, represented at its quintessence by the concept of

the immortal soul. Human logic finds it almost impossible to come to terms with the concept of nonexistence. In religion, the human mind finds a larger dimension and is relieved of the ordeal of a confrontation with non-existence.

Even without respect to religion, the idea of suicide has been abhorrent 7 throughout history. Some societies have imposed severe penalties on the families of suicides in the hope that the individual who sees no reason to continue his existence may be deterred by the stigma his self-destruction would inflict on loved ones. Other societies have enacted laws prohibiting suicide on the grounds that it is murder. The enforcement of such laws, of course, has been an exercise in futility.

Customs and attitudes, like individual themselves, are largely shaped by the 8 surrounding environment. In today's world, life can be prolonged by science far beyond meaning or sensibility. Under these circumstances, individuals who feel they have nothing more to give to life, or to receive from it, need not be applauded, but they can be spared our condemnation.

The general reaction to suicide is bound to change as people come to 9 understand that it may be a denial, not an assertion, of moral or religious ethics to allow life to be extended without regard to decency or pride. What moral or religious purpose is celebrated by the annihilation of the human spirit in the triumphant act of keeping the body alive? Why are so many people more readily appalled by an unnatural form of dying than by an unnatural form of living?

"Nowadays," the Van Dusens wrote in their last letter, "it is difficult to die. We 10 feel that this way we are taking will become more usual and acceptable as the years pass.

"Of course, the thought of our children and our grandchildren makes us sad, 11 but we still feel that this is the best way and the right way to go. We are both increasingly weak and unwell and who would want to die in a nursing home?

"We are not afraid to die. . . ." 12

Pitney Van Dusen was admired and respected in life. He can be admired and 13 respected in death. "Suicide," said Goethe, "is an incident in human life which, however much disputed and discussed, demands the sympathy of every man, and in every age must be dealt with anew."

Death is not the greatest loss in life. The greatest loss is what dies inside us 14 while we live. The unbearable tragedy is to live without dignity or sensitivity.

Questions about Meaning

1. This article discusses many different people's points of view on suicide. Try to put them in your own words. Make specific reference to the text (including what paragraph(s) you took your information from).

2. Why did the Van Dusens take their own lives?

3. What are the dominant religious attitudes towards suicide?

4. What is the legal attitude towards suicide?

5. Cousins suggests that suicide has been universally condemned, but are there situations or periods in history when suicide is or has been condoned or even encouraged in some societies?

Questions about Rhetorical Strategy and Style

1. Where in the article is the author's clearest explanation of his own point of view on suicide? What is the effect of suspending his judgment?

2. How does Cousins persuade the reader to support the possibility of assisted suicide?

3. The author uses several rhetorical questions in his article. There is one in paragraph 2, two in paragraph 9, and one in paragraph 11. What answer is the author hoping for to each of those questions? What are the pros and cons of using rhetorical questions in an argument or opinion piece?

Deficits

Michael Ignatieff

Michael Ignatieff (1947–) became leader of the Liberal Party of Canada late in 2008. He has spent most of his adult life, however, outside of politics—as a journalist, historian, teacher, and novelist. "Deficits" is taken from Scar Tissue, *a work that focuses in large part on the relationship between a son and his mother who is dying of Alzheimer's disease, the disease which Ignatieff's own mother suffered from before she died. That Ignatieff published* Scar Tissue *as fiction should be kept in mind.*

It begins the minute Dad leaves the house.   1

"Where is George"?

"He is out now, but he'll be back soon."

"That's wonderful," she says.

About three minutes later she'll look puzzled: "But George…"   5

"He's away at work, but he'll be back later."

"I see."

"And what are you doing here? I mean it's nice, but…"

"We'll do things together."

"I see."   10

Sometimes I try to count the number of times she asks me these question but I lose track.

I remember how it began, five or six years ago. She was 66 then. She would leave a pot to boil on the stove. I would discover it and find her tearing through the house, muttering, "My glasses, my glasses, where the hell are my glasses"?

I took her to buy a chain so that she could wear her glasses around her neck. She hated it because her mother used to wear *her* glasses on a chain. As we drove home, she shook her fist at the windscreen.

"I swore I'd never wear one of these damned things."

I date the beginning to the purchase of the chain, to the silence that descended 15 over her as I drove her home from the store.

The deficits, as the neurologists call them, are localized. She can tell you what it felt like when the Model T Ford ran over her at the school gates when she was a girl of seven. She can tell you what her grandmother used to say, "A genteel sufficiency will suffice," when turning down another helping at dinner. She remembers the Canadian summer nights when her father used to wrap her in a blanket and take her out to the lake's edge to see the stars.

But she can't dice an onion. She can't set the table. She can't play cards. Her grandson is five, and when they play pairs with his animal cards, he knows where the second penguin will be. She just turns up cards at random.

He hits her because she can't remember anything, because she keeps telling him not to run around quite so much.

Then I punish him. I tell him he has to understand.

20 He goes down on the floor, kisses her feet, and promises not to hit her again.

She smiles at him, as if for the first time, and says, "Oh, your kiss is so full of sugar."

After a week with him, she looks puzzled and says, "He's a nice little boy. Where does he sleep? I mean, who does he belong to"?

"He's your grandson."

"I see." She looks away and puts her hand to her face.

25 My brother usually stays with her when Dad is out of town. Once or twice a year, it's my turn. I put her to bed at night. I hand her the pills—small green ones that are supposed to control her moods—and she swallows them. I help her out of her bra and slip, roll down her tights, and lift the nightie over her head. I get into the bed next to hers. Before she sleeps she picks up a Len Deighton and reads a few paragraphs, always the same paragraphs, at the place where she has folded down the page. When she falls asleep. I pick the book off her chest and I pull her down in the bed so that her head isn't leaning against the wall. Otherwise she wakes up with a crick in her neck.

Often when I wake in the night, I see her lying next to me, staring into the dark. She stares and then she wanders. I used to try to stop her, but now I let her go. She is trying to hold on to what is left. There is a method in this. She goes to the bathroom every time she wakes, no matter if it is five times a night. Up and down the stairs silently, in her bare feet, trying not to wake me. She turns the lights on and off. Smooths a child's sock and puts it on the bed. Sometimes she gets dressed, after a fashion, and sits on the downstairs couch in the dark, clutching her handbag.

When we have guests to dinner, she sits beside me at the table, holding my hand, bent forward slightly to catch everything that is said. Her face lights up when people smile, when there is laughter. She doesn't say much any more; she is worried she will forget a name and we won't be able to help her in time. She doesn't want anything to show. The guests always say how well she does. Sometimes they say, "You'd never know, really." When I put her to bed afterward I can see the effort has left her so tired she barely knows her own name.

She could make it easier on herself. She could give up asking questions.

"Where we are now, is this our house"?

30 "Yes,"

"Where is our house"?

"In France."

I tell her: "Hold my hand, I'm here. I'm your son."

"I know."

35 But she keeps asking where she is. The questions are her way of trying to orient herself, of refusing and resisting the future that is being prepared for her.

She always loved to swim. When she dived into the water, she never made a splash. I remember her lifting herself out of the pool, as sleek as a seal in a black swimsuit, the water pearling off her back. Now she says the water is too cold and taking off her clothes too much of a bother. She paces up and down the poolside, watching her grandson swim, stroking his towel with her hand, endlessly smoothing out the wrinkles.

I bathe her when she wakes. Her body is white, soft, and withered. I remember how, in the changing-huts, she would bend over as she slipped out of her bathing suit. Her body was young. Now I see her skeleton through her skin. When I wash her hair, I feel her skull. I help her from the bath, dry her legs, swathe her in towels, sit her on the edge of the bath and cut her nails: they are horny and yellow. Her feet are gnarled. She has walked a long way.

When I was as old as my son is now I used to sit beside her at the bedroom mirror watching her apply hot depilatory wax to her legs and upper lip. She would pull her skirt up to her knees, stretch her legs out on the dresser, and sip beer from the bottle, while waiting for the wax to dry. "Have a sip," she would say. It tasted bitter. She used to laugh at the faces I made. When the wax had set, she would begin to peel it off, and curse and wince, and let me collect the strips, with fine black hairs embedded in them. When it was over, her legs were smooth, silky to touch.

Now I shave her. I soap her face and legs with my shaving brush. She sits perfectly still; as my razor comes around her chin we are as close as when I was a boy.

She never complains. When we walk up the hill behind the house, I feel her 40 going slower and slower, but she does not stop until I do. If you ask her whether she is sad, she shakes her head. But she did say once, "It's strange. It was supposed to be more fun than this."

I try to imagine what the world is like for her. Memory is what reconciles us to the future. Because she has no past, her future rushes toward her, a bat's wing brushing against her face in the dark.

"I told you. George returns on Monday."

"Could you write that down"?

So I do. I write it down in large letters, and she folds it in her white cardigan pocket and pats it and says she feels much less worried.

In half an hour, she has the paper in her hand and is showing it to me. 45

"What do I do about this"?

"Nothing. It just tells you what is going to happen."

"But I didn't know anything of this."

"Now you do," I say and I take the paper away and tear it up.

It makes no sense to get angry at her, but I do. 50

She is afraid Dad will not come back. She is afraid she has been abandoned. She is afraid she will get lost and never be able to find her way home. Beneath the fears that have come with the forgetting, there lie anxieties for which she no longer has any names.

She paces the floor, waiting for lunch. When it is before her, she downs it before anyone else, and then gets up to clear the plates.

"What's the hurry"? I ask her.

She is puzzled. "I don't know," she says. She is in a hurry, and she does not know why. She drinks whatever I put before her. The wine goes quickly.

"You'll enjoy it more if you sip it gently." 55

"What a good idea," she says and then empties the glass with a gulp.

I wish I knew the history of this anxiety. But I don't. All she will tell me is about being sprawled in the middle of Regent Street amid the blood and shop glass during an air raid, watching a mother sheltering a child, and thinking: I am alone.

In the middle of all of us, she remained alone. We didn't see it. She was the youngest girl in her family, the straggler in the pack, born cross-eyed till they straightened her eyes out with an operation. Her father was a teacher and she was dyslexic, the one left behind.

In her wedding photo, she is wearing her white dress and holding her bouquet. They are side by side. Dad looks excited. Her eyes are wide open with alarm. Fear gleams from its hiding place. It was her secret and she kept it well hidden. When I was a child, I thought she was faultless, amusing, regal. My mother.

60   She thinks of it as a happy family, and it was. I remember them sitting on the couch together, singing along to Fats Waller records. She still remembers the crazy lyrics they used to sing:

> There's no disputin'
> That's Rasputin
> The high-falutin loving man.

I don't know how she became so dependent on him, how she lost so many of the wishes she once had for herself, and how all her wishes came to be wishes for him.

     She is afraid of his moods, his silences, his departures, and his returns. He has become the weather of her life. But he never lets her down. He is the one who sits with her in the upstairs room, watching television, night after night, holding her hand.

     People say: it's worse for you, she doesn't know what is happening. She used to say the same thing herself. Five years ago, when she began to forget little things, she knew what was in store, and she said to me once, "Don't worry. I'll make a cheerful old nut. It's you who'll have the hard time." But that is not true. She feels everything. She has had time to count up every loss. Every night, when she lies awake, she stares at desolation.

     What is a person? That is what she makes you wonder. What kind of a person are you if you only have your habits left? She can't remember her grandson's name, but she does remember to shake out her tights at night and she never lets a dish pass her by without trying to clean it, wipe it, clear it up, or put it away. The house is littered with dishes she is putting away in every conceivable cupboard. What kind of a person is this?

     It runs in the family. Her mother had it. I remember going to see her in the house with old carpets and dark furniture on Prince Arthur Avenue. The windows were covered with the tendrils of plants growing in enormous Atlas battery jars, and the parquet floors shone with wax. She took down the giraffe, the water buffalo, and the leopard—carved in wood—that her father had brought back from Africa in the 1880s. She sat in a chair by the fire and silently watched me play with them. Then—and it seems only a week later—I came to have Sunday lunch with her and she was old and diminished and vacant, and when she looked at me she had no idea who I was.

65   I am afraid of getting it myself. I do ridiculous things: I stand on my head every morning so that the blood will irrigate my brain; I compose suicide notes, always some variant of Captain Oates's: "I may be gone for some time." I never stop thinking about what it would be like for this thing to steal over me.

     She has taught me something. There are moments when her pacing ceases, when her hunted look is conjured away by the stillness of dusk, when she sits in the garden, watching the sunlight stream through all the trees they planted together over 25 years in this place, and I see something pass over her face which might be serenity.

     And then she gets up and comes toward me looking for a glass to wash, a napkin to pick up, a child's toy to rearrange.

     I know how the story has to end. One day I return home to see her and she puts out her hand and says: "How nice to meet you." She's always charming to strangers.

People say I'm already beginning to say my farewells. No, she is still here. I am not ready yet. Nor is she. She paces the floor, she still searches for what has been lost and can never be found again.

She wakes in the night and lies in the dark by my side. Her face, in profile, 70 against the pillow has become like her mother's, the eye sockets deep in shadow, the cheeks furrowed and drawn, the gaze ancient and disabused. Everything she once knew is still inside her, trapped in the ruined circuits—how I was when I was little, how she was when I was a baby. But it is too late to ask her now. She turns and notices I am awake too. We lie side by side. The darkness is still. I want to say her name. She turns away from me and stares into the night. Her nightie is buttoned at the neck like a little girl's.

Questions about Meaning

1. Based on Ignatieff's account, what are the effects of Alzheimer's on people who have the disease? What are the effects on their family members? Who has a harder time dealing with the disease? Support your answer with specific reference to the text.

2. What is the fear that Ignatieff says "was her secret"? What does this teach us about the effects of childhood experiences?

3. What is the author's relationship to his mother? How is it different from their relationship when he was a child?

4. Why does the author make the comparison between his mother and a little girl in the last line of the essay? Is this an effective ending for the essay? Why or why not?

Questions about Rhetorical Strategy and Style

1. Why does the author introduce this essay with a dialogue between himself and his mother? What effect does it have on the reader?

2. Why would Ignatieff choose to relate so many intimate details about how he cares for his mother? What does this level of detail contribute to his essay?

3. This narrative relies heavily on concrete, sensory detail. List at least one example each of the author's appeal to sight, sound, taste, touch and smell. What emotions do these sensory details evoke?

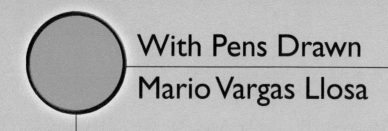

With Pens Drawn
Mario Vargas Llosa

This essay was published in the May 1997 issue of Prospect Magazine, and is based on a speech that Mario Vargas Llosa gave in 1985. The writer discusses the issue of whether literature has a greater function than simply entertainment. Llosa argues that, unlike television and cinema, literature has the responsibility of addressing the pertinent challenges of its time. Literature must remain current and confront uncomfortable truths.

1   My vocation as a writer grew out of the idea that literature does not exist in a closed artistic sphere but embraces a larger moral and civic universe. This is what has motivated everything I have written. It is also, alas, now turning me into a dinosaur in trousers, surrounded by computers.

2   Statistics tell us that never before have so many books been published and sold. The trouble is that hardly anybody I come across believes any longer that literature serves any great purpose beyond alleviating boredom on the bus or the underground, or has any higher ambition beyond being transformed into telly- or cine-scripts. Literature has gone for light. That is why critics such as George Steiner have come to believe that literature is already dead, and how novelists such as VS Naipaul have come to proclaim that they will not write another novel because the genre now fills them with disgust.

3   But amid this pessimism about literature, we should remember that many people still fear the writer. Look at the criminal clique which governs Nigeria and executed Ken Saro-Wiwa; at those who persecuted Taslima Nasreen in Bangladesh; at the imams who declared a fatwa on Salman Rushdie; at the Muslim fundamentalists in Algeria who have cut the throats of dozens of journalists, writers and thespians; at those in Cairo who financed the attack which could have cost the

life of Naguib Mahfouz; and at all those regimes in North Korea, Cuba, China, Laos, Burma and elsewhere where censorship prevails and prisons are full of writers.

So in those countries which are supposed to be cultivated—and which are the most free and democratic—literature is becoming a hobby without real value, while in those countries where freedom is restricted, literature is considered dangerous, the vehicle of subversive ideas. Novelists and poets in free countries, who view their profession with disillusionment, should open their eyes to this vast part of the globe which is not yet free. It might give them courage. 4

I have an old-fashioned view: I believe that literature must address itself to the problems of its time. An author must write with the conviction that what he is writing can help others become more free, more sensitive, more clear-sighted; yet without the self-righteous illusion of many intellectuals that their work helps contain violence, reduce injustice or promote liberty. I have erred too often myself, and I have seen too many writers I admired err—even put their talents at the service of ideological lies and state crimes—to delude myself. But without ceasing to be entertaining, literature should immerse itself in the life of the streets, in the unravelling of history, as it did in the best of times. This is the only way in which a writer can help his contemporaries and save literature from the flimsy state to which it sometimes seems condemned. 5

If the only point of literature is to entertain, then it cannot compete with the fictions pouring out of our screens, large or small. An illusion made of words requires the reader's active participation, an effort of the imagination and sometimes, in modern literature, complex feats of memory, association and creativity. Television and cinema audiences are exempt from all this by virtue of the images. This makes them lazy and increasingly allergic to intellectually challenging entertainment. 6

I say this without animosity towards the audiovisual media; indeed, I am a self-confessed cinema addict—I see two or three films a week—and also enjoy a good television programme. But from personal experience, I have to say that all the great films I have enjoyed have not helped me understand the labyrinth of human psychology as well as the novels of Dostoevsky, or helped reveal the mechanisms of society as the novels of Tolstoy and Balzac, or charted the peaks and chasms of experience like Mann, Faulkner, Kafka, Joyce or Proust. 7

Screen fiction is intense on account of its immediacy and ephemeral in terms of effect: it captivates us and then releases us almost instantly. Literary fiction holds us captive for life. To say that the works of the authors I have mentioned are entertaining would be to insult them. For, while they are usually read in a state of high excitement, the most important effect of a good book is in the aftermath, its ability to fire memory over time. The afterglow is still alive within me because without the books I have read, I would not be who I am, for better or worse, nor would I believe what I believe, with all the doubts and certainties that keep me going. Those books shaped me, changed me, made me. And they still keep on changing me, in step with the life I measure them against. In those books I learned that the world is in bad shape and that it will always be so-which is no reason to refrain from doing whatever we can to keep it from getting worse. They taught me that in all our diversity of cultures, races and beliefs, as fellow actors in the human comedy, we deserve equal respect. They also taught me why we so rarely get it. There is nothing like good literature to help us detect the roots of the cruelty human beings can unleash. 8

9   Without a committed literature it will become even more difficult to contain all those outbreaks of war, genocide, ethnic and religious strife, refugee displacement and terrorist activity, which threaten to multiply and which have already smashed the hopes raised by the collapse of the Berlin Wall. The stupor with which the EU witnessed the Balkan tragedy—200,000 dead and ethnic cleansing now legitimised by elections—provides dramatic evidence for the need to rouse the lethargic collective will from the complacency which holds it down. Removing blindfolds, expressing indignation in the face of injustice and demonstrating that there is room for hope under the most trying circumstances, are all things literature has been good at, even though it has occasionally been mistaken in its targets and defended the indefensible.

10   The written word has a special responsibility to do these things because it is better at telling the truth than any audiovisual medium. These media are by their nature condemned to skate over the surface of things and are much more constrained in their freedom of expression. The phenomenal sophistication with which news bulletins can nowadays transport us to the epicentre of events on all five continents has turned us all into voyeurs and the whole world into one vast theatre, or more precisely into a movie. Audiovisual information—so transient, so striking and so superficial—makes us see history as fiction, distancing us by concealing the causes and context behind the sequence of events that are so vividly portrayed. This condemns us to a state of passive acceptance, moral insensibility and psychological inertia similar to that inspired by television fiction and other programmes whose only purpose is to entertain.

11   That is a perfectly legitimate state to be in, we all like to escape from reality; indeed, that is one of the functions of literature. But making the present unreal, turning actual history into fiction has the effect of demobilising the citizen, making him or her feel exempt from any civic responsibility, encouraging the conviction that it is beyond anyone's reach to intervene in a history whose screenplay is already written. Along this path we may well slide into a world where there are no citizens, only spectators, a world where, although formal democracy may be preserved, we will be resigned to the kind of lethargy dictatorships aspire to establish.

12   The other big problem with the audiovisual medium is the extremely high cost of production. This hangs unavoidably over every producer's choice of subject matter and over the way to tell the story. The hunger for success is not a manifestation of a filmmaker's vanity, it is the prerequisite for any opportunity to make a film (or the next film). The conformity of the audiovisual medium arises not just from the need to reach the widest possible audience, it also results from the fact that as mass media with an immediate impact on huge sectors of public opinion, television and the cinema are more controlled by the state than any other media, even in the most liberal of countries. Not that they are explicitly censored, although that can happen; rather they are under surveillance, regulated and guided. They are discouraged from tackling certain issues and encouraged to be merely entertaining.

13   This is the cause of literature's responsibility. Freedom is precious, but no country can be assured that it will last unless it is exercised and defended. Literature, which owes its life to freedom, helps us to understand that freedom does not come out of a clear blue sky; it is a choice, a conviction, a train of thought that needs to be constantly enriched and tested. Literature can also make us understand that democracy is the best means we have invented to prevent war; Kant's thesis is even more true today than when he wrote it. For at least a century now, wars have always been waged between dictatorships, or by totalitarian regimes

against democracies. It is almost unknown for two democratic countries to wage war. There can be no clearer lesson. For free countries, the best way to promote peace is to promote democracy.

A writer who is engaged does not need to abandon his adventures with the imagination or experimentations with language; he does not need to abandon risk; nor does he need to give up laughing or playing, because his duty to entertain need not be incompatible with his social responsibility. To amuse, enchant, dazzle- that is what the great poems, the great tragedies, the great novels and essays have always done. No idea or character in literature can last if it does not fascinate us, like a rabbit from a magician's hat.

During his years in exile in France, while Europe was threatened by the advance of Nazism, Walter Benjamin devoted himself to the poetry of Charles Baudelaire. He wrote a book about him which he did not finish, but the fragments he left are read with fascination. Why Baudelaire? Why choose this subject during such a time? When we read Benjamin, we discover that Les Fleurs du Mal contained answers to such questions as how urban civilisation would develop and the plight of the individual in mass societies. The image of Benjamin poring over Baudelaire, while the circle of oppression which cost him his life closed in on him, is a moving one. At the same time the philosopher Karl Popper, in exile on the other side of the world, in New Zealand, began to learn ancient Greek and immerse himself in Plato in order to make his own contribution to the fight against totalitarianism. A crucial book emerged: The Open Society and its Enemies. Benjamin and Popper, the Marxist and the liberal, two engaged and original figures inside big currents of thought that they renewed, illustrate that it is possible, through writing, to oppose adversity. They show that dinosaurs can work through difficult times-and remain useful.

Questions about Meaning

1. What is the true purpose of literature, according to Mario Vargas Llosa, and how does that purpose contrast with what literature's purpose has become?

2. Why, according to the author, do some people fear the writer of literature? Give examples from the text of the possible consequences of good literature.

3. According to the author, in what ways do some writers and intellectuals become guilty of "self-righteous illusion" (p. 219). What does the writer mean by that phrase?

4. Explain the contrast that the author draws between the effect of what is referred to in the reading as "screen fiction" and "literary fiction" (p. 219).

Questions about Rhetorical Strategy and Style

1. Mario Vargas Llosa alludes to dinosaurs at the beginning and the end of the essay. Is this allusion effective in advancing the writer's main ideas, and does the author prove that "good literature" is still relevant in advancing discussion and action in response to real and urgent social problems?

2. The writer uses the metaphor of theatrical drama to suggest that the audio visual medium has turned people into "voyeurs", and this makes people superficial and passive. Is the use of the metaphor effective in the argument that an audiovisual medium, such as cinema, causes people to escape from reality and lose the desire for effective civic response to real problems?

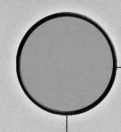

No Allusions in the Classroom

Jaime M. O'Neill

In light of the recent episode of the Jimmy Kimmel show in which he turned up evidence of complete ignorance of the fact that Obamacare and the Affordable Care Act are the same thing, I thought of this old essay I wrote almost three decades ago. We ain't gettin' no smarter. The article was published in Newsweek Magazine in September of 1985. The essay addresses the communication challenges between professors and students, as well as students' lack of basic general knowledge that prevents effective teaching and learning.

1   Josh Billings, a 19th-century humorist, wrote that it is better "not to know so much than to know so many things that ain't so." Recently, after 15 years of teaching in community colleges, I decided to take a sampling to find out what my students know that ain't so. I did this out of a growing awareness that they don't always understand what I say. I suspected that part of their failure to understand derived from the fact that they did not catch my allusions. An allusion to a writer, a geographical locality or a historical episode inevitably produced telltale expressions of bewilderment.

2   There is a game played by students and teachers everywhere. The game goes like this: the teacher tries to find out what students don't know so that he can correct these deficiencies; the students, concerned with grades and slippery self-images, try to hide their ignorance in every way they can. So it is that students seldom ask pertinent questions. So it is that teachers assume that students possess basic knowledge which, in fact, they don't possess.

3   Last semester I broke the rules of this time-honored game when I presented my English-composition students with an 86-question "general knowledge" test on the first day of class. There were 26 people in the class; they ranged in age from 18 to 54. They had all completed at least one quarter of college-level work.

Here is a sampling of what they knew that just ain't so: 4

Creative: Ralph Nader is a baseball player. Charles Darwin invented gravity. 5 Christ was born in the 16th century. J. Edgar Hoover was a 19th-century president. Neil Simon wrote "One Flew Over the Cuckoo's Nest"; "The Great Gatsby" was a magician in the 1930s. Franz Joseph Haydn was a songwriter during the same decade. Sid Caesar was an early roman emperor. Mark Twain invented the cotton gin. Heinrich Himmler invented the Heimlich maneuver. Jefferson Davis was a guitar player for The Jefferson Airplane. Benito Mussolini was a Russian leader of the 18th century; Dwight D. Eisenhower came earlier, serving as a president during the 17th century. William Faulkner made his name as a 17th-century scientist. All of these people must have appreciated the work of Pablo Picasso, who painted masterpieces in the 12th century.

My students were equally creative in their understanding of geography. They 6 knew, for instance, that Managua is the capital of Vietnam, that Cape Town is in the United States and that Beirut is in Germany. Bogota, of course, is in Borneo (unless it is in China). Camp David is in Israel, and Stratford-on-Avon is in Grenada (or Gernada). Gdansk is in Ireland. Cologne is in the Virgin Islands. Mazatlan is in Switzerland. Belfast was variously located in Egypt, Germany, Belgium and Italy. Leningrad was transported to Jamaica; Montreal to Spain.

And on it went. Most students answered incorrectly far more than they 7 answered correctly. Several of them meticulously wrote "I don't know" 86 times, or 80 times, or 62 times.

They did not like the test. Although I made it clear that the test would not be 8 graded, they did not like having their ignorance exposed. One of them dismissed the test by saying, "Oh, I get it; it's like Trivial Pursuit." Imagining a game of Trivial Pursuit among some of today's college students is a frightening thought; such a game could last for years.

But the comment bothered me. What, in this time in our global history, is 9 trivial? And what is essential? Perhaps it no longer matters very much if large numbers of people in the world's oldest democratic republic know little of their own history and even less about the planet they inhabit.

But I expect that it does matter. I also suspect that my students provide a fairly 10 good cross section of the general population. There are 1,274 two-year colleges in the United States that collectively enroll nearly 5 million students. I have taught at four of those colleges in two states, and I doubt that my questionnaire would have produced different results at any of them. My colleagues at universities tell me that they would not be surprised at similar undergraduate answers.

My small sampling is further corroborated by recent polls which disclosed 11 that a significant number of American adults have no idea which side the United States supported in Vietnam and that a majority of the general populace have no idea which side the United States is currently supporting in Nicaragua or El Salvador.

Less importantly, a local marketing survey asked a sampling of your computer 12 whizzes to identify the character in IBM's advertising campaign that is based on an allusion to Charlie Chaplin in "Modern Times." Few of them had heard of Charlie Chaplin; fewer heard or knew about the movie classic.

Common Heritage: As I write this, the radio is broadcasting the news about 13 the Walker family. Accused of spying for the Soviets, the Walkers, according to a U.S. attorney, will be the Rosenbergs of the '80s. One of my students thought Ethel Rosenberg was a singer from the 1930s. The rest of them didn't know.

Communication depends, to some extent, upon the ability to make (and catch) allusions, to share a common understanding and a common heritage. Even preliterate societies can claim the shared assessment of their world. As we enter the postindustrial "information processing" age, what sort of information will be processed? And, as the educational establishment is driven "back to the basics," isn't it time we decided that a common understanding of our history and our planet is most basic of all?

14   As a teacher, I find myself in the ignorance-and-hope business. Each year hopeful faces confront me, trying to conceal their ignorance. Their hopes ride on the dispelling of that ignorance.

15   All our hopes do.

16   We should begin servicing that hope more responsibly and dispelling that ignorance with a more systematic approach to imparting essential knowledge.

17   Socrates, the American Indian chieftain, would have wanted it that way.

Questions about Meaning

1. What is Jaime O'Neill's main argument in the essay, and does he defend it convincingly?

2. The writer says that students and teachers play a game about knowledge, a game that hampers effective teaching and learning. What is that game?

3. According to the writer, why do students try to hide gaps and any deficiencies in their general knowledge? What are other possible reasons why people may try to hide their ignorance?

4. According to the author, why is it important to learn, understand and share allusions in the classroom?

Questions about Rhetorical Strategy and Style

1. Identify and comment on the writer's literary style and tone, and state whether that style and tone are effective in advancing his main idea.

2. In paragraph 6 of the reading, the writer presents some test findings of what his students "...knew that just ain't so." Comment on the writer's tone, and discuss the fairness of that tone in the light of the students' so-called lack of knowledge.

Bringing a Daughter Back from the Brink with Poems

Betsy MacWhinney

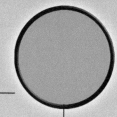

Betsy MacWhinney, an ecologist in Duvall, Washington, is working on a memoir about single parenthood. The article is part of a mother's project to remind her teenager that life is worth living. A version of this article appeared in print on March 1, 2015 on page ST6 of the New York edition of the New York Times with the headline: A Poem in a Shoe Helps Secure a Child's Footing.

When George W. Bush was re-elected in 2004, my 13-year-old daughter, Marisa, was so angry that she stopped wearing shoes. 1

She chose the most ineffective rebellion imaginable: two little bare feet against the world. She declared that she wouldn't wear shoes again until we had a new president. 2

I had learned early in motherhood that it's not worth fighting with your children about clothes, so I watched silently as she strode off barefoot each morning, walking down the long gravel driveway in the cold, rainy darkness to wait for the bus. 3

The principal called me a few times, declaring that Marisa had to start wearing shoes or she would be suspended. I passed the messages on, but my daughter continued her barefoot march. 4

After about four months, she donned shoes without comment. I didn't ask why. I wasn't sure if wearing shoes was a sign of failure or maturity; asking her seemed like it could add unnecessary insult to injury. 5

But all of her rebellion that year wasn't quite so harmless. I feared she was acting out in dangerous ways. 6

7   As we walked through the grocery store one day, she reached out for an avocado, causing her sleeve to fall back, revealing a scary-looking scab on her wrist along the meridian where a watchband would be.

8   I grabbed her hand. "Oh, Marisa. You must be in a lot of pain."

9   She looked away, saying nothing.

10   I tried to squelch a wave of nausea, chilled by the knowledge that my daughter was harming herself.

11   I did what parents do: I engaged with professionals and took their advice. Marisa went to a counselor alone, and we went to a different one together.

12   I felt a pit of horror in my stomach as a psychiatrist told me, in front of Marisa: "She shouldn't be left alone, and she shouldn't be allowed to handle anything dangerous. No knives. If you have any medication in the home, keep it locked up and away from her."

13   Later that evening we were unloading the dishwasher together, her on one side, me on the other. I unconsciously passed her a sharp knife to put away.

14   "Mom, are you sure you can trust me with this?" she said jokingly.

15   I had held it together pretty well up to that point, at least in front of her, but started sobbing uncontrollably when she said that.

16   She looked surprised, and gave me a hug. "I'll be O.K.," she promised.

17   I started Tuesday Night Dinners, to which I'd invite everyone we knew who would be fine with the chaotic scene of a weekday family dinner.

18   Sometimes three people would show, sometimes 20, and we would eat the kind of simple food that a working mother can throw together between getting home at 5 p.m. and having people arrive at 5:30.

19   The parents of her friends would come with their teenagers, and at least for that one evening the house was lively with people. I wanted life to come to her. I wanted her to float on the current of rich connections.

20   Other evenings were filled with sullen, delicate silences punctuated by minor conflicts: me resisting the urge to ask how she was doing, because I was afraid of what I might learn, and her courageously struggling to understand teenage-hood.

21   As she played the guitar in her bedroom, I tried not to lurk outside the closed door, but when the music stopped, I had to breathe through my panic, wondering if she was still safe.

22   It wasn't clear to her whether she should bother growing up. She would ask me, "Do you like your life?" Her tone implied judgment of my life without her having to spell it out: You drive, work in a cubicle, do chores and are terminally single. What's the point?

23   One day my son came home from school talking about vandalism that had occurred at the elementary school. "Someone spray-painted stuff all over the schoolyard," he said. "Things like, 'Too many Bushes, not enough trees.' "

24   I glanced sideways at Marisa. She met my eyes and looked down, confirming my suspicions. I'm no fan of vandalism, but I was actually glad to learn she cared that much about something.

25   It turns out, she did the deed with a boy, who was caught and required to pay a fine. I asked my daughter to call the boy's family and confess, which she did, and offered to pay half the fine, which they accepted.

26   I started leaving poems in her shoes in the morning. She had used the shoes as a form of quiet protest, so I decided I would use them to make a quiet stand for hope. When one of your primary strategies as a parent involves leaving Wendell Berry's "Mad Farmer Liberation Front" in your child's shoe, it's clear things aren't going well.

What I wanted her to know is: People have been in pain before, struggled to find hope, and look what they've done with it. They made poetry that landed right in your shoe, the same shoe you didn't wear for four months because of your despair. 27

Before she went to school in the morning, I wanted her to read the poem "Wild Geese" by Mary Oliver that talks about not having to be good and not having to walk on your knees for miles, repenting. As Ms. Oliver writes, "You only have to let the soft animal of your body love what it loves." 28

Or this, from Mr. Berry: "Be joyful, though you have considered all the facts." 29

Would that matter to her? Would she get my message that the world loved her and she should really try to start loving it back? 30

I wasn't going to talk her out of how dire things were on the planet, but could she, even so, find reasons to put shoes on each day? Raising a child who had no hope for the future seemed like my biggest failure ever. 31

I normally don't invite poetry into my daily life. As an ecologist, I embrace science. But all I had to offer her at that point were the thoughts of others who struggled to make a meaningful life and had put those thoughts into the best, sparest words they could. 32

It suddenly struck me — I the one who loves science, data, facts and reason — that when push comes to shove, it was poetry I could count on. Poetry knew where hope lived and could elicit that lump in the throat that reminds me it's all worth it. Science couldn't do that. 33

I believed, inexplicably, that it was urgent to deliver the perfect words in her shoe each day. It felt like her life depended on it. 34

One day I called in late to work so I could purchase scissors and a glue stick from a gas station minimart. I took the supplies and a stack of discarded magazines into a cheap Mexican restaurant to drink bad coffee and assemble poems in the form of a ransom note, as if my daughter had been kidnapped and I had to disguise the writing to get her back. 35

I frantically searched for the word "bones" so I could nod to her budding sexuality with Roethke's "I knew a woman, lovely in her bones," but superstitiously didn't want to clip the word "bones" from a grizzly headline. I hoped no one would ask why I was late, because I had no idea where to begin, how to explain. 36

For a few weeks she didn't comment on the poems. She had to know I was doing it because she had to remove the poems from her shoe before putting them on in the morning. I felt encouraged, though, when I'd find a well-worn, many-times-folded poem in her pocket as I did laundry. 37

As the days grew longer, she became more involved in life. She made plans, took up running, planted seeds, decorated her room. I could see that her putting on the shoes wasn't defeat, but maturity. 38

At some point, I knew she had come out of a long dark tunnel. I also knew it wouldn't be her last tunnel. 39

The most optimistic people often struggle the hardest. They can't quite square what's going on in the world with their beliefs, and the disparity is alarming. 40

She was temporarily swamped at the intersection of grief over a bleak political landscape, transition to a mediocre high school, and the vast existential questions of a curious adolescent. 41

In retrospect, my poetry project was a harmless sideline that kept me benevolently out of her way as she struggled not just to see the horizon but to march bravely toward it. 42

43   A few years ago, she was interviewed to join a group of students on a long trip to Sierra Leone. The professor explained that it was likely to be a very difficult time, far from home, with physical and mental hardship.

44   "What would you do," he asked Marisa, "if you get to the abyss, and it begins talking?"

45   "Well," she replied, "I would have a lot of questions for the abyss, indeed."

Questions about Meaning

1. According to Betsy MacWhinney, the mother chooses not to fight her daughter over how she chooses to dress. Do you think that the mother makes the right decision? Explain your answer.

2. In paragraph 15, the mother breaks down in tears in response to her daughter's humorous question as to whether it is safe for the mother to hand her a knife. With close reference to the reading, why do you think that the mother breaks down in tears?

3. Why does the mother start "Tuesday night dinners", and whose interest is being served by this activity?

4. The mother draws a contrast between the art of poetry and the science of ecology (see paragraph 32). In the light of what unfolds in the relationship between mother and daughter, how effective is poetry in helping to bring them closer to understanding each other? Explain your answer.

Questions about Rhetorical Strategy and Style

1. Discuss the mother's overriding tone in the reading, and explain how this tone reflects her mood and attitude.

2. Is the writer's narrative style effective in the telling of the story? Explain its effectiveness.

Part III:
Writing Analytical Essays

Analyzing Your Reading and Writing Context

It is like the rubbing of two sticks together to make a fire, the act of reading, an improbable pedestrian task that leads to heat and light.

—ANNA QUINDLEN

Here is this chapter's point in a nutshell: Writers write for a purpose to an audience within a genre. Together, these three factors—purpose, audience, and genre—create what we call **"rhetorical context."** The more aware you are of these factors, the more efficient you will be as a reader and the more effective you will be as a writer. Analyzing a text's rhetorical context as you read will enable you to frame a response in terms of your own rhetorical context: What will be your purpose, audience, and genre? Your answers will influence not only what you write but also the way you read and use additional texts.

In this chapter, you will learn

- To analyze a text's original rhetorical context (purpose, audience, and genre)

- To analyze your own rhetorical context for reading

- To adapt experts' reading strategies and make your reading more efficient

  - By using genre knowledge

  - By analyzing the text's original social/historical context

- To recognize the major role reading plays in different types of college writing assignments

Rhetorical Context: Purpose, Audience, and Genre

Recognizing the influence of rhetorical context helps rhetorical readers reconstruct the strategy behind an author's choices about content (for example, what to include and exclude), structure (for example, what to say first, when to reveal the thesis, how to arrange the parts, how to format the document), and style (whether to use big words or ordinary words, complex or easy sentence structure, lots of jargon or no jargon, and so forth).

Analyzing an Author's Purpose

We noted that writers have designs on readers—that is, writers aim to change a reader's view of a subject in some way. They might aim to enlarge a reader's view of a subject, clarify that view, or restructure that view. This motive to reach out to an audience through language inevitably stems from some problem or perceived misunderstanding or gap in knowledge that an author wishes to remedy. Rhetorician Lloyd F. Bitzer used the term **exigence** for a flaw that an author believes can be altered by a text presented to an audience.[1] This flaw might be a circumstance that is other than it should be, a situation in need of attention, or perhaps an occasion in need of special recognition. Your ability as a reader to pinpoint an author's sense of a flaw, a problem, or some other situation in need of change will enable you to zero in on that author's purpose. Furthermore, when you are ready to write about what you have read, thinking of your purpose as writing in order to remedy a flaw will help you focus sharply. Such "flaws" or problems may be as simple as the need to provide information or as complex as the need to advocate for standardizing a set of medical procedures in order to reduce infections. For example, you might need to inform a potential employer of your availability and qualifications for a particular job, so you submit a letter and résumé. Or you could need to demonstrate to a history professor that you do, indeed, have a good grasp of the economic system that dominated during China's Ming dynasty, so you answer an exam question with careful detail.

A set of categories for conceptualizing the ways that writers aim to change readers' minds is summarized in Table 1.1 (see pp. 232–233). Based on a scheme developed by rhetoricians to categorize types of discourse in terms of a writer's aim or purpose, the table identifies eight **rhetorical aims** or purposes that writers typically set for themselves. This framework offers a particularly powerful way of thinking about both reading and writing because each row zeroes in on how a writer might envision a purpose that connects subject matter to audience in a given rhetorical situation. In the table, we describe how texts in each category work, what they offer readers, and the response their authors typically aim to bring about. The table illustrates the differences among the aims with examples of texts that a college student might compose in response to assignments in a variety of courses.

We have labeled the table's third column "Desired Response" because we want to emphasize that a writer can only desire a certain response from a reader; they cannot assume or force that response. The reader is in charge because it is the reader who decides whether to accede to the writer's intentions or to resist them. Because writers try to persuade an intended audience to adopt their perspective, they select and arrange evidence, choose examples, include or omit material, and

---

[1] Bitzer's concept of an exigence within a *rhetorical situation*, modified over the years, was first described in his essay, "The Rhetorical Situation," *Philosophy and Rhetoric* 1.1 (1968): 1–14. EbscoHost. Web. 3 June 2012.

TABLE 1.1	**A Spectrum of Purposes**		
Rhetorical Aim	**Focus and Features**	**Desired Response**	**Examples**
Express and Reflect **Offers Readers:** Shared emotional, intellectual experience	**Focus:** Writer's own life and experience **Features:** Literary techniques such as plot, character, setting, evocative language	**Readers** can imagine and identify with writer's experience. **Success** depends on writer's ability to create scenes, dialog, and commentary that engage readers.	Nursing student reflects on her semester of Service Learning at a school for young children with developmental delays and disabilities.
Inquire and Explore **Offers Readers:** Shared intellectual experience, new information, new perspectives	**Focus:** Puzzling problem seen through narration of writer's thinking processes **Features:** Delayed thesis or no thesis; examination of subject from multiple angles; writer's thinking is foregrounded.	**Readers** will agree question or problem is significant, identify with writer's thinking, and find new insights. **Success** depends on writer's ability to engage readers with question or problem and the exploration process.	Students in an honors seminar taught by a physicist and philosopher write papers that explore the question: "What makes study of the origins of the universe significant to daily life in the twenty-first century?"
Inform and Explain (also called *expository writing*) **Offers Readers:** Significant, perhaps surprising, new information; presentation tailored to readers' interest and presumed knowledge level	**Focus:** Subject matter **Features:** Confident, authoritative stance; typically states point and purpose early; strives for clarity; provides definitions and examples; uses convincing evidence without argument	**Readers** will grant writer credibility as expert, and be satisfied with the information's scope and accuracy. **Success** depends on writer's ability to anticipate readers' information needs and ability to understand.	Economics intern is assigned to track 10 years of the rise and fall of mortgage interest rates and report on experts' current explanations of the trends.
Analyze and Interpret **Offers Readers:** New way of looking at the subject matter	**Focus:** Phenomena that are difficult to understand or explain **Features:** Relatively tentative stance; thesis supported by evidence and reasoning; new or unsettling analyses and interpretations must be convincing; doesn't assume that evidence speaks for itself	**Readers** will grant writer credibility as analyst and accept insights offered, or at least acknowledge value of approach. **Success** depends on writer's ability to explain reasoning and connect it with phenomena analyzed.	Literature student analyzes the definition of justice employed by various characters in Sophocles' play Antigone with the goal of interpreting the author's understanding of the concept.
Persuasion: Take a Stand **Offers Readers:** Reasons to make up or change their minds about a question at issue	**Focus:** Question that divides a community **Features:** States a firm position, provides clear reasons and evidence, connects with readers' values and beliefs, engages with opposing views	**Readers** will agree with writer's position and reasoning. **Success** depends on writer's ability to provide convincing support and to counter opposition without alienating readers.	For an ethics class, an architecture student decides to write an argument in favor of placing certain buildings in his community on the historic preservation register, thus preserving them from demolition or radical remodeling

TABLE 1.1	A Spectrum of Purposes (Continued)		
Rhetorical Aim	**Focus and Features**	**Desired Response**	**Examples**
Persuasion: **Evaluate and Judge** **Offers Readers:** Reasons to make up or change their minds about a focal question regarding worth or value	**Focus:** Question about worth or value of a phenomenon **Features:** Organized around criteria for judgment and how phenomenon matches them	**Readers** will accept writer's view of the worth or value of the phenomenon. **Success** depends on writer's ability to connect subject to criteria that readers accept.	Political theory students are asked to evaluate and choose between the descriptions of an ideal ruler embodied in Plato's philosopher king and Machiavelli's prince.
Persuasion: **Propose a Solution** Offers Readers: A recommended course of action	**Focus:** Question about what action should be taken **Features:** Describes problem and solution, then justifies solution in terms of values and consequences; level of detail depends on assumptions about readers' knowledge	**Readers** will assent to proposed action and do as writer suggests. **Success** depends on readers' agreement that a problem exists and/or that the recommended action will have good results.	A group of seniors majoring in social welfare collaborates on a grant proposal to a community foundation interested in improving health education in a rural area.
Persuasion: **Seek Common Ground** Offers Readers: New perspectives and reduced intensity regarding difficult issues	**Focus:** Multiple perspectives on a vexing problem **Features:** Lays out the values and goals of the various stakeholders so that others can find commonalities to build on; does not advocate	**Readers** will discover mutuality with opponents; conflict may not be resolved; discussion could lead to cooperative action. **Success** depends on readers' discovery of mutual interests.	An environmental studies student designs a thesis project to interview advocates and stakeholders who are divided over a proposal to remove a dam from a major river; her goal is to find and highlight points of agreement.

select words and images to best support their perspective. But readers are the ones who decide—sometimes unconsciously, sometimes deliberately—whether the presentation is convincing. Your awareness of how a text is constructed to persuade its intended audience will enable you to decide how you want to respond to that text and use it in your own writing.

● For Writing and Discussion

To explore the spectrum of aims presented in Table 1.1, choose an issue or situation that interests you and fill in the grid of a similar table with sample writing scenarios and purposes for each of the table's eight rows of rhetorical aims. Working alone or with others, fill in as many cells in the example column as you can. Choose from the following hypothetical writers or another writer-reader combination that intrigues you in connection with the topic you choose.

- College students in a variety of courses
- A single writer (perhaps an entertainment columnist or a sports writer) seeking publication in a variety of venues, including the Web, about the same subject matter

- People in a variety of roles writing with different aims about the same topic (perhaps a family matter such as pets or divorce, or a public matter such as green energy or human rights) ●

Identifying an Author's Intended Audience

Audience plays a major role in guiding an author's choices. As you analyze a text, watch for cues in the author's language and use of detail that reveal assumptions about the intended audience.

For example, suppose a writer wants to persuade legislators to raise gasoline taxes in order to reduce fossil fuel consumption. Her strategy might be to persuade different groups of voters to pressure their congressional representatives. If she writes for a scientific audience, her article can include technical data and detailed statistical analyses. If she addresses the general public, however, her style will have to be less technical and more lively, with storylike anecdotes rather than tabular data. If she writes for an environmental publication, she can assume an audience already supportive of her pro-environment values. However, if she writes for a business publication such as the *Wall Street Journal*, she will have to be sensitive to her audience's pro-business values—perhaps by arguing that what is good for the environment will be good for business in the long run.

Analyzing a Text's Genre

As writers respond to rhetorical situations by adapting content, structure, and style to different purposes and audiences, they must also adapt to the conventions of a text's **genre**, a term that refers to a recurring category or type of writing based on identifiable features such as structure (for example, a thesis-driven argument or an informal reflection) and document design (for example, the format of academic papers, Web pages, or promotional brochures). These genre-based decisions about format include whether to add visual images, and, if so, what kind will be appropriate and effective. Because particular textual features are expected in particular situations, a writer's effort to follow or modify genre conventions can become a valuable tool for engaging readers and moving them toward desired responses such as those indicated in Table 1.1.

You may be familiar with the concept of genre from literature classes where you studied an assortment of genres, such as plays, novels, and poems. Within each of these broad literary genres are subgenres such as the sonnet and haiku or tragedy and comedy. Similarly, workplace writing has a number of subgenres (memos, marketing

---

Analyzing an Author's Designs on Your Thinking

One way to analyze an author's purpose is to consider the kind of change the author hopes to bring about in readers' minds. Try using this formula to quiz yourself about the author's desire to change your mind:

At the beginning of the text, the writer assumes that the reader believes
_____.

By the end of the text, the writer hopes that the reader believes
_____.

These questions will help you, as a rhetorical reader, to analyze your own response to the text—whether you are going to think or do what the writer apparently hopes you will.

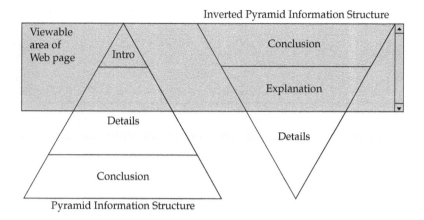

FIGURE 1.1 Diagram of inverted pyramid structure recommended for organizing Web content

proposals, financial reports, progress reports) as does academic writing (laboratory reports, field notes, article abstracts, literature reviews). As the descriptions of typical college writing assignments later in this chapter show, even familiar academic assignments have subgenres (informal response papers, essay exams, article summaries, or researched arguments that present a semester's worth of work).

Consider one commonly encountered genre: the **inverted pyramid** of a news article, in print or online. These reports begin with the key facts of a news event—*who, what, when, where, why,* and *how*—before offering background information and details. As Figure 1.1 shows, a similar structure is recommended for Web writing, where it is necessary to capture readers' attention quickly, in the limited amount of space immediately visible on a screen.

In both cases, someone in a hurry or with only a passing interest in the subject matter should be able to glean the gist of the news or of the Web site's purpose by reading just the initial sentences. Furthermore, on Web sites, putting the essential facts first makes it easier for search engines to spot and report on the page's content.

Genre differences in written texts frequently become evident through visual cues, and these cues in turn create reader expectations. The Web site of the *New York Times* uses typefaces and layout that resemble those of its paper edition, but the home page of a veterinary clinic (interested in inviting new patients) will likely be different from the home page of an advice blog about caring for exotic birds. Similarly, genre differences influence the look of print documents. If you were browsing publications in the current periodicals rack at a library, you could quickly distinguish popular magazines such as *Popular Science* and *Business Week* from scholarly journals such as the *American Journal of Human Genetics* or the *Journal of Marketing Research*. The glossy covers of the magazines, often adorned with arresting photographs, distinguish them from sober-looking scholarly journals, the covers of which typically display a table of contents of the articles within. (These genre distinctions are less apparent when you are browsing through articles in a computerized periodicals database.) As you develop your ability to recognize genres and the ways that their conventions shape content, you will also sharpen your ability to decide whether and how to use particular texts for your own purposes.

As illustration, consider the distinctive differences between the genres of the two articles introduced by the images in Figures 1.2 and 1.3. As the captions

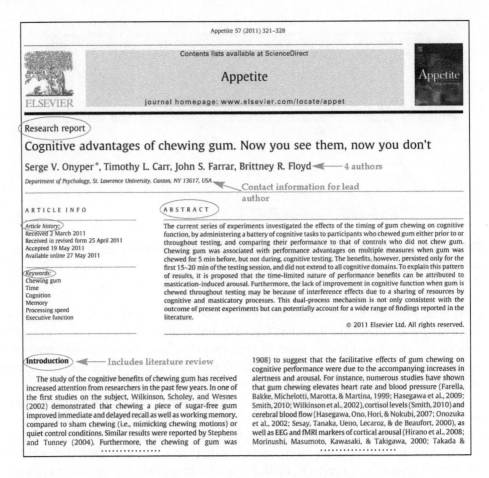

Appetite 57 (2011) 321–328

Contents lists available at ScienceDirect

Appetite

journal homepage: www.elsevier.com/locate/appet

ELSEVIER

Research report

Cognitive advantages of chewing gum. Now you see them, now you don't

Serge V. Onyper*, Timothy L. Carr, John S. Farrar, Brittney R. Floyd ◄— 4 authors

Department of Psychology, St. Lawrence University, Canton, NY 13617, USA ↗ Contact information for lead author

ARTICLE INFO

Article history:
Received 2 March 2011
Received in revised form 25 April 2011
Accepted 19 May 2011
Available online 27 May 2011

Keywords:
Chewing gum
Time
Cognition
Memory
Processing speed
Executive function

ABSTRACT

The current series of experiments investigated the effects of the timing of gum chewing on cognitive function, by administering a battery of cognitive tasks to participants who chewed gum either prior to or throughout testing, and comparing their performance to that of controls who did not chew gum. Chewing gum was associated with performance advantages on multiple measures when gum was chewed for 5 min before, but not during, cognitive testing. The benefits, however, persisted only for the first 15–20 min of the testing session, and did not extend to all cognitive domains. To explain this pattern of results, it is proposed that the time-limited nature of performance benefits can be attributed to mastication-induced arousal. Furthermore, the lack of improvement in cognitive function when gum is chewed throughout testing may be because of interference effects due to a sharing of resources by cognitive and masticatory processes. This dual-process mechanism is not only consistent with the outcome of present experiments but can potentially account for a wide range of findings reported in the literature.

Introduction ◄— Includes literature review

The study of the cognitive benefits of chewing gum has received increased attention from researchers in the past few years. In one of the first studies on the subject, Wilkinson, Scholey, and Wesnes (2002) demonstrated that chewing a piece of sugar-free gum improved immediate and delayed recall as well as working memory, compared to sham chewing (i.e., mimicking chewing motions) or quiet control conditions. Similar results were reported by Stephens and Tunney (2004). Furthermore, the chewing of gum was

1908) to suggest that the facilitative effects of gum chewing on cognitive performance were due to the accompanying increases in alertness and arousal. For instance, numerous studies have shown that gum chewing elevates heart rate and blood pressure (Farella, Bakke, Michelotti, Marotta, & Martina, 1999; Hasegawa et al., 2009; Smith, 2010; Wilkinson et al., 2002), cortisol levels (Smith, 2010) and cerebral blood flow (Hasegawa, Ono, Hori, & Nokubi, 2007; Onozuka et al., 2002; Sesay, Tanaka, Ueno, Lecaroz, & de Beaufort, 2000), as well as EEG and fMRI markers of cortical arousal (Hirano et al., 2008; Morinushi, Masumoto, Kawasaki, & Takigawa, 2000; Takada &

FIGURE 1.2 Image from page 1 of a research report the scholarly journal Appetite about the fleeting cognitive benefits of gum-chewing

indicate, the first is taken from the scholarly journal *Appetite* and the second was originally published in a monthly health newsletter, the *UC Berkeley Wellness Letter*. A quick glance makes evident the differences in these texts' rhetorical contexts, from the different page layouts to the contrasts between casual language and formal vocabulary.

The article from *Appetite* depicted in Figure 1.2 is one of two studies from the October 2011 issue that were used by a staff writer for the *Wellness Letter* to produce "Chew on This"—a short, easy-to-read summary of recent research on gum-chewing (presented in full in Figure 1.3). This piece was written to catch the attention of casual readers whose curiosity might be piqued by the clever title and the questions about the effects of chewing gum placed in bold-face headings, questions that readers will discover do not have definitive answers. Contrast this informal article with the formality and detail evident on the first page of the *Appetite* article in Figure 1.2. Despite the playful wording in the title—"Cognitive Advantages of Chewing Gum. Now You See them, Now You Don't"—the overall presentation of the opening page signals that it is a scholarly research report, including the label at the upper left labeling it as such. Scholarly elements highlighted by the labels and circles in the figure include the names of four authors (with an asterisk indicating the one to whom correspondence may be sent), a history of the article's submission to the journal, an abstract, a keywords list, and an introduction reviewing the literature from previous studies on the topic. The

Chew on This ◄————————— Punning Title

Most people chew gum for pleasure or out of habit; others to freshen breath or stop a food or cigarette craving. Does gum provide any real benefits? There have been lots of studies on gum over the years, including two recent ones.

Informal language in attention-getting questions

The best evidence concerns gum's ability to prevent cavities by boosting saliva flow and neutralizing acid produced by mouth bacteria. Sugar-free gums are best for this, notably those with the sugar alcohol xylitol, which suppresses the growth of cavity-producing bacteria. Still, gum can't replace brushing and flossing.

Closes with scholarly quote followed by joking paraphrase.

Can gum make you thinner? Gum chewing burns only about 11 calories an hour. But if it keeps you from eating a candy bar, that's a big plus. Studies on whether gum reduces appetite have produced conflicting findings. The latest study, in the journal *Appetite*, found that when women chewed gum (15 minutes, once an hour, for three hours), they ate about 30 fewer calories when subsequently offered a snack compared to when they hadn't chewed gum. The women also said they felt less hungry and fuller after chewing the gum. Gum manufacturers have helped publicize these results. But each piece of gum had 5 to 10 calories, so the women didn't actually cut down on calories significantly. Would sugarless gum have had the same effect? Maybe, maybe not.

Make you smarter? Some early research found that gum chewing improved performance on memory tests, perhaps by boosting blood flow to the brain and stimulating a part of the brain where information is processed. But more recent studies have failed to find any brain benefit—or have noted that gum sometimes worsens performance.

Another recent study in *Appetite* found that gum improved performance on certain cognitive tests, but only when it was chewed before, not during, the tests. The benefit lasted just 15 to 20 minutes. According to the researchers, gum doesn't help thinking—and possibly even impairs it—during a task because of "interference due to a sharing of metabolic resources by cognitive and masticatory processes." In other words, some people can't think (or walk) and chew gum at the same time.

FIGURE 1.3 Text of the "Last Word" column on the last page (p. 8) of the UC Berkeley Wellness Letter, Feb. 2012. Note that the journal that published the original research, Appetite, is mentioned only briefly (as highlighted in the figure).

article's remaining seven pages describe in detail the methodology of two studies about gum-chewing and test-taking behaviors, present charts and graphs of the results, and discuss the significance of those results.

Casual readers are likely to respond positively to the newsletter's brief summary of the research, but the readers of the scholarly journal are looking for more than lighthearted advice about gum-chewing. The *Appetite* article's intended audience is other researchers, not the general public. The keywords list will help those researchers find this article so that they can read about both its findings and methodology. As is customary, the article's last page suggests what work needs to be done by subsequent researchers: "In summary, the current study demonstrates that the discrepancies in research findings of the burgeoning literature on the effect of gum chewing on cognitive function can be attributed to the timing of chewing....further studies are needed to provide a more complete picture of the relationship between physiological changes and cognitive functioning due to the chewing of gum." (Onyper et al., 327—see full citation below).[2]

---

[2]Serge V. Onyper, et al., "Cognitive Advantages of Chewing Gum. Now You See Them, Now You Don't." Appetite 57.2 (2011): 321–328. Science Direct. Web. 9 June 2012.

From dense scientific research reports like this, the unnamed author of "Chew on This" used expert reading skills to dig out key points of information—and ambiguity—and transform them into a lively little article designed to spark a few smiles as well.[3] This reader-writer might have been trained as a journalist, or might be a graduate student in psychology or public health who will go on to build a career by publishing in journals like *Appetite*. In the pages ahead, we suggest strategies for you as both reader and writer for developing your own abilities to work with and for a variety of audiences, purposes, and genres.

● **For Writing and Discussion**

Both of the scholarly articles about gum-chewing from the October 2011 issue of *Appetite* (see full citations in footnotes 2 and 3) should be available through your school library, probably electronically. We invite you to explore in more detail the genre differences between them and the newsletter article in Figure 1.3. If your library also subscribes to the *UC Berkeley Wellness Letter*, you will have an opportunity to note contrasting genre features in that publication as well. ●

Analyzing Your Own Rhetorical Context as Reader/Writer

When you are assigned to read texts of any type (a textbook, a scholarly article, data on a Web site, historical documents, or other kinds of readings), think not only about the authors' rhetorical context, but also about your own.

Determining Your Purpose, Audience, and Genre

When you write about various texts or use them in your own arguments, you will be writing for a purpose to an audience within a genre. In college, your purpose will be determined by your assignment. (See the final section of this chapter, "Typical Reading-Based Writing Assignments Across the Curriculum," pp. 242–247.) Your audience may range from yourself to your professor and your classmates, to readers of a certain newspaper or blog, even to participants in an undergraduate research conference. Your assigned genre might come from a wide range of possibilities: summary, Web posting, rhetorical analysis, reader-response reflection, source-based argument, or a major research paper.

Identifying your purpose at the outset helps you set goals and plan your reading accordingly. Your purpose for reading may seem like a self-evident matter—"I'm reading this sociology book because it was assigned for tomorrow." That may be, but what we have in mind is a more strategic consideration of your purpose. Ask yourself how the reading assignment ties in with themes established in class. How does it fit with concepts laid out on the course syllabus? Is this your first course in sociology? If so, you might set a purpose for yourself of gathering definitions of the foundational concepts and specialized vocabulary used by sociologists. These basic but strategically stated goals might lead you to allow extra time for the slowed-down reading that students usually need in order to get their bearings at the beginning of introductory courses.

---

[3]The Appetite article about gum-chewing and snacking is by Marion M. Hetherington and Martin F. Regan, "Effects of Chewing Gum on Short-Term Appetite Regulation in Moderately Restrained Eaters." Appetite 57.2 (2011): 475–482. *Science Direct*. Web. 9 June 2012.

To illustrate the importance of establishing purposes for your reading, let's move farther into the semester and assume you are skimming articles to select some for closer reading and possible use in an annotated bibliography for this first course in sociology. Further, imagine that your assignment is to choose and summarize articles that demonstrate how sociological research can shed light on a current public controversy. An important first step in an assignment like this is to identify a clear and compelling **research question**. A strong research question will enable you to know what you're looking for, and it will guide you to read more purposefully and productively. Let's say you are interested in whether pop culture has a negative effect on family values. You want to think that it doesn't, but from sometimes intense discussions among family and friends, you realize that the answer might be "it depends." Maybe sociological research has laid out some systematic ways of thinking about this issue, and a more productive question would be "How does pop culture impact family values?" or "What is known about how pop culture impacts family values?"

Following the demands of your research question, you will need to define both "pop culture" and "family values" and narrow your focus as you find articles related to your controversy. Some sources will report research findings contrary to your own views; others will tend to confirm your views. To summarize them fairly, you will have to pay careful attention to the way these authors articulate their own research questions and present their results. Setting goals ahead of time for both your writing and your reading will help you know what to look for as you select and read articles.

Matching Your Reading Strategies to Your Purpose as Reader/Writer

Although all readers change their approach to reading according to their audience, purpose, and the genre of the text at hand, most readers do so without thought or reflection, relying on a limited set of strategies. By contrast, experienced readers vary their reading process self-consciously and strategically. To see how one accomplished undergraduate, Sheri, contrasts her "school" reading with her "reading-for-fun" process, see the box on the next page. You will no doubt notice that her strategies combine idiosyncratic habits (the blue pen and cold room) with

Preparing to Read: Sheri's Process

"When I am reading for class, for starters I make sure that I have all of my reading supplies. These include my glasses, a highlighter, pencil, blue pen, notebook paper, dictionary, and a quiet place to read, which has a desk or table. (It also has to be cold!) Before I read for class or for research purposes I always look over chapter headings or bold print words and then formulate questions based on these. When I do this it helps me to become more interested in the text I am reading because I am now looking for answers.

"Also, if there are study guide questions, I will look them over so that I have a basic idea of what to look for. I will then read the text all the way through, find the answers to my questions, and underline all of the study guide answers in pencil.

"When I read for fun, it's a whole other story! I always take off my shoes and sit on the floor/ground or in a very comfortable chair. I always prefer to read in natural light and preferably fresh air. I just read and relax and totally immerse myself in the story or article or whatever!"[4]

[4]Sheri's description of her reading process is quoted in Paula Gillespie and Neal Lerner, *The Allyn and Bacon Guide to Peer Tutoring* (Boston: Allyn & Bacon, 2000), 105. Print. Preparing to Read: Sheri's Process

sound, widely used academic reading habits (looking over chapter headings, checking for study guide questions, and so on).

What personal habits or rituals do you combine with your more purposeful reading behaviors? The awareness and flexibility evident in the way Sheri talks about her reading are valuable because planning as she does would enable you to work efficiently and maximize the use of your time. Furthermore, thinking about your purpose as Sheri does will help you maintain a sense of your own authority as you read, a notion that is very important for college writing.

Sheri's self-awareness and deliberate reading strategies are not typical. When we ask students to describe the behaviors of good readers, many initially say "speed" or "the ability to understand a text in a single reading." Surprisingly, most experienced readers don't aim for speed reading, nor do they report that reading is an easy, one-step process. On the contrary, experienced readers put considerable effort into reading and rereading a text, adapting their strategies and speed to its demands and to their purpose for reading. Because your purposes for reading academic assignments will vary considerably, so must your academic reading strategies. You will read much differently, for example, if your task is to interpret or analyze a text than if you are simply skimming it for its potential usefulness in a research project. Contrary to popular myth, expert readers are not necessarily "speed" readers. Experienced readers pace themselves according to their purpose, taking advantage of four basic reading speeds:

- *Very fast:* Readers scan a text very quickly if they are looking only for a specific piece of information.
- *Fast:* Readers skim a text rapidly if they are trying to get just the general gist without worrying about details.
- *Slow to moderate:* Readers read carefully in order to get complete understanding of an article. The more difficult the text, the more slowly they read. Often difficult texts require rereading.
- *Very slow:* Experienced readers read very slowly if their purpose is to analyze a text. They take elaborate marginal notes and often pause to ponder over the construction of a paragraph or the meaning of an image or metaphor. Sometimes they reread the text dozens of times.

As your expertise grows within the fields you study, you will undoubtedly learn to vary your reading speed and strategies according to your purposes, even to the point of considering "efficient" reading of certain texts to involve slowing way down and rereading.

How Expert Readers Use Rhetorical Knowledge to Read Efficiently

This section illustrates two strategies used by expert readers to apply rhetorical knowledge to their reading processes.

Using Genre Knowledge to Read Efficiently

Besides varying reading speed to match their purpose, experienced readers also adjust their reading strategies to match the genre of a text. It is clear that the articles represented in Figures 1.2 and 1.3 (pp. 236–237) call for different kinds of reading strategies, but you may be surprised to learn that many scientists wouldn't read the scholarly article straight through from beginning to end. Instead,

Physicists' Techniques for Efficient Reading

Researchers who studied the way that physicists read articles in physics journals found that the physicists seldom read the article from beginning to end but instead used their knowledge of the typical structure of scientific articles to find the information most relevant to their interests. Scientific articles typically begin with an abstract or summary of their contents. The main body of these articles includes a five-part structure: (1) an introduction that describes the research problem, (2) a review of other studies related to this problem, (3) a description of the methodology used in the research, (4) a report of the results, and (5) the conclusions drawn from the results. The physicists in the study read the abstracts first to see if an article was relevant to their own research. If it was, the experimental physicists went to the methodology section to see if the article reported any new methods. By contrast, the theoretical physicists went to the results section to see if the article reported any significant new results.

depending on their purpose, it is likely that they would read different sections in different order. The material in the following box describes how a group of physicists were guided both by their purpose for reading and by their familiarity with the genre conventions of scientific research reports. We invite you to read the material in the box before proceeding to the next paragraph.[5]

Considering how scientists with different interests read specialized articles in their discipline, we can surmise that some researchers would read the results section of the *Appetite* article very carefully, whereas others would concentrate on the methodology section. Still another reader, perhaps a graduate student interested in finding a dissertation topic, might read it to see what research the authors say still needs to be accomplished. With sharply narrow interests and purposes, these readers would probably not find the article difficult to read. In contrast, nonspecialists might find it daunting to read, but as experienced readers, they would recognize that it is not necessary to understand all the details in order to understand the article's gist. They might read the abstract, then skip directly to the discussion section, where the authors analyze the meaning and the significance of their results.

Using a Text's Social/Historical Context to Make Predictions and Ask Questions

Recognizing that a text is part of a larger conversation about a particular topic, experienced readers can also use textual cues—such as format, style, and terminology—as well as their own background knowledge to speculate about the original context of a text, make predictions about it, and formulate questions.

These strategies for actively engaging with a text's social or historical context are illustrated in Ann Feldman's report of interviews with expert readers reading texts within their own areas of expertise. For example, Professor Lynn Weiner, a social historian, describes in detail her behind-the-scenes thinking as she prepared to read a chapter entitled "From the Medieval to the Modern Family" from Philippe Aries's *Centuries of Childhood: A Social History of Family Life*, written in 1962. Quotations from Professor Weiner's description of her thinking are shown in the box below. As Professor Weiner reads, she continues to elaborate this context, confirming and revising predictions, asking new questions, evaluating what Aries has to say in light of the evidence he can provide, and assessing the value of his ideas to her own work

[5]Research reported by Cheryl Geisler, *Academic Literacy and the Nature of Expertise* (Hillsdale, NJ: Erlbaum, 1994), 20–21. Print.

Building a Context for Reading

"This work isn't precisely in my field and it is a difficult text. I also know it by its reputation. But, like any student, I need to create a context in which to understand this work. When the book was written, the idea of studying the family was relatively new. Before this time historians often studied kings, presidents, and military leaders. That's why this new type of social history encouraged us to ask, 'How did ordinary people live?' Not the kings, but the families in the middle ages. Then we have to ask: 'Which families is [Aries] talking about? What causes the change that he sees? ... For whom is the change significant?' ... I'll want to be careful not ... to assume the old family is bad and the new family is good. The title suggests a transition so I'll be looking for signs of it." [6]

as a social historian. She concludes by saying, "A path-breaking book, it was credited with advancing the idea that childhood as a stage of life is historically constructed and not the same in every culture and every time. In my own work I might refer to Aries as I think and write about families as they exist today."

Professor Weiner's description of creating a context for understanding the Aries book suggests that the ability to recognize what you do not know and to raise questions about a text is as important as identifying what you do know and understand. Sometimes readers can reconstruct context from external clues such as a title and headings; from a text's visual appearance; from background notes about the author, including the date and place of publication; or from what a book's table of contents reveals about its structure and scope. But readers often have to rely on internal evidence to get a full picture. A text's context and purpose may become evident through some quick spot reading (explained in the next chapter), especially in the introduction and conclusion. Sometimes, however, the full rhetorical and social context can be reconstructed only through a great deal of puzzling as you read. It's not unusual that a whole first reading is needed to understand exactly what conversation the writer is joining and how she or he intends to affect that conversation. Once that context becomes clear, rereading of key passages will make the text easier to comprehend.

Typical Reading-Based Writing Assignments Across the Curriculum

In college, a reading assignment is often only the first step in a complex series of activities that lead toward writing something that will be graded. In many cases, the material you are asked to read and respond to may include visual elements that demand attention, such as charts and graphs, photographs, drawings, or specific features of document or Web design. What you write will naturally vary according to the situation, ranging from a quick answer on an essay exam to an extensive source-based paper. In this section, we discuss five types of common college assignments in which reading plays a major role:

1. Writing to understand course content more fully
2. Writing to report your understanding of what a text says
3. Writing to practice the conventions of a particular type of text
4. Writing to make claims about a text
5. Writing to extend the conversation

---

[6]Ann Feldman, *Writing and Learning in the Disciplines* (New York: Harper, 1996), 16–17, 25–29. Print.

The role that reading plays in connection with these different purposes for writing can be placed along a continuum, starting at one end with assignments in which the ideas in the texts you read predominate and moving to assignments in which the content is subordinate to your own ideas and aims. The first two assignment types ask you to write in order to learn course subject matter and to practice careful listening to texts. The last three ask you to compose your own analyses and arguments for specific audiences. Writing teachers sometimes distinguish these two categories of assignment goals by referring to them as "writing to learn" and "learning to write."

Writing to Understand Course Content More Fully

"Writing-to-learn" assignments aim to deepen your understanding of materials you read by asking you to put the author/creator's ideas into your own words or to identify points of confusion for yourself. The primary audience for writing in this category is often yourself, although teachers may sometimes ask you to submit them so that they can check on your understanding and progress. The style is informal and conversational. Organization and grammatical correctness are less important than the quality of your engagement with the content of the reading. These assignments typically take one of the following forms.

In-Class Freewriting

The point of freewriting is to think rapidly without censoring your thoughts. It is often assigned in class as a way to stimulate thinking about the day's subject. A typical in-class freewrite assignment might be this:

> Choose what for you personally is the single most important word in what we read for today. You need not speculate about which word the author or your instructor or any other classmate would choose. Just choose the word that seems most important to you, and then explore in writing why you chose it. This word may occur only once or many times.[7]

Reading or Learning Logs

Reading or learning logs are informal assignments, usually organized chronologically, in which you record your understanding, questions, and responses to a reading or image. Some teachers give specific prompts for entries, whereas others just ask that you write them with a certain regularity and/or of a certain length. A typical prompt might be "How would you describe the author's voice in this essay?" If a teacher asks you simply to write your own reflections in a log, you might use some of the questions rhetorical readers ask (pp. 238–239) to examine the text's method and your response to it.

Double-Entry Journals

Double-entry journals are like reading logs but formatted so that you may conduct an ongoing dialogue with your own interpretations and reactions to a text. Once again, the audience is primarily yourself. Although the double-entry system was originally designed for lined notebook paper, it can work equally well—or even better—on screen. Here is how the system works: Divide a notebook page with a line down the middle, or set up a two-column layout in your word processing

---

[7]We thank Joan Ruffino, an instructor at the University of Wisconsin–Milwaukee, for this freewriting assignment.

program. On the right side of the page, record reading notes—direct quotations, observations, comments, questions, objections. On the left side, record your later reflections about those notes—second thoughts, responses to quotations, reactions to earlier comments, answers to questions or new questions. Skip lines as necessary so that your dialogue on the left lines up with your original notes on the right. Another option is to use a commenting function to create a sidebar column for your responses to your original notes; but in our experience, students find the spatial alignment difficult to track. Rhetorician Ann Berthoff, who popularized the double-entry approach, says that it provides readers with a means of conducting a "continuing audit of meaning."[8] In a double-entry journal, you carry on a conversation with yourself about a text.

Short Thought Pieces or Postings to a Discussion Board

Sometimes written for an instructor, sometimes for a specified group of peers, short (250–300 words) response papers or "thought" pieces are somewhat more formal than the assignments discussed so far, but they are still much more informal than essay assignments. They call for a fuller response than the previous types of writing, but the purpose is similar—to articulate an understanding of a particular text by identifying significant points and offering a personal response or interpretation of them. Teachers will often provide a specific prompt for these assignments, sometimes as a way to generate a series of short pieces that will build to a larger paper. When the piece is written for a discussion forum, instructors may ask that you include a question or respond to a classmate's questions.

Here is a sample response piece that was posted to an online class forum. The teacher asked the students to write about the insights they gleaned regarding obsessive-compulsive disorder (OCD) from reading Lauren Slater's essay "Black Swans," in which the author narrates the onset of her ongoing battle with it.

Student Posting to a Class Forum

Reading "Black Swans" taught me some basic information about OCD, but more importantly, it taught me how terrifying this disease can be. It begins with a single obsessive thought that leads to a cycle of anxiety, repetitive behaviors, and avoidance of situations that produce the obsessive thoughts. In severe cases, like Slater's, the person completely avoids life because the obsessive thoughts invade every aspect of life.

What impressed me most about this essay, however, was Slater's ability to put me in her shoes and make me feel some of the terror she felt. She vividly describes her experience at being stricken with this condition without warning. A single thought—"I can't concentrate"—suddenly blocked out all other thoughts. Even her own body seemed foreign to her and grotesque: "the phrase 'I can't concentrate on my hand' blocked out my hand, so all I saw was a blur of flesh giving way to the bones beneath, and inside the bones the grimy marrow, and in the grimy marrow the individual cells, all disconnected." I see why Max says it was the most terrifying aspect of the disease to him. I can't imagine being disconnected from my own body. More horrifying to me, though, was her sense of being completely unable to control her mind: "My mind was devouring my mind." I will be interested to see what others think.

---

[8]Ann Berthoff, *The Making of Meaning* (Montclair, NJ: Boynton Cook, 1981), 45. Print.

Writing to Report Your Understanding of What a Text Says

Another common reading-based assignment asks you to report your understanding of what a text says. Here, your goal is to summarize the text rather than respond to it. Reports like this are necessary, for example, when essay exam questions ask students to contrast the ideas of several authors. Another example would be an **annotated bibliography** summarizing sources related to a particular topic or question, or a literature review at the beginning of a report for a science class. A summary can be as short as a single sentence (when, for example, you want to provide context for a quotation in a paper) or longer and more detailed (when, for example, you are summarizing an opposing view that you intend to refute in your own argument.) Although summaries or reports of your understanding of a text will vary in length and purpose, they are always expected to be accurate, fair, and balanced.

Writing to Practice the Conventions of a Particular Type of Text

Assignments that ask you to practice the conventions of a particular type of writing—its organizational format, style, ways of presenting evidence, and so on—use readings as models. Such assignments are common in college courses. In a journalism class, for example, you would learn to write a news report using the inverted pyramid structure; in a science course, you would learn to write up the results of a lab experiment in a particular scientific report format. Novices in a discipline learn to write in specialized genres by reading examples and practicing their formats and rhetorical "moves."

Generally, using readings as models of a genre or subgenre involves the following activities:

- Identifying the features that characterize a particular type of text
- Noting the ways in which a rhetorical situation affects the features identified in model texts
- Deciding on your own topic and reason for writing this particular type of text
- Using the features of the model text (or texts) and your own rhetorical situation to guide your writing

Let's say, for example, that you've been asked to write a **proposal argument**. Proposals typically include three main features: description of the problem, proposal of a solution, and justification of that solution. As you read sample proposals, you will find that in different contexts, authors deal with these features differently, depending on their audience and purpose. In some cases, for example, there is a great deal of description of the problem because the intended audience is unfamiliar with it or doesn't recognize it as a problem. In other cases, it is presumed that the intended reading audience already recognizes the problem. The key to success is to adapt a model text's structural and stylistic characteristics to your own rhetorical purpose, not to follow the model slavishly. (For more details about proposal arguments, see Table 1.1 on pp. 232–233.)

In courses across the curriculum, your ability to analyze and adopt the conventions particular to a given discipline's ways of writing will help you write successful papers. For example, when you are asked in a philosophy class to write an argument in response to Immanuel Kant's *Critique of Pure Reason*, you are primarily being asked to engage with the ideas in the text. But secondarily, you are also being asked to practice the conventions of writing a philosophical argument in which counterexamples and counterarguments are expected. Thus, in any field of study, it pays to be alert not only to the ideas presented in material you are assigned to read, but also to its structure and style.

Writing to Make Claims About a Text

Assignments in this category ask you to analyze and critique texts, including texts in which images and layout are key elements of rhetorical effect. Such papers must go beyond a summary of what a text says to make claims about that content and how it is presented. Many academic writers take as their field of study the texts produced by others. Literary critics study novels, poems, and plays; cultural critics analyze song lyrics, advertisements, cereal boxes, and television scripts; historians analyze primary source documents from the past; theologians scrutinize the sacred texts of different religions; lawyers analyze the documents entered into court proceedings, the exact wording of laws and statutes, and the decisions of appellate courts. In all these cases, the analysis and critique involve examining small parts of the whole to understand, explain, and perhaps object to, overall points and success.

Many college composition courses ask students to write rhetorical analyses of texts. To **analyze**—a word that at its root means "take apart"—a text, you need to identify specific rhetorical methods and strategies used by the author, show how these rhetorical choices contribute to the text's impact, and evaluate those elements in light of the author's evident purpose. In assignments like this, the text and your ideas about it are of equal importance. These assignments asking for analysis are not invitations for you to refer briefly to the text and then take off on your own opinions about the topic, nor are they invitations merely to summarize or rehearse what the text has said. Rather, analysis assignments expect you to engage critically with a specific text. On the one hand, you will be expected to represent what the text said accurately and fairly. On the other hand, you will be expected to offer your own analysis, interpretation, or critique in a way that enables readers to see the text differently. Further guidance about engaging with texts this way appears, which includes guidelines for writing a rhetorical analysis along with a sample assignment and student paper as illustration.

Writing to Extend the Conversation

These assignments treat texts as voices in a conversation about ideas. They typically ask writers to read and synthesize material from several sources. Here, your own ideas and aims take center stage; your source texts play important but less prominent backup roles. The most familiar form this assignment takes is the research or seminar paper. A key difference between these assignments and high school research papers is that college instructors expect the paper to present your own argument, not simply to report what others have said. In other words, you are expected to articulate a significant question or problem, research what published authors have said about it in print or on the Web, and formulate your own argument. To write these multisource papers successfully, you must use your source texts primarily to position yourself in the conversation and to supply supporting data, information, or testimony. The argument—your main points—must come from you.

A helpful way to approach these assignments is to treat the texts you have read as springboards for further research and discovery. Think of the readings you encounter in your research as voices in a conversation that your essay will join. By giving you the opportunity to define your own purposes for writing in dialog with other texts, such assignments prepare you for the research assignments typical of many college courses, where your goal is to synthesize material from a number of sources and then produce your own paper, inserting another voice—your own—into the ongoing conversation.

Chapter Summary

This chapter has focused on the three major elements of rhetorical context—purpose, audience, and genre. In the first part of the chapter, we explained how to analyze these three factors for a text that you are reading. We then showed you how to analyze your own rhetorical context as a reader/writer. In particular, we showed you how

- To analyze a text's original rhetorical context
- To determine your own rhetorical context and to match your reading strategies to your own purposes
- To use rhetorical knowledge to make your reading more efficient
  - By using genre knowledge to read more efficiently
  - By analyzing the text's original social/historical context

Finally, we explained five different ways that assignments across the curriculum might ask you to use readings.

Part IV:
Structure and Mechanics

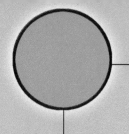

Chapter 1:
The Essay

Each body paragraph begins with a topic sentence.

The introductory paragraph introduces the essay's topic and contains its thesis statement.

The title gives a hint about the essay's topic.

The thesis statement contains the essay's topic and its controlling idea.

What Is an Essay?

An *essay* is a series of paragraphs that support one main or central idea. Essays differ in length, style, and subject, but the structure of an essay generally consists of an *introductory paragraph*, several *body paragraphs*, and a *concluding paragraph*.

Before you begin reading the following chapters, become familiar with the parts of the common five-paragraph essay.

Alternative Culture

In an era when alternative has become mainstream, what's an angst-ridden teenager to do? Dyeing hair punk colors has become passé. Goths with white face powder, dark lipstick, and lots of eyeliner no longer attract even a second glance. Everyone listens to "alternative" music. It has become increasingly hard for a teenager to rebel against the mainstream.

In other eras, youths had something to rebel about. The 1960s had the hippie era, as young adults rebelled by protesting against injustice, the Vietnam War, and the restrictions of society. LSD, marijuana, and free love reigned. Flash forward to the 1970s, when the punk movement came into existence with bands such as the Sex Pistols, and unemployed youths railed against consumerism. Kurt Cobain in the early 1990s became the rallying cry for a new generation of teenagers disillusioned with the confines of society. But what is happening now? Nobody is in the streets. Nobody is rising up.

Furthermore, bizarre fashion statements have become acceptable. Previously, rebellious teenagers had to resort to shopping in thrift stores or making their own clothes to attain their desired fashion statement. Luckily (or unluckily) for them, society now makes it easy to dress like an individual. Companies make jeans that already have holes in them so they do not have to wait around to have that punk look. If they want to look different, they can try Urban Outfitters, the trendy chain store for people who are fed up with trendy chain stores, where they can look "unique" just like everyone else who shops there.

With this watering down of alternative culture, it has become harder and harder to shock anyone or gain any notorious press. Marilyn Manson, the press's former whipping boy and scapegoat for music as a cause of violence in society (witness the aftermath of the Columbine shootings), has faded from the public's view. Then Eminem became a strange symbol for the increasingly difficult quest to be different from everyone else and to shock society into paying attention. He got some press for his song about killing his wife, but today, nobody is paying attention.

Today's teens, with little to rebel against, find themselves wearing clothing that is mainstream and espousing ideas that shock no one. Perhaps to be truly alternative, adolescents must think for themselves. Authentic is best, no matter what that might be. They can dress as punk or as preppy as they like. They should not let society's version of "alternative" control their actions. The truly cool can think for themselves.

The concluding paragraph brings the essay to a satisfactory close.

Each body paragraph contains details that support the thesis statement.

—*Veena Thomas, student*

Taken from *The Canadian Writer's World: Paragraphs and Essays,* First Canadian Edition.

Writing the Essay

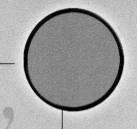

> *Without words, without writing, and without books there would be no history, and there could be no concept of humanity.*
>
> —HERMANN HESSE
> *German author (1877–1962)*

CONTENTS

Completed in 1973, the Sydney Opera House in Australia has tonnes of concrete, steel, and glass supporting its structure. In the same way, an essay is a sturdy structure that is supported by a strong thesis statement and solid body paragraphs held together by plenty of facts and examples.

EXPLORING

Explore Topics

There are limitless topics for writing essays. Your knowledge and personal experiences will help you find topics and develop ideas when you write your essay.

When you are planning your essay, consider your topic, audience, and purpose. Your **topic** is who or what you are writing about. Your **audience** is your intended reader, and your **purpose** is your reason for writing. Do you hope to entertain, inform, or persuade the reader?

Narrowing the Topic

Your instructor may assign you a topic for your essay, or you may need to think of your own. In either case, you need to narrow your topic (make it more specific) to ensure that it suits your purpose for writing and fits the size of the assignment. To narrow your topic, you can use some exploring methods such as questioning or brainstorming.

When you narrow your topic, keep in mind that an essay contains several paragraphs; therefore, an essay topic can be broader than a paragraph topic. In the following examples, you will notice that the essay topic is narrow but is slightly larger than the paragraph topic.

Broad Topic	Paragraph Topic	Essay Topic
Job interview	Dressing for the interview	Preparing for the interview
Rituals	College orientation week	Initiation rituals

Hint Choosing an Essay Topic

Paragraphs and essays can also be about the same topic. However, an essay has more details and concrete examples to support its thesis.

Do not make the mistake of choosing an essay topic that is too broad. Essays that try to cover a large topic risk being superficial and overly general. Make sure that your topic is specific enough that you can cover it in an essay.

DAVID NARROWS HIS TOPIC

Student writer David Raby-Pepin used both brainstorming and questioning to narrow his broad topic, "music." His audience was his English instructor, and the purpose of his assignment was to persuade.

- Should street performers be required to have a licence?
- downloading music
- difference in earning power between classical and pop musicians
- Why do some rock bands have staying power?
- how to be a successful musician
- What is hip-hop culture?
- the popularity of shows like *So You Think You Can Dance*
- difference between poetry and song lyrics

The Writer's Desk Narrow the Topics

Practise narrowing five broad topics.

EXAMPLE:

Money: *– reasons it doesn't make you happy*

– teach children about value of money

– best ways to be financially successful

1. Crime: _____

_____

_____

2. Volunteer work: _____

_____

_____

3. Fashion: _____

_____

_____

4. Advertising: _____

_____

_____

5. Education: _____

_____

_____

DEVELOPING

The Thesis Statement

Once you have narrowed the topic of your essay, develop your thesis statement. The **thesis statement**—like the topic sentence in a paragraph—introduces the topic of the essay and arouses the interest of the reader.

Characteristics of a Good Thesis Statement

A thesis statement has three important characteristics.

- It expresses the main topic of the essay.
- It contains a controlling idea.
- It is a complete sentence that usually appears in the essay's introductory paragraph.

Here is an example of an effective thesis statement.

      topic   controlling idea

Marriage has lost its importance for many young people in our society.

Writing an Effective Thesis Statement

When you develop your thesis statement, ask yourself the following questions.

1. **Is my thesis statement a complete statement that has a controlling idea?**
   Your thesis statement should always reveal a complete thought and make a point about the topic. It should not announce the topic or express a widely known fact.

Incomplete:	Gambling problems.
	(This statement is not complete.)
Announcement:	I will write about lotteries.
	(This statement announces the topic but says nothing relevant about the topic. Do not use expressions such as *I will write about . . .* or *My topic is . . .*)
Thesis statement:	A lottery win will not necessarily lead to happiness.

2. **Does my thesis statement make a valid and supportable point?** Your thesis statement should express a valid point that you can support with evidence. It should not be a vaguely worded statement, and it should not be a highly questionable generalization.

Vague:	Workplace relationships are harmful.
	(For whom are they harmful?)
Invalid point:	Women earn less money than men.
	(Is this really true for all women in all professions? This generalization might be hard to prove.)
Thesis statement:	Before co-workers become romantically involved, they should carefully consider possible problems.

3. **Can I support my thesis statement in an essay?** Your thesis statement should express an idea that you can support in an essay. It should not be too broad or too narrow.

Too broad:	There are many museums in the world.
	(It would be difficult to write an essay about this topic.)
Too narrow:	The Canadian War Museum is in Ottawa.
	(What more is there to say?)
Thesis statement:	Ottawa's Canadian War Museum contains fascinating artifacts related to the secret world of espionage.

 **Give Specific Details**

Give enough details to make your thesis statement focused and clear. Your instructor may want you to guide the reader through your main points. To do this, mention both your main point and your supporting points in your thesis statement. In other words, your thesis statement provides a map for the readers to follow.

Weak:	My first job taught me many things.
Better:	My first job taught me about responsibility, organization, and the importance of teamwork.

PRACTICE I

Identify the problem in each thesis statement. Then revise each statement to make it more interesting and complete.

Announces	Invalid	Broad
Incomplete	Vague	Narrow

EXAMPLE:

I will write about human misery on television news.

Problem: _Announces_

Revised statement: _Television news programs should not treat personal tragedies as big news._

1. I think that college friendships are important.

   Problem: _____

   Revised statement: _____

   _____

2. Scholarships go to athletes, so academic excellence is not appreciated in colleges.

   Problem: _____

   Revised statement: _____

   _____

3. Scientific discoveries have changed the world.

   Problem: _____

   Revised statement: _____

   _____

4. The streets are becoming more dangerous.

   Problem: _____

   Revised statement: _____

   _____

5. How to use a digital camera.

   Problem: _____

   Revised statement: _____

   _____

6. This essay will talk about security and privacy on the Internet.

   Problem: _____

   Revised statement: _____

   _____

The Writer's Desk   **Write Thesis Statements**

For each item, choose a narrowed topic from the Writer's Desk on pages 252–253. Then write an interesting thesis statement. Remember that each thesis statement should contain a controlling idea.

EXAMPLE: Topic: Money

Narrowed topic: *Winning a lottery*

Thesis statement: *Rather than improving your life, a lottery win can lead to feelings of guilt, paranoia, and boredom.*

1. Topic: Crime

   Narrowed topic: _____

   Thesis statement: _____

   _____

2. Topic: Volunteer work

   Narrowed topic: _____

   Thesis statement: _____

   _____

3. Topic: Fashion

   Narrowed topic: _____

   Thesis statement: _____

   _____

4. Topic: Advertising

   Narrowed topic: _____

   Thesis statement: _____

   _____

5. Topic: Education

   Narrowed topic: _____

   Thesis statement: _____

   _____

The Supporting Ideas

The thesis statement expresses the main idea of the entire essay. In the following illustration, you can see how the ideas flow in an essay. Topic sentences relate to the thesis statement, and details support the topic sentences; therefore, every single idea in the essay is unified and supports the thesis.

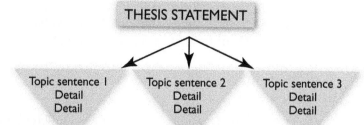

THESIS STATEMENT

Topic sentence 1
Detail
Detail

Topic sentence 2
Detail
Detail

Topic sentence 3
Detail
Detail

PRACTICE 2

Read the following essay. After you have finished reading, do the following:

1. Create an effective thesis statement. It should sum up the point of the entire essay.

2. Write a topic sentence at the beginning of each body paragraph. The topic sentence should sum up the main point of the paragraph in an interesting way.

Introduction:
Danger has always been synonymous with travel. In past centuries, pirates on the high seas attacked passing ships. Land travellers were not much safer; bandits could attack their covered carriages. Even trains were not safe; in 1904 the outlaw Billy Miner held up a train in Mission Junction and robbed it. Today, with modern communication and with high-speed trains and planes, travel is quick and relatively risk-free. Nonetheless, there are still certain hazards inherent in travelling. **Thesis statement:** _____

_____

Body paragraph 1 topic sentence: _____

_____

For example, before you arrive in a new town, find an address and phone number for affordable lodging, and book a room for your first night. If you are a budget traveller, you can always find cheaper accommodations the next day. If you are going to visit a large city, plan to arrive during the daylight hours. It is dangerous to arrive at night and then try to find your way around. Also, make sure that you have a map of your destination. You can download maps on the Internet.

Body paragraph 2 topic sentence: _____

_____

Do not flash your money in public places. You might wear a money belt under your clothing. One innovative solution is to sew long, extended pockets on the insides of your clothes; you could keep your cheques and passport there. In a small, easily accessible purse or wallet, keep small amounts of local currency for your daily spending.

Body paragraph 3 topic sentence: _____
_____

For example, you could bring along a first aid kit that includes bandages and pain relievers. Wear hats in very hot, sunny places. If you are visiting a tropical country, make sure you have the proper vaccinations. Be careful about where you eat and what you eat, and buy bottled drinking water. Your health is important. Obviously, if you get sick, you are not going to enjoy your trip.

Conclusion:

Although robberies can happen, it is unlikely that someone will physically hurt you. If you take risks with your health, if you are careless with your money and passports, or if you underestimate thieves, you may have an unpleasant experience. Of course, if you are careful, you should have a perfectly safe and exciting trip.

Generating Supporting Ideas

An effective essay has **unity** when the body paragraphs support the thesis statement. When you develop supporting ideas, make sure that they all focus on the central point that you are making in the thesis statement. To generate ideas for body paragraphs, you could use exploring strategies such as brainstorming, clustering, or freewriting.

DAVID'S SUPPORTING IDEAS

David created a list to support his thesis statement. Then he reread his supporting points and removed ideas that he did not want to develop in his essay.

THESIS STATEMENT: Rap and hip-hop artists use their music to share their positive cultural values with others.

- use lyrics to reveal their religious opinions
- Christian lyrics
- ~~hip hop inspired breakdancing~~
- praise Allah
- want to promote peace
- some address issues of violence
- ~~some hip hop artists have been jailed~~
- advise fans about healthy lifestyles
- warn about drugs
- talk about AIDS

The Writer's Desk List Supporting Ideas

Choose two of your thesis statements from the previous Writer's Desk on page 256, and create two lists of possible supporting ideas.

Thesis 1: _____   Thesis 2: _____

_____   _____

Support: _____   Support: _____

_____   _____

_____   _____

_____   _____

_____   _____

_____   _____

_____   _____

_____   _____

_____   _____

_____   _____

Organizing Your Ideas

After you have examined your list of supporting ideas, choose three or four that are most compelling and most clearly support your statement. Highlight your favourite ideas, and then group together related ideas. Finally, make your essay as clear and coherent as possible by organizing your ideas in a logical manner using time, space, or emphatic order.

DAVID'S EXAMPLE

David underlined his three best supporting points, and he grouped related ideas using emphatic order.

3 — use lyrics to reveal their religious opinions
  — Christian lyrics
  — hip hop inspired breakdancing
  — praise Allah

1 — want to promote peace
  — some address issues of violence
  — some hip hop artists have been jailed

2 — advise fans about healthy lifestyles
  — warn about drugs
  — talk about AIDS

The Writer's Desk   **Organize Your Ideas**

Look at the list you produced in the previous Writer's Desk, and then follow these steps.

1. Highlight at least three ideas from your list that you think are most compelling and most clearly illustrate the point you are making in your thesis statement.

2. Group together any related ideas with the three supporting ideas.

3. Organize your ideas using time, space, or emphatic order.

The Essay Plan

An **essay plan** or an **outline** can help you organize your thesis statement and supporting ideas before writing your first draft. To create an essay plan, follow these steps.

- Look at your list of ideas and identify the best supporting ideas.
- Write topic sentences that express the main supporting ideas.
- Add details under each topic sentence.

In the planning stage, you do not have to develop your introduction and conclusion. It is sufficient to simply write your thesis statement and an idea for your conclusion. Later, when you develop your essay, you can develop the introduction and conclusion.

DAVID'S ESSAY PLAN

David wrote topic sentences and supporting examples and organized his ideas into a plan. Notice that he begins with his thesis statement, and he indents his supporting ideas.

THESIS STATEMENT:	Rap and hip-hop artists use their music to share their positive cultural values with others.
Body paragraph 1:	Many musicians shout out a powerful message of nonviolence. — They promote peace. — Some artists address the issue of violence.
Body paragraph 2:	Some advise fans about responsible and healthy lifestyles. — They discuss the importance of good parenting. — They talk about drug addiction or AIDS.

Body paragraph 3:   These urban musicians use their poetry to reveal
                           their religious beliefs.
                           — Some show their Christian faith through the
                             lyrics.
                           — Others praise Allah.

Concluding sentence: Finally, music is a way for rap musicians to share
                           their personal culture with the world.

Writing a Formal Essay Plan

Most of the time, a basic essay plan is sufficient. However, in some of your courses, your instructor may ask you to make a formal plan. A formal plan uses Roman numerals and letters to identify main and supporting ideas.

Thesis statement: _____

  I. _____

    A. _____

    B. _____

 II. _____

    A. _____

    B. _____

III. _____

    A. _____

    B. _____

Concluding idea: _____

PRACTICE 3

Create an essay plan based on Veena Thomas's essay "Alternative Culture" on page 250.

_____

_____

_____

_____

_____

_____

_____

_____

_____

_____

_____

_____

_____

_____

PRACTICE 4

Complete the following essay plan. Add details under each supporting point. Make sure that the details relate to the topic sentence.

Thesis statement: Rather than improving your life, a lottery win can lead to feelings of guilt, paranoia, and boredom.

I.   Feelings of guilt are common in newly rich people.

Details: A. _____

_____

B. _____

_____

C. _____

_____

II. Lottery winners often become paranoid.

Details: A. _____

_____

B. _____

_____

C. _____

_____

III. After lottery winners quit their jobs, they commonly complain of boredom and loneliness.

Details: A. _____

_____

B. _____

_____

C. _____

_____

Concluding idea: _____

_____

_____

The Writer's Desk **Write an Essay Plan**

Write an essay plan using one of your thesis statements and supporting details you came up with in the previous Writer's Desk.

Thesis statement: _____

_____

I. _____

Details: A. _____

B. _____

C. _____

II. _____

Details: A. _____

B. _____

C. _____

III. _____

Details: A. _____

B. _____

C. _____

Concluding idea: _____

_____

The Introduction

After you have made an essay plan, you develop the sections of your essay by creating an effective introduction, linking paragraphs, and writing a conclusion.

The **introductory paragraph** introduces the subject of your essay and contains the thesis statement. A strong introduction will capture the reader's attention and make him or her want to read on. Introductions may have a lead-in, and they can be developed in several different ways.

The Lead-In

You can begin the introduction with an attention-grabbing opening sentence, or lead-in. There are three common types of lead-ins.

- Quotation
- Surprising or provocative statement
- Question

Introduction Styles

You can develop the introduction in several different ways. Experiment with any of these introduction styles.

- **Give general or historical background information.** The general or historical information gradually leads to your thesis. For example, in an essay about winning a lottery, you could begin by giving a brief history of lotteries.
- **Tell an interesting anecdote.** Open your essay with a story that leads to your thesis statement. For example, you might begin your lottery essay by telling the story of a real-life lottery winner.
- **Present a vivid description.** Give a detailed description, and then state your thesis. For example, you might describe the moment when a lottery winner realizes that he or she has won.
- **Present an opposing position.** Open your essay with an idea that contradicts a common belief, and build to your thesis. For instance, if most people want to win the lottery, you could begin your essay by saying that you definitely do not want to be a millionaire.
- **Give a definition.** Define a term, and then state your thesis. For example, in an essay about the lottery, you could begin by defining *happiness*.

 **Placement of the Thesis Statement**

Although a paragraph often begins with a topic sentence, an introduction does not begin with a thesis statement. Rather, most introductory paragraphs are shaped like a funnel. The most general statement introduces the topic. The following sentences become more focused and lead to a clear, specific thesis statement. Therefore, the thesis statement is generally the last sentence in the introduction.

PRACTICE 5

In introductions A through E, the thesis statement is underlined. Read each introduction and then answer the questions that follow. Look at David's example for some guidance.

DAVID'S INTRODUCTION

Can hip-hop, with its obscene lyrics and violent culture, have any redeeming qualities? Hip-hop and rap music originated from poor, minority-inhabited neighbourhoods located in New York City. Since the residents did not have enough money to buy musical instruments, they began creating beats with their mouths. This raw form of music rapidly became popular within these communities because it gave people a way to express themselves and to develop their creative abilities. Rap and hip-hop artists use their music to share their positive cultural values with others.

1. What type of lead-in does David use?   _**Question**_

2. What introduction style does he use?
    a. Description   b. Definition
    (c.) Background information   d. Opposing position

3. What is his essay about?   _**The positive message of hip-hop and rap music**_

A. "I never saw the blow to my head come from Huck. Bam! And I was on all fours, struggling for my equilibrium." These are the words of Kody Scott, a former member of a Los Angeles street gang. Kody is describing part of the initiation ritual he endured in order to join a local branch (or "set") of the Crips. First, he stole an automobile to demonstrate his "street smarts" and willingness to break the law. Then he allowed himself to be beaten, showing both that he was tough and that he was ready to do whatever the gang required of him. He completed the process by participating in a "military action"—killing a member of a rival gang. Initiations like this are by no means rare in today's street gangs. Kody, by the way, was just eleven years old.

—Linda L. Lindsey and Stephen Beach, "Joining the Crips," *Essentials of Sociology*

1. What type of lead-in does the author use? _____

2. What introduction style does the author use?
    a. Anecdote   b. Definition
    c. Background information   d. Opposing position

3. What is this essay about? _____

B. Many practices in conventional medicine are safe and effective. There are, arguably, many that, while effective in the short term, can also have serious adverse consequences. Integrative medicine invites us to look outside our self-imposed box and to begin to understand how there really are no *conventional* and *alternative* distinctions, except in our own minds. Healing is healing. Should not our primary interest be helping our patients to heal safely and effectively? If this is our goal, then we will soon realize that all healing practices, orthodox or alternative, can be complementary if used appropriately and judiciously. This is the goal of integrative medicine. In order to reach this goal, we need to begin a dialogue with other healing practitioners and with our patients, the public, and governments. We need to inform ourselves about other practices and their potential benefits and limitations with an open mind and a healthy scepticism. And we need to encourage appropriate research in these fields in order to evaluate scientifically their potential use in a more holistic model of care.

—Mark Sherman, MD CM, CCFP, "Integrative Medicine: Model for Health Care Reform,"
Canadian Family Physician

4. What type of lead-in does the author use? _____

5. What introduction style does the author use?
   a. Anecdote   b. Definition
   c. Description   d. Opposing position

6. What is this essay about? _____

> **C.** High school is a waste of time. In fact, it is a baby-sitting service for teens who are too old to be baby-sat. In England, fifteen-year-olds graduate and can choose technical or university streams of education. They are free to choose what to study, or they can stop schooling and get jobs. In short, they are treated like mature adults. In our country, we prolong the experience of forced schooling much longer than is necessary. We should abolish high schools and introduce a system of technical or pre-university schooling.
>
> —Adelie Zang, Student

7. What type of lead-in does the author use? _____

8. What introduction style does the author use?
   a. Anecdote   b. Definition
   c. Background information   d. Opposing position

9. What is this essay about? _____

> **D.** When I was 8 years old, I read a story about a boy who built a robot out of junkyard scraps. The robot in the story could move, talk, and think, just like a person. For some reason, I found the idea of building a robot very appealing, so I decided to build one of my own. I remember optimistically collecting body parts: pipes for arms and legs, motors for muscles, light bulbs for eyes, and a big tin can for the head, fully expecting to assemble the pieces into a working mechanical man. After nearly electrocuting myself a few times, I began to get my parts to move, light up, and make noises. I felt I was making progress. If I only had the right tools and the right parts, I was sure that I could build a machine that could think.
>
> —Danny Hillis, "Can They Feel Your Pain"?

10. What introduction style does the author use?
    a. Anecdote   b. Definition
    c. Background information   d. Opposing position

11. What is this essay about? _____

> **E.** The story of how Christianity ultimately conquered the Roman Empire is one of the most remarkable in history. Christianity faced the hostility of the established religious institutions of its native Judea and had to compete not only against the official cults of Rome and the sophisticated philosophies of the educated classes, but also against "mystery" religions like the cults of Mithra, Isis, and Osiris. The Christians also suffered formal persecution, yet Christianity finally became the official religion of the empire.
>
> —Albert M. Craig et al., *The Heritage of World Civilizations*

12. What introduction style does the author use?
    a. Description
    b. Definition
    c. Historical information
    d. Opposing position

13. What is this essay about? _____

The Writer's Desk Write Three Introductions

In the previous Writer's Desk, you made an essay plan. Now, write three different styles of introductions for your essay. Use the same thesis statement in all three introductions. Later, you can choose the best introduction for your essay.

The Conclusion

A **conclusion** is a final paragraph that rephrases the thesis statement and summarizes the main points in the essay. To make your conclusion more interesting and original, you could close with a prediction, a suggestion, a quotation, or a call to action.

DAVID'S CONCLUSION

David concluded his essay by restating his main points.

> Finally, music is a way for hip-hop and rap musicians to share their personal culture with the world. This cultural facet can be reflected through different values, religious beliefs, and ways of life.

He could then close his essay with one of the following:

Prediction: If you are concerned about hip-hop portraying negative images, don't abandon the music yet. There are many artists who promote and will continue to promote positive values through upbeat lyrics.

Suggestion: Hip-hop fans should encourage musicians to continue to give a positive message through their music.

Call to action: If you are concerned by the negative message of hip-hop music, make your opinions heard by joining the debate on hip-hop blogs and buying CDs from musicians who only write positive lyrics.

Quotation: According to hip-hop artist Doug E. Fresh, "Hip Hop is supposed to uplift and create, to educate people on a larger level, and to make a change."

PRACTICE 6

Read the following conclusions and answer the questions.

A. As soon as smoking is banned in all public places, we will see the benefits. Our hospitals will treat fewer smoking-related illnesses, and this will save money. Non-smokers will be saved from noxious fumes, and smokers, who will be forced to smoke outdoors, might feel a greater desire to give up the habit. In the future, we will have a world where a non-smoker can go through life without having to breathe in someone else's cigarette smoke.

—Jordan Lamott, "Butt Out!"

1. What method does the author use to end the conclusion?
    a. Prediction   b. Suggestion
    c. Quotation   d. Call to action

B. Ultimately, spam is annoying, offensive, time consuming, and expensive. There is nothing good to say about it. Spam marketers will argue that we get junk in our mail, and that cannot be denied, but we do not get crates of junk mail every week. If we did, paper junk mail would be banned in a hurry. The only real solution is for governments around the world to work together in order to make spam production illegal. Governments should actively hunt down and prosecute spammers.

—Adela Fonseca, "Ban Spam"

2. What method does the author use to end the conclusion?
    a. Prediction   b. Suggestion
    c. Quotation   d. Call to action

C. Every once in a while the marketing wizards pay lip service to today's expanding career options for women and give us a Scientist Barbie complete with a tiny chemistry set as an accessory. But heaven forbid should little Johnnie plead for his parents to buy him that Scientist Barbie. After all, it is acceptable for girls to foray, occasionally, into the world of boy-style play, but for boys the opposite "sissified" behavior is taboo. Why is this? One commentator, D. R. Shaffer, says, "The major task for young girls is to learn how not to be babies, whereas young boys must learn how not to be girls."

—Dorothy Nixon, "Put GI Barbie in the Bargain Bin"

3. What method does the author use to end the conclusion?
    a. Prediction   b. Suggestion
    c. Quotation   d. Call to action

 **Avoiding Conclusion Problems**

In your conclusion, do not contradict your main point, and do not introduce new or irrelevant information. David initially included the next sentences in his conclusion.

> The rap and hip-hop movement is not restrained only to the musical scene. It influences many other facets of art and urban culture as well. It can be found in dance and fashion, for instance. Thus, it is very versatile.

He revised his conclusion when he realized that some of his ideas were new and irrelevant information. His essay does not discuss dance or fashion.

The Writer's Desk **Write a Conclusion**

In previous Writer's Desks, you wrote an introduction and an essay plan. Now write a conclusion for your essay.

The First Draft

After creating an introduction and conclusion, and after arranging the supporting ideas in a logical order, you are ready to write your first draft. The first draft includes your introduction, several body paragraphs, and your concluding paragraph.

The Writer's Desk **Write the First Draft**

In previous Writer's Desks, you wrote an introduction, a conclusion, and an essay plan. Now write the first draft of your essay.

REVISING AND EDITING

Revising and Editing the Essay

Revising your essay is an extremely important step in the writing process. When you revise your essay, you modify it to make it stronger and more convincing. You do this by reading the essay critically, looking for faulty logic, poor organization, or poor sentence style. Then you reorganize and rewrite it, making any necessary changes.

Editing is the last stage in writing. When you edit, you proofread your writing and make sure that it is free of errors.

Revising for Unity

To revise for **unity,** verify that all of your body paragraphs support the thesis statement. Also look carefully at each body paragraph: ensure that the sentences support the topic sentence.

 **Avoiding Unity Problems**

Here are two common errors to check for as you revise your body paragraphs.

- **Rambling paragraphs.** The paragraphs in the essay ramble on. Each paragraph has several topics, and there is no clearly identifiable topic sentence.
- **Artifical breaks.** A long paragraph is split into smaller paragraphs arbitrarily, and each smaller paragraph lacks a central focus.

To correct either of these errors, revise each body paragraph until it has *one* main idea that supports the thesis statement.

Revising for Adequate Support

When you revise for adequate **support,** ensure that there are enough details and examples to make your essay strong and convincing. Include examples, statistics, quotations, or anecdotes.

Revising for Coherence

When you revise for **coherence,** ensure that paragraphs flow smoothly and logically. To guide the reader from one idea to the next, or from one paragraph to the next, try using **paragraph links.**

You can develop connections between paragraphs using three methods.

1. **Repeat words or phrases from the thesis statement in each body paragraph.** In the next example, *violent* and *violence* are repeated words.

Thesis statement:	Although some will argue that <u>violent</u> movies are simply a reflection of a <u>violent</u> society, these movies actually cause a lot of the <u>violence</u> around us.
Body paragraph 1:	Action movie heroes train children to solve problems with <u>violence</u>.
Body paragraph 2:	<u>Violent movies</u> are "how to" films for many sick individuals.

2. **Refer to the main idea in the previous paragraph, and link it to your current topic sentence.** In body paragraph 2, the writer reminds the reader of the first point (the newly rich feel useless) and then introduces the next point.

Thesis statement:	A cash windfall may cause more problems than it solves.
Body paragraph 1:	The newly rich often lose their desire to become productive citizens, and they end up <u>feeling useless</u>.
Body paragraph 2:	Apart from <u>feeling useless</u>, many heirs and lottery winners also tend to feel guilty about their wealth.

3. **Use a transitional word or phrase to lead the reader to your next idea.**

   Body paragraph 2:   <u>Furthermore</u>, the newly rich often feel guilty about their wealth.

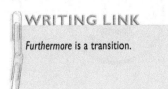

WRITING LINK

Furthermore is a transition.

Expository Writing

Chapter Objectives

After completing this chapter you will be able to

1. take advantage of rhetorical modes to shape ideas in expository writing;

2. write an expository essay informing readers about an academic subject;

3. provide reasoned support for your opinions in an expository essay;

4. draw a timeline to help you in developing your thesis statement;

5. improve your writing by appropriate placement of transitional words and phrases.

Introduction

Expository writing informs readers by explaining ideas. The writer may choose to write using opinions, but they must be reasoned out and supported. As a student, most of the writing you will do for courses will be expository. A nursing student may be asked to write an essay about nursing principles; a biology student may be asked to write an essay about ecosystems; a history student may be asked to write about the first administrator of British Columbia.

As a student using expository writing for many of your course assignments, you want to know about the rules and guidelines, or the **conventions of writing**, connected to this kind of writing. This chapter will help you focus on the conventions of expository essay writing.

Taken from *Spotlight on Critical Skills in Essay Writing with 2009 MLA updates*, Second Edition, by Carole Anne May.

Using Common Rhetorical Modes in Expository Writing

Rhetoric is a term originally used by the ancient Romans and Greeks to refer to the powers of oration. The ancient Greek orators, known for their eloquent use of language, gave moving, persuasive speeches about important themes many centuries before text was widely available. To be a brilliant orator in those times meant a life of study of rhetoric, dialectics, and grammar. Today rhetoric has just as much to do with argumentative and persuasive writing as with great speeches.

Rhetoric is the effective use of persuasive language. Some of the tools used in rhetoric to organize ideas are still valuable today. These tools, often referred to as rhetorical modes, develop ideas by arranging them into patterns: by time, definition, cause and effect, comparison and contrast, classification and division, and so forth.

Expository writing also takes advantage of rhetorical modes to shape ideas in a variety of ways, depending on the writer's purpose. For example, if you wanted to write about child care in Canada, you could organize your ideas with the use of different rhetorical modes: a historical view of child care in Canada, for example, employs a time order or process approach. But if you look for similarities and differences between traditional Aboriginal child care and 18th century European child care, then you are using a comparison and contrast mode. If, on the other hand, you want to consider the range of child care in Canada in 2009, you might put the services into groupings; in other words, you would be using a classification approach. Should you wish to define what child care is, then your approach would use a definition rhetorical mode. You might also decide to use a blended approach in which you mix two modes, perhaps historical (time or chronological) and contrast. Whichever mode you choose will depend on your purpose and sometimes the nature of the assignment.

Process Analysis

A process analysis is a piece of writing that describes something that happens over time. It deals with the stages of something or the sequence of events that take place in an activity of some sort. Process analysis writing is used in many subject areas. For example, much writing within a course in one of the technologies will include how to do something: how to program a computer using a special new computer language, how to measure something, or how to design something. Many science courses and health courses also use the process pattern. In a nursing course, students might read how to change a dressing, how to give an injection, how to chart, or how to communicate with a worried patient. In chemistry, much of the writing within the texts and the writing done by students will involve some sort of process design. Your process pattern could be made up of

- stages,
- a sequence or set of sequences,
- steps,
- dates,
- points of separation.

Tips for Writing Process Pieces

Tip 1.   *Have a clear purpose in mind.* To use a process pattern in an essay, you must have a clear idea of the process, how it is arranged or how you want to arrange it, and why you want to talk about it. The thesis statement plays a key role in the construction of an essay by rhetorical mode. If you choose to use the process pattern, you must let the reader know in the thesis statement the point of telling the reader about the process in the first place. Are you trying to be interesting? Are you trying to compare one process with another? Are you attempting to help the reader understand something by analyzing a process? Keep this in mind when you write an essay that is going to describe a process. There must be some angle of interest in the thesis statement; otherwise, the reader could simply look up the information in a reference book. Ask yourself, "Why am I telling the reader this? Am I merely stating the obvious"?

EXAMPLES:

1. Here's how I make my own clothes!

(Poor thesis statement. True, it shows process analysis. But there is no angle of interest. Why would anyone want to bother reading this?)

2. Any woman can make herself a dress that is glamorous and trendy yet relatively inexpensive compared to designer labels.

(Better: Now there is a point to writing the essay. The writer will talk about making a garment and show through the description of the process how the dress will save the maker money without sacrificing style.).

Tip 2.   *Use a timeline.* You may choose to employ a timeline, used for arranging stages over a duration. As you do your thinking or arranging, you will have some sort of framework in which to put your ideas. The arrangement may be a sequence of events, so the events themselves can be charted out on a line. However, not all events are clear when trying to describe something, so often you are forced to cluster smaller sets of events into stages, which is, in effect, categorizing ideas. We cluster small steps into larger stages, and we may then choose to chart these stages on a timeline. Timelines help us to arrange our ideas clearly.

Another advantage of drawing a timeline is that it can also help you to develop your thesis statement. For example, if you drew a timeline with four stages shown by four important dates in Canadian history, you might then develop the following thesis: *Canada has gone through four distinct stages during its journey from colony to independent nation.* After you have charted the sequence on the timeline and developed a good working thesis, you might start thinking about other keywords or phrases that you would want to include in your essay.

Tip 3.   *Use key words and phrases.* Key words and phrases help the reader follow the passage of time throughout the essay. You might choose actual dates to mark the time, but if you are simply putting forth phases, you will probably use transitions, such as *next, later, after that, soon, by this time,* and so forth. (Refer to the detailed list of transitions in chapter 4 for a more complete listing of process or time-order transitions.) In addition, you may want to repeat key phrases in the process itself. This repetition not only reminds the reader of your thesis, but also lets the reader follow the overall process more easily. A caution, though: do not make your writing sound *too* repetitive. Sometimes you can use synonyms for terms rather than using the same word over and over again. Using synonyms can help keep the reader's interest and will also help you expand your written expression and style.

Comparison and Contrast

Throughout your life you have learned by comparing and contrasting things. You might have discovered more about apartments by comparing them to houses; you might also have known which dogs on your street to pet and which ones to leave alone through the use of comparison/contrast; you may have decided important life choices based on this mode.

Tips for Writing Comparison and Contrast Pieces

Tip 1.   *Choosing the items.* The first stage of carrying out a comparison could not be more straightforward. Take two people, events, ideas, books, works of art, or two of anything, and ask yourself, "How are these two things the same? How are they different"? By so doing, you are conducting a comparative analysis.

A well-planned comparison/contrast essay will almost write itself, but its initial construction takes some thought. Deciding which two things to compare broadly is quite an easy task. But then you must decide how to compare them. A point of comparison is a characteristic that you choose that is common to both items being compared, and to be effective it must be clear and logical. For example, let's suppose you wanted to compare children living in Canada with children living in China. One point of comparison might be education because both groups of children attend school. Another point of comparison might be entertainment because children all over the world love to play. Finally, the last point of comparison you might choose is responsibility in the family. Most children are responsible for helping out the family to lesser or greater degrees.

Tip 2.   *Make the items relate.* It is unproductive and confusing to talk about points that do not relate in some way to the two broad categories you are writing about, and so well-thought-out points are critical to a good essay using a comparison/contrast pattern. Also remember that each point of comparison must be distinct; do not overlap these major points because your writing will become repetitious.

Here is a further example. Suppose you want to discuss Calgary and Vancouver in relation to one another because you want to determine which place to live. Perhaps you have decided on four points of comparison:

1. population
2. industry
3. climate
4. architecture

Thus you would not include harbours in your discussion because Calgary has none. If you added a point of comparison like annual rainfall, you would find it overlaps with climate. However, if you did decide to discuss Vancouver's harbour because you believed it to be a very important feature, then you might invent a point of comparison like transportation systems. Similarly, if annual rainfall seemed vital to your discussion, then you could include it in the discussion of climate.

Tip 3. *Develop a clear framework for discussing the items.* Once you have thought out your points of comparison and sketched out a few notes for each point or planned some of the discussion, then you must decide the actual structure of the comparison/contrast essay. Will you discuss each city separately? Will you use the points of comparison for each paragraph and include both cities under each point? The choice is yours: block format or point-by-point. Sometimes it is good practice to include both cities in the discussion throughout the essay because the points of comparison become the feature of the paper. But at the same time this type of set-up can become rather tedious to read if the writer is not paying attention to style. Here are two possible models of the structure of the essay:

Model 1: Block Format

Introductory paragraph

   Body paragraph 1: Calgary

   – population

   – industry

   – climate

   – architecture

   Body paragraph 2: Vancouver

   – population

   – industry

   – climate

   – architecture

   Concluding paragraph

Model 2: Point-by-Point

Introductory paragraph

   Body paragraph 1: population

   – Calgary

   – Vancouver

   Body paragraph 2: industry

   – Calgary

   – Vancouver

   Body paragraph 3: climate

   – Calgary

   – Vancouver

   Body paragraph 4: architecture

   – Calgary

   – Vancouver

Concluding paragraph

Both of these models will work; however, each has different characteristics. Model 1 contains only two large body paragraphs and so would be structurally awkward. It would not really be a conventional essay because it would not fit the expected number of body paragraphs. Besides that, it requires the reader to remember the points made in the first half of the essay in order to compare them to the information given in the second portion. Obviously, the longer an essay is, the more difficult it will be for the reader to hold pertinent ideas in mind. The writer could add body paragraph 3 to discuss differences.

In Model 2, points of comparison are arranged by paragraph so that they are emphasized and are easier for the reader to retain. Its structure seems to balance points, so the discussion itself "feels" more balanced upon reading. To help make ideas cohere, use transitions. Keywords to use in comparison/contrast essays are words like *similarly, same, different, on the other hand, conversely*, and so forth.

Tip 4. *Use comparison and contrast to help develop your critical thinking and reading.* Most experts agree that comparing and contrasting are two of the most important of the critical skills. One composition professor observes just how relational this skill is: "I ask my students to think about people, places, and things, as well as ideas. I ask them to explore the connections between time and space, between global and local concerns, between divergent lifestyles and cultures, between events and ideas, between individualism and independence" (V.P. Stephen, "Hello, out there . . . Is anybody thinking"? *Teaching* Fall 2004: 54).

The following example shows how one student wrote about an important event in his life—whether to buy or to rent.

TO BUY OR TO RENT?

Recently couples have been having a hard time deciding whether to own or rent a home. Because interest rates have risen, potential homeowners have had to weigh the benefits of owning against those of renting. This problem is even more confusing because of the high rents that are now being charged. In some aspects renting may seem more secure, but owning has far more benefits.

First, the investment in land has always been the safest. A mortgage may seem like a large debt, but property value does increase, and the opportunity of selling can mean receiving more money than has been paid. For example, homes in 2004 have increased in value by at least 150% since 1984. In fact, paying rent is paying someone else's mortgage, and receiving no investment or property in return. Also, owners can borrow money on their equity, the value of their home less the debt still owing, for emergencies or new investments.

Subsequently, owners can use the money made available through these loans toward renovations, increasing the value of their home. Renovation is sometimes necessary when there is a new member in the family and an extra room is needed. On the other hand, renters have no alternative but to move. Along with renovations, owners can paint or wallpaper without having to ask permission. Renters must, and are usually denied permission because landlords (owners) do not trust the quality of work or the taste of the renter. If landlords do agree, usually renters are not reimbursed for the supplies and work they have put in. Additionally, this increases the value of the home or property for the owners, but it does nothing for renters except perhaps make a difficult situation a little more liveable.

With the threat of having to move at the request of the landlord, renters must consider many problems that can arise from moving often. First, moving is expensive: truck rental and connection fees for hydro, telephone, and cable add up to a great deal of money, not including the damage deposit. If renters have children, they must also think about the adjustments they will have to make. Moving from school and friends can be quite a psychological trauma for children, and they may become shy and evasive. Children who do not have this threat can feel secure, making good, long-lasting friendships.

Is owning a home better than renting? Owning allows people to renovate, invest, and feel secure in the family's well being, whereas renting means moving, having to ask permission to paint or wallpaper, and possibly causing anxiety in children. With all this taken into account, the benefits of owning far outweigh those of renting.

Definition

The definition rhetorical pattern explores what something is or what the nature of something is. Definitions look at what characteristics define something. Many writing assignments are based on conceptualizing some idea or quality through definition. Read the following to get an idea of how definition works.

Tips for Writing a Definition Piece

Tip 1.   *Choose the concept wisely.* Try to select a topic, idea, or concept with some depth. An abstract idea generally offers the potential for a richer discussion. For example, talking about the nature of something can lead to interesting deliberation. Think of the nature of violence, the nature of family kinships, the nature of a contest, or the nature of research. Aren't you really thinking of what could constitute each of them?

Tip 2.   *Use a technique that gets at your purpose.* You can structure your definition using one of the following techniques:

- Define by how something works.

- Define by how something is put together.

- Define by what distinguishes the term or idea.

- Define by how something is different from something else.

- Define by what something is not.

- Define by where something comes from.

EXAMPLES:

- How something works: A defibrillator is a device that actually uses the body's energy in an unusual way.
- How something is put together: An ideology is a theory organized around a single common purpose.
- What distinguishes the term or idea: Space travel is unlike ground or sea transport.
- What something is not: Desire is not love.
- Where something comes from: Canadian social democracy has its roots in the Prairies and in the region's work ethic.

Tip 3. *Plan carefully.* When defining a quality, issue, idea, or object, be sure your definition essay has the following elements:

In the introduction:

- the term or idea you are defining
- a sentence that contains your definition
- a clear thesis with definition as a clear rhetorical mode

In the body:

- paragraphs that explore distinguishing features
- clarification, using supporting examples or anecdotes

In the conclusion:

- a renaming of your term or idea
- your summary definition

EXAMPLES:

What is a friend?

A friend is a person who trusts you to tell the truth, laughs at your jokes, and helps you build the new porch you need.

For the writer, a friend has three characteristics that distinguish friendship from non-friendship.

In the following paragraph, the writer gets at the idea of a pessimist by attempting to define one.

Pessimists are people with a problem. Their negative attitudes towards most things follow them everywhere they go; they see shadows instead of light, sadness instead of joy, and anger instead of laughter. Convinced that they have been born with "bad karma," they journey through life as if a permanent black cloud were over their heads. Scornful, self-pitying, sarcastic, they surround themselves with others who share their doom-and-gloom philosophy. Together, they revel in the misfortunes of others, natural catastrophes, and destruction wrought by humans, using these events to reinforce their belief that life is a cruel trick invented by a sadistic deity for its own amusement. As self-proclaimed experts, pessimists recount utopian visions of living, absent from the "real" world. Their cynical nature prevents them from feeling enjoyment and relaxation. Their credo is Murphy's Law—what can go wrong will go wrong—and they await the next misfortune. They have little ambition because ambition prefigures hope, and hope is for optimists—fools who live to try to find happiness in their days. Bitterness and resentment become pessimists' constant companions, and sadly, their predictions come true—loneliness follows.

What characteristics define a pessimist in this writer's view? How is a pessimist distinguished from an optimist? Has definition helped you to think through some ideas about pessimism?

Cause and Effect

Cause and effect are relational. When you write an essay using this rhetorical mode, you must show how something influences or is influenced by something else. You consider impact, results, consequences, and outcomes in thinking through a cause-and-effect relationship.

Tips for Writing a Cause-and-Effect Piece

Tip 1. *Choose two items that relate.* When you select the items for discussion, be sure that you are able to discuss how they relate. You can find the relationship between ideas, but the connections may not always be visible. Try to find something interesting to say about the relationship. Do not simply state what is obvious. Sometimes you may have to do some research to determine the nature of the relationship.

Tip 2. *Use creative questioning.* Ask questions about the nature of the relationship in order to generate and deepen discussion. Here are some examples:

- Do children view depictions of violence as real?

- How do small children view such representations on television?

- Do children copy what they see?

- Do depictions of violence in television programming influence children? How?

- What effects does television watching have on young viewers?

Tip 3. *Select items of interest.* If possible, choose something that interests you. Read the following examples. In the paragraph about walking, the writer was interested in finding connections between wellness and fitness. In the paragraph about stress, the writer wanted to establish what kind of impact it has. There may be more to these relational ideas than is first obvious. Also, ongoing research on topics of interest often changes what people once believed about them. Assumptions are challenged by the research, and new knowledge emerges.

- Moderate exercise improves wellness.
  (Something influences something else.)

- Cheating on exams results in failure.
  (Something is a result of something else.)

- Good advertising brings in business.
  (Something is the consequence of something else.)

In the following paragraph, the writer explores the benefits of walking by relating walking to its positive effects.

> Walking can have positive effects on the body, mind, and spirit. Beginners can start easily and feel the benefits quickly. Fitness levels can be improved by just walking around the block a few times a week. Walking helps to encourage the strengthening of bones and to reduce bone porosity, especially important to women in later life because the loss of bone density results in bone breaks. In fact, walking stimulates bone cells to build more bone. Walking on a regular basis can also decrease the need for some medications, and it can help

people who have just had heart surgery with their recovery. Moreover, circulation is improved by walking, and pumping more blood through the body benefits energy levels, improves muscle tone, and generates a feeling of well-being that radiates into other aspects of a person's life. Furthermore, a powerful benefit is an increase of energy, which brings on a feeling of well-being. In a study carried out in 2007 at the University of Eastern Ontario, people reported that, after taking walks after supper, they felt more relaxed and happy than they did before the walk. Serotonin builds up in the blood and is carried to the brain; this natural chemical makes people feel happier. Also, walking promotes safe and healthy weight loss which, in turn, makes walkers feel better about themselves. When people feel discouraged or overwhelmed by life, they feel their spirits lifted as they walk, and they seem to find solutions to many problems. The link between walking and improved health is clear; people simply have to take responsibility for their own fitness and get started.

What cause-and-effect connections does the writer make? What examples are used? Is the relationship between walking and health clearly established? Is it convincing? Why or why not?

In the following essay, the writer examines the relationship between stress and its results. Notice her clear thesis statement, which establishes a cause-and-effect mode and three distinct areas of effect.

THE EFFECTS OF STRESS ON EVERYDAY LIVING

Modern life has made people more anxious and rushed. Getting to work on time or finishing a paper can leave a person frustrated. Stress, the adjustment period to any change in life, physically, mentally, or spiritually, varies from day to day. If too many changes occur, and there is not enough time to absorb these alterations, a person will suffer from chronic stress. Stress will eventually affect family life, work capabilities, and health.

When parents are pressured to get a job done, whether it be at school, work, or even at home, their actions affect those around them. While parents are at their busiest, the children are vying for attention, negative or positive. Caught in this vicious circle, the parents become angry and impatient, which then causes the children to become more upset and erratic. For teenagers, drugs and vandalism can become their way of coping with the lack of attention and understanding. Studies done on the reasons why teenagers became delinquent found that, in most cases, it was because of a bad family situation. Rheinhold (2008) suggests that family break-up was the cause of teenagers acting out against authority in 83.5% of the cases studied. Stress causes people to say things and act differently. Husbands and wives lose communication, and the home becomes a place of tensions rather than relaxation.

Because stress affects sleep, it also affects how alert and energetic people are. If individuals are tired and lack motivation, the quality of work will deteriorate. In the report, "On the Job: Workers, Employers, and the Cost of Stress," the Canadian Association of Workplace Safety claims that absenteeism and safety on the job cost Canadian companies about $3.4 billion annually (2007, p. 27.) In addition, production slows down. Jobs that were once completed easily now take days to finish. Fellow workers also notice changes. Where they once saw a good-natured person, they now see a tired and irritable ogre. Eventually, with the lack of contact from fellow workers, the workload seems greater and becomes a burden for the employee until he or she does not care anymore.

The relationship between stress and health has also been chronicled since the beginning of the twentieth century. Hans Selye (1974), a Canadian pioneer in stress research, called it "the new modern silent disease" (p. 12). Although researchers are still conducting studies on this relationship, most evidence has shown that when people are mentally worn down they are more susceptible to disease and illness. Stress can cause a loss of appetite or an increase, and the effect on the body can be hazardous. Obesity is one of the major causes of strokes. In contrast, if a person is not eating, he or she begins to lack the essential vitamins and minerals that are necessary to fight off illness. Terminally ill patients have found that exercising regularly releases stress, improves their tolerance for pain, and for some, extends their lives.

The family, the workplace, and the individual are all susceptible to the serious effects of stress. Whatever the causes of stress are, be it a death in the family, a heavy workload, or a lack of money, people should find positive ways of releasing it. Taking walks, exercising, or working on a relaxing hobby are very essential and should be done every day so that stress is kept to a minimum. Learning to cope with stress will not only improve people's lives but also the lives of those around them.

Classification and Division

This rhetorical mode groups ideas. A classification pattern puts things into groups, categories, or types. A division pattern describes what parts or elements make up something. For example, you may want to discuss parenthood. If you ask, "What types of parents are there"? you would be using a classification pattern. If you ask, "What makes up a good parent"? you would be using a division type of pattern. This rhetorical mode is a useful one in the natural sciences, in social sciences, and in philosophy discussions.

Tips for Writing a Classification and Division Piece

Tip 1.   *Consider your specific purpose.* This rhetorical mode may suit various purposes. You might be trying to consider ideas in a new way, perhaps to create new classifications of things. By the same token, you may find that you are asked to consider the components of something. For example, in a literature essay you may decide to define a hero as someone who is loyal, stands up for his own convictions, and sacrifices for others. Then, you might consider the main character of a novel and attempt to fit him into your definition. This division pattern is commonly used because it asks a writer, thinker, or reader to consider what constitutes something. This is a fairly straightforward pattern to use and is effective because once your categories or parts have been decided, most of the organization of the essay has been taken care of.

Tip 2.   *Do not overgeneralize or stereotype.* When using this type of pattern, be careful of grouping people into categories and then making sweeping definite statements about their characteristics. This is a form of stereotyping that can be racist or sexist. Be sure your statements about people are fair and well supported.

Tip 3.   *Try to classify in an interesting way.* If you choose classification, try to think of new and engaging ways of grouping your ideas. Do not simply state the obvious. Instead of re-hashing categories, try to invent new ones. For example, could you devise new categories for fashion? Could you invent another way of looking at the movies?

Tip 4. *Use transitions that indicate a classification and division mode.* These transitions will reinforce the mode for the reader and will help to unify your piece of writing. Use keywords and phrases like *type*, *division*, *group*, *kind*, etc.

Read the following essay example based on classification and division. Look over the thesis statement, the categories the writer invents, and the support for each category. What do you think the writer's purpose was in writing the piece?

EXAMPLE: CLASSIFICATION AND DIVISION
Three Kinds of Drivers

Since cars were invented, western society deals with the problems and harm stemming from a variety of driving habits. Most drivers seem unaware of the potentially damaging power of the ordinary automobile. Others drive by the rules. Three types of drivers—the reckless, who is a danger; the inconsistent, who is a menace; and the circumspect, who is an exemplar of safe driving—dominate Canadian roadways.

The first type, the reckless driver, causes harm. Since most drivers in this category are male and 18–35 years of age, according to accident data, this type of driver will be referred to as "he." Largely, he does not obey posted signs and speed limits. He is caught speeding more than drivers in any other age group. He speeds while ignoring road conditions and drives according to how he feels. Secondly, this driver respects neither drivers nor pedestrians. He is seldom aware of pedestrian crosswalks or walkers, bikers, or joggers on the road. According to a 2008 Alberta Council for Road Safety report, pedestrian deaths in crosswalks is on the rise. The Insurance Alliance of British Columbia also confirms this evidence in a 2007 study of fatal accidents. Property is also damaged by this driver. Some estimates claim insurance rates increase by 10 percent a year due to damage to vehicles and real property. The reckless driver causes the most harm, but another type is also dangerous.

The inconsistent driver is unpredictable. Driving habits change, depending on the driver's stress levels. Most of the time, this person obeys the road signs and the speed limits, but sometimes, he or she will take undue chances. He or she may run an amber light because he or she is late. This driver may carelessly ignore speed limits because of inattention. The inconsistent driver may suddenly change lanes without giving other drivers proper signals. He or she may weave all over the lane as the individual fumbles with a coffee cup, a cigarette, or the stereo system. This driver may like to socialize as he or she is driving down the road, paying more attention to the conversation than the road conditions. Moreover, this driving type is totally distractible. If there is a scene alongside the road, this driver will "rubberneck" in order to get a glimpse, completely unaware that by doing so, he or she has slowed traffic or made the driver behind come to a screeching halt. This driver does not intend to drive recklessly; he or she is simply unmindful, in contrast to the third type of driver.

The circumspect driver is the most reliable and is generally accident-free. This driver obeys signs, attends to speed limits, and is attentive of the road conditions. He or she drives defensively, taking in the "big picture" on the road, including construction zone speed limits, school zones, dangerous drivers in other lanes, black ice, detours, and other roadway hazards. This driver respects the road rights of others and pays close attention to pedestrians. He or she drives for safety: In rush hour traffic, this is the driver who will allow another driver to access a lane or make a lane change. He or she also respects the need to give opportunities to commercial drivers like bus or cab drivers, or truckers who drive as their livelihood. Because the circumspect driver is so expert, he or she rarely gets into collisions or causes harm on the road.

These three types of drivers are on Canadian roadways night and day. Two types create problems and harm, while the last makes driving pleasant and safe. All in all, some drivers are uneducated as to the potential damage of careless driving, and as NRW news reports, 72 percent of people killed on the roads were killed by reckless, ruthless drivers. Each driver on the road chooses the type of driver to be. With more consideration and thought, every driver could become the circumspect one.

Using a Blended Approach in Expository Writing

Generally speaking, you will find that writers use a combination of rhetorical modes when they write, although one mode may dominate. Different modes are better suited to different purposes, so it is not unusual to see body paragraphs in different modes.

Sometimes your topic requires this flexibility. It will depend on your purpose, your audience, and your tone to some extent. For example, if your audience is a group who might require further explanation, then you may decide to define some key ideas in your first body paragraph. In the second and third body paragraphs, you might decide to compare and contrast your definitions to other popular ones, considering what is different and what is the same about them. In the paragraphs following, you might decide to discuss the impact of certain ways of representing something through the definitions—a cause-and-effect rhetorical mode.

Sometimes you will be assigned one particular mode to work with, but in many other writing situations, you will decide the design of your paper. A history course, for instance, may have three or four written assignments in it. Your professor or instructor will be interested in how you make your ideas relate. You may choose cause and effect, classification, and process analysis as tools to organize and design one paper. You may choose another set for another paper, depending on your purpose. If you wish to explore how ideas contrast in two different periods of Canadian social history—ideas of marriage, for example—then you will use this tool mainly, but you may also want to bring in definitions of marriage as part of your paper's discussion. You may also want to divide the idea of marriage into the component parts that have traditionally comprised it. Therefore, as a matter of critical thinking and writing, you will choose the appropriate rhetorical modes and thinking tools to develop your topic and to suit your specific purpose in writing.

The following article comes from a popular Canadian magazine. The writer uses a blended approach in the organization of the piece. Read the article, paying attention to the rhetorical modes Jennifer Quist uses. Since the piece is written for a magazine, you will notice some differences in paragraphing style between this article and academic writing. For example, the last part of the article is a single sentence only. In academic writing, you must use complete paragraphs in all sections of your paper.

EXAMPLE: BLENDED APPROACH
It's All in the Bag
by Jennifer Quist

> Jennifer Quist, her husband, and three young sons live in Fort McMurray, Alta., where she writes a weekly newspaper column.

It looks like a shrunken, leather Noah's ark with a long shoulder strap sewn onto its ends. It can still be found slumped on the third step up to the second floor of my parents' house. Inside, it's crammed with credit cards, hand lotions, tissues, gum, makeup, half a dozen pens (some that actually work), a cellophane rain hat from decades past, and a cellular phone from the cutting edge of technology. It's always been an institution of motherhood in our family—the Big Purse.

My mother isn't a cruel woman, but she is merciless when it comes to the primacy of the Purse. She has forced her own children to fetch it for her, sit crowded in shopping carts with it, and feel it tossed heavily onto our feet in the front seat of her car. She has even made us carry it in public. The loss-prevention sentinels that "greet" shoppers at discount stores bristle with even greater suspicion than usual when a teenager skulks sheepishly through the automatic doors with a behemoth handbag half-tucked under her jacket. I could almost hear the surveillance cameras zooming in to see that the bulging purse stayed shut. It was with us everywhere—the Big Purse.

It was one of those mothering institutions that I dreaded as a young girl, like varicose veins and zippered housecoats. In my younger days, as I peered at it over the tops of my sociology textbooks, the Big Purse looked exactly like a shackle of male oppression. It slouched on the stairs embodying the injustices of a society where women must be weighed down by huge, ugly sacs in order to maintain social order. In those early days, I assured myself that it must be possible for me to someday have a family of my own and at the same time resist the powerful gravity of the Big Purse.

It was also in the midst of my liberal feminist education that I decided that male power in modern society has a major seat that has been overlooked in all the excitement over pay equity and patrilineal nomenclature: the unfair allocation of pockets between the sexes.

Even in an age that has seen practical fashion movements like "cargo" clothing, there are still times when women are expected to dress in clothes that are completely devoid of pockets. This is especially true when women need to dress in formal wear or maternity clothing. Women are consistently deprived of pockets in the clothes that are designed and merchandised for us. Maybe someone is afraid that a pregnant woman with pockets would be too socially powerful. After all, a fruitful womb is the ultimate pocket known to humankind.

Regardless, most women, pregnant or not, find themselves often relying on the charity of the many-pocketed opposite sex to carry our car keys and bank cards. Men's clothing is slathered in pockets. While women teeter around dress-up affairs juggling ridiculous, shiny clutch purses and glorified wallets on strings, men tuck what they need into the nine pockets sewn into most of their suits.

Growing up is full of surprises. As my life unfolded, it turned out that things aren't quite as unfair as I had once thought. I didn't find this out all at once. It crept up on me little by little as I started having my own children. It seems that with every new phase my kids pass through, I find myself back in the accessories sections of cheap department stores rifling through tables full of cavernous, discount purses. Every time I visit the sales racks I come away with a bigger purse than the I one I brought in with me.

Now it sits in a corner of my bedroom—my very own Big Purse. It holds water bottles, baby wipes, diapers of two different sizes, Aspirin, toddler-bribing treats, half a dollar in pennies, and even something my own mother was never neurotic enough to carry herself: a coupon file.

I admit that I was wrong about the Big Purse. With my Big Purse at my side I'm almost completely self-sufficient. I can blow my nose whenever I want to because I always have a tissue. I'm the only one at noisy amusement parks with access to Aspirin. And when the baby spits up I'm the heroine, with a perpetual stash of baby wipes within arms' reach.

The Big Purse is probably not a symptom of male oppression. Instead, it might just be part of the cure for it. In the lives of women like myself and my mother, the Big Purse makes it possible for us to be independent, adaptable, in control and functional in a world that is more focussed on meeting the needs of the many-pocketed. The Big Purse doesn't embody the whimper of a defeated sex but the war cry of a resourceful gender with a workable alternative to simply mimicking its oppressors.

I lug my Big Purse with pride. It doesn't weigh me down. It helps to set me free.

Source: *Jennifer Quist, "It's All in the Bag," Maclean's 1 Apr. 2002: 12.*
By permission of Jennifer Quist.

Parallel Structure

Section Theme **PSYCHOLOGY**

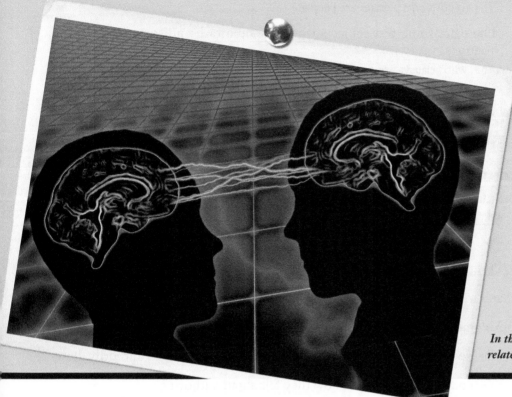

In this chapter, you will read about topics related to psychological experiments.

The Writer's Desk Warm Up

Write a short paragraph comparing your personality to that of a family member or friend. Describe how your personalities are similar and different.

What Is Parallel Structure?

Parallel structure occurs when pairs or groups of items in a sentence are balanced. In the following sentences, the underlined phrases contain repetitions of grammatical structure but not of ideas. Each sentence has parallel structure.

> <u>Internet sites</u>, <u>magazines</u>, and <u>newspapers</u> published the results of the experiment.
>
> (The nouns are parallel.)

Taken from *The Canadian Writer's World: Paragraphs and Essays*, by Lynne Gaetz, Suneeti Phadke, and Rhonda Sandberg.

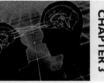

Psychologists <u>observe</u> and <u>predict</u> human behaviour.
(The present tenses are parallel.)

The experiment was <u>fascinating</u>, <u>groundbreaking</u>, and <u>revolutionary</u>.
(The adjectives are parallel.)

To get to the psychology department, go <u>across the street</u>, <u>into the building</u>, and <u>up the stairs</u>.
(The prepositional phrases are parallel.)

There are some test subjects <u>who develop a rash</u> and some <u>who have no reactions</u>.
(The "who" clauses are parallel.)

PRACTICE I

All of the following sentences have parallel structures. Underline the parallel items.

EXAMPLE:

Students in my psychology class <u>listened to the instructor</u>, <u>took notes</u>, and <u>asked questions</u>.

1. Professor Stanley Milgram taught at Yale, conducted a famous experiment, and wrote a book about his research.

2. Milgram's experiment was controversial, provocative, and surprising.

3. His experiment tried to understand how humans reacted to authority, how they obeyed authority, and how they felt about authority.

4. For his experiment, Milgram used one actor in a lab coat, one actor with glasses, and one unsuspecting subject in street clothes.

5. The psychologist told the subject to sit at the desk, to watch the "patient" behind the glass, and to listen to the experiment "leader."

6. The leader told the subject when to start electric shocks, when to increase the level of shocks, and when to stop the experiment.

7. Milgram's experiment raised important questions, ended in astonishing results, and gave valuable insight into human behaviour.

8. Psychologists continue to perform experiments, give lectures, and debate issues.

Identify Faulty Parallel Structure

It is important to use parallel structure when using a series of words or phrases, paired clauses, comparisons, and two-part constructions.

Series of Words or Phrases

Use parallel structure when words or phrases are joined in a series.

Not parallel:	Students, administrators, and people who teach sometimes volunteer for psychology experiments.
Parallel:	<u>Students</u>, <u>administrators</u>, and <u>teachers</u> sometimes volunteer for psychology experiments. (The nouns are parallel.)
Not parallel:	I plan to study for tests, to attend all classes, and listening to the instructor.
Parallel:	I plan <u>to study</u> for tests, <u>to attend</u> all classes, and <u>to listen</u> to the instructor. (The verbs are parallel.)

Paired Clauses

Use parallel structure when independent clauses are joined by *and, but,* or *or.*

Not parallel:	The experimenter placed two probes on her head, and her wrist is where he attached a monitor.
Parallel:	The experimenter placed two probes <u>on her head</u>, and he attached a monitor <u>to her wrist.</u> (The prepositional phrases are parallel.)
Not parallel:	She felt dizzy, and she also had a feeling of fear.
Parallel:	She felt <u>dizzy</u>, and she also felt <u>afraid</u>. (The adjectives are parallel.)

 **Use Consistent Voice**

When a sentence has two independent clauses and is joined by a coordinating conjunction, use a consistent voice. In other words, if one part of the sentence is active, the other should also be active.

Not parallel:	The researcher conducted the experiment, and then a report was written by him.
Parallel:	The researcher <u>conducted the experiment</u>, and then <u>he wrote a report.</u> (Both parts use the active voice.)

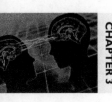

PRACTICE 2

Correct the faulty parallel structure in each sentence.

EXAMPLE:

Some psychology experiments are bold, pioneering, and ~~show their~~ ~~originality.~~   *original.*

1. Ivan Pavlov was a Russian physiologist, a research scientist, and he won a Nobel prize.

2. Pavlov became interested in dog salivation, and digestion also interested him.

3. To get to his lab, Pavlov walked through the door, up the stairs, and the department is where he entered.

4. Pavlov used many sound-making devices to stimulate his dogs, such as metronomes, whistles, and he also used tuning forks.

5. Pavlov noticed that the dogs heard the noise, saw the food dish, and were salivating.

6. Some of the dogs were excited, nervous, and expressed enthusiasm.

7. Western scientists found Pavlov's experiments to be astounding, innovative, and thought they were important.

8. Ivan Pavlov worked quickly and was very efficient.

Comparisons

Use parallel structure in comparisons containing *than* or *as*.

Not parallel:	Creating new experiments is more difficult than to re-create an earlier experiment.
Parallel:	<u>Creating a new experiment</u> is more difficult than <u>re-creating an earlier experiment.</u> (The *-ing* forms are parallel.)
Not parallel:	His home was as messy as the way he kept his laboratory.
Parallel:	His <u>home</u> was as messy as his <u>laboratory</u>. (The nouns are parallel.)

Two-Part Constructions

Use parallel structure for the following paired items.

either . . . or	not . . . but	both . . . and
neither . . . nor	not only . . . but also	rather . . . than

Not parallel:	My psychology class was both informative and a challenge.
Parallel:	My psychology class was both <u>informative</u> and <u>challenging</u>. (The adjectives are parallel.)
Not parallel:	I would rather finish my experiment than leaving early.
Parallel:	I would rather <u>finish</u> my experiment than <u>leave</u> early. (The verbs are parallel.)

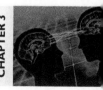

PRACTICE 3

Correct ten errors in parallel construction.

EXAMPLE:

interesting.
Philip Zimbardo is creative and ~~an interesting person.~~

1. Philip Zimbardo created an experiment that was both unique and startled others. The Stanford Prison Experiment examined how ordinary people would react when placed in positions of power. He chose twenty-four students who were healthy, stable, and they abided by the law. Each subject would be either a guard or a prisoner for a two-week period.

2. On the first day of the experiment, each guard was told to wear a uniform, carry a baton, and sunglasses were put on. Ordinary people who had committed no crime, who had broken no laws, and been honest were placed in a cold room. The prisoners were not only arrested but the guards also deloused them.

3. Immediately, the experimenters observed shocking behaviour. Some of the guards started to act controlling, sadistic, and they abused the prisoners. On the second day, the prisoners rioted and the guards attacked.

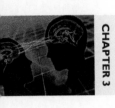

Some prisoners decided that they would rather leave than continuing with the experiment.

4.   During the next few days, officials, priests, and teachers observed the experiment. Nobody questioned the morality of the proceedings. Then, on the sixth day, another psychologist arrived. She was appalled and she felt horror when she realized what was happening.

5.   Zimbardo realized that his student actors were taking the experiment too seriously. Both the prisoners and the people playing the guards had to stop the experiment. Zimbardo worried that the student actors would be seriously hurt, distressed, and suffer from depression.

PRACTICE 4

Correct the errors in parallel construction.

EXAMPLE:

Information about bystander apathy is surprising and ~~of interest.~~ *interesting.*

1.   Bystander apathy is the unwillingness of an individual to help another in an emergency. In the 1960s, psychologists started to collect data, investigate behaviours, and proposing theories about bystander apathy. Many incidents have occurred that appear to demonstrate how people assume it is someone else's responsibility to respond in an emergency.

2.   In several large Canadian cities, homelessness is widespread. People on their way to work or when they go to school walk right past individuals sitting or lying down on cold, damp, urban streets. Often people step over huddled, quivering, homeless persons without glancing at their eyes or to see if they are okay. This is an example of bystander apathy.

3.   Sadly, people tend to react to out-of-the ordinary events like these by doing what everyone else is doing: not acting. Groups of bystanders often hold back (more so than individuals on their own do) and resist helping others, thinking that someone else will react. This is called "pluralistic ignorance."

4.   Many psychologists have studied the phenomenon of bystander apathy, and the results have been published by them. There are many reasons a bystander may not help someone in trouble. Bystanders may not want to risk their own lives, they may not have the skills to help in an emergency, or legal problems could be incurred. In addition, many people do not want to look stupid or be seen as being foolish if there is no real emergency. Psychologists believe that these are only some possible reasons for bystander apathy.

Sentence Errors

CONTENTS

Sentence Fragments

Writing sentence fragments is unacceptable. Fragments may look like sentences, but they are not sentences. Like a sentence, a fragment will begin with a capital and end with a final punctuation mark. But for a word group to function as a sentence, it must have at least one *independent clause*—that is, a subject and a verb, usually referred to as a *predicate*, and be able to stand alone as a complete thought.

Some fragments are *dependent clauses*, which means they can't stand alone. A dependent clause has a subject and a predicate but begins with a subordinating conjunction. Other fragments are merely phrases that lack subjects, predicates, or both.

Revise a sentence fragment in one of two ways: Make the fragment part of a sentence, or rephrase the fragment so it functions as a sentence.

Dependent Clause Fragments

Dependent clauses begin with words that indicate they can't stand alone, even though they have subjects and predicates like independent clauses. All the following words can introduce dependent clauses:

after	if	until
although	so that	when
because	that	where
before	though	who
even though	unless	which

You can usually combine a dependent clause fragment with a sentence:

■ Driving is still cheap. ~~Even~~ though gas prices have skyrocketed. The price of flying, in contrast, is out of reach.

If a dependent clause fragment can't be combined with a sentence, rewrite it as a sentence. The most direct way to do so is to eliminate the subordinating words and add any words necessary to complete the sentence:

■ The elderly poor live each day in fear of starvation. ~~Which~~ Some psychologists claim it kills more of them than disease.

Phrase Fragments

A word group without a subject or verb is called a phrase. When such a word group is capitalized and punctuated like a sentence, it is a phrase fragment. You can usually revise a phrase fragment by combining it with another sentence:

■ We saw Marla and Joe at the Cinco de Mayo party. Dancing the cha-cha.

■ Start your essay now. To have it ready by Friday.

■ The newspaper carried the story. About hackers changing grades.

■ The college is looking for a new president. A person with a warm personality and patience.

If you can't combine a phrase fragment with a sentence, turn it into a sentence. To do so, you may need to add a subject, a verb, or both:

■ Fourteen thousand angry demonstrators attended the rally. They were waving ~~Waving~~ signs and marching into the night.

Stylistic Fragments

Writers sometimes use fragments for dramatic effect or emphasis.

How many middle-income families does the reduction in luxury tax help? Frankly, none. Families earning less than $40,000 a year have trouble paying for groceries, clothes, education, and medical and dental care. They do not buy half-million-dollar speed boats, private jets, and German limousines.

EXERCISE

Correcting Sentence Fragments

Correct each of the following sentence fragments by integrating the dependent clause with the independent clause or by rewriting the dependent clause as an independent clause. Keep in mind that each corrected sentence should read smoothly and be punctuated accurately.

1. Dragons appear in a variety of roles. Symbolizing evil to some cultures, wisdom to others, and power to still others.
2. The Sumerians thought of dragons as embodiments of evil. A concept later attached to the devil.
3. The Gnostics, early religious sects of Europe and Asia, used a figure of a dragon biting its own tail. To symbolize the cyclic nature of time and the continuity of life.
4. To convince the people that their leaders had the dragonlike qualities of strength and goodness. Early Chinese emperors adopted the dragon as a symbol of imperial power.
5. Although you may not believe they ever existed, images of dragons have survived in art, fiction, stories, and dreams. In every corner of the world.

EXERCISE

Correcting Sentence Fragments

Rewrite each of the following sentences to correct the sentence fragments. Either integrate the dependent clause or phrase with the independent clause or rewrite the fragment as an independent clause. Keep in mind that each corrected sentence should read smoothly and be punctuated accurately.

1. Belief in dragons has persisted into the twentieth century. Although no scientific evidence has been found to support the belief.
2. Dragons' teeth and dragons' bones, believed to have nearly miraculous curative powers, could be purchased in China in this century. If one had sufficient money.
3. In Europe, the demand has been less for bones and teeth than for dragons' blood. A sure-fire love potion when burned while reciting the proper incantation.
4. Sightings of dragons continue to this day. In somewhat remote areas that have a long tradition of dragon stories.
5. The Loch Ness monster is perhaps the most famous contemporary dragon. Attracting journalists and investigators in great numbers. First seen in AD 565, this aquatic monster is extremely selective about public appearances. Defying the efforts of scientists using the latest equipment to locate it.
6. Other dragons inhabit other lakes in both Scotland and Ireland. Unfortunately, like the Loch Ness monster, they seldom show themselves to more than one person at a time.
7. In the United States, a few sightings have been made in several of the Great Lakes. The location for earlier Native American stories of dragonlike beasts.
8. What explains the popular belief in dragons? In the absence of any scientific evidence that they ever existed.
9. The problem with this theory is that dinosaurs and similar animals that could have been the ancestors of dragons ceased to exist millions of years ago. Before human beings appeared on the earth.
10. Can belief in dragons be explained? At least to everyone's satisfaction? Probably not.

Run-On Sentences

A *run-on sentence* is composed of two or more independent clauses that have been written incorrectly as one sentence. Remember, an *independent clause* is a word group that has a subject and a predicate—that is, the main verb—and can stand alone as a complete thought. When you write two or more independent clauses as one sentence, they must be joined in one of two ways:

ro

1. With a comma, followed by a coordinating conjunction: *and, but, or, nor, for, so, yet*
2. With a semicolon, or, if appropriate, a colon or a dash

There are two types of run-on sentences. The first, called a *fused sentence*, occurs when two independent clauses are joined without any punctuation:

FUSED

Primitive people have myths that reflect group consciousness modern people have television.

A second type of run-on sentence is called a *comma splice*. It occurs when two or more independent clauses are joined by a comma without a coordinating conjunction:

COMMA SPLICE

Primitive people have myths that reflect group consciousness, modern people have television.

As you can see, there is very little difference between the two types of run-on sentences. Both types, moreover, can be corrected in one of four ways:

1. Use a comma and a coordinating conjunction.
2. Use a semicolon.
3. Separate the clauses.
4. Subordinate the clauses.

None of these four ways is necessarily better than the others. How you decide to revise a run-on sentence should be determined by the meaning of the passage it appears in and by the effect you wish to create:

- Primitive people have myths that reflect group consciousness, ^and^ modern people have television.

- Primitive people have myths that reflect group consciousness; modern people have television.

- Primitive people have myths that reflect group consciousness, ~~modern~~ ^Modern^ people have television.

- ^Although primitive^ Primitive people have myths that reflect group consciousness, modern people have television.

Use a Comma and a Coordinating Conjunction

If your intent is to give ideas equal emphasis, use a comma and coordinating conjunction to revise a run-on sentence. Keep in mind that there are only seven coordinating conjunctions: *and, but, or, nor, so, for,* and *yet.*

■ Barbara French is a rare book collector ^and^ her brother Tom is a librarian.

Use a Semicolon

Use semicolons sparingly to show the meanings of the independent clauses are closely related and to achieve a stylistic balance:

■ American adolescence ended at the Pacific ^;^ American maturity began with a turn toward the Atlantic.

Always use a semicolon to revise a run-on sentence that contains a conjunctive adverb—such as *however, therefore, moreover,* and *furthermore*—and be sure to follow the conjunctive adverb with a comma:

■ Portland is the largest city in Oregon ^;^ however ^,^ Salem is the state capital.

Separate Independent Clauses into Sentences

If the run-on sentence is exceptionally long or if you don't want to give independent clauses equal emphasis, recast them as separate sentences:

■ Every age is dramatically affected by televised violence ^.^ ^Now^ some nine-year-olds carry guns to school.

Subordinate Clauses

Subordinate clauses to one of the dependent clauses for two reasons: if one idea is more important than the other or if you wish to create sentence variety:

■ ^Because the^ The ultimate effect of emphysema on the body is deprivation of oxygen, it kills by suffocating.

EXERCISE

Correcting Run-On Sentences and Comma Splices

Correct the run-on sentences and comma splices in the following paragraph. Use the most appropriate of the four ways in each case.

It is a summer weekend you have worked all day and want to relax "Time for the movies," you decide. The nearby theater that features classic and international films has been turned into a sixplex, the old theater had good popcorn and a nice-size screen. The new sixplex has small screens with a motel-room charm at least it offers five more movies.

What are the movies? Well, there is the picture about a scowling superhero who makes caustic remarks as he kills the bad guys in the latest cop thriller it stars a generally shirtless, muscle-bound action hero and the latest international model. There is the teen comedy about a nerdy, fast-talking, fifteen-year-old who anxiously chews on floppy disks he wears glasses upside down and suffers from anguish he's too skinny to make the Ping-Pong team it stars the latest teen heartthrob in baggy clothes and an unknown starlet. Then there is the latest catastrophe movie, it stars everyone, muscle men, heartthrobs, and, of course, plenty of models and starlets (catastrophe movies have plenty of cameos).

The remaining theaters are rerunning the other three movies what's a film buff to do go to the nearest Blockbuster, what else?

Subject/Verb Agreement

Remember: When a word refers to one person or thing, it is *singular* in number. When a word refers to more than one person or thing, it is *plural* in number. For instance:

agr

SINGULAR	PLURAL
person	people
woman	women
ox	oxen
this	these
either	both
he, she, it	they

A verb must always agree with its subject in number. Singular subjects take singular verbs:

A jet lands every four minutes.

The winner was carried from the field.

Plural subjects take plural verbs:

Jets land every four minutes.

The winners were carried from the field.

If a verb immediately follows a subject, you will probably have little trouble making them agree. But sometimes, you will write a sentence that's a little more tricky. Either the subject or its number will be hard to identify.

Intervening Words

Words that come between a subject and its verb often obscure an agreement error. Usually, these words will modify a subject and include a noun that seems to be the subject but isn't. By reading the sentence without the modifying words (shown in brackets below), you will usually be able to spot the agreement error:

- Archery [as practiced by Zen masters] take concentration. *(takes)*

■ A solution [for the city's many problems] do not exist.

(does)

■ The mayor [surrounded by hundreds of supporters] were singing.

(was)

Expressions such as *together with*, *as well as*, *in addition to*, *accompanied by*, and *along with* don't make a singular noun plural:

The major [accompanied by four scouts] are traveling west.

(was)

Compound Subjects

When two or more subjects are joined by a coordinating conjunction, such as *and* and *or*, they form a *compound subject*. Subjects joined by *and* usually take a plural verb. Compound subjects joined by *and* are usually plural:

■ Spiritual growth and psychological insight among artists is not uncommon.

(are)

An exception to this guideline comes when the parts of a compound subject function as a single idea or refer to a single person or thing. In these cases, the subject should take a singular verb:

■ Ham and eggs, once America's traditional breakfast, are banished from lowfat diets.

(is)

■ The Stars and Stripes wave over the battlefield.

(waves)

When a compound subject is preceded by *each* or *every*, the verb should be singular. Although these words refer to more than one, they imply consideration of one at a time. And when a compound subject is followed by *each*, the verb is singular, too:

■ Every hotel, bed and breakfast, and campground are filled.

(is)

■ Diplomacy and threat each require skilled execution.

(requires)

When a compound subject is joined by *or* or *nor*, the verb should agree with the part of the subject nearest to the verb:

■ The James Boys or Billy the Kid are the Wild West's most written-about outlaw.

(is)

Even though the preceding sentence is now correct, it still doesn't sound right. It's better to correct such a sentence by rearranging the order of the compound subject so it rings truer in a reader's mind:

Billy the Kid or the James Boys are the Wild West's most written-about outlaws.

Neither the atomic bomb nor space flights have influenced human events as powerfully as the Bill of Rights.

Indefinite Pronouns as Subjects

Generally, use singular verbs with indefinite pronouns. *Indefinite pronouns* refer to unspecified subjects. Most indefinite pronouns—such as *everyone*, *someone*, *no one, everything, anybody, neither,* and *something*—are singular and take singular verbs:

- Most everyone in Utah support keeping twenty-two million acres of ^supports^ wilderness.

- Neither partner, GM nor IBM, are discussing the agreement. ^is^

A few indefinite pronouns—such as *all, any, none,* and *some*—may be singular or plural. Whether you use a singular or plural verb depends on the noun or the indefinite pronoun it refers to:

The judge announced that all of the jury were present.

The judge said that all of the report was helpful.

Collective Nouns and Nouns Ending in -s as Subjects

Collective nouns take singular or plural verbs, depending on how they are used. Collective nouns—like *army, audience, class, committee, faculty, group, herd, public,* and *team*—are singular even though they name groups of individuals. When referring to a group as a single unit, a collective noun takes a singular verb:

- The American public eventually see the truth. ^sees^

When you wish to draw attention to individual members of the group, a collective noun should take a plural verb:

- The faculty argue among themselves in meetings, hallways, and offices. ^argues^

Treat units of measurement like singular collective nouns when they refer to a single unit:

By midgame, one-third of the crowd was gone.

Five dollars is the cost of a ticket.

Most nouns that are plural in form but singular in meaning take singular verbs. For example, nouns like *athletics, civics, economics, mathematics, measles, mumps, news, physics,* and *species* are singular and take singular verbs:

- Measles are irritating but relatively harmless. ^is^

Words like *trousers* and *scissors* are regarded as plural and take plural verbs, except when used after *pair*:

These socks have holes in the toes.

- This pair of socks have holes in the toes. ^has^

Miscellaneous Subject/Verb Agreement Problems

A verb must agree with its subject, even when the verb precedes the subject. (Verbs generally *follow* subjects.) When the subject/verb word order is reversed, check to see that the subject and verb still agree:

- In the back of his mind is the pain of abuse and the joy of recovery.

Don't mistake the expletives *there* and *here* for subjects. They merely signal that the subject follows the verb:

- There is several deceptive techniques card magicians use.

Be sure the verb following *who, which,* and *that* agrees with its subject. *Who, which,* and *that* are *relative pronouns* that refer to other words called *antecedents.* When a relative pronoun serves as a subject, the verb must agree with the pronoun's antecedent:

- Wind that blow over the peaks create massive snow plumes.

In a sentence that uses *one of the,* look carefully at the meaning to determine if the verb should be singular or plural:

- He is one of the critics who is joining the argument.

The antecedent of *who* is *critics,* not *one*:

- He is the only one of the critics who care.

The antecedent of *who* is *one*.

Use a singular verb when its subject is a title or words named as words:

- *Six Days and Seven Nights* seem to last at least that long.
- *Chitlins* refer to pigs' intestines used as food.

EXERCISE

Correcting Subject/Verb Agreement

Correct the errors in subject/verb agreement in each of the following sentences.

1. In baseball, slugging percentage as well as batting average is considered in judging a batter's worth.
2. The use of automatic pitching machines make batting practice more efficient.
3. Alert fielding, consistent hitting, and reliable pitching leads to success for a baseball team.
4. Neither the first baseman nor the infielders expects a bunt.
5. Many stories about the "good old days" of baseball probably exaggerate the feats of players.
6. Neither of the batters swing hard enough to belt it over the fence.
7. The team play an opponent from Nebraska on Friday.

8. The secret of our victories are efficient practices.
9. Two dollars are a small enough price to pay for admission.
10. Here in the locker room is the new uniforms.

Verb Tense

Verb tense reveals when—in the past, present, or future—an action has taken place or will take place. When you begin a passage in one tense, keep using it unless you have good reason to shift:

> Economists hope the budget will continue to be balanced in the year 2011. They are projecting an even more dramatic increase in employment and foreign exports.

These sentences move logically from the present, *hope*, to the future, *will continue*, and back to the present, *are projecting* and *increase*. This shift from present to future and back to present tense is logical and thus appropriate. When you shift tense inappropriately, though, the sense of the time sequence is disrupted:

■ Outside the rain stopped and the clouds opened. The truck is reflecting sunlight from its wet surface. The driver dashed from the store to the driver's cab, opens the door, and leaps in.

[handwritten annotations: *was* above "is reflecting"; *opened* above "opens"; *leaped* above "leaps"]

Here, the time sequence shifts from the past to the present tense inappropriately. When correcting a passage such as this, select one dominant tense—usually, the past tense—and stick to it.

Always use the present tense, often referred to as the *historical present*, as the dominant tense when writing about subjects in literature, film, and art. The logic behind this convention is that even though such works were created in the past, the action or image still exists in the immediate present.

Even so, using the historical present can sometimes create difficulty. For example, when referring to an artist, you should write in the past tense; when referring to an artwork, write in the present tense:

> Shakespeare wrote *Hamlet* near the turn of the seventeenth century. The plot conveys an ancient message: Revenge is a powerful human motive.

Also use the present tense when writing about habitual action or beliefs:

> Even today, the rule of law reflects the desire for revenge.

EXERCISE

Correcting Verb Tense

Recast the verb sequence in the following paragraph. The first sentence is correct as it stands, but several of the subsequent sentences are incorrect.

> Properly speaking, human life began with hunting. The eating of meat is at the heart of humanity's rise to world dominion. War is not

with other humans but with animals, and it is waged for meat. In hunting societies, choice of mates by women depends on the capability of men to provide meat for them and their children. The amount of flesh food establishes the standard of living for hunting societies, just as it did for the modern societies descended from them. It was not essential for modern humans to eat meat as long as they made a concerted effort to compensate for it nutritionally; however, it was doubtful that a healthy nonmeat diet was possible for most people.

Pronoun Case

Pronouns take the places of nouns. In the following example, the pronoun *her* takes the place of the noun *Joan*; the pronoun *him* takes the place of the noun *grandfather*; and the pronoun *they* takes the place of the noun *family*:

> Joan photographed her grandfather. When the family saw her portrait of him, they all wanted copies.

The word that a pronoun replaces is called the *antecedent* of the pronoun. *Joan* is the antecedent of *her*; *grandfather* is the antecedent of *him*; and *family* is the antecedent of *they*.

Generally, which pronoun to use for an antecedent won't take much thought, but in some situations, you will have to give the choice careful consideration.

I versus *Me* and *She* versus *Her*

You must select the accurate case of a personal pronoun depending on how the pronoun functions in the sentence. Pronouns functioning as subjects, or *subject complements*, function in the *subjective case*. Pronouns functioning as objects function in the *objective case*. Finally, pronouns indicating possession function in the possessive case.

SUBJECTIVE CASE	OBJECTIVE CASE	POSSESSIVE CASE
I	me	my
we	us	our
you	you	your
he / she / it	him / her / it	his / her / its
they	them	their

Pronouns as Subjects and Predicate Nominatives

Always use a subjective case pronoun when the pronoun functions as the subject of a clause. You need to be especially cautious in selecting the proper case when the subject of the clause is compound:

- The president and her attended the dedication ceremony. *(she)*

- Since Roberto and me returned from Europe, the phone hasn't stopped ringing. *(I)*

Always use the subjective case pronoun when the pronoun functions as a predicate nominative. A *predicate nominative* is a noun or pronoun that follows the main verb in a clause. A predicate nominative renames or identifies the subject of the main verb, usually following *be, am, is, are, was, were, being,* or *been*:

■   The contestants who had the most points were Raul and ^me.

> In speech, it's common practice to use objective case pronouns as predicate nominatives in expressions beginning with *it is* or *it's*:

>> It's me.

>> It is him.

>> It's them.

> Such uses of the objective case are unacceptable in writing, however. Instead, use these forms:

>> It is I.

>> It is he.

>> It is we.

>> It is they.

Pronouns as Objects

Always use the objective case pronoun when the pronoun functions as an *object*. There are three kinds of objects: direct objects, indirect objects, and objects of prepositions.

A *direct object* receives the action of a verb. (Recall that a predicate nominative renames or identifies the subject of a main verb.) For instance:

> Betty hit the ball.

Ball is the direct object. It was *hit*.

In the following example, both *Dr. Naga* and *her* (not *she*) are the direct objects of *interest*:

> All forms of life interest Dr. Naga and her.

An *indirect object* always precedes the direct object and usually indicates to whom or for whom the action is done:

> Betty hit John the ball.

John is the indirect object. The action was done for him.

In the following example, the direct object is *good news*. The correct indirect objects are *him* and *the family*, not *he* and *the family*. *Him* is the objective case of the subjective pronoun *he*:

■   The doctor gave the family and he ^good news.
      him

Always use the objective case pronoun when the pronoun functions as the *object of a preposition*. Prepositions include such words as *of, with, by, near, above, under, be-*

hind, next to, between, and *for.* A *preposition* always begins a prepositional phrase—that is, a word group that begins with a preposition and ends with a noun or pronoun. The noun or pronoun becomes the object of the preposition:

- This is a secret between you and I. [*me*]

Appositives

Appositives are phrases that rename nouns and pronouns and have the same functions as the words they rename. If an appositive phrase follows a subject, then use a subjective case pronoun; if it follows an object, use an objective case pronoun:

- The team leaders, Dr. Fillmore and him, disagree. [*he*]
- The hiring committee interviewed only three candidates: John Williams, Van Zinberg, and I. [*me*]

Pronouns after *Than* or *As*

Because a comparison often omits the verb at the end of a sentence, choose the appropriate subject case pronoun if a verb can be added or if the appropriate objective case pronoun if a verb can't be added. Look at these examples:

- Soyon Lee has played cello longer than me. [*I*]

The completed sentence would read . . . *than I have played cello.*

- Le Bon devoted as much energy to the project as her. [*she*]

The completed sentence would read . . . *as she devoted.*

- Students respected no other professor on campus as much as she. [*her*]

In this sentence the meaning "as much as they admired her" is understood.

We or Us before Nouns

Always choose the appropriate pronoun by first reading the sentence *without* the noun (in brackets below):

> We [seniors] deserve to have early enrollment privileges.

> Rising fees are threatening those of us [students] who are existing on limited incomes.

Pronouns before Gerunds

A *gerund* is the *-ing* form of a verb that functions like a noun. Use the possessive case for a pronoun that comes before a gerund:

- Me running up the hill took all my energy. [*My*]

Also use the possessive case for a noun before a gerund:

■ Tani running up the hill took all his energy.

Who and Whom

Writers frequently confuse the use of *who* and *whom*. If you keep the following in mind, you will use them correctly: *Who* is a subjective case pronoun and can only be used as a subject or subject complement. *Whom* is an objective case pronoun and can only be used as an object. Use *who* and *whom* in dependent clauses and questions.

You can decide which word is correct by answering the stated or implied question in the *who* or *whom* part of the sentence. If a subjective case pronoun answers the question, use *who*; if an objective case pronoun answers the question, use *whom*. For instance:

Whom did you see at the crime scene?

The answer to this stated question is *I saw **him** or **her** or **them*** (all objective case pronouns) *at the crime scene*.

The police want to know who should be considered as suspects.

The answer to the implied question is ***They*** (a subjective case pronoun) *should be considered as suspects*.

EXERCISE

Correcting Pronoun Case

In the following paragraph, correct any errors you find in pronoun case. (Keep in mind that some pronouns are used correctly.)

> Last Saturday, Dylan and Warren invited Jamie and I to go shopping with them for birthday presents for Reza. First we went to the sporting goods department to buy him some golf balls. The clerk, who we recognized from political science class, showed us all the different brands he had in stock. We bought the cheapest ones. Then Jamie wanted a Coke. Dylan and her went to the snack bar while Warren and me looked at sport shirts. The clerk showed us several racks of shirts, but them didn't look good to us. Warren and me decided to join Dylan and Jamie at the snack bar. After we finished our drinks, we decided to try a different store. The clerk in the men's department didn't want to help us, but we saw a pale-blue sweater that was just right for Reza. Jamie couldn't resist telling the clerk, "You helping us is really appreciated." I was embarrassed and said I wanted to head back to the parking lot to find our car. On the way home, we argued to see whom would wrap the presents, and, as always happens in arguments, Dylan gave in, so the task fell to him.

Pronoun/Antecedent Agreement

The *antecedent* of a pronoun is the word or words the pronoun refers to. An antecedent and its pronoun must agree, whether they are singular or plural:

SINGULAR

The anthropologist took her vacation in Mexico with a group of students.

PLURAL

The students piled their suitcases on top of the anthropologist's van.

For compound antecedents joined by *and*, always use a plural pronoun:

Ramon and Rachel gave their best effort in the tango contest.

For compound plural or singular antecedents joined by *or* or *nor*, use a pronoun that agrees with the nearest antecedent:

■ Every evening, the singers or Tracy perform their favorite songs.
  performs her

When a sentence that follows this convention sounds awkward or puzzling, recast it:

Every evening, Tracy or the singers perform their favorite songs.

Indefinite Pronouns

Generally, use a singular pronoun to refer to an indefinite pronoun that functions as an antecedent. *Indefinite pronouns* refer to nonspecific persons or things:

anybody	either	everything	no one
anyone	everybody	neither	someone
each	everyone	none	something

Although they seem to be plural, they should be treated as singular antecedents in writing:

■ Every one of the women canceled their subscription to Vanity Fair.
  her

■ Everybody in the president's cabinet offered their advice.
  his or her

Traditional grammar calls for the use of the masculine pronoun *his* (*he*) to refer to a person of either sex when the gender of the antecedent is unknown. This practice, however, reflects a gender bias in English. To offset the bias, use *his or her* (*he* or *she*) in place of a masculine pronoun. Or rewrite the sentence in the plural to reflect the same meaning:

Each student was expected to furnish his or her own supplies.

Students were expected to furnish their own supplies.

Collective Nouns

Generally use a singular pronoun to refer to a collective noun. *Collective nouns* include words such as *army, audience, class, committee, group, herd, jury, public,* and *team*. Even though they identify classes or groups with many members, collective nouns are usually singular because the members are acting as a single unit:

- The jury of five women and seven men spoke with one voice. They declared *(It)*

  the defendant guilty as charged.

If a passage makes clear that the members of a group are acting individually, then use a plural pronoun:

- The jury members could not agree. It deliberated for three days before the *(They)*

  judge declared a mistrial.

Generic Nouns

Use a singular pronoun to refer to a generic noun. *Generic nouns* refer to typical members of groups. They are always singular:

- A law student must study hours every night if they are to graduate. *(he or she is)*

Such a sentence can also be recast to reflect the same meaning:

- A law student must study hours every night if they are to graduate. *(Law students)*
- A law student must study hours every night if they are to graduate.

Who, Whom, Which, and That

Who refers to persons and sometimes to animals that have been named in the passage:

> Fahid, who had lived in Rome, once worked as a guide to the catacombs.

> Lassie was the first Hollywood dog who had a fan club.

Which refers to things or places and unnamed animals:

> Death Valley, which is an austere wasteland, is located on the California/Nevada border.

> Carla's German shepherd, which is highly spirited, would have been restless in the van.

Whose, the possessive form of *who*, can be used to refer to animals and things to avoid awkward constructions using *of which*:

- *Humongous* is a word the origin of which puzzles me. *(whose)*

That also refers to things or places, unnamed animals, and sometimes to persons, when they are collective or anonymous:

> The hills that border Acapulco are dotted with expensive homes.

> Acapulco is heaven for tourists that love tropical beaches.

> **EXERCISE**
>
> **Correcting Pronoun Case**

Select the correct pronoun in each of the following sentences.

1. That noise must be either the radio or the coffee pot falling out of (their, its) box.
2. Claire and Bonnie forgot (their, her) homework.
3. The group is planning to rent (their, its) boat tomorrow.
4. Her canary, Sunshine, was the one (which, who) flew out the window.
5. Acapulco, (who, which) is less than 250 miles from Mexico City, offers good fishing all year.
6. Each of the women had (their, her) speech prepared.
7. Valerie's puppy, (which, who) stayed at the dog hotel, would have been unbearable on the sailboat.
8. The creek (which, that) flowed into the pasture is dry.
9. Every one of the poets read (their, his or her) best poem.
10. Sailfish, (who, which) are most plentiful in winter, are known for their swiftness.

Pronoun Reference

A pronoun must clearly refer to its antecedent—that is, the word or words it stands for. If the reference is unclear, revise the sentence to clarify it.

Vague Pronoun Reference

Pronouns such as *this*, *they*, and *which* should not refer vaguely to word groups that appear earlier in the sentence:

- Travelers, especially to rural areas, are more and more becoming targets for crime. Vacationers must accept this ^fact when making travel plans.

- *Silence of the Lambs* is a classic thriller that chronicles the pursuit of a serial killer referred to as "Buffalo Bill" ^which was very chilling. ^The film

Indefinite Pronoun Reference

The pronouns *they*, *you*, and *it* should refer to specific antecedents. Don't use *they* to refer to an antecedent that has not been clearly stated:

- Often, guidelines to saving money on auto repairs are discussed on *The Car Show*. For example, they ^point out that having an oil change every 3,000 miles may lead to driving an extra 25,000 miles before the valves need work. ^the hosts

Don't use *it* indefinitely in such constructions as *It says that* . . . For example:

- In the Preamble to the Declaration of Independence, it says that everyone is created equal. ^The

Don't use the pronoun *you* unless addressing the reader directly:

- When beginning to write, ~~you~~ a writer should first create a list of ideas.

The indefinite *you* is considered very informal and thus inappropriate for most writing:

- Most people do well if they are personally engaged in learning. ~~You~~ They find that losing ~~yourself~~ themselves intellectually in a problem is exhilarating.

Ambiguous Pronoun Reference

Avoid writing passages in which single pronouns have two antecedents:

- When the Bulls and the Jazz meet, ~~they~~ the Bulls are predicted to win by eight points.

Also avoid *implied* pronoun references. A pronoun must have a specific antecedent, not a word that's implied but not actually stated in the sentence:

- After General Custer circled his troops, he discovered that doing so was a useless defense against the attack.
- ~~In~~ Deidre's biography of Beckett~~, she~~ implies that Beckett was haunted by memories of his mother.

A pronoun ending in *-self* or *-selves* is a *reflexive* pronoun that refers directly to an antecedent in the same sentence:

- The hunter shot himself in the foot.

Don't use a reflexive pronoun to replace a grammatically appropriate pronoun:

- The secret is between Riley and ~~myself~~ me.

EXERCISE

Correcting Pronoun Reference

Rewrite each of the following sentences to correct faulty pronoun references.

1. They said the sun would shine tomorrow.
2. Lena watched a television movie and ate a TV dinner. She enjoyed that.
3. The farm had a rabbit and gopher snake, but it died.
4. The council must budget to build a foundation for the city's statue of Martin Luther King, Jr. It is crumbling.
5. I blame me for sending the wrong report.
6. When you drive on Cliff Road after dark, it can be dangerous.
7. Although Al had neither read the novel nor seen the film, he said that he didn't like it.
8. Vandals are setting fires in the park. They concern nearby neighbors.
9. After he saw the first half, he turned it off.
10. The checks must be countersigned by you and myself.

Commas

The *comma* is the most frequently used—and misused—punctuation mark. Learn comma use, and you will be well on your way to controlling punctuation errors. To do so, it might help to divide comma use according to two applications: commas functioning within sentences and commas functioning within conventional constructions.

Commas Functioning within Sentences

Commas function within sentences to help readers group words that belong together. For example:

- Although grizzly bears like to eat hikers, campers, and picnickers seldom become meals.

Without a comma separating *eat* and *hikers*, the sentence will confuse readers for a moment. Your goal is to keep readers moving through your writing by avoiding disruptions like this.

Before a Coordinating Conjunction Joining Independent Clauses

When a coordinating conjunction (*and, but, or, nor, yet, for, so*) links independent clauses—that is, word groups that can stand alone as sentences—a comma must precede the conjunction. The comma and coordinating conjunction show readers that one independent unit of thought has ended and another is beginning:

- The helicopter buzzed overhead, and the police sirens wailed in the distance.

- The crowd shouted, but the senator continued to speak.

If, however, the independent clauses are short and there is no chance of misreading the sentence, then you may omit the comma:

The sky is gray and the sea is rough.

Remember that not every coordinating conjunction in a sentence joins independent clauses. (See also Misuses of Commas, pp. 000–000.)

Taken from *Four in One: Rhetoric, Reader, Research Guide, and Handbook*, Fifth Edition,

After Introductory Word Groups

A comma after a phrase or clause that begins a sentence shows readers that the subordinate information has ended and the main information is beginning:

- Off the San Francisco coast, Great White sharks breed.

- Beaten by relentless winds, the caravan returned to the oasis.

- Whenever heavy rains hit Southern California, hillside homes slide down into valleys.

If a brief word group begins a sentence, you may omit the comma, as long as doing so doesn't create misreading:

> By December the plan will be complete.

Between Items in a Series

Use commas to separate words, phrases, and clauses in a series of three or more items:

- George Washington, Abraham Lincoln, and Franklin Roosevelt are our best-known presidents.

- You must clarify the goal, define the objectives, and establish a deadline to plan successfully.

- He did not know who he was, where he had been, or what would happen next.

Although some writers omit the comma before the last item in a series, we recommend that you always include it to avoid any chance of misreading:

- The cabin is primitive, but it does have electricity, hot and cold running water and gas heat.

Adding the comma avoids the silly misreading that the cabin has *hot and cold running water* and *hot and cold gas heat.*

Between Coordinate Adjectives

If two or more descriptive words describe a noun separately, they are coordinate adjectives. Always separate *coordinate adjectives* with commas:

- Intelligent sensitive witty films are seldom made in Hollywood.

You can tell coordinate adjectives because they can be joined by the word *and—intelligent and sensitive and witty.*

Don't use commas between cumulative adjectives—that is, descriptive words that don't separately modify a noun:

> A flock of large colorful birds flew across the bay.

With Restrictive and Nonrestrictive Word Groups

Never set off a restrictive word group with commas, but always set off a nonrestrictive word group with commas. A *restrictive* word group determines the meaning of the word it modifies by defining or identifying it; it is essential to the meaning of the sentence. A *nonrestrictive* word group adds information but is not essential to the meaning of a sentence:

> A student who sets academic goals will graduate in four years.

In this sentence, the word group beginning with *who* is essential to the meaning: *Only* students who set academic goals will graduate in four years. Without the word group, the sentence would mean something else: *Any* student will graduate in four years.

Here's an example of a nonrestrictive word group:

> Sharon Lever, who studies five hours each day, will graduate in four years.

In this sentence, the word group beginning with *who* adds information but not essential information. The basic meaning of the sentence is clear without the word group: Sharon will graduate in four years. The information that she studies five hours each day is nonessential.

Look at a few more restrictive examples:

> Citizens who are interested in politics should run for office.

The meaning here is that *only* those citizens who are interested in politics should run for office; no one else should run.

> The mechanic working on the Volkswagen lost his temper.

In this sentence, *only* the mechanic working on the Volkswagen lost his temper; the mechanics working on other cars did not.

> Now look at a few more nonrestrictive examples:

> Paris, which is flooded with tourists each summer, has always embraced American jazz musicians.

The amount of tourist traffic is nonessential to the information that Parisians like jazz.

> The right to free speech, like breathing itself, is essential to a democratic society.

Like breathing itself adds color to the sentence but is not essential to its meaning.

With Transitional and Parenthetical Expressions, Absolute Phrases, and Contrasting Elements

Transitional and Parenthetical Expressions.   Use commas to set off transitional and parenthetical expressions that interrupt the flow of a sentence. *Transitional expressions* include such words and phrases as *on the one hand, on the other hand, for example, in fact, first, second,* and so on. Transitional expressions also include conjunctive adverbs such as *however, furthermore, nevertheless, and moreover.*

Here are some examples of using commas with transitional expressions:

- On the one hand, she liked the color; on the other hand, she hated the design.

- Stephen King is the undisputed master of the horror novel; soon, however, he may become the master of the horror film.

Parenthetical expressions often add afterthoughts or supplemental information to sentences:

- If life is a bowl of cherries, as I have heard said, then why am I in the pits?

Absolute Phrases. Use a comma to set off an *absolute phrase*—that is, a phrase that modifies an entire sentence:

- The doberman leaped at Kurt's throat, teeth snapping, eyes flashing anger.

- Their feet aching from the climb, the four campers crawled into their sleeping bags.

Be sure that by adding a comma, you have not written a comma splice, mistakenly treating an absolute phrase as an independent clause:

- Their feet were aching from the climb, *when* the four campers crawled into their sleeping bags.

Contrasting Elements. Use commas to set off words that signal sharp contrasts in thought in a sentence:

- Love, not hate, is the essence of self-renewal.

- Existential thought, unlike communist practice, maintains that the individual has responsibility for his or her life.

With Direct Addresses, Interrogative Tags, the Words Yes and No, Mild Interjections, and Direct Quotations with Identifying Phrases

DIRECT ADDRESSES

- Friends, please have patience.

INTERROGATIVE TAGS

- People have to accept responsibility for their own decisions, don't they?

THE WORDS YES AND NO

- Yes, they have bananas.

MILD INTERJECTIONS

- You see films like *The Mummy* become cult classics.

IN DIRECT QUOTATIONS WITH IDENTIFYING PHRASES

- In *The Island Stallion*, Walter Farley writes, "Time should be reckoned by events that happen to a person, not by the lapse of hours."

- "We are all strong enough," a French philosopher said, "to bear the misfortunes of others."

Commas within Conventional Constructions

Dates

In a date, the year is set off from the rest of the sentence with commas:

- Do you remember that July 19, 2001, was the first time we went on a date together?

Don't use commas if the date is inverted or if only the month and the year are given:

> The concert is 29 December 2007.

> The salesman said we should not expect a new software release until September 2012.

Addresses

Use commas to set off elements of an address or a place name. Do not, however, set off a zip code with a comma:

- The campus is located at 2701 Fairview Drive, Costa Mesa, California 92926.

Titles

If a title comes after a name, set it off from the rest of the sentence with commas:

- Ruth Bellow, PhD, is department chairwoman.

Numbers

Use a comma to separate long numbers into groups of three, beginning from the right:

> Over 12,000 people attended the performance.

In a four-digit number, the comma is optional–5,675 or 5675. Never add commas, however, in numbers that indicate addresses, pages, or years:

> Report to work at the warehouse on 4424 Broadway.

> The assignment starts on page 1204 of your textbook.

> The year 2003 was not good for buying stocks and bonds.

Salutations and Closes to Friendly Letters

In a friendly letter, add commas following the salutation (or greeting) and following the close:

> Dear Uncle Joe,

> Yours truly,

Misuses of Commas

The most common misuse of commas comes when writers mistake a compound element in an independent clause for an independent clause. The comma error usually takes place when a sentence has a compound predicate:

- Galileo wrote extensive notes\ and drew detailed images.

    The word group before the comma is an independent clause because it has a subject, *Galileo*, and a predicate, *wrote*. It can stand alone as a sentence. The word group following the comma has a predicate, *drew*, but shares the subject *Galileo* with the preceding independent clause. This word group can't stand alone as an independent clause. The comma separating the two word groups is incorrect.
    Other common misuses of commas include the following:

BETWEEN SUBJECTS AND THEIR VERBS

- First contact between humans and celestial aliens\ is the subject of many science fiction writers.

BETWEEN CUMULATIVE ADJECTIVES
- The snail has a soft\ slimy body.

WITH RESTRICTIVE ELEMENTS

- The belief\ that comets are the fiery messages of the gods, is an ancient one.

AFTER COORDINATING CONJUNCTIONS

- Live performances are dramatic, but, CDs can be played over and over.

AFTER *SUCH* **AS AND** *LIKE*

- Some writers, such as\ Virginia Wolfe and James Joyce, were significant innovators.

BEFORE *THAN*

- Watching a powerful play is more moving\ than watching a film of the play.

TO SET OFF PARENTHESES

- Suarez\ (the last of the big-time gamblers)\ hit Vegas with $102 and a lucky charm.

WITH END PUNCTUATION IN QUOTATIONS

- "To be or not to be? Isn't that the question"?, Philip mused.

EXERCISE

Using Commas Correct comma errors in the following sentences. Keep in mind that there may be more than one error in a sentence or none at all. Identify any correct sentences, and be able to state which guideline applies to each corrected sentence.

1. Citizens of the United States refer to themselves as *American* but seldom remember that citizens from other Western countries are also *American*.

2. In spite of early Hollywood resistance stunt women are now accepted and do everything from rolling cars at seventy miles per hour to leaping from helicopters.

3. Grammarians say we are not supposed to use *ain't* yet people still do.

4. A Zen master wrote "A person should live as if he were walking on the beach at low tide."

5. Glass sparkled in the sunlight for the clouds had drifted north.

6. Chasing gangsters at break-neck speeds is a standard sequence in cop films.

7. The aging process is relentless but most people dread growing old.

8. James Fenimore Cooper an American writer created the first espionage novel.

9. Bulging biceps rippled stomach and yes even sinewy necks are the new physical features people yearn for.

10. Advertising is often no more than a deceptive dull appeal to consumers' insecurities.

11. "A writer writes out of one thing only" says James Baldwin "personal experience."

12. The new chef praises muskrat chili which is certainly not as common as Texas chili right?

13. Early colonists brought such words as *bandit robber highwayman* and *outlaw* with them from England.

14. Presidential news conferences offer more entertainment than information because reporters do not ask pointed questions.

15. Handicapped by low budgets authorities seem to be losing the battle against poachers.

16. Professional athletes begin their careers out of a love for sports and a few of them keep loving sports.

17. If you are tempted to spend $54000 for a leopard skin coat remember that each coat requires the pelts of seven animals.

18. Ernest Hemingway who had a fine art collection claimed to have learned to write description from studying Impressionist paintings.

19. Natural meat also called game (not the kind you play on ballfields) includes a variety of wildlife found in America.

20. Seals are fun to swim with, but sharks are thrilling.

Semicolons

The *semicolon* can join independent clauses, but the clauses should be closely related in meaning and not be joined by a coordinating conjunction, such as *and* or *but*. You can also use a semicolon instead of a comma in a very limited number of situations. Remember, the semicolon is not as frequently used as a comma; in fact, you should use it only in formal writing.

Between Main Clauses

Use a semicolon between main clauses that are closely related in meaning and not joined by a coordinating conjunction:

- Some moths escape bats by not flying; ~~and~~ others confuse bat radar.

  Use a semicolon to distinguish main clauses joined by conjunctive adverbs, such as *therefore*, *however*, and *nevertheless*:

- The 1950s inspired fantastic science fiction movies; however, most of them carried a realistic social message.

When a conjunctive adverb immediately follows a semicolon, as in the previous example, always follow it with a comma. When a conjunctive adverb does not immediately follow a semicolon, put commas before and after it:

- Bicycle touring is a healthy way to see England; riding in a constant drizzle, unfortunately, is not.

To Separate Items in a Space

Commas are typically used to separate items in a series, but not always. If any of the items themselves contain commas or if any of the items are long, then use semicolons to separate them:

- Effective lawyers can become first, realistic legal advisors; second, wise business consultants; and third, close friends who know their clients from a variety of perspectives.

Misuse of Semicolons

Don't use a semicolon to join a dependent clause or phrase to an independent clause:

- If you want to cool down a potato, cut it into smaller pieces.

  Don't use a semicolon between clauses joined by *and* or *but*:

- There are almost two thousand kinds of ants, and all live in ant colonies.

EXERCISE

Using Semicolons   In the following sentences, insert and delete semicolons and commas as needed.

1. The state police improved their record of citizen complaints however the city police received more citizen complaints than ever.
2. Summit meetings are seldom more than media events they are opportunities where world leaders thump their chests and scowl.
3. Jogging increases endurance, swimming conditions the entire body.
4. For you to excel as a police officer requires hard work, long hours, and physical strength, an ability to think fast, write reports, and talk with strangers and a taste for black coffee and fast food.
5. Through hard work; we can achieve our goals, reap our rewards, and benefit humankind; but, our descendants will neither appreciate our efforts nor credit our successes.

Colons

: The *colon* should be used only after a complete sentence to clarify, illustrate, or specify detail in what follows, such as a list or long quotation.

To Indicate Lists

Use a colon at the end of a complete sentence that sets up a list:

> John Fowles has written several novels that have been made into films: *The Collector, The Magus,* and *The French Lieutenant's Woman.*

To Emphasize Snetences

Use a colon to set off a sentence that should be emphasized, such as a conclusion or general principle:

> Kevin Cestra has no doubts about his future: He will attend medical school and then train as a psychiatrist.

To Introduce Illustrations

Use a colon at the end of a complete sentence to set off a series of illustrations or examples:

> Climbing in subzero temperatures is life threatening: hypothermia sets in; concentration drifts; flesh numbs.

To Specify Details

Similarly, use a colon to identify a series of details or specific points:

> They stood on the bridge and watched the crowd escape: women clutching infants, men lugging suitcases, and children dragging blankets.

To Introduce Long Quotations

Use a colon to introduce a long quotation, which is broken out from the regular text:

> In 1962, Rachel Carson's *Silent Spring* sounded this warning:
>
>> The most alarming of all man's assaults upon the environment is the contamination of air, earth, rivers, and the sea with dangerous and even lethal materials. The pollution is for the most part irrecoverable.

Remember: Only use a colon after a sentence. If the lead-in to a quotation is not a complete sentence, add as *follows* or the *following* and then a colon to announce the quotation:

- In *Silent Spring*, Rachel Carson writes the following:

Conventional Uses of Colons

Here are some conventional uses of colons:

After formal salutations	*Dear Sir:*
Between hours and minutes	*1:20 p.m.*
In proportions	*The ratio of cats to dogs is 3:1.*
Before subtitles	*Homicide: Life on the Streets*
In bibliographic entries	*Los Angeles: Angel City Books, 2007*

A colon is traditionally used in Biblical references between the chapter and verse, as in *Matthew 4:6*. However, the Modern Language Association, in its current style guidelines, recommends using a period, as in *Matthew 4.6*.

EXERCISE

Using Colons Rewrite each of the following sentences or groups of sentences by using colons accurately. Sometimes, you must drop words or combine sentences to rewrite effectively.

1. Propaganda devices have catchy names. They are *glittering generalities, bandwagon, testimonial, plain folks,* and *poisoning the well.*
2. The sky was full of death. Jets were strafing the hills. Artillery shells were whistling overhead. Toxic fumes were drifting from the oil fields.

3. Our forests, our hills, and our prairies all have one thing in common. They will soon succumb to land development.

4. The town meeting broke up after Simpson's fiery outburst. He said, "Either clean up the streets or declare this town a health hazard!"

5. Jonathan Swift in *Gulliver's Travels* introduced the Yahoos. They are a race of brutish, degraded creatures who have the form and all the vices of humans.

Apostrophes

The *apostrophe* shows possession or ownership and indicates contractions. It also has several other conventional uses.

To Show Possession

Use an apostrophe to show that a noun is in the possessive case, as in *the King's men* and *Truman's decision*. Possession is often loosely applied, however, as in *the island's inhabitants* and the *dog's bark*. An apostrophe shows possession in one of two ways: by adding an *'s* or by adding only an apostrophe.

Singular Nouns

For a singular noun, a plural noun not ending in *-s* (such as *men, women, oxen*), and an indefinite pronoun (such as *no one, someone,* and *anybody*), add an *'s*:

> The officer's revolver lay on the floor.
>
> Terrorism is Israel's biggest problem.
>
> The women's forum meets once a week.
>
> Someone's car alarm is blaring.
>
> Declaring war is outside the commander-in-chief's powers.

Plural Nouns and Singular Nouns Ending in *-s*

For a plural noun ending in *-s* and a singular noun ending in *-s*, add only an apostrophe if adding an *'s* makes pronunciation difficult:

> The sports announcers' banquet is Saturday night.
>
> The circus' snake has disappeared.
>
> The sisters' birthdays are on the same date.

When a possessive sounds awkward or is difficult to read, revise it for clarity:

> A snake from the circus disappeared.

To show joint possession, make the last noun in the series possessive; to show individual possession, make each noun possessive:

> Ralph, Cherie, and Rene's business is profitable.
>
> Ralph's, Cherie's, and Rene's businesses are profitable.

When such constructions become confusing or awkward sounding, revise them:

> Ralph's bicycle shop, Cherie's pizza parlor, and Renee's consulting practice are all profitable.

To Form Contractions

Use an apostrophe in a contraction to mark an omission of letters:

it is	it's	do not	don't
cannot	can't	does not	doesn't
will not	won't	are not	aren't
you will	you'll	we will	we'll

Do not confuse the contraction *it's (it is)* with the possessive pronoun its.

Conventional Uses of Apostrophes

An apostrophe may be used to make the following plurals: numbers mentioned as numbers, letters mentioned as letters, and words mentioned as words. Consider these examples:

> When speaking publicly, don't use *well's*, *huh's*, and you *know's*.

> Multiplication is a mystery, especially the *8's* and *9's*.

When using a year to indicate a decade, add an -*s* without an apostrophe: *the 1980s*. When omitting the first two digits of a year, mark the omission with an apostrophe: *the '80s*.

EXERCISE

Using Apostrophes Correct the use of apostrophes in each of the following sentences.

1. Is this Rexs final offer?
2. No matter what the circumstances, anyones tale of woe interests Zoe Ann.
3. The Mothers Crusade, founded in the early 90s, begins its peace march in June.
4. Cameron's, Rod's, and Allison's fish tank cracked last night.
5. The tire companies attempts to scuttle mass transportation ignore the citys gridlock problem.
6. Zenas strength is cunning, not muscle.
7. *Mississippi* is spelled with four ss and four is.
8. Whose classic 57 Ford is that?
9. His *what ifs* make the world sound gloomy.
10. Santa Cruzs city center is sensational.

Delivering Presentations

CONTENTS

The best speakers draw their inspiration from their audience, and they maintain contact with their audience, communicating with body language and presentation style in addition to the content. Audience members leave feeling like they've had a conversation with the speaker even if they have been silent through the presentation.

Plan a Presentation

A successful presentation, like successful writing, requires careful planning. Look closely at what you are being asked to present and how long you will have. Decide early on what kind of presentation you will give and what visuals you will incorporate.

Select your topic

Choosing and researching a topic for a presentation is similar to choosing and researching a topic for a written assignment. Ask these questions:

- Will you enjoy speaking on this topic?
- Does the topic fit the assignment?
- Do you know enough to speak on this topic?
- If you do not know enough, are you willing to do research to learn more about the topic?

Remember that if your presentation requires you to do any research, then you will need to develop a written bibliography as you would for a research assignment. You will need to document the sources of your information and provide those sources in your presentation.

Think about your audience

Unlike writing, when you give a speech you have your audience directly before you. They will give you concrete feedback during your presentation by smiling or frowning, by paying attention or losing interest, by asking questions or sitting passively. Ask these questions:

- Will your audience likely be interested in your topic?
- Are there ways you can get them more interested?
- What is your audience likely to know or believe about your topic?
- What does your audience probably not know about your topic?
- What key terms will you have to define or explain?
- Where is your audience most likely to disagree with you?
- What questions are they likely to ask?

Organize your presentation

Make a list of your key points	Think of the best way to order your key points.
Plan your introduction	You have to get the audience's attention, introduce your topic, convince the audience that it is important to them, present your thesis, and give your audience either an overview of your presentation or a sense of your direction.
Plan your conclusion	End on a strong note. Simply summarizing is a dull way to close. Think of an example or an idea that your audience can take away with them.

Design Effective Visuals

Visual elements can both support and reinforce your major points. They give you another means of reaching your audience and keeping them stimulated. Visuals should communicate content and not just be eye candy. Some of the easier visuals to create are outlines, statistical charts, flow charts, photographs, and maps.

At a minimum, consider putting an outline of your talk on a transparency or on a PowerPoint slide. An outline allows an audience to keep track of where you are in your talk and when you are moving to your next point.

Create visuals
Follow these guidelines to create better visuals.

Keep the text short	You don't want your audience straining to read long passages on the screen and neglecting what you have to say. Except for quotations, use short words and phrases on transparencies and slides.
Always proofread	Typos and misspelled words make you look careless and can distract the audience from your point.
Use dark text on a white or light-coloured background	Light text on a dark background is hard to read.

Use graphics that reproduce well	Some graphics do not show up well on the screen, often because there isn't enough contrast.
Plan your timing when using visuals	Usually you can leave a slide on the screen for one to two minutes, which allows your audience time to read the slide and connect its points to what you are saying.

Know the advantages and disadvantages of presentation software

Presentation software allows you to combine text, images, sounds, animations, and even video clips on *computer-generated* slides, which can be projected onto a large screen. Presentation software, such as Microsoft PowerPoint, allows you to import charts and other graphics that you have created in other programs, and it gives you several options for presentation, including printed handouts and Web pages.

The major drawback of presentation software is perhaps that it is too easy to use. An attractive presentation can be empty of content. You can quickly get carried away with all the special effects possible—such as fade-ins, fade-outs, and sound effects. Presentations with many special effects often come off as heavy on style and light on substance. They also can be time-consuming to produce.

Give a Memorable Presentation

What makes an effective presentation?

Usually more effective	Usually less effective
Talk	Read
Stand	Sit
Make eye contact	Look down
Move around	Stand still
Speak loudly	Mumble
Use visual elements	Lack visual elements
Focus on main points	Get lost in details
Give an overview of what you are going to say in the introduction	Start your talk without indicating where you are headed
Give a conclusion that summarizes your main points and ends with a key idea or example	Stop abruptly
Finish on time	Run overtime

The following sample essay was written by Audrey McKenzie, a COMM 170 student, in the final two-hour exam. She wrote the essay in response to the following question:

Identify and explain three types of support used by Dallaire in "Cri de Coeur." Be sure to explain how each works to support Dallaire's main idea.

Throughout the ages, wars have begun and been fought because of greed, religion, and vanity, among other reasons. It is, however, those who are caught in the middle who suffer the ultimate price. The United Nations was formed after World War II partly to ensure that the tragedies that can befall the innocents don't occur. Since its formation, it is evident that the senseless destruction of innocent civilians cannot always be stopped. In this excerpt of his memoir, "Cri de Coeur," Romeo Dallaire (2010) uses narration, contrast, and descriptive detail to showcase the shortcomings and failures that befell all those involved during the UN peace-keeping mission in Rwanda.

Dallaire's use of narration makes his excerpt all the more heart-breaking, by using first-person accounts of the horrors that occurred. The reader is drawn in by his telling of the stress and heartache. This is evident in his account of finding the lost boy. In paragraph six, Dallaire (2010) mentions the "dense canopy of foliage," and the "deserted huts" that surrounded him and his small group of men (p. 67). His use of narration sets the stage, the "anxious knot in [Dallaire's] stomach" (p. 67) is also felt by the reader. Later in his account, Dallaire tells of the effects he felt years after his return: "It's as if someone has sliced into my brain and grafted this horror called Rwanda frame by blood-soaked frame directly on my cortex. I could not forget even if I wanted to" (p. 68). His open and brutally honest first-person depictions invite the reader in to share in Dallaire's failures and struggles to bring himself to retell the events he lived.

Dallaire (2010) also uses the mode of contrast to depict how the world viewed the situation in Rwanda with what was actually happening. In paragraph nine, after seeing the small boy's decomposing family and after holding the boy, Dallaire describes the contrasts in the boy's state, "alive yet terribly hungry, beautiful but covered in dirt, bewildered but not fearful" (p. 68). It was during this embrace that Dallaire realized that the agreements he had made concerning the export of orphans had been "eradicated" (p. 68). The contrast of how he had felt and what he had believed at the beginning of the mission, with what his mind and heart were feeling after holding the child, who filled Dallaire "with a peace and serenity that elevated [him] above the chaos" (p. 68), is evident and shattering, as we soon discover that Dallaire's "dream was abruptly destroyed" (p. 68) after the boy was taken away from him. In paragraph eighteen, the contrast is clear between what the UN was supposed to do and what actually happened. The people of Rwanda believed the UN was intervening to help them, to "stop the extremism...[and] killings" and to guide them "through the perilous journey to a lasting peace" (p. 69). Instead, the red tape, bureaucracy, and indifference were all that greeted the Rwandans. Dallaire could not be clearer when he states, "That mission, UNAMIR, failed" (p. 69).

Lastly, the mode that best supports his story is that of description. Dallaire's graphic imagery illuminates the failures of the mission and the fact that it was the innocent who suffered, "the butchery of children barely out of the womb, the stacking of severed limbs like cordwood, the mounds of decomposing bodies being eaten by the sun" (Dallaire, 2010, p. 70). Dallaire's description of the hut in which the small boy's deceased family lay instantly shocks the reader. Dallaire describes how "it was so dark inside that at first [he] smelled rather than saw the horror that lay before [him]" (p. 67). He goes on to graphically detail the decaying bodies with "stark white bone poking through the...leather-like covering that had once been skin" (p. 67). It is through these details that the failures of the mission are so clear: the people who were let down, either those who had been massacred or those who remain, the living dead.

By using these three forms of rhetorical mode, Dallaire (2010) makes the reader fully aware of the devastation of all who were involved. Dallaire's story depicts the failures of himself, the failures of the United Nations, and the failures on behalf of the innocent in Rwanda. "Cri de Coeur" is a chilling example of how the failures of one become the failures of many.

Reference

Dallaire, R. (2010). Cri de coeur. In Pearson Learning Solutions (Ed.), *Effective reading and writing for COMM 170 and beyond* (pp. 67–70). Toronto: Pearson Education.

The following sample take-home essay was written by Darlene Cunningham, another COMM 170 student. She wrote in response to the following prompt: *Assess "Grinning and Happy" as an attempt to make a particular historical event or experience compelling for readers decades after that event or experience happened.*

The Power of Anger

In *The Power of Now* (1999) Eckhart Tolle says that "where there is anger, there is always pain underneath." (p.32) Nowhere is this idea more evident than in Joy Kogawa's "Grinning and Happy." While reading through this excerpt from her novel *Obasan*, you are almost instantly bombarded by her sense of anger about the events which she writes of, and by the end you can almost feel her pain as if it were your own. But does her anger make the piece more compelling to a new generation of readers? I believe it does. During my research for this essay, I have read a few other firsthand accounts of this same event and of other equally horrendous experiences, and I have found Kogawa's "Grinning and Happy" to be the most interesting account because of the overall angry tone, the use of repetition, and the vivid mental pictures the words create.

In paragraph seven, Kogawa (2010) says "The fact is I never got used to it and I cannot, I cannot bear the memory. There are some nightmares from which there is no waking, only deeper and deeper sleep" (p. 123). The repetition here of "cannot" and "deeper" is used to hammer the words home and to add stress to the words, which in turn tells the reader that this is an important point that Kogawa is trying to make. It allows the reader to feel her pain as opposed to a dry textbook version of events that does not evoke any emotion in the reader whatsoever.

In a collection of historical documents compiled by the Japanese Canadian Centennial Project (1978), Hideo Kukubo tells of his similar experience in such a manner that does not evoke anger or as much interest in his readers:

> I was in that camp for four years. When it got cold the temperature went down to as much as 60 below. The buildings stood on flat land beside a lake. We lived in huts with no insulation. Even if we had the stove burning the inside of the windows would be all frosted up and white, really white. I had to lie in bed with everything on that I had . . . [A]t one time there were 720 people there, all men, and a lot of them were old men. (p. 90)

While this account gives details of the same event, it is far less interesting because the language used is so flat.

In paragraph 20, Kogawa (2010) paints a very vivid picture of what it was like for her to be working in the beet fields during the harsh Alberta winter:

> And then it's cold. The lumps of clay mud stick on my gumboots and weight my legs and the skin under the boots beneath the knees at the level of the calves grows red and hard and itchy from the flap flap of the boots and the fine hairs on my legs grows coarse there and ugly. (p. 125)

The detail in the way the author describes exactly what the cold and mud weighing her boots do to her legs paints such a vivid image in the reader's head that they can picture themselves right there alongside her in the fields and can almost feel the chaffing on their own legs. In a world that thrives on the here and now, this is a very important factor that many take into consideration when judging the effectiveness of a literary work.

In 1997, Reiko Komoto (1997) penned his memories of what it was like in an internment camp in the U.S.:

> Our sleeping quarters consisted of two white-washed horse stalls. All bathrooms, the dining room and similar rooms were located in other buildings. School was held in the dining room with all grades and dining tables in the place of desks . . . Topaz was located in the Sevier Desert, near the small town of Delta, Utah. As a consequence I missed the flowers, trees, and green plants that grew so abundantly in California. Can you imagine being thrilled to see a living green tree?!

While Komoto goes into detail explaining his surroundings and such, the language he uses does not bring forth vivid mental pictures, which in turn makes it less interesting to read than Kogawa's piece.

Starting in paragraph 13 and continuing through paragraph 22, Kogawa (2010) lists the things about the internment camp that she took offence to. She repeats the terms "I mind" and "It's the" to highlight all the bad things she had to go through (Kogawa, pp. 124-125). She begins with "Yes, I mind. I mind everything. Even the flies" (Kogawa, p. 124) and goes on to list many things such as "It's the bedbugs and my having to sleep on the table to escape the nightly attack, and the welts over my body . . . I mind growing ugly"(Kogawa, pp.124-125). And with each new sentence you read you can feel her anger building up at the indignities that she was faced with and that come pouring out of her soul. Raw human emotion pulls the readers in and grasps their attention firmly in its fist. One cannot read this piece without feeling entranced by this poor woman and what she went through, and it is the directness and vividness of her language than make this telling of those events so compelling. Kogawa states, "Grinning and happy and all smiles standing around a pile of beets. That is one telling. It's not how it was" (p. 125). You know that it is a living breathing person who actually faced these atrocities telling you her story instead of just some random person telling you the events in the way that he or she perceives them to have happened.

So, in short, yes this piece is compelling to a new generation of readers because of the repetitive language, the vivid imagery, and, most importantly, the anger that lets you know the emotion is as real as the events that caused it. The best advice I can give to write an article or story or essay that resonates inside the next generation of readers is to make sure that the concept is real to you and that you are connected to it personally because the raw emotion behind it will make it relatable to almost anyone.

References

Japanese Canadian Centennial Project. (1978). *A dream of riches: The Japanese Canadians 1877-1977* (p. 90). Vancouver, Canada: Author.

Kogawa, J. (2010). Grinning and happy. In Pearson Learning Solutions (Ed.), *Effective reading and writing for COMM 170 and beyond* (pp. 123-125). Toronto, Canada: Pearson Learning Solutions.

Komoto, R. *Japanese internment camps: A personal account.* Retrieved November 23, 2011 from http://www.uwec.edu/geography/ivogeler/w188/life.htm

Tolle, E. (1999) *The power of now.* San Fancisco: New World Library.

Using Sources in Your Writing

APPENDIX
3 A

Quick Points   You will learn to

➤ Use quotations effectively (see 1B).
➤ Integrate sources using paraphrasing and summarizing (see 1C–1E).

1A How can I integrate sources into my writing?

You integrate sources into your writing when you combine information or ideas from other writers with your own. To do this well, you use three techniques: quotation (see 1B), paraphrase (see 1C), and summary (see 1D). Mastering these techniques allows you to write smooth, effective papers that avoid plagiarism: stealing or representing someone else's words or ideas as your own (see Section 2).

1B How can I use quotations effectively?

A quotation is the exact words of a source enclosed in quotation marks. Well-chosen quotations can lend a note of authority and enliven a document with someone else's voice. Watch the Video

Avoid adding too many quotations, however. If more than a quarter of your paper consists of quotations, you've probably written what some people call a "cut-and-paste special." Doing so gives your readers—including instructors—the impression that you haven't bothered to develop your own thinking and that you're letting other people do your talking. Quick Box 1.1 provides guidelines for using quotations.

■ Making quotations fit smoothly with your sentences

When you use quotations, the greatest risk you take is that you'll end up with incoherent, choppy sentences. You can avoid this problem by making the words you quote fit smoothly with three aspects of your writing: grammar, style, and

Quick Box 1.1

Guidelines for using quotations

- Use quotations from authorities on your subject to support or challenge what you've written.
- Never use a quotation to present your thesis statement or a topic sentence.
- Select quotations that fit your message. Choose a quotation only for the following reasons.
    Its language is particularly appropriate or distinctive.
    Its idea is particularly hard to paraphrase accurately.
    The source's authority is especially important for support.
    The source's words are open to interpretation.
- Never allow quotations to make up a quarter or more of your paper. Instead, rely on paraphrase (see 1C) and summary (see 1D).
- Quote accurately. Always check a quotation against the original source—and then recheck it.
- Integrate quotations smoothly into your writing.
- Avoid plagiarism (Section 2).
- Document quotations carefully.

logic. Here are some examples of sentences that don't mesh well with quotations, followed by a revised version. All examples are in MLA documentation style.

Source

Turkle, Sherry. Alone Together: Why We Expect More from Technology and Less from Each Other. New York: Basic, 2011. Print.

Original (Turkle's Exact Words)

Digital connections and the sociable robot may offer the illusion of companionship without the demands of friendship. Our networked life allows us to hide from each other, even as we are tethered to each other.   [from page 1]

Grammar Problem

Turkle explains how relying on network communication "illusion of companionship without the demands of friendship" (1).

Style Problem

Turkle explains that the digital connections and lives of robots "offer the illusion of companionship without the demands of friendship" (1).

Logic Problem

Turkle explains networked connections "without the demands of friendship" (1).

Acceptable Use of the Quotation

Turkle explains that networked connections "may offer the illusion of companionship without the demands of friendship" (1).

■ Using brackets to add words

What do you do when a quotation doesn't fit smoothly with your writing? You can add a word or very brief phrase to the quotation, in brackets—[ ]—so that it fits seamlessly with the rest of your sentence. Make sure, however, that your bracketed additions don't distort the meaning of the quotation.

Original (Turkle's Exact Words)

If we divest ourselves of such things, we risk being coarsened, reduced.

Quotation with Explanatory Brackets

"If we divest ourselves of such things [as caring for the sick], we risk being coarsened, reduced".

■ Using ellipsis to delete words

Another way to fit a quotation smoothly into your sentence is to use ellipsis. Delete the part of the quotation that seems to be causing the problem, and mark the omission by using ellipsis points. When you use ellipsis to delete troublesome words, make sure that the remaining words accurately reflect the source's meaning and that your sentence still flows smoothly.

Original (Turkle's Exact Words)

The idea of addiction, with its one solution that we know we won't take, makes us feel hopeless.

Quotation Using Ellipsis

Turkle notes that "the idea of addiction . . . makes us feel hopeless" .

■ Integrating author names, source titles, and other information

A huge complaint instructors have about student papers is that sometimes quotations are simply stuck in, for no apparent reason. Without context-setting information, your readers can't know exactly why you included a particular quotation. Furthermore, your readers need to know who said each group of quoted words.

Source

Wright, Karen. "Times of Our Lives." Scientific American Sept. 2002: 58–66. Print.

Original (Wright's Exact Words)

In human bodies, biological clocks keep track of seconds, minutes, days, months and years.

Incorrect (Disconnected Quotation)

The human body has many subconscious processes. People don't have to make their hearts beat or remind themselves to breathe. "In human

---

Quick Box 1.2

Strategies for introducing quotations

- Mention in your sentence (before or after the quotation) the name of the author you're quoting.
- Mention in your sentence the title of the work you're quoting from.
- Give additional authority to your material. If the author of a quotation is a noteworthy figure, refer to his or her credentials.
- Add your own introductory analysis to the quotation, along with the name of the author, the title of the source, and/or the author's credentials.

---

bodies, biological clocks keep track of seconds, minutes, days, months and years" (Wright 66).

Correct

The human body has many subconscious processes. People don't have to make their hearts beat or remind themselves to breathe. However, other processes are less obvious and perhaps more surprising. Karen Wright observes, for example, "In human bodies, biological clocks keep track of seconds, minutes, days, months and years" (66).

Another strategy for working quotations smoothly into your paper is to integrate the author's name, the source title, or other information, as shown in Quick Box 1.2.

Here are some examples, using a quotation from Karen Wright, that apply techniques from Quick Box 1.2.

Author's Name

Karen Wright explains that "in human bodies, biological clocks keep track of seconds, minutes, days, months and years" (66).

Author's Name and Source Title

Karen Wright explains in "Times of Our Lives" that "in human bodies, biological clocks keep track of seconds, minutes, days, months and years" (66).

Author's Name and Credentials

Karen Wright, an award-winning science journalist, explains that "in human bodies, biological clocks keep track of seconds, minutes, days, months and years" (66).

Author's Name with Student's Introductory Analysis

Karen Wright reviews evidence of surprising subconscious processes, explaining that "in human bodies, biological clocks keep track of seconds, minutes, days, months and years" (66).

1C   How can I write a good paraphrase?

Watch
the Video

A paraphrase precisely restates in your own words the written or spoken words of someone else. Paraphrase only passages that carry ideas you need to reproduce in detail to explain a point or support an argument. Avoid trying to paraphrase

Quick Box 1.3

Guidelines for writing paraphrases

- Never use a paraphrase to present your thesis statement or a topic sentence.
- Say what the source says, but no more.
- Reproduce the source's sequence of ideas and emphases.
- Use your own words, phrasing, and sentence structure to restate the material. If some technical words in the original have only awkward synonyms, quote the original words—but do so sparingly.
- Read your sentences over to make sure they don't distort the source's meaning.
- Expect your material to be as long as the original or even slightly longer.
- Integrate your paraphrase into your writing so that it fits smoothly.
- Avoid plagiarism (Section 2).
- Document your paraphrase carefully.

more than a paragraph or two; for longer passages, use summary (see 1D). Quick Box 1.3 offers advice for paraphrasing.

Here is an example of an unacceptable paraphrase and an acceptable one.

Source

Bringhurst, Robert. The Solid Form of Language. Kentville, NS: Gaspereau, 2004. Print.

ORIGINAL (BRINGHURST'S EXACT WORDS)

A script is not a language—and the classification of scripts is as different from the classification of languages as the classification of clothes is from the classification of people. Writing, nevertheless, is many things, used by different people in many different ways. In itself, it is both less and more than language. More because it can develop into rich and varied forms of graphic art. Less because, much as we love it, it is not an inescapable part of the human experience or the perennial human condition. If language is lost, humanity is lost. If writing is lost, certain kinds of civilization and society are lost, but many other kinds remain—and there is no reason to think that those alternatives are inferior. Humans lived on the earth successfully—and so far as we know, quite happily—for a hundred thousand years without the benefit of writing. They have never lived, nor ever yet been happy, so far as we know, in the absence of language.

Unacceptable Paraphrase (Highlighted Words are Plagiarized)

Script is not the same as language, and the classification of scripts is different from the classification of languages. A script is like the garment in which a language is clothed. Writing, nevertheless, has many uses and forms. In one sense, it is more than language because it can evolve into rich and varied forms of graphic art. In another sense, writing is less than language because, even if we are attached to it, human experience and the human condition do not depend on it. There is no humanity without language, but if writing is lost, not all civilization or society is lost. What remains may not even be inferior to literate civilization. For most of their time on earth, human beings lived successfully—and perhaps even happily—without the benefit of writing. However, we have never lived, much less been happy, in the absence of language (Bringhurst 69).

Acceptable Paraphrase

Script is not the same as language. Bringhurst points out that scripts are classified differently from the languages that use them just as clothes are classified differently from the people who wear them. In one sense, he explains, writing is more than language because it can evolve into a variety of artistic forms. In another sense, writing is less than language because, even if we are attached to it, writing can be separated from what it means to be human. There is no humanity without language, but civilization and human society can survive without writing. What remains may not even be inferior to literate civilization. For most of their time on earth, human beings had no writing and, Bringhurst claims, they still lived successfully and even happily. However, he concludes, we have never lived, much less been happy, without language (69).

The first attempt to paraphrase is unacceptable because the writer has simply changed a few words. What remains is plagiarized: It retains much of the original language, has the same sentence structure, and uses no quotation marks.

The second paraphrase is acceptable. It captures the meaning of the original in the student's own words.

1D   How can I write a good summary?

Watch
the Video
A summary differs from a paraphrase (see 1C) in an important way: Whereas a paraphrase restates the original material in its entirety, a summary states only the main points of the original source in a much briefer fashion. A summary doesn't include supporting evidence or details. As a result, a summary is much shorter than a paraphrase. Summarizing is the technique you'll probably use most frequently to integrate sources. Quick Box 1.4 explains how to summarize effectively.

Here's an example of an unacceptable summary and an acceptable one.

Source

Klein, Naomi. No Logo: Taking Aim at the Brand Bullies. Toronto: Knopf, 2000. Print.

Quick Box 1.4

Guidelines for summarizing

- Identify the main points, and take care not to alter the meaning of the original source.
- Don't be tempted to include your opinions; they don't belong in a summary.
- Never use a summary to present your thesis statement or a topic sentence.
- Keep your summary as short as possible to accomplish your purpose.
- Integrate summarized material smoothly into your writing.
- Use your own words. If you need to use key terms or phrases from the source, include them in quotation marks.
- Document the original source accurately.
- Avoid plagiarism (Section 2).

ORIGINAL (KLEIN'S EXACT WORDS)

Many brand-name multinationals, as we have seen, are in the process of transcending the need to identify with their earthbound products. They dream instead about their brands' deep inner meanings—the way they capture the spirit of individuality, athleticism, wilderness or community. In this context of strut over stuff, marketing departments charged with the managing of brand identities have begun to see their work as something that occurs not in conjunction with factory production but in direct competition with it. "Products are made in the factory," says Walter Landor, president of the Landor branding agency, "but brands are made in the mind."   [from pages 195–196]

Unacceptable Summary (Highlighted Words are Plagiarized)

We have seen that many multinational corporations are transcending the need to think about their relationship to their products. Instead, they think of strut over stuff and about individuality, athleticism, and other brand attributes. This seems superficial. Marketing departments today see branding as competing with factory production: The brand is an idea of the mind, while the product is manufactured in a factory (Klein 195–96).

Acceptable Summary

According to Naomi Klein, many multinational corporations no longer identify with their products as such. Instead, they think of their brands and the desirable attributes that the brands represent. Marketing departments today see branding as competing with factory production: They claim that the brand is an idea that must not be confused with the manufactured product (195–96).

The unacceptable summary has several major problems: It doesn't isolate the main point clearly. It plagiarizes by taking much of its language directly from the source. Finally, it includes the writer's interpretation ("This seems superficial") rather than objectively representing the original. The acceptable summary concisely isolates the main point, puts the source into the writer's own words, calls attention to the author by including her name in the summary, and remains objective throughout.

■ Degrees of summary

The degree to which your summary compresses the original source depends on your situation and assignment. For example, you can summarize an entire 500-page book in a single sentence, in a single page, or in five or six pages. Following are two different levels of summary based on the same source, a 3000-word article too long to reprint here.

Source

Schwartz, Barry. "The Tyranny of Choice." Chronicle of Higher Education (23 Jan. 2004): B6. Web. 3 Apr. 2014.

Summary in a Single Sentence

Research finds that people with large numbers of choices are actually less happy than people with fewer choices (Schwartz).

Summary in 50 to 100 Words

Research finds that people with large numbers of choices are actually less happy than people with fewer choices. Although the amount of wealth and number of choices have increased during the past thirty years, fewer people report themselves as being happy, and depression, suicide, and mental health problems have increased. Although some choice is good, having too many choices hinders decision making, especially among "maximizers," who try to make the best possible choices. Research in shopping, education, and medical settings shows that even when people eventually decide, they experience regret, worrying that the options they didn't choose might have been better (Schwartz).

Notice that the longer summary begins with the same sentence as the short one; leading a summary with the reading's main idea is effective. Notice that both summaries put ideas in the writer's own words and capture only the main idea.

1E   Which verbs help weave source material into sentences?

Use the verbs in Quick Box 1.5 appropriately according to their meanings in your sentences. For example, says and states are fairly neutral introductory verbs; you're just reporting the source's words. On the other hand, while still fairly neutral, claims or contends introduces a slight skepticism; you're suggesting that you may not share the source's certainty. Demonstrates or, even stronger, proves indicates that you find the source conclusive on a particular point.

Quick Box 1.5

Useful verbs for integrating quotations, paraphrases, and summaries

acknowledges	contrasts	illustrates	recommends
agrees	declares	implies	refutes
analyzes	demonstrates	indicates	rejects
argues	denies	insists	remarks
asserts	describes	introduces	reports
begins	develops	maintains	reveals
believes	discusses	means	says
claims	distinguishes	notes	shows
comments	between	notices	specifies
compares	among	observes	speculates
complains	emphasizes	offers	states
concedes	establishes	points out	suggests
concludes	explains	prepares	supports
confirms	expresses	promises	supposes
considers	finds	proves	wishes
contends	focuses on	questions	writes
contradicts	grants	recognizes	

2 AVOIDING PLAGIARISM.

Quick Points   You will learn to

➤   Identify plagiarism (see 2A).
➤   Use techniques to avoid the different types of plagiarism
    (see 2B).

2A   What is plagiarism?

To use sources well, you need to learn how to incorporate others' words and
ideas into your own papers accurately, effectively, and honestly. This last skill is Watch
the Video
especially important, so that you avoid plagiarism, which is presenting another
person's words, ideas, or visual images as if they were your own. Plagiarizing,
like stealing, is a form of academic dishonesty or cheating. It's a serious offence
that can be grounds for a failing grade or expulsion from a college or university.
Beyond that, you're hurting yourself. If you're plagiarizing, you're not learning.

Plagiarism isn't just something that professors get fussy about. In the
workplace, it can get you fired. Plagiarism at work also has legal implications;
using someone else's intellectual property without permission or credit is a form
of theft that may land you in court. Furthermore, plagiarism in any setting—
academic, business, or civic—hurts your credibility and reputation. Quick Box 2.1
lists the major types of plagiarism.

ESL Tip: Perhaps you come from a country or culture that considers it
acceptable for students to copy the writing of experts and authorities, even without
citing them, as a sign of respect or learning. Please bear in mind that this practice
is unacceptable in Canadian and most Western settings.

Quick Box 2.1

Types of plagiarism

You're plagiarizing if you . . .
- Buy a paper from an Internet site, another student or writer, or any other source.
- Turn in any paper that someone else has written, whether the person has given it
  to you, you've downloaded it from the Internet, or you've
  copied it from any other source.
- Change selected parts of an existing paper and claim the paper as your own.
- Neglect to put quotation marks around words that you quote directly from a
  source, even if you list the source in your Works Cited or References.
- Type or paste into your paper any key terms, phrases, sentences, or
  longer passages from another source without using documentation to tell precisely
  where the material came from.
- Use ideas or reasoning from a source without correctly citing and
  documenting that source, even if you put the ideas into your own words. (See 2E.)
- Combine ideas from many sources and pass them off as your own without
  correctly citing and documenting the sources.
- Use photographs, charts, figures, or other visual images from anyone (colleagues,
  organizations, websites, and so on) without crediting and documenting them.

Quick Box 2.2

Strategies for avoiding plagiarism

- Acknowledge when you're using the ideas, words, or images of others. Always document the sources.
- Become thoroughly familiar with the documentation style your instructor requires you to use (see Appendix 3C).
- Follow a consistent notetaking system. Use different colours, or some other coding system, to distinguish three different types of material.
    1. **Quotations** from a source: write clear, even oversized quotation marks so you can't miss them later (documentation required)
    2. **Material you have paraphrased, summarized**, or otherwise drawn from a source (documentation required)
    3. **Your own thoughts**, triggered by what you have read or experienced (no documentation required; see 2D)
- When you quote, paraphrase, or summarize in your draft, include the appropriate in-text citation right away, and add the source to your Works Cited or References. Don't wait to do this later. The danger of forgetting or making a mistake is too great.
- As part of editing and proofreading, look carefully at your paper for any places that might need documentation.
- Consult your instructor if you're unsure about any aspect of the documentation process.

2B How do I avoid plagiarism?

Watch the Video

The first step in avoiding plagiarism is to learn the techniques of quoting (see 1B), paraphrasing (see 1C), and summarizing (see 1D) source materials. The second step is to document sources correctly. A third step is to take advantage of the learning opportunities your instructor may build into assignments. Many instructors require students to hand in a working bibliography (see 19F) or annotated bibliography (see 19H). Your instructor may ask to see your research log (see 19E), your working notes, copies of your sources, or working drafts of your paper. Quick Box 2.2 suggests some practical steps you can take to avoid plagiarism.

2C How do I avoid plagiarism when using Internet sources?

Watch the Video

You might be tempted to download a paper from the Internet. Don't. That kind of intellectual dishonesty can get you into real trouble. We've been dismayed to hear that some students believe if they buy a paper or hire someone else to write it, the paper is "theirs." No. It's not. This is clearly plagiarism.

Even if you have absolutely no intention of plagiarizing, being careless can easily lead to trouble. Quick Box 2.3 suggests some ways you can avoid plagiarism when you're working on the Internet.

Quick Box 2.3

Guidelines for avoiding plagiarism
  when using Internet sources

- Never copy material from an online source and paste it directly into your paper without taking great care. You can too easily lose track of what is your own and what comes from a source.
- Keep material that you downloaded or printed from the Internet separate from your own writing, whether you intend to quote, summarize, or paraphrase the material. Be careful how you manage copied files. Use another colour or a much larger font as a visual reminder that this isn't your work.
- Copy or paste downloaded or printed material into your paper only when you intend to use it as a direct quotation or visual. Immediately place quotation marks around the material (later you may decide to set off a long passage as a block quotation; only then would you remove the quotation marks). Be sure to document the source at the same time as you're copying or pasting the quotation into your paper, or you may forget to do it later or do it incorrectly.
- Summarize or paraphrase materials before you include them in your paper. Document the sources of summarized passages at the same time as you insert them in your paper.
- Use an Internet service to check a passage you're not sure about. If you're concerned that you may have plagiarized by mistake, use Google to search one or two sentences that concern you. To make this work, always place quotation marks around the sentences you want to check when you type them into the search window.

2D   What don't I have to document?

You don't have to document common knowledge or your own thinking. Common knowledge is information that most educated people know, although they might need to remind themselves of certain facts by looking them up in a reference book. For example, you would not need to document statements like these:

- Newfoundland entered Confederation in 1949.

- Mercury is the planet closest to the sun.

- Water boils at 100°C.

- All the oceans on our planet contain salt water.

2E   How do I document ideas?

You need to document everything that you learn from a source, including ideas or reasoning. Expressing others' ideas in your own words doesn't release you from the obligation to tell exactly where you got them. Consider the following example.

Source

Silberman, Steve. "The Placebo Problem." The Best American Science Writing 2010. Ed. Jerome Groopman and Jesse Cohen. New York: Ecco, 2010. 31–44. Print.

Original (Silberman's Exact Words)

The fact that an increasing number of medications are unable to beat sugar pills has thrown the industry into crisis. The stakes could hardly be higher. In today's economy, the fate of a long-established company can hang on the outcome of a handful of tests.

Plagiarism Example

The fact that more and more drugs are unable to beat sugar pills has caused problems. Much is at stake. Currently, the future of established companies can depend on the outcome of a handful of tests.

Even though the writer changed some wording in the preceding example, the ideas aren't original. The highlighted phrases are especially problematic examples of plagiarism because they're Silberman's exact wording. To avoid plagiarism the student needs both to document the source and to use quotation marks to show Silberman's wording.

1. Correct Example Using Quotation, Paraphrase, and Documentation

Steve Silberman claims that the increasing success of placebos "has thrown the [drug] industry into crisis." The market is so competitive that even "a handful of tests" can determine whether a company survives (33).

2. Correct Examples Using Summary and Documentation

A.   Steve Silberman argues that the success of placebos challenges drug company profits (33).

B.   The success of placebos challenges drug company profits (Silberman 33).

In correct example 1, the writer has properly integrated Silberman's ideas through quotation and paraphrase, and she has included an in-text citation that points to her Works Cited page. In correct example 2A, the writer summarizes the idea, including the author's name in the sentence and a parenthetic citation. In correct example 2B, she also summarizes, but here she includes the author's name as part of the parenthetical citation.

3   WRITING ABOUT READINGS

Quick Points   You will learn to

➤   Write summary and response essays (see 3B and 3C).
➤   Use analysis and synthesis in your writing (see 3D).

3A   What are typical assignments for writing about readings?

Although much academic writing requires using techniques for integrating sources (quotation, paraphrase, and summary, which we explained in Section 1), some assignments focus entirely on writing about reading. Some common types of papers are summary essays (see 3B), response essays (see 3C), analysis essays, and synthesis essays (see 3D). Research paper assignments require finding and synthesizing multiple sources. Appendix 3B give extensive advice about research writing.

3B   How do I write a summary essay?

For papers that consist entirely of summary, you might get an assignment like "Write a 500-word summary of the article by Newmann," or "Write a one-page summary of Appendix 3B." Writing good summary essays takes practice and skill. We offered several techniques for summarizing within a longer essay in 1D. Following is specific advice for writing a summary essay.

Watch the Video

Generating ideas for a summary essay

- Identify topic sentences or main ideas, separating them from examples or illustrations. You want to focus on the main ideas.

- Take notes in your own words, and then put the source away. Write from your notes, going back to check the original only after you've written a first draft.

Shaping and drafting a summary essay

- Begin with a sentence that summarizes the entire reading, unless you're writing a long summary.

- Follow the order of the original.

- Summarize proportionally. Long and important aspects of the original source need to get the most space and attention in your summary.

- Include a Works Cited or References page, depending on the required documentation style.

◼ A student's summary essay

Brian Jones received the assignment to write a 200-word summary of an article.

                                                      Jones 1

Brian Jones

Economics 101

Professor Connolly

15 Jan. 2014

    Summary of "Losing the Land Again: The Risks of Privatizing Property on First Nations Reserves"

    In "Losing the Land Again: The Risk of Privatizing Property on First Nations Reserves," Kyle Carsten Wyatt argues that the federal government proposal to privatize reserve lands holds several risks, including the loss of the lands to outsiders. Wyatt examines the nineteenth-century Dawes Act in the United States as a cautionary example.

Jones 2

Wyatt notes that the Assembly of First Nations and most First Nations communities and Native studies specialists oppose privatization. He debates journalist John Ibbitson, who believes that because the law will let reserves opt out, unlike the Dawes Act, sales of Native lands will be voluntary. Wyatt counters that desperate people do not make voluntary economic choices and predicts that this law will be one more stage in a 500-year-long "coercive land grab."

According to Wyatt, the Dawes Act also began as a voluntary measure but led to a sell-off to farmers and ranchers, railroads, and resource companies. Natives were poorly compensated and by 1934 had lost more than half their land, with the remainder entangled in legal complexities. Although reserves in Canada are not as economically productive as they could be, Wyatt emphasizes the land's religious and cultural value. He warns that defining Native status and band membership will complicate the plan, and cautions that the definitions may change some day. Above all, he warns that lands will be lost.

Work Cited

Wyatt, Kyle Carsten. "Losing the Land Again: The Risk of Privatizing

Property on First Nations Reserves." TheWalrus.ca. Walrus Foundation, 28 Jan. 2013. Web. 10 Jan. 2014.

1C   How do I write a response essay?

Watch the Video

A response essay has two missions: to provide a summary of a source and to make statements—supported by reasons—about the source's ideas or quality. Responses may

1. Comment on a work's accuracy, logic, or conclusions ("Is this history of hip-hop music accurate?" "Is this argument about requiring off-campus internships convincing?")

2. Present the writer's reaction to a source ("I found the ideas in the reading shocking/intriguing/confusing/promising, etc.")

3. Focus on a work's form, or genre ("How well does this poem satisfy the requirements of a sonnet?")

> **Quick Box 3.1**
>
> *Effective response essays*
>
> - Include a clear and concise summary of the source.
> - State agreements, disagreements, or qualified agreements. (In a qualified agreement, you accept some points but not others.)
> - Provide reasons and evidence for your statements.

4. Explain a reading's relation to other works ("Is this novel better than that novel?") or to the "real" world ("To what extent does this article accurately portray student life?")

Quick Box 3.1 explains additional elements of effective response essays.

Generating ideas for a response essay

- Use active reading (see 4C) and critical reading (see 4A) to identify the main points and generate reactions to the source.
- Use techniques for analyzing (see 4B), drawing inferences (see 4B), and assessing reasoning processes (see 3C).
- Discuss the source with another person. Summarize its content and ask the other person's opinion or ideas. Debate that opinion or challenge the ideas. Discussions and debates can get your mind moving. (If in your writing you use that other person's ideas, be sure to give the person credit as a source.)
- Respond to the source relying on your prior knowledge and experience, your reading, or your research.

■ A student's response essay

Here is student Kristin Boshoven's short response to Barry Schwartz's essay, "The Tyranny of Choice"; we included Kristin's summary of that essay in 1D. Note that she incorporates the summary before using her own experience and her general knowledge to respond.

                                                              Boshoven 1

Kristin Boshoven

English 101

Professor Lequire

12 Apr. 2014

     Too Much Choice: Disturbing but Not Destructive

     Barry Schwartz argues that people with large numbers

of choices are actually less happy than people with fewer

choices. Although the amount of wealth and choice has

increased during the past thirty years, studies show that

fewer people report themselves as being happy. Depression,

suicide, and mental health problems have increased. While

---

some choice is good, too many choices hinder decision making, especially among people who Schwartz calls "maximizers," people who try to make the best possible choices. Research in shopping, education, and medical settings shows that even when people eventually decide, they experience regret, worrying that the options they didn't choose might have been better.

Although Schwartz cites convincing evidence for his claims, he ultimately goes too far in his conclusions. Excessive choice does seem to make life harder, not easier, but it alone can't be blamed for whatever unhappiness exists in our society.

My own experience supports Schwartz's finding that people who have thirty choices of jam as opposed to six often don't purchase any. A week ago I decided to buy a new smart phone. When we went to the store, we were confronted with twenty different models, and even though a helpful salesperson explained the various features, I couldn't make up my mind. I decided to do more research, which was a mistake. After weeks of reading reviews and product reports, I am close to making a decision. However, I have a sinking feeling that as soon as I buy a phone, I'll learn that another choice would have been better, or mine will drop $50 in price. I could relate similar experiences trying to choose which movie to see, which dentist to visit, and so on. I suspect others could, too, which is why I find Schwartz's argument convincing at this level.

However, when he suggests that the increase of choice is a source of things like depression and suicide, he goes too far. Our society has undergone tremendous changes in the past forty or fifty years, and many of those changes are more likely to cause problems than the existence of too much choice. For example, workers in the 1950s through the 1970s could generally count on holding jobs with one company as long as they wanted, even through retirement. A 1950s autoworker, for example, might not have been thrilled with his job (and these were jobs held almost exclusively by men), but at least he could count on it, and it paid enough

Boshoven 3

to buy a house and education for his family. The economic uncertainties of the past decades have meant that workers—and now women as well as men—do not have the same job stability they once did.

Although I agree that too many choices can lead to anxiety and even unhappiness, there are larger factors. If people report more depression and suicide than previously, a more likely candidate is economic and social uncertainty, not having too many kinds of cereal on the grocery store shelves.

Work Cited

Schwartz, Barry. "The Tyranny of Choice." Chronicle of Higher

Education (23 Jan. 2004): B6. Web. 3 April 2014.

1D How do I write synthesis essays?

A synthesis weaves ideas together. Unsynthesized ideas and information are like separate spools of thread, neatly lined up, possibly coordinated, but not woven together or integrated. Synthesized ideas and information are like threads woven into a tapestry. By synthesizing, you show evidence of your ability to bring ideas together.

Watch
the Video

One common synthesizing task is to connect two or more readings or source materials into a single piece of writing. Another common type of synthesis is to connect material to what you already know, as the student did in 3C.

Your goal in synthesizing multiple sources is to join two or more texts together into a single piece of writing that is your own. The resulting text needs to be more than just a succession of summaries. That is, avoid merely listing who said what about a topic. Such a list isn't a synthesis—it doesn't create new connections.

Quick Box 3.2 suggests additional approaches for writing a synthesis.

Quick Box 3.2

Effective syntheses

- Compare or contrast ideas and information. Do the sources generally agree or generally disagree? What are the bases of their agreement or disagreement? Are there subtle differences or shades of meaning or emphasis?
- Create definitions that combine and extend definitions you encounter in the separate sources.
- Use examples or descriptions from one source to illustrate ideas in another.
- Use processes described in one source to explain those in others.
- Truly synthesize the sources, and don't just write about one source and then the other.

The following example shows how student Tom Mentzer synthesized two sources. First read Source 1 and Source 2, and then read Tom's synthesis.

Source 1

In Shishmaref, calamity has already arrived. The village of 600 Inupiaq lies on the fragile barrier island of Sarichef, where sea ice forms later each year, exposing the land to autumn storms that carve away 50 feet or more of shoreline a season. Two houses have slipped into the sea; 18 others have been moved back from the encroaching ocean; others buckle from the melting permafrost. Ten million dollars has been spent on seawalls, to no avail. Residents have concluded permanent resettlement is their only option.

—Julia Whitty and Robert Knoth, "Sea Change"

Source 2

Global temperatures have risen by about 0.6 degrees Celsius since the nineteenth century. Other measures of climate bolster the theory that the world is getting warmer: satellite measurements suggest that spring arrives about a week earlier now than in the late 1970s, for example, and records show that migratory birds fly to higher latitudes earlier in the season and stay later.

—John Browne, "Beyond Kyoto"

Now read Tom's synthesis. Notice how he used summary and paraphrase to synthesize the two sources. Also notice how the first sentence in his synthesis weaves the sources together with a new concept.

Example of a Synthesis of Two Sources

Global warming is affecting both the natural and artificial worlds. Rising temperatures have accelerated spring's arrival and changed the migration patterns of birds (Browne 20). They have also changed life for residents of Arctic regions. For example, eighteen families in Shishmaref, Alaska, had to move their houses away from the coast because the permafrost under the beaches had thawed (Whitty and Knoth).

—Tom Mentzer, student

Notice how the student used summary (see 1D) and paraphrase (see 1C) to synthesize the two sources. Also observe how the first sentence in his synthesis weaves the sources together with a new concept. The student also used in-text citations (in MLA style) to signal to the reader which information he borrowed from the two sources. In his Works Cited list at the end of his paper, he listed full source information for both sources.

Sources Listed In Works Cited Page

Browne, John. "Beyond Kyoto." Foreign Affairs 83.4 (2004): 20–32. Print.

Whitty, Julia, and Robert Knoth. "Sea Change." Mother Jones. Foundation for National Progress, Sept.–Oct. 2007. Web. 2 Jan. 2014.

■ **EXERCISE 3-1**   Find two short passages on related topics by different authors, each passage no more than two paragraphs long; alternatively, use two passages that your instructor assigns. Write a one-paragraph synthesis of the two passages. ■

Quick Points   You will learn to

➤ Choose a research topic and refine a research question
   (see 1B and 1C).
➤ Identify two main types of research papers (see 1D).

1A   What is research?

Research is a systematic process of gathering information to answer a question. You're doing research when you're trying to decide which college or university to attend or which smart phone to buy. Even these everyday tasks have things in common with academic research: finding, evaluating, and synthesizing information. Research is an absorbing, creative activity. It lets you come to know a subject deeply, leads to fresh insights, and shapes you into a self-reliant learner.

How much research you will do for a writing assignment can vary, depending on your *audience*, *purpose*, and type of writing. Commonly, you might need to write a *research or term paper*,* and Section 6 will help you with such long projects. However, any writing might benefit from a little research. Consider the original and revised sentences that follow.

ORIGINAL	Most young people use the Internet these days.
RESEARCHED	According to the website of the Media Research Clearinghouse, 95 percent of Canadian youth had Internet access in 2012.

In the second version, the writer specifically answers the question, "How many young people have access to the Internet?" Whenever writing has a vague language like "a lot" or "many" or "some," research can improve it with more precise information. Your *ethical appeals* are stronger because readers respect you as someone who takes the time to find facts. Specific details persuade readers.

Here are major reasons writers do research:

▪ **To find a single fact.** Sometimes you simply need to answer a direct question of "How much?" or "When?" or "Where?" or "Who?"

* Words printed in SMALL CAPITAL LETTERS are discussed elsewhere in the text and are defined in the Terms

- How does the cost of university today compare to the cost twenty years ago?
- To understand an issue or situation more broadly. Sometimes you need to learn basic information as well as the range of viewpoints or opinions on a particular topic.
    - What are the effects of globalization?
- **To gather current information.** You may need to bring together the most current information. A **review of the literature** is a comprehensive synthesis of the latest knowledge on a particular topic.
    - What treatments are possible for diabetes?
- **To identify a specific opinion or point of view.** You might want to find out what the people who disagree with you believe—and why. You can then defend your position. You might also look for experts who support your view.
    - What are the arguments for restricting student Internet downloads?
- **To create new knowledge.** Researchers can also make new knowledge. Chemists and biologists do this kind of research, of course, but so do psychologists, sociologists, journalists, and others. They do experiments, surveys, interviews, and observations. For instance, if you were writing a guide to coffeehouses in a certain area, you'd need to visit all of them, take notes, and present your findings to readers. Field research (see 2C) is a general name for research that creates new knowledge.
    - What are the current political views of 18- to 25-year-olds?

1B   How do I choose a research topic?

Watch
the Video
Sometimes instructors assign specific topics; other times you get to choose (see 2F). Here's advice for selecting your own research topic.

- Select a topic that interests you. It will be your companion for quite a while, perhaps most of a term.
- Choose a sufficiently narrow topic that will allow you to be successful within the time and length given by the assignment. Avoid topics that are too broad.

NO	Emotions
YES	How people respond to anger in others
NO	Social networking
YES	The effect of Facebook on job applications

- Choose a topic that your readers will perceive as significant. Avoid trivial topics that prevent you from investigating ideas, analyzing them critically, or synthesizing complex concepts.

NO	Kinds of fast food
YES	The relation between fast food and obesity

If the freedom to choose any topic leads to research-topic block, don't panic. Instead, try some of the following strategies for generating ideas.

- **Talk with others.** Ask instructors or other experts in your area of interest what issues currently seem important to them. Ask them to recommend readings or the names of authorities on those issues.
- **Browse the Internet.** Some Web search engines provide SUBJECT DIRECTORIES (see 3E). Browsing those and their categories and subcategories can turn up an interesting topic.

- **Pay attention to news and current events.** Regularly browsing newspapers or magazines (print or online), blogs, or social network channels can furnish a wealth of issues and topics.
- **Browse textbooks in your area of interest.** Read the table of contents and major headings in a textbook related to your topic. Note the names of important books and experts, often mentioned in reference lists at the end of chapters or at the back of the book.
- **Read encyclopedia articles.** Read online and, if available, print encyclopedias about your area of interest. Notice subcategories for possible ideas for investigation. Never, however, stop with encyclopedias—they are too basic for academic research. Be very cautious about using information from Wikipedia because it can be seriously unreliable (see the Alert in 3H).
- **Browse the library or a good bookstore.** Stroll through the shelves to find subjects that interest you. Look at books as well as popular magazines. Skim academic journals in fields that interest you.

1C   What is a research question?

A **research question** provides a clear focus for your research and a goal for your WRITING PROCESS. Without such a question, your research writing can become an aimless search for a haphazard collection of facts and opinions. For example, you can more successfully research the question "How do people become homeless?" than you can research the broad topic of "homelessness." Some questions can lead to a final, definitive answer (for example, "How does penicillin destroy bacteria?"). Others can't because they involve an argument that has two or more sides (for example, "Is softball a better sport than volleyball?").

The answer to your research question usually, but not always, appears in your THESIS STATEMENT (see 2G) of your research essay. Sometimes the thesis statement simply alludes to your answer, especially when the answer is long or complicated.

1D   What are two main types of research papers?

Most research papers are either informative or argumentative. Informative research papers explain a topic by SYNTHESIZING several sources (see 3D). Your goal is to gather and clarify scattered information for your readers. Informative research papers answer questions like "What is the current state of knowledge about X?" or "What are the current controversies or positions about Y?" We devote Section 5 to synthesizing and integrating sources in research papers.

In section 6C, we present a FRAME for writing an informative research paper. It is much like the frame for an informative essay in, and the sample student essay in section 10E serves as a useful example of informative writing.

Argumentative research papers go a step further to argue a point. In these papers, you choose a topic on which intelligent people have different positions, identify and analyze sources, and argue the position that appears best. You back reasons with support. Argumentative research papers answer questions like, "What is the best course of action regarding X?" or "Why should I believe Y?"

In section 3C, we present a frame for an argumentative research paper along with a sample student paper. That example is a companion to the frame and sample argumentative student essay, as well as to the frame and sample proposal-solution student essay.

2 DEVELOPING A SEARCH STRATEGY

Quick Points You will learn to

➤ Use search strategies appropriate for your research project (see 2A–2C).
➤ Do field research (see 2C).
➤ Maintain a research log and bibliographies (see 2E–2H).
➤ Take effective notes (see 2I).

2A What is a search strategy?

A SEARCH STRATEGY is an organized procedure for locating and gathering sources to answer your research question. Using a search strategy helps you work more systematically and quickly. Following are three frequently used search strategies. You can switch or combine strategies or create your own.

QUESTIONING METHOD	Useful when you have a topic. Think of a research question and brainstorm to break it into several smaller questions. Then find sources to answer each of them. This allows you to see if your sources cover all the areas important to your research question. This can give your search a direction and purpose.
EXPERT METHOD	Useful when your topic is specific and narrow. Start with articles or books by an expert in the field. You might want to interview an expert on the topic. Then pursue key sources mentioned.
CHAINING METHOD	Useful when your topic is general. Start with reference books and bibliographies in current articles or WEBSITES. Use them to link to additional sources. Keep following the links until you reach increasingly expert sources. You might also talk with people who have some general knowledge of your topic and ask them to refer you to experts and/or sources they might know.

Start and complete your search as soon as possible after you get your assignment. This gives you time early in your process to discover sources that take time to obtain (for example, through an interlibrary loan).

One more piece of advice: Rather than spend endless hours simply gathering sources, take time to read and analyze some of your materials to make sure your topic will work. Your research log (see 2E) can be useful for this purpose.

2B   What is a source?

A SOURCE is any form of information that provides ideas, examples, or evidence. Sources are either primary or secondary.

Watch
the Video

- A PRIMARY SOURCE is original work that can take one of two forms. One is FIELD RESEARCH (see 2C) that you carry out yourself, such as experiments, observations, interviews, and surveys. Another form is original documents such as letters, diaries, novels, poems, short stories, autobiographies, original reporting, findings from a research study, speeches, journals, and so on. In addition to physical copies in libraries or elsewhere, copies of original documents often exist online in digital form.

- A SECONDARY SOURCE reports, describes, comments on, or analyzes someone's original work. That is, someone other than the primary source relays the information, adding a layer between you and the original material. This happens online all the time; someone summarizes a news article in a blog (or maybe only includes a link) but then comments on it. Secondary sources aren't necessarily weak, but be sure to evaluate them to check that what's being reported to you isn't distorted or biased.

Suppose you wish to research student attitudes toward dietary supplements. Surveying several students would be primary research. Consulting scholars' books and articles about student attitudes toward foods and pharmaceuticals would be secondary research. Your decision to use primary and/or secondary sources depends on your research question or the nature of your assignment. For her paper in Appendix 4, Leslie Palm conducted primary research by analyzing several video games and secondary research by reading scholarly articles about them.

2C   What is field research?

Field research involves going into real-life situations to observe, survey, interview, or participate in some activity firsthand. As a field researcher, you might go to a factory, a lecture, a day-care centre, or a mall—anywhere that people engage in everyday activities. You might also interview experts and other relevant individuals. Finally, you might observe and describe objects, such as paintings or buildings, or performances and events, such as concerts or television shows. Field research yields original data.

■ Surveying

Surveys use questions to gather information about people's experiences, situations, or opinions. Multiple-choice or true/false questions are easy for people to complete and for researchers to summarize and report. Open-ended questions, in which people are asked to write responses, require more effort to summarize. However, they sometimes provide more complete or accurate information. For advice on developing a survey, see Quick Box 2.1.

Watch
the Video

When you report findings from a survey, keep within your limitations. For example, if the only people who answer your survey are students at a particular campus, you can't claim they represent "all students."

❶   Alert: Online tools can help you distribute and analyze surveys easily. Two popular free services for small surveys are Zoomerang and SurveyMonkey. You go to the service's website, enter your survey questions, and then receive a

Quick Box 2.1

Guidelines for developing a survey

1. Define what you want to learn.
2. Identify the appropriate types and numbers of people to answer your survey so that you get the information you need.
3. Write questions to elicit the information.
4. Phrase questions so that they are easy to understand.
   NO Recognizing several complex variables, what age generally do you perceive as most advantageous for matrimony?
   YES What do you think is the ideal age for getting married?
5. Make sure that your wording doesn't imply what you want to hear.
   NO Do irresponsible and lazy deadbeats deserve support from hardworking and honest taxpayers?
   YES Should we provide benefits to unemployed people?
6. Decide whether to include open-ended questions that allow people to write their own answers.
7. Test a draft of the questionnaire on a small group of people. If any question is misinterpreted or difficult to understand, revise and retest it.

URL to send to participants. After you receive responses, you can go back to the site to download the results or do some analysis. ●

▣ Interviewing

Watch the Video

Instead of surveying, you might interview people in the general population to gather data or opinions. You might also interview experts, who can offer valuable information and viewpoints. One good place to start is with the faculty at your school, who may also suggest additional sources. Also, corporations, institutions, or professional organizations often have public relations offices that can answer questions or make referrals.

Make every attempt to conduct interviews in person so that you can observe body language and facial expressions. However, if distance is a problem, you can conduct interviews over the phone or online. Quick Box 2.2 provides suggestions for conducting interviews.

Quick Box 2.2

Conducting research interviews

- Arrange the interview well in advance, do background research, prepare specific questions, and arrive on time.
- Rehearse how to ask your questions without reading them (perhaps highlight the key words). Looking your interviewee in the eye as you ask questions establishes ease and trust. If you're interviewing on the telephone, be organized and precise.
- Take careful notes, listening especially for key names, books, websites, or other sources.
- Create a shortcut symbol or letter for key terms you expect to hear during the interview. This cuts down on the time needed to look away from your interviewee.
- Use standard paper so that you have room to write. (Many people are annoyed when others type while they're talking.)
- Bring extra pens or pencils.
- Never depend on recording an interview, because people have become reluctant to be recorded.

Notes	Comment/Analyses
Small conference room; round table covered with papers	
JP suggests fundraising plan	JP seems nervous. Her normal behaviour, or is it this situation?
AR and CT lean forward; SM leans back	
SM interrupts JP's plan, asks for more; CT silent	The fact that JP and AR are women might explain SM's response. Or is it that he's more senior?
JP continues proposal	
SM looks out window, taps pencil	Seems to have made up his mind. A power move?

Figure 2.1   A double-column set of notes.

◼ Observing people and situations

Anthropologists, education and marketing researchers, sociologists, and other scholars conduct research by observing people and situations. For observations of behaviour (for example, fans at a game or tourists at a museum), take notes during the activity. Try to remain objective so that you can see things clearly. One strategy is to take notes in a two-column format. On the left, record only objective observations; on the right, record your comments or possible interpretations. Figure 2.1 is an example of a double-column note strategy.

2D   What documentation style should I use?

A DOCUMENTATION STYLE is a system for providing information to your readers about each source you use. Documentation styles vary from one academic discipline to another.

MLA (Modern Language Association) STYLE (Appendix 3C): Humanities

APA (American Psychological Association) STYLE (Appendix 3C): Social sciences

CM (*Chicago Manual*) STYLE: Various disciplines, generally in the humanities

CSE (Council of Science Editors) style: Many natural sciences

IEEE (Institute of Electrical and Electronics Engineers) style: Engineering and technology, computing

If you don't know which style to use, ask your instructor. Use only one documentation style in each piece of writing.

Determine the required documentation style at the start so that you keep a list of the exact details you need to document your sources. You need to document all primary sources and secondary sources. If you're doing primary research, your instructor may ask you to submit notes or results from observations, questionnaires, surveys, or interviews.

2E What is a research log?

A **research log**—a diary of your research process—can be useful for keeping yourself organized and on track. With long projects it's easy to waste time retracing what you've done and figuring out where you're headed next. Research logs can also show instructors and others how carefully you've worked. Here's how to set one up:

- Create a "Research Log" file or folder on your computer or notebook.
- Record each step in your search for information. Enter the date, your search strategies, the gist of the information you discovered, the documentation details of exactly where you found it, and exactly where you have filed your detailed notes, if any, on the source.
- Decide on the next step you should take with your research.
- Realize when you're ready to move away from gathering material to organizing it or writing about it.
- Keep notes on your thoughts and insights as you move through the research, organizing, and writing processes.

Although much of what you write in your research log will never find its way into your paper, it will greatly increase your efficiency. Figure 2.2 shows a page from Andrei Gurov's research log for his paper in Appendix 3C.

2F What is a working bibliography?

A WORKING BIBLIOGRAPHY is a preliminary list of the sources you gather in your research. It contains information about each source and where your readers can find it. As a rough estimate, your working bibliography needs to be about twice as long as the list of sources you end up using. Following is a list of basic elements to include (for more detailed information about documenting specific types of sources, see Appendix 3C–4).

Begin your working bibliography as soon as you start identifying sources. If your search turns up only a very few sources, you may want to change your topic.

Figure 2.2 A selection from the research log of Andrei Gurov, who wrote the paper in Apppendix 3C.

November 17: Finished reading Brown's book, <u>The Déjà Vu Experience</u>. Great source. I wonder if he's published anything more recently. Will meet with reference librarian this afternoon to identify sources.

November 18: Followed librarian's suggestion and searched the PsycINFO database for more recent articles. Found a chapter by Brown in a 2010 book that looks promising.

Elements of a Citation to Record

Books	Periodical Articles	Online Sources
Author(s)	Author(s)	Author(s) (if available)
Title of book	Title of article; digital object identifier (doi), if any	Title of document
Publisher and place of publication	Name of periodical, volume number, issue number	Name of website or database; editor or sponsor of site
Year of publication	Date of issue	Date of electronic publication
Call number	Page numbers of article	Electronic address (URL)
Print or Web version?	Print or Web version?	Date you accessed the source

Figure 2.3   Bibliographic entry in MLA format.

Brown, Alan S. and Elizabeth J. Marsh. "Digging into Déjà Vu:
   Recent Research on Possible Mechanisms." The Psychology of
   Learning and Motivation: Advances in Research and Theory.
   Ed. Brian H. Ross. Burlington: Academic P, 2010, 33–62. Web.
   20 Nov. 2014.

If it reveals a vast number, you'll want to narrow your topic or choose a different one. Expect to add and drop sources throughout the research process.

You can record your working bibliography on note cards or on a computer. On the one hand, note cards are easy to sift through and rearrange. At the end of your writing process, you can easily alphabetize them to prepare your final bibliography. Write only one source on each card (see Figure 2.3).

On the other hand, putting your working bibliography on a computer saves having to type your list of sources later. If you do this, clearly separate one entry from another alphabetically, by author, or by subtopics.

Whichever method you use, when you come across a potential source, immediately record the information exactly as you need it to fulfill the requirements of the *documentation style* your assignment requires. Spending a few extra moments at this stage can save you hours of work and frustration retracing your steps later on.

2G   Can social networking software help me create or organize bibliographies?

Several software programs allow you to store bibliographic information about your sources and then access this information to organize it in many ways. For example, a program like NoodleBib or RefWorks lets you type in information (author, title, publisher, and so on) about each source you find. Then, with a click of a button, you can generate an MLA-style Works Cited page, an APA-style

References page, or a bibliography in many other formats. You can export the bibliography into the paper you're writing, without having to retype. Of course, you're still responsible for the accuracy of any bibliography you generate with this software.

These programs also allow you to import citations directly from many databases, which means you never have to type them. Because you store your source information online, you can access it from any computer. Check to see if your library gives you access to bibliographic software.

Other online tools can help you collect, store, access, and organize materials you find on the Web. For example, Diigo <http://www.diigo.com> allows you to store URLs or even copies of webpages so you always have access to them from any device that connects to the Internet. You can tag each entry by adding descriptive words so that you can search for particular topics later. You can also highlight or add notes. You can share your bibliographies with others, which can be helpful for group projects.

There's one disadvantage, however. Because this software makes it so easy to gather materials, it can be tempting to merely record information and avoid analysis. Analysis is vital to making sources your own.

2H   What is an annotated bibliography?

View
the Model
Document

An ANNOTATED BIBLIOGRAPHY includes not only documentation information about your sources but also a commentary. Instructors sometimes require annotated bibliographies as a step in research projects, or they sometimes assign them as separate projects in their own right.

Most annotations contain.

1. The thesis or a one-sentence summary
2. The main points or arguments in support of the thesis
3. The kinds of evidence used in the source (For example, does the source report facts or results from formal studies? Are these primary or secondary? Does the source contain stories? Interviews?)

Figure 2.4 shows part of an annotated bibliography using MLA-style documentation.

2I   How do I take content notes?

Watch
the Video

When you write **content notes**, you record information from your sources.

- For content notes on index cards, put a heading (title and author) on each card that gives a precise link to one of your bibliography items.
- For content notes on your computer, keep careful track of what ideas came from each source. One strategy is to open a new file for each source. Later, after you determine what topics are important for your paper, open a new file and type a heading for each topic. Copy and paste notes from all your sources under the headings they best fit.
- For all content notes, always include the page numbers from which you're taking notes. If an electronic source has no page numbers, use chapter, section, or paragraph numbers, if any.

Figure 2.4   Section from an annotated bibliography in MLA style.

Brown, Alan S., and Elizabeth J. Marsh. "Digging into Déjà Vu: Recent

Research on Possible Mechanisms." *The Psychology of Learning*

and Motivation: Advances in Research and Theory. Ed. Brian

H. Ross. Burlington: Academic P, 2010, 33-62. Web. 20 Nov. 2014.

This chapter summarizes laboratory research that tried

to explain déjà vu. The authors discuss three theories.

"Split perception" refers to people seeing part of a scene

before seeing the whole. "Implicit memory" refers to people

having had a previous experience that, however, is stored in

their memories imprecisely, so they remember only the

sensation and not the scene. "Gestalt familiarity" refers to

having experienced something very familiar to the present

setting.

Carey, Benedict. "Déjà Vu: If It All Seems Familiar, There May Be

a Reason." *New York Times* 14 Sept. 2004: F1+. *LexisNexis*.

Web. 11 Nov. 2014.

Scientific research shows that déjà vu is a common and real

phenomenon, even if its causes are unclear. Perhaps the best

explanation is that people have had a similar previous

experience that they have since forgotten.

- For every note, do one of three things: (1) copy the exact words from a source, enclosing them in quotation marks; (2) write a paraphrase; or (3) write a summary. Keep track of the kind of note you're taking to avoid plagiarism. You might use the code Q for quotation, P for paraphrase, and S for summary.

- As you take notes, separately record your own reactions and ideas. Use critical thinking skills. For example, what are the strengths and weaknesses of the source? What are its implications? Also include a note about what might be useful from the source. Does it provide an example? An idea? A fact? Take care to differentiate your ideas from those in your sources. You might write your own thoughts in a different colour ink (note card) or font (computer); you might use a computer's "Comment" feature.

Figure 2.5 shows one of Andrei Gurov's note cards for his research paper in 26B.

2J   How do I plan a research project?

If you feel overwhelmed by the prospect of research writing, you're not alone. Dividing your project into steps makes the process less intimidating, and target deadlines along the way keep you on track. Quick Box 2.3 suggests how to plan a research project. (The numbers in parentheses tell you where to find more information in this book.)

Figure 2.5 Handwritten content note card in MLA style.

Brown, Alan S. "The Déjà Vu Illusion." *Current Directions in*
     Psychological Science 13.6 (2004): 256–59. Print.

Summary: Recent advances in neurology and the study of cognitive illusions
reveal that two seemingly separate perceptual events are indeed one.

Comment: This is the part that grabs my attention. How could this be?

Quick Box 2.3

Sample schedule for a research project

Assignment received _____

    Assignment due date _____

	FINISH BY (DATE)
PLANNING	
1. Start my research log (2E).	_____
2. Choose a topic suitable for research (1B).	_____
3. Draft my research question (1C).	_____
4. Understand my writing situation and type of research paper (2D and 2D).	_____
5. Determine what documentation style I need to use (2D).	_____
RESEARCHING	
6. Plan my search strategy, but modify as necessary (2A).	_____
7. Decide the kinds of research I need to do:	
a. Conduct field research (2C)? If yes, schedule tasks.	_____
b. Find published sources?	_____
8. Locate and evaluate sources (3, 4).	_____
9. Compile a working bibliography (2F) and/or annotated bibliography (2H).	_____
10. Take content notes from sources I find useful (2I).	_____
WRITING	
11. Draft my thesis statement (2G).	_____
12. Review content notes and determine relations between sources (5).	_____
13. Create an outline, as required or useful (2H).	_____
14. Draft my paper (3B).	_____
15. Use correct in-text citations.	_____
16. Compile my final bibliography (Works Cited for MLA; References for APA) or any other documentation style required.	_____
17. Revise my paper (6E).	_____
18. Edit and proofread my paper for content, plagiarism, in-text citations, bibliography, and format (6E, 6F).	

Quick Points   You will learn to

➤ Identify the different types of published sources (see 3A).
➤ Locate sources using libraries, databases, and online tools (see 3B–3J).

3A   What kinds of published sources are there?

Published sources refer to books, articles, documents, and other writings that appear online or in print. Because most academic research writing relies on published sources—material for you to read—we've written this chapter to explain how to find them. The sheer number and types of published sources today can be confusing. However, you can clarify your research by asking two questions: Is the source scholarly or popular? Quick Box 3.1 helps you decide. Is the source edited or unedited? Quick Box 3.2 explains the differences.

Popular sources can be high quality, especially if they're edited and from serious publishers or periodicals (such as *the Globe and Mail* or *the Literary Review of Canada*). Unedited sources can be useful too, but because no editor has selected or reviewed them, you should judge them carefully before you use them. Section 4 explains how to evaluate all your sources.

Quick Box 3.1

Scholarly sources versus popular sources

Scholarly Sources	**Popular Sources**
Examples: Journal articles; books published by university presses; professional organization websites	**Examples:** Newspapers and magazines; general websites and blogs
Audience: Scholars, experts, researchers, students	**Audience:** General readers; people who may be interested but don't necessarily have specific knowledge or expertise
Purpose: To provide cutting-edge ideas and information supported by research	**Purpose:** To entertain; to translate expert information for general readers; to persuade
Authors: Researchers; professors; content experts; professionals	**Authors:** Journalists or freelance writers; hobbyists or enthusiasts; people from all walks of life
Characteristics: Citations and bibliographies show sources of ideas; sources explain research methods and limitations of conclusions	**Characteristics:** Rarely include citations or bibliographies; might refer to people or sources in the body of the work
Where published: Appear in scholarly books and periodicals or on sites maintained by professional organizations	**Where published:** Appear in popular books and periodicals; blogs; personal or informal sites
How you find them: Mainly through DATABASES	**How you find them:** Sometimes through databases; often through SEARCH ENGINES

Quick Box 3.2

Edited versus unedited sources

Edited	Unedited
Examples: Periodicals; books from a publisher; organizational or professional websites	**Examples:** Personal blogs and websites; online comments or discussion postings; self-published books
Selection: An editor or other professional has evaluated and chosen the work to publish	**Selection:** The individual publishes his or her work (for example, in a blog)
Accuracy/Quality: Reviewed by an editor or expert readers	**Accuracy/Quality:** Not reviewed by others before publication
Publisher: A periodical or book publisher, or a professional organization	**Publisher:** The author him- or herself (as in blogs or discussion posts) or perhaps a special-interest group
How you find them: Mainly through databases or catalogues	**How you find them:** Mainly through search engines; unedited works almost never appear in databases

3B   How can libraries help me?

Watch the Video

In an age when the Web contains billions of pages of information, it might seem almost prehistoric to talk about libraries. After all, the library is where generations of students have traditionally gone to find books and PERIODICALS organized by CATALOGUES, INDEXES, and DATABASES, but today so much is now available online. Still, many sources, especially scholarly ones, are available only through the library. Notice that we've said "through" the library, not necessarily "in" it. That's because many library sources and services are available through the Internet to students or registered users.

Storing books in a physical building is only one of a library's functions. Just as importantly, librarians and scholars systematically gather and organize sources so that you can find the best ones efficiently and reliably. You can access and search electronic catalogues, indexes, and databases from computers in the library itself or, in many cases, by connecting to the library via the Internet. If you have remote access, you'll probably need to log in with an ID and password.

Still, the building itself continues to be a vital place for all research. One key advantage of going to the library is your chance to consult with librarians face-to-face. Never hesitate to ask how to proceed or where to find a resource. Quick Box 3.3 lists ten useful questions librarians are used to answering.

3C   What are search engines and databases?

Search engines and databases are two related, but different, ways to find published sources.

■ Search engines

Watch the Video

Search engines are programs designed to hunt the Web for sources on specific topics by using KEYWORDS (see 3D) or subject directories (see 3E). Once you use a BROWSER (a program like Internet Explorer, Firefox, or Safari) to get on the

Quick Box 3.3

Top ten questions to ask a librarian

1. Do I need to log in to use the library's computer system? If so, how?
2. Can I access the library's computer system from home or off campus?
3. How do I search the library's catalogue?
4. Can I look for books directly on the shelves, or do I need to request them from a central place? How do I check out materials?
5. How do I use an electronic version of a library book?
6. What databases would you recommend if I'm looking for scholarly sources on topic X?
7. What might be the best keywords or search strategy to use when I'm searching databases for sources on topic X?
8. How can I best keep track of sources I find? Can I e-mail them to myself? Print a list of citations?
9. How can I get copies of articles or other sources I need?
10. If our library doesn't own a source I need, is there a way for me to access or order a copy?

Web, you can use a search engine like Google <http://www.google.ca> or Yahoo! <http://ca.yahoo.com>. Of course, if you know a specific Web address—called a **URL,** for Universal (or Uniform) Resource Locator—you can type it directly into a search box. Quick Box 3.4 offers tips for using search engines.

Anyone can put anything on the Web. This makes the Web a rich source of information, but it also makes finding what you need difficult, and it opens the possibility of encountering inaccurate or biased materials. Searching the Web will produce hits: links to specific sites or materials. However, many articles and documents, especially those published in scholarly journals or some edited periodicals, can't be found on the Web through search engines. To find them, you need to use databases.

▧ Databases

Watch
the Video

databases are collections of sources that experts or librarians have gathered. You find databases mostly in libraries or through library websites, and you search them mainly by using keywords. We explain how in section 3D. Sources that you identify through databases are usually more reliable and appropriate than sources you find by simply browsing the Web. Therefore, we recommend that you search a database as part of any college or university research project.

Quick Box 3.4

Tips on using Web search engines

■ Use keyword combinations or boolean expressions if you need to narrow your search (see Quick Box 3.5).

■ Try using more than one search engine because different search engines will provide different results for the same search.

■ To be able to return to a good source easily, go to the toolbar at the top of the screen, click on "Bookmark," and then click on "Add." Or use social networking software (see 2G) to gather your sources.

■ Use the "History" function in your search engine to revisit sites you've been to before.

■ Be prepared to find sources in various formats. Most common are webpages in html (Hypertext Markup Language) format. However, you may also encounter Word or Excel documents, PowerPoint slides, or PDF (portable document format) files.

❗ Alert: Google Scholar is a site within Google that does pretty much what it announces: It lists scholarly sources, including books and articles, that are on the Web. It functions somewhat like a database. ⬤

Most academic libraries subscribe to one or more database services, such as EBSCO, ProQuest, and FirstSearch. Your library's website will show the resources it has available. Because the school pays for these services, you don't have to, but you'll need an ID or password to use them. Commonly, your student number serves as your ID, but check with a librarian.

GENERAL DATABASES include sources from a broad range of periodicals and books, both popular and scholarly. General databases are suitable for academic research projects. However, take care to focus on scholarly sources and well-regarded popular publications. Large libraries have many general databases. A common one is *Academic Search Premier*.

SPECIALIZED DATABASES focus on specific subject areas or disciplines. They list books and articles published by and for expert readers. Some examples include *Art Abstracts, MLA International Bibliography, PsycINFO,* and *Business Abstracts*. Many specialized databases include the abstract, or summary, that is printed at the beginning of each scholarly article.

Each source in a DATABASE contains bibliographic information, including a title, author, date of publication, and publisher (in the case of books or reports) or periodical (in the case of articles). The entry might also provide a summary or list of contents.

3D   How do I use search engines and databases?

Watch the Video

keywords (also called *descriptors or identifiers*) are your pathways to finding sources in databases, catalogues, and websites. Keywords are the main words in a source's title or words that an author or editor has identified as most important to its topic and content. Figure 3.1 shows three screens from a keyword search of *PsycINFO* on *déjà vu*. While working on the research paper that appears in section 26B the student consulted this database.

You can search the Web with a single keyword, but usually that generates far too many or far too few hits. Combinations of keywords using BOOLEAN EXPRESSIONS or ADVANCED SEARCHES can solve both problems.

■ Using Boolean expressions

Using BOOLEAN EXPRESSIONS means that you search a database or search engine by typing keyword combinations that narrow and refine your search. To combine keywords, use the words *AND, OR,* and *NOT* (or symbols that represent those words). Quick Box 3.5 explains how.

■ Using advanced searches

Advanced searches (sometimes called *guided searches*) allow you to search by entering information in an online form. A typical search involves selecting a range of dates of publication (for example, after 2010 or between 1990 and 1995) and specifying only a certain language (such as English) or a certain format (such as books). Figure 3.3 shows an example of a search for sources that have *déjà vu* in their titles and use *false memory* as another keyword but are not about *crime*.

Figure 6.1   Keyword search of déjà vu in a database.

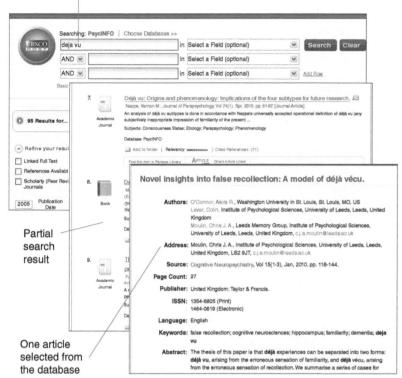

Keyword Search

Partial
search
result

One article
selected from
the database

Quick Box 3.5

Boolean expressions for refining keyword searches

AND or the + ("plus") symbol: Narrows the focus of your search because both keywords must be found. If you research the topic of the APA paper in 29B (how women characters are depicted in video games), the expression video games AND women AND characters works. Many search engines and databases don't require the word AND between terms. Figure 3.2 illustrates the results.

NOT or the − ("minus") symbol: Narrows a search by excluding texts containing the specified word or phrase. If you want to eliminate women playing games from your search, type video games AND women AND characters NOT players.

OR: Expands a search's boundaries by including more than one keyword. If you want to expand your search to include sources about women characters who are either heroes or villains in games, try the expression video games AND women AND characters AND heroes OR villains.

Quotation marks (" "): Direct the search to match your exact word order. For example, a search for "role playing games" will find sources that contain the exact phrase "role playing games." If, for example, you search for James Joyce without using quotation marks, search engines will return all pages containing the words James and Joyce anywhere in the document; however, a search using "James Joyce" brings you closer to finding websites about the Irish writer.

Figure 3.2 A Venn diagram showing overlaps among video games, women, and characters.

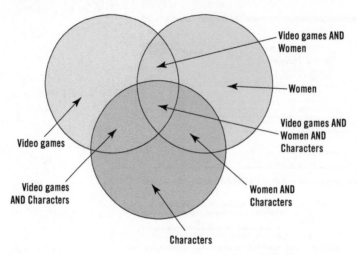

Figure 3.3 Advanced keyword search.

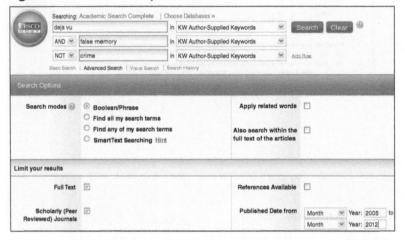

3E How do I use subject directories?

Subject directories provide an alternative to keyword searches. These directories are lists of topics (education, computing, entertainment, and so on) or resources and services (shopping, travel, and so on), with links to sources on those topics and resources. Many search engines, and some library catalogues or databases, have one or more subject directories. In addition, there are independent subject directories. Some examples are

Educator's Reference Desk <http://www.eduref.org>

Librarians' Index to the Internet <http://lii.org>

Library of Congress <http://www.loc.gov>

Refdesk.com <http://www.refdesk.com>

UBC Library Research Guides <http://guides.library.ubc.ca>

University of Toronto Libraries Portal <http://discover.library.utoronto.ca/resources-research>

Clicking on a general category in a subject directory will take you to lists of increasingly specific categories. Eventually, you'll get a list of webpages on the most specific subtopic you select. These search engines also allow you to click on a category and enter keywords.

3F   How do I find books?

A library's CATALOGUE, which lists its holdings (its entire collection), exists as a computer database in almost every modern library. To find a book, you can search by author, by title, by subject, or by keyword. Some catalogues let you search by CALL NUMBER, search particular indexes, or search using Boolean expressions.

Suppose you want to find a book by Naomi Klein, but you don't know its title. You can search the online catalogue for books by this author. In the space for "author" on the computer screen, you type in "klein, naomi." (Usually you enter the last name first, but check to see how your library's system works.) If your library owns any books by Naomi Klein, the catalogue will show you their titles and other information, such as the call number. Among the books you might find is No Logo: Taking Aim at the Brand Bullies (Toronto: Knopf Canada, 2000). Or suppose you know this title and want to see if your library owns the book. In the space for "title," you type in "no logo." (Usually you do not need to include the full title or words like the or a.)

Suppose, however, you don't know an author's name or a book title. You have only a research topic. In this case, you need to search by subject, using the terms listed in the *Library of Congress Subject Headings (LCSH)*. The *LCSH* is a multivolume catalogue available, primarily in book form, in the reference section of every library. An abridged version of the information in the *LCSH* is online at <http://authorities.loc.gov>. If you are researching a Canadian topic, consult Library and Archives Canada's Canadian Subject Headings (CSH) at <http://www.collectionscanada.ca/csh/index-e.html>. Suppose you are researching the topic "brand name products—public opinion." If you enter that term in the space for subject searches, No Logo: Taking Aim at the Brand Bullies by Naomi Klein will be listed—if your library owns that book.

Finally, you may wish to search by keyword in your library's holdings. You could find Klein's book using the keywords logo, brand, advertising, and so on. A sample book catalogue keyword search is shown in Figure 3.4.

Scan the results to identify promising sources. When you select a record (usually by clicking on it or a box next to it), you encounter detailed information about the source, often including a table of contents, a brief summary of the contents, and information on the book's location in the library system and availability.

Some libraries allow you to print out this information, send it to your e-mail account or a social networking site, or download it (see 2G). Whether you choose one of these options or copy the information directly into your WORKING BIBLIOGRAPHY, it's crucial to record the CALL NUMBER exactly as it appears, with all numbers, letters, and decimal points. The call number tells where the book is located in the library's stacks (storage shelves). If you're researching in a library with open stacks (shelves that are accessible without special permission), the call number leads you to the area in the library where all books on the same subject can be found.

A call number is especially crucial in a library or special collection with closed stacks, which is a library where you hand in a slip at the call desk (or submit a

Figure 3.4   A book catalogue search using keywords.

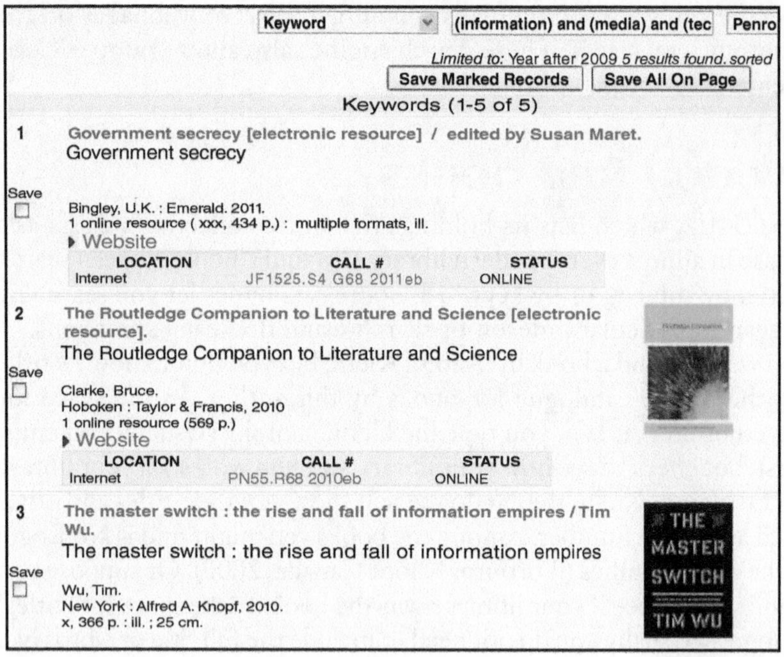

request online) and wait for the book to arrive. Such libraries don't permit you to browse the stacks, so you have to rely entirely on the book catalogue.

■ Electronic books

You're probably familiar with electronic books and readers like the Kindle, Nook, and iPad. Many books have electronic versions that you can access—and without paying, if you go through a library.

Google has scanned many books and put them on the Web. You can find them by searching Google Books. Even if you find a book you want online, only a portion of it will probably be available. If you're lucky, it will be the part you want; otherwise, you'll need to find the book through other means such as Interlibrary Loan.

3G   How do I find periodicals?

PERIODICALS are edited magazines, journals, and newspapers published periodically, that is, at set intervals. Many of them have websites or publish electronic versions. An increasing number of periodicals appear only online. You find periodicals by searching databases. Quick Box 3.6 describes several types of periodicals.

■ Locating articles themselves

Databases help you find information about sources, but how do you get your hands on the source itself? Often you can find an online full-text version of the article to read, download, or print. A full-text version may be either in HTML format or PDF; the listing will tell you which one. If you have a choice, we recommend using the PDF version, which is easier to cite because it has the layout of a print article. However, if you want to copy a section and paste it in your notes, only HTML allows this (but be careful to avoid plagiarism).

Quick Box 3.6

Types of periodicals

Type	Characteristics	Useful for
Journal	Scholarly articles written by experts for other experts; usually focus on one academic discipline; published relatively infrequently; examples are *Canadian Journal of Public Health* and *The Canadian Journal of Sociology*	The most reliable expert research on a particular subject; detailed articles and extensive bibliographies that can point to other sources or experts; may also have book reviews
News magazines	Short to mid-length articles on current events or topics of interest to a broad readership; lots of photos and graphics; may have opinions or editorials, as well as reviews; generally are published weekly; examples are *Time* and *Maclean's*	Easily understandable and timely introductions to current topics; often can point to more expert sources, topics, and keywords
Special-interest or "lifestyle" magazines	Written for audiences (including fans and hobbyists) interested in a particular topic; include news and features on that topic; generally published monthly, with entertainment as an important goal; examples include *Zoomer and Wired*	Providing "how-to" information on their topics of focus, as well as technical information or in-depth profiles of individuals, products, or events; many include reviews; the more serious examples are well written and reliable
"Intellectual" or literary magazines	Publish relatively longer articles that provide in-depth analysis of issues, events, or people; may include creative work as well as nonfiction; aimed at a general, well-educated audience; usually published monthly; examples include *The Walrus and Literary Review of Canada*	Learning about a topic in depth but in a way that's more accessible than scholarly journals; becoming aware of major controversies and positions; learning who experts are and what books or other sources have been published; reading arguments on topics
Trade magazines	Focus on particular businesses, industries, and trade groups; discuss new products, legislation, or events that will influence individuals or businesses in that area; examples include *Canadian Poultry and Broadcaster*	Specialized information focusing on applying information or research in particular settings; seeing how specific audiences or interest groups may respond to a particular position
Newspapers	Publish articles about current news, sports, and cultural events; contain several sections, including opinions and editorials, lifestyle, sports; most appear daily	Very current information; national newspapers cover world events and frequently have analysis and commentary; local newspapers cover small happenings you likely won't find elsewhere; opinion sections and reviews are sources of ideas and positions

Sometimes, however, you need to find a print copy of the periodical. Often the listing in the database will say whether your library owns a copy and what its call number is. Otherwise, you'll need to check if the periodical is listed in the library's CATALOGUE.

In either case, search for the periodical by name, not the article's author or title. Then use its call number to find it in the library. To find the specific article you want, look for the issue in which the article you need appears. For advice on locating sources that your library doesn't own, see the alert that ends this chapter.

3H How do I use reference works?

Reference works include encyclopedias, almanacs, yearbooks, fact books, atlases, dictionaries, biographical reference works, and bibliographies. *General* reference works provide information on a vast number of subjects, but without much depth. *Specialized* reference works provide information on selected topics, often for more expert or professional audiences.

■ General reference works

GENERAL REFERENCE WORKS are the starting point for many researchers—but they're no more than a starting point. They help researchers identify useful keywords to use to search for subject headings and online catalogues. They're also good for finding examples and verifying facts.

Most widely used general reference works are available online. Check your library's website to see what it has subscribed to. Be aware that often you have to pay a fee for works you don't access through a library.

General Encyclopedias

Articles in multivolume general encyclopedias, such as the *Encyclopaedia Britannica*, can give you helpful background information, the names of major experts in the field, and, often, a brief BIBLIOGRAPHY on a variety of subjects.

❶ **Alert:** A Note on *Wikipedia*. *Wikipedia* is an unedited source that almost anyone can modify. Obviously, then, the accuracy and quality of information it contains isn't always reliable. There's always the possibility that a *Wikipedia* source is flawed. Still, *Wikipedia* can be a useful starting place for some quick information on a topic. When students use *Wikipedia* extensively, however, readers realize they haven't taken the time or responsibility to do thorough research on their topic. ●

Almanacs, Yearbooks, and Fact Books

Often available both in print and online, almanacs, yearbooks, and fact books are huge compilations of facts and figures. Examples include the *World Almanac*, *Facts on File*, The Canadian Global Almanac, Canada Year Book, and the *United Nations Statistical Yearbook*.

Atlases and Gazetteers

Atlases, such as the *Times Atlas of the World*, contain maps of our planet's continents, seas, and skies. Gazetteers, such as the *Columbia Gazetteer of the World* and the Canadian Atlas Online gazetteer, provide comprehensive geographical information on topography, climates, populations, migrations, natural resources, and so on.

Dictionaries

Dictionaries define words and terms. The Canadian Oxford Dictionary is in wide use here. In addition to general dictionaries, specialized dictionaries focus exclusively on many academic disciplines.

Biographical Reference Works

Biographical reference books, such as the *Who's Who* series and the *Dictionary of Canadian Biography*, give brief factual information about famous people—their accomplishments along with pertinent events and dates in their lives.

Bibliographies

BIBLIOGRAPHIES are guides to sources on particular topics. They list books, articles, documents, films, and other resources along with publication information so that you can find them. Annotated or critical bibliographies describe and evaluate the works that they list.

■ Specialized reference works

SPECIALIZED REFERENCE WORKS provide authoritative, specific information on selected topics, often for more expert researchers. These works are usually appropriate for university- and college-level research. Examples include the Encyclopedia of Banking and Finance, Encyclopedia of Chemistry, Encyclopedia of Religion, Encyclopedia of the Biological Sciences, Canadian Annual Review of Politics and Public Affairs, International Encyclopedia of Film, New Grove Dictionary of Music and Musicians, and Oxford Companion to Canadian Literature.

3I   How can I find images?

If you need or want to include images in a research paper, you have three options. A keyword search through the "Images" menu on Google or Yahoo! will generate links to images as they appear in sites and documents across the Internet. However, there are ethical and, sometimes, even legal concerns in using what you find this way. Although Canadian copyright law generally lets students use sources once for a classroom project, you are behaving ethically if you get written permission from the photographer or site where you found the image. Always be sure to cite the source properly.

A good alternative is to use a "stock photo" website. These are services like iStockphoto and Getty Images that have gathered thousands, even millions, of photographs, which you can browse by category or keyword. For a small fee you can purchase the one-time use of an image from these sites. (There are a few "free" sites, too.)

Finally, your library may provide access to image archives or databases. Ask a librarian. Once again, always cite images properly.

3J   How do I find government documents?

Canadian government publications are available in astounding variety. You can find information on laws, regulations, populations, weather patterns, agriculture, parks, education, health, and many other topics.

A federal government website known as the Canada Site, <http://www.canada.gc.ca>, is an excellent starting point for online research into current Canadian government publications. It provides direct access to federal departments, boards, and agencies and their publications; to public records, including parliamentary debates and hearings; and to databases. You can also follow its links to provincial and territorial government websites. Statistics Canada <http://www.statcan.gc.ca> collects and analyzes a wide range of data.

🛈 **Alert:** Almost no library will contain every source that you need. However, many libraries are connected electronically to other libraries' book catalogues, giving you access to additional holdings. The Canadian Library Gateway, a project of Library and Archives Canada <http://www.collectionscanada.gc.ca/index-e.html>, coordinates an interlibrary loan system linking the catalogues of university and other large libraries throughout the country. Often you or a librarian can request materials from other libraries through interlibrary loan (generally free of charge).●

4 EVALUATING SOURCES

Quick Points You will learn to

➤ Identify reliable sources.

Watch
the Video

Not all sources are created equal. Sources differ in quality. Some present information that has been carefully gathered and checked. Others report information, even rumour, that is second- or thirdhand or, worse, perhaps not even based in fact.

Some sources make claims that are accompanied by strong evidence and reasoning. Others make claims based only on opinion, or they use information illogically. Some are written by experts wanting to advance knowledge. Others are produced by people wanting to promote special interests however they can, even if it means ignoring data, oversimplifying issues, or overpromising results. Some sources have been reviewed by experts and published only after passing standards. Others appear without anyone judging their quality.

As an academic writer, you don't want to use weak sources that hurt your ETHOS and ruin your paper. Therefore, evaluate each source you find by asking the questions in Quick Box 4.1.

4A How did you find the source?

Sources that you find through DATABASES, especially databases you access through a library website (see Section 3), are more likely to be useful than sources found through a general Google or Yahoo! search. A source in a database has been edited and checked for quality. The more scholarly a database is, the more confident you can be that its sources are reliable.

For example, suppose you want to research the safety of vaccines. A Google search produces thousands of sources. Some of them are reliable; many are not. If you search a library database like Academic Search Premier, you'll find hundreds of sources, mainly of higher quality. Still, the most authoritative sources come from an academic library's CATALOGUE or a scholarly database like Medline, which is created for physicians, researchers, and other medical professionals.

4B Is the publisher authoritative?

The publisher is the company or group ultimately responsible for a book, periodical, or website.

Quick Box 4.1

Five questions for evaluating sources

1. How did you find the source? (See 4A.)
2. Is the publisher authoritative? (See 4B.)
3. Is the author qualified to write about the topic? (See 4C.)
4. Does the source have sufficient and credible evidence? (See 4D.)
5. Does the source pass other critical thinking tests? (See 4E.)

Is the Publisher Authoritative?

Reliable sources are . . .	Questionable sources are . . .
■ **From reputable publishers.** Generally, encyclopedias, textbooks, and academic journals, such as the Canadian Journal of Family Law, are authoritative. Books from university and other established presses are authoritative. Sources published in major newspapers and in general-readership magazines, and textbooks, such as those from Pearson, are reliable, too.	■ **From special-interest groups.** Some groups exist only to advance a narrow interest or political viewpoint. Examples would be a group existing only to stop all immigration. Special-interest groups might publish useful sources, but you want to check their facts and reasoning by asking "Why does the group exist?" Be sure to question its motives, especially if it asks you to take a specific action, such as donate money. See if materials published by the group are included in scholarly databases, and apply other tests listed in this chapter.
■ **Websites from educational, not-for-profit, or government organizations.** Websites from professional associations, such as the Canadian Medical Association, are reliable. If you don't recognize an organization, you need to investigate how long it has existed, whether it is not-for-profit, who its members and leaders are, and so on.	■ **Websites from commercial enterprises** may or may not provide evidence or list sources for claims they make. If they fail to do so, or if the evidence and sources seem weak, don't use them. Be sure the site is not one that encourages illegal activities.
■ **Direct online versions of authoritative print sources.** Many journals, newspapers, and book publishers release online versions of print publications. Online versions of authoritative publications are reliable.	■ **Secondhand excerpts, quotations, and references.** Materials that appear in a source that is not the official site of the publisher (such as a quotation taken from a magazine) may have been edited in a biased or inaccurate manner. Always check the original.

4C   Is the author qualified to write about the topic?

Anyone can express an opinion or argue for an action, but the only writers worth quoting or summarizing in your writing have knowledge and expertise about their topics. Often, their credentials appear in a note in an introduction, at the bottom of the first page, or at the end of an article. In a book, look for an "About the Author" statement, on a website a short biography or a "Contributors" note. Sometimes you might need to do some research to learn about the author.

Is the Author Qualified to Write About the Topic?

Reliable sources are . . .	Questionable sources are . . .
■ **From expert authors.** Experts have degrees or credentials in their field. Bio-graphical material in the source may list these credentials. If in doubt, look up the author in a biographical dictionary, search online for a list of publications or bio, or search a database. Check if the author's name appears in other reliable sources. Check whether there is contact informa-tion for questions or comments.	■ **From authors with dubious credentials.** A warning sign should flash when you can't identify who has produced a source. Discussion threads, anonymous blogs, and similar online post-ings are questionable when they don't give information about the writer's qualifications. Check to make sure that listed credentials fit the topic.

ESL Tip: The definition of "authority" can differ across cultures. In Canada, a source has authority only if it meets specific criteria. It must appear in a scholarly book or journal; its author must have a degree, title, or licence; or other authorities must seek his or her knowledge. A source is not reliable simply because the author or speaker is an influential or well-known member of the community or claims to have knowledge about a topic.

4D Does the source have sufficient and accurate evidence?

If an author expresses a point of view but offers little evidence to back up that position, reject the source. See Figure 4.1 for an example of how sources use evidence.

Figure 7.1 Source that cites evidence and source that does not.

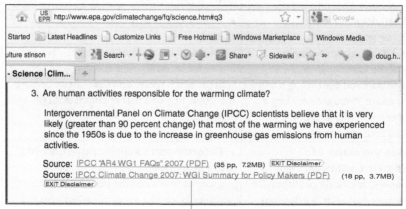

The US Environmental Protection Agency provides specific facts, and the source of those facts.

RedDawn [6/13/2012]
So it's been hot and the global warming clones are screaming again. Big deal. many scientists show that theres no proof we're making the world warmer, just google it if you want to know the truth. If the temperatures increasing, its because of natural causes not pollution, smoke, etc. Politicians wont give money to real scientists to prove it. Common sense, people!

This posting, from a blog, makes claims but provides no evidence, simply telling readers to "just google it."

The source has some proofreading errors, substitutes name-calling for reasoning, and has other logical fallacies.

Does the Source Have Sufficient and Accurate Evidence?

Reliable sources are . . .	Questionable sources are . . .
▪ **Well supported with evidence.** The source's writer provides clear and plentiful facts and reasons to support assertions.	▪ **Unsupported or biased.** They carry assertions that have little or no supporting evidence.
▪ **Factually accurate.** The sources for statistics, quotations, and other information are listed. You or anyone can look them up to check their accuracy.	▪ **Factually questionable.** They may include statistics or other information, but they fail to identify who generated it. You have no way to check facts.
▪ **Current.** Information is recent or, in the case of websites, regularly updated.	▪ **Outdated.** They may give 20-year-old medical advice or base political analyses on a website last updated in 2009.

4E   Does the source pass other critical thinking tests?

Use CRITICAL THINKING skills when you evaluate a source. Distinguish sources that show critical thinking through use of a balanced tone from sources that are biased in tone.

Does the Source Pass Other Critical Thinking Tests?

Reliable sources are . . .	Questionable sources are . . .
■ **Balanced in tone.** The source is respectful of others and creates a sense of fairness.	■ **Biased in tone.** Some warning signs of biased tone are name-calling, sarcasm, stereotyping, or absolute assertions about matters that are open to interpretation. For example, if a source declares, "Television programs are never worth watching" or that "women are always better than men at writing," you are encountering bias.
■ **Balanced in treatment.** The author advocates a credible position but also acknowledges different viewpoints. For example, the author summarizes contradictory evidence.	■ **One-sided.** The author omits any mention or fair summary of competing views or gives unreliable information.
■ **Logical.** The source draws fair conclusions from evidence. The reasoning is clear.	■ **Full of logical fallacies.**
■ **Well edited.** The source has been proofread and is free of grammatical errors.	■ **Marked by errors.** Beware of any source that has typos or sloppy errors.

5   SYNTHESIZING SOURCES IN RESEARCH PAPERSES

Quick Points   You will learn to

➤ Connect the different sources you use in your writing.
➤ Synthesize source material and integrate it into your writing.

5A   What is synthesizing sources in research papers?

When you SYNTHESIZE sources, you connect them to one another and to your own thinking. Often, you do this in an original paper. Your CRITICAL THINKING skills help you synthesize, as do QUOTING, SUMMARIZING, and PARAPHRASING (Appendix 3A). We also explained synthesizing in 3E. We've found that a useful question to help you synthesize multiple sources in a research paper is "How do the sources I've found relate to one another?" The rest of Section 5 explains how to define relationships between sources.

Watch
the Video

5B What are possible relationships between sources?

Knowing five relationships can help you go beyond simply listing or summarizing your sources, a practice that usually results in a weak paper. Those relationships are

- **Different Subtopic:** Sources are on the same broad subject but about different subtopics.
- **Agreement:** Two sources make the same basic point, though perhaps in different words.
- **Part Agreement:** Two sources mostly agree but differ a little bit.
- **Disagreement:** Two sources disagree.
- **General and Specific:** One source offers specific information that either supports or contradicts a more general point in another source.

We suggest that you begin by reading through your content notes and sorting them into groups by subtopic. Next, within each group, choose one pair of sources and ask which relationship in the list just given best describes them. Repeat this process with additional sources until you've identified the relationships between all of them.

5C What can I do when sources are about different subtopics?

You will likely find sources that present different subtopics of the same broad subject. For example, as you research career options, one source might discuss salaries, another might discuss workplace environments, and a third might discuss expectations for job openings. When one student was researching how the Internet has affected the way we get information, among the sources he found were these.

Source A	Source B
"While new technology eases connections between people, it also, paradoxically, facilitates a closeted view of the world, keeping us coiled tightly with those who share our ideas. In a world that lacks real gatekeepers and authority figures . . . conspiracy theories, myths, and outright lies may get the better of many of us." (3–4)	"CNN used to be a twenty-four-hour news outlet shown only on TV. The *New York Times* and the *Wall Street Journal* were simply newspapers. But on the Internet today, they are surprisingly similar. . . . Online, the lines between television and newspapers have blurred— and soon the same will be said about books, movies, TV shows, and more." (1)
Manjoo, Farhad. *True Enough: Learning to Live in a Post-Fact Society.* Hoboken, NJ: Wiley. 2008. Print.	Bilton, Nick. *I Live in the Future & Here's How It Works.* New York: Crown Business, 2010. Print.
Student's Content Note	Student's Content Note
Manjoo 3–4 although technology can connect us to others, it can also allow us to communicate only with people that agree with us; we might be susceptible to lies [paraphrase]	Bilton 14 TV network and newspaper sites have become similar on the Internet. Examples: CNN and *NY Times, WSJ* [summary]

Notice how in the student's content notes, he specified the kind of note he took in brackets (see 2I). Here is a possible sentence/paragraph guide for sources on different subtopics:

Sentence and Paragraph Guides

There are (one, two, or however many) important considerations for (aspects of, reasons for, etc.) _____ . One is _____ [from Source A] _____ . A second is _____ [from Source B] _____ .

Example

There are two important developments in the way we receive news online. One is that, even though it is easier to connect to information, we tend to seek people with whom we already agree (Manjoo 3–4). A second, as Nick Bilton notes, is that distinctions between types of news sources on the Internet are disappearing (14).

As you write your content notes, consider making each source a separate section, paragraph, or sentence of your paper, depending on how much information each source contains.

5D   What can I do when sources agree?

Sources agree when they present similar information or make the same point. If sources are truly repetitious, you might use only one. Sometimes, however, including multiple similar sources strengthens your point. Here is an example:

Source A	Source B
"Our study confirmed the well-known gender gap in gaming, verifying that this overall trend also occurs among college students. Seventy percent of male undergraduates had played a digital game the week of the survey, compared to only one quarter of the females. The majority of women fell in the category of non-gamers, those who had not played a game in over 6 months, or never." (Winn 10)	"Women proportionally were more likely than men to only play an hour or less per week. . . . Twenty-one percent of the women and 68% of the men played two or more hours per week." (Ogletree 539)
Winn, Jillian, and Carrie Heeter. "Gaming, Gender, and Time: Who Makes Time to Play?" *Sex Roles* 61 (2009): 1–13. Web. 9 May 2011.	Ogletree, Shirley Matile, and Ryan Drake. "College Students' Video Game Participation and Perceptions: Gender Differences and Implications." *Sex Roles* 56 (2007): 537–42. Web. 9 May 2011.
Student's Content Note	Student's Content Note
Winn 10 70% of male students played video games; 25% of female [summary]	Ogletree 539 68% of men and 21% of women played 2 or more hours per week [summary]

Here is a possible sentence/paragraph guide for synthesizing sources that agree:

Sentence and Paragraph Guides

A and B reach the same conclusion (provide similar information, argue the same point, reach the same conclusion, etc.) about _____. A explains that _____. B found that _____.

Example

Two studies show that men play video games more extensively than women. Winn and Heeter found that 70% of male students but only 25% of females regularly play games (10). In a study of how many hours per week students play, Ogletree learned that 68% of men and only 21% of women play two or more hours per week (539).

5E   What can I do when sources partly agree?

Often sources generally agree with each other but use different evidence or emphasize slightly different conclusions. Here is an example:

Source A	Source B
"[M]ore males reportedly developed leadership skills as a result of playing video games as opposed to females. More males also reported that playing video games helped them develop skills that will help them in the workplace, such as the ability to work as a team member, to collaborate with others and the ability to provide directions to others." (Thirunarayanan 324)	"The study of video games is a new and emerging field and much more research needs to be done. However, my preliminary findings suggest that it is our desire to interact with others that drives us to spend a lot of time online. Just as people desire to see friends and maintain those relationships, people desire to maintain their social bonds online." (Seaton 36)
Thirunarayanan, M. O., Manuel Vilchez, Liala Abreu, Cyntianna Ledesma, and Sandra Lopez. "A Survey of Video Game Players in a Public, Urban Research University." *Educational Media International* 47.4 (2009): 311–27. Web. 9 May 2011.	Seaton, J. X. "Understanding Online Social Bonding in Gaming Environments: Conclusions and Concerns." MA Thesis. Athabasca U, 2011. Web. 25 May 2014.
Student's Content Note	Student's Content Note
Thirunarayanan 324 more men said they learn leadership and team member skills than women said they did [summary]	Seaton 36 gamers want to build and maintain social bonds online [summary]

Here is a possible sentence or paragraph guide to use when sources partly agree:

Sentence and Paragraph Guides

Observers generally agree (conclude, share the opinion, or demonstrate, etc.) that _____. However, a difference between them is _____. A emphasizes (asserts, believes, etc.) _____. B, on the other hand, emphasizes _____.

Example

Observers generally agree that playing video games can have some positive social effects. However, they differ as to who benefits most. Seaton asserts that games build and maintain social connections, suggesting this is true for all players (36). Thirunarayanan et al., on the other hand, found that men believe they learn leadership and team member skills more than women say they do (324).

5F   What can I do when sources disagree?

Because people can disagree on everything from whether certain laws should be passed to whether certain movies are any good, it's no surprise that sources can disagree, too. Here is an example:

Source A	Source B
"Imagine that everything stays 99 percent the same, that people continue to consume 99 percent of the television they used to, but I percent of that time gets carved out for producing and sharing. The connected population still watches well over a trillion hours of TV a year; I percent of that is more than one hundred Wikipedias' worth of participation per year." (Shirky 23)	"With hundreds of thousands of visitors a day, Wikipedia has become the third most visited site for information and current events; a more trusted source for news than the CNN or BBC Web sites, even though Wikipedia has no reporters, no editorial staff, and no experience in news-gathering. It's the blind leading the blind—infinite monkeys providing infinite information for infinite readers, perpetuating the cycle of misinformation and ignorance." (Keen 4)
Shirky, Clay. *Cognitive Surplus, Creativity and Generosity in a Connected Age.* Toronto: Penguin, 2010. Print.	Keen, Andrew. *The Cult of the Amateur.* New York: Doubleday, 2007. Print.
Student's Content Note	Student's Content Note
Shirky 23 If people used even 1% of time they spend watching TV instead to produce content for the Web they'd create "one hundred Wikipedias' worth" each year [paraphrase and quotation]	Keen 4 Wikipedia used more for information and current events than CNN or the BBC no professionals writing for W. writers are "infinite monkeys" who create "misinformation and ignorance" [summary and quotation]

Here is a possible sentence/paragraph guide to use for sources that disagree:

Sentence and Paragraph Guides

There are two different perspectives (positions, interpretations, or opinions, etc.) about _____. A says _____. B, on the other hand, says _____.

However, your writing will be stronger if you go a step further and use critical thinking to understand the nature of the disagreement. For example:

- Writers might disagree because they use different facts or information (or no information at all!).

- Writers might disagree when they use the same information but interpret it differently.

- Writers might operate with different assumptions or perspectives.

Here is a stronger sentence/paragraph guide for sources that disagree:

Sentence and Paragraph Guides

There are two different perspectives (positions, interpretations, or opinions, etc.) about _____. A says _____. B, on the other hand, says _____. They disagree mainly because they cite different facts (interpret information differently, operate with different assumptions). A points to _____, while B _____. On this point, B's [or A's] perspective is more convincing because _____.

EXAMPLE

Some writers find Wikipedia a reason for celebration, while others declare it a cause for despair. Clay Shirky hopes people will divert just 1% of their TV watching time to writing for the Web, which could generate "one hundred Wikipedias' worth" of content each year (23). That possibility would trouble Andrew Keen, who characterizes those writers as "infinite monkeys" who only spread "misinformation and ignorance" (4). They assume quite different things about quality of knowledge on Wikipedia. Keen has little faith in the ability of crowd sourcing to filter and produce accurate information.

5G What can I do when sources aren't equally specific?

■ 1. When a specific source supports a more general idea in another source

Sometimes a source provides examples, illustrations, or evidence that support a more general point in another. Here is an example:

Source A	Source B
"Old media is facing extinction." (Keen 9)	"The Canadian newspaper industry is still facing circulation woes with nearly all of the Canadian daily newspapers that are members of Audit Bureau of Circulations (ABC) showing declines in ABC's latest top-line report. The report covers average daily circulation for Canadian newspapers for the six months ending Sept. 30, 2011. Its unaudited total paid circulation data shows that 5 of the 9 Canadian newspapers saw a decrease in circulation." (Androich)
Keen, Andrew. *The Cult of the Amateur.* New York: Doubleday, 2007. Print.	Androich, Alicia. "Canada's Newspaper Circulation Numbers Still Dropping." *Marketing.* Rogers Digital Media, 1 Nov. 2011. Web. 19 May 2014.
Student's Content Note	Student's Content Note
Keen 9 "Old media is facing extinction" [quotation]	Androich 19 of 23 Canadian newspapers surveyed lost circulation April through September 2011 [summary]

Here are useful sentence/paragraph guides when a specific source supports a general one:

Sentence and Paragraph Guides

A observes (claims, argues, concludes, etc.) that _.
B provides an example (a set of data, some information, etc.) to support this observation. B states that _____.

or

According to B, _____. This illustrates A's concept (point, claim, conclusion) that _____.

Example

According to Alicia Androich, 19 of 23 Canadian newspapers surveyed lost circulation from April through September 2011. Her figures illustrate Andrew Keen's observation that "Old media is facing extinction" (9).

■ 2. When a specific source contradicts a more general idea in another source

Sources can disagree with each other at the level of ideas or claims. Sometimes, however, the disagreement is more subtle. Specific information in one source can contradict a more general point made in another. This can happen when writers make a claim but offer no proof or when they offer partial or different evidence. Here's an example:

Student's Content Note	Student's Content Note
Gladwell 16 hockey in Canada is a "meritocracy," with the best minor league players being selected and promoted to higher levels [summary]	Ormsby playing minor hockey is a "luxury item" that is out of reach for some kids; one-third of Canadian parents say they haven't been able to afford to enrol their children in organized sports when they wanted [summary]

Here is a useful sentence/paragraph guide when specific information contradicts a general claim:

Sentence and Paragraph Guides

Evidence suggests (proves, demonstrates, etc.) that A's claim that _____ is wrong (incomplete, overstated, etc.). B shows that _____.

Example

Although Malcolm Gladwell demonstrates convincingly in his example how the best minor hockey players are selected and promoted, minor hockey does not appear to be a "meritocracy," as he calls it (16). Reporter Judith Ormsby has shown that minor hockey has actually become a "luxury item" that many kids can no longer afford, regardless of their talent level. She says that one-third of Canadian parents report that organized sports were too expensive to enrol their children in when they wanted to.

6   DRAFTING AND REVISING A RESEARCH PAPER

Quick Points   You will learn to

➤ Write and refine a research paper.

6A   How does the writing process apply to research papers?

DRAFTING and REVISING a research paper is like drafting and revising any piece of writing. Yet to write a research paper, you need extra time because you need to demonstrate that:

- You've followed the steps of the research process (see Appendix 3B).

- You've evaluated your SOURCES (see Appendix 3A).

- You haven't plagiarized (see Appendix 3A).

- You've correctly employed QUOTATIONS, PARAPHRASES, and SUMMARIES (see Appendix 3A).

- You've moved beyond summary to SYNTHESIS so that your sources are interwoven with each other and with your own thinking, not merely listed one by one (see Section 5).

- You've used DOCUMENTATION accurately. (For MLA STYLE, see Appendix 3C; for APA STYLE, see Appendix 4; for other documentation styles.)

6B   How do I draft a research paper?

Expect to write several drafts of your research paper. The first draft is a chance to discover new insights and fresh connections. Here are some ways to write your first draft.

Watch the Video

- **Some researchers work from a source map or cluster diagram.** They organize their notes into topics and determine the relationship between sources. They use frames and sentence and paragraph guides to generate a first draft.

- **Some research writers work with their notes at hand.** They organize the notes into broad categories so that each category becomes a section of the first draft. This method can reveal any gaps in information that call for additional research. It can also show that some of your research doesn't fit into your paper. However, don't throw it out because it might be useful in a later draft.

- **Some research writers generate a list of questions that their paper needs to address.** Then they answer each question, one at a time, looking for the content notes that will help them. For example, on the topic of déjà vu, some possible questions might be, "What is déjà vu? What are possible explanations for it? Does everyone experience it the same way or with the same frequency?" Generating and answering questions can turn a mass of information into manageable groupings.

- **Some research writers stop at various points and use** FREEWRITING **to get their ideas into words.** They say that it helps them to recognize when they need to adjust their research question or adjust their search. After a number of rounds of researching and freewriting, they find that they can write their complete first draft relatively easily.

- **Some research writers review their sources and create an** OUTLINE **before drafting.** Some find a FORMAL OUTLINE helpful, whereas others use a less formal approach.

6C   What are frames for research papers?

Although all research papers seek to answer a question, some are mainly informative, others are mainly persuasive, and still others are a mix. We offer here two possible frames to adapt to the specifics of your assignment. The first frame is for an informative research paper; the second for an argumentative research paper.

Frame for an Informative Research Paper

Introductory paragraph(s)

- Establish why your topic is important or interesting. Consider, "Why does this matter? To whom does this matter? What might happen if we resolve this issue one way versus another?"
- Your THESIS STATEMENT needs to make clear how you will answer your research question.

Body paragraph(s): Background information

- Provide the history or background of your topic. Why is it a problem or concern at this time?

Body paragraphs: Explanations of topics

- Discuss the main subtopics of your general topic in a paragraph with a clear TOPIC SENTENCE.
- If a subtopic is lengthy, it may require more than one paragraph.

Body Paragraphs: Complications

- Discuss what is controversial or in dispute. What do people disagree about? Why? Do they dispute facts? Interpretations? Causes? Effects or implications? Solutions?

Conclusion

- Wrap up your topic. What questions or issues remain? What are areas for further research or investigation? What might readers do with this information?

Works Cited or References

- If you are using MLA style, include a list of Works Cited (Chapter 25); if you are using APA style, include a References list (Chapter 28).

Frame for an Argumentative Research Paper

Introductory paragraph(s)

- Establish why your topic is important or interesting. Consider, "Why does this matter? To whom does this matter? What might happen if we resolve this issue one way versus another?"
- Your THESIS STATEMENT needs to make clear how you will answer your research question.

Body paragraph(s): Background information

- Provide the history or background of your topic. Why is it a problem or concern at this time?

Body paragraph(s): Agreement among sources

- Discuss points of agreement. What is uncontroversial or widely accepted?
- Depending on the size or nature of the topic, this may be one or several paragraphs.

Body paragraph(s): Complications

- Discuss what is controversial or in dispute. What do people disagree about? Why? Do they dispute facts? Interpretations? Causes? Effects or implications? Solutions?

Body paragraph(s): Arguments

- Present your arguments. What reasons do you have for your position or proposed action? State each reason as a TOPIC SENTENCE, and provide evidence and support in the paragraph.
- If you have extensive support for a particular reason, you might need more than one paragraph.

Conclusion

- Wrap up your argument. Why is your position or proposal best? What actions should follow?

Works Cited or References

- If you are using MLA style, include a list of Works Cited (Chapter 25); if you are using APA style, include a References list (Chapter 28).

6D   A student's argumentative research paper.

Here's a short research paper in which a student uses the argumentative frame to organize his argument about the effects of digital information on democracy. For a longer argumentative research paper in MLA style, see 12E. For an informative research paper in MLA style, see 26B.

View the Model Document

Yan 1

Matthew Yan

Professor Daniels

WRIT 1133

5 May 2014

Cautions about Information in the Digital Age

Consider how typical middle class city people in the 1970s learned about the world around them. A newspaper arrived on the doorstep each morning, and the small number of major television networks summarized major events each evening. After dinner people might have read a magazine, perhaps checking background information in a family encyclopedia. Occasionally they visited the library to consult expert materials housed there.

Forty years later this daily pattern would still be true for a small group of people—a very small group. Most of us now get news from a wide range of digital sources, from websites to social networks to on-demand television networks, and they get it 24/7. Paul Sagan and Tom Leighton point out that people now "listen to podcasts on their way to work; check for news updates on their cell phones; watch, pause, and rewind live video newsfeeds on the Internet; and read and comment on blogs at the office, the gym, or the corner coffee shop" (119). Clearly the amount of easily accessed information is useful and convenient. However, there are troubling signs that the nature of digital information is eroding important aspects of our democracy.

There is wide agreement on the lessening popularity of traditional print media. Alicia Androich of Marketing magazine describes the continuing troubles that the newspaper industry in Canada is experiencing. From April to September 2011, she says, 19 of the 23 Canadian daily papers that belong to the Audit Bureau of Circulations had declines in paid circulation. A study by the US-based Pew Research Center characterizes people's news habits as "foraging and opportunism. They seem to access news when the spirit moves them or they have a chance to check up on headlines" (Purcell 2).

> This two-paragraph INTRODUCTION explains the topic, points to an important question, and ends with the paper's thesis statement.

> paraphrase

> quotation

Yan 2

Although everyone agrees that people are getting less information through professional reporters through traditional pipelines, there is a heated debate whether this is positive or negative, especially when it comes to the Internet. Clay Shirky is a strong advocate for common people generating knowledge. He hopes people might divert just 1% of their TV watching time to writing for the Web, which could generate "one hundred Wikipedias' worth" of content each year (23). That possibility would trouble Andrew Keen, who characterizes those writers as "infinite monkeys" who only spread "misinformation and ignorance" (4). These two men assume quite different things about quality of knowledge on Wikipedia. Keen has considerably less faith than Sharky in the ability of people to write accurately. James Fallows points out common fears that ours will become "an age of lies and idiocy," although he ultimately decides that common people posting tweets and blogs and videos strengthens our knowledge of emerging events (44).

Despite the positive contributions of amateur reporters, there are three reasons why traditional sources of expert information are important. First, the amount of misinformation online is extensive and troubling. Second, many Internet postings tend to reduce complex ideas to slogans or oversimplifications. Last, people increasingly tend to select themselves into interest groups, which makes it harder to understand other points of view and to consider ideas rationally.

There is convincing evidence that the nature of digital information and how people read it have the potential to erode our democracy. What, then, should we do? Obviously, it would be impossible to restrict online publishing only to experts. It would be undesirable, too; the Internet contains huge amounts of good information, and access for all to contribute means that diverse voices and experiences can be heard. Instead of restricting readers and writers, the answer is to educate them. With such a flood of information coming from so many channels, schools now need more than ever to teach students how to recognize information that is questionable or biased. Beyond that, however, is the personal responsibility that we all have as readers and writers. We need to pursue the truth and to form judgments based on sound evidence and reasoning, especially when important issues are at stake. This can take effort, but it leaves plenty of time for online entertainment, for silly pictures of cats and Facebook stories of last night's celebration.

Yan 3

Works Cited

Androich, Alicia. "Canada's Newspaper Circulation Numbers Still Dropping." Marketing. Rogers Digital Media, 1 Nov. 2011. Web. 19 May 2014.

Fallows, James. "Learning to Love the (Shallow, Divisive, Unreliable) New Media." Atlantic. Atlantic Monthly Group, April 2011: 34–49. Web. 24 Apr. 2014.

Keen, Andrew. The Cult of the Amateur. New York: Doubleday, 2007. Print.

Purcell, Kristen, Lee Rainie, Amy Mitchell, Tom Rosenstiel, and Kenny Olmstead. "Understanding the Participatory News Consumer: How Internet and Cell Phone Users Have Turned News into a Social Experience." Pew Internet and American Life Project. Pew Research Center, 1 Mar. 2010. Web. 24 Apr. 2014.

Sagan, Paul, and Tom Leighton. "The Internet & the Future of News." Daedalus 139.2 (2010): 119–25. Academic Search Premier, Web. 24 Apr. 2014.

Shirky, Clay. Cognitive Surplus, Creativity and Generosity in a Connected Age. Toronto: Penguin, 2010. Print.

6E   How do I revise a research paper?

Before you write each new draft, read your previous draft with a sharp eye. Assess all the features listed in Quick Box 6.1. For best results, take a break of a few days (or at least a few hours) before beginning this process to get some distance from

Quick Box 6.1

Revision checklist for a research paper

Writing
✓ Do your one or two introductory paragraphs lead effectively into the material? (4B)
✓ Have you met the basic requirements for a thesis statement? (2G)
✓ Do your thesis statement and the content of your paper address your research question(s)? (4C)
✓ Have you developed effective body paragraphs? (4D–4F)
✓ Do your ideas follow sensibly and logically within each paragraph and from one paragraph to the next? (4E)
✓ Does the concluding paragraph end your paper effectively? (4G)
Research
✓ Have you fully answered your research question? (4C)
✓ Have you evaluated the quality of your sources? Have you used sources that are appropriate for ACADEMIC WRITING? (7)
✓ Have you used QUOTATIONS, PARAPHRASES, and SUMMARIES well?
✓ Have you integrated your source material well without PLAGIARIZING?

your material and a clearer vision of what you need to revise. You might consider asking a few people you respect to read and react to a draft.

One key to revising any research paper is to examine carefully the evidence you've included. EVIDENCE consists of facts, statistics, expert studies and opinions, examples, and stories. Use RENNS (see 4D) to see if you can develop paragraphs more fully. Identify each of the points you have made in your paper, including your THESIS STATEMENT and all your subpoints. Then ask yourself the following questions.

- **Is the evidence sufficient?** To be sufficient, evidence can't be thin or trivial. As a rule, the more evidence you present, the more convincing your thesis will be to readers.

- **Is the evidence representative?** Representative evidence is customary and normal, not based on exceptions.

- **Is the evidence relevant?** Relevant evidence relates directly to your thesis or topic sentence. It illustrates your reasons straightforwardly and never introduces unrelated material.

- **Is the evidence accurate?** Accurate evidence is correct, complete, and up to date. It comes from a reliable source. Equally important, you present it honestly, without distorting or misrepresenting it.

- **Is the evidence reasonable?** Reasonable evidence is not phrased in extreme language and avoids sweeping generalizations. Reasonable evidence is free of LOGICAL FALLACIES (see 3D).

6F   How do I edit and format a research paper?

Quick Box 6.2 lists questions to ask when you edit your research paper.

Quick Box 6.2

Editing checklist for a research paper

✓ Is the paper free of errors in grammar, punctuation, and mechanics?
✓ Are your style and tone effective?
✓ Is the format correct in your parenthetical references? (Appendix 3C or 4)
✓ Does each of your parenthetical references tie in to an item in your Works Cited list (MLA style) or References list (APA style) at the end of your paper or follow CM, CSE, or IEEE styles? (Appendix 3C or 4)
✓ Does your format exactly match what you've been assigned to follow? Check margins, spacing, title, headings, page numbers, font, and so on. (Appendix 3C or 4)

MLA Documentation

APPENDIX
3C

Quick Points   You will learn to

➤   Cite sources in your writing using MLA style.

1A   What is MLA documentation style?

A DOCUMENTATION STYLE* is a standard format that writers follow to tell readers what sources they used and how to find them. Different disciplines follow different documentation styles. The one most frequently used in the humanities is from the Modern Language Association (MLA).

MLA style requires you to document your sources in two connected, equally important ways.

1. Within the body of the paper, use parenthetical documentation, as described in this chapter.
2. At the end of the paper, provide a list of the sources you used in your paper. Title this list "Works Cited," as described in Section 2.

The guidelines and examples in this chapter are based on the Seventh Edition of *The MLA Handbook for Writers of Research Papers* (2009), which is the most current edition. If you need more information regarding MLA style updates, check <http://www.mla.org>. See Quick Box 2.1 for more guidance on these requirements.

1B   What is MLA in-text parenthetical documentation?

MLA-style parenthetical documentation (also called in-text citations) places source information in parentheses within the sentences of your research papers. This information—given each time that you quote, summarize, or paraphrase source materials—signals materials used from outside sources and enables readers to find the originals. (See Appendix 3A for information on how to quote, paraphrase, and summarize.)

Author name cited in text; page number cited in parentheses   If you include an author's name (or, if none, the title of the work) in the sentence to introduce the source material, you include in parentheses only the page number where you found the material:

> According to Brent Staples, IQ tests give scientists little insight into intelligence (293).

For readability and good writing technique, try to introduce the names of authors (or titles of sources) in your own sentences.

Author name and page number cited in parentheses   If you don't include the author's name in your sentence, you need to insert it in the parentheses, before the page number. There is no punctuation between the author's name and the page number:

> IQ tests give scientists little insight into intelligence (Staples 293).

■ Placement of parenthetical reference

When possible, position a parenthetical reference at the end of the quotation, summary, or paraphrase it refers to—preferably at the end of a sentence, unless that would place it too far from the source's material. When you place the parenthetical reference at the end of a sentence, insert it before the sentence-ending period.

If you're citing a quotation enclosed in quotation marks, place the parenthetical information after the closing quotation mark but before sentence-ending punctuation.

> Coleman summarizes research that shows that "the number, rate, and direction of time-zone changes are the critical factors in determining the extent and degree of jet lag symptoms" (67).

Block quotations: Longer than four lines   The one exception to the rule of putting parenthetical information before sentence-ending punctuation concerns quotations that you set off in block style, meaning one inch (about 2.5 cm) from the left margin. (MLA requires that quotations longer than four typed lines be handled this way.) For block quotations, place the parenthetical reference after the period.

> Bruce Sterling worries that people are pursuing medical treatments in other countries, and not always for good reasons:
>
> > Offshore docs offer medical services that are faster, cheaper, and safer than anything available at home. . . . Medical tourism is already in full swing. Thailand is the golden shore for wealthy, sickly Asians and Australians. Fashionable Europeans head to South Africa for embarrassing plastic surgery. Crowds of scrip-waving Americans buy prescription drugs in Canada and Mexico. (92)

If you quote more than one paragraph, indent the first line of each paragraph—including the first if it's a complete paragraph from the source—an additional quarter inch (0.5 cm).

1C What are MLA examples for parenthetical citations?

The directory at the beginning of this tab corresponds to the numbered examples in this section. Most of these examples show the author's name or the title included in the parenthetical citation, but remember that it's usually more effective to include that information in your sentence.

1. One Author—MLA

Give an author's name as it appears on the source: for a book, on the title page; for an article, directly below the title or at the end of the article.

IQ tests give scientists little insight into intelligence (Staples 293).

2. Two or Three Authors—MLA

Give the names in the same order as in the source. Spell out *and*. For three authors, use commas to separate the authors' names.

As children get older, they begin to express several different kinds of intelligence (Todd and Taylor 23).

Another measure of emotional intelligence is the success of inter- and intrapersonal relationships (Voigt, Dees, and Prigoff 14).

3. More Than Three Authors—MLA

If your source has more than three authors, you can name them all or use the first author's name only, followed by *et al.*, either in a parenthetical reference or in your sentence. *Et al.* is an abbreviation of the Latin *et alii*, meaning "and others." In MLA citations, don't underline or italicize *et al.* No period follows *et*, but one follows *al*.

Emotional security varies, depending on the circumstances of the social interaction (Carter et al. 158).

4. More Than One Source by an Author—MLA

When you use two or more sources by the same author, include the relevant title in each citation. In parenthetical citations, use a shortened version of the title. For example, in a paper using two of Howard Gardner's works, *Frames of Mind: The Theory of Multiple Intelligences* and "Reflections on Multiple Intelligences: Myths and Messages," use *Frames* and "Reflections." Shorten the titles as much as you can without making them ambiguous to readers, and start with the word by which the work is alphabetized in your WORKS CITED list. Separate the author's name and the title with a comma, but don't use punctuation between the title and page number.

Although it seems straightforward to think of multiple intelligences as multiple approaches to learning (Gardner, *Frames* 60–61), an intelligence is not a learning style (Gardner, "Reflections" 202–03).

When you incorporate the title into your own sentences, you can omit a subtitle. After the first mention, you can shorten the main title as well.

5. Two or More Authors with the Same Last Name—MLA

Use each author's first initial and full last name in each parenthetical citation. If both authors have the same first initial, use the full name in all instances.

According to Anne Cates, psychologists can predict how empathetic an adult will be from his or her behaviour at age two (41), but other researchers disagree (T. Cates 171).

6. Group or Corporate Author—MLA

Use the corporate name just as you would an individual's name.

> In a five-year study, the Canadian Institute of Child Health reported that these tests are usually unreliable (11).

> A five-year study shows that these tests are usually unreliable (Canadian Institute of Child Health 11).

7. Work Cited by Title—MLA

If no author is named, use only the title. If the title is long, shorten it. Here's an in-text citation for an article titled "Are You a Day or Night Person?"

> The "morning lark" and "night owl" descriptions typically are used to categorize the human extremes ("Are You" 11).

8. Multivolume Work—MLA

If you use more than one volume of a multivolume work, include the relevant volume number in each citation. Separate the volume number and page number with a colon followed by a space.

> Rand believes that Borneo forest dwellers escaped illnesses from retroviruses until the 1960s (1: 543).

> By 1900, the Amazon forest dwellers had been exposed to these viruses (Rand 3: 202).

9. Novel, Play, Short Story, or Poem—MLA

Literary works frequently appear in different editions. When you cite material from literary works, providing the part, chapter, act, scene, canto, stanza, or line numbers usually helps readers locate what you are referring to better than page numbers alone. Unless your instructor tells you not to, use arabic numerals for these references, even if the literary work uses roman numerals. For novels that use them, give part and/or chapter numbers after page numbers. Use a semicolon after the page number but a comma to separate a part from a chapter.

> Flannery O'Connor describes one character in *The Violent Bear It Away* as "divided in two—a violent and a rational self" (139; pt. 2, ch. 6).

For plays that use them, give act, scene, and line numbers. Use periods between these numbers. For short stories, use page numbers.

> Among the most quoted of Shakespeare's lines is Hamlet's soliloquy beginning "To be, or not to be: that is the question" (3.1.56).

> The old man in John Collier's "The Chaser" says about his potions, "I don't deal in laxatives and teething mixtures . . ." (79).

For poems and songs, give canto, stanza, and/or line numbers. Use periods between these numbers.

> In "To Autumn," Keats's most melancholy image occurs in the lines "Then in a wailful choir the small gnats mourn / Among the river swallows" (3.27–28).

10. Bible or Sacred Text—MLA

Give the title of the edition you're using, the book (in the case of the Bible), and the chapter and verse. Spell out the names of books in sentences, but use abbreviations in parenthetical references.

He would certainly benefit from the advice in Ephesians to "get rid of all bitterness, rage, and anger" (*New International Version Bible*, 4.31).

He would certainly benefit from the advice to "get rid of all bitterness, rage, and anger" (*New International Version Bible*, Eph. 4.31).

11. Work in an Anthology or Other Collection—MLA

You may want to cite a work you have read in a book that contains many works by various authors and that was compiled or edited by someone other than the person you're citing. Your in-text citation should include the author of the selection you're citing and the page number. For example, suppose you want to cite the poem "La Belle Dame sans Merci" by John Keats, in an anthology edited by R. S. Gwynn and Wanda Campbell. Use Keats's name and the title of his work in your sentence and the line numbers (see item 9) in a parenthetical citation.

Keats opens "La Belle Dame sans Merci" with a dark, eerie scene: "O, what can ail thee, Knight at arms, / Alone and palely loitering? / The sedge has withered from the Lake / And no birds sing!" (1–4).

12. Indirect Source—MLA

When you want to quote words that you found quoted in someone else's work, put the name of the person whose words you're quoting into your own sentence. Give the work where you found the quotation either in your sentence or in a parenthetical citation beginning with *qtd. in*.

Pierre Trudeau makes a notably populist statement: "The ordinary person can be appealed to through common sense. Beyond the effects of technology. My grandfather, for instance, was not especially literate but he was able to reason choices out" (qtd. in Powe 126).

Powe quotes Pierre Trudeau as having made a notably populist statement: "The ordinary person can be appealed to through common sense. Beyond the effects of technology. My grandfather, for instance, was not especially literate but he was able to reason choices out" (126).

13. Two or More Sources in One Reference—MLA

If more than one source has contributed to an idea, opinion, or fact in your paper, cite them all. An efficient way to credit all is to include them in a single parenthetical citation, with a semicolon separating each block of information.

Once researchers agreed that multiple intelligences existed, their next step was to try to measure or define them (West 17; Arturi 477; Gibbs 68).

14. An Entire Work—MLA

References to an entire work usually fit best into your own sentences.

In *Convergence Culture*, Henry Jenkins explores how new digital media create a culture of active participation rather than passive reception.

15. Electronic Source with Page Numbers—MLA

The principles that govern in-text citations of electronic sources are exactly the same as the ones that apply to books, articles, or other sources. When an electronically accessed source identifies its author, use the author's name for parenthetical references. If no author is named, use the title of the source. When an electronic source has page numbers, use them exactly as you would the page numbers of a print source.

Learning happens best when teachers truly care about their students' complete well-being (Anderson 7).

16. Electronic Source without Page Numbers—MLA

Many online sources don't number pages. Simply refer to those works in their entirety. Include the name of the author, if any, in your sentence.

> In "What Is Artificial Intelligence?" John McCarthy notes that the science of artificial intelligence includes efforts beyond trying to simulate human intelligence.

2   MLA WORKS CITED LIST

Quick Points   You will learn to

➤ Cite your sources at the end of your paper in an MLA Works Cited list.

2A   What are MLA guidelines for a Works Cited list?

Watch the Video

In MLA-style DOCUMENTATION, the WORKS CITED list gives complete bibliographic information for each SOURCE used in your paper. Include only the sources from which you quote, paraphrase, or summarize. Quick Box 2.1 gives general information about the Works Cited list. The rest of this chapter gives models of many specific kinds of Works Cited entries.Quick Box 2.1

Quick Box 2.1

Guidelines for an MLA-style Works Cited list

See the student essay in Section 3 for a sample student Works Cited list.

TITLE
Use "Works Cited" (without quotation marks), centred, as the title.

PLACEMENT OF LIST
Start a new page numbered sequentially with the rest of the paper, following the Notes pages, if any.

CONTENT AND FORMAT
Include all sources quoted from, paraphrased, or summarized in your paper. Start each entry on a new line and at the regular left margin. If the entry uses more than one line, indent the second and all following lines one-half inch (about 1.25 cm) from the left margin. Double-space all lines.

SPACING AFTER PUNCTUATION
Use one space after a period, unless your instructor asks you to use two. Always put only one space after a comma or a colon.

ARRANGEMENT OF ENTRIES
Alphabetize by author's last name. If no author is named, alphabetize by the title's first significant word (ignore *A, An,* or *The*).

AUTHORS' NAMES

Use first names and middle names or middle initials, if any, as given in the source. Don't reduce to initials any name that is given in full. For one author or the first-named author in multiauthor works, give the last name first. Use the word *and* with two or more authors. List multiple authors in the order given in the source. Use a comma between the first author's last and first names and after each complete author name except the last, which ends with a period: Fein, Ethel Andrea, Bert Griggs, and Delaware Rogash.

Include *Jr., Sr., II,* or *III* but no other titles or degrees before or after a name. For example, an entry for a work by Edward Meep III, MD, and Sir Richard Bolton would start like this: Meep, Edward, III, and Richard Bolton.

CAPITALIZATION OF TITLES

Capitalize all major words and the first and last words of all titles and sub-titles. Don't capitalize ARTICLES (*a, an, the*), PREPOSITIONS, COORDINATING CONJUNCTIONS, or *to* in INFINITIVES in the middle of a title.

SPECIAL TREATMENT OF TITLES

Use quotation marks around titles of shorter works (poems, short stories, essays, articles). Use italics for the titles of longer works (books, periodicals, plays).

When a book title includes the title of another work that is usually in italics (such as a novel, play, or long poem), the preferred MLA style is not to italicize the incorporated title: *Decoding* Jane Eyre.

If the incorporated title is usually enclosed in quotation marks (such as a short story or short poem), keep the quotation marks and italicize the complete title of the book: *Theme and Form in "I Shall Laugh Purely": A Brief Study.*

Drop *A, An,* or *The* as the first word of a periodical title.

PLACE OF PUBLICATION

If several cities are listed for the place of publication, give only the first. MLA doesn't require a province, territory, state, or country name to accompany an unfamiliar city, but your instructor may ask you to include their abbreviations.

PUBLISHER

Use shortened names as long as they're clear: *Random* for *Random House*. For companies named for more than one person, name only the first: *Prentice* for *Prentice Hall*. For university presses, use the capital letters *U* and *P* (without periods): Oxford UP, U of Chicago P. If there is no publisher, use "N.p."

PUBLICATION MONTH ABBREVIATIONS

Abbreviate all publication months except *May, June,* and *July*. Use the first three letters followed by a period (*Dec., Feb.*) except for *Sept.*

PAGE RANGES

Give the page range—the starting page number and the ending page number, connected by a hyphen or a short dash—of any paginated electronic source and any paginated print source that is part of a longer work (for example, a chapter in a book, an article in a journal). A range indicates that the cited work is on those pages and all pages in between. If that is not the case, use the style shown next for discontinuous pages. In either case, use numerals only, without the word *page* or *pages* or the abbreviation *p.* or *pp.*

Use the full second number through 99. Above that, use only the last two digits for the second number unless it would be unclear: 103-04 is clear, but 567-602 requires full numbers.

DISCONTINUOUS PAGES

When the source is interrupted by material that's not part of the source (for example, an article beginning on page 32 but continued on page 54), use the starting page number followed by a plus sign (+): 32+.

MEDIUM OF PUBLICATION

Include the medium of publication for each Works Cited entry. Every entry for a print source must include "Print," followed by a period. Supplementary bibliographic information like the original publication information for a work cited in translation, name of a book series, or the number of volumes in a set should follow the medium of publication. Every source from the World Wide Web must include *Web*, followed by a period and the date of access. Broadcast sources (*Television, Radio*), sound recordings (*CD, Podcast, LP, Audiocassette*), films, DVDs, live performances, musical scores, works of visual art, and so on are also noted.

VOLUME AND ISSUE NUMBERS FOR SCHOLARLY JOURNALS

Include both a volume and issue number for each Works Cited entry for scholarly journals. This applies both to journals that are continuously paginated through each annual volume and those that are not.

WORKS CITED INFORMATION FOR INTERNET SOURCES

For online sources, provide as much of the following information as you can.

1. The author's name if given, or the compiler, editor, director, performer, etc.
2. Title of the work (italicized if the work is independent; in quotation marks if the work is part of a larger work). If the work has no title, describe it: for example, *Home page, Introduction, Online posting* (not italicized and without quotation marks).
3. The italicized title of the website, if distinct from the title of the work.
4. The version or edition used, if relevant.
5. The publisher or sponsor of the site (if not available, use *N.p.*).
6. The date of electronic publication or the most recent update (if not given, use *n.d.*).
7. The medium of publication (*Web*).
8. The date you accessed the site.

If you are also citing publication information for a print version of the online source, begin the entry with that information but omit the original medium (*Print*). Then provide the following information.

9. The italicized title of the website or database.
10. The medium of publication you consulted (*Web*).
11. The date you accessed the site.

Give any supplementary information that normally follows the medium of publication in a print citation immediately before the title of the website or database.

URLs IN ELECTRONIC SOURCES

Entries for online citations should include the URL *only when the reader probably could not locate the source without it.* If the entry requires a URL, enclose the URL in angle brackets <like this> following the access date, and end it with a period. If your computer automatically creates a hyperlink when you type a URL, format the URL to look the same as the rest of the entry. If a URL must be divided between two lines, break the URL only after a slash and do not use a hyphen.

2B   What are MLA examples for sources in a Works Cited list?

The directory at the beginning of this tab corresponds to the numbered examples in this section. Not every possible documentation model is here. You may find that you have to combine features of models to document a particular source. You will also find more information in the *MLA Handbook for Writers of Research Papers.* This section follows the *MLA Handbook* in starting with periodicals in print, and then moving on to books in print, followed by online periodicals, online books, and then by additional common sources in different media and formats. Figure 2.1 provides another tool to help you find the Works Cited model you need: a decision-making flowchart.

Figure 2.1   Decision-making flowchart for finding the right MLA citation format.

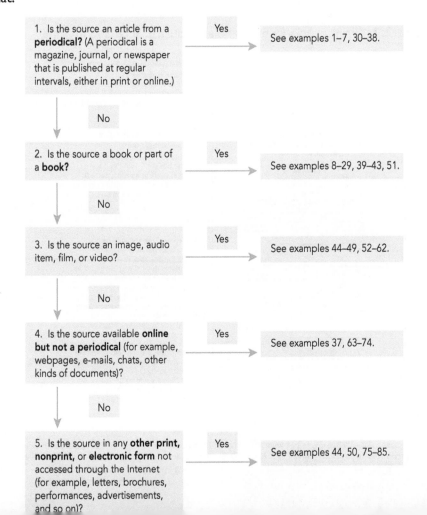

Periodicals

You can read periodical articles in four different formats. Some articles appear in all print and electronic versions; others are published in only one or two formats.

1. **Print**
2. **Digital version in a database.** You most commonly access these sources through a DATABASE such as EBSCO or Academic Search Premier, which your library purchases.
3. **Digital version with direct online access.** Without going through a database, you access these sources directly on the Web, either by entering a specific URL or clicking on links provided by a search. Of course, many other Web sources are not from periodicals; we explain them in examples 68–80.
4. **Digital version on a digital reader.** Many devices allow you to access online content. These include e-readers like Kobo or Kindle, tablet computers (like iPads), or smart phones (like BlackBerry or Android devices).

A citation for a periodical title contains three major parts: author, title of article, and publication information, including the medium in which you access the source—usually print or Web—and for Web sources, your date of access as well. MLA also identifies some types of sources, such as editorials or letters, in citations.

Figure 2.2 shows how to cite a print article from a scholarly journal.

Figure 2.2 Print article from a scholarly journal, accessed in print.

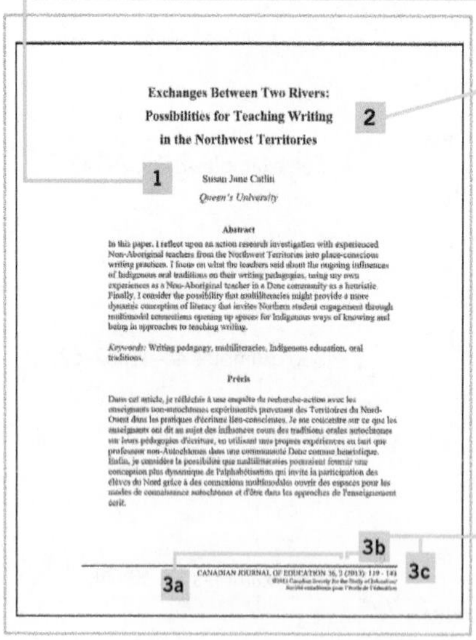

1 AUTHOR INFORMATION

Name of Author
Write the author's last name, followed by a comma, the author's first name, and the middle initial (if given). End with a period.

2 TITLE INFORMATION

2 Article Title
Begin with a quotation mark, write the title (with subtitle, if there is one), include a period, and end with a closing quotation mark. Capitalize all major words.

3 PUBLICATION INFORMATION

3a Journal Title and Volume
Italicize the title. Capitalize all major words. Include the volume number and issue number, separated by a period.

3b Date of Publication
Include the year of publication in parentheses, followed by a colon.

3c Page Numbers
Provide the page numbers on which the article begins and ends, separated by a hyphen. For numbers up to 99, include both digits. For higher numbers, include only the last two digits (145-57) unless doing so would be unclear (295-307). End with a period followed by the medium of publication, Print.

CITATION

1 2

Catlin, Susan Jane. "Exchanges Between Two Rivers: Possibilities for Teaching Writing in the Northwest Territories." *Canadian Journal of Education / Revue canadienne de l'éducation* 36.2 (2013): 119–43. Print.

2 3

Figure 2.4 (on page 405) shows how to cite an article from a scholarly journal that was accessed in a database.

Periodicals—Print

1. Article in a Scholarly Journal: Print

Williams, Bronwyn T. "Seeking New Worlds: The Study of Writing beyond Our Classrooms." *College Composition and Communication* 62.1 (2010): 127–46. Print.

Provide both volume and issue number, if available.

2. Article in a Newspaper: Print

Omit *A*, *An*, or *The* as the first word in a newspaper title. Give the day, month, and year of the issue (and the edition, if applicable). If sections are designated, give the section letter as well as the page number. If an article runs on nonconsecutive pages, give the starting page number followed by a plus sign (for example, 23+ for an article that starts on page 23 and continues on page 42).

McCarthy, Shawn. "Sale Puts Ottawa out of Nuclear Business." *Globe and Mail* 28 June 2011: A1+ Print.

If no title is listed, begin with the title of the article. If the city of publication is not part of the title, put it in square brackets after the title, not italicized.

"Judge Bars Public from CNR Building in Interim Order." *Beacon Herald* [Stratford] 24 July 2004: A1. Print.

3. Article in a Weekly or Biweekly Magazine: Print

Johnson, Brian D. "Why Six Dylans Are Better Than One." *Maclean's* 26 Nov. 2007: 43–46. Print.

If there is no author given, begin with the title of the article.

"Too Many Suits, and Not Enough Skirts in the Boardrooms." *Economist* 26 Nov. 2011: 73–74. Print.

4. Article in a Monthly or Bimonthly Magazine: Print

Fallows, James. "The 1.4 Trillion Question." *Atlantic* Jan.–Feb. 2008: 36–48.

5. Editorial, Letter to the Editor, or Review: Print

After the author's name or title, provide information about the type of publication.

"London Doomed to Repeat Its History on Heritage." Editorial. *London Free Press* 20 July 2011: B8. Print.

Martens, Janice. "Lipstick in Kindergarten." Letter. *Winnipeg Free Press* 23 Mar. 2013: A14. Print.

Voyer, Graeme. "Great War Started One Policy at a Time." Rev. of *The Sleepwalkers*, by Christopher Clark. *Winnipeg Free Press* 23 Mar. 2013: J9. Print.

6. Article in a Collection of Reprinted Articles: Print

Brumberg, Abraham. "Russia after Perestroika." *New York Review of Books* 27 June 1991: 53–62. Rpt. in *Russian and Soviet History*. Ed. Alexander Dallin. New York: Garland, 1992. 300–20. Print. Vol. 14 of *The Gorbachev Era*.

7. Abstract in a Collection of Abstracts: Print

If the journal title does not indicate that what you are citing is an abstract, write the word *Abstract*, not italicized, followed by a period, after the publication information for the original article. Give publication information about the collection of abstracts. For abstracts identified by item numbers rather than page numbers, use the word *item* before the item number.

Marcus, Hazel R., and Shinobu Kitayamo. "Culture and the Self: Implications for Cognition, Emotion, and Motivation." *Psychological Review* 88.2 (1991): 224–53. *Psychological Abstracts* 78.2 (1991): item 23878. Print.

Books

You can read books these days in four different formats.

1. **Print**
2. **Digital version through an e-book.** E-books are electronic versions of books for digital readers like the Kindle, Nook, iPad, and so on.
3. **Digital version from a database.** Some books are available through library databases; in a sense, you're "checking out the books" online.
4. **Digital version through direct online access.** Versions of some older books, whose copyrights have expired, are available directly on the Web. Portions of several more recent books are also available directly on the Web, through sites like Google Books. However, the section you might need for your research is frequently not available.

Figure 2.3 shows how to cite a single-author print book.

Books—Print

8. Book by One Author: Print

Trudeau, Pierre E. *Federalism and the French Canadians*. Toronto: Macmillan, 1968. Print.

9. Book by Two or Three Authors: Print

Doob, Anthony, and Carla Cesaroni. *Responding to Youth Crime in Canada*. Toronto: U of Toronto P, 2004. Print.

Scardamalia, Marlene, Carl Bereiter, and Bryant Fillion. *Writing for Results: A Sourcebook of Consequential Composing Activities*. Toronto: OISE, 1981. Print.

10. Book by More Than Three Authors: Print

Give only the first author's name, followed by a comma and the phrase *et al.* ("and others"), or list all names in full and in the order in which they appear on the title page.

Saul, Wendy, et al. *Beyond the Science Fair: Creating a Kids' Inquiry Conference*. Portsmouth: Heinemann, 2005. Print.

11. Two or More Works by the Same Author(s): Print

Give author name(s) in the first entry only. In the second and subsequent entries, use three hyphens and a period to stand for exactly the same name(s). If the person served as editor or translator, put a comma and *ed.* or *trans.* after the three hyphens. Arrange the works in alphabetical (not chronological) order according to book title, ignoring labels such as *ed.* or *trans.*

Atwood, Margaret. *The Handmaid's Tale*. Toronto: McClelland, 1985. Print.

---. *Survival*. Toronto: Anansi, 1972. Print.

---. *Writing with Intent: Essays, Reviews, Personal Prose 1983–2005*. New York: Carroll, 2005. Print.

12. Book by Group or Corporate Author: Print

When a corporate author is also the publisher, use a shortened form of the corporate name in the publication information. (The CBC Massey Lectures Series is considered the corporate author of the book in the second item.)

American Psychological Association. *Publication Manual of the American Psychological Association*. 6th ed. Washington: APA, 2009. Print.

CBC Massey Lectures Series. *The Lost Massey Lectures: Recovered Classics from Five Great Thinkers*. Toronto: Anansi, 2007. Print.

Figure 2.3 Two-author print book.

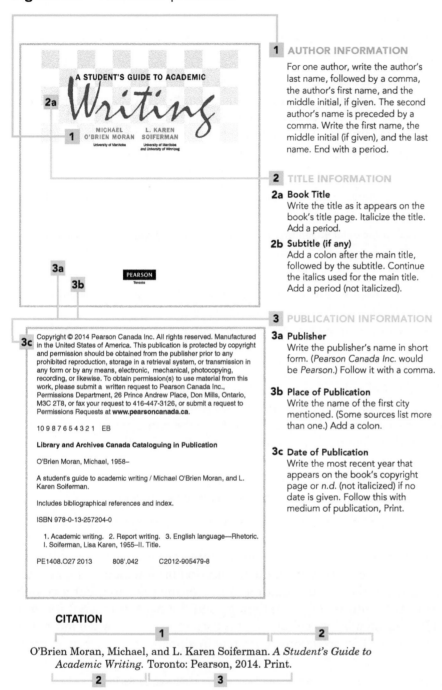

1 AUTHOR INFORMATION

For one author, write the author's last name, followed by a comma, the author's first name, and the middle initial, if given. The second author's name is preceded by a comma. Write the first name, the middle initial (if given), and the last name. End with a period.

2 TITLE INFORMATION

2a Book Title
Write the title as it appears on the book's title page. Italicize the title. Add a period.

2b Subtitle (if any)
Add a colon after the main title, followed by the subtitle. Continue the italics used for the main title. Add a period (not italicized).

3 PUBLICATION INFORMATION

3a Publisher
Write the publisher's name in short form. (*Pearson Canada Inc.* would be *Pearson.*) Follow it with a comma.

3b Place of Publication
Write the name of the first city mentioned. (Some sources list more than one.) Add a colon.

3c Date of Publication
Write the most recent year that appears on the book's copyright page or *n.d.* (not italicized) if no date is given. Follow this with medium of publication, Print.

Copyright © 2014 Pearson Canada Inc. All rights reserved. Manufactured in the United States of America. This publication is protected by copyright and permission should be obtained from the publisher prior to any prohibited reproduction, storage in a retrieval system, or transmission in any form or by any means, electronic, mechanical, photocopying, recording, or likewise. To obtain permission(s) to use material from this work, please submit a written request to Pearson Canada Inc., Permissions Department, 26 Prince Andrew Place, Don Mills, Ontario, M3C 2T8, or fax your request to 416-447-3126, or submit a request to Permissions Requests at **www.pearsoncanada.ca.**

10 9 8 7 6 5 4 3 2 1 EB

Library and Archives Canada Cataloguing in Publication

O'Brien Moran, Michael, 1958–

A student's guide to academic writing / Michael O'Brien Moran, and L. Karen Soiferman.

Includes bibliographical references and index.

ISBN 978-0-13-257204-0

1. Academic writing. 2. Report writing. 3. English language—Rhetoric. I. Soiferman, Lisa Karen, 1955–II. Title.

PE1408.O27 2013   808'.042   C2012-905479-8

CITATION

O'Brien Moran, Michael, and L. Karen Soiferman. *A Student's Guide to Academic Writing.* Toronto: Pearson, 2014. Print.

13. Book with No Author Named: Print

If there is no author's name on the title page, begin the citation with the title. Alphabetize the entry according to the first significant word of the title, ignoring *A*, *An*, or *The*.

The Chicago Manual of Style. 16th ed. Chicago: U of Chicago P, 2010. Print.

14. Book with an Author and an Editor: Print

If your paper refers to the work of the book's author, put the author's name first; if your paper refers to the work of the editor, put the editor's name first.

Trudeau, Pierre Elliott. *The Essential Trudeau.* Ed. Ron Graham. Toronto: McClelland, 1998. Print.

Graham, Ron, ed. *The Essential Trudeau*. By Pierre Elliott Trudeau. Toronto: McClelland, 1998. Print.

15. Translation: Print

Tremblay, Michel. *Assorted Candies for the Theatre*. Trans. Linda Gaboriau. Vancouver: Talonbooks, 2007. Print.

16. Work in Several Volumes or Parts: Print

If you cite only one volume, put the volume number before the publication information. If you wish, you can give the total number of volumes at the end of the entry. Use arabic numerals for volume numbers, not roman numerals.

Chrisley, Ronald, ed. *Artificial Intelligence: Critical Concepts*. Vol. 1. London: Routledge, 2000.
Print. 4 vols.

If you are using more than one volume, include the total number of volumes before the publication information.

Chrisley, Ronald, ed. *Artificial Intelligence: Critical Concepts*. 4 vols. London: Routledge, 2000.
Print.

17. Anthology or Edited Book: Print

Use this model if you are citing an entire anthology. In the following example, *ed.* stands for "editor"; use *eds.* for more than one editor.

Nurse, Donna Bailey, ed. *Revival: An Anthology of the Best Black Canadian Writing*. Toronto:
McClelland, 2006. Print.

18. One Selection from an Anthology or an Edited Book: Print

Give the author and title of the selection first and then the full title of the anthology. Information about the editor starts with *Ed.* (for "Edited by"), so don't use *Eds.* when there is more than one editor. Give the name(s) of the editor(s) in normal order rather than reversing first and last names. Give the page range after the publication date.

Clarke, George Elliott. "King Bee Blues." *Revival: An Anthology of the Best Black Canadian
Writing*. Ed. Donna Bailey Nurse. Toronto: McClelland, 2006. 229–30. Print.

19. More Than One Selection from the Same Anthology or Edited Book: Print

If you cite more than one selection from the same anthology, you can list the anthology as a separate entry with all the publication information. Also, list each selection from the anthology by author and title of the selection, but give only the name(s) of the editor(s) of the anthology and the page number(s) for each selection. Here, *ed.* stands for "editor," so it is correct to use *eds.* when more than one editor is named. List selections separately in alphabetical order by author's last name.

Davies, Robertson, "The Charlottetown Banquet." Ioannou and Missen 40–52. Print.

Ioannou, Greg, and Lynne Missen, eds. *Shivers: An Anthology of Canadian Ghost Stories*. Toronto:
McClelland, 1989. Print.

Mistry, Rohinton. "The Ghost of Firozsha Baag." Ioannou and Missen 198–216. Print.

20. Article in a Reference Book: Print

If the articles in the book are alphabetically arranged, you don't need to give volume and page numbers.

Shadbolt, Doris. "Carr, Emily." *The Canadian Encyclopedia*. 2nd ed. Edmonton: Hurtig, 1988. Print.

If no author is listed, begin with the title of the article. If you're citing a widely used reference work, give only the edition, year of publication, and medium of publication.

"Ireland." *The New Encyclopaedia Britannica: Macropaedia.* 15th ed. 2002. Print.

21. Second or Later Edition: Print

If a book isn't a first edition, the edition number appears on the title page. Place the abbreviated information (*2nd ed.*, *3rd ed.*, etc.) between the title and the publication information. Give only the latest copyright date for the edition you're using.

Pratt, E. J. *The Collected Poems of E. J. Pratt.* Ed. Northrop Frye. 2nd ed. Toronto: Macmillan, 1958.
   Print.

22. Introduction, Preface, Foreword, or Afterword: Print

Give first the name of the writer of the part you're citing and then the name of the cited part, capitalized but not italicized or in quotation marks. After the book title, write *By* or *Ed.* and the full name(s) of the book's author(s) or editor(s), if different from the writer of the cited material. If the writer of the cited material is the same as the book author, include only the last name after *By*. If a single author has written the entire book including the introduction, preface, and so forth, and there is no editor listed, cite the entire book instead of creating a separate entry for this part. Following the publication information, give inclusive page numbers for the cited part, using roman or arabic numerals as the source does.

Hesse, Doug. Foreword. *The End of Composition Studies.* By David W. Smit. Carbondale: Southern
   Illinois UP, 2004. ix–xiii. Print.

When the introduction, preface, foreword, or afterword has a title, include it in the citation before the section name.

Fox-Genovese, Elizabeth. "Mothers and Daughters: The Ties That Bind." Foreword. *Southern
   Mothers.* Ed. Nagueyalti Warren and Sally Wolff. Baton Rouge: Louisiana State UP, 1999. iv–
   xviii. Print.

23. Reprint of an Older Book: Print

Republishing information can be found on the copyright page.

Epp, Marlene. *Women Without Men: Mennonite Refugees of the Second World War.* 2000. Toronto: U
   of Toronto P, 2003. Print.

24. Book in a Series: Print

Steinberg, Blema S. *Women in Power: The Personalities and Leadership Styles of Indira Gandhi, Golda
   Meir, and Margaret Thatcher.* Montreal: McGill-Queen's UP, 2008. Print. Arts Insight Ser.

25. Book with a Title Within a Title: Print

Lumiansky, Robert M., and Herschel Baker, eds. *Critical Approaches to Six
   Major English Works: Beowulf through Paradise Lost.* Philadelphia: U of Pennsylvania P, 1968.
   Print.

MLA also accepts a second style for embedded titles.

Lumiansky, Robert M., and Herschel Baker, eds. *Critical Approaches to Six
   Major English Works: "Beowulf" through "Paradise Lost."* Philadelphia: U of Pennsylvania P,
   1968. Print.

26. Bible or Sacred Text: Print

Bhagavad Gita. Trans. Juan Mascaro. Rev. ed. New York: Penguin, 2003. Print.

The Holy Bible. New International Vers. New York: Harper, 1983. Print.

The Qur'an. Trans. Abdullah Yusuf Ali. 13th ed. Elmhurst: Tahrike Tarsile Qur'an, 1999. Print.

27. Government Publication: Print

For publications that name no author, start with the name of the government (such as Canada). Then name the branch of government or the agency (such as Department of Finance or Task Force on Program Review).

Canada. Indian and Northern Affairs Canada. *An Aboriginal Book List for Children.* Ottawa: Indian and Northern Affairs Canada, 2000. Print.

When the author is known, the author's name may either come first or follow the title.

Savoie, Donald J. *Horizontal Management of Official Languages. Reports.* Canada. Office of the Commissioner of Official Languages. Ottawa: Minister of Public Works and Government Services Canada, 2008. Print.

Canada. Office of the Commissioner of Official Languages. *Horizontal Management of Official Languages. Reports.* By Donald J. Savoie. Ottawa: Minister of Public Works and Government Services Canada, 2008. Print.

28. Published Proceedings of a Conference: Print

Smith, Donald B., ed. *Forging a New Relationship: Proceedings of the Conference on the Report of the Royal Commission on Aboriginal Peoples.* 31 Jan.–2 Feb. 1997. Montreal: McGill Institute for the Study of Canada, 1997. Print.

29. Unpublished Dissertation or Essay: Print

Treat published dissertations as books. Put the title in quotation marks and follow it with a descriptive label (such as *Diss.*, *MA thesis*, or *Unpublished essay*). In the following example, the title of the television series is italicized.

Byers, Michele. "*Buffy the Vampire Slayer:* The Insurgence of Television as a Performance Text." Diss. U of Toronto, 2000. Print.

Periodicals—Web

30. Article in a Scholarly Journal with a Print Version: Direct online access

Archibald, W. Peter. "Small Expectations and Great Adjustments: How Hamilton Workers Most Often Experienced the Great Depression." *Canadian Journal of Sociology* 21.3 (1996): 359–402. Web. 22 Feb. 2014.

31. Article in a Scholarly Journal with a Print Version: Database

Williams, Bronwyn T. "Seeking New Worlds: The Study of Writing beyond Our Classrooms." *College Composition and Communication.* 62.1 (2010): 127–46. Proquest. Web. 24 Oct. 2014.

32. Article in a Scholarly Journal Published Only Online: Direct online access

Rutz, Paul X. "What a Painter of 'Historical Narrative' Can Tell Us about War Photography." *Kairos* 14.3 (2010). Web. 11 Nov. 2014.

33. Article in a Newspaper: Direct online access

The name of the website is italicized. The sponsor of the website precedes the date of publication.

El Akkad, Omar. "New Identification Rules Bar Some Canadians from Casting Ballots." *Globe and Mail. Globe and Mail,* 15 Oct. 2008. Web. 20 Nov. 2014.

34. Article in a News Site Published Only Online: Direct online access

Perkins, Tara. "Conrad Black's Chicago Court Date Set for Tuesday: U.S. Attorney's Office." *CP Online.* Canadian Press, 18 Nov. 2005. Web. 22 Nov. 2014.

35. Article in a Weekly or Biweekly Magazine: Direct online access

Johnson, Brian D. "Why Six Dylans Are Better Than One." *Maclean's. Maclean's,* 26 Nov. 2007. Web. 24 Nov. 2014.

Figure 2.4   Article from a scholarly journal accessed in a database.

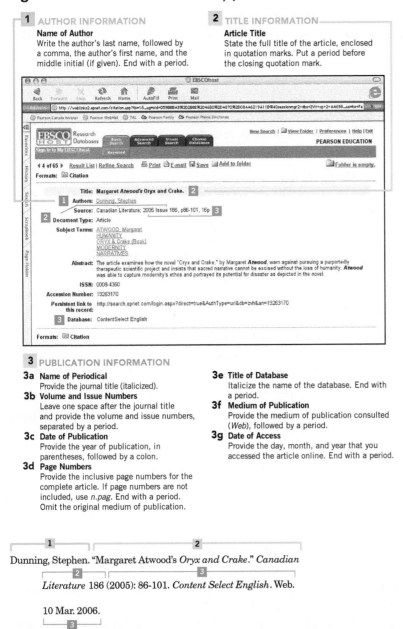

1 AUTHOR INFORMATION

Name of Author
Write the author's last name, followed by a comma, the author's first name, and the middle initial (if given). End with a period.

2 TITLE INFORMATION

Article Title
State the full title of the article, enclosed in quotation marks. Put a period before the closing quotation mark.

3 PUBLICATION INFORMATION

3a Name of Periodical
Provide the journal title (italicized).

3b Volume and Issue Numbers
Leave one space after the journal title and provide the volume and issue numbers, separated by a period.

3c Date of Publication
Provide the year of publication, in parentheses, followed by a colon.

3d Page Numbers
Provide the inclusive page numbers for the complete article. If page numbers are not included, use *n.pag.* End with a period. Omit the original medium of publication.

3e Title of Database
Italicize the name of the database. End with a period.

3f Medium of Publication
Provide the medium of publication consulted (*Web*), followed by a period.

3g Date of Access
Provide the day, month, and year that you accessed the article online. End with a period.

Dunning, Stephen. "Margaret Atwood's *Oryx and Crake*." *Canadian Literature* 186 (2005): 86-101. *Content Select English*. Web. 10 Mar. 2006.

36. Article in a Monthly or Bimonthly Magazine: Direct online access

Fallows, James. "The 1.4 Trillion Question." *The Atlantic.com*. Atlantic Monthly Group, Jan.–Feb. 2008. Web. 2 May 2014.

An editorial, letter to the editor, or review begins like its print equivalent (item 5).

Baird, Daniel. Rev. of Once, by Rebecca Rosenblum. *Walrusmagazine.com*. The Walrus Foundation, Oct./Nov. 2008. Web. 20 July 2014.

37. Abstract: Database

Marcus, Hazel R., and Shinobu Kitayamo. "Culture and the Self: Implications for Cognition, Emotion, and Motivation." Abstract. *Psychological Abstracts* 78.2 (1991): item 23878. *PsycINFO*. Web. 10 Apr. 2014.

38. Abstract: Direct online access

This abstract's location is a journal accessed online.

McIntyre, John W. R., and C. Stuart Houston. "Smallpox and Its Control in Canada." *CMAJ* 161.12 (1999): 1543–47. Abstract. Web. 14 Aug. 2014.

Books—Web

39. Book by One Author: E-Book

Trudeau, Pierre E. *Federalism and the French Canadians.* Toronto: Macmillan, 1968. Web. Kobo file.

40. Book by One Author: Database

With a book published before 1900, you may omit the publisher after the place of publication.

Eaton, Arthur W. *Acadian Legends and Lyrics.* London, 1889. *Early Canadiana Online.* Web. 25 May 2014.

41. Book by Two or Three Authors: Direct online access

Thomson, A. B. R., and E. A. Shaffer, eds. *First Principles of Gastroenterology.* 3rd ed. Gastroenterology Resource Centre, 2005. Web. 22 Mar. 2014.

42. Book in a Scholarly Project: Direct online access

Herodotus. The History of Herodotus. Trans. George Rawlinson. *Internet Classics Archive.* Ed. Daniel C. Stevenson. MIT, 11 Jan. 1998. Web. 15 May 2014.

43. Government Publication: Direct online access

The title of the work (*Report*) is followed here by the name of the website (italicized) and the sponsoring agency.

Canada. Royal Commission on Bilingualism and Biculturalism. *Report. Commissions of Inquiry.* Library and Archives of Canada, 12 Apr. 2005. Web. 12 Sept. 2014.

Additional Common Sources

44. Television or Radio Program

Include at least the title of the program (italicized), the network, the local station and its city, the date of the broadcast, and the medium of broadcast.

"Chasing Pavements: Part 2." *Degrassi: The Next Generation.* Perf. Charlotte Arnold, Luke Bilyk, and Stefan Brogren. CTV. CFTO, Toronto. 8 Apr. 2013. Television.

For a series, supply the title of the specific episode (in quotation marks) before the title of the program or series (italicized).

45. Television or Radio Program: Direct online access

Omit the local station (unless it is important information) and the broadcast medium, and add the name of the website, the medium on which you accessed the program (*Web*), and the date of access.

Walsh, Mary. "Regeneration Trilogy by Pat Barker." *Mary Walsh: Open Book.* CBC, 29 Sept. 2002. *CBC.ca.* Web. 15 Nov. 2014.

46. Sound Recording

Put first the name most relevant to what you discuss in your paper (performer, conductor, work). Include the recording's title, the artist(s) (if distinct from the first item), the issuer, the year of issue, and the medium (*CD, LP, Audiocassette*).

Smetana, Bedrich. *My Country.* Czech Philharmonic Orch. Cond. Karel Ancerl. Vanguard, 1975. LP.

Cohen, Leonard. "Tower of Song." *I'm Your Man.* Sony, 1988. CD.

47. Sound Recording, Podcast, or Clip: Direct online access

Atwood, Margaret. "Writing Women's Fiction." *CBC Digital Archives*. CBC, 9 Apr. 1981. Web. 12
    June 2014.

48. Video, Film, DVD, etc.

Give the title first, and include the director, the distributor, and the year of release
and medium. The screenwriter may follow the title. For a DVD or video, give its
year; as an option, you may also give the original year of release before the name
of the distributor. Other information (writer, producer, major actors) is optional;
it follows the title and precedes the distributor. Put first names first.

Calendar. Screenplay by Atom Egoyan. Dir. Atom Egoyan. Prod. Ego Filmarts/ZDF. Perf. Atom
    Egoyan and Arsinée Khanjian. 1993. Alliance Atlantis, 2001. DVD.

Stories We Tell. Dir. Sarah Polley. Prod. Anita Lee and Silva Basmajian. Perf. Rebecca Jenkins.
    Mongrel Media, 2012. Film.

49. Video or Film Clip: Direct online access

Reeves, Matt, dir. *Cloverfield*. Trailer. Bad Robot, 2008. Web. 18 Jan. 2014.

50. Live Performance

Twelfth Night. By William Shakespeare. Dir. Des McAnuff. Perf. Suzy Jane Hunt, Brian Dennehy,
    and Tom Rooney. Festival Theatre, Stratford. 3 July 2011. Performance.

Cohen, Leonard. "Old Ideas Tour." Rogers Arena, Vancouver. 12 Nov. 2012. Performance.

51. Musical Score

Cite a published score as a book. Italicize any work that has a title, such as an opera
or ballet or a named symphony. Don't italicize or put in quotation marks music
identified only by form, number, and key.

Schubert, Franz. Symphony No. 8 in B minor (*Unfinished Symphony*). 1822. Ed. Martin Cusid. New
    York: Norton, 1971. Print.

52. Work of Visual Art

Give creator, title, creation date, medium of composition, the museum or
individual who owns it, and its location.

Pratt, Christopher. *Shop on an Island*. 1969. Oil on canvas. London Regional Art Gallery, London.

53. Work of Visual Art: Direct online access

Add to the standard information for a work of visual art the name of the database or
website (italicized) on which you accessed it. Then list the medium of publication
(*Web*) and access date.

Anghik, Abraham. *Kittigazuti—1918*. 2000. Lithograph. Winnipeg Art Gallery. *The Inuit Shaman*.
    Web. 18 Nov. 2014.

54. Work of Visual Art in a Periodical: Print

Give complete publication information, as for an article.

Greene, Herb. "Grace Slick." 2004. Photograph. *Rolling Stone* 30 Sept. 2004: 102. Print.

55. Comic or Cartoon: Direct online access

Turner, Jason. "Jason and the Comics." Cartoon. *Broken Pencil*. Broken Pencil Magazine, Winter
    2011. Web. 9 May 2014.

56. Map, Chart, or Graphic

Gibsons-Sechelt Sunshine Coast. Map. Coquitlam: Canadian Cartographics, 1996. Print.

57. Map, Chart, or Graphic: Direct online access

"+15 Walkway System." Graphic. *DowntownCalgary.com*. Calgary Downtown Assn., 2010. Web. 21
    May 2014.

58. Photo Essay: Direct online access

"Gallery: G8 and G20 summits." *National Post*. Photo essay. 29 June 2010. Web. 5 July 2014.

59. Image from a Social Networking Site

Gristellar, Ferdinand. *The Gateway Arch*. Photograph. *Ferdinand Gristellar*. Facebook, 7 Aug. 2009. Web. 3 Sept. 2014.

60. Image from a Service or Distributor

Nova Scotia Stock Photos. *Stonehurst South, Lobster Traps and Seascape*. Photograph. Getty Images #427498-001. Web. 3 Apr. 2014.

61. Podcast

Include as much of the following information as you can: author, title, sponsoring organization, website, date posted, medium of publication, and date accessed.

Karchut, Paul. "Parkour Turns the Urban Jungle into a Jungle Gym." Podcast. *Extreme Canada*. CBC Radio, 25 July 2011. Web. 26 July 2011.

62. Slide Show: Direct online access

Erickson, Britta, narr. *Visionaries from the New China*. Slide show. July 2007. Web. 11 Sept. 2014.

63. Entire Website

WebdelSol.Com. Ed. Michael Neff. Web del Sol, 2008. Web. 4 Aug. 2008.

Figure 2.5 shows how to cite a page from a website.

64. Professional Home Page

Provide as much of the following information as you can find:

1. The name of the person who created or put up the home page.
2. The name of the sponsoring organization and the date the page was posted.
3. The date you accessed the material.

Mountain Culture. Banff Centre for Continuing Education, 2006. Web. 22 Nov. 2014.

This is the home page of an institute based at the Banff Centre.

65. Personal Home Page

Hesse, Doug. Home page. 2013. Web. 1 Apr. 2014. <http://portfolio.du.edu/dhesse>.

Provide the URL when a page might be difficult to find.

66. Page from a Website

Provide as much information as you can.

"About the Manitoba Geocaching Association." *Manitoba Geocaching Association*. 2007. Web. 29 Nov. 2012.

Statistics Canada. "Hours Worked and Labour Productivity in the Provinces and Territories." *Daily* 27 Jan. 2010. Web. 14 July 2014.

67. Academic Department Home Page

English Department. Home page. Simon Fraser U, 2014. Web. 26 Feb. 2014.

68. Course Home Page

Cramer, Peter. "Studies in Rhetoric." *Undergraduate Courses*: Fall 2013. Dept. of English, Simon Fraser U, 2013. Web. 15 June 2013.

69. Government or Institutional Website

The Banff Centre. Banff Centre for Continuing Education, 2006. Web. 22 Nov. 2014.

Figure 11.5   Page from a website.

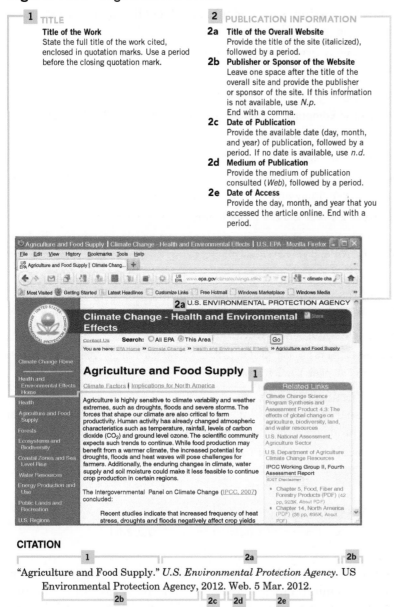

The title of the home page of the Banff Centre for Continuing Education is *The Banff Centre*.

70. Discussion Posting

The name of the bulletin board or discussion list and its sponsor follows the author (if any), title, and type of source.

Firrantello, Larry. "Van Gogh on Prozac." Online posting. *Salon Table Talk*. Salon Media, 23 May 2005. Web. 7 June 2014.

71. Chat or Real-Time Communication

Give the name of the speaker or writer, a title for the event (if any), the webpage or forum, date, publication medium, access date, and URL if needed.

Berzsenyi, Christyne. Online discussion of "Writing to Meet Your Match: Rhetoric, Perceptions, and Self-Presentation for Four Online Daters." *Computers and Writing Online*. AcadianaMoo. 13 May 2007. Web. 14 Feb. 2014.

72. E-mail Message
Start with the name of the writer. Give the title or subject line in quotation marks. Then describe the message and identify the recipient.

Parks, George. "Atwood's Library Tweets: What the Mayor Didn't Know." Message to Mike Liston. 26 July 2011. E-mail.

73. Posting on a Blog

Male, Mack D. "Potholes in Edmonton." *Mastermaq*. N.p., 5 Apr. 2013. Web. 7 Feb. 2014. *N.p.* indicates that the site has no sponsor.

74. Posting on Facebook or Twitter

Adler-Kassner, Linda. "Conversations toward Action." *Council of Writing Program Administrators*. Facebook, 5 Feb. 2010. Web. 6 May 2014.

Reproduce the full text of a tweet and the posted time.

Paikin, Steve (@spaikin). "the demonstration on the esplanade was peaceful. it was like an old sit in. no one was aggressive. and yet riot squad officers moved in." 26 June 2010, 8:42 p.m. Tweet.

75. Published or Unpublished Letter
Note the author and the recipient. Unpublished letters include a description of the format, either *MS* (manuscript, meaning handwritten) or *TS* (typescript).

Irvin, William. Letter to Lesley Osburn. 7 Dec. 2007. TS.

Williams, William Carlos. Letter to his son. 13 Mar. 1935. *Letters of the Century: America 1900–1999*. Ed. Lisa Grunwald and Stephen J. Adler. New York: Dial, 1999. 225–26. Print.

76. Microfiche Collection of Articles
A microfiche is a transparent sheet of film that is read through a special magnifier. Each fiche holds several pages, with each page designated by a grid position.

Smith, David. "Creators Ready to Unveil Super Tape." *Vancouver Sun* 6 Apr. 1988: C12. Microform, *BCARS Newspaper Index* 32 (1990): fiche 2, grid D12.

77. Report or Pamphlet
Use the format for books, to the extent possible.

Assembly of First Nations. *Annual Report 2009–2010*. Ottawa: AFN, 2010. Print.

78. Legal Source
If you are writing for a general audience, use only familiar abbreviations in citing laws, bills, and cases. At a minimum, give the name of a law or case, or the number of a bill and the parliamentary session at which the bill was debated, and the date.

Bill C-50, An Act to Amend the Criminal Code in Respect of Cruelty to Animals. 1st Sess. 38th Parl., 2005. Print.

Legal writers follow the *Canadian Guide to Uniform Legal Citation* (7th edition, 2010) and include abbreviated publication information for laws and court cases.

Canada Labour Code. R.S.C. 1985, c. L-2, S. 12. Print.

Delgamuukw v. British Columbia, [1997] 3 S.C.R. 1010. Print.

79. Interview
Note the type of interview, for example "Telephone" or "Personal" (face-to-face). For a published interview, give the name of the interviewed person first, identify the source as an interview, and then give details as for any published source.

Brooks, Max. Telephone interview. 30 Aug. 2014.

Kettlitz, Nicola. "C-Suite: Interviews with Canada's Top Decision Makers." By Mary Teresa Bitti. *Financial Post* 28 June 2011: FP14. Print.

Pope, Carol. Interview by Amy Standen. *Salon.com*. Salon Media Group, 29 Apr. 2002. Web. 27 Jan. 2014.

80. Lecture, Speech, or Address

Barlow, Maude, Council of Canadians. "Public Health Care." Victoria. 16 Jan. 2012. Speech.

81. Advertisement

McCord Museum. Advertisement. *Walrus* July/Aug. 2011: 24. Print.

BlackBerry PlayBook. Advertisement. *Edmonton Journal*. Postmedia Network,
    2 May 2011. Web. 24 July 2012.

WestJet Airlines. Advertisement. CTV. 24 June 2011. Television.

82. Video Game or Software

Tom Clancy's Splinter Cell Trilogy. Montreal: Ubisoft, 2011. Game.

83. Digital File

To cite a digital file in a version that has not been published on the Web or as a CD (such as a PDF file stored on a computer, a word-processed document, a PowerPoint presentation, an image received as an e-mail attachment, or an MP3 file), follow the guidelines for the kind of work being cited. For an unknown file type, use *Digital file*.

Cite more facts about the file (such as date of last modification), if needed, in the place reserved for version or edition.

Leung, Valerie. "The New Canadian Graphic Novel." File last modified on 24 Feb. 2013. *Microsoft Word* file.

Bayrakdarian, Isabel, perf. "Che Tango Che." *Tango Notturno*. CBC Records, 2006. MP3 file.

Laursen, Finn. "European Union Centre of Excellence (EUCE) Dalhousie University." EUCE Directors Meeting, Ottawa. 18 Jan. 2007. *PowerPoint file*.

84. Nonperiodical Publication on CD, DVD, or Tape

Follow the guidelines for print publications, with these additions: give the vendor's name and the publication date as shown in the source; the publication date or update, if available, if the source is a database; and the publication medium.

Perl, Sondra. *Felt Sense: Guidelines for Composing*. Portsmouth: Boynton, 2004. CD.

85. Work in More Than One Publication Medium

Follow the format for the medium of the component or version that you primarily used. For medium of publication, list all the media you consulted in alphabetical order.

Thomson, A. B. R., and E. A. Shaffer, eds. *First Principles of Gastroenterology*. 3rd ed. Gastroenterology Resource Centre, 2005. Print, Web. 12 Feb. 2014.

This entry follows the format for citing a book that appears independently on the Web, as the online version was the one primarily consulted.

2C   What are MLA guidelines for content or bibliographic notes?

In MLA STYLE, footnotes or endnotes serve two specific purposes: (1) You can use them for ideas and information that do not fit into your paper but are still worth relating; and (2) you can use them for bibliographic information that would intrude if you were to include it in your text. See 3A for advice about formatting notes.

Text Of Paper

Ronald Wright's *Stolen Continents* surprises us by telling the story of the European conquest of North and South America "through Indian eyes."[1]

Content Note—Mla

1. Wright, who was born and educated in England, brings an outsider's point of view to his adopted country, Canada. This may explain his willingness to examine the post-conquest history of the First Nations from a new and disturbing perspective.

Text Of Paper

Barbara Randolph believes that enthusiasm is contagious (65).[1] Many psychologists have found that panic, fear, and rage spread more quickly in crowds than positive emotions do, however.

Bibliographic Note—Mla

1. Others who agree with Randolph include Thurman 21, 84, 155; Kelley 421–25; and Brookes 65–76.

3 A STUDENT'S MLA-STYLE RESEARCH PAPER

Quick Points   You will learn to

➤ Format your paper according to MLA guidelines.

3A What are MLA format guidelines for research papers?

Watch the Video

Check whether your instructor has special instructions for the final draft of your research paper. If there are no special instructions, you can use the MLA STYLE guidelines here. The student paper in 3B was prepared according to MLA guidelines.

■ General formatting instructions—MLA

Use 8½-by-11-inch white paper. Double-space throughout. Use a one-inch margin (2.5 cm) on the left, right, top, and bottom. Don't justify the type.

Drop down ½ inch (1.25 cm) from the top edge of the paper to the name-and-page-number line described below. Then drop down another ½ inch (1.25 cm) to the first line, whether that is a heading, a title, or a line of the text of your paper. For an example, see 3B.

Paragraph indents in the body of the paper and indents in Notes and Works Cited are ½ inch (1.25 cm), or about five characters. This is equivalent to the indent in Microsoft Word for "first line." The indent for a set-off quotation (3B) is 1 inch (2.5 cm), or about ten characters.

Order of parts—MLA

Use this order for the parts of your paper: body of the paper; endnotes, if any (headed "Notes," without quotation marks); Works Cited list; and attachments, if any (such as questionnaires, data sheets, or any other material your instructor tells you to include). Number all pages consecutively.

Name-and-page-number header for all pages—MLA

Use a header consisting of a name-and-page-number line on every page of your paper, including the first, unless your instructor requires otherwise. Most word-processing programs have an "insert header" or "view header" function that automatically places a header ½ inch (1.25 cm) from the top edge of the page. In the header, type your last name, then a one-character space, and then the page number. Align the header an (2.5 cm) inch from the right edge of the paper; in most word-processing programs, this is a "flush right" setting.

First page—MLA

Use a name-and-page-number line. MLA doesn't require a cover page but understands that some instructors do, in which case you should follow your instructor's prescribed format.

If your instructor does not require a cover page, use a four-line heading at the top of the first page. Drop down 1 inch (2.5 cm) from the top of the page. Start each line at the left margin, and include the following information.

Your name (first line)

Your instructor's name (second line)

Your course name and section (third line)

The date you hand in your paper (fourth line)

For the submission date, use either day-month-year form (26 Nov. 2014) or month-day-year style (Nov. 26, 2014) if your instructor prefers it.

On the line below this heading, centre the title of your paper. Don't underline the title or enclose it in quotation marks. On the line below the title, start your paper.

❶ Capitalization Alerts: (1) Use a capital letter for the first word of your title and the first word of a subtitle, if you use one. Start every NOUN, PRONOUN, VERB, ADVERB, ADJECTIVE, and SUBORDINATING CONJUNCTION with a capital letter. Capitalize the last word of your title, no matter what part of speech it is. In a hyphenated compound word (two or more words used together to express one idea), capitalize every word that you would normally capitalize: Father-in-Law.

(2) Don't capitalize an article (*a, an, the*) unless one of the preceding capitalization rules applies to it. Don't capitalize any PREPOSITIONS, no matter how many letters they contain. Don't capitalize COORDINATING CONJUNCTIONS. Don't capitalize the word *to* used in an INFINITIVE. ●

Notes—MLA

If you use a note in your paper (2C), try to structure the sentence so that the note number falls at the end. The ideal place for a note number, which appears slightly raised above the line of words, is after the sentence-ending punctuation. Don't leave a space before the number. Word processing programs have commands for inserting "references" such as notes, and you'll want to choose endnotes rather than footnotes. If you use the references feature to insert a note, the program will generally open a box in which you type the words of your note. The program then saves all your notes together, in order.

Your notes should come on a separate page after the last page of the body of your paper and before the Works Cited list. You may have to cut and paste your notes file into the proper position. Centre the word *Notes* at the top of the page, using the same 1-inch (2.5 cm) margin; don't underline it or enclose it in quotation marks.

Number the notes consecutively throughout the paper, except for notes accompanying tables or figures. Place table or figure notes below the table or illustration. Instead of note numbers, use raised lowercase letters: a, b, c.

■ Works Cited list—MLA

The Works Cited list starts on a new page that has the same name-and-page-number heading as the previous pages. One inch (2.5 cm) below the top edge of the page, centre the words "Works Cited." Don't underline them or put them in quotation marks.

One double space after the Works Cited heading, start the first entry in your list at the left margin. If an entry takes more than one line, indent each subsequent line after the first by ½ inch (1.25 cm). Use no extra spacing between entries.

3B A student's MLA-style research paper

View
the Model
Document

MLA style doesn't require an outline before a research paper. Nevertheless, many instructors want students to submit them. Most instructors prefer the standard traditional outline format that we discuss in 5H. Unless you're told otherwise, use that format.

Some instructors prefer what they consider a more contemporary outline format. Never use it unless it's explicitly assigned. It differs because it outlines the content of the INTRODUCTORY and CONCLUDING PARAGRAPHS, and full wording of the THESIS STATEMENT is placed in the outline of the introductory paragraph. We show an example of this type in the topic outline of Andrei Gurov's paper that follows.

1″ ↕   ½″ ↕
Gurov i

Outline ⟵ Double-space

I. Introduction

    A. The meaning of the term déjà vu

    B. Thesis statement: Although a few people today still believe that feelings of déjà vu have mysterious and supernatural origins, recent research in cognitive

       psychology and the neurosciences has produced laboratory experiments that could explain the phenomenon rationally.

II. Percentage of people who report experiencing déjà vu

III. Misunderstandings of the phenomenon of déjà vu

    A. Precognition

    B. False memory

IV. New psychological and medical theories of déjà vu

    A. Human sight's two pathways

    B. Implanted memories

       1. Natural: from old memories long forgotten

       2. Manipulated: from subliminal stimulation

       3. Inattentional blindness

V. Conclusion

    A. Many years of paranormal explanations of déjà vu

    B. Scientific research after 1980

    C. Much promise for further research

1"   ½"

Gurov 1

Andrei Gurov

Put identifying information in upper left corner.

Professor Ryan

English 101, Section A4

12 Dec. 2014

Use ½-inch top margin, 1-inch bottom and side margins; double-space throughout.

Centre title.

Déjà Vu: At Last a Subject for Serious Study

"Brain hiccup" might be another name for *déjà vu*, French for "already seen." During a moment of déjà vu, a person relives an event that in reality is happening for the first time. The hiccup metaphor seems apt because each modern scientific explanation of the déjà vu phenomenon involves a doubled event, as this paper will demonstrate. However, such modern scientific work was long in coming. In his article "The Déjà Vu Illusion," today's leading researcher in the field, Alan S. Brown at Southern Methodist University, states that "for over 170 years, this most puzzling of memory illusions has intrigued scholars" but was hampered when "during the behaviorist era . . . the plethora of parapsychological and psychodynamic interpretations" multiplied rapidly (256). Thus, notions of the supernatural and magic halted the scientific study of déjà vu in the twentieth century when it was considered an unscientific topic. Although a few people today still believe that feelings of déjà vu have mysterious or supernatural origins, recent research in cognitive psychology and the neurosciences has produced laboratory experiments that could explain the phenomenon rationally.

Quotation marks around phrases show they appeared separately in the source.

The ellipsis indicates words omitted from a quotation.

(Proportions shown in this paper are adjusted to fit space limitations of this book. Follow actual dimensions discussed in this book and your instructor's directions.)

Gurov 2

Some people report never having experienced déjà vu, and the percentages vary for the number of people who report having lived through at least one episode of it. In 2004, Brown reports that of the subjects he has interviewed, an average of 66 percent say that they have had one or more déjà vu experiences during their lives (*Experience* 33). However, in early 2005 in "Strangely Familiar," Uwe Wolfradt reports that "various studies indicate that from 50 to 90 percent of the people [studied] can recall having had at least one such déjà vu incident in their lives."

Perhaps part of the reason for this variation in the range of percentages stems from a general misunderstanding of the phrase *déjà vu*, even by some of the earlier scientific researchers twenty or more years ago. Indeed, in today's society, people throw around the term *déjà vu* without much thought. For example, it is fairly common for someone to see or hear about an event and then say, "Wow. This is déjà vu. I had a dream that this exact same thing happened." However, dreaming about an event ahead of time is a different phenomenon known as *precognition*, which relates to the paranormal experience of extrasensory perception. To date, precognition has never been scientifically demonstrated. As Johnson explains about dreams, however,

> . . . there is usually very little "data," evidence, or documentation to confirm that a Precognition has taken place. If a person learns about some disaster and THEN [author's emphasis] tells people that he/she has foreseen it the day before, that may or may not be true, because there is usually not corroborative confirmation of what the person claims.

Header has student's last name and page number.

This Web source has no page numbers or paragraph numbers.

Use block indent of 1 inch (or about ten spaces) for a quotation longer than four typed lines.

continued >>

Gurov 3

Thus, precognition, a phenomenon talked about frequently but one that has never held up under scientific scrutiny, is definitely not the same as déjà vu.

False memory is another phenomenon mislabelled *déjà vu*. It happens when people are convinced that certain events took place in their lives, even though the events never happened. This occurs when people have strong memories of many unrelated occurrences that suddenly come together into a whole that's very close to the current experience. It seems like a déjà vu experience. This occurs from the

Introductory phrase smoothly leads into direct quotation.

> converging elements of many different but related experiences. When this abstract representation, which has emerged strictly from the melding together of strongly associated elements, happens to correspond to the present experience, a déjà vu may be the outcome.
> (Brown, *Experience* 160)

To illustrate lab-induced false memory, Brown in *The Déjà Vu Experience* cites investigations in which subjects are shown lists of words related to sleep; however, the word *sleep* itself is not on the list. In recalling the list of words, most subjects insist that the word *sleep* was indeed on the list, which means that the memory of a word that was never there is false memory. This is exactly what happens when well-intentioned eyewitnesses believe they recall certain criminal acts even though, in fact, they never saw or experienced the events at all (159).

Put only page number in parentheses when author is named in text.

In the last twenty years especially, new theories have come to the fore as a result of rigorous work from psychological and medical points of view. In *Experience*, Brown surveys the literature and concludes that this relatively young field of investigation is dividing itself into four categories: (1) dual

Gurov 4

processing, (2) memory, (3) neurological, and (4) attentional. This paper briefly discusses the first and second as each relates to the third. Next, I discuss the first as it relates to the second.

Brain-based studies of the human sense of sight are one heavily researched theory of déjà vu that has been partially explained in the last two decades. Such studies focus on the dual pathways by which the sight of an event reaches the brain (Glenn; Carey F1). For example, the left hemisphere processes information from the right eye and the right hemisphere processes information from the left eye. The brain is incapable of storing data with respect to time and is only able to "see" events in relation to others. Each eye interprets data separately, at the same precise time. According to research, the human brain can perceive two visual stimuli at one instant as long as they are "seen" less than 25 milliseconds apart. Since the human brain is capable of interpreting both signals within this time, when events are perceived normally, they are seen and recognized by the brain as one single event (Weiten 69, 97–99, 211).

Put author and page number in parentheses when author is not named in the sentence.

Occasionally, however, the neurological impulses that carry data from each eye to the brain are delayed. As Johnson explains, the person might be fatigued or have had his or her attention seriously distracted (as when crossing the street at a dangerous intersection). As a result, one signal may reach the brain in under 25 milliseconds, while the other signal is slowed and reaches the brain slightly more than 25 milliseconds later. Even a few milliseconds' delay makes the second incoming signal arrive late—and, without fail, the brain interprets the stimuli as two separate events rather than one event. The person thus has the sensation of having seen the event before because the brain has recognized the milliseconds-later event as a memory.

Paragraph summarizes several pages of source material, as parenthetical citation shows.

continued >>

Implanted memories are another well-researched explanation for the déjà vu phenomenon. Examples of implanted memories originate in both the natural and the lab-induced experiences of people. For instance, perhaps a person walks into the kitchen of a new friend for the first time and, although the person has never been there before, the person feels certain that he or she has. With hypnosis and other techniques, researchers could uncover that the cupboards are almost exactly like those that the person had forgotten were in the kitchen of the person's grandparents' house and that the scent of baking apple pie is identical to the smell the person loved when walking into the grandparents' home during holidays (Carey F1). Professor Anne Cleary and her colleagues conducted an experiment in which students studied images of simple scenes and then were shown a second set of images. Some of the second set were made to resemble the original study images. Students tended to "remember" those scenes that had elements in common, even if these elements were not identical (1083).

Thomas McHugh, a researcher at MIT, believes he has even discovered the specific "memory circuit" in the brain that is the source of this kind of déjà vu (Lemonick). This circuit allows people to complete memories with just a single cue. For example, you can remember much about a football game you saw even if someone just mentions the two teams involved. Sometimes, however, the circuit "misfires," and it signals that a new memory is actually part of the pattern of an old one. Researchers Akira O'Connor, Colin Lever, and Chris Moulin claim that the false sensations of memory differ from those of familiarity. They call the former "déjà vécu," and

Gurov 6

note serious cases in which people live much of their life in this state. It remains to be seen whether their distinction will be confirmed.

Wolfradt describes a lab-induced experiment in which psychologist Larry L. Jacoby in 1989 manipulated a group of subjects so that he could implant a memory that would lead to a déjà vu experience for each of them. He arranged for his subjects to assemble in a room equipped with a screen in front. He flashed on the screen one word so quickly that no one was consciously aware they had seen the word. Jacoby was certain, however, that the visual centres of the brain of each subject had indeed "seen" the word. Later, when he flashed the word leaving it on the screen long enough for the subjects to consciously see it, everyone indicated they had seen the word somewhere before. All the subjects were firmly convinced that the first time they had seen the word, it absolutely was not on the screen at the front of the room they were in. Some became annoyed at being asked over and over. Since Jacoby's work, lab-induced memory research has become very popular in psychology. In fact, it has been given its own name: *priming*. Alan Brown and Elizabeth Marsh confirmed Jacoby's findings in three follow-up studies (38–41).

Inattention, or what some researchers call "inattentional blindness," is also an extensively researched explanation for the déjà vu experience. Sometimes people can see objects without any impediment right before them but still not process the objects because they're paying attention to something else (Brown, *Experience* 181). The distraction might be daydreaming, a sudden lowering of energy, or simply being drawn to another

continued >>

object in the environment. As David Glenn explains in "The Tease of Memory":

> Imagine that you drive through an unfamiliar town but pay little attention because you're talking on a cellphone. If you then drive back down the same streets a few moments later, this time focusing on the landscape, you might be prone to experience déjà vu. During your second pass, the visual information is consciously processed in the hippocampus [of the brain] but feels falsely "old" because the images from your earlier drive still linger in your short term memory.

The busy lifestyle today would seem to lead to many distractions of perception and thus to frequent experiences of déjà vu; however, these are no more frequently reported than any other causes reported concerning déjà vu.

One compelling laboratory experiment studying inattention is described by Carey in "Déjà Vu: If It All Seems Familiar, There May Be a Reason." He recounts a test with many college students from Duke University in Durham, North Carolina. The students were asked to look at a group of photographs of the campus of a university in another US state, that were flashed before them at a very quick speed. A small black or white cross was superimposed on each photograph, and the students were instructed to find the cross and focus on it (F6). Brown in *Experience* explains that the researchers assumed that the quick speed at which the photographs had been shown would result in no one's having noticed the background scenes. A week's time passed, and the same students were shown the pictures once again, this

Gurov 8

time without the crosses. Almost all insisted that they had been to the college campus shown in the photos, which was physically impossible for that many students since they lived in Durham, North Carolina, and the college in the photographs was in Dallas, Texas (182–83). This means that the scenes in the photographs did indeed register in the visual memories of the students in spite of the quick speed and the distraction of looking only for the crosses.

The worlds of psychology and neurology have learned much since the age of paranormal interpretations of déjà vu experiences, starting around 1935. That is when rational science energetically began its disciplined investigations of brain-based origins of the déjà vu phenomenon. Concepts such as dual processing of sight, implanted memories, and inattentional blindness, among other theories, have gone far in opening the door to the possibilities of many more inventive theories to explain incidents of déjà vu. The leading researcher in the field today, Alan S. Brown, is among the strongest voices urging a vast expansion of investigations into this still relatively unexplored phenomenon. He is optimistic this will happen, given his whimsical remark to Carlin Flora of *Psychology Today:* "We are always fascinated when the brain goes haywire." Researchers conducting these studies might watch for the unsettling experiences of other investigators who "have had déjà vu about having déjà vu" (Phillips 29).

Concluding paragraph summarizes paper.

continued >>

Gurov 9

Works Cited

Brown, Alan S. *The Déjà Vu Experience: Essays in Cognitive Psychology*. New York: Psychology, 2004. Print.

---. "The Déjà Vu Illusion." *Current Directions in Psychological Science* 13.6 (2004): 256–59. Print.

--- and Elizabeth J. Marsh. "Digging into Deja Vu: Recent Research on Possible Mechanisms." *The Psychology of Learning and Motivation: Advances in Research and Theory*. Ed. Brian H. Ross. Burlington: Academic, 2010, 33–62. *LexisNexis*. Web. 20 Nov. 2014.

Carey, Benedict. "Déjà Vu: If It All Seems Familiar, There May Be a Reason." *New York Times* 14 Sept. 2004: F1+. *LexisNexis*. Web. 11 Nov. 2014.

Cleary, Anne M., Anthony J. Ryals, and Jason S. Nomi. "Can Déjà Vu Result from Similarity to a Prior Experience? Support for the Similarity Hypothesis of Déjà Vu." *Psychonomic Bulletin & Review* 16.6 (2009): 1082–88. Web. 3 Dec. 2014.

Flora, Carlin. "Giving Déjà Vu Its Due." *Psychology Today* Mar.–Apr. 2005: 27. *Academic Search Premier*. Web. 7 Nov. 2014.

Glenn, David. "The Tease of Memory." *Chronicle of Higher Education* 23 July 2004: A12. Print.

Johnson, C. "A Theory on the Déjà Vu Phenomenon." *MB-soft.com*, 8 Dec. 2001. Web. 20 Nov. 2014.

Lemonick, Michael D. "Explaining Déjà Vu." *Time* 20 Aug. 2007. *Academic Search Premier*. Web. 5 Dec. 2014.

O'Connor, Akira R., Colin Lever, and Chris J. A. Moulin. "Novel Insights into False Recollection: A Model of Déjà Vécu." *Cognitive Neuropsychiatry* 15.1–3 (2010): 118–44. Web. 14 Nov. 2014.

Phillips, Helen. "Looks Familiar." *New Scientist* 201.2701 (2009): 28–31. Web. 20 Nov. 2014.

Weiten, Wayne. *Psychology: Themes and Variations*. Belmont: Wadsworth, 2005. Print.

Wolfradt, Uwe. "Strangely Familiar." *Scientific American Mind* 16.1 (2005): 32–37. *Academic Search Elite*. Web. 7 Nov. 2014.

Works Cited begins on a new page. Note that heading is centred.

Three hyphens indicate same author as entry above.

Double-space throughout.

List sources in alphabetical order.

The APA Style of Documentation

1 APA IN-TEXT CITATIONS.

Quick Points   You will learn to

➤ Cite sources in your writing using APA style.

1A   What is APA documentation style?

The American Psychological Association (APA) sponsors the APA STYLE,* a DOCUMENTATION system widely used in the social sciences. APA style has two equally important features that need to appear in research papers.

1. Within the body of your paper, use IN-TEXT CITATIONS, in parentheses, to acknowledge your SOURCES. Sections 1B and 1C explain the proper way to provide in-text citations.
2. At the end of the paper, provide a list of the sources you used—and only those sources. Title this list, which contains complete bibliographic information about each source, "References." Section 2 provides examples.

See Section 3 for a sample student paper in APA style.

1B   What are APA in-text parenthetical citations?

APA style requires parenthetical in-text citations that identify a source by the author's name and the copyright year. If there is no author, use a shortened version of the title. In addition, APA style requires page numbers for DIRECT QUOTATIONS, but it recommends using them also for PARAPHRASES and SUMMARIES. Find out your instructor's preference to avoid any problems. Put page numbers in parentheses, using the abbreviation *p.* before a single page number and *pp.* when the material you're citing falls on more than one page. Separate the parts of a parenthetical citation with commas. End punctuation always follows the citation unless it's a long quotation set in block style.

   If you refer to a work more than once in a paragraph, APA style recommends giving the author's name and the date at the first mention and then using only the

---

* Words printed in SMALL CAPITAL LETTERS are discussed elsewhere in the text and are

name after that. However, if you're citing two or more works by the same author, include the date in each citation to identify which work you're citing. When two or more sources have the same last name, use both first and last names in the text or first initial(s) and last names in parentheses.

If you refer to a work more than once in a paragraph, APA style recommends giving the author's name and the date at the first mention and then using only the name after that. However, if you're citing two or more works by the same author, include the date in each citation to identify which work you're citing. When two or more sources have the same last name, use both first and last names in the text or first initial(s) and last names in parentheses.

1C   What are APA guidelines for in-text citations?

This section shows how to cite various kinds of sources in the body of your paper. The directory at the beginning of this tab corresponds to the numbered examples in this section.

1. **Paraphrased or Summarized Source**

   Modern technologies and social media tend to fragment individual identities (Conley, 2009).

   Author name and date cited in parentheses.

   Dalton Conley (2009) contends that modern technologies and social media fragment individual identities.

   Author name cited in text; date cited in parentheses.

2. **Source of a Short Quotation**

   Approaches adopted from business to treat students as consumers "do not necessarily yield improved outcomes in terms of student learning" (Arum & Roksa, 2011, p. 137).

   Author names, date, and page reference cited in parentheses.

   Arum and Roksa (2011) find that approaches adopted from business to treat students as consumers "do not necessarily yield improved outcomes in terms of student learning" (p. 137).

   Author names cited in text, followed by the date cited in parentheses incorporated into the words introducing the quotation; page number in parentheses immediately following the quotation.

3. **Source of a Long Quotation**

When you use a quotation of forty or more words, set it off in block style indented ½ inch (1.25 cm) from the left margin. Don't use quotation marks. Place the parenthetical reference one space after the end punctuation of the quotation's last sentence.

   Although some have called for regulating online games, others see such actions as unwarranted:

   > Any activity when taken to excess can cause problems in a person's life, but it is unlikely that there would be legislation against, for example,

people excessively reading or exercising. There is no argument that online gaming should be treated any differently. (Griffiths, 2010, pp. 38–39)

Author name, date, and page reference are cited in parentheses following the end punctuation.

4. One Author

One of his questions is, "What actually happened in Walkerton?" (O'Connor, 2002, p. 2).

In a parenthetical reference in APA style, a comma and a space separate a name from a year and a year from a page reference.

5. Two Authors

Give both names in each citation.

One report describes 2123 occurrences (Krait & Cooper, 2003).

The results that Krait and Cooper (2003) report would not support the conclusions Davis and Sherman (1999) draw in their review of the literature.

When you write a parenthetical in-text citation naming two (or more) authors, use an ampersand (&) between the final two names, but write out the word *and* for any reference in your own sentence.

6. Three, Four, or Five Authors

Use all the authors' last names in the first reference. In all subsequent references, use only the first author's last name followed by *et al.* (meaning "and others"). No period follows *et*, but one always follows *al.*

First Reference

In one study, only 30% of the survey population could name the most commonly spoken languages in five Middle Eastern countries (Ludwig, Rodriquez, Novak, & Ehlers, 2008).

Subsequent Reference

Ludwig et al. (2008) found that most people surveyed could identify the language spoken in Saudi Arabia.

7. Six or More Authors

Name the first author followed by *et al.* in all in-text references, including the first.

These injuries can lead to an inability to perform athletically, in addition to initiating degenerative changes at the joint level (Mandelbaum et al., 2005).

8. Author(s) with Two or More Works in the Same Year

If you use more than one source written in the same year by the same author(s), alphabetize the works by title for the REFERENCES list, and assign letters in alphabetical order to each work: (2007a), (2007b), (2007c). Use the year–letter combination in parenthetical references. Note that a citation of two or more such works lists the year extensions in alphabetical order.

> Most recently, Torrevillas (2007c) draws new conclusions from the results of eight experiments conducted with experienced readers (Torrevillas, 2007a, 2007b).

9. Two or More Authors with the Same Last Name

Include first initials for every in-text citation of authors who share a last name. Use the initials appearing in the References list. (In the second example, a parenthetical citation, the name order is alphabetical, as explained in item 12.)

> R. A. Smith (2008) and C. Smith (1999) both confirm these results.

> These results have been confirmed independently (C. Smith, 1999; R. A. Smith, 2008).

10. Group or Corporate Author

If you use a source in which the "author" is a corporation, agency, or group, an in-text reference gives that name as author. Use the full name in each citation, unless an abbreviated version of the name is likely to be familiar to your audience. In that case, use the full name and give its abbreviation at the first citation; then, use the abbreviation for subsequent citations.

> After 1949 the federal government took over responsibility for most public housing projects (Canada Mortgage and Housing Corporation [CMHC], 1990).

> In subsequent citations, use the abbreviated form alone.

11. Work Listed by Title

If no author is named, use a shortened form of the title for in-text citations. Ignoring *A*, *An*, or *The*, make the first word the one by which you alphabetize the title in your References list. The following example refers to an article fully titled "Are You a Day or Night Person?"

> Scientists group people as "larks" or "owls" on the basis of whether individuals are more efficient in the morning or at night ("Are You," 1989).

12. Two or More Sources in One Reference

If more than one source has contributed to an idea or opinion in your paper, cite them alphabetically by author in one set of parentheses; separate each source of information with a semicolon.

> Conceptions of personal space vary among cultures (Morris, 1977; Worchel & Cooper, 1983).

13. Personal Communication, Including E-Mail and Other Nonretrievable Sources

Telephone calls, personal letters, interviews, and e-mail messages are "personal communications" that your readers can't access or retrieve. Acknowledge personal communications in parenthetical references, but never include them in your References list at the end of your paper.

Recalling his first summer at camp, one person said, "The proximity of 12 other kids made me—an only child with older, quiet parents—frantic for eight weeks" (A. Weiss, personal communication, January 12, 2011).

14. Retrievable Online Sources

When you quote, paraphrase, or summarize an online source that is available to others, cite the author (if any) or title and the date as you would for a print source, and include the work in your References list.

It is possible that similarity in personality is important in having a happy marriage (Luo & Clonen, 2005, p. 324).

15. Sources with No Page Numbers

If a source doesn't provide page numbers, use the paragraph number preceded by the abbreviation *para*. If there are no printed paragraph numbers, count down from the beginning of the document, or cite the closest subheading and count down paragraphs from that.

(Daniels, 2010, para. 4)

(Sanz, 2009, Introduction)

(Herring, 2011)

16. Source Lines for Graphics and Table Data

If you use a graphic from another source or create a table using data from another source, provide a note at the bottom of the table or graphic, crediting the original author and the copyright holder. Here are examples of two source notes, one for a graphic using data from an article, the other for a graphic reprinted from a book.

Graphic Using Data from an Article

Note. The data in columns 1 and 2 are from "Advance Organizers in Advisory Reports: Selective Reading, Recall, and Perception," by L. Lagerwerf et al., 2008, *Written Communication, 25*(1), p. 68. Copyright 2008 by Sage Publications.

Graphic from a Book

Note. Figure 36.7, "Locating and citing source information for an online video," from *Simon & Schuster Handbook for Writers*, 6th Canadian ed. (p. 496), by L. Q. Troyka and D. Hesse, with C. Strom, 2013, Toronto: Pearson. Copyright 2013 by Pearson Canada Inc. Reprinted with permission.

2 APA REFERENCES LIST

Quick Points You will learn to

➤ Cite sources in your writing using APA style.

Watch
the Video

The REFERENCES list at the end of your research paper provides complete bibliographic information for readers who may want to access the SOURCES you drew on to write your paper.

Include in the References list all the sources you quote, paraphrase, or summarize in your paper so that readers can find the same sources with reasonable effort. Never include in your References list any source that's not generally available to other people (see item 13 in 1C).

2A What are APA guidelines for a References list?

An APA References list needs to meet specific requirements in terms of its title, placement, contents and format, spacing, arrangement, type and order of elements included for each kind of entry, punctuation, capitalization, and so on. Quick Box 2.1 provides details.

Quick Box 2.1

Guidelines for an APA-style References list

TITLE
The title is "References," centred, without quotation marks, italics, or underlining.

PLACEMENT OF LIST
Start a new page numbered sequentially with the rest of the paper, immediately after the body of the paper.

CONTENTS AND FORMAT
Include all quoted, paraphrased, or summarized sources in your paper that are not personal communications; your instructor may tell you also to include all the references you have simply consulted. Start each entry on a new line, and double-space all lines. Use a *hanging indent* style: The first line of each entry begins flush left at the margin, and all other lines are indented ½ inch (1.25 cm).
Wolfe, C. R. (2011). Argumentation across the curriculum. *Written Communication, 28,* 193–218.

SPACING AFTER PUNCTUATION
APA calls for one space after commas, periods, question marks, and colons. However, in draft papers submitted for publication, it recommends double-spacing after punctuation that ends a sentence.

ARRANGEMENT OF ENTRIES
Alphabetize by the author's last name. If no author is named, alphabetize by the first significant word (ignore *A, An,* or *The*) in the title of the work.

AUTHORS' NAMES
Use last names, first initials, and middle initials, if any. Reverse the order for all authors' names, and use an ampersand (&) before the last author's name: Mills, J. F., & Holahan, R. H.

Give names in the order in which they appear on the work. Use a comma between each author's last name and first initial and after each complete name except the last. Use a period after the last author's name. If there are eight or more authors, give the first six authors' names, insert a comma and an ellipsis, and end with the last author's name, but don't use an ampersand. When the author name is the same as the publisher, write "author" at the end of the citation.

DATES
Date information follows the name information and is enclosed in parentheses. Place a period followed by one space after the closing parenthesis.

For books, articles in journals that have volume numbers, and many other print and nonprint sources, the year of publication or production is the date to use. For articles from most general-circulation magazines and newspapers, use the year followed by a comma and then the exact date that appears on the issue (month, month and day, or season, depending on the frequency of the publication). Capitalize any words in dates, and use no abbreviations.

CAPITALIZATION OF TITLES
For book, article, and chapter titles, capitalize the first word, the first word after a colon between a title and subtitle, and any proper nouns. For names of journals and proceedings of meetings, capitalize the first word; all nouns, verbs, adverbs, and adjectives; and any other words four or more letters long.

SPECIAL TREATMENT OF TITLES
Use no special treatment for titles of shorter works (poems, short stories, essays, articles, webpages). Italicize titles of longer works (books, newspapers, journals, or websites). If an italic typeface is unavailable, underline the title and the end punctuation using one unbroken line.

Do not drop any words (such as *A*, *An*, or *The*) from the titles of periodicals such as newspapers, magazines, and journals.

ABBREVIATIONS OF MONTHS
Do not abbreviate the names of months in any context.

PAGE NUMBERS
Use all digits, omitting none. For references to books and newspapers only, use *p.* and *pp.* before page numbers. List all discontinuous pages, with numbers separated by commas: pp. 32, 44–45, 47–49, 53.

PUBLICATION INFORMATION
See 2B for how to cite articles from periodicals (both print or online), books (both print or digital), images and video, other Web sources, and miscellaneous sources.

2B   What are APA examples for sources in a References list?

The directory at the beginning of this tab corresponds to the numbered examples in this section. For quick help deciding which example you should follow, see the decision flowchart in Figure 2.1. You can find other examples in the *Publication Manual of the American Psychological Association* (6th edition) or at the APA website, <http://www.apastyle.org>.

Citations for periodical articles contain four major parts: author, date, title of article, and publication information (usually, the periodical title, volume number, page numbers, and sometimes a DOI, or digital object identifier).

Quick Box 2.2 summarizes the basic entries for periodical entries. Variations on the basic entries follow the Quick Box.

Quick Box 2.2

Basic entries for periodical articles—APA

1. Articles with a DOI: Print or online

A DOI (digital object identifier) is a numerical code sometimes assigned to journal articles. The DOI for an article will be the same even if the article appears in different versions, including print and online. (To see where you can find an article's DOI, refer to Figure 2.2.) If a source contains a DOI, simply conclude the citation with the letters "doi" followed by a colon, then the number. Always use this citation method with a source that has a DOI.

AUTHOR · DATE · ARTICLE TITLE

Agliata, A. K., Tantelff-Dunn, S., & Renk, K. (2007). Interpretation of

PUBLICATION INFORMATION

teasing during early adolescence. *Journal of Clinical Psychology, 63*(1), 23–30.

DOI

doi: 10.1002/jclp.20302

2. Articles with no DOI: Print

For print articles without a doi, use this format.

AUTHOR · DATE · ARTICLE TITLE

Wood, W., Witt, M. G., & Tam, L. (2005). Changing circumstances,

PERIODICAL TITLE · VOLUME NUMBER · PAGE RANGE

disrupting habits. *Journal of Personality and Social Psychology*, 88, 918–933.

3. Articles with no DOI: Online

For online articles without a DOI, retrieval information begins with the words "Retrieved from," then the URL of the periodical's Web home page, and, occasionally, additional information. If you found the article through an online subscription database, do a Web search for the URL of the periodical's home page, and include the home page URL. If you can't find the periodical's home page, then name the database in your retrieval statement: Abstract retrieved from Psyc-INFO database. (See citation 17.) If a URL must be divided between two or more lines, break the address only before slashes or punctuation marks.

Retrieval date: Include the date you retrieved the information only if the item does not have a publication date or is likely to be changed in the future (such as a prepublication version of an article or a wiki; see citation 6).

AUTHOR · DATE · ARTICLE TITLE

Eagleman, D. (2011, July/August). The brain on trial.

MAGAZINE TITLE · ONLINE RETRIEVAL INFORMATION

The Atlantic. Retrieved from http://www.theatlantic.com

Do not add a period after a URL. APA keeps *The, A,* and *An* in titles.

Figure 2.1   Decision-making flowchart for APA References citations.

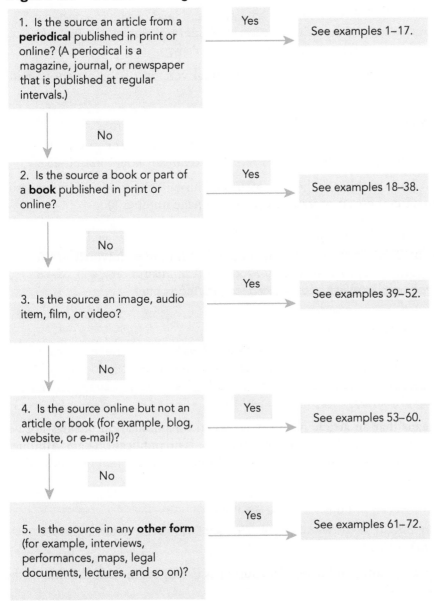

1. Is the source an article from a **periodical** published in print or online? (A periodical is a magazine, journal, or newspaper that is published at regular intervals.)

Yes → See examples 1–17.

No ↓

2. Is the source a book or part of a **book** published in print or online?

Yes → See examples 18–38.

No ↓

3. Is the source an image, audio item, film, or video?

Yes → See examples 39–52.

No ↓

4. Is the source online but not an article or book (for example, blog, website, or e-mail)?

Yes → See examples 53–60.

No ↓

5. Is the source in any **other form** (for example, interviews, performances, maps, legal documents, lectures, and so on)?

Yes → See examples 61–72.

Periodicals—APA References

1. **Article in a Journal with Continuous Pagination: Print**

Williams, B. T. (2010). Seeking new worlds: The study of writing beyond our classrooms. *College Composition and Communication, 62,* 127–146.

Continuous pagination means that page numbers in each issue of a volume begin where the page numbers in the previous issue left off. So, for example, if issue one stopped at page 125, issue two would start at page 126. Just give the volume number, italicized, after the journal title.

2. **Article in a Journal with Continuous Pagination: Online, with DOI**

Gurung, R., & Vespia, K. (2007). Looking good, teaching well? Linking liking, looks, and learning. *Teaching of Psychology, 34,* 5–10. doi: 10.1207/s15328023top3401_2

3. Article in a Journal with Continuous Pagination: Online, no DOI

Pollard, R. (2002). Evidence of a reduced home field advantage when a team moves to a new stadium. *Journal of Sports Sciences, 20,* 969–974. Retrieved from http://www.tandf.co.uk/journals/rjsp

No retrieval date is included because the final version of the article is being referenced.

4. Article in a Journal That Pages Each Issue Separately: Print

Peters, B. (2011). Lessons about writing to learn from a university–high school partnership. *WPA: Writing Program Administration, 34*(2), 59–88.

Give the volume number, italicized, with the journal title, followed by the issue number in parentheses (not italicized), and the page number(s).

5. Article in a Journal That Pages Each Issue Separately: Online, with no DOI

Peters, B. (2011). Lessons about writing to learn from a university–high school partnership. *WPA: Writing Program Administration, 34*(2), 59–88. Retrieved from http://wpacouncil.org/journal/index.html

6. In-press Article: Online

George, S. (in press). How accurately should we estimate the anatomical source of exhaled nitric oxide? *Journal of Applied Physiology.* doi:10.1152 /japplphysiol.00111.2008. Retrieved February 2014 from http://jap.physiology.org/papbyrecent.shtml

In press means that an article has been accepted for publication but has not yet been published in its final form. Therefore, there is no publication date. Although the article has a DOI, it also has a "retrieved from" statement that includes a date, in case anything changes.

7. Article in a Weekly or Biweekly Magazine: Print

Johnson, B. D. (2007, November 26). Why six Dylans are better than one. *Maclean's, 120,* 43–46.

Give the year, month, and date. If no author is listed, begin with the title of the article.

Too many suits, and not enough skirts in the boardrooms. (2011, November 26). *The Economist, 401,* 73–74.

8. Article in a Weekly or Biweekly Magazine: Online

MacQueen, K. (2011, June 8). The case for a national drug plan. *Macleans. ca.* Retrieved from http://www.macleans.ca

9. Article in a Monthly or Bimonthly Periodical: Print

Goetz, T. (2011, July). The feedback loop. *Wired, 19*(7), 126–133.

Give the year and month(s). Insert the volume number, italicized with the periodical title. Put the issue number in parentheses; do not italicize it.

10. Article in a Newspaper: Print

McCarthy, S. (2011, June 28). Sale puts Ottawa out of nuclear business. *The Globe and Mail,* pp. A1–A2.

Figure 2.2   Journal article available (a) online and (b) in print, with a DOI.

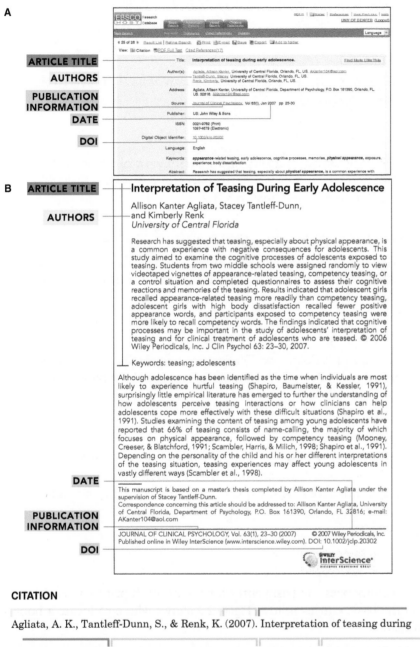

CITATION

Agliata, A. K., Tantleff-Dunn, S., & Renk, K. (2007). Interpretation of teasing during

early adolescence. *Journal of Clinical Psychology, 63*(1), 23–30. doi: 10.1002/jcpl.2302

Use the abbreviation *p.* (or *pp.* for more than one page) for newspapers. If no author is listed, begin with the title of the article.

Private water may violate Constitution. (2002, November 27). *The Ottawa Citizen*, pp. A1, A7.

11. **Article in a Newspaper: Online**

Perkins, T. (2005, November 22). Conrad Black's Chicago court date set for Tuesday: U.S. Attorney's office. *CP Online*. Retrieved from http://www. thecanadianpress.com

12. **Unsigned Editorial**

    London doomed to repeat its history on heritage [Editorial]. (2011, July 20). *The London Free Press*, p. B8.

13. **Letter to the Editor**

    Nichols, G. (2013, April). [Letter to the editor]. *The Walrus*. Retrieved from http://www.thewalrus.ca

14. **Book Review**

    Toews, W. (1995, August 26). Politics of the mind [Review of the book *They say you're crazy: How the world's most powerful psychiatrists decide who's normal*]. *Winnipeg Free Press*, p. C3.

15. **Article in a Looseleaf Collection of Reprinted Articles**

    Hayden, T. (2002). The age of robots. In E. Goldstein (Ed.), *Applied Science 2002. SIRS 2002*, Article 66. (Reprinted from *U.S. News & World Report*, pp. 44–50, 2001, April 23).

16. **Online Magazine Content Not Found in Print Version**

    Smith, D. (2013, April 10). Politics on TV: The menace of temporary foreign pilots. [Supplemental material]. *Macleans.ca*. Retrieved from http://www2.macleans.ca

17. **Abstract as a Secondary Source: Online**

    Walther, J. B., Van Der Heide, B., Kim, S., Westerman, D., & Tong, S. (2008). The role of friends' appearance and behavior on evaluations of individuals on Facebook: Are we known by the company we keep? *Human Communication Research, 34(1)*, 28–49. Abstract retrieved from PsycINFO database.

Books—APA References

Quick Box 2.3 summarizes the basic entry for books, both print and electronic. Variations on the basic entries follow. Figure 2.3 shows where to locate a book's citation information.

Quick Box 2.3

Basic entries for books—APA

All citations for books have four main parts: author, date, title, and publication information. For traditional print books, publication information includes place of publication and the name of the publisher. For electronic versions of books, publication information also includes retrieval information.

PLACE OF PUBLICATION

For US publishers, give the city and state, using two-letter postal abbreviations listed in most dictionaries. For Canadian cities, Canadian writers normally add the two-letter postal abbreviation for the province or territory. For publishers in other countries, give city and country spelled out. However, if the state or country is part of the publisher's name, omit it after the name of the city.

PUBLISHERS

Use a shortened version of the publisher's name except for an association, corporation, or university press. Drop Co., Inc., Publishers, and the like, but retain *Books* or *Press*.

AUTHOR	DATE	TITLE	PUBLICATION INFORMATION

Kingwell, M. (1999). *Marginalia: A cultural reader.* Toronto, ON: Penguin Books.

RETRIEVAL INFORMATION FOR ELECTRONIC BOOKS

If a book has a DOI (Digital Object Identifier), include that number after the title, preceded by *doi* and a colon. Most electronic books do not have a DOI. When there is no DOI, use "Retrieved from" followed by the URL where you accessed the book.

Figure 2.3   Citation information for a print book—APA.

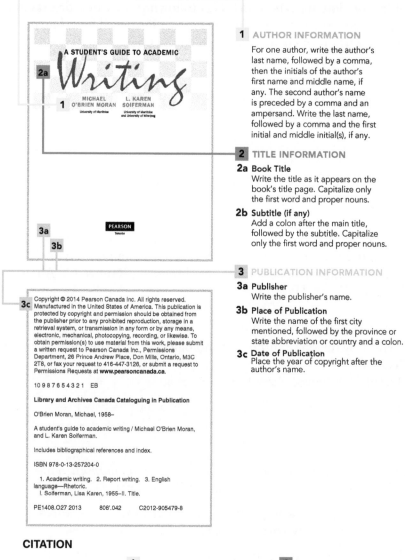

1 AUTHOR INFORMATION
For one author, write the author's last name, followed by a comma, then the initials of the author's first name and middle name, if any. The second author's name is preceded by a comma and an ampersand. Write the last name, followed by a comma and the first initial and middle initial(s), if any.

2 TITLE INFORMATION

2a Book Title
Write the title as it appears on the book's title page. Capitalize only the first word and proper nouns.

2b Subtitle (if any)
Add a colon after the main title, followed by the subtitle. Capitalize only the first word and proper nouns.

3 PUBLICATION INFORMATION

3a Publisher
Write the publisher's name.

3b Place of Publication
Write the name of the first city mentioned, followed by the province or state abbreviation or country and a colon.

3c Date of Publication
Place the year of copyright after the author's name.

CITATION

O'Brien Moran, M., & Soiferman, L.K. (2014). *A student's guide to academic writing.* Toronto, ON: Pearson Canada.

18. **Book by One Author: Print**

Trudeau, P. E. *Federalism and the French Canadians*. Toronto, ON: Macmillan Canada.

19. **Book by One Author: Online**

Eaton, A. W. (1889). *Acadian legends and lyrics*. Retrieved from http://www.canadiana.org

Some books are increasingly available through library databases. APA does not include the name or location of the publisher in citations for online books.

20. **Book by One Author: E-book or E-reader**

Trudeau, P. E. *Federalism and the French Canadians*. [Kobo version]. Retrieved from http://www.kobo.com

The name of the version appears in brackets following the title, for example [Kobo version], [Kindle version], or [Nook version]. "Retrieved from" precedes the URL of the site from which you downloaded the book.

21. **Book by Two Authors**

Doob, A., & Cesaroni, C. (2004). *Responding to youth crime in Canada*. Toronto, ON: University of Toronto Press.

22. **Book by Three to Seven Authors**

Lynam, J. K., Ndiritu, C. G., & Mbabu, A. N. (2004). *Transformation of agricultural research systems in Africa: Lessons from Kenya*. East Lansing, MI: Michigan State University Press.

For a book by three to seven authors, include all the names. For a book by eight or more authors, use the first six names followed by a comma, three ellipsis points, and the last author's name: Smith, A., Jones, B., Ramos, C., Abrams, D., Sagan, E., Chin, F., . . . Havel, J.

23. **Two or More Books by the Same Author(s)**

Arrange references by the same author chronologically, with the earlier date of publication listed first.

Atwood, M. (1972). *Survival*. Toronto, ON: Anansi.

Atwood, M. (1981). *True stories*. Toronto, ON: Oxford University Press.

24. **Book by a Group or Corporate Author**

American Psychological Association. (2009). *Publication manual of the American Psychological Association* (6th ed.). Washington, DC: Author.

CBC Massey Lectures Series. (2007). *The Lost Massey Lectures: Recovered classics from five great thinkers*. Toronto, ON: Anansi.

Cite the full name of the corporate author first. If the author is also the publisher, use the word *Author* as the name of the publisher. (The CBC Massey Lectures Series is considered the corporate author of the book in the second item.)

25. **Book with No Author Named**

   The Chicago manual of style (16th ed.). (2010). Chicago, IL: University of Chicago Press.

Ignoring *The*, this would be alphabetized under *Chicago*, the first important word in the title.

26. **Book with an Author and an Editor**

   Trudeau, P. E. (1998). *The Essential Trudeau* (R. Graham, Ed.). Toronto, ON: McClelland & Stewart.

27. **Translation**

   Tremblay, M. (2007). *Assorted candies for the theatre* (L. Gaboriau, Trans.). Vancouver, BC: Talonbooks.

28. **Work in Several Volumes or Parts**

   Chrisley, R. (Ed.). (2000). *Artificial intelligence: Critical concepts* (Vols. 1–4). London, UK: Routledge.

29. **Anthology or Edited Book**

   Nurse, D. B. (Ed.). (2006). *Revival: An anthology of the best Black Canadian writing*. Toronto, ON: McClelland & Stewart.

30. **Selection in an Anthology or an Edited Book**

Give the author, date, and title of the selection first. The word *In* introduces the larger work from which the selection is taken. Note that names are inverted only in the author position; in all other circumstances, they are written in standard form.

   Clarke, G. E. (2006). King bee blues. In D. B. Nurse (Ed.), *Revival: An anthology of the best Black Canadian writing* (pp. 229–230). Toronto, ON: McClelland & Stewart.

31. **Selection in a Work Already Listed in References**

Provide full information for the cited anthology (second example), along with information about the individual selection. Put entries in alphabetical order.

   Bond, R. (2004). The night train at Deoli. In A. Chaudhuri (Ed.), *The Vintage book of modern Indian literature* (pp. 415–418). New York, NY: Vintage Books.

   Chaudhuri, A. (Ed.). (2004). *The Vintage book of modern Indian literature*. New York, NY: Vintage Books.

32. **Second or Later Edition**

   Gibaldi, J. (2009). *MLA handbook for writers of research papers* (7th ed.). New York, NY: Modern Language Association.

An edition number, if it is not the first edition, appears on the title page.

33. Introduction, Preface, Foreword, or Afterword

First give the name of the writer of the item you're citing. After the year, give the name of the item cited. If this writer isn't also the author of the book, use the word *In* and the author's name before the title of the book.

Hesse, D. (2004). Foreword. In D. Smit, *The end of composition studies* (pp. ix–xiii). Carbondale: Southern Illinois University Press.

34. Reprint of an Older Book

Epp, M. (2003). *Women without men: Mennonite refugees of the Second World War*. Toronto, ON: University of Toronto Press. (Original work published 2000)

35. Government Publication

Use the complete name of a government agency as author when no specific person is named.

Indian and Northern Affairs Canada. (2000). *An Aboriginal book list for children*. Ottawa, ON: Author.

Savoie, D. J. (2008). *Horizontal management of official languages. Reports, Office of the Commissioner of Official Languages*. Ottawa, ON: Minister of Public Works and Government Services Canada.

36. Published Proceedings of a Conference

Smith, D. B. (Ed.). (1997). *Forging a new relationship: Proceedings of the conference on the Report of the Royal Commission on Aboriginal Peoples*. Montreal, QC: McGill Institute for the Study of Canada.

When citing a specific department or other university facility, put the name of the university first.

37. Thesis or Dissertation

Byers, M. (2000). Buffy the Vampire Slayer: *The insurgence of television as a performance text* (Unpublished doctoral dissertation), University of Toronto, Toronto, ON.

The title of the television series is taken out of italics when it is part of the italicized title of an independent work.

Stuart, G. A. (2006). *Exploring the Harry Potter book series: A study of adolescent reading motivation*. Retrieved from ProQuest Digital Dissertations. (AAT 3246355)

The number in parentheses at the end is the accession number.

38. Entry from Encyclopedia: Print or Online

Shadbolt, D. (1988). Emily Carr. In *The Canadian encyclopedia* (2nd ed., Vol. 1, p. 366). Edmonton, AB: Hurtig.

Turing test. (2008). In *Encyclopædia Britannica*. Retrieved February 9, 2008, from http://www.britannica.com/bps/topic/609757/Turing-test

Because the reference is to a work that may change, a retrieval date is included.

Images, audio, film, and video

39. Photograph, Painting, Drawing, Illustration, etc.: Original

Pratt, C. (1968). *Shop on an island* [Painting]. London, ON: London Regional Art Gallery.

McMillan, D. (2001). *Village grave. Commemoration Day, April, 1995* [Photograph]. Winnipeg, MB: Winnipeg Art Gallery.

40. Photograph, Painting, Drawing, Illustration, etc. in a Periodical

Greene, H. *Grace Slick.* (2004, September 30). [Photograph]. *Rolling Stone,* 102.

41. Photograph, Painting, Drawing, Illustration, etc. in a Book

Figurine of a seated goddess. (1997). [Illustration]. In S. D. Campbell (Ed.), *The Malcove collection* (p. 98). Toronto, ON: University of Toronto Press.

42. Comic or Cartoon

Sutton, W. (2011, May 2). *Ryan's a late adopter.* [Cartoon]. *The New Yorker, 87*(11), 64.

43. Photo Essay

Gallery: G8 and G20 summits. (2010, June 29). [Photo essay]. *The National Post.* Retrieved from http://www.nationalpost.com

44. Image from a Social Networking Site

Gristellar, F. (2009, August 7). *The Gateway Arch.* [Photograph]. Retrieved from https://www.facebook.com/qzprofile.php?id=7716zf92444

45. Map, Chart, or Other Graphic: Online

+15 walkway system. (2010). [Graphic]. *DowntownCalgary.com.* Retrieved from http://www.calgarydowntown.com

46. Audio Book

Turkle, S. (2011). *Alone together: Why we expect more from technology and less from each other.* [MP3-CD]. Old Saybrook, CT: Tantor Media.

47. Sound Recording

Cohen, L. (Performer). (1988). Tower of song. On *I'm your man* [CD]. Toronto, ON: Sony Music Canada.

Verdi, G. (1874). Requiem. [Recorded by R. Muti (Conductor) and the Chicago Symphony Orchestra and Chorus]. On *Requiem* [CD]. Chicago: CSO Resound. (2010)

48. Audio Podcast

Suzuki, D. (2010, July 5). *The bottom line* [Audio podcast]. Retrieved from http://www.cbc.ca /thebottomline/2010/07

49. Film, Videotape, or DVD

Ego Filmarts/ZDF (Producer), & Egoyan, A. (Director). (1993). *Calendar* [Motion picture]. Canada/Armenia/Germany: Zeitgeist Films.

Madden, J. (Director), Parfitt, D., Gigliotti, D., Weinstein, H., Zwick, E., & Norman, M. (Producers). (2003). *Shakespeare in love* [DVD]. United States: Miramax. (Original motion picture released 1998)

50. Video: Online

For video downloads, include the download date and the source.

Capra, F. (Director/Producer). (2010). *It happened one night* [Motion Picture]. United States: Columbia Pictures. Retrieved from Netflix. (Original motion picture released 1934)

Wesch, M. (2007, January 31). *Web 2.0 . . . the machine is us/ing us* [Video file]. Retrieved from http://www.youtube.com/watch?v=6gmP4nk0EOE

51. Broadcast Television or Radio Program

Moore, Y., & Schuyler, L. (Writers), & Deacon, C. (Director). (2011, April 8). Chasing pavements: Part 2 [Television series episode]. In L. Schuyler & S. Stohn (Producers), *Degrassi: The Next Generation*. Toronto, ON: Epitome Pictures.

If you're citing a television series produced by and seen on only one station, cite its call letters.

52. Television or Radio Program: Online

Mercer, R. (Writer/Actor). (2011, January 18). Season 8—episode 12 [Television series episode]. In G. Lunz (Producer), *The Rick Mercer Report*. Retrieved from http://www.cbc.ca/video/#/Shows/1221254309/ ID=1750748073

If writers or directors can be identified, list them in the author position. Producers go in the editor position. Include the episode title, if any, and the title of the series. If it is a one-time program, list only the title. The URL is listed because the source may be hard to find.

Other online sources

Because websites may change, the retrieval statement includes the date retrieved as well as the URL. This example has no author.

ARTICLE TITLE   DATE

Think again: Men and women share cognitive skills. (2006).

PUBLICATION INFORMATION   RETRIEVAL INFORMATION

American Psychological Association. Retrieved January 18, 2013,

URL

from http://www.psychologymatters.org/thinkagain.html

53. Entire Website

Association for the Advancement of Artificial Intelligence. (2008, March). Retrieved March 17, 2013, from http://www.aaai.org

Neff, M. (Ed.). (2011). WebdelSol. Retrieved August 4, 2013, from http://webdelsol.com

Because material on a website may change, use a "retrieved from" date.

54. Page from a Website

Think again: Men and women share cognitive skills. (2006). *American Psychological Association*. Retrieved January 18, 2013, from http://www.psychologymatters.org/thinkagain.html

The Banff Centre. (2010, July). Parks Canada's youth videography project. Retrieved March 4, 2013, from http://www.banffcentre.ca

55. Real-Time Online Communication

Berzsenyi, C. (2007, May 13). Writing to meet your match: Rhetoric, perceptions, and self-presentation for four online daters. *Computers and Writing Online*. [Synchronous discussion]. Retrieved from http://acadianamoo.org

If a chat, discussion, or synchronous (meaning available as it is happening) online presentation can be retrieved by others, include it in your References list.

56. E-Mail Message

Because e-mails to individuals cannot be retrieved by others, they should not appear in the References list. Cite them in the body of your paper, as in this example:

The wildfires threatened several of the laboratory facilities at our Saskatchewan research site (T. Martin, personal communication, June 20, 2012).

57. Posting on a Blog

Phillips, M. (2011, June 15). Need to go to the ER? Not until the game's over. [Web log post]. Retrieved from http://www.freakonomics.com/2011/06/15/need-to-go-to-the-er-not-until-the-games-over

58. Wiki

NASCAR Sprint Cup series [Wiki]. (2011). Retrieved April 6, 2014, from http://nascarwiki.com

Machine learning. (n.d.) Retrieved January 5, 2013, from Artificial Intelligence Wiki: http://www.ifi.unizh.ch/ailab/aiwiki/aiw.cgi

N.d. means "no date." Because a wiki can change by its very nature, always include a retrieval date.

59. Posting on Facebook

Adler-Kassner, L. (2011, May 6). Conversations toward action. [Facebook group]. Retrieved from Council of Writing Program Administrators at https://www.facebook.com/groups/106575940874

Include the citation in your References list only if it is retrievable by others. If it's not, cite it only in the body of your paper, as in example 56.

60. **Message on a Online Forum, Discussion Group,**
    or Electronic Mailing List

Firrantello, L. (2005, May 23). Van Gogh on Prozac. *Salon Table Talk*. [Online forum posting]. Retrieved February 15, 2013, from http://www.salon.com

Boyle, F. (2002, October 11). Psyche: Cemi field theory: The hard problem made easy [Discussion group posting]. Retrieved from news://sci.psychology.consciousness

Haswell, R. (2005, October 17). A new graphic/text interface. [Electronic mailing list message]. Retrieved May 20, 2013, from http://lists.asu.edu/archives /wpa-l.html

APA advises using *electronic mailing list*, as Listserv is the name of specific software.

Other Sources

61. **Letters**

Williams, W. C. (1935). [Letter to his son]. In L. Grunwald & S. J. Adler (Eds.), *Letters of the century: America 1900–1999* (pp. 225–226). New York, NY: Dial Press.

In the APA system, unpublished letters are considered personal communications inaccessible to general readers, so they do not appear in the References list. They are cited only in the body of the paper (see example 56). Letters that have been published or can be retrieved by others are cited as above.

62. **Report, Pamphlet, or Brochure**

In Vancouver Web Services. (2010). *Website design and hosting in Vancouver* [Brochure]. Retrieved from http://www.invancouver.com

63. **Legal Source**

Give the name of a law, the name and number of a case, or the number of a bill and the parliamentary session at which the bill was debated, and the date. Also give the published source where the law is codified or the case is reported. See Appendix 7.1 of the APA *Publication Manual* for other types of legal citations.

Bill C-50. An Act to amend the Criminal Code in respect of cruelty to animals, 1st Sess., 38th Parl., 2005.

Legal writers follow the *Canadian Guide to Uniform Legal Citation* (7th edition, 2010), and include abbreviated publication information for laws and cases.

Canadian Labour Code, R.S.C. 1985, c.L.-2, s.12.

Delgamuukw v. British Columbia, [1997] 3 S.C.R. 1010.

64. **Advertisement**

An appeal [Advertisement]. (2005). *Canadian Journal of Communication, 30*(3), 435.

BlackBerry PlayBook [Advertisement]. (2011, May 2). Retrieved from
http://www.edmontonjournal.com

65. Computer Software or Video Game

Tom Clancy's splinter cell trilogy [Video game]. (2011). Montreal, QC:
Ubisoft.

Provide an author name, if available. Standard software (Microsoft Word) and
program languages (C++) don't need to be given in the References list. The name
of a software program is not italicized.

66. Presentation Slides or Images

Laursen, F. (2007). *European Union Centre of Excellence (EUCE) Dalhousie
University* [PowerPoint slides]. Retrieved from http://euce.dal.ca/Files /
EUCE-January2007.pdf

67. Interview

In APA style, a personal interview is not included in the References list. Cite the
interview in the text as a personal communication.

Max Brooks (personal communication, August 30, 2014) endorses this view.

68. Lecture, Speech, or Address

Hawking, S. (2010, June 20). Address given at the Perimeter
Institute, Waterloo, ON. Retrieved from http://www.youtube.com/
watch?v=IpT1ANHlXpk

69. Live Performance

APA style does not require a live performance to be listed in the References list.
You can follow this model, however, if it is essential to include the details of a
performance.

Shakespeare, W. (Author), McAnuff, D. (Director), Hunt, S. J., Dennehy,
B., & Rooney, T. (Performers). (2011, July 3). *Twelfth night* [Theatrical
performance]. Stratford ON: Festival Theatre.

70. Microfiche Collection of Articles

Wenzell, R. (1990, February 3). Businesses prepare for a more diverse work
force [Microform]. *St. Louis Post Dispatch*, p. 17. *NewsBank: Employment
27*, fiche 2, grid D12.

A microfiche is a transparent sheet of film (a *fiche*) with microscopic printing that
needs to be read through a special magnifier. Each fiche holds several pages, with
each page designated by a grid position. A long document may appear on more
than one fiche.

71. Musical Score

Schubert, F. (1971). *Symphony in B Minor (Unfinished)*. M. Cusid (Ed.).
[Musical score]. New York, NY: Norton. (Original work composed 1822)

72. Nonperiodical Publications on CD, DVD, or Magnetic Tape

Perl, S. (2004). *Felt Sense: Guidelines for Composing*. [CD]. Portsmouth, NH: Boynton.

3   A STUDENT'S APA-STYLE RESEARCH PAPER

Quick Points   You will learn to

➤   Format your paper according to APA guidelines.

3A   What are APA format guidelines for research papers?

⊙ Ask whether your instructor has instructions for preparing a final draft. If not,
Watch you can use the APA guidelines here. For an illustration of these guidelines, see
the Video the student paper in 3B.

◼ General instructions—APA

Print on 8½-by-11-inch (standard size) white paper and double-space. Set at least a 1-inch (about 2.5 cm) margin on the left, and leave no less than 1 inch on the right and at the bottom.

Leave ½ inch (about 1.25 cm) from the top edge of the paper to the title-and-page-number line (also known as a running head). Leave another ½ inch (or 1 inch from the top edge of the paper) before the next line on the page, whether that's a heading (such as "Abstract" or "Footnotes") or a line of your paper.

Indent the first line of all paragraphs ½ inch, except in an abstract, the first line of which isn't indented. Do not justify the right margin. Indent footnotes ½ inch.

◼ Order of parts—APA

Number all pages consecutively. Use this order for the parts of your paper:

1. Title page
2. Abstract (if required)
3. Body of the paper
4. References
5. Footnotes, if any
6. Appendixes, if any (questionnaires, data sheets, or other material your instructor asks you to include)

◼ Title-and-page-number line (running head) for all pages—APA

Use a title-and-page-number line on all pages of your paper. Place it ½ inch (1.25 cm) from the top edge of the paper, typing the title (use a shortened version if necessary). Place the page number 1 inch (2.5 cm) from the right edge of the paper. Ask whether your instructor wants you to include your last name in the running head. The "header" tool on a word processing program will help you create the title-and-page-number line easily. See the sample student paper in 3B.

Title page—APA

Use a separate title page. Include your running head. Centre your complete title horizontally and place it in the top half of the page. (Don't italicize, underline, or enclose your title in quotation marks.) On the next line, centre your name, and below that centre the course title and section, your professor's name, and the date. See the sample student paper in 3B.

Alerts: (1) Use the guidelines here for capitalizing the title of your own paper and for capitalizing titles you mention in the body of your paper, but not in the REFERENCES list; see Quick Box 2.1.

(2) Use a capital letter for the first word of your title and for the first word of a subtitle, if any. Start every NOUN, PRONOUN, VERB, ADVERB, and ADJECTIVE with a capital letter. Capitalize each main word in a hyphenated compound word (two or more words used together to express one idea): *Father-in-Law, Self-Consciousness*.

(3) Do not capitalize ARTICLES (*a, an, the*) unless one of the other capitalization rules applies to them. Do not capitalize PREPOSITIONS and CONJUNCTIONS unless they're four or more letters long. Do not capitalize the word to used in an INFINITIVE. ●

Abstract—APA

An abstract is a summary of your paper in 150 to 250 words. Type the abstract on a separate page, using the numeral 2 in the title-and-page-number line. Centre the word *Abstract* 1 inch (2.5 cm) from the top of the paper. Do not italicize or underline it or enclose it in quotation marks. Double-space below this title, and then start your abstract, double-spacing it. Do not indent the first line.

Set-off quotations—APA

Set off (display in block style) quotations of forty words or more. See 27C for a detailed explanation and example.

References list—APA

Start a new page for your References list immediately after the end of the body of your paper. One inch (2.5 cm) from the top of the paper centre the word *References*. Don't italicize, underline, or put it in quotation marks. Double-space below it. Start the first line of each entry at the left margin, and indent any subsequent lines five spaces or ½ inch (1.25 cm) from the left margin. Use this hanging indent style unless your instructor prefers a different one. Double-space within each entry and between entries.

Notes—APA

Put any notes on a separate page after the last page of your References list. Centre the word *Footnotes* one inch (2.5 cm) from the top of the paper. Do not italicize or underline it or put it in quotation marks.

On the next line, indent ½ inch (1.25 cm) and begin the note. Raise the note number slightly (you can use the superscript feature in your word-processing program), and then start the words of your note, leaving no space after the number. If the note is more than one typed line, do not indent any line after the first. Double-space throughout.

3B A student's APA-style research paper

View the Model

Leslie Palm wrote the following paper in response to an assignment that asked students to research how gender was portrayed in a specific circumstance.

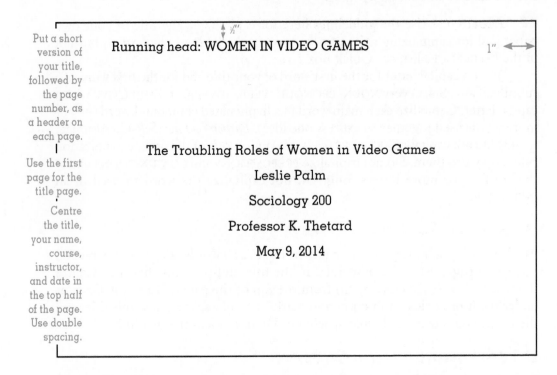

Put a short version of your title, followed by the page number, as a header on each page.

Running head: WOMEN IN VIDEO GAMES   1"

The Troubling Roles of Women in Video Games

Leslie Palm

Sociology 200

Professor K. Thetard

May 9, 2014

Use the first page for the title page.

Centre the title, your name, course, instructor, and date in the top half of the page. Use double spacing.

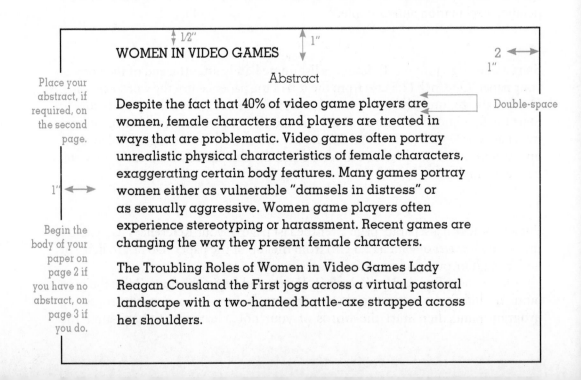

WOMEN IN VIDEO GAMES   2

Abstract

Despite the fact that 40% of video game players are women, female characters and players are treated in ways that are problematic. Video games often portray unrealistic physical characteristics of female characters, exaggerating certain body features. Many games portray women either as vulnerable "damsels in distress" or as sexually aggressive. Women game players often experience stereotyping or harassment. Recent games are changing the way they present female characters.

The Troubling Roles of Women in Video Games Lady Reagan Cousland the First jogs across a virtual pastoral landscape with a two-handed battle-axe strapped across her shoulders.

Place your abstract, if required, on the second page.

Begin the body of your paper on page 2 if you have no abstract, on page 3 if you do.

WOMEN IN VIDEO GAMES   3

She is the Player Character in a play-through of *Dragon Age: Origins*, a 2009 single-player role-play game, and she is trying to progress through the main quest. However, other characters taunt her. "I have never seen a woman Grey Warden before," says one skeptically. Lady rolls her eyes before sharply answering, "That's because women are too smart to join."

"So what does that make you?" asks the interrupter.

"Insane," she replies.

This exchange exemplifies how women have frequently been portrayed and treated in video games for over two decades. Gaming has long been inaccurately considered an activity pursued almost solely by reclusive males caricatured as "pale loners crouched in the dark among Mountain Dew bottles and pizza boxes" (Wong, 2010). Game producers have mostly catered to this stereotypical player, with discouraging results. Despite evidence that large numbers of women play video games, and despite some important changes, women game characters continue to be physically objectified, represented either as passive or sexually aggressive, and even harassed.

According to the Entertainment Software Association of Canada (2012), 58% of Canadians are gamers, and 46% of all players are women. US data show that "women over 18 years of age are one of the industry's fastest growing demographics, [representing] a greater portion of the game-playing population (33 percent) than boys age 17 or younger (20 percent)" (Entertainment Software Association, 2011). And yet, studies show that both male and female gamers believe games to be a "particularly masculine pursuit" (Selwyn, 2007, p. 533).

Physical Characteristics of Female Characters

The most obvious gender stereotyping in many games comes from the nature of the characters' bodies or avatars. A 2007 content analysis of images of video game characters from top-selling gaming magazines showed that male characters (83%) are more likely than female characters (62%) to be portrayed as aggressive; however, female characters are more likely to be sexualized (60 vs. 1%) and scantily clad (39 vs. 1%) (Dill & Thill, 2007, p. 851–864). Even female characters that are considered strong or dominant in personality (such as Morgainn in *Dragon Age: Origins* or Sheva in *Resident Evil 5*) routinely dress in tops that are essentially strips of fabric and skin-tight leather pants. In fact, the reward for beating

---

Introductory paragraphs create interest.

Paragraph 2 provides background information.

Thesis statement gives paper's focus.

Paragraph 3 gives data.

Brackets show the writer added language.

Citation with page number for direct quotation.

First heading.

Paragraph 4 starts to develop the first main point.

Resident Evil 5 is that you get to dress the avatar Sheva in a leopard-print bikini.

Paragraph 5 summarizes research related to the first main point.

Author and date are included in sentence, so only page numbers are in parentheses.

In *Gender Inclusive Game Design*, S. G. Ray (2003) outlined the physical traits seen in both male and female avatars: females are characterized by "exaggerated sexual features such as large breasts set high on their torso, large buttocks, and a waist smaller than her head" (pp. 102–104). Dickerman, Christensen, and Kerl-McClain (2008) found similar qualities. Analyzing characters in 60 video games, Downs and Smith (2010) found that women were more likely to be "hypersexualized" than men, depicted with unrealistic body proportions, inappropriate clothing, and other qualities (p. 728).

Paragraph 6 extends the first main point.

If the source had page numbers, a page reference would appear in parentheses.

Direct quotation embedded in a sentence.

Even non-human females receive this treatment. Game designer J. Rubenstein (2007) questions why females of non-human races in the popular game *World of Warcraft* are so much smaller and more feminine than their male counterparts. Of one species she notes, "The male is massive: tall with unnaturally large muscles and equally large hooves. . . . It would not be unreasonable to expect the female of the species to be similar." Apparently in *World of Warcraft's* earliest designs, the genders were far more similar; however, when screened to a pool of test gamers, complaints that the females were "ugly" resulted in their being changed to their current form. One scholar notes, "Since gamers and the like have been used to video representations of scantily-clad females and steroid-enhanced males," it is understandable that they would design non-human races in a similar way (Bates, 2005, p. 13).

Gender and Character Behaviour

Second heading.

Topic sentence of paragraph 7 announces the second main point.

In-text citation for a source by two authors.

No page number because examples are names of video games.

The personalities of the characters also demonstrate the gender bias in many games. Dietz's 1998 study of 33 games found that most did not portray women at all. Even 10 years later, 86% of game characters were male (Downs & Smith, 2010). Only five of the games in Dietz's study portrayed women as heroes or action characters. The second most common portrayal in this study was as "victim or as the proverbial 'Damsel in Distress'" (Dietz, 1998, pp. 434–435). Examples of vulnerable women stretch from the 1980s to today, from Princess Peach (Nintendo's *Mario*) and Princess Zelda (Nintendo's *The Legend of Zelda*) to Alice Wake (Remedy Entertainment's *Alan Wake*), Ashley Graham (Capcom's *Resident Evil 4*), and Alex Roivas (Nintendo's *Eternal Darkness: Sanity's Requiem*). The helpless woman, simply put, is a video game staple, as undergraduates overwhelmingly recognized in one study (Ogletree & Drake, 2007).

WOMEN IN VIDEO GAMES   5

A different staple role gaining popularity is that of the aggressive but sexy woman who will seduce you at night and then shoot you in the morning. Bayonetta, Jill Valentine (in *Resident Evil 3* and *Resident Evil 5*) and, of course, Lara Croft of the *Tomb Raider* series are all examples of this archetype. There is some debate as to whether these examples are evidence of new female power and liberation or simply a new form of exploitation. Dill and Thill (2007) argue that an aggressive female is not necessarily a liberated one and that "many of these images of aggressive female video game characters glamorize and sexualize aggression." Eugene Provenzo agrees, pointing out the contradiction between "the seeming empowerment of women, while at the same time . . . they're really being exploited in terms of how they're shown, graphically" (as cited in Huntemann, 2000).

Lara Croft is perhaps the epitome of the energetic, aggressive character as an over-exaggerated sexual object. Lead graphic artist Gard went through five designs before arriving at her final appearance, and he began with the desire to counter stereotypical female characters, which he describes as "either a bimbo or a dominatrix" (as cited in Yang, 2007). Gard's inspirations included Swedish pop artist Neneh Cherry and comic book character Tank Girl, both feminist icons. Croft's original incarnation was as the South American woman Lara Cruz. Gard disavows accusations of sexism in the design, and insists that the character's iconic breasts were a programming accident that the rest of the team fought to keep (McLaughlin, 2008).

The Treatment of Women Gamers

Video game culture reinforces negative gender roles for female players. Many multiplayer games encourage players to use headsets and microphones, a gender-revealing practice that is intended for easy strategizing. However, it often leads to sexual harassment and lewd commentary that also carries over to message boards, comments sections, and Internet forums. Technology blogger Kathy Sierra was forced to abandon her website after multiple misogynistic comments and e-mails. Ailin Graef, who has made millions in the 3D chat-platform Second Life, was "swarmed by flying pink penises" during an interview in that virtual world (McCabe, 2008).

A study by psychologists at Nottingham Trent University in England determined that 70% of female players in massively multiplayer online games chose to "construct male characters when given the option," presumably in an attempt to avoid such actions as female posters on gaming message boards

---

Paragraph 8 introduces a slightly different aspect of the second main point.

Ellipses dots show that the writer has removed language from the quotation.

Paragraph 9 provides a specific example.

Third heading.

Topic sentence of paragraph 10 explains third main point.

Specific examples illustrate the point.

being asked to post pictures of their breasts or "get the f*** off" (McCabe, 2008). Women gamers are considered so rare (which is surprising, given that they make up nearly 50% of players) that it's a common occurrence for male gamers to respond with a degree of shock any time a female shows up in a game—even if that shock is complimentary or respectful. Sarah Rutledge, a 25-year-old female med student, said of her gaming on *World of Warcraft*,

> On the one hand, you get a lot of help and attention from guys playing the game, which can be helpful. You get invitations to join groups. But it's clear this has less to do with my ability than the fact I'm that curious creature: a woman. (personal communication, April 29, 2014)

One team of researchers found significant differences between men and women game players in gaining positive effects from gaming. They found males more likely than females to develop leadership, teamwork, and communicative skills, and they suggest this demonstrates games' biases toward males (Thirunarayanon, Vilchez, Abreau, Ledesma, & Lopez, 2010, p. 324).

Gradual Changes in Gender Roles and Gaming

In recent years gender roles have somewhat shifted. Often role-playing games permit the user to choose various characteristics of the Player Character, including making her female. Aside from appearance and responses from Non-Player Characters, the gender rarely affects a character's actual skills or attributes. More games have been released with females as the sole protagonists, including *Silent Hill 3* (Heather Mason), *No One Lives Forever* (Cate Archer), *Mirror's Edge* (Faith), and *Heavenly Sword* (Nariko). Jade, the protagonist of *Beyond Good and Evil* (released in 2003), has been praised for being strong and confident without being overtly sexualized. So have characters like Alyx Vance (co-protagonist of 2004's *Half-Life 2*) and Chell (protagonist of *Portal*, 2007, and *Portal 2*, 2011).

Chell in particular was heralded as a massive step forward in gender dynamics. People were surprised that "as the player, you're never even aware that you're a woman until you catch a glimpse of yourself in the third person" (*iVirtua*, 2007). In this way, Chell echoes the "original" feminist character Samus Aran of Nintendo's 1986 *Metroid*; one only discovers that Aran is female when she removes her bulky robot-armour during the ending scene, after twenty-plus hours of first-person gameplay. *Portal*, despite being an indie game produced by

WOMEN IN VIDEO GAMES   7

students as their thesis, became a hit, was wildly acclaimed by critics, and won multiple awards.

These developments don't satisfy all fans. Some argue that a more inclusive focus actually threatens the quality of experience for stereotypically straight male gamers. Bioware, a gaming company based in Edmonton, came under fire during the releases of two major titles for featuring romance and dialogue options that cater not only to women, but to gays and lesbians. The release of *Dragon Age 2* in 2011 caused an uproar on its own message boards for allowing romantic options to be bisexual. One fan, "Bastal" (2011), protested that

> the overwhelming majority of RPG gamers are indeed straight and male. . . . That's not to say there isn't a significant number of women who play Dragon Age and that BioWare should forgo the option of playing as a women [*sic*] altogether, but there should have been much more focus on making sure us male gamers were happy.

He and others then go on to propose a mode, which, if activated, would force male companions to flirt only with female PCs, and vice versa. However, such views disturb game creators like Gaider (2011), who argued that people like Bastal are

> so used to being catered to that they see the lack of catering as an imbalance. . . . The person who says that the only way to please them is to restrict options for others is, if you ask me, the one who deserves it least.

"If we just continue to cater to existing (male) players, we're never going to grow," says Beth Llewellyn, senior director of corporate communications for Nintendo (as cited in Kerwick, 2007). Video game companies have begun producing a new generation of games that give women the opportunity to grab a laser gun or broadsword and duke it out in billion-dollar franchises like *Halo, Fallout, Mass Effect, World of Warcraft,* and *Guild Wars.* However, depicting women more accurately and favourably in games reaches a goal more important than mere entertainment. "Video-simulated interfaces" are being used to train people for various professions (Terlecki et al., 2011, p. 30), and it is crucial that these environments are suitable for all. The promising news is that while there is still extensive gender stereotyping (in both the gaming and the real world), game makers are taking giant strides—in both boots and heels.

Paragraph 14 explains some fans' responses.

Quotations longer than 40 words are set off block style, with no quotation marks. They're both from online sources with no page numbers; other source information appears in the sentences introducing the quotations.

Concluding paragraph.

Key quotation begins the concluding paragraph based on idea in previous paragraph.

Sentence helps answer the "so what?" question.

Because there are more than 6 authors for this citation, student uses the first author and "et al."

References

Bastal. (2011, March 22). Bioware neglected their main demographic: The straight male gamer [Online discussion posting]. Retrieved May 3, 2014, from http://social.bioware.com/forum/1/topic/304/index/6661775&lf=8 (Topic 304, Msg. 1)

Bates, M. (2005). *Implicit identity theory in the rhetoric of the massively multiplayer online role-playing game (MMORPG)* (Doctoral Dissertation, Pennsylvania State University.) Available from ProQuest Dissertations and Theses database. (AAT 3172955)

Dickerman, C., Christensen, J., & Kerl-McClain, S. B. (2008). Big breasts and bad guys: Depictions of gender and race in video games. *Journal of Creativity in Mental Health, 3*(1), 20–29. doi: 10.1080/15401380801995076

Dietz, T. L. (1998). An examination of violence and gender role portrayals in video games: Implications for gender socialization and aggressive behavior. *Sex Roles, 38,* 433–435.

Dill, K. E., & Thill, K. P. (2007, October 17). Video game characters and the socialization of gender roles: Young people's perceptions mirror sexist media depictions. *Sex Roles, 57,* 861–864.

Downs, E., & Smith, S. L. (2010). Keeping abreast of hypersexuality: A video game character content analysis. *Sex Roles, 62,* 721–733. doi: 10:1007/s11199-009-9637-1

Dragon Age: Origins [Video game]. (2009). Edmonton, AB: Bioware Studios.

Entertainment Software Association. (2011). *Essential facts about the computer and video game industry 2010: Sales, demographic and usage data.* Washington, DC: Author. Retrieved from http://theesa.com

Entertainment Software Association of Canada. (2012). *Essential facts 2012.* Retrieved from http://theesa.ca

Gaider, D. (2011, April 2). Re: Bioware neglected their main demographic [Online forum comment]. Retrieved May 3, 2014, from http://social.bioware.com/forum/1/topic/304/index/6661775&lf=8 (Topic 304, Msg. 2)

Huntemann, N. (Producer & Director). (2000). *Game over: Gender, race & violence in video games* [Video file]. USA: Media Education Foundation. Retrieved from http://www.mediaed.org

Begin References on a new page, with hanging indent.

Dissertation from a database, with accession number.

Journal article online, with document object identifier (doi).

Journal article in print.

Video game.

Report available online. Because the author is the same as the publisher, the publisher is listed as "Author."

Comment in an online discussion.

Online video.

WOMEN IN VIDEO GAMES   9

iVirtua Editorial Team. (2007, December 9). Portal is a feminist masterpiece. London, England: iVirtua Media Group. Retrieved from http://www.ivirtuaforums.com/ portal-is-a-feminist-masterpiece-great-read-media-studies-t14-61

Kerwick, M. (2007, May 13). Video games now starring strong female characters. *The Record*. Retrieved from http://www.popmatters.com/female-characters

McCabe, J. (2008, March 6). Sexual harassment is rife online: No wonder women swap gender. *The Guardian*, p. G2. Retrieved from http://www.guardian.co.uk/

McLaughlin, R. (2008). The history of Tomb Raider. IGN Entertainment, Inc. Retrieved from http://m.ign.com/ articles/856183

Ogletree, S. M., & Drake, R. (2007). College students' video game participation and perceptions: Gender differences and implications. *Sex Roles, 56,* 537–542. doi: 10.1007 /s11199-007-9193-5

Ray, S. G. (2003). *Gender inclusive game design: Expanding the market*. Hingham, MA: Charles River Media.

Rubenstein, J. (2007, May 26). Idealizing fantasy bodies. *Iris Gaming Network*. Retrieved from http://theirisnetwork.org

Selwyn, N. (2007). Hi-tech = Guy-tech? An exploration of undergraduate students' gendered perceptions of information and communication technologies. *Sex Roles, 56,* 525–536. doi: 10.1007/s11199-007-9191-7

Terlecki, M., Brown, J., Harner-Steciw, L., Irvin-Hannum, J., Marchetto-Ryan, N., Ruhl, L., & Wiggins, J. (2011). Sex differences and similarities in video game experience, preferences, and self-efficacy: Implications for the gaming industry. *Current Psychology, 30,* 22–33. doi: 10.1007/s12144-010-9095-5

Thirunarayanon, M. O., Vilchez, M., Abreu, L., Ledesma, C., & Lopez, S. (2010). A survey of video game players in a public, urban research university. *Educational Media International, 47,* 311–327. doi: 10.1080/09523987-2010.535338

Wong, D. (2010, May 24). Five reasons it's still not cool to admit you're a gamer. *Cracked*. Retrieved from http:// www.cracked.com/article_18571

Yang, R. (2007). The man behind Lara [Interview]. *GameDaily*. Retrieved from http://gamedaily.com/articles/ features/the-man-behind-lara

Newspaper article available online.

Book.

Reading Index